Survey Research in the Social Sciences

Survey Research in the

Social Sciences

Edited by Charles Y. Glock

Russell Sage Foundation

NEW YORK 1967

With Contributions by

JOHN W. BENNETT   HERBERT MCCLOSKY
CHARLES Y. GLOCK   JAMES N. MORGAN
DANIEL KATZ   EDWARD A. SUCHMAN
FRED MASSARIK   GUSTAV THAISS
MARTIN TROW

© 1967
RUSSELL SAGE FOUNDATION
Printed in the United States of America

Library of Congress Catalog Card Number: 67–25911

Designer: Asher T. Applegate
CONNECTICUT PRINTERS, INC., HARTFORD, CONNECTICUT

Contents

For
PAUL F. LAZARSFELD

Introduction*

SIGNIFICANT breakthroughs in methods of scientific inquiry are remarkably rare. And, when they do arise, they seldom emerge full flower. It takes years, often decades, and sometimes centuries for the full implications of an innovating idea to be understood and more time still for understanding to become commonly shared in the relevant scientific community. Contributions are overlooked at the time of their introduction, only to be rediscovered many years later. Innovations lie fallow because they threaten established ways of doing things, or are resisted because they contradict a "sacred" societal belief. The work of one man is unknown to the work of another, though joint knowledge would have enhanced the work of both.

Such observations seem more appropriate for the past than for the present. Ideas are no longer as "sacred" as they used to be, nor are there any longer, in Western society at least, scientific or other groups with the power to suppress new ideas. Modern communications insure that scientists will learn quickly what others are doing. Moreover, knowledge of an innovating idea seems likely to produce concentrated effort toward its formalization.

Survey research, at first glance, appears to resemble more closely the second of these sets of observations than the first. In the 1930's and 1940's, social scientists were quick to seize upon the idea of using data collected from a sample of a universe in scientific inquiry. Since then, not only have the initial ideas been extended, but survey research has become, in some disciplines at least, the most widely used tool of empirical investigation. The proliferation of studies based on survey data and the large number of

* Individual authors have made their acknowledgements at appropriate places throughout this book. As editor, I should like here to express my particular gratitude to Hanan Selvin, now of the University of Rochester, and Gertrude J. Selznick of the Survey Research Center, Berkeley, for all the help and counsel they have provided along the way. My debt to the authors of individual chapters is unbounded. They were patient, understanding, and cooperative during the long period of our mutual effort. The Russell Sage Foundation provided the financial support for the volume, and we are all grateful for this help. We owe a personal debt to the Foundation's president, Orville G. Brim, Jr., for his encouragement and his patience. Finally, to Toni Brown and Shirley Manning, who assisted me in editing the volume, my sincere thanks for extraordinary service in the final days of completing the task.

technical books and articles written on survey methods are further testimony that survey research has quickly changed the landscape of social inquiry.

More careful scrutiny, however, of the quality of the literature, of the degree that training in survey research has infiltrated into social science curricula and, indeed, of the amount of consensus which exists about what constitutes a survey suggest that the outward signs of widespread diffusion, acceptance, and use of survey research may be, in part, misleading. Survey research may not be the exception to the tendency for new methodological ideas to evolve, to be disseminated, and to be internalized slowly that it initially appears to be.

That some of the most significant monographs of the last decades have emerged from the analysis of survey data would seem to belie this more conservative view. Such works as *Union Democracy,*[1] *The People's Choice,*[2] *The American Voter,*[3] *Social Class and Mental Illness,*[4] *The Adolescent Society,*[5] and the first two volumes on *The American Soldier,*[6] among others, cannot be faulted on their quality. But for every significant study, there are many more which are theoretically sterile, technically incompetent, or simply "non-studies" in the sense that they do not describe a population of interest or engage in an examination of causal relations.

That survey research is not taught to any extent in many disciplines and is frequently mistaught in others is further evidence that survey research has not really penetrated deeply into the social science consciousness. The number of universities which provide systematic training in survey research can almost be counted on the fingers of one hand. And, in even these universities, training tends to be concentrated in one or two departments. Certainly considerably fewer social science students are trained in survey research than in experimental method.

1. Lipset, S. M., Martin Trow, and J. S. Coleman, *Union Democracy:* The Internal Politics of the International Typographical Union. Free Press, Glencoe, Ill., 1956.
2. Lazarsfeld, P. F., B. R. Berelson, and Hazel Gaudet, *The People's Choice:* How the Voter Makes Up His Mind in a Presidential Campaign. Columbia University Press, New York, 1948.
3. Campbell, Angus, P. E. Converse, and W. E. Miller, *The American Voter.* John Wiley & Sons, New York, 1960.
4. Hollingshead, A. deB. and F. C. Redlich, *Social Class and Mental Illness:* A Community Study. John Wiley & Sons, New York, 1958.
5. Coleman, J. S., *The Adolescent Society:* The Social Life of the Teenager and Its Impact on Education. Free Press of Glencoe, New York, 1961.
6. Stouffer, S. A., *et al., The American Soldier:* Vol. 1, Adjustment During Army Life; Vol. 2, Combat and its Aftermath. Princeton University Press, Princeton, 1949; 1950.

Survey research, to be sure, is now practiced in all of the social sciences and in most related professional disciplines. The amount and quality of its use, however, varies considerably from field to field and, in every field, the contributions which have been made, both to using survey research imaginatively to deal with substantive problems and to advancing survey methods technically, have come from the very few rather than the many. Furthermore, there is little communication across disciplines and creative innovations made in one tend not to be known in another.

Additionally, there are widespread misconceptions among social scientists who consider themselves informed, as to what it means to use survey methods in scientific research. Sometimes, survey research is conceived of too narrowly as being solely a data collection device, as being capable of generating data only on individuals but not larger entities, or as being unsuitable for studying problems involving social processes or change. More serious misconceptions are located at the analytical level. The problems range from a failure to comprehend the logic of survey analysis to misuse of that logic through the application of inappropriate statistics. Survey research is often rejected as a possible method because of these misconceptions. At other times, it is pursued within them to the detriment of both the individual investigator and the general image of survey research as a scientific method.

Different observers are likely to offer different explanations of the situation. There are undoubtedly some who would argue that it merely reflects inherent deficiencies in the method—that survey research, in effect, has had the fate it deserves. To be correct, however, such an interpretation would require social scientists to be effectively informed about survey research and, being so informed, to reject it rationally as a method. The evidence is all too clear that an understanding of survey research has not been that widely diffused in the social science community.

Why this should be is puzzling. Perhaps insufficient time has passed since the introduction of modern survey research in the 1930's. Perhaps, too, it is due to the relative absence of communication across disciplines. Certainly, survey research has penetrated more deeply into some disciplines than others. The fact of the matter is, however, that survey research is far from being universally understood, even in the disciplines which have used it most widely and effectively. Here, a possible explanation is that the internal logic of survey research—particularly of survey analysis—is not easily comprehended. The kind of elementary introductory statement from which the novice might gain comprehension is missing from the literature.

To a large extent, those who understand and use survey research were initially persuaded by what they heard in lectures rather than what they read in the literature.

Whatever the cause, it has seemed to this observer unfortunate that survey research is not more widely understood and effectively used. Even acknowledging its present shortcomings, survey research is a ubiquitous method, offering possibilities for application to a wide range of problems in both the core social sciences and in related professional disciplines. Presumably, in the natural course of events, this will slowly come to be understood, and eventually the potential for survey research will be realized. This book, in effect, represents an effort to accelerate this process.

Insofar as the present situation can be accounted for by a failure in communication, it seemed worthwhile to conceive of a volume which would make explicit the characteristics which distinguish survey research from other modes of inquiry—a volume that would communicate the elementary logic of survey design and analysis, and provide, for each discipline, an evaluation of how survey research has been used and conceivably may be used to deal with the central problems of each field. Such a volume might not generate wholesale conversions to survey research, but it could help reduce the present tendency of the social scientist to overlook or to avoid survey research because he is uninformed or misinformed about its applicability to his own research. A comprehensive volume should also encourage a profitable exchange of ideas across disciplines. Contributions to the technical advancement of survey research have come from many sources, and each discipline has innovated unique applications. Thus, the practitioner of an applied social science discipline and the investigator in a more theoretically oriented one might find as much stimulation from reading about the use of survey research in other fields as in his own.

Informed by this conception, the book considers the uses of survey research in each of the five academic social sciences—sociology, political science, psychology, economics, and anthropology—and in three related professional disciplines—education, social work, and public health and medicine. Law, business administration, journalism, and other professional fields are omitted not because survey research is considered irrelevant to work in these areas, but because basic orientations to survey research are not as unique to these fields as they are to the academic disciplines. This warranted some selectivity to avoid repetition. Education, public health, and social work were selected to represent the professional fields primarily because they appear to allow exemplification of uses of survey research on a greater range of applied problems.

The tasks of providing a brief history of survey research and of describing its character are taken up later in this introductory chapter. This might also have been the appropriate place to discuss the underlying logic of survey design and analysis, since there is no need to repeat this in each of the chapters. However, it is difficult to communicate the logic without examples. Consequently, it was decided that the author of one of the field chapters should assume the double task of introducing the logic and also of reviewing survey research applications in his discipline. Sociology was chosen to carry this burden because of its greater experience with survey research and because a majority of the refinements in survey design have emanated from it. The essay on survey applications in sociology, therefore, is the first chapter of the book.

The chapter on political science follows. Its author has complemented the methodological discussion included in the chapter on sociology with a further elaboration on problems of data collection. However, this chapter, like all succeeding chapters, is primarily concerned with assessing the ways survey research has been used and may potentially be used in the discipline.

The chapters, understandably, vary in the relative attention given to present as against potential uses. The emphasis in chapters 1 and 2 is on present uses; survey research has penetrated most deeply into sociology and political science. Chapter 3, on psychology, balances the two emphases. Chapters 4 and 5 are devoted to economics and anthropology, respectively. These disciplines have been the most resistant to adopting the survey as an empirical tool. The authors, while differing in optimism, advance a persuasive case for more effective use of surveys in the two fields.

More so, perhaps, than in the basic disciplines, there are widespread misconceptions about survey research in applied fields. In chapter 6, on education, the author examines the prevailing misconceptions and suggests how they have derailed the successful adoption of the survey methods in much educational research. Chapter 7, on social work, pursues the same theme, but emphasizes the particular failure in social work to comprehend the possibilities of using surveys for pursuing explanations. Chapter 8, the last chapter in the book, considers the changing uses of survey methods in public health and medicine.

At the time the essays were commissioned, the authors were asked to emphasize the uses of survey research and to forego as much as possible an obvious temptation to be didactic about how to conduct surveys. The available technical literature is highly adequate in this latter respect and the reader will find appropriate references made to it as he goes along.

There is always a danger of excessive repetition in a book of this kind. By and large, however, the authors have succeeded remarkably well in avoiding it; what repetition remains was thought to be necessary to the continuity of each essay.

A Brief History of Survey Research

Survey research is to be understood as a mode of inquiry which combines a distinct method of data collection with a distinct form of analysis. Modern survey research dates back to the 1930's when the two were first juxtaposed in an explicit way. Independently, however, the data collection and analytical components of survey research are much older than this.

Viewing survey research only as a data collection device, its roots can be traced back at least to the ancient Egyptians, who developed systematic accounting procedures for foreign and domestic trade.[7] Since then, at various times in the history of man, rulers and their administrators have done population counts, or taken crude surveys of crop production, these data being gathered for practical purposes such as taxation.

The idea of systematically gathering quantitative materials for more scientific purposes is, of course, a later development. However, there are examples in the nineteenth century of efforts in this direction, most notably Charles Booth's encyclopaedic collection of data from all of the poor districts of London,[8] and Frédéric Le Play's exacting study of family income and expenditures in France.[9] There is no record that Karl Marx's questionnaire on the conditions of workers was ever filled out by those to whom it was sent.[10] That the questionnaire was constructed, however, is evidence that questionnaire studies were not alien to Marx's times.

These early attempts at mass data collection did not have the benefit, of

7. This brief discussion of the history of survey research owes much to Glazer, Nathan, "The Rise of Social Research in Europe," in *The Human Meaning of the Social Sciences*. Edited by Daniel Lerner. Meridian Books, New York, 1959.
8. Booth, Charles, ed., *Life and Labour of the People of London,* 17 volumes. Macmillan, London and New York, 1892–1893.
9. Le Play, Pierre Guillaume Frédéric, *La Reforme Sociale En France,* 2 volumes. E. Dentu, Paris, 1866.
10. Referred to in Glazer, Nathan, *op. cit.,* p. 63.

course, of probability sampling theory. By the early twentieth century, ideas about sampling had developed to the point where they might have been applied to the collection of data from human populations. The connection was not made in any significant way, however, until the 1930's when George Gallup and Elmo Roper began their public opinion studies based on interviews collected from a sample of the national population.

The studies of Gallup and Roper and the earlier studies of Booth and Le Play were methodologically significant primarily because of their contribution to the evolution of methods of data collection. On the analytical level, these studies were essentially descriptive; no attempt was made to test causal propositions through the statistical manipulation of the data obtained.

Modern survey research is also characterized by a distinct mode of analysis—a special version of multivariate analysis—which allows "the study and interpretation of complex interrelationships among a multiplicity of characteristics."[11] The character of these analytical ideas will be discussed in chapter 1. From whence, however, did they come? No one has sought to pull all of the threads together. The ideas existed in the work of such statisticians as Yule and Kendall.[12] Yule, in fact, had worked out at least part of the elementary logic of survey analysis by 1911. Hanan Selvin[13] has pointed out that many of the basic steps of multivariate analysis were also used by Durkheim in his intricate analysis of the statistics of suicide done in the 1890's.[14] Durkheim, however, apparently thought so little of his innovations that he never again tried out the same kind of analysis on a different subject, although his publications extend in an unbroken line for another quarter of a century.

The broader implications of Durkheim's work and of the work of Yule and Kendall were not perceived until the 1930's when Lazarsfeld combined an elaboration of their analytical ideas with the data collection procedures

---

11. Quoted from Lazarsfeld, P. F. and Morris Rosenberg, eds., *The Language of Social Research:* A Reader in the Methodology of Social Research. Free Press, Glencoe, Ill., 1955, p. 111. The book also includes a discussion of the general idea of multivariate analysis, pp. 115–147.
12. Yule, G. Udny, *An Introduction to the Theory of Statistics.* Charles Griffin, London, 1911.
13. Selvin, H. C., "Durkheim's *Suicide* and the Problems of Empirical Research," *Journal of Sociology,* Vol. 63, 1958, pp. 607–619.
14. Durkheim, Emile, *Suicide: A Study in Sociology.* Translated by J. A. Spaulding and George Simpson. Free Press, Chicago, 1951.

of Gallup and Roper to initiate the modern era of survey research.[15] Lazarfeld's seminal contribution was to perceive and to make explicit the potential for using survey research in the social scientist's search for explanations.

The most notable immediate application of the new methodology, aside from Lazarsfeld's own studies, was in the studies done on the American soldier during World War II under the direction of Samuel Stouffer.[16] These studies solidified Lazarsfeld's contributions and demonstrated the versatility of survey research to deal with a wide variety of theoretical as well as applied problems in the social sciences. In a commentary on Stouffer's studies, Kendall and Lazarsfeld took the occasion to formalize the logic of survey analysis in what has since become a classic statement.[17] It was this statement which later stimulated the still most comprehensive treatment of survey research from a technical point of view, Herbert Hyman's *Survey Design and Analysis*.[18]

Survey research, once launched, was not a methodology to be carried on by the individual scholar working alone. Facilities in the form of data collection and data processing machinery were a necessary adjunct to the effective conduct of survey research. These requirements have stimulated a proliferation of university-based institutes and centers devoted to survey research and equipped to foster its pursuit. Among the earliest of these, and all by and large still thriving, were the Bureau of Applied Social Research at Columbia University, the Survey Research Center at the University of Michigan, the National Opinion Research Center at the University of Chicago, and the Washington Public Opinion Laboratory at the University of Washington. Since World War II, each of these centers has contributed to the continued refinement of survey methods and to their introduction in varying degrees into all the social sciences.

Sparked by these innovators, other universities have followed suit and there are active and substantial centers now at the University of California, Berkeley, at U.C.L.A., and at the Universities of Wisconsin and Illi-

15. Lazarsfeld's ideas were given concrete expression in *The People's Choice, op. cit.* The formalization of the analytical strategy was presented first in an address to the American Sociological Society (now Association) in 1946; this address was subsequently published in Lazarsfeld, P. F. and Morris Rosenberg, *op. cit.,* pp. 115–147.
16. Stouffer, S. A., *et al., op. cit.*
17. Kendall, P. L. and P. F. Lazarsfeld, "Problems of Survey Analysis," *Continuities in Survey Research:* Studies in the Scope and Method of "The American Soldier." Edited by R. K. Merton and P. F. Lazarsfeld. Free Press, Chicago, 1950.
18. Hyman, H. H., *Survey Design and Analysis:* Principles, Cases and Procedures. Free Press, Chicago, 1955.

nois. Because of the investment required, such centers are still not common to all universities. However, at every major university, some facilities exist to aid in the conduct of survey research.

At once a strength and weakness of these centers has been a tendency for them to be associated with a single department of instruction. This has significantly stimulated the growth of training in survey research in the particular department. At the same time, it has undoubtedly been an obstacle to the establishment of needed interdisciplinary courses in survey research. The Survey Research Centers at the Universities of Michigan and California are the notable exceptions to the tendency toward single-department affiliation, both being located organizationally in their respective universities to serve all of the social sciences. This has stimulated more widespread interest in survey research, though not to the extent of involving all social science departments and related professional disciplines.

Perhaps the major factor inhibiting the wider use of survey research is its cost. Even simple surveys are not inexpensive and more ambitious ones frequently involve expenditures upwards of $100,000. An important innovation in this respect is the recent establishment of archives of survey data. These archives give recognition to the possibilities of using survey data for secondary analysis long after the primary analysis has been completed. Data which cost thousands of dollars to collect are thus made available for a pittance. Scholars using these archives must tailor their problems to the data at hand, of course. By now, however, such rich and varied data have been accumulated as to allow a wide range of choice, and the pursuit of survey research at very small cost indeed. There are now over a score of such archives at American universities, most notably the Roper Public Opinion Center at Williams College, the Inter-University Consortium for Political Research with headquarters at the University of Michigan, and the International Data Library and Reference Service at the University of California. In 1965, the national importance of this development was recognized with the establishment of the Council of Social Science Data Archives.

All this activity has still not produced an integrated view of survey research. Variations persist in the way it is practiced both within and between disciplines. There is still considerable progress to be made to gain consensus about whether survey research ought to be taught, to whom, and in what way. And there are still unresolved methodological issues both with respect to data collection and to analysis. There is no doubt, however, that survey research is here to stay and that the future will witness its expanded use as a means of social inquiry.

The Character of Survey Research

Given the fact that survey research is now widely practiced, considerable consensus might be expected about how to define it. In point of fact, however, there are almost as many definitions of the word "survey" as there are people who have written about surveys. One author, Moser, even refuses to offer a definition, arguing that a "straightforward definition . . . would have to be so general as to defeat its purpose . . ."[19] In apparent agreement, Hyman[20] gives no explicit definition, but instead points to an array of case studies ranging from Durkheim's analysis of official statistics on suicide[21] to Kinsey's *Sexual Behavior in the Human Male*.[22] Clearly, any definition that attempts to encompass everything that has been called a survey would be, as Moser claims, too general to be useful. This lack of consensus is reflected to a degree in the present volume; there are different shades of meaning and understanding in the authors' conceptions of survey research.

The relative absence of a wholly integrated view, however, makes it necessary in further introduction of the book to be explicit about what the differences are. This will not add to the independent contribution each chapter makes to an examination of survey research in its field. It can, however, sensitize the reader to the problem of integration and make more profitable his reading of the chapters on disciplines other than his own.

To begin, there is consensus among the authors that survey research is a quantitative rather than a qualitative method, requiring standardized information from and/or about the subjects being studied. Who these subjects are, how they are selected, what data are collected from or about them and in what way, and how the collected data are to be analyzed are subject to variation. Whatever the differences in these respects, however, the starting point for all the authors is that the collected data be standardized.

None of the authors confront the issue directly of the minimum number of cases required to constitute a survey. The authors of the chapters on psychology and social welfare would countenance a rather small number— both cite studies in which the n is less than 100. The prevailing view, however, is that a substantial number of cases is required and, while the precise number is nowhere specified, it is understood implicitly that there be sufficient cases to allow their being extensively analyzed statistically.

19. Moser, C. A., *Survey Methods in Social Investigation.* Macmillan, London, 1958.
20. Hyman, H. H., *Survey Design and Analysis, op. cit.*
21. Durkheim, Emile, *op. cit.*
22. Kinsey, A. C., W. B. Pomeroy, and C. E. Martin, *Sexual Behavior in the Human Male.* W. B. Saunders, Philadelphia, 1948.

As to who or what may be the subject of surveys, again the issue is not faced directly in all chapters. Judging from the examples used as illustrations, individuals are seen most often as the appropriate subjects of survey research. Undoubtedly none of the authors would deny that larger entities than persons might be the subjects of survey research. Only in the chapter on sociology, however, is this issue dealt with in any detail, and there the author acknowledges that the unit of analysis may range from the individual to a wide variety of larger entities—groups, organizations, communities—so long as information is collected from or about a sufficient number of these entities to meet the requirement of statistical treatment.

As to how the subjects of a study are to be selected and what they are to represent, the common assumption running through all of the chapters is that the subjects represent a pre-defined universe as, for example, all adults in the population of the United States, or all students attending the nation's colleges and universities, or all clientele over a designated period of a social welfare agency. Representativeness might be secured by drawing a sample of this universe, or by collecting data from or about all members of that universe. There is implicit agreement that the data must be available in a form to allow primary manipulation by the analyst. The manipulation of published data as available, for example, in census reports, would not be included as survey research, but rather consigned to demographic analysis.

Little attention is given to collecting data from non-representative samples but, in some chapters, the possibility is considered of over-representing certain categories of subjects in order to include them in sufficient numbers for analysis. It is also recognized that studies which are primarily concerned with relationships between variables rather than with projecting findings descriptively to a pre-defined universe might be desirable and necessary under certain conditions. Such exceptions, however, are rare. By and large, the view which dominates most of the chapters is that survey research is concerned with data collected from a sample of a pre-defined universe.

Whether respondents to surveys are to be viewed as subjects and/or informants is also not dealt with explicitly in most chapters. Most frequently, the respondent is conceived of as a subject rather than an informant. It can be assumed, however, that no author would rule out using respondents as informants and this is recognized explicitly in some chapters.

The authors would impose no restrictions on how the data are collected. The data collection method most commonly assumed is the personal interview. However, collecting data by sending questionnaires through the mails, or by telephone interviews, would be countenanced. Indeed, there is no requirement that questionnaires be used at all; standardized information collected by other methods as, for example, examining records, would be equally acceptable.

By standardized information, the authors have in mind that questions, if a questionnaire is used, be uniformly asked of all subjects. No author would limit the form of the question, closed and open-ended questions being equally acceptable. It is assumed, however, that responses to open-ended questions would be quantified through coding before analysis. Branch questions which call for a response only under special conditions as, for example, when a question is relevant only to male respondents, are also permissible so long as all respondents meeting the special condition are asked the question.

The authors uniformly avoid such technical questions as means for dealing with non-responses, standards of coding, and modes of data processing. Here, the common assumption is that such matters are treated adequately in the technical literature and are not the concern of the present volume. Nevertheless, the authors proceed presuming that technical standards are necessarily to be met.

It is at the analytical level, perhaps, that differences in the perspectives of different disciplines are most in evidence. The differences are not, however, to be understood as stemming from disagreement about survey analysis *per se*. Rather, they arise primarily because of differences in the kinds of analytical questions asked. In chapter 1, a distinction is made between survey analysis directed to answering descriptive questions, what may be called correlational questions, and explanatory questions.

Descriptive questions ask simply about the distribution of some datum in a population or among subgroups of a population. Here, the analyst's concern is simply to describe a distribution or to make comparisons between distributions—for example, to learn how respondents answered a question on birth control and to compare the responses of men and women. Analysis stimulated by descriptive questions is meant to ascertain facts, not to test theory.

Correlational questions, unlike descriptive ones, ask about the relations between variables and do so from a theoretically-grounded expectation as to why the variables ought to be related. The theory, however, does not include an element of cause and effect. Rather, it is assumed that the variables ought to be related because they are each a component of some larger entity. Thus, for example, it may be assumed that verbal and mechanical ability will be correlated because they are both components of a larger phenomenon—intelligence. Correlational questions, as this example illustrates, are primarily raised in analysis at the point of concept and index formation.

Explanatory questions, like correlational ones, ask about the relation between variables; but unlike correlational questions, the informing theory suggests that the reason for the relation is that one variable is causally related to another—for example, in political science, the hypothesis that political ideology is a determinant of voting behavior. Explanatory questions may extend not only to establishing the existence of a causal relation but also to asking why the relationship exists.

Survey analysis, all authors implicitly agree, may be pursued to answer all three kinds of questions. The authors differ, however, in how much emphasis they give to the three questions in their review of survey applications in their own fields. Except in chapter 1, little explicit attention is given to the use of survey data to answer correlational type questions, i.e. in concept and index formation, though this would have been a relevant topic in all disciplines. As between descriptive and explanatory questions, the latter tend to be emphasized but the chapters vary in how far the explanatory questions raised are pursued. And, in some chapters, notably anthropology and social welfare, descriptive questions tend to be highlighted.

These differences in emphasis reflect, in part, basic differences in the research orientations of the various fields. For example, whether they use survey methods or not, anthropologists are inherently more interested in description than are other social scientists. The chapters also reflect the aforementioned differences in the extent to which the logic of survey analysis has permeated different fields. From the reader's point of view, by keeping in mind the purposes to which surveys may be put, these differences in emphasis should pose no problem. Indeed, by highlighting the variety and richness of survey analysis, they heighten the rewards to be gained by peering into the other fellow's back yard.

Survey Design and Analysis in

Sociology

by Charles Y. Glock
Survey Research Center
University of California
Berkeley

Survey Design and Analysis in Sociology*

As THIS volume attests, survey research has now become a major tool of empirical research in all of the social sciences. No discipline can claim credit for this. Contributions to the development of survey methods have come from many quarters. Yet, defining sociology broadly, there is no other discipline that has adopted survey methods as enthusiastically or used them as extensively. As a result, it is possible to exemplify from sociological applications of survey methods almost the full range of variations in the ways that surveys have been designed and that survey data have been analyzed. Beginning the book with the chapter on sociology, therefore, allows the accomplishment of two tasks—to review and evaluate the uses, both present and potential, of survey methods explicitly in sociological research, and also to introduce the reader more generally to what survey research is all about.

The strategy that has been adopted to organize the chapter is to attempt to codify the uses to which surveys may be put in sociological research within what are considered to be the principal variations in survey designs. The chapter moves progressively from simple to more complex designs, pausing at each point to delineate both abstractly and through examples the kinds of questions which each design has answered or may potentially answer. No attempt has been made to be comprehensive about including and commenting upon all of the surveys that have been conducted by sociologists. The chapter is intended, however, to be reasonably exhaustive in its coverage of types of design and their uses and to illustrate them by appropriate reference to the sociological literature.

It is to be further noted that the chapter is concerned primarily with setting forth the elementary logic of survey design and survey analysis; problems of sampling, of instrument construction, of data collection and processing, and, indeed, of the advanced use of statistics in analysis, have been,

* This chapter is dedicated to the many persons whose ideas and work it summarizes. I was immensely helped in the organization of the chapter by Hanan Selvin, Martin Trow, and William L. Nicholls. Earl Babbie, Rodney Stark, Stephen Steinberg, and Paul Wong offered constructive criticism along the way. I also owe a debt to Robert Wenkert for editorial assistance.

relatively speaking, ignored. This emphasis was chosen, in part, because there exists an adequate literature on these latter problems, reference to which is made at appropriate points along the way. Mostly, however, it was chosen because it seemed the better way to meet the primary purpose of this volume, namely, to demonstrate the potential of survey research in social inquiry.[1]

The design of a survey is inextricably linked to the analytical operations which are to be performed and which, in turn, are a function of the investigator's purposes. Generally speaking, sociologists use surveys with one or both of two purposes in mind.[2] They may be interested in what we shall call *description,* in finding out how one or more characteristics are distributed in a population, as for example, to learn the distribution of broken homes in the population of a community, or of the response to a political crisis on a university campus of students and faculty, or of attitudes toward matters of governmental policy in the national U.S. population. Rather than description, the goal may be *explanation*—to find out why a distribution takes the form that it does. What makes for broken homes? What accounts for the support and opposition which a political movement on campus generates? What brings about favorable and unfavorable attitudes toward government policy? A sociologist may have only one of these two kinds of purposes in mind as he plans his inquiry, or he may be interested in serving both simultaneously; for example, he may want to learn both how students and faculty feel and why they feel the way they do.

Descriptive and explanatory purposes of surveys may be further distinguished according to whether they include or exclude the element of change.

Thus, existing survey designs in sociology can be meaningfully catalogued according to whether their purpose is description and/or explanation, and according to whether or not they include an interest in change. This cataloguing forms the basis for this chapter's organization.

Static designs are discussed first; those invented to deal with change presented second. Within static designs, initial attention is given to one—

1. In the existing literature, the most comprehensive statement on logical problems in survey design and analysis is contained in Hyman, H. H., *Survey Design and Analysis: Principles, Cases and Procedures.* Free Press, Chicago, 1955. This work has not been revised since its initial publication. Yet, though now over ten years old, it continues to be the standard reference work in the field.
2. A third purpose—answering correlational questions—was mentioned in the Introduction. This purpose is seldom the ground for launching a survey, but will be treated later in the chapter.

the cross-sectional survey—which is capable of serving both descriptive and explanatory purposes simultaneously. Then variations on this design, generated to meet more specialized descriptive or explanatory conditions, are presented. In the subsequent discussion of designs geared to studying change, two designs—trend and panel—are described.

The Cross-sectional Survey: The Basic Survey Design

The earliest and still most commonly used design in survey research is one which involves the collection of standardized information from or about a sample chosen to represent the component units of a pre-defined universe.[3] This design, as all survey designs, allows for variation in the form of the instrument used, in the method of its administration, in the mode of sampling, in the definition of the universe, and in the unit of analysis. So long, however, as the design meets the criteria of collecting standardized information from or about a sample representative of a universe, it falls within that category of design which we shall call the basic survey design.

This design is popularly illustrated by the Gallup poll. Here, the universe is defined ordinarily as all Americans of voting age. The instrument is a questionnaire administered through personal interviews with a probability sample of that universe. The unit of analysis is the person. The basic survey design, however, does not require that the universe constitute a population of people. It may be a population of groups or of organizations or of communities; for example, all formally constituted fraternities on American college campuses, all American corporations employing 500 or more persons, or all communities with a population of 5,000 or more. Where the universe is defined in such terms, the unit of analysis is defined in parallel terms, with the group, the organization, or the community becoming the focus of analysis rather than the person.

Standardized information may be collected, as in the Gallup poll, by personal interview. The basic survey design also allows for the collection of data through other means—through questionnaires sent through the mail, through interviewing people over the telephone, or through retrieving data from records.

Finally, respondents in a survey employing the basic design may serve as

3. Or from and/or about all of the component units of a pre-defined universe. The latter, of course, constitutes a census. However, because census data is subject to the same kind of analysis as sample survey data, censuses might appropriately be included in this definition of the basic survey design.

subjects, supplying information only about themselves; as informants, furnishing information about entities with which they are familiar (for example, about the organizations which employ them or the groups to which they belong); or as both, supplying a combination of information about themselves and about relevant contexts.

Most commonly, though not uniquely, the unit of analysis in surveys using the basic design is the person. This is not because the design is any the less suited for studying larger entities. The use of surveys for such purposes is less well developed, however, and on the occasions where larger entities than the person have been studied, the definition of the problem has frequently required some variation from the basic survey design. What these variations have been in the sociological use of surveys will be reported later.

The data which are produced by a survey comprise the answers to the questions which the subjects of the survey have been asked, or which have been collected through secondary sources. These questions may all refer to one point in time, for example, the present. More typically, however, the questions asked vary with respect to the point in time to which they refer. Some will ask about the present, some about the immediate past, still others about the distant past; and in some instances, questions may be asked about anticipated behavior or events. It is usually not possible to decide unequivocally the time order of the various bits of information collected in a cross-sectional survey. To take a simple example: if a survey collects data both about general attitudes toward the President of the United States and about specific attitudes to current policies which he is pursuing, it would be difficult to decide which came first—the general or the more specific attitudes. The logic of survey analysis, however, has been developed in large measure on the assumption that the time order of data can be established. For didactic purposes, we shall assume that time order is known in the first part of our discussion. Later we shall return to the problem of what may be done when time order cannot be established.

Making this assumption, then, the data produced by a typical cross-sectional survey constitute the answers to a uniform and time-orderable series of questions asked of a sample of a pre-defined universe of subjects. Chart 1 depicts these data symbolically with the numbers heading each column representing the time dimension (point in time) of the information represented by the letters falling under them. The letters, then, each represent a different question asked in a survey. Thus, all questions symbolized by the designation A are of the same time order—*1*—which is the earliest

CHART 1

SYMBOLIC REPRESENTATION OF THE DATA
PRODUCED BY A CROSS-SECTIONAL SURVEY

Time Dimension

Questions	*1*	*2*	*3*	*4*	*5*
	A	B	C	D	E
	A_1	B_1	C_1	D_1	E_1
	A_2	B_2	C_2	D_2	E_2
	A_3	B_3	C_3	D_3	E_3
	etc.	etc.	etc.	etc.	etc.

time order about which data have been collected. At the opposite extreme, all questions symbolized by the designation E fall into the fifth time dimension—which is the latest point in time about which data were collected.

Given a body of data of this kind, three basic statistical operations can be performed on them. First, the distribution of the subjects' answers to each individual question can be tabulated. Two, distributions of answers to questions located at the same point in time can be related to each other. Three, distributions of answers to questions located in different time dimensions can be related to each other. We shall call the first of these statistical operations *marginal tabulations,* the second *time-bound association,* and the third *time-ordered association.* Within these three statistical operations, the basic uses of cross-sectional survey data can be ordered and illustrated.

MARGINAL TABULATIONS

The simplest way in which survey data can be used is to discover how the subjects are distributed in their answers to each question. Such distributions, called the marginals, report how many of the subjects chose each of the possible answers to a question. If, for example, "E" represents a question asking subjects whether or not they support the United Nations, the marginal tabulation would show how many subjects support the U.N., how many oppose it, and how many have no opinion. Where the survey has used an "area" or "probability" sample, inferences with a desired level of precision can be made from discovered distributions in the sample to actual distributions in the population from which it is drawn.[4]

4. See Stephan, F. F. and P. J. McCarthy, *Sampling Opinions:* An Analysis of Survey Procedure. John Wiley & Sons, New York, 1958; and Kish, Leslie, *Survey Sampling.* John Wiley & Sons, New York, 1965: for useful discussions of sampling theory and practice in survey research.

It is highly unlikely that a sociological survey would be undertaken only to produce purely descriptive information on how one or more variables are distributed in a population. Such information, a by-product of cross-sectional surveys, is nevertheless useful in building basic knowledge of population characteristics over and above those produced by censuses. Moreover, such data accumulated in successive surveys conducted at different points in time are grist for the mill of the sociologist who is concerned with documenting changes in social attitudes or beliefs or in social characteristics. Among contemporary sociologists, Lipset, Hyman and Sheatsley have made particularly good use of comparing marginal data from different surveys of the national population of the United States to point to changing trends in American life.[5] Hyman and Sheatsley, for example, have recently used such data to document shifts in the attitudes of white Americans toward Negro Americans. Marginal data is also essential in helping to decide what data to interrelate in further analysis. By and large, however, collecting marginal data is never the primary *raison d'etre* for conducting a sociological survey. Invariably, the objectives transcend these purely descriptive functions which a survey can serve.

TIME-BOUND ASSOCIATION

Analysis *per se* of survey data begins when advantage is taken of the possibility of relating the distributions of answers to one question to the distribution of answers to one or more other questions. The purposes served, however, are drastically different when the two or more datum being related are in the same time dimension than when they are time-orderable. As mentioned above, we shall call analysis of the first kind time-bound association and analysis of the second time-ordered association.[6]

Referring back to Chart 1, time-bound association is that analytical step which involves examination of the joint distribution of answers to two or more questions within a column but not between columns. Thus, relating the distribution of answers to question C to the answers to question C_2 would be time-bound association; relating the answers to question C_2 to the answers to question D would not. The crucial attribute of time-bound association, then, is that the data being related are of the same time order.

5. Lipset, S. M., *Political Man:* The Social Bases of Politics. Doubleday, New York, 1960; Hyman, H. H. and P. B. Sheatsley, "Attitudes Toward Desegregation," *Scientific American*, Vol. 211, July, 1964, pp. 16–23.
6. The correlational type questions referred to in the Introduction are pursued through time-bound association.

In practice, this means that it can be established or reasonably inferred that one variable is in the same time dimension as another.

The hypotheses, or if you will, intimations which motivate a sociologist to engage in time-bound association are to be sharply distinguished from those which motivate time-ordered association. The latter, explicitly or implicitly, assumes a causal connection between the variables being examined—that the distribution of answers to one question is in some way and to some degree caused by the distribution of answers to another question. The hypotheses which inform time-bound association have a quite different quality and may take one of two different forms. One form postulates an association between variables because they are each thought to be measures or indicators of the same phenomenon. The second assumes that the phenomena being measured by two or more variables are different, but postulates that the occurrence of one is likely to be accompanied by the occurrence of one or more others. In both cases, however, no inference is made that the distribution on one variable is causally related to the distribution on another.

Time-bound association is principally engaged in by sociologists in that part of the analytic process which requires the operationalization of concepts—the construction of scales, indices, and typologies.[7] It is possible in survey analysis to rely on the answers to a single question as a satisfactory way to operationalize a concept. On occasion, for example, sociologists have been known to rely on a question asking a subject's occupation to classify his socio-economic status. Or, answers to a single question asking the subject's opinion on governmental control of business might be used to classify subjects as liberal or conservative.

Generally, however, it is not considered particularly reliable or valid to use only one indicator to operationalize a concept. In the interests of precision, a more satisfactory procedure is to combine the answers to a number of questions to form a scale or typology. In such instances, it is hypothesized that the answers to several or more questions are each indicators of the same underlying concept and may be appropriately combined to form a

7. For a general discussion of the principles of concept and index formation, see Lazarsfeld, P. F. and Morris Rosenberg, eds., *The Language of Social Research: A Reader in the Methodology of Social Research.* Free Press, Glencoe, Ill., 1955, particularly pp. 15–108; Boudon, Raymond and P. F. Lazarsfeld, *Le Vocabulaire Des Sciences Sociales:* Concepts et Indices. Mouton, Paris, 1965; and Hempel, C. G., "Classification." Chapter in *Fundamentals of Concept Formation in Empirical Science.* University of Chicago Press, Chicago, 1952.

summary measure of that concept. The procedure used to test the hypothesis may range from simple cross-tabulation to elaborate factor analysis
or latent structure analysis of the variables involved.[8] However sophisticated the procedure, the analytic operation is time-bound not time-ordered
association. No causal connection between the variables being examined is
inferred or assumed.

Sociologists rarely, if ever, undertake a survey for the express and exclusive purpose of operationalizing a concept. The construction of scales,
indices, and typologies is a step taken in preparation for time-ordered association. They provide, in effect, more refined independent and dependent
variables for time-ordered analysis than do the answers to individual questions.

The number of scales, indices, and typologies which may be generated
in analysis will vary with investigator, with subject matter, and with the
character of the inquiry. Some analyses make very little use of such summary measures, relying primarily on responses to individual questions.
Other studies base most of the analysis on such more refined measures. The
point made here, however, is that the construction of refined measures constitutes one of the uses of time-bound association.

The consequence of time-bound association of this kind for Chart 1 is
to change its character somewhat. Answers to individual questions remain,
of course, for possible use in time-ordered association. However, the step
of time-bound association will have contributed additional data in the form
of new variables at all or some time dimensions. Chart 2 is a revision of
Chart 1, adding the variables produced by time-bound association. As in
Chart 1, the unitary symbols (A, A_1, A_2, B, B_1, etc.) represent the responses
to individual questions asked in a survey, arranged according to their respective time orders. The compounded symbols (AA_3, $B_1B_2B_5$, etc.) each
represent a scale, index, or typology produced by the step of time-bound
association. Thus, AA_3 may be a measure of social class, and EE_4E_5 a
measure of political liberalism. Note that the number of summary measures

8. On factor analysis, see Thurstone, L. L., *Multiple-Factor Analysis*. University of
Chicago Press, Chicago, 1947, and Harman, Harry H., *Modern Factor Analysis*. Uni-
versity of Chicago Press, Chicago, 1960. On latent structure analysis, see Lazarsfeld,
P. F., "A Conceptual Introduction to Latent Structure Analysis," in *Mathematical
Thinking in the Social Sciences*. Edited by P. F. Lazarsfeld. Free Press, Chicago, Ill.,
1954, pp. 347–387, and Lazarsfeld, P. F., "Latent Structure Analysis." In *Psychology,
A Study of a Science, Conceptual and Systematic*. Edited by Sigmund Koch. McGraw-
Hill, New York, 1959, pp. 476–573.

CHART 2

SYMBOLIC REPRESENTATION OF THE DATA
PRODUCED BY A CROSS-SECTIONAL SURVEY
AFTER THE STEP OF TIME-BOUND ASSOCIATION

Data in the form of:	*Time Dimension*				
	1	*2*	*3*	*4*	*5*
Questions (as in Chart 1)	A	B	C	D	E
	A_1	B_1	C_1	D_1	E_1
	A_2	B_2	C_2	D_2	E_2
	A_3	B_3	C_3	D_3	E_3
	etc.	etc.	etc.	etc.	etc.
Scales, Indices and	(AA_3)	$(B_1B_2B_5)$	(CC_1)	(DD_2)	(EE_4E_5)
Typologies (as produced					
by time-bound association)	(A_2A_4)	(B_6B_8)	$(C_2C_3C_4)$	$(D_2D_6D_7)$	(E_1E_8)
	etc.	etc.	etc.	etc.	etc.

produced within each time dimension may be none, one, or several, depending in actual practice on the nature of the survey. However, not all individual questions need contribute to the construction of a summary measure.

A second use of time-bound association is to determine whether two or more variables *measuring different phenomena* tend to co-vary. To be subsumed under analysis of this kind are (1) conditions where it is relatively clear that the variables under consideration are on the same dimension, and (2) situations where the variables may in reality be time-ordered, but there is no way for the investigator to determine what that time order is. In both cases, the analytical step does no more than establish the extent of a descriptive relation between the variables. Since the variables, by definition, are neither time-ordered nor time-orderable, no possible causal connection exists or can be decided.

Time-bound association of this kind is practiced much more frequently where the time order of variables is ambiguous than where it is clear that their time order is the same. This is because there are very few instances where it can be established, using cross-sectional survey data, that the time order of variables measuring different phenomena are precisely on the same time dimension. To illustrate the ambiguous situation: an investigator has collected information on his subjects' attitudes toward Negroes and on the amount of their social contact with Negroes, and wishes now to assess whether or not attitudes are improved with greater social contact. If his data have been collected in a cross-sectional survey, this assessment may not be possible because of the ambiguity of the time order of the two measurements. The best that the investigator can do, under the circumstances, is to determine how the two measures co-vary, in effect, to engage in time-bound association. He is then placed in a position to say how much co-variation exists. He cannot, however, establish that one factor led to the other, or vice versa.

While it is often impossible to undertake time-ordered association using cross-sectional survey data, the kind of time-bound association just described can nevertheless be highly useful in research. Given the practical difficulties of undertaking longitudinal or panel studies (see pp. 50–57) which constitute the most effective means for resolving the time-order problem, the cross-sectional survey becomes a useful device for deciding whether a panel study would be worth the effort. In the case illustrated, a finding that there is absolutely no relation between contact and attitude, though important information in its own right, would hardly justify a panel study on the topic. On the other hand, to find a high degree of co-variation would not only be useful knowledge but would in addition justify taking additional steps to establish the time order correctly.

All of which is to say that time-bound association of this second kind is frequently the refuge which users of cross-sectional surveys must take because the time order of the variables under examination cannot be established.

TIME-ORDERED ASSOCIATION

Once analysis turns to examining the association between variables which are temporally ordered relative to each other, there is an imputation—sometimes manifest, sometimes latent—of a causal connection between them. That is to say, the analysis assumes explicitly or implicitly that the distribution of answers on one question or scale (the dependent variable) can in some way and to some degree be accounted for by the distribution of answers to another question or scale (the independent variable).[9]

Referring to Chart 2, time-ordered association involves examining the relation between variables located at different time dimensions. Relating

9. Many sociological analyses do not make explicit whether a causal connection between two variables is being asserted or not. It is suggested, however, that such an assertion is implied where the variables whose association is being examined are of different time orders. See discussion of "differentiated description" below.

the distribution on C to the distribution on C_3 would be time-bound association in these terms, whereas relating variables located at different horizontal points across the chart would be time-ordered association.

In time-ordered association, the investigator is obliged to establish which of the variables he is considering are to be treated as dependent and which are to be treated as independent. Independency or dependency are not inherent or fixed properties of variables. Rather, they are properties determined by the use made of a given variable in analysis—by whether it is earlier or later in time order than the variable(s) to which it is related. Thus, a given variable would be defined as dependent when it is related to other variables of an earlier time order. These other variables would be independent variables. The dependent variable in one relationship, however, may become an independent variable in another when the new variable to which it is related is of a later time order.

The purposes and design of a study place limitations, of course, on how different variables may be used in time-ordered association. A study done in the model represented by Chart 2 would allow variables of time order *1* to be treated independently only. This is because no data of an earlier time order were collected. Similarly, variables of time order *5* could only be treated dependently since they are at the latest time order for which data were collected. Because they are intermediate, variables of time orders *2, 3,* and *4* can be treated both independently and dependently. Variables of time order *2,* for example, would be dependent variables when they are related to variables of time order *1.* In turn, they would be independent variables when they are related to variables of a later time order—*3, 4,* or *5.* Chart 3 summarizes how variables at each of the points in time depicted in Chart 2 may be treated relative to variables at each other point in time.

The form which time-ordered association may take when the data have been collected using the cross-sectional survey design will depend on the investigator's purposes; on whether or not he has a hypothesis to test and, if so, on whether it is formulated in advance or *ex post facto* as the analysis proceeds. It will also depend on how well he can establish the time order of the variables he is examining.

From among the possible variations, two basic uses of time-ordered association may be distinguished. The first of these, what we shall call differentiated description, uses time-ordered association simply in order to see how different subgroups in a sample are distributed on another variable. While the variables examined are on different time dimensions, the analysis is not pursued to test a hypothesis. Rather, having seen how his total

CHART 3

THE TIME ORDER OF VARIABLES DETERMINES THEIR USE
AS INDEPENDENT AND/OR DEPENDENT VARIABLES IN ANALYSIS[a]

		Designation of Variables of Time Order				
		1	*2*	*3*	*4*	*5*
When they are related	*1*	X	D	D	D	D
to variables of time order	*2*	I	X	D	D	D
	3	I	I	X	D	D
	4	I	I	I	X	D
	5	I	I	I	I	X

[a] Variables of the time order heading each column vary with respect to whether they may be treated as independent, dependent, or neither, according to the time order of variables to which they are related. Where they are related to variables of an earlier time order, they are dependent. They are independent where the variables to which they are related are of a later time order. They are neither independent nor dependent when the time order of the related variables is the same.

X signifies that only time-bound association is possible because the variables being related are of the same time order; no identification of variables as being independent or dependent is warranted.

I = Independent variable.
D = Dependent variable.

sample is distributed on a variable, the analyst, more often routinely than purposively, looks further to see how the distribution varies among subdivisions of the sample. Frequently, this involves the production of *stratified marginals*—the distribution of responses to all questions asked on a survey broken down by standard demographic factors, e.g., age, sex, income, and education. Differentiated description of this kind may be an initial step to explanatory analysis, or it may be an end in itself. In either case, however, it is different from time-ordered association pursued for explanatory purposes. There, the analytical goal is not only to discover the strength of a relation, but to learn what brought it about, i.e., to explain it. Unlike differentiated description, *explanation* is explicitly grounded in theory, and research is designed and analysis pursued to test it.

Because analysts do not make explicit what their analytical purposes are, or because they are themselves not cognizant of the alternatives, it is not always possible to distinguish clearly between differentiated description and explanation. For example, analysis sometimes goes beyond differentiated description to enter into explanation, but stops short of completing the process. Despite the ambiguities in practice, it is nevertheless useful to distinguish the two uses of time-ordered association in formal terms.

Differentiated description is most clearly illustrated by the kinds of tabulations which characterize census reports.[10] A usual pattern in such reports is to first present marginal tabulations, for example, the distribution of the population at issue by sex, by age, by size of family, by ethnic background, and the like. Such simple marginal tabulations are then usually followed by cross-tabulations showing how the marginal distributions vary for different subgroups. Thus, a census report may first show an age pyramid for the population as a whole and then go on to depict its form for women as compared to men, or a table presenting a breakdown of the ethnic composition of the national population will be followed by another one showing how the breakdown varies for different regions of the country. The variables used to make such comparisons are chosen because the census people feel that they will be of interest and use to their clientele, not because they are explicitly concerned with testing a hypothesis. Implicitly, however, the choice is likely to be influenced by theoretical considerations, however vaguely defined. Thus, age pyramids for men and women are compared because it is believed that sex will produce a meaningful difference. No such tabulations are presented for people with blue, brown, and grey eyes because there is no reason to presume that eye color would make a meaningful difference.

Like census data, the data produced by a cross-sectional survey lend themselves to differentiated description. The range of variables on which comparisons can be made is usually wide indeed, and is limited only by the necessity that the variables to be used in subgroup comparisons are represented in adequate numbers in the sample.

Differentiated description is a form of social bookkeeping which is of major importance in sociology, and many sociological surveys have no aim other than this. One significant function of such surveys is to substitute fact for fancy. All sorts of images prevail in popular folklore about the values, beliefs, attitudes, and behavioral patterns of different groups. Surveys provide a means to check on such images, to refine them if they are true, and to refute them if they are not. Knowledge of what particular publics are like, how different social classes vary in social attitudes and behavior, what it means to be well or poorly educated or an older or younger person, and so

10. Census data may, of course, be subjected to the same kind of analysis as sample survey data.

forth, has been largely contributed to by sociological surveys which have gone no further analytically than differentiated description.[11]

Surveys of this kind are also an important tool in applied sociological studies. Efforts at public education can be more effectively guided, for example, if one knows beforehand what the existing level of information and understanding is among different segments of the public. Schools can be more effectively planned if it is known whether the number of pre-school children in a community is increasing or declining. Such information is useful irrespective of whether or not fluctuations in the level of information can be explained or changes in the number of pre-school children can be accounted for.

Sociologists disagree among themselves as to the appropriateness of engaging in research to the end of social criticism. For those who do, however, information gained from analyzing survey data to the point of differentiated description is often relevant to their purposes. Social criticism of contemporary mass media, for example, is supported, in part, by survey data on the characteristics of audiences.[12] Similarly, criticism of America's Viet Nam policies has been based, in part, on results of a survey demonstrating that superficial evidence of support for such policies was not confirmed by a more careful assessment of public opinion.[13]

Finally, it is important to note that it is at the point of differentiated description that the theoretical and explanatory functions of survey research are first manifested. Differentiated description, whenever it reveals differences among subgroups, almost inevitably stimulates the question of why this should be so. Why, for example, should air corps officers be more dissatisfied with the Army's promotion system during World War II than officers in the military police? Why should tolerance for non-conformity be greater among the more than the less educated? Why should church-goers exhibit more prejudice toward minority groups than non-church goers?

Many sociological surveys aim only at description, whether simple or differentiated. Most, however, have a theoretical and explanatory purpose in mind. The cross-sectional survey design lends itself to pursuing explana-

11. Among studies built wholly or in large part on differentiated description are Havemann, Ernest and P. S. West, *They Went to College*. Harcourt, Brace, New York, 1952; Steiner, G. A., *The People Look at Television:* A Study of Audience Attitudes. Alfred A. Knopf, New York, 1963; and Gurin, Gerald, *et. al., Americans View Their Mental Health:* A Nationwide Interview Survey. Basic Books, New York, 1960.

12. Steiner, G. A., *op. cit.;* Lazarsfeld, P. F. and P. L. Kendall, *Radio Listening in America:* The People Look at Radio—Again. Prentice-Hall, New York, 1948.

13. *New York Times,* March 15, 1966, p. 1, col. 6.

tory analysis to a variety of ends—presuming, of course, that the appropriate data have been collected.

Reviewing the literature, sociologists turn to using surveys when they confront the following types of theoretical problems.[14] Note that the first three problems on the list focus on the relation between only two variables, while the others are concerned with more complicated relationships; also note that a survey analysis may be concerned exclusively with one of these problems or may confront a combination of them simultaneously:—

1. Testing a hypothesis that two variables are "causally" related.
2. Understanding the process which produces a relation between two variables.
3. Specifying the conditions that maximize or minimize a relationship.
4. Accounting for the "total" distribution on a dependent variable.
5. Following out the implications of the distribution on an independent variable.
6. Exploring the causes and the consequences of the distribution on a variable.[15]

Testing a hypothesis that two variables are "causally" related.[16] A hypothe-

14. The following discussion of the analytical operations performed to deal with the first three problems is based largely on Hyman, H. H., *Survey Design and Analysis, op. cit.,* particularly chapter 7. The notion of *replication* is not included in Hyman's discussion. It was suggested to the author by Hanan Selvin. The discussion of the last three problems has been contributed to by William Nicholls, Hanan Selvin, and Martin Trow, all of whom have shared responsibility with the author in teaching a graduate methods course at the University of California (Berkeley). The labeling of the analytical strategies discussed—accounting studies, implications studies, and phenomenon studies—is attributable to Trow.

15. These theoretical problems do not call necessarily for a cross-sectional design. However, that design does lend itself to pursuing these problems analytically and in the present context, to an exposition of the elementary logic of analysis. With minor modifications to be noted, this logic is also applicable to other designs which call for the collection of data at one point in time. Greater modification is required when the design provides for the collection of data at more than one point in time—as will also be noted in the later discussion.

16. It is not possible, as will be discussed, to prove a causal relation between two variables using survey data. The most that can be done is to establish that a relation between two variables is not explained away by any known antecedent variable. There is always the possibility that an antecedent variable or set of variables may be subsequently found to explain away the relationship. The word "causal" is used in the present discussion to convey the thrust of the kind of analyses described rather than what is possible of achievement.

sis that two variables are causally related is of the kind that ordinarily informs experiments. When such a hypothesis informs the analysis of survey data, it must first be established that there is what we shall call a descriptive relation between the two variables. Referring to Chart 2 (p. 11), assume that the two variables in question are C and E, with the former, by reason of its earlier time order, being defined as the independent and the latter as the dependent variable. Further assume that relating C to E produces a positive result: E occurs more frequently when C is present than when it is absent.

At this stage in an experiment, the relationship between C and E would be assumed to be both descriptively *and* causally true.[17] That is to say, it is descriptively true, presuming that C and E are both dichotomous, that E occurs more frequently among subjects possessing attribute C than among those without this attribute. In an experiment, the relationship is also thought to be causal because the design of the experiment—random assignment to experimental and control groups—strongly limits the possibility that the relationship may be spurious.

Such is not the case in survey analysis because of the absence of experimental and control groups. In a survey, two variables which are found to be descriptively related may or may not be causally related. In his efforts to determine whether or not the relationship is also causal—or, more appropriately, to establish that the relationship is *not* spurious—the survey analyst looks for variables *antecedent* to both C and E which might explain away the original relation. Within the limits set by our chart, the antecedent variables which he may consider are limited to those falling under time orders *1* and *2*. Individually or in combination, these variables may be introduced to determine what effect they have on the original relation.

The result of this procedure may be *explanation* or *replication*. Explanation occurs when an antecedent third variable *explains away* the original relation. Replication occurs when the original relation is *repeated* when the third variable is taken into account. If the relation between C and E is explained by, let us say, A, the statistical result will be that the original relation disappears in what are called the partial tables. Such a result is de-

17. In the sense of leaving absolutely no room for doubt, even an experiment cannot prove causality. It can, however, come closer to that goal than a survey. For an excellent introduction to problems of causal inference, see Blalock, H. M., Jr., *Causal Inferences in Nonexperimental Research.* University of North Carolina Press, Chapel Hill, 1964.

TABLE 1

A EXPLAINS THE RELATION BETWEEN C AND E

	Original Relation			*Partial Relations*			
				A		Ā	
	C	C̄		C	C̄	C	C̄
E	65%	50%	=	70%	70%	40%	40%
Ē	35	50	+	30	30	60	60
	100%	100%		100%	100%	100%	100%
	(600)	(600)		(500)	(200)	(100)	(400)

picted hypothetically in Table 1.[18] Note that in the original relation, subjects possessing attribute C are more likely to be E than those without this attribute. In the partial tables, however, the relationship disappears. Under condition A, and under condition Ā, E occurs as frequently among C̄ as among C.

What this result tells the analyst, in effect, is that the original relation between C and E is spurious—that the distribution on both C and E is produced by the antecedent factor A.[19] C and E are indeed descriptively related; they are not, however, causally related.

18. This example is an ideal typical one in that the test factor (the variable, in this case A, introduced into the original relation) completely explains the original relationship away. In actual practice, such total explanation occurs only infrequently. The more typical pattern is for the strength of the relation to be reduced in the partials indicating that the original relation is explained in part by the test factor.

19. It is to be noted that Hyman, H. H., in *Survey Design . . . , op. cit.,* pp. 254–260 suggests that results as depicted in Table 1 may be interpretable as a developmental configuration or sequence rather than as spuriousness. The distinction between spuriousness and developmental sequence, according to Hyman, cannot be decided on statistical grounds but requires an interpretation of the qualitative relationship between the test factor and the independent variable. The idea of a developmental configuration can best be conveyed perhaps by an example.

A common illustration of spuriousness is to cite the high positive correlation between the number of fire engines at the scene of a fire and the amount of damage done by the blaze. Knowledge of such a correlation, taken at face value, may suggest that fire engines cause damage; hence, the more trucks, the worse for the property owner. Obviously, however, these two phenomena are highly related because each is caused by the same variable, so far unmentioned—the size of the fire. Statistically, the original positive correlation between the number of trucks and the amount of damage

Analysis whose aim is to test the hypothesis that C and E are causally related would be discontinued at this point. The hypothesis has been shown to be false and there would be no purpose in proceeding further in exploring the relation between C and E. The analyst may, of course, shift his analytical question and go on to assess the causality of the relation between A and C and A and E. The character of such further elaboration will occupy our attention later.

"Confirmation" of a hypothesis that two variables are causally related occurs when replication is the result of introducing a third variable into the original relation.[20] Here, the statistical result is that the original relation is more or less repeated in the partials (Table 2). Under both condition A and condition Ā, a relation between C and E persists.

What this result tells us, of course, is only that A does not explain away the relation between C and E. It does not guarantee that C and E are causally related. Actually, there is no way with survey data, or with any

---

disappears (or is reversed) when size of the fire is introduced as a test factor and controlled.

In this example, it is true that the number of fire trucks is not a cause of the amount of damage and, in this sense, the original relation is spurious. At the same time, how many fire engines go to a fire is part of a developmental sequence which begins with the size of the fire. Hyman would restrict spuriousness to apply only where an antecedent test factor is not an *intrinsic* part of the developmental sequence essential to the distribution on the independent variable. Thus, in his terms, the fire truck example illustrates a developmental sequence, not spuriousness. Spuriousness would occur, presumably, if a factor like the average age of firemen "explained" both how many fire engines went to a fire and how much damage was produced.

Hyman makes a useful contribution in introducing the concept of developmental configuration. However, he does not clearly establish that there are cases where spuriousness can occur independently of a developmental configuration. Thus, if it were the average age of firemen which explained both the number of fire trucks and the amount of damage, this would have to be because the age of firemen has something to do with the number of trucks sent to the fire.

While the issue warrants further study, we shall, for present purposes, assume that spuriousness is indeed established by a result such as that presented in Table 1, in the sense that it demonstrates that C is not a cause of E. Whether or not a developmental configuration is also present we shall leave to the reader to decide, offering, however, the assertion—still to be confirmed—that a developmental configuration is always present in the sense that Hyman defines it.

20. "Confirmation" in the sense only that the original relation is not explained away by the particular test factor introduced. The possibility that other test factors may prove the original relation to be spurious remains.

TABLE 2

THE RELATION BETWEEN C AND E IS REPLICATED
UNDER CONDITION A

	Original Relation			Partial Relations			
				A		Ā	
	C	C̄		C	C̄	C	C̄
E	65%	50%		70%	55%	60%	45%
			=			+	
Ē	35	50		30	45	40	55
	100%	100%		100%	100%	100%	100%
	(600)	(600)		(300)	(300)	(300)	(300)

form of data to guarantee that a relationship is causal. The best that the analyst can do with survey data is to introduce all of the factors which he conceives might prove the relation to be spurious. If replication rather than explanation is the consistent result, the probability is increased that the relationship is causal. It is always possible, however, that a test factor exists which would explain away the relation, had the analyst had the knowledge and foresight to collect data on it and to introduce it into his analysis. Thus, the survey analyst, as analysts of any other form of data, can never conclude absolutely that two variables are indeed causally related.

There are, of course, many situations in sociology where it is important to test hypotheses that two variables are causally related. Such situations are not confined to studies where survey data have been or may be used. They may arise whatever methodology is used. Looking into the conditions giving rise to the development of capitalism, Max Weber was as concerned to establish a causal link between his independent and dependent variables as many a modern survey researcher.[21] Weber, of course, had no survey data with which to work. Nevertheless, he went to great lengths in his comparative studies and through other means to establish that the link he discerned between the content of Calvin's theology and the ethics of capitalism was causal and not spurious.

The use of a cross-sectional survey to test a causal hypothesis requires

21. Weber, Max, *Protestant Ethics and the Spirit of Capitalism*. Charles Scribner's Sons, New York, 1930.

that the investigator design his survey to include data on his independent and dependent variables and on such antecedent variables as theory would suggest might explain away the expected original relation. Analysis, then, involves introducing these antecedent variables into the two-variable relation to test the null hypothesis.

A recent study of Christian beliefs and anti-Semitism provides a relevant case example of a sociological analysis pursued to test a causal hypothesis.[22] The authors, having established to their satisfaction a descriptive relationship between a syndrome of specified religious beliefs and anti-Semitism, confront the problem of causality.[23] Does religious belief produce anti-Semitism or is there some antecedent factor or factors which explain both belief and anti-Semitism?

Adopting the null hypothesis that the relation is spurious, the investigators turn to theory to suggest possible explanations of the relation. In effect, they ask themselves what common factor may lead people to a particular kind of religious belief and also lead them to be anti-Semitic. To illustrate, the authors postulate, among other things, that older people are more likely to hold to more traditional religious beliefs. Moreover, in these changing times, the lingering anti-Semitism in American life might be a residue remaining only in the older generation. Thus, it is possible that the empirical relation between belief and anti-Semitism is simply an artifact of uncontrolled age differences.

Both the expectations, that adherence to traditional belief and that anti-Semitism will be greater among the aged, are confirmed by their data. Moreover, when the relation between belief and anti-Semitism is examined with age controlled, it is found that at each belief level, the older person is more likely to be anti-Semitic (this is an example of *specification,* about which more will be said later). But the age trends do not explain away the original relation. Religious belief is found still to be related to anti-Semitism whatever a subject's age.

22. Glock, C. Y. and Rodney Stark, *Christian Belief and Anti-Semitism.* Harper & Row, New York, 1966.
23. The syndrome of religious beliefs referred to includes what the authors call orthodoxy, a commitment to a literal interpretation of religious dogma; particularism, a disposition to see Christian truth as the only religious truth; specifically religious hostility toward Jews, as manifested in an invidious interpretation of the Crucifixion story; and religious illibertarianism, as indicated by an unwillingness to grant religious liberty to outsiders. In their study, the authors combine these various components of their syndrome of religious beliefs into a measure of religious bigotry.

Following the same logic, the investigators then proceed to test other alternative explanations of the original relation. In the end, nothing that they introduce explains the relation away. Under all conditions, religious belief continues to be independently related to anti-Semitism.

The investigators recognize that their failure to find support for the null hypothesis does not prove causality. The nagging question remains, as it does in all surveys designed to test a causal hypothesis, that the causality is more apparent than real; that the true explanation for the relation has simply been overlooked. On this matter, there is ordinarily no alternative but to leave it to subsequent investigations to provide further tests of the hypothesis.

In the present instance, the nature of the subject matter and the design of the study allowed for testing the causal hypothesis in an additional way. The investigators reasoned that it would greatly strengthen their case if it could be shown that religious belief *does not* predict racial prejudice. To be sure, different kinds of prejudices tend to go together; and, in their sample, anti-Semitism is related to prejudice against Negroes. However, their study does not attempt to account for anti-Semitism in general, but to uncover and isolate specifically religious causes for prejudice against Jews. Since Negroes are largely Christians, these same religious factors should not operate to generate hostility toward them. To the degree, they argue, that they have successfully uncovered purely religious sources of prejudice, their model ought to fail to account for racial prejudice. By and large, this is their finding. While religious ideology remains massively related to anti-Semitism, it bears no significant relationship to prejudice against Negroes.

This additional test increases the confidence with which they can assert that religious belief is a cause of anti-Semitism. In the end, however, despite the persuasiveness of their evidence, they are obliged to acknowledge that their proof is incomplete. The possibility that the explanatory factor has been overlooked remains. Nevertheless, through their analysis, they have increased the probability that the relationship is causal.

The anti-Semitism example illustrates what happens when a causal hypothesis is "confirmed" through survey analysis. Other examples of analysis pursued to the same end using cross-sectional survey data are Hollingshead and Redlich's study to establish a causal nexus between social class and mental illness, Selvin's effort to prove that the leadership climate of army training companies causally affects the off-duty behavior of recruits, and Miller and Swanson's investigation of the causal consequences of "bureaucratic" and "entrepreneurial" value orientations of parents on their patterns of child training.[24]

There are considerably fewer examples in the literature where disconfirmation occurs; that is, cases where sociologists locate an antecedent variable or variables which clearly explain away an original relation. The absence of examples is undoubtedly due to a natural tendency to focus on relationships for which there are good theoretical grounds for expecting causality. It may also be that disconfirmations tend not to get reported in the literature. Or, it may be that the social world is so complex that there are few occasions where a relationship can be explained away by a single or by several antecedent factors. There are, however, exceptions to the rule.

An example is contained in an unpublished manuscript, *Right Wing Radicalism,* by Martin Trow.[25] Trow's survey, done during the McCarthy period, was based on a probability sample of the population of Bennington, Vermont, and was concerned with examining the sources of support for McCarthy's methods. Among other things, Trow hypothesized that support for McCarthy would be greater among persons whose general tolerance for political dissent was low. To test his hypothesis, he developed a scale of tolerance for political dissent and compared the extent of support for McCarthy's methods among those who scored high and low on this scale. His result is presented in Table 3, which appears to confirm the hypothesis; those with low political tolerance were indeed more likely to support McCarthy's methods than those with high political tolerance.

TABLE 3

SUPPORT FOR MCCARTHY'S METHODS AMONG SUBJECTS WITH
HIGH AND LOW TOLERANCE FOR POLITICAL DISSENT

	Tolerance for Political Dissent	
	High	*Low*
Support McCarthy's Methods	35%	60%
Oppose McCarthy's Methods	65	40
	100%	100%
	(419)	(257)

24. Hollingshead, A. deB. and F. C. Redlich, *Social Class and Mental Illness: A Community Study.* John Wiley & Sons, New York, 1958; Selvin, H. C., *The Effects of Leadership.* Free Press, Glencoe, Ill., 1960; Miller, D. R. and G. E. Swanson, *The Changing American Parent.* John Wiley & Sons, New York, 1958.
25. Unpublished doctoral thesis, Columbia University, 1954.

Knowing that political tolerance was highly associated with his subjects' educational levels (Table 4), Trow was led to consider the possibility that the original relationship between tolerance and support, while descriptively true, might not be causally true. In effect, he postulated that both tolerance and support for McCarthy might be a result of education, in which case the original relation between tolerance and support ought to disappear or be drastically reduced when education is taken into account. As can be seen in Table 5, this is substantially what happens. When education is introduced into the original relationship, degree of tolerance is no longer found to be

TABLE 4

SUBJECTS HIGH ON POLITICAL TOLERANCE ARE ON THE AVERAGE
MORE HIGHLY EDUCATED THAN THOSE WITH
LOW POLITICAL TOLERANCE

	Level of Political Tolerance	
	High	*Low*
Some College +	47%	12%
High School Graduate	27	24
Some High School	13	27
Some Grade School	13	37
	100%	100%
	(419)	(257)

TABLE 5

RELATIONSHIP BETWEEN POLITICAL TOLERANCE AND SUPPORT FOR
MCCARTHY'S METHODS, CONTROLLING FOR EDUCATION

	Some Grade School		*Some High School*		*High School Graduate*		*Some College*	
	High	*Low*	*High*	*Low*	*High*	*Low*	*High*	*Low*
Support McCarthy's Methods	51%	63%	44%	44%	43%	45%	23%	18%
Oppose McCarthy's Methods	49	37	56	56	57	55	77	82
	100%	100%	100%	100%	100%	100%	100%	100%
	(54)	(94)	(55)	(68)	(113)	(62)	(197)	(33)

associated with support for McCarthy's methods. Degree of education, in this instance, explains away the original relationship.[26]

Understanding the process which produces a relation between two variables. Thus far, we have illustrated the way in which a sociologist may use survey data to test a hypothesis that two variables are causally related. If the hypothesis is disconfirmed, i.e., if an antecedent variable is found which explains the original relationship away, the analyst, in effect, has exhausted his interest in the original relation. Such is not the case, however, where the hypothesis is "confirmed." Here, the "fact" that the original relation is not spurious raises the additional question of how to interpret the relation. What are the links that bind the two variables together? Efforts made to answer this question have come to be called *interpretation*.

The logic underlying the effort to interpret a relation is that there is something which follows from an independent variable which ties it to the dependent variable. Interpretation, however, can only occur where the test factor is intervening between, rather than antecedent to, the independent and dependent variables. Referring once again to Chart 2, and assuming that the original variables with which one is concerned are C (time order *3*) and E (time order *5*), the variables of time order *4* are the only variables which intervene and which, consequently, may be used in the quest for interpretation.

The statistical result of interpretation is the same as when explanation occurs; the original relation disappears or is sharply reduced in the partials. This is shown hypothetically in Table 6. Note first the positive relation between C and E in the total table. Note in the partial tables, however, that the original relation has disappeared when the intervening variable D is taken into account.

While explanation and interpretation produce the same result statistically, the two have a radically different meaning. Explanation signified in Table 1 that the imputation that C causes E is spurious; the "real" meaning is that variations in both C and E are a result of the antecedent variable A; in effect, A leads both to C and E. Interpretation as exemplified in Table 6

---

26. This is another example of a developmental configuration (see footnote 19). Tolerance for political dissent does not cause opposition to McCarthy's methods. It is nevertheless true that the test factor—education—and level of tolerance are intrinsically related.

TABLE 6

D INTERPRETS THE RELATION BETWEEN C AND E

| | Original Relation | | | Partial Relations | | | |
| | | | | D | | D̄ | |
	C	C̄		C	C̄	C	C̄
E	68%	39%		75%	75%	35%	35%
			=			+	
Ē	32	61		25	25	65	65
	100%	100%		100%	100%	100%	100%
	(1,200)	(1,000)		(1,000)	(100)	(200)	(800)

means that D, which intervenes between C and E, is the link that binds C and E together.[27] D is part of a causal chain C----> D ----> E.

It is relatively common in sociological inquiry, based on surveys or otherwise, that the analyst confronts the task of trying to interpret what is or is thought to be a causal relation. This is because the original relation itself does not make manifest the process which produces it. For example, social class may be found to be consistently related to certain acts of crime; the higher the class, the less the crime. Efforts to explain away the relation may prove unsuccessful, leading to a conclusion that the relation is probably causal. If this should occur, however, the result affords no interpretation of why it should occur. To resolve the issue, the analyst is inexorably led to ask what characterizes the lower classes, in contrast to the higher classes, which makes them more prone to the specified crimes. So it is with any causal relation between two variables.

It would seem, given the relative frequency that interpretation is a logical step in analysis, that it would be relatively easy to find examples of it in the sociological literature. At the theoretical and speculative level, the task is indeed easy. Almost any sociological monograph contains examples of speculative efforts to interpret an association between two variables as being the result of some specified intervening third variable or set of variables. Examples to illustrate successful empirical tests of interpretative hypotheses are much more difficult to locate.

27. The reader will recall that interpretation is to be pursued only if the relationship to be interpreted was not spurious in the first place.

The paucity of examples appears to be a result, at least in part, of the failure of many analysts to internalize this particular aspect of analytic logic. Even as astute an analyst as Stouffer missed many opportunities, in both *The American Soldier,* and in *Communism, Conformity, and Civil Liberties,* to subject interpretations to full empirical test.[28] The volumes are rife with speculations about why two variables are found to be related but, at best, these are subjected to only partial empirical test.

The relative failure of sociologists to use survey data to test interpretative hypotheses is scarcely evidence, however, for denying the utility of this analytical step. Properly used, it can prove highly illuminating to our understanding of social processes. One example of a successful interpretation is found in the aforementioned study of Christian belief and anti-Semitism.[29] At one point in their analysis, the investigators find a relatively strong association between being more orthodox and particularistic in religious belief and holding prejudiced secular attitudes toward Jews.[30] The relevant table for Protestants in their sample is reproduced as Table 7.

Confronted with this evidence, the investigators asked themselves, in effect, how does the relation come about? What is there about an orthodox and particularistic faith which is predisposing to secular anti-Semitism? Their hypothesis is that the link which binds the two together is specifically religious hostility against the Jews. The reasoning is this: orthodox and particularistic Christians, because of their traditional beliefs and their view that salvation can only be achieved through Christ, are led to view the Jews as religious outsiders and to be religiously hostile toward them. It is, then, this religious hostility which leads to secular anti-Semitism. Introducing a

28. Stouffer, S. A., *et. al., The American Soldier:* Vol. 1, Adjustment During Army Life. Princeton University Press, Princeton, 1949; Stouffer, S. A., *Communism, Conformity, and Civil Liberties:* A Cross Section of the Nation Speaks Its Mind. Doubleday, New York, 1955.
29. Glock, C. Y. and Rodney Stark, *op. cit.* The author apologizes for his parochialism in choosing examples. However, this example of *interpretation* was thought to illustrate its meaning in a particularly clear way.
30. Orthodoxy is defined as holding to be inviolate traditional Christian belief in God, in Jesus Christ, in the Biblical miracles, etc. Particularism constitutes a set of beliefs which sees Christianity as the only true faith and a belief in Christ as Savior to be absolutely necessary for salvation. Prejudiced secular attitudes toward Jews refers to holding negative stereotypes toward Jews which make no reference to Judaism as a religion.

TABLE 7

RELIGIOUS BELIEF AND PREJUDICE TOWARD JEWS
AMONG PROTESTANTS

Index of Anti-Semitic Prejudice	*Propensity to Orthodox and Particularistic Belief*		
	High	*Medium*	*Low*
High	29%	13%	7%
Medium High	23	21	13
Medium	39	48	53
None	9	18	27
	100%	100%	100%
	(522)	(421)	(310)

TABLE 8

RELIGIOUS BELIEF, RELIGIOUS HOSTILITY,
AND PREJUDICE TOWARD JEWS AMONG PROTESTANTS

Index of Religious Hostility toward Jews		*Per Cent High or Medium on Anti-Semitism* *Propensity to Orthodox and Particularistic Belief*					
		High		*Medium*		*Low*	
High	4	77%	(97)	62%	(50)	—	(7)
	3	53	(75)	54	(73)	56%	(32)
	2	35	(79)	34	(93)	38	(92)
	1	19	(21)	21	(96)	15	(151)
Low	0	5	(19)	16	(82)	10	(217)

measure of religious hostility into the original relation produced the result reported in Table 8.[31]

Reading across the table, the relationship between orthodoxy and particularism has vanished into meaningless patterns. On the other hand, within each religious belief category, the effect of religious hostility is powerful indeed (reading down the columns of the table). As interpretations go, this

31. Religious hostility is defined as perceiving the Jews as responsible for the Crucifixion and conceiving of the contemporary Jew as subject to God's continuing punishment for this perceived act of his forbears.

is as close to a classic example as we were able to find. It provides, for our present didactic purposes, a germane example of how interpretation in the analysis of cross-sectional survey data proceeds.

Specifying the conditions that maximize or minimize a relationship. A third kind of hypothesis which may be formulated about a two-variable relationship concerns the conditions under which it is more or less true. Here, the introduction of a test factor is motivated by the expectation that the strength of the original relation will not be uniform under all conditions. Hypotheses of this kind may be referred to as specifying hypotheses and when they are confirmed, the statistical result is called *specification*.

Specification may take a variety of forms. The crucial distinction to be made is between specifications which involve no change in the direction of the original relation in the partials and those which do. To illustrate the former possibility, let us assume that we have found a positive association between C and E and wish now to test the proposition that the association will be stronger when B is also present and weaker when it is absent.[32] Table 9 illustrates a possible result which would confirm the proposition.

In both partials, we find that C is positively related to E. However, under condition B, the association is considerably stronger than under condition B̄. Epsilon, the percentage point difference between the proportion of C w/a E and the proportion of C̄ w/a E, is 36 in the original relation. Under condition B, epsilon is raised to 60. Under condition B̄, however, it is reduced to 10. C, then, is more strongly related to E when B is present than when it is absent.

Specification of this kind occurs very frequently in sociological analysis of survey data. An example is contained in the 1948 study of voting be-

---

32. Unlike explanation, replication, and interpretation, there are no restrictions concerning the time order of the third variable which may be introduced to specify a two-variable relation. Such a relation may be specified by an antecedent factor, an intervening one, by a factor of the same time order as the original independent variable or the original dependent variable, or, as is often the case, by a factor whose time order relative to the original variables is indeterminate. Thus, variables of the time order *1* through *5* in Chart 2 might be used to specify an original relation between C and E. For the examples of specification presented in Tables 9 and 12, we have arbitrarily chosen an antecedent variable B as the test factor. The reader should recognize, however, that we might have equally as well used any or all of the variables symbolized in Chart 2 with the exception, of course, of C and E, the two variables used to characterize the original relation.

TABLE 9

B Specifies the Relation between C and E

	Original Relation				Partial Relations			
					B		B̄	
	C	C̄		C	C̄		C	C̄
E	68%	32%		80%	20%		50%	40%
			=			+		
Ē	32	68		20	80		50	60
	100%	100%		100%	100%		100%	100%
	(500)	(500)		(300)	(200)		(200)	(300)
Epsilon:	36				60		10	

TABLE 10

Religion and Vote Intention

	Religion	
Vote Intention	Protestant	Catholic
Republican	78%	35%
Democratic	22	65
	100%	100%
	(435)	(191)
Epsilon:	43	

havior in Elmira, New York.[33] Looking at the relation between religion and vote, the investigators found that Protestants were much more likely to have a Republican vote intention than Catholics (Table 10).

When the same relationship was examined controlling for age, the direction of the original relation was sustained in all of the partials. However, its strength is specified by age. Religion makes considerably more of a difference in the voting behavior of older than of younger voters (Table 11).

Sometimes, a test factor may specify the direction of the original relation to be different in one of the partials though the same in the other. This

33. Berelson, B. R., P. F. Lazarsfeld, and W. W. McPhee, *Voting: A Study of Opinion Formation in a Presidential Campaign.* Chicago University Press, Chicago, 1954, pp. 64–69. The data from *Voting* are presented here in a somewhat revised format to heighten the relevancy of the illustration.

TABLE 11

RELIGION AND VOTE INTENTION
AMONG DIFFERENT AGE GROUPS

	|	*Age*			
Vote Intention	*55 and Over*		*35 to 54*		*Under 35*	
	Prot.	*Cath.*	*Prot.*	*Cath.*	*Prot.*	*Cath.*
Republican	88%	18%	82%	41%	66%	38%
Democratic	12	82	18	59	34	62
	100%	100%	100%	100%	100%	100%
	(126)	(40)	(185)	(80)	(124)	(71)
Epsilon:	70		41		28	

TABLE 12

B SPECIFIES THE RELATIONSHIP BETWEEN C AND E

	Original Relation			*Partial Relations*			
				B		B̄	
	C	C̄		C	C̄	C	C̄
E	68%	50%		80%	30%	30%	60%
			=			+	
Ē	32	50		20	70	70	40
	100%	100%		100%	100%	100%	100%
	(800)	(600)		(600)	(200)	(200)	(400)
Epsilon:	18			50		—30	

effect is illustrated in Table 12. Note that under condition B, the relation between C and E is strengthened but is in the same direction as in the original relation. Under condition B̄, however, the original relation is reversed.

An example of this kind of specification is to be found in a recent study of the impact of the Eichmann trial on public opinion.[34] At one point in the analysis, the investigators find a negative association between being informed about the details of the trial and perceiving the trial as legal; the

34. Glock, C. Y., Gertrude Selznick, and J. L. Spaeth, *The Apathetic Majority:* A Study Based on Public Responses to the Eichmann Trial. Harper & Row, New York, 1966.

more informed are the more critical. When the same relationship is examined separately for Negro and white subjects, it is found to be reversed for Negroes and strengthened for whites.

Specification, whatever its form, has the effect of changing mildly or drastically the analytic question being addressed. In the Eichmann example, the analytic question raised by the original relation between knowledge and legality was why should greater knowledge lead to greater skepticism about the trial's legality. Once the test factor—race—is introduced into the relationship, the analytic question assumes a quite different character. Now, one has to ask why knowledge has an effect in one direction among subjects of one race and the opposite effect among subjects of another race. Similarly, but less drastically, in the earlier voting-intention example, the analytic question is confounded by the information that religion counts more in the voting intention of the aged than of the young. It is no longer sufficient to explain religion's effect on vote. The partials raise the additional question of why its effect should be particularly strong among the aged.

Earlier, it was noted that there are no restrictions as to the time order of the variables which may be introduced as test factors in specification. The time order of the test factor relative to the original variables does, however, influence both the meaning attached to the specification and the further course of analysis. Where the test factor is antecedent and specification occurs, for example, it is usually because the test factor represents social contexts which differ in their influence on the original relation. The succeeding analytic question, therefore, is why the relation is stronger in one context than in another. When the test factor is intervening, it is evident that where the link between the independent and dependent variables is of one kind it has a different effect than when it is of another kind. This raises the question, then, of what accounts for the relation between the independent and the intervening variables. Where the test factor is of the same time order as the independent variable, the effect is to call for a confounding of the independent variable in further analysis, that is, an examination of the meaning of the joint effect of the independent and intervening variables on the dependent variable. Finally, where the test factor is of the same time order as the dependent variable, a confounding of the dependent variable may be called for in further analysis.

In actual practice, there are few occasions where sociologists have followed through on a specification in any of these ways, partly because of the complexity of doing so with the often small samples that survey research must work with, and partly because the logic has not been completely worked out as yet. It is clear, however, that on logical grounds, specification ought to have a significant effect on subsequent analysis, and therefore ought to be attempted systematically in explanatory analysis.

Accounting for the "total" distribution on a dependent variable. Cross-sectional surveys may be undertaken with no other theoretical purpose than to test a hypothesis concerning the relation between a single independent and a single dependent variable; or, as suggested earlier, they may be conducted merely to produce a simple or differentiated description. The cross-sectional design also allows for dealing with more complex problems.

One class of more complex problems relates to maximally accounting for the distribution on a dependent variable. Social life being as complex as it is, it is hardly ever possible to find any single independent variable which will account for all of the variation on a dependent variable. A logical next step is to look for other factors to account for what remains unexplained, and in the end, to trace out the network of causal relations which are involved. We shall call studies pursued to this end *accounting studies.*

Viewed ideal-typically in the terms represented by Chart 2, an accounting study would first settle on a dependent variable whose distribution is to be accounted for. This would presumably be a variable of the most recent time order on which data have been collected—in the example, a variable of time order 5.[35] Variables of an earlier time order—*1* through *4*—would then constitute independent variables which the investigator has postulated to be components of the causal chain contributing to the distribution on his dependent variable. Analysis would proceed by seeking to discover how the independent variables, alone or in combination, are related to the dependent variable. The result might look like the depiction in Chart 4. Here, the dependent variable is E_2. The arrows between variables signify their involvement in the causal chain which produces the distribution on E_2. The circled variables are those which are found to be irrelevant to the causal chain.

This ideal-typical representation can only be approximated in any actual accounting analysis. On most problems, sociological theory is not likely to be sufficiently advanced to allow the formulation of such a complex model.

35. This need not necessarily be the case, however. It would also be possible to focus on a dependent variable at an earlier time order and to restrict the analysis to examining how variables of still earlier time orders affect its distribution.

Moreover, on the technical side, it can be anticipated both that the size of the sample will not be large enough to allow for handling this many variables simultaneously, and that it will not be possible to establish the time order of variables with this much precision. For present purposes, the representation illustrates what an accounting analysis aspires to rather than what it can ordinarily achieve.

Many sociological studies using survey data have sought to go beyond examining how and why a single independent variable affects the distribution on a dependent one. Usually, however, this has meant studying the mutual effects of a limited number of independent variables on the dependent variable rather than seeking to work out all of the implications of the accounting model.

Studies done in this mode proceed to examine, first individually and then in combination, how a series of independent variables relate to a dependent variable. The implicit conception is an additive one; the distribution is conceived to be a function of the relative presence or absence of a number of predisposing characteristics.

One study whose analysis followed this pattern is *The People's Choice*.[36] In that study, the authors establish that each of three key independent variables—socio-economic status, religious affiliation, and rural-urban background—is independently related to their dependent variable, political predisposition. However, the effect is also additive. In combination, the three variables account for much more of the variation on political predisposition than any one of them does individually.

Stouffer comes slightly closer to approximating the idealized model (Chart 4) in his *Communism, Conformity, and Civil Liberties*.[37] Like Lazarsfeld *et al.*, he successfully accounts for a large part of the variation in his dependent variable—tolerance of non-conformity—as being due to the mutual influence of independent variables, in this case, age, education, religion, and region of country. However, he goes one step further to suggest that the way in which his subjects perceive the Communist threat in the United States is one link which binds these background variables and his dependent variable together.

36. Lazarsfeld, P. F., B. R. Berelson, and Hazel Gaudet, *The People's Choice:* How the Voter Makes Up His Mind in a Presidential Campaign. Columbia University Press, New York, 1948.
37. Stouffer, S. A., *op. cit.*

CHART 4

IDEAL TYPICAL REPRESENTATION OF AN ACCOUNTING ANALYSIS

Time Dimension

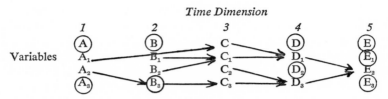

However incomplete, the Lazarsfeld and Stouffer studies and others done in a similar vein illustrate the utility of the cross-sectional survey to deal with accounting type problems.[38] However, these investigations were working implicitly, not explicitly, within the accounting model as it is conceptualized in Chart 4. Bearing the model in mind, there is the potential for more fully approximating it in future studies, even within the limitations which the cross-sectional design imposes, and even though problems of sample size and time order will continue to be inhibiting factors.

There exists no formula to guide an accounting analysis; the course of analysis will be determined more by theoretical and substantive considerations than by formal methodological rules. Analysis may proceed, using only the relatively simple statistical technique of cross tabulation, as illustrated in earlier tables, or it may combine cross tabulation with more advanced statistical techniques such as multiple regression and analysis of variance.[39] There is still debate as to what is the best combination of techniques. For the present, the most successful analyses appear to be those

38. Other studies using cross-sectional survey data which have been analyzed more or less in this mode are Lipset, S. M., "Opinion Formation in a Crisis Situation," *Public Opinion Quarterly,* Vol. 17, No. 1, 1953, pp. 20–46, Campbell, Angus, P. E. Converse, and W. E. Miller, *The American Voter.* John Wiley & Sons, New York, 1960; McPhee, William and W. A. Glazer, eds., *Public Opinion and Congressional Elections.* Free Press, Chicago, 1962; Lerner, Daniel, *The Passing of Traditional Society: Modernizing the Middle East.* Free Press, Chicago, 1958; Stouffer, Samuel, *The American Soldier, op. cit.;* Glock, C. Y., Gertrude Selznick, and J. L. Spaeth, *op. cit.;* Srole, Leo, *et al., Mental Health in the Metropolis:* The Midtown Manhattan Study. McGraw-Hill, New York, 1962; Trow, Martin, *op. cit.*

39. For a discussion of the possibilities for using such techniques in survey analysis, see Selvin, H. C., *The Logic of Survey Analysis,* Research Monograph 12, Survey Research Center, University of California, (Berkeley), 1965. This monograph represents a preliminary version of a book on survey analysis currently in preparation.

which artfully combine all forms of elaboration—explanation, replication, interpretation, and specification.

The implications of the distribution on an independent variable. Another class of problems for which the cross-sectional survey design is applicable is one in which primary attention is focused on an independent rather than a dependent variable. Here, the investigator's concerns are with the range of consequences which follow from the distribution on an independent variable, rather than the effects of a number of independent variables on a dependent one. In sociology, this kind of concern arises where, on theoretical and/or empirical grounds, it is postulated that some social characteristic will have significant and widespread effects; for example, that social class has implications for a wide range of values, beliefs, and attitudes. We shall call studies of this order *implications studies.*

A typical implications study progressively examines how one independent variable is related to a series of dependent variables with antecedent test factors introduced to establish the causality of the relationships. In effect, implications studies utilize, in a repeated way, the logic discussed earlier for testing a proposition that two variables are causally related. Chart 5 shows the structure of an implications analysis in the terms set by Chart 2.

In this example, variable C_1 at time order 3 is the independent variable whose implications are to be traced. The solid arrows point to the dependent variables on which it is postulated that C_1 will have an effect. The broken arrows refer to the variables antecedent to C_1 which are introduced to test for spuriousness.

Sociological studies done in this mode are relatively uncommon—a sign perhaps that there exist few single variables which can generate the widespread effects which the model assumes. At the same time, the infrequent

CHART 5

IDEAL TYPICAL REPRESENTATION OF AN IMPLICATIONS ANALYSIS

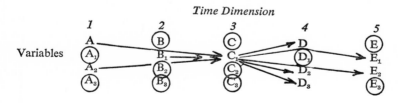

use of the model may result from its not having been made explicit in the literature. From among the examples which can be cited, Lenski's *The Religious Factor* is perhaps the most ambitious.[40]

Lenski's study tests the hypothesis that religion is an independent source of a variety of economic, political, and family values and attitudes. Using interviews with a cross-sectional sample of the population of Detroit as data, he proceeds systematically to examine the relationships between his independent variable—religion—and each of a large number of dependent variables.[41] He almost invariably finds a descriptive relation between religion and each of his dependent variables. To establish that the relationships are also causal, he demonstrates that they are replicated rather than explained away when theoretically appropriate test factors are introduced.

Exploring the causes and consequences of the distribution on a variable. Survey data also allow for combining an accounting and an implications analysis in the same study. *Phenomenon studies,* as we shall call them, involve seeking to account for the distribution on a variable which is first treated as dependent, then redefined as the independent variable. Analysis proceeds by studying its consequences on a number of dependent variables.

Phenomenon studies require that data be collected which are both antecedent to and posterior to the variable on which analytical attention is focused. In Chart 3, only variables of time orders *2, 3,* or *4* can be made the subject of a phenomenon analysis. How such an analysis might look is shown in Chart 6.

In this depiction, C_3 is the key variable. The arrows leading to it from antecedent variables of time orders *1* and *2* indicate that they are involved in the causal chain which contributes to the distribution on C_3. The arrows leading from C_3 to variables of time orders *4* and *5* indicate the dependent variables to which C_3 is found to be related.

One example of a cross-sectional study done in this mode is Selvin and Wenkert's study of school spirit based on interviews with a sample of stu-

40. Lenski, G. E., *The Religious Factor:* A Sociological Study of Religion's Impact on Politics, Economics, and Family Life. Doubleday, New York, 1961.
41. Religion is defined by Lenski both in terms of denomination, i.e., Protestant, Catholic, Jewish and in terms of a number of different kinds of religious involvement —associational, communal, doctrinal, devotional. In the course of his analysis, he shifts in which of these definitions he uses as his independent variable, often replicating the same analysis with different independent variables. In this sense, his analysis may be said to comprise a series of implications studies.

CHART 6

IDEAL TYPICAL REPRESENTATION OF A PHENOMENON ANALYSIS

Time Dimension

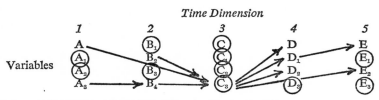

dents at the University of California, Berkeley.[42] They seek first to account for variation in the amount of school spirit which students exhibit. They then shift ground, treat school spirit as an independent variable, and study its implications for a variety of dependent variables, e.g., drop-out rate, school performance, leisure time pursuits.

A recent study of church involvement also used the phenomenon model to inform the analysis.[43] Here, the authors first seek to test a theory of social deprivation to account for variations in church involvement. Once this analysis is exhausted, they then proceed to examine various presumed consequences of differential involvement—what effect it has on perceptions of the church's role in society, on identification with church-advocated social attitudes, and on churchgoers' attitudes toward the ecumenical movement.

As these examples demonstrate, phenomenon analysis is most appropriate where it is possible to identify a key variable as the link between a set of antecedent and a set of posterior variables. In effect, a phenomenon study is a variation on the simpler step, described earlier, of interpretation.

With phenomenon studies, we bring to a close our discussion of the ways cross-sectional surveys have been used in sociological inquiry. We suspect that there are still other generic ways that surveys have been used which we have not detected. Our list, however, is probably complete enough to demonstrate the versatility of the cross-sectional design in dealing with a range of theoretical and empirical problems. Where we have been less complete is in covering the range of substantive problems in sociology which

42. Selvin, H. C., and Robert Wenkert, "School Spirit in Context of a Liberal Education." In *Social Problems,* Fall, 1962.
43. Glock, C. Y., Benjamin Ringer, and Earl Babbie, *To Comfort and to Challenge: A Dilemma of the Contemporary Church.* University of California Press, Berkeley and Los Angeles, 1967.

the cross-sectional survey has helped to illuminate. The reader will undoubtedly have noted that the subjects of religion and politics have dominated the examples which have been cited. This is, in part, a reflection of the author's particular interests and is also due to the fact that studies in these fields have contributed germane examples of the analytic points which we have wanted to make. These two subject matters, of course, far from exhaust past uses of the cross-sectional survey. Aside from the studies already cited, sociological surveys have been conducted on such diverse topics as the ethics of lawyers,[44] the training of physicians,[45] the effects of mass media,[46] the paths of the elderly to the psychiatric ward,[47] the values of college youth,[48] occupational prestige,[49] the motivations to vacationing in the wilderness,[50] the role response of ministers' wives,[51] the response of Puerto Rican migrants to New York life,[52] the role of the school superintendency,[53] and public attitudes toward voluntary charitable organizations.[54]

Because it can simultaneously serve both descriptive and explanatory purposes, the cross-sectional survey design is probably more widely used than any other design in sociology and all other social science disciplines. There are, however, limitations which restrict its usefulness. We have al-

44. Carlin, J. E., *Lawyers' Ethics:* A Survey of the New York City Bar. Russell Sage Foundation, New York, 1966.
45. Merton, R. K., George Reader, and P. L. Kendall, eds., *The Student Physician.* Harvard University Press, Cambridge, 1957.
46. Klapper, J. T., *The Effects of Mass Communication.* Free Press, Glencoe, Ill., 1960.
47. Lowenthal, M. F., *Lives in Distress.* Basic Books, New York, 1964.
48. Goldsen, R. K., *et al., What College Students Think.* Van Nostrand, New York, 1960.
49. Inkeles, Alex and P. H. Rossi, "National Comparisons of Occupational Prestige," *American Journal of Sociology,* Vol. 61, 1956, pp. 329–339.
50. Glock C. Y., G. J. Selznick, and Jacqueline Wiseman, "The Wilderness Vacationist," in *Wilderness and Recreation:* A Report on Resources, Values and Problems to the Outdoor Recreation Resources Review Commission by the Wildland Research Center, University of California, 1962, chap. 5.
51. Douglas, William, *Ministers' Wives.* Harper & Row, New York, 1965.
52. Mills, C. W., Clarence Senior, and R. K. Goldsen, *The Puerto Rican Journey.* Harper, New York, 1950.
53. Gross, Neal, W. S. Mason, and A. W. McEachern, *Explorations in Role Analysis:* Studies of the School Superintendency Role. John Wiley & Sons, New York, 1958.
54. Sills, D. L., *The Volunteers:* Means and Ends in a National Organization. Free Press, Glencoe, Ill., 1957.

ready noted the problems of time order and sample size.[55] These problems are not troublesome where the analytic goals are description or time-bound association; they do, however, raise difficulties in time-ordered association.[56] Less a criticism than an observation is that a cross-sectional survey is more suited to social psychology than to purely sociological inquiry. This is undoubtedly the impression which has been conveyed by the examples cited in this section. There is no inherent reason why surveys cannot collect data on larger units of analysis than the individual.[57] Parishes may be studied instead of parishioners. Or, corporations instead of employees. By and large, however, it is considerably easier to make the individual the unit of analysis and most often this is what has been done. That this produces a tendency to frame problems in social psychological terms is indisputable. It is possible, of course, to ask individuals questions about their social contexts and such information frequently allows inferences to be drawn about larger entities than the individual. However, what the individual can accurately report about his milieu is highly circumscribed. He can report his occupation, for example, but he is likely to have only an incomplete idea about the climate of opinion which characterizes his place of work.

Sociologists have recognized these and other limitations in the cross-sectional survey design and have invented ingenious design variations to get around them. These variations retain and indeed extend the analytical possibilities already discussed. They permit the direct confrontation of more purely sociological problems and they provide some resolution of the time order and sample size problems. The balance of our chapter will be devoted to describing these variations on the cross-sectional design and demonstrating how they extend the utility of survey research in sociological inquiry.

55. A useful discussion of the steps which may be taken to estimate time order may be found in Hyman, H. H., *op. cit.*, pp. 193–226.
56. A criticism which may be made of many theoretically oriented studies is that they deal too lightly with the time order problem. At the same time, imposing too rigid requirements that time order be firmly established would be dysfunctional to exploratory inquiry.
57. Among studies which have used a unit of analysis other than the person are: Swanson, G. E., *The Birth of the Gods.* University of Michigan Press, Ann Arbor, 1960; and Udy, S. H., *Organization at Work:* A Comparative Analysis of Production among Non-industrial Peoples. Human Relations Area Files Press, New Haven, Conn. 1959. Swanson's unit of analysis was the primitive tribe, Udy's was production organizations in a sample of non-industrial societies.

Variations on the Cross-sectional Design

OVER-REPRESENTATION

Much of survey analysis relies on comparisons between different subgroups in the sample—Negroes compared to whites, Protestants to Catholics and Jews, upper class to middle and working class. It is important, therefore, that the sample of subjects include sufficiently large numbers of each relevant subgroup for comparisons to be made. The cross-sectional survey, of course, represents each subgroup in proportion to its distribution in the population being studied. Consequently, it is not an efficient design if analytic attention is to be given to comparing subgroups, one or another of which is a small minority of the total population.

An obvious solution to this problem is to over-represent the subgroup or groups which would be under-represented if a strict probability sample were employed. This is relatively easy, however, only when a reliable estimate exists of how the groups are distributed in the population, and where the characteristic at issue is easily recognizable by interviewers.

Suppose that a study seeks to compare the consumption patterns of Negroes and whites in a large metropolitan community. The census indicates that the ratio of Negroes to whites in the community is one to nine. A strict probability sample of the community would obviously be inefficient since it would produce many more whites than are needed for comparison and too few Negroes. It is simple, however, to stratify by race (i.e., consider the two races separately) and draw probability samples of equal size from the Negro and white populations. By over-representing the Negroes, sufficient numbers are included in the study for efficient Negro-white comparisons.

On many occasions, however, the conditions present in this example are not met; the distribution is not known, and the characteristic to be over-represented is not visible. For example, an investigator is not likely to know in advance what proportion of a population holds to a particular attitude, has been exposed to a particular communication, is informed about a particular event, has recently migrated into the community, etc. Not only is the distribution unknown, but the characteristics are not readily observable. In such instances, a solution used in some sociological studies is to undertake a preliminary "locator" study to provide the necessary information.

An example is provided by a study in which persons who had participated in adult education programs during the previous year were to be compared with individuals who had not had such an experience.[58] The researchers wanted to interview a probability sample of both groups, but there was no available information in the community on which to judge how many people had been participants in an adult education program. In this case, a large probability sample of the entire population was interviewed briefly to locate a smaller sample of participants and to assess their prevalence.[59] Subjects for more intensive study were drawn from the lists compiled in the locator interviews.

Sometimes the proportion of the population having the designated attribute is so small that even a screening interview would be too costly. If one person out of a thousand, for example, possesses the attribute in question, a total of 100,000 screening interviews would theoretically be required to locate a sample of 100. In such instances, one solution which has been tried is to use the respondents of a screening interview also as informants, asking them both about themselves and about anyone they know with the designated characteristic.[60] This technique does pose statistical problems, since the relation of the sample characteristics to the population characteristics is unknown. However, in certain cases, sample unreliability may be tolerated in the interest of exploring a problem on which no reliable information exists.

These simple modifications of the cross-sectional design impose certain restrictions on the way the data may be analyzed. At a descriptive level, results must be weighted to allow projection of the findings back to the total population. Within categories of the over-represented characteristic, however, the data may be examined descriptively simply as if two universes had been sampled. Similarly, time-bound association may be pursued either with a combined weighted sample or for the two samples separately.

Where the over-represented characteristic is to be used as an independent variable, the modifications require that this characteristic be controlled con-

58. London, Jack, Warren Hagstrom, and Robert Wenkert, *Adult Education and Social Class*. Monograph 9, Survey Research Center, University of California, Berkeley, 1963.

59. In this instance, locator interviews were done, where possible, by telephone and otherwise by personal interview.

60. Bigman, S. K., *Methodological Considerations in International Broadcasting Research* (mimeographed), Bureau of Applied Social Research, Columbia University, 1951. Bigman reports a study of Voice of America listeners in Norway in which this technique was used to locate the listeners.

sistently in any explanatory use which is made of the data. This would, of course, be the natural thing to do or else over-representation would not have been adopted in the first place. Should the over-represented characteristic not produce the expected effect, however, there would be no warrant for combining the two samples to explore other problems, except under the condition that the data are appropriately weighted to represent the two groups in the same proportions as they occur in the universe.

Where the over-represented characteristic is to be used as a dependent variable—as was, for example, the case in the aforementioned study of adult education—analysis could proceed along any of the lines appropriate to analyzing a straight cross-sectional sample. The adult education study pursued an accounting analysis using participation as a dependent variable. The one reservation to be borne in mind, however, is that the results cannot be interpreted descriptively. Thus, if only 10 per cent of the population are participants while 50 per cent of the sample are participants, and it is found that among blue collar workers in the sample 30 per cent are participants whereas among white collar workers the equivalent figure is 70 per cent, it is not descriptively accurate to say that 30 per cent of blue collar workers and 70 per cent of white collar workers have participated in adult education. The only interpretation that can be made of such a finding is that social class is related to participation. To obtain a descriptive assessment of the rate of participation of the two worker groups, the participant and non-participant samples would have to be weighted to their proper representation in the universe.

CONTEXTUAL DESIGNS

A more significant variation on the cross-sectional design has grown out of an understandable sociological interest in studying social contexts and their influence on individual behavior. The cross-sectional survey, as noted earlier, has some capability for generating contextual information. Necessarily, however, this is limited to what the individual subject is capable of reporting himself. Here, the problem is that individuals have only incomplete information about the various groups in which they function and the amount and accuracy of such information is likely to vary considerably from subject to subject. Everyone interviewed in a cross-sectional survey is undoubtedly capable of reporting the size and composition of his family. Some may be able to report accurately on how many people are employed at their place of work or how many members there are in their church.

Few, if any, however, will be able to describe accurately the social structure of their place of work, what their co-workers feel about working conditions, or the range of salaries that their co-workers are paid. Theoretically, some information of this kind is obtainable from independent sources. Employers of respondents could be contacted to furnish contextual information about the firm. In a survey, however, where a randomly drawn population sample of, say, 2,000 people has been interviewed, it is obviously impractical to track down every employer for this purpose.

The difficulties of using a straight cross-sectional survey approach for studies of social contexts have stimulated the invention of a number of alternative strategies. These strategies, while not applicable to all situations, have been found highly useful where the subjects of an inquiry share the same context and where information about this context is crucial to pursuing the study's objectives.

Lazarsfeld and Thielen's study, *The Academic Mind,* is a relevant case in point.[61] These investigators were concerned with examining the impact of the McCarthy period on academic freedom among social scientists. They hypothesized that the degree to which a professor felt personally threatened and, as a result, was led to be careful about what he said in class, would be highly influenced by the climate of opinion in the institution at which he taught. Given the same external pressures, it was expected that greater resistance to pressures to conform would be exhibited in some college contexts than in others.

"Climate of opinion" was defined in this study as the proportion of the faculty at an individual faculty member's college who were apprehensive to the point of "toning down" lectures or not assigning "controversial" books. In order to include "climate of opinion" as a contextual variable, a two-stage sampling design was adopted. First, a probability sample of the nation's colleges and universities was drawn, with the chance of a particular college being drawn proportional to the size of its social science faculty. A sample of individual faculty members was then drawn from each of the chosen colleges. Enough cases were selected from each school so that individual responses on apprehension could be combined to yield an estimate of the climate of opinion surrounding the individual respondents at each college.

61. Lazarsfeld, P. F. and Wagner Thielens, Jr., *The Academic Mind.* Free Press, Chicago, 1958.

This contextual design produces data which can be used to make descriptive projections from the sample to the universe.[62] Moreover, it extends the analytic possibilities beyond those which the cross-sectional design allows. It is a fortunate accident when a cross-sectional survey happens to include enough people from a particular context so that this context can be described statistically on the basis of the distribution of individual responses. However, since this is the very *raison d'etre* of a contextual design, this kind of statistical description of the context is always possible. Since this design includes data on both the individual and his context, it is also possible to study the joint influence of the individual's characteristics and of the contextual characteristics on the individual's behavior; for example, it is possible to contrast the apprehensiveness of politically liberal professors in institutions where most professors are politically liberal with the behavior of such professors in institutions where they are in a minority. Finally, this kind of design makes it possible to pursue an analysis at the level of the context itself; for example, to compare colleges with high and low proportions of "productive" professors.

The contextual design utilized by Lazarsfeld and Thielens can be adapted to studies of any institution with distinct subdivisions—hospitals, business corporations, churches, unions, and so forth. It is also possible to elaborate on the design. For example, a study of Episcopalian parishioners began with the same kind of two-stage sampling used by Lazarsfeld and Thielens.[63] First, a sample of Episcopal parishes was chosen, taking into account the size of the parish. Then the sample of parishioners was drawn in such a way that it not only represented the universe of parishioners but also provided enough respondents in each parish to construct contextual variables. The significant addition here was an interview with the rector of each parish sampled. It thus became possible to analyze the data at the level of the parish, of the individual parishioners, and of the individual priest, and

---

62. Within, of course, defined statistical limits. The ability of the design to do this derives from the fact that it uses, in effect, a probability sample of the universe.
63. Glock, C.Y., Benjamin Ringer, and Earl Babbie, *op. cit.* In this instance, it was not possible to execute the study in full accordance with the design because of a shortage of funds. Consequently, all of the analytical possibilities could not be taken up in actual analysis. Nevertheless, under more favorable circumstances, this kind of design would be eminently feasible and would produce the analytic advantages noted in the text.

to treat the last as either an individual respondent or as part of the context of the parishioner.[64]

SOCIOMETRIC DESIGN

There is a class of problems in sociology whose study requires a consideration of networks of interpersonal relations and their influence on behavior. The flow of information through a community or an organization is one example. Another is the way that members of a group interact to produce the social structure of the group. The cross-sectional survey is not well suited to such problems. When respondents are chosen by means of a probability sample, the chance that any one person will know and be interacting with any other person is remote indeed. This is not the case using a contextual design where at least some respondents would probably turn out to know each other. For example, in the Lazarsfeld-Thielens study, some information was obtained about the interaction of respondents with other faculty members at their college. However, in this study, many respondents were not in interaction with each other, particularly at larger schools.

The need in some instances for studying interaction patterns has given rise to a further variation on the cross-sectional survey design which we shall call the sociometric design. The procedures to be followed in such a case are not wholly different from those used in the contextual design. Subtle differences, however, warrant the identification of a separate type.

The distinguishing characteristic of the sociometric design is that it entails collecting information from *all* persons in a given context so that the network of interpersonal relations may be described and its influence on

64. Further examples of the adroit use of contextual designs are Lipset, Seymour M., Martin Trow, and J. S. Coleman, *Union Democracy:* The Internal Politics of the International Typographical Union. Free Press, Chicago, 1956; and Wilson, A. B., "Residential Segregation of Social Classes and Aspirations of High School Boys," *American Sociological Review,* Vol. 24, December, 1959, pp. 836–845. The former study concerns the membership of the International Typographical Union. Rather than drawing a straight probability sample of members, the investigators first sampled shops and then drew samples within shops. They were thus able to study the contextual effect of the climate of opinion in the shop on the attitudes and behavior of its members. Wilson gathered information on students in 13 high schools in and around the San Francisco-Oakland Bay Area, choosing his schools to represent variations in the class composition of students. His analysis focuses on examining the effect of the social class composition of his schools on the aspirations of students.

individual behavior examined. A good example is a recent study by Coleman, Katz, and Menzel of the processes by which physicians come to adopt innovations in medical practice.[65] Coleman *et al.* assume that the readiness of a physician to adopt a medical innovation will depend, in part, on such factors as the nature of the physician's practice, his background and formal training, and his exposure to information about the innovation from both professional and non-professional sources. Had their conceptualization of the project gone no further than this, a cross-sectional design would probably have been adequate.

The investigators went on to suggest, however, that the physician's "place" in the general community of physicians would also exert an important influence on his adoption practices. They expected physicians to be concerned about, and to be influenced by, the interpretation other physicians might make of their use of medical innovations. The nature and extent of this concern would depend, it was postulated, on the physician's position in the social structure of the medical community. These considerations led the investigators to adopt a research design that called for interviewing *all* physicians serving patients in four communities, providing the advantage that findings in one community could be checked in others to test their consistency and generalizability, while at the same time allowing the investigators to obtain an important independent and objective measure of adoption through examination of pharmacists' prescription records. Had the sample been distributed over a larger area, such information would have been impractical to obtain.

Using this design, the task of obtaining information to assess physicians' relative standing in the medical community was met by asking each physician sociometric questions about his interaction with other physicians. The physician's location in the medical social structure then became an important independent variable in trying to account for variations in adoption patterns. A significant conclusion of the study is that the structure of the medical community and the individual doctor's place in it do indeed have an important bearing on his adoption of new drugs.

65. See Coleman, J. S., Elihu Katz, and Herbert Menzel, "The Diffusion of an Innovation Among Physicians," *Sociometry,* Vol. 20, 1957, pp. 253–269; Menzel, Herbert, "Innovation, Integration, and Marginality: A Survey of Physicians." *American Sociological Review,* Vol. 25, October, 1960, pp. 704–713; and Coleman, J. S., Elihu Katz, and Herbert Menzel, *Medical Innovation:* A Diffusion Study. Bobbs-Merrill, New York, 1966.

The use of sociometric questions poses special problems of analysis over and above those already discussed. With the advent of the computer, it has become possible to plot sociograms of the interactions of a large number of people. Making sense of the computer output is another matter, however, and so far, this has not been successfully done except where the number of cases is relatively small.

Coleman *et al.* used a sociogram to analyze data collected in a pilot study to their larger project. Here, however, they had to deal with the interaction patterns of only 36 physicians interviewed in the small pilot community. They found it necessary to virtually abandon this mode of analysis in their final project because of the complexities introduced by the larger number of cases. This occasioned the invention of the alternative strategies which are reported in the publications of this project.[66]

Systematic discussion of the special analytic problems which arise in studying sociometric data is still to come. It is likely that further experience with sociometric studies will be required to produce it, but that it will eventually prove worthwhile seems demonstrated by the ability of such studies to deal not only with problems of individual behavior but with larger units of analysis as well.[67]

PARALLEL-SAMPLE DESIGNS

Overlapping the contextual design is a more loosely defined class of studies that might be called "parallel-sample designs." These involve complementing a conventional cross-sectional survey with auxiliary surveys of special publics. In his study, *Communism, Conformity, and Civil Liberties,* Stouffer combined a cross-sectional design—a national sample of the general U.S. population—with a special sample of community leaders in selected

---

66. A further example of the use of a sociometric design is Coleman, J. S., *The Adolescent Society:* The Social Life of the Teenager and its Impact on Education. Free Press of Glencoe, New York, 1961. Coleman administered a questionnaire to *all* students of ten schools in varying types of communities, of varying sizes, and with apparent differences in their status systems. See also Coleman, J. S., "Relational Analysis: The Study of Social Organizations with Survey Methods," in *Complex Organizations:* A Sociological Reader. Edited by Amatai Etzioni. Holt, Rinehart, & Winston, New York, 1961.

67. Coleman, J. S., and Duncan MacRae, Jr., "Electronic Processing of Sociometric Data for Groups Up to 1,000 in Size," *American Sociological* Review, Vol. 25, October, 1960, pp. 722–727.

cities.[68] This enabled him to compare the values and attitudes of leaders with those of the general public both in the selected cities and in the country as a whole. A similar instance occurs in Herbert McClosky's study of political values.[69] He supplemented a sample of the general population with samples of the delegates to the Democratic and Republican National Conventions in 1956. Here, again, the use of auxiliary samples facilitated comparisons between leaders and followers.

Klausner and Kincaid, in a study done in 1956 of a New England flood disaster, were interested in examining some of the problems that arise when disaster victims are temporarily housed in the homes of neighbors spared by the flood.[70] They began with a cross-sectional sample of flood victims but then interviewed their hosts as well. In this way, they were able to compare two different perceptions of the same situation.

Over-representation, and the contextual, sociometric, and parallel-sample designs clearly do not exhaust the possible variations of the cross-sectional survey. They illustrate, however, the versatility of the survey method in dealing with a variety of sociological problems, whether they be concerned with the influence of social variables on individual behavior or with the investigation of larger units of analysis, such as organizations.

Studies of Short and Long-term Change

Although all of the survey designs discussed thus far provide for collecting data at one point in time only, this does not mean that the data refer only to that point. Almost always, they include reference to past as well as present events. Consequently, the use of these designs is not restricted to static problems; they can be, and have been, used for the studies of social process and social change.

These survey designs are not, however, ideally suited to these purposes. Respondents to an interview find it difficult to remember past behavior and attitudes and what they can recall is often unconsciously distorted by their present beliefs. Moreover, studies of process and change require that the time order of events be established with considerable precision. This is not

68. Stouffer, S. A., *op. cit.*
69. McClosky, Herbert, *et al.*, "Issue Conflict and Consensus Among Party Leaders and Followers," *American Political Science Review,* Vol. 54, June, 1960, pp. 406–427.
70. Klausner, S. Z. and H. V. Kincaid, *Social Problems of Sheltering Flood Evacuees.* Bureau of Applied Social Research, Columbia University, New York, 1956.

something that people can be relied upon to report accurately, and making inferences on logical grounds is often an unsatisfactory substitute.

Survey methods have been adapted for studying process and change through the relatively simple, albeit costly device of repeating the same study at different periods of time. Studies may do this by repeatedly asking the same questions of equivalent samples of different individuals—trend studies, or of the same individuals—panel studies. In theory, the repeated studies may take any of the forms already discussed. In practice, they have primarily involved repetitions of cross-sectional surveys.

TREND STUDIES

To exemplify studies done in this mode we must turn to sources other than sociology. Sociologists, while they have used other people's data to pursue the kind of analysis which this design allows, have not had the financial resources to plan and execute such studies *de novo*. The primary motive for engaging in periodic surveys on the same topic is to study trends and the agency having the broadest interest in trends is the federal government. It is not surprising, therefore, to find many government agencies engaging in research of this kind. Periodic surveys to study changes in population characteristics are regularly conducted by the Bureau of the Census; the Department of Agriculture uses the same device to study changes in consumption habits; studies of employment, health, production, manufacturing facilities, etc. are done repeatedly by other government agencies. Business firms are also prone to use repeated surveys to study changes in their public images and most public opinion polling organizations repeat at least some of the same questions in successive studies which they undertake.

All of these studies collect their information from samples which are equivalently drawn for each repeated survey. The equivalency of the samples allows, within statistically defined limits, the assessment of change during the time between surveys. Using an equivalent rather than the same sample assures also that successive samples are always representative of the possibly changing universe.

Trend studies are primarily useful in *describing* changes over shorter or longer periods of time. The data they produce have only limited value in seeking explanations of change. To illustrate their potentialities and limitations, consider the following shift in voting intention between August and October, as revealed by two successive surveys of the national population.

	August	October
Prefer candidate "x"	47%	53%
Prefer candidate "y"	53	47

Between August and October the net preference for candidate "x" increased by 6 percentage points, giving him a majority. Such a shift would ordinarily stimulate speculation about its cause. Let us say that one speculation accounts for the shift as a result of the fact that candidate "x" proved as the campaign progressed to have a particular appeal for women. One way to test this speculation is to compare shifts in party preferences separately for men and women, as for example:—

	Men		Women	
	Aug.	*Oct.*	*Aug.*	*Oct.*
"x"	49%	50%	45%	56%
"y"	51	50	55	44

The table lends support to the speculation. The overall net increase in support for candidate "x" is largely accounted for by net shifts in the voting intentions of women. Men showed little difference in their net preference for the candidates at the two time periods. Armed with this evidence, the data could be examined further to discover whether older women were more likely to exhibit a net shift than younger women, and so forth.

Some understanding of the factors underlying net change can be gained through this procedure. Explanatory analysis of trend data, however, is inevitably frustrated because the data allow no estimate of the amount of individual change that produced the observed overall shifts in distributions, i.e., the net change. The change of 11 percentage points in the proportion of women favoring candidate "x", for example, might have come about through all of the women originally for "x" in August remaining faithful to him in October with the additional 11 per cent being recruited from those who had been for "y" in August. However, it is equally possible that "x" lost a small or a large proportion of his August supporters but that this defection was counterbalanced by a shift to "x" that was greater by 11 percentage points. Repeated studies with equivalent samples offer no way to determine the patterns of defection and faithfulness that lead to the observed shifts in distribution.

In sum, this survey design is useful in identifying change, in plotting trends, and in helping to specify differential rates of change among subgroups. It is not suited to pursuing explanatory analysis of change except that, insofar as it pinpoints the subgroups which change most, it can lead to more sophisticated speculation.

Whatever inspirations sociologists may have had to launch substantial trend studies have been frustrated until now by the prohibitive costs. There have been efforts, however, to influence the content of ongoing data collection operations. For example, attempts have been made to persuade public opinion polling agencies to repeat key questions in successive surveys. There have also been efforts to inform the content of continuing government surveys. Paralleling such activities has been a growing recognition of opportunities for secondary analysis of existing data in the sociological study of change.

To date, probably the most ambitious study based on secondary analysis is Alford's *Party and Society*.[71] Alford was concerned with testing the proposition that voting along class lines has declined substantially in Western democracies over the last decades. To this end, he assembled and re-analyzed 39 past national surveys of voting behavior conducted in Great Britain, the United States, Australia, and Canada between 1936 and 1962. Because of the aforementioned limitations, his analysis is essentially descriptive rather than explanatory. However, he makes adroit use of the possibilities for examining differential rates of change among subgroups of his populations. Alford's study also illustrates the potential for using survey data for comparative international research about which we shall have more to say shortly.

Panel studies, to which we now turn, overcome some of the analytical difficulties of trend studies. Practical considerations, however, make panel studies suitable only for the study of relatively short-run change. The one major advantage of trend studies is that they can be carried on over an indefinite period of time.

PANEL STUDIES

Panel studies, as we have previously indicated, call for interviewing the same subjects at two or more points in time. Their principal analytic advantage over trend studies is that they allow the investigation of *turnover,* i.e. shifts in the behavior or attitudes of individual units from one period to the next.

71. Alford, Robert, *Party and Society:* The Anglo-American Democracies. Rand McNally, Chicago, 1963.

Consider the same political example that illustrated the discussion of trend studies. Now, however, assume that the data refer to successive interviews with the same respondents. With trend type data, it is only possible to study shifts in the total distribution of preferences. Panel studies make it possible to study these shifts *and* to show how they result from shifts in individual preferences, as in this typical turnover table:

	August		
	Favorite Candidate		
October	"x"	"y"	Total
Favor candidate "x"	40%	13%	53%
Favor candidate "y"	7	40	47
Total	47%	53%	100%

The bottom row of figures gives the distribution of candidate preference in August. The figures are the same as those provided by the trend study. The "Total" column of figures at the far right shows the distribution in October, again corresponding to the trend study figures, creating the impression that only 6 per cent shifted. Looking at the figures in the body of the table, however, the diagonals tell us that 80 per cent were consistent in their candidate preference for August and October (40 per cent for "x" both times and 40 per cent for "y" both times), and that the balance of 20 per cent shifted (13 per cent from "y" to "x" and 7 per cent from "x" to "y"). By making it possible to see gross as well as net change, panel studies provide a means for inquiring into a number of questions concerning the dynamics of social change:[72]

1. *What kinds of people are most likely to change and in what direction?* Following along with our political example, we may ask then whether women are more likely to change than men, the rich more than the poor, the educated more than the uneducated, politically alert more than the politically apathetic, etc.

2. *Under what conditions do changes come about?* In studies of political behavior, it has been repeatedly demonstrated that people under cross pressures are least stable in their voting intentions.[73] Those, for example,

72. For examples of some of these uses, see Glock, C. Y., "Some Applications of the Panel Method to the Study of Social Change," in *The Language of Social Research.* Edited by P. F. Lazarsfeld and Morris Rosenberg, *op. cit.,* pp. 242–250. The most extensive extant discussion of the logic of panel analysis is Levenson, Bernard, *Panel Analysis Workbook,* Bureau of Applied Social Research, Columbia University, 1955.
73. See for example, Berelson, B. R., P. F. Lazarsfeld, and W. W. McPhee, *op. cit.*

whose colleagues at work are Democratic but whose families are traditionally Republican are more prone to shift than those for whom the two situations reinforce each other. A panel study not only enables a comparison to be made of the behavior of those who are facing cross pressures and those who are not, but it allows assessment of which of the several influences operating in a cross pressure situation is most likely to determine behavior.

3. *What is the effect of a particular stimulus in producing change?* Here, panel studies are useful in identifying factors leading to exposure to particular stimuli as well as their efficacy in producing change. In effect, with appropriate controls, the panel provides a means to approximate the situation of the experiment in field studies.

4. *What are the conditions which produce differential changes in attitudes and behavior?* As we have previously suggested, not everyone who changes his vote during an election campaign does so in the same direction. The same stimulus may affect different people in different ways. The panel is suited to studying such differential change.

5. *What attitudes and behavior patterns are likely to change simultaneously over time?* The mutual interaction between variables is, of course, highly relevant to any study of change. Changes in one variable often imply changes in another. The panel method is unique in allowing the specification of such mutual interaction.

6. *What is the relationship between present attitudes and future behavior?* Panel studies provide a means to test predictive hypotheses in sociology. Are those who are liberal in college likely to remain so when they reach middle age? To what degree is anticipated behavior confirmed in later actual behavior?

It has been suggested that panel studies are most applicable to the study of short-run social change. This is a consequence of practical limitations in the execution of panel studies rather than of any innate quality of the design.[74] The difficulties of persuading people to agree to become panel members and, more important, of locating them at successive interview points are inevitable, but not impossible to overcome. It is important to note, perhaps, that impediments are fewer where the subjects of study are institutions, churches, labor unions, and the like; problems of non-response or re-location of respondents are not so likely to arise in panel studies in

---

74. For a discussion of some of the difficulties, see Kendall, Patricia L., *Conflict and Mood:* Factors Affecting Stability of Response. Free Press, Chicago, 1954, and also Glock, C. Y., *Participation Bias and Re-Interview Effect in Panel Studies,* unpublished doctoral thesis, Columbia University, 1952.

which, for example, the sample is of the nation's colleges and universities rather than a sample of individuals.

Of all the variations in survey designs we have discussed, this one has the most promise for sociological inquiry. Panel studies provide a means to study social change and the social processes which underly it, the central concerns of sociology. They largely solve the problem of time order and, consequently, broaden opportunities for explanatory analysis. They are especially suited to studying units of analyses larger than the individual and to building indices which require that account be taken of change. Yet, despite these and other advantages, sociologically inspired panel studies are relatively rare.

There have been several panel studies of political behavior during national presidential campaigns and congressional elections.[75] The method has been used in a study of changes in occupational choice.[76] Panel studies have also been done in a few instances to assess the impact of information or educational programs.[77] And, a study using panel data has been made of patterns of personal influence.[78] At most, however, fewer than ten panel studies have been reported in the sociological literature. All of these are studies of short-run social change and none have applied the method to studying larger entities than individuals.

The discrepancy between potential and actual use is undoubtedly a result, in part, of practical difficulties in conducting panel studies. The fact that social change is often a slow process and requires data collected over an extended period of time is also a contributing factor, as is the matter of cost. We suspect, however, that the discrepancy is also due to the fact that

75. Lazarsfeld, P. F., B. R. Berelson, and Hazel Gaudet, *op. cit.,* and Berelson, B. R. and P. F. Lazarsfeld, and W. W. McPhee, *op. cit.*

76. Rosenberg, Morris, "Factors Influencing Change of Occupational Choice," in *The Language of Social Research.* Edited by P. F. Lazarsfeld and Morris Rosenberg, *op. cit.,* pp. 250–260.

77. Pratt, Lois V., "An Evaluation of an Industry Promotional Campaign," mimeographed, Bureau of Applied Social Research, Columbia University, New York, 1953; and Hyman, H. H., C. R. Wright, and T. K. Hopkins, *Applications of Methods of Evaluation:* 4 Studies of the Encampment for Citizenship. University of California Press, Berkeley and Los Angeles, 1962; and Davis, J. A., *Great Books and Small Groups.* Free Press, Glencoe, Ill., 1961. Davis' study combines a panel design with contextual design.

78. Katz, Elihu and P. F. Lazarsfeld, *Personal Influence:* The Part Played by People in the Flow of Mass Communication. Free Press, Chicago, 1955.

the logic of panel analysis has still to be wholly codified, a necessary element, apparently, to the widespread diffusion of any methodological innovation.

Conclusions

We began this chapter with the observation that survey research has been extensively used in sociology. What we have reported testifies to the observation. It cannot be concluded, however, that the logic of survey research has penetrated deeply into the sociological consciousness or that the potential for applying the method to sociological problems has been exhausted. Survey research, after all, has been a sociological tool only for several decades and, while considerable progress has been made both substantively and methodologically, the promise for the future looms much larger than the accomplishments of the past.

Speculating about this promise, there are a number of grounds for optimistically assuming that we are on the horizon of significant new breakthroughs in the use of survey methods in sociological inquiry. An inhibiting influence of the past has been the social-psychological bias of the cross-sectional survey. Recent innovations in survey design such as the contextual and the sociometric are significant signs that the method is being effectively adapted to more strictly sociological problems.

A second inhibiting factor has been the absence of a fully worked out logic of survey analysis. Though the logic of elaborating on two-variable relations has been effectively worked out for some time, sociologists interested in working on more complex problems have had to rely on their artfulness in analysis without the benefit of fully understanding the logical implications of their procedures. Solutions are still not immediately at hand. However, pioneering work now underway to introduce mathematics into survey analysis as well as the progress being made in using more advanced statistical procedures as analytical tools are slowly shifting the burden of analysis from art to science.[79]

The cost of survey research has also been a significant element in restricting its use, but the growing recognition that it is not always necessary to collect new data for every problem—that creative use can be made of exist-

79. Coleman, J. S., *Introduction to Mathematical Sociology*. Free Press of Glencoe, New York, 1964; Selvin, H. C., *The Logic of Survey Analysis, loc. cit.*; and Blalock, H. M., Jr., *op. cit.*

ing survey data—promises to be a partial solution to the problem of cost. The viability of this solution is indicated by the spectacular growth of social science data archives over the last few years and their intensive use, particularly by sociologists at smaller institutions without resources for conducting survey research *de novo*. Also contributing to a solution is an increasing awareness on the part of fund granting agencies that social science research is expensive and is likely in the future to require investments of the same magnitude as are now commonplace in the physical sciences. Certainly the gap between investments in the two kinds of research is still large. Nevertheless, a change is in process, indicated by the increasing interest and investment of the federal government in social science research.

A final indication of the promise for expanding use of survey research in sociology is, of course, the rapidly growing interest in comparative international research, particularly in the developing countries. Survey methods are especially appropriate to such research because they afford an effective and efficient means for collecting social data where none existed before. There will be problems, of course, in applying a technology which has been largely developed in the United States to other cultures. Yet, it is already clear that this will be an important new way in which survey research will be used in the future.

Bibliography

Alford, Robert, *Party and Society:* The Anglo-American Democracies. Rand McNally, Chicago, 1963.

Berelson, B. R., P. F. Lazarsfeld and W. W. McPhee, *Voting:* A Study of Opinion Formation in a Presidential Campaign. Chicago University Press, Chicago, 1954.

Bigman, S. K., *Methodological Considerations in International Broadcasting Research* (mimeographed). Bureau of Applied Social Research, Columbia University, New York, 1951.

Blalock, H. M., Jr., *Causal Inferences in Nonexperimental Research.* University of North Carolina Press, Chapel Hill, 1964.

Booth, Charles, ed., *Life and Labour of the People in London,* 17 vols. Macmillan, London and New York, 1892–1893.

Boudon, Raymond and P. F. Lazarsfeld, *Le Vocabulaire Des Sciences Sociales:* Concepts et Indices. Mouton, Paris, 1965.

Campbell, Angus, P. E. Converse, and W. E. Miller, *The American Voter.* John Wiley & Sons, New York, 1960.

Carlin, J. E., *Lawyers' Ethics:* A Survey of the New York City Bar. Russell Sage Foundation, New York, 1966.

Coleman, J. S., *The Adolescent Society:* The Social Life of the Teenager and its Impact on Education. Free Press of Glencoe, New York, 1961.

Coleman, J. S., "Relational Analysis: The Study of Social Organizations with Survey Methods," in *Complex Organizations:* A Sociological Reader. Edited by Amatai Etzioni. Holt, Rinehart & Winston, New York, 1961.

Coleman, J. S., *Introduction to Mathematical Sociology.* Free Press of Glencoe, New York, 1964.

Coleman, J. S. and Duncan MacRae, Jr., "Electronic Processing of Sociometric Data for Groups Up to 1,000 in Size," *American Sociological Review,* Vol. 25, October, 1960, pp. 722–727.

Coleman, J. S., Elihu Katz, and Herbert Menzel, "The Diffusion of an Innovation Among Physicians," *Sociometry* Vol. 20, 1957, pp. 253–269.

Coleman, J. S., Elihu Katz, and Herbert Menzel, *Medical Innovation:* A Diffusion Study. Bobbs-Merrill, New York, 1966.

Davis, J. A., *Great Books and Small Groups.* Free Press, Glencoe, Ill., 1961.

Douglas, William, *Ministers' Wives,* Harper & Row, New York, 1965.

Durkheim, Emile, *Suicide:* A Study in Sociology. Translated by J. S. Spaulding and George Simpson. Free Press, Chicago, 1951.

Glazer, Nathan, "The Rise of Social Research in Europe," in *The Human Meaning of the Social Sciences.* Edited by Daniel Lerner. Meridian Books, New York, 1959.

Glock, C. Y., "Participation Bias and Re-interview Effect in Panel Studies," unpublished doctoral thesis, Columbia University, 1952.

Glock, C. Y., "Some Applications of the Panel Method to the Study of Social Change," in *Language of Social Research*. Edited by P. F. Lazarsfeld and Morris Rosenberg. Free Press, Glencoe, Ill., 1955, pp. 242–250.

Glock, C. Y. and Rodney Stark, *Christian Belief and Anti-Semitism*. Harper & Row, New York, 1966.

Glock, C. Y., Benjamin Ringer, and Earl Babbie, *To Comfort and to Challenge:* A Dilemma of the Contemporary Church. University of California Press, Berkeley and Los Angeles, 1967.

Glock, C. Y., Gertrude Selznick, and J. L. Spaeth, *The Apathetic Majority:* A Study Based on Public Responses to the Eichmann Trial. Harper & Row, New York, 1966.

Glock, C. Y., Gertrude Selznick and Jacqueline Wiseman, "The Wilderness Vacationist," in *Wilderness and Recreation:* A Report on Resources, Values and Problems to the Outdoor Recreation Resources Review Commission by the Wildland Research Center, University of California, 1962, chap. 5.

Goldsen, R. K., *et al., What College Students Think*. Van Nostrand, New York, 1960.

Gross, Neal, W. S. Mason, and A. W. McEachern, *Explorations in Role Analysis:* Studies of the School Superintendency Role. John Wiley & Sons, New York, 1958.

Gurin, Gerald, *et al., Americans View Their Mental Health:* A Nationwide Interview Survey. Basic Books, New York, 1960.

Harman, H. H., *Modern Factor Analysis*. University of Chicago Press, Chicago, 1960.

Havemann, Ernest and P. S. West, *They Went to College:* The College Graduate in America Today. Harcourt, Brace, New York, 1952.

Hempel, C. G., "Classification." In *Fundamentals of Concept Formation in Empirical Science*. University of Chicago Press, Chicago, 1952.

Hollingshead, A. deB. and F. C. Redlich, *Social Class and Mental Illness:* A Community Study. John Wiley & Sons, New York, 1958.

Hyman, H. H., *Survey Design and Analysis:* Principles, Cases and Procedures. Free Press, Chicago, 1955.

Hyman, H. H. and P. B. Sheatsley, "Attitudes Toward Desegregation," *Scientific American*, Vol. 211, July, 1964, pp. 16–23.

Hyman, H. H., C. R. Wright, and T. K. Hopkins, *Applications of Methods of Evaluation:* 4 Studies of the Encampment for Citizenship. University of California Press, Berkeley and Los Angeles, 1962.

Inkeles, Alex and P. H. Rossi, "National Comparisons of Occupational Prestige," *American Journal of Sociology*, Vol. 61, 1956, pp. 329–339.

Katz, Elihu and P. F. Lazarsfeld, *Personal Influence:* The Part Played by People in the Flow of Mass Communications. Free Press, Chicago, 1955.

Kendall, P. L., *Conflict and Mood:* Factors Affecting Stability of Response. Free Press, Chicago, 1954.

Kendall, P. L. and P. F. Lazarsfeld, "Problems of Survey Analysis," in *Continuities in Survey Research:* Studies in the Scope and Method of "The American Soldier." Edited by R. K. Merton and P. F. Lazarsfeld. Free Press, Chicago, 1950.

Kinsey, A. C., W. B. Pomeroy, and C. E. Martin, *Sexual Behavior in the Human Male*. W. B. Saunders, Philadelphia, 1948.

Kish, Leslie, *Survey Sampling.* John Wiley & Sons, New York, 1965.

Klapper, J. T., *The Effects of Mass Communication.* Free Press, Glencoe, Ill., 1960.

Klausner, S. Z. and H. V. Kincaid, *Social Problems of Sheltering Flood Evacuees.* Bureau of Applied Social Research, Columbia University, New York, 1956.

Lazarsfeld, P. F., ed., *Mathematical Thinking in the Social Sciences.* Free Press, Chicago, 1954.

Lazarsfeld, P. F., "Latent Structure Analysis," in *Psychology:* A Study of Science, Conceptual and Systematic. Edited by Sigmund Koch. McGraw-Hill, New York, 1959, pp. 476–573.

Lazarsfeld, P. F. and P. L. Kendall, *Radio Listening in America:* The People Look at Radio—Again. Prentice-Hall, New York, 1948.

Lazarsfeld, P. F. and Wagner Thielens, Jr., *The Academic Mind.* Free Press. Chicago, 1958.

Lazarsfeld, P. F., B. R. Berelson, and Hazel Gaudet, *The People's Choice:* How the Voter Makes Up His Mind in a Presidential Campaign. Columbia University Press, New York, 1948.

Lazarsfeld, P. F. and Morris Rosenberg, eds., *The Language of Social Research:* A Reader in the Methodology of Social Research. Free Press, Glencoe, Ill., 1955.

Lenski, G. E., *The Religious Factor:* A Sociological Study of Religion's Impact on Politics, Economics, and Family Life. Doubleday, New York, 1961.

Le Play, P. G. F., *La Reforme Sociale en France,* 2 vols. E. Dentu, Paris, 1866.

Lerner, Daniel, *The Passing of Traditional Society:* Modernizing the Middle East. Free Press, Chicago, 1958.

Levenson, Bernard, *Panel Analysis Workbook.* Bureau of Applied Social Research, Columbia University, New York, 1955.

Lipset, S. M., "Opinion Formation in a Crisis Situation," *Public Opinion Quarterly,* Vol. 17, No. 1, 1953, pp. 20–46.

Lipset, S. M., *Political Man:* The Social Bases of Politics. Doubleday, New York, 1960.

Lipset, S. M., Martin Trow, and J. S. Coleman, *Union Democracy:* The Internal Politics of the International Typographical Union. Free Press, Chicago, 1956.

London, Jack, Warren Hagstrom and Robert Wenkert, *Adult Education and Social Class.* Monograph 9, Survey Research Center, University of California, Berkeley, 1963.

Lowenthal, M. F., *Lives in Distress.* Basic Books, New York, 1964.

McClosky, Herbert, *et al.,* "Issue Conflict and Consensus Among Party Leaders and Follower," *American Political Science Review,* Vol. 54, June, 1960, pp. 406–427.

McPhee, William and W. A. Glazer, eds., *Public Opinion and Congressional Elections.* Free Press, Chicago, 1962.

Menzel, Herbert, "Innovation, Integration, and Marginality: A Survey of Physicians," *American Sociological Review,* Vol. 25, October, 1960, pp. 704–713.

Merton, R. K., George Reader, and P. L. Kendall, eds., *The Student Physician.* Harvard University Press, Cambridge, 1957.

Miller, D. R. and G. E. Swanson, *The Changing American Parent.* John Wiley & Sons, New York, 1958.

Mills, C. W., Clarence Senior, and R. K. Goldsen, *The Puerto Rican Journey*. Harper. New York, 1950.

Moser, C. A., *Survey Methods in Social Investigation*. Macmillan, London, 1958.

Pratt, L. V., "An Evaluation of an Industry Promotional Campaign" (mimeographed). Bureau of Applied Social Research, Columbia University, New York, 1953.

Rosenberg, Morris, "Factors Influencing Change of Occupation," in *Language of Social Research*. Edited by P. F. Lazarsfeld and Morris Rosenberg. Free Press, Glencoe, Ill., 1955, pp. 250–260.

Rossi, P. H., *Why Families Move*. Free Press, Glencoe, Ill., 1955.

Selvin, H. C., "Durkheim's *Suicide* and the Problems of Empirical Research," *Journal of Sociology*, Vol. 63, 1958, pp. 607–619.

Selvin, H. C., *The Effects of Leadership*. Free Press, Glencoe, Ill., 1960.

Selvin, H. C., *The Logic of Survey Analysis*. Monograph 12, Survey Research Center, University of California, Berkeley, 1965.

Selvin, H. C. and Robert Wenkert, "School Spirit in Context of a Liberal Education." In *Social Problems,* Fall, 1962.

Sills, D. L., *The Volunteers:* Means and Ends in a National Organization. Free Press, Glencoe, Ill., 1957.

Srole, Leo, *et al.*, *Mental Health in the Metropolis:* The Midtown Manhattan Study. McGraw-Hill, New York, 1962.

Steiner, G. A., *The People Look at Television:* A Study of Audience Attitudes. Alfred A. Knopf, New York, 1963.

Stephan, F. F. and P. J. McCarthy, *Sampling Opinions:* An Analysis of Survey Procedure, John Wiley & Sons, New York, 1958.

Stouffer, S. A., *Communism, Conformity, and Civil Liberties:* A Cross Section of the Nation Speaks Its Mind. Doubleday, New York, 1955.

Stouffer, S. A., *et al.*, *The American Soldier,* Vol. 1 and Vol. 2. Princeton University Press, Princeton, 1949, 1950.

Swanson, G. E., *The Birth of Gods*. University of Michigan Press, Ann Arbor, 1960.

Thurstone, L. L., *Multiple-Factor Analysis:* A Development and Expansion of the Vectors of Mind. University of Chicago Press, Chicago, 1947.

Trow, Martin, "Right Wing Radicalism," unpublished doctoral thesis, Columbia University, New York, 1954.

Udy, S. H., *Organization at Work:* A Comparative Analysis of Production among Non-industrial Peoples. Human Relations Area Files Press, New Haven, Conn., 1959.

Weber, Max, *Protestant Ethics and the Spirit of Capitalism*. Charles Scribner's Sons, New York, 1930.

Whelpton, P. K. and C. V. Kiser, "Social and Psychological Factors Affecting Fertility," *Melbank Memorial Fund Quarterly,* Vol. 23, October, 1945.

Wilson, A. B., "Residential Segregation of Social Classes and Aspirations of High School Boys," *American Sociological Review,* Vol. 24, December, 1959, pp. 836–845.

Yule, G. U., *Introduction to the Theory of Statistics*. Charles Griffen, London, 1911.

Survey Research in

Political Science

by Herbert McClosky
Survey Research Center
University of California
Berkeley

Nature and Types of Surveys

Survey Methods and the Science of Politics
> Establishing the Facts
> Increasing the Range and Amount of Information
> Adoption of a Scientific Posture

The Substantive Contributions of Surveys
> Public Opinion
> Participation
> Voting
> Political Elites and Leadership
> Political Ideology and Extreme Belief
> Political Socialization, Stability, and Change
> Psychology and Politics
> Political Institutions and Systems
> Comparative and International Studies

New Applications for Survey Research
> Political Leadership
> Internal Party Affairs
> Relation of Belief to Action
> Historical and Trend Analysis

The Contribution of Surveys to Theory

Limitations and Problems in the Use of Political Surveys

Survey Research in Political Science

THE APPLICATION of survey methods to the study of politics is approximately as old as the study of political behavior. Although they refer to different things—one is a technique for gathering data while the other is an intellectual orientation toward a field of study—the progress of the one has promoted the advancement of the other. Within two decades the survey method has become the most important research procedure in the "behavioral" study of politics, and is being increasingly adopted by "non-behaviorists" as well.

The growing reliance upon survey analysis in political science is one aspect of a pervasive change that has been transforming the study of politics for the past two decades. Traditionally a discipline concerned mainly with legal, institutional, historical, and normative questions, political science has been shifting its focus toward such phenomena as role, process, group, personality, ideology, elites, political recruitment, socialization, social stratification, mobility, function, political stability, decision-making, and political change. Whereas traditional political science has relied principally upon documentary sources, reportage, anecdotal data, subjective and unsystematic observation, individual interpretations, narrative treatment, and the philosophical examination of analytical and normative statements, the behavioral study of politics has stressed direct observation, objective measurement, systematic data collection, the operationalizing of concepts, quantification, a deliberate search for regularities and variations, and systematic comparison across groups and cultures in an effort to ascertain the limits of generalization. The new political science also differs from the old in being interested in classes of phenomena rather than in individual (or unique) events and institutions.

Political science journals now contain articles on community power and decision-making; functional analyses of political systems; legislative roll calls and constituency characteristics; mathematical analyses of choice behavior; experiments in leadership, influence, communication, and conformity; clinical studies of the relations between personality and attitudes; applications of game theory to international phenomena; simulation studies of international or organizational processes; psychoanalytic studies of renowned political leaders; and studies of the political impact of the mass media. As these topics suggest, political scientists are drawing on the same research techniques employed by the other social sciences: laboratory experiments, surveys, participant observation, clinical and attitude testing, case studies (both of individuals and institutions), content analysis, mathematical models, game theory, systems analysis, macro-studies of the informal and formal features of political communities, simulation studies, and so forth. Not all of these are equally useful to political science, and none of them has so far displaced documentary or institutional studies as the prevailing mode of inquiry; but the proportion is rapidly changing and the trend is unmistakable.

Among the new research techniques employed by political scientists, survey research is perhaps the most common and, up to now, the most useful. Surveys are now being used in almost every branch of political science and, in some areas of inquiry, such as voting, they have become virtually the exclusive method of investigation. Although voting is a form of political behavior that is especially amenable to survey research, survey procedures can be adapted to a wide range and variety of political activities.

In the pages that follow, we first set forth the nature and types of surveys, the different ways in which surveys may be used, variations in the design and purpose of surveys, and the multiple objectives that the survey method can serve. In the second section, we examine the ways in which surveys help to promote the scientific study of politics by forcing improvements in the rigor of research procedures, the quality of measures, and the techniques for certifying facts. The third and largest section reviews the major survey research and findings on such topics as public opinion, political participation, voting, political socialization, psychological aspects of politics, political change, and comparative politics. In the fourth section, we consider the potential application of surveys to subjects that have so far been little explored, such as political leadership, internal party affairs, the relation of political belief to action, and historical and trend analysis. In the fifth section, we examine the contribution of surveys to political theory, including the modifications that are being suggested in theories about democracy, parties, and extreme belief and affiliation. Finally, we address some of the limitations and problems that beset the survey method, and some of the criticisms aimed at the use of surveys to study politics.

Nature and Types of Surveys

A survey may be defined as any procedure in which data are systematically collected from a population, or a sample thereof, through some form of direct solicitation, such as face-to-face interviews, telephone interviews, or mail questionnaires. Surveys, of course, are not the only devices political scientists can use to collect systematic data on populations. They can also consult ecological reports for information on consumption, industrialization, and other indices of "modernization," state and county publications for aggregative data on party registration and voting preferences, or census and other government reports for figures on population changes, income levels, and number and size of voting districts. The utility of these sources, however, is severely limited. Aggregative data, for example, can tell us little about the political attitudes and motivations of the population or its subgroups; official election returns can furnish only a crude estimate of which groups have voted for whom;[1] and comparisons of gross voting figures in various elections cannot specify which voters have shifted their preference for a candidate or party from one election to the next. These and scores of similar questions can usually be answered only through surveys. Surveys can, of course, be justified "only when the desired information cannot be obtained more easily and less expensively from other sources."[2]

The survey investigator may be interested in the individuals or groups who compose his "sample" not for themselves but for what they "represent." Usually, in fact, he chooses for study persons who collectively possess in miniature the same characteristics as the "universe" of persons he wishes to investigate. That universe may be the adult population of the entire nation or of a smaller unit. It may consist of active party members, political officer holders, or some other special group, such as state legislators, judges, or young people attending high school. There is no inherent restriction on either the size or composition of the universe. These are determined by the

---

1. Robinson, W. S., "Ecological Correlation and the Behavior of Individuals," *American Sociological Review,* Vol. 15, June, 1950, pp. 351–357; and Ranney, Austin, "The Utility and Limitations of Aggregate Data in the Study of Electoral Data," in *Essays on the Behavioral Study of Politics.* Edited by Austin Ranney. University of Illinois Press, Urbana, 1962, pp. 91–102, at p. 91.
2. Campbell, Angus and George Katona, "The Sample Survey: A Technique for Social Science Research," in *Research Methods in the Behavioral Sciences.* Edited by Leon Festinger and Daniel Katz. Dryden Press, New York, 1953, p. 16.

investigator's interest, and by the questions he wishes to answer. The universe may be small enough to permit the investigator to interview all of its members (this would be the case, for example, if one were doing a survey of national committeemen of the American parties); or it may be so large and geographically far-flung that the sample selected for study will number only a tiny fraction of the whole. Not all samples employed in political studies need to be "representative" in the sense of being cross-section miniatures of the general population; ordinarily they need only to mirror the characteristics of the particular universe being studied. A cross-section sample of the general population is essential only if one is actually investigating the general population. If one is studying political leaders, it would be wasteful to draw a sample of the general population in order to cull the small number of leaders to be found among them.

The accuracy with which a sample reflects the characteristics of the universe, and the number and type of characteristics represented in the sample, can vary somewhat with the nature of the inquiry. In general, a sample must more perfectly reflect the characteristics of the universe being studied if the investigator wishes to describe that universe than if his main concern is to discover or test relationships among variables. A scholar seeking to ascertain the number of Democratic voters in the general population will need a sample whose characteristics approximate quite closely those of the general population itself. This requirement becomes still more urgent if he also intends to predict the magnitude of the Democratic vote in an election, for even a small misrepresentation in the sample may lead to an erroneous forecast of the outcome. If, however, he is seeking to discover what the approximate correlation is between, say, belief in democracy and personality characteristics, he may be able to get by with a less perfect sample, for the correlation between these variables is not likely to be severely altered by the over-representation of certain groups—providing, of course, the errors are not extremely large.

Fulfilling the requirements of representative sampling may in some political studies be hindered by the fact that the characteristics of the universe are not known, and no practicable procedure may be available for ascertaining them. For example, no adequate description of the universe of persons active in politics is presently available, and an investigator who wishes to sample this universe cannot be certain that he has achieved an appropriate likeness. In such cases he may attempt to reduce systematic bias and undesired over-representation by casting a wide net and drawing his sample from many party units at different levels of activity in widely separated localities. Given sufficient funds, he might also employ a procedure known as "double sampling," in which a preliminary survey would first be carried out merely to locate and learn the characteristics of the party actives throughout the nation—merely, in other words, to determine the nature of the universe to be sampled.

The discovery that one can, by scientific sampling, reproduce in miniature and with remarkable accuracy the characteristics of a given universe is the *sine qua non* of the survey procedure, and holds out immense opportunities for the study of politics. Since political science is concerned with institutional and group phenomena involving thousands or even millions of people, procedures are needed for making the observation of such multitudes manageable. Without sampling, the study even of a local election, or of special groups such as Negroes, farmers, and political leaders, would require countless observations of many thousands of people. Through sampling, however, these and dozens of other groups can be reproduced in miniature, reduced to manageable proportions, and studied directly, closely, and in detail. The potential value of this procedure is incalculable, for it has now become possible simultaneously to study one or many political sub-cultures, to collect detailed information on millions of people by sampling only one or two thousand of them, to gather evidence systematically on a large number of questions and hypotheses and, by virtue of these possibilities, to advance the scientific study of politics in a way that could not have been imagined even fifty years ago.

Before the development of survey methods and scientific sampling, the political analysis of mass responses rested upon the observational skills and intuition of the individual investigator. He was often compelled to gather evidence on a hit or miss basis, relying on published articles or books, on such letters or diaries as he could find, and on discussions with persons whose opinions seemed to him worthwhile. Whether the political responses yielded by these sources were truly representative of a larger universe or were opinions unique to the individuals who expressed them was rarely known. Generalizations about slave owners or debtors or Northerners or those who voted for Wilson were, as a result, inadequately grounded and lacking in warranty. As retrospective empirical studies of past elections and other political events indicate, many historical inferences formerly regarded as "settled" turn out, in the light of contemporary survey knowledge, to be suspect.[3] They reflect not only the biases of the investigator, but the fortuitous character of his data-gathering procedures.

With the aid of surveys, some of these difficulties can now be mitigated. In principle, we can accurately compare and contrast individuals and groups from every part of the society, occupants of every kind of political role, persons or groups holding every type of political belief, political leaders and followers, Northerners and Southerners, Democrats and Republicans, rich and poor, debtors and creditors, supporters and opponents of various public policies, and every combination of these that interest us. We are thus able to test generalizations that until now have been loosely grounded in impressions gathered from anecdotal and other unsystematic evidence. This potentiality is essential for the development of a scientific understanding of politics.

Survey methods can be used in the comparative study of institutions, nations, and political practices as well as in the study of individuals and groups. One might, for example, discover much about the practices of bureaucratic agencies by surveying samples of their officials. One might learn how their decisions are actually made, whether their procedures differ according to the size of the agency, the degree of "modernization," and the types of training received by their functionaries, how they relate in practice to the legislative branches, and whether executive policies are in fact dominated by permanent civil servants. Comparable studies could be done on the institutional practices of judicial bodies, legislatures, or political parties —all with a degree of scientific refinement rarely possible heretofore.

Just as political surveys differ in the types of universes they investigate, so do they also vary in their design and purpose. The term "survey" usually conjures up the image of an interviewer canvassing house to house, asking direct opinion questions and receiving direct answers. While this is the classic pattern of the public opinion poll, many other kinds of political surveys are possible. The primary concern of some surveys has been to describe the beliefs of the general population or certain of its segments, while others have sought to test hypotheses and to investigate the relations among variables. Some have used randomly drawn samples, while others have deliberately over-sampled certain groups in order to study them more closely. Some have merely ascertained surface opinions, while others have probed

3. Truman, D. B., "Research in Political Behavior," *American Political Science Review,* Vol. 46, December, 1952, pp. 1003–1006.

deeply into the underlying attitude structure and personality characteristics of the respondents. Some have focused upon beliefs and others upon actions, some upon opinion-makers and others upon opinion-consumers. Most surveys have been one-shot affairs, collecting all of their data at a single point in time, but others have employed a "panel" of respondents who are interviewed and reinterviewed at different points in time in order to assess their shifts in opinion and party preference, or their response to changing political events.

The adaptability of the survey method is also illustrated by the range of subjects to which surveys may be addressed. They can, for example, be employed either for omnibus political studies or for studies that are narrowly restricted in subject matter. An investigator may be interested in a single political outcome, such as voting turnout, but if he is to explore adequately even this one variable, he will need information on many different kinds of people. He will require samples of regular voters, occasional voters, and non-voters, and on each of these he will doubtless want information on their group, psychological, political, and intellectual characteristics. He can collect such data in a single survey, and can use the results to explore his respondents' behavior either intensively or extensively. He can use the information yielded by the survey to construct indices and scales that will permit him to examine, from various points of view and with considerable thoroughness and refinement, the relationships in which he is interested. Although a survey utilizing large samples may seem an uneconomical way to collect data on a single dependent variable, it often turns out to be the most efficient and economical method possible. Among the most striking examples of this are the handful of large-scale voting surveys that have in three decades taught us more about the act of voting than was learned in all previous history.[4] These survey studies have shown that even the apparently simple act of voting is in reality the behavioral manifestation of extraordinarily complex forces.

Surveys offer the further advantage of furnishing information simultaneously on more than one set of dependent and independent variables. A survey that is primarily focused on voting can also collect information

4. Lazarsfeld, P. F., B. R. Berelson and Hazel Gaudet, *The People's Choice:* How the Voter Makes up his Mind in a Presidential Campaign. Duell, Sloan, and Pearce, New York, 1944; Berelson, B. R., P. F. Lazarsfeld, and W. W. McPhee, *Voting: A Study of Opinion Formation in a Presidential Campaign.* Chicago University Press, Chicago, 1954; Campbell, Angus, *et al., The American Voter.* John Wiley & Sons, New York, 1960.

on a number of related behaviors, any one of which may be treated as a dependent variable and explored in its own right. Party affiliation, level of political participation, and political ideology may, in relation to voting, be considered as independent variables; but from other perspectives they can obviously be treated as dependent variables. A large-scale survey that measures and collects data on many dimensions at once permits the investigator an extraordinary measure of flexibility not only in the manipulation of variables but in the selection of hypotheses he may wish to test. He can observe the same dimension from different perspectives and he can control or vary particular factors so that their relation to certain behavioral outcomes can be assessed more precisely.

Omnibus surveys also permit the investigator to undertake new lines of inquiry or even new studies that were not expressly provided for in the original design. If certain lines of analysis prove fruitless, the investigator often has on hand the information he needs to shift the direction of the inquiry and to test alternative explanations. Every survey of any magnitude contains far more data than the original investigator is likely to use. Indeed, recent scholarship has shown that survey data can often be exploited by investigators who had nothing to do with the original study but who find that it contains information they can readily adapt to their own inquiries. Secondary analysis of the data accumulated by opinion polls has often provided more significant results than were yielded by the initial analysis.

The impression is common, though erroneous, that political surveys have been used almost exclusively to assess public opinion. Although political surveys began as opinion polls, public opinion is only one of many subjects to which they are now addressed. Surveys are being adapted to almost every area of political study and to many different types of problems. They have been used to skim off the opinions of respondents and to interview them in depth, focusing intensively on certain aspects of behavior or on complex systems of belief. While surveys, of course, cannot usually investigate these matters as thoroughly as they can be explored in repeated psychiatric interviews, they can employ clinical personality keys, attitude scales, and other sophisticated measuring devices to achieve a fairly detailed profile of the personality and attitude characteristics of respondents.

Flexibility is also possible in the design of the survey questionnaire and procedure. The questionnaire may be open-ended or focused, loosely or highly structured, intensive or extensive, probing or concerned with surface responses, addressed to a single question or to many questions. It may, in its level of language and conceptualization, be fashioned either for particular classes of people or for people of many different kinds. The procedure may consist entirely of face-to-face interviews, telephone interviews, mail questionnaires, questionnaires delivered by interviewers that are self-administered by respondents and then returned by mail (or alternatively picked up, when completed, by interviewers), or some combination of these. Each method has its advantages and disadvantages.

Survey Methods and the Science of Politics

Reliance upon surveys in political science roughly coincides with the emergence of the behavioral emphasis and the growing desire to make the study of politics more scientific. By tradition a documentary, discursive, and intuitive discipline, political science has compiled vast amounts of information on political institutions and practices and has furnished legal, moral, and philosophical criticism of great value to statecraft. Inspired by the examples of the major political philosophers—Aristotle, Plato, Hobbes, Locke, Machiavelli, Rousseau, *et al.*—students of politics have produced instructive essays on such philosophic and speculative subjects as the nature of political obligation, the optimal balance between order and political freedom, the moral presuppositions of democracy, and the relation of the state to human nature.

Nevertheless, political scientists have characteristically neglected certain practices that distinguish scientific enquiry from other forms of observation, particularly the effort to accrete and link up data in a way that will yield a unified body of principles. A science aims to fashion a coherent structure of knowledge, in which each empirical proposition is systematically and consistently connected with the rest, and all facts can in principle be "explained." It approaches phenomena not as idiosyncratic events but as instances of a class whose regularities and variations can in principle be mapped and assessed. To accomplish this, it must employ rigorous methods for verifying the status of "facts" and for testing the validity of its explanations. It must develop procedures for discovering and correcting its own errors, and it must be prepared to abandon theories or explanations, no matter how cherished, that conflict with the evidence. A science grows by a cumulative process in which certain observations can be regarded as "settled" and new efforts can be devoted to studies at the margins of what is already "known." The value of achieving a cumulative discipline can scarcely be overestimated. In contrast to the discursive forms of inquiry, it promotes an economy of effort, for the same problems do not need in each instance to be restudied or approached as though for the first time. Instead, they can be understood as aspects of familiar problems whose nature has in part already been fathomed. An investigator can proceed step by step, from the known to the unknown, linking each new finding to the body of established knowledge. In this way, the progress of a discipline can be greatly accelerated, for the potential acquisition of new knowledge expands exponentially as the perimeters of what has been established grow continually larger. This accelerating capacity is one of the most remarkable features of the natural sciences, and lies at the heart of the modern scientific and industrial "explosion." The comparative backwardness of the social and humanistic disciplines can in part be traced to their slowness in adopting methods for systematic, cumulative research.

The attainment of a scientific form of social inquiry depends, in part, on the desire to achieve it; but it also depends on the "state of the art," on the availability of appropriate techniques and opportunities for conducting rigorous empirical research. One needs not only reliable and valid measures for appraising potentially relevant factors, but also analytic and statistical devices for observing, manipulating, and testing the influence of variables. One, likewise, requires procedures for expressing data in quantitative form so that they may be handled statistically. Failing these, one is compelled to fall back upon inexact descriptions and comparisons ("more than," "less than," "for the most part," "in most instances"), and one can assess only vaguely the impact of a given factor on a given outcome.

The scientific study of politics is designed to uncover, observe, and explain certain regularities and variations in political phenomena. To do this well, an investigator must aim to achieve maximum objectivity and precision. He is obliged to reveal his assumptions, to state his hypotheses explicitly, and to employ his data in a manner that will most rigorously test his claims. He must also make his constructs "operational" so that he can assess their validity (i.e., their ability to measure what he says they are measuring) and ascertain their effects precisely. Failure to operationalize concepts tempts the investigator to substitute metaphorical for exact language, to claim objective warranty for what are only subjective impressions, and to perpetuate errors that, under more rigorous definitions, might quickly be flushed out and corrected. Scholars who seek to build upon work done by scientific procedures know what has and has not been confirmed, and are less likely to be diverted into blind alleys and wasted efforts by the false information, misleading claims, or unwarranted inferences of their predecessors. Behavioral scientists therefore place great emphasis on the methods employed to verify explanations. By their standards, it is no longer sufficient for a theory or explanation to be persuasive, elegant, aesthetic, interesting, or brilliant; it must also be valid. An explanation is accepted or rejected depending upon its ability to account for the evidence and to meet the most critical statistical tests. Unlike the intuitive scholar who argues his thesis in persuasive essays, the behavioral scientist takes special pains to erect barriers against his own biases and convictions. He conducts his research in a conscious, deliberate manner that reveals rather than obscures the structure of the research design, the nature of the procedures employed, and the strength and consistency of the findings. His ultimate aim is to achieve a body of systematic theory adequate to explain political phenomena of the broadest possible range and variety.[5]

Among the procedures so far available for achieving a science of politics, the survey has been the most useful. The magnitude of its contribution can be gleaned from a summary of the ways in which it serves the several important requirements of science.

ESTABLISHING THE FACTS

The primary function of a political survey is to collect and certify the facts. What do voters believe about the candidates? What are their opinions on issues? Do individuals at different levels of the society differ in their political attitudes? Before surveys came into use, even such simple questions often could not be answered accurately, or the accuracy of the answer could not be certified by reference to an objective procedure.

The ability to establish the facts is, of course, a *sine qua non* of any scholarly field of inquiry. Yet traditional political and historical studies have tended to pay less attention than they should to the task of certifying the evidence needed to confirm their conclusions. Many of their claims, therefore, are intuitive or conjectural rather than factual—the products of partial, anecdotal, and haphazard observation. They are given, for example, to

5. Dahl, R. A., "The Behavioral Approach in Political Science: Epitaph for a Monument to a Successful Protest," *American Political Science Review*, Vol. 55, December, 1961, pp. 763–772; Kirkpatrick, E. M., "The Impact of the Behavioral Approach on Traditional Political Science," in *Essays on the Behavioral Study of Politics*. Edited by Austin Ranney, *op. cit.*, pp. 24–25; and Alpert, Harry, "Public Opinion Research as Science," *Public Opinion Quarterly*, Vol. 20, Fall, 1956, pp. 493–500, at pp. 495–497.

infer a nation's climate of opinion from a relatively small number of books, articles, speeches, editorials, or legislative acts. They are likely to take isolated events—a demonstration, a violent incident, a sharp conflict, a protest by a vociferous group—as signifying major trends in political belief and preference. When one observes political phenomena anecdotally, one's eye is drawn to whatever is dramatic and exciting, which means, often, to whatever is idiosyncratic and atypical. The tendency to overstress the unusual and to ignore the everyday occurrence or the modal opinion is characteristic not only of journalists but also of scholars who fail to adopt rigorous research techniques.

The habit of generalizing from mere impressions or isolated instances may still be observed in current social and political analysis. Contemporary writing, for example, is ridden with assertions that modern man is alienated, conformist, escaping from freedom, frustrated about his status, other-directed, psychologically disoriented by reason of rapid social mobility, class conscious, hungry for meaning, overwhelmed by a debilitating sense of aimlessness and drift, bothered by conflicting norms and frantic for guidance, separated from meaningful work, oppressed by mechanization, and dehumanized by the anonymities of mass society. I cite these not to contest their validity but only to observe that the facts they allege have not been adequately established and that the magnitude and pervasiveness of the conditions they profess to find have rarely been investigated by their proponents in the thorough, empirical, systematic manner they deserve. Yet many of the facts needed to assess the warranty of such allegations are accessible through survey methods. One can use surveys to map a range and variety of responses bearing on these matters. In place of sweeping generalizations about modern man's anxiety or aimlessness or conformity, one might substitute fairly precise estimates of the frequency and extent of these states. Exactly what proportion of men and women feel this way? Do the old exhibit these responses more than the young? The uneducated more than the educated? Workers more than managers? Rural residents more than urban residents? Non-believers more than those who attend church? Persons in conflicting status roles more than those in congruent roles? One can, if one chooses, also ascertain through cross-cultural comparisons of survey results the essential facts concerning the relation of these attitude states to the level of industrialization and state of political culture.

While surveys are not the only procedures for searching out vital political and social facts, they can often furnish information that is both more precise and more varied than the information supplied by other sources. Surveys, for example, can substantially augment aggregative types of data such as election statistics. Official voting returns can tell us who won an election, which districts voted for which candidates, and whether the turnout was large or small. But they cannot tell us what motivated the voters, why they divided as they did, how much they knew about issues, and whether they were significantly affected by the personalities of the candidates. A careful assessment of the facts on these questions requires a survey of some type. Even if a shrewd observer could, by intuitive observation, correctly divine the answers to such questions, a survey would still be needed to confirm his conclusions since, inevitably, an equally shrewd observer will have been led by *his* intuitive observation to a very different set of conclusions. Even if surveys were employed solely to confirm "what everybody knows" (a widely repeated charge that is patently false), they would still be essential. As it turns out, "what everybody knows" is almost invariably contradicted by an opposing and equally "well-known" conclusion. Unless we can verify which of the two "well-known" claims is correct, we can never resolve the conflict and separate truth from error.

It has become fashionable in some intellectual circles to deplore "fact-grubbing" and to exalt "theory." But the polarity implied by this distinction is spurious. While theory, of course, is vital to scientific advancement, facts are the building blocks of every science, essential to both the construction and testing of theory. Their verification, therefore, is essential to the progress of a science. In the study of politics, survey methods are often indispensable for this purpose.

INCREASING THE RANGE AND AMOUNT OF INFORMATION

Surveys also make it possible to collect in a single effort vast amounts of information on large numbers of people. Their potentiality in this regard is probably greater than that of any alternative method. Studies using aggregative data, for example, may supply information on many people, but the range of the information is usually narrow and little or nothing can be learned about any individual. Laboratory or field experiments are in some respects superior to surveys in their power to confirm or disconfirm hypotheses, but they are generally compelled for reasons of cost, manpower, and the nature of the research design, to limit themselves to a small number of subjects and a severely restricted set of variables. Documentary studies of political phenomena can encompass many people and many topics, but are deficient in the ability to portray those phenomena accurately in all their range and variety. They can, furthermore, supply detailed personal information only on the few individuals on whom biographical data are available. Anthropological studies of communities come closest to surveys in their capacity for collecting large amounts and varieties of detailed data on large numbers of people. Many of these studies, however, are in reality crude surveys, less systematic and quantitative than the standard survey, but superior in their ability to observe how men act, how they relate to each other, and how they are affected by institutional practices.

In a single political survey that utilizes a one- or two-hour interview of a sample of, say, 1500 persons, skilled interviewers can collect vast amounts of data on personal and social background factors (e.g., age, sex, education, religion, income, occupation, residence, marital status, organizational memberships) and on such political matters as party preference, political interest and participation, nature and frequency of political discussions, family political background, opinions on issues, attitudes on conservatism, internationalism, equalitarianism, and democratic beliefs and practices. Even psychological information can be collected by using personality scales, questions about primary group involvement, measures of behavioral conformity and non-conformity, and the like. Much can also be learned about the reaction of individuals and groups to current political developments, their response to conflicting political choices, and their predictions about political trends.

Even these questions and answers do not exhaust the data-gathering potential of the survey procedure. Various questions (and their answers) can be combined and recombined into indices and scales that will furnish information on entirely new variables. Consider a simple illustration: if we ask a respondent for his own party preference and that of his father, we can, by combining the answers, simultaneously learn whether the respondent has shifted from or remained loyal to his father's party. This datum may be useful in answering a number of questions that interest political scientists. Do people shift their party preference because of changes in economic status, life style, or geographic location? Are they more likely to shift if their families lack cohesiveness or possess conflicting status characteristics? Are there personality differences between shifters and non-shifters? Is the rejection of the parental party preference an aspect of a generalized rebellion against parents? Thus, even this simple example opens the possibility of exploring many questions that were not specifically asked in the initial questionnaire. Our illustration contains only two variables that were combined into a third, but indices can be constructed that consist of three, four, or even more elements. A questionnaire containing 25 questions, hence, may yield measures several times that number.

The number of findings yielded by a survey can be further augmented by manipulating variables in the course of the analysis so as to vary, in effect, the conditions under which behavior occurs. The sample, for example, can be divided by education and the less educated compared with the more educated. Or college graduates with high incomes can be compared with college graduates of low income. Numerous other combinations involving occupation, religion, age, rural-urban residence, party membership, and so forth, are equally possible. Nor is the survey investigator restricted to an analysis of the so-called "marginals," i.e. the figures resulting from the *prima facie* answers of the total sample to the questions used. The marginals reported in public opinion polls, for example, represent only the first approximation of the knowledge uncovered by the survey. Much more can be learned, some of it of great significance and subtlety, by comparing various subgroups of the population.

New knowledge may also result from unexpected findings that are sometimes turned up by surveys. Such findings usually set off a train of questions and conjectures that lead the investigator to redirect his inquiry. How are the unanticipated findings to be explained? Do they appear to be related to some special circumstance, to the unsuspected influence of some variable, or to the interaction effect produced by the joining of two variables? The survey method frequently provides the information needed to explore and to resolve such questions.

Using survey methods to study politics furnishes more and better answers to old questions as well as new answers to new questions. It is characteristic of a science that each improvement in research techniques inspires new questions that had either never been thought of before or were dismissed for want of a method for finding the answers. Surveys have encouraged political scientists to ask and to investigate numerous questions they would scarcely have raised a few decades ago, including, for example, questions about the effects of personality on leader preference, the relation of cognitive habits to political attitudes, the group process by which political beliefs are transmitted and sustained, the degree of correspondence between leader and follower opinions, and scores of other problems that involve social and psychological mechanisms. As answers to these questions are found, they inspire, in turn, new questions, and sometimes new research techniques as well. There is thus a continual interplay between advances in research technique and the acquisition of scientific knowledge.[6]

ADOPTION OF A SCIENTIFIC POSTURE

The increasing use of survey methods is one aspect of a many-sided development toward a science of politics. Surveys have contributed to that development not only by the quality and range of data they make possible, but also by their effect on the investigator himself. They compel him, for example, to pay attention to requirements of scientific inquiry that he might otherwise be tempted to ignore. To begin with, he is forced to define his concepts in operational terms. Such political concepts as power, consent, accountability, liberal-conservative, right wing, freedom, and equality have characteristically been employed so imprecisely as to impede the accumulation of knowledge about them. Survey research, like other forms of systematic, empirical inquiry, forces the investigator to decide exactly what he means by these terms and how he intends to measure them. He cannot settle for a nominal definition, but must specify the empirical criteria he will use as indicators of the phenomenon. If he is measuring, say, liberalism-conservatism, he must decide which actions or verbal responses he will employ in classifying one individual as more (or less) conservative than another. He must also consider whether his measure is valid and whether it can be distinguished from other measures that bear different names.

Similar requirements hold for the many terms employed by political science that describe *relationships* such as conformity, deviation, homogeneity, agreement, support, affiliation, defection, and loyalty. The survey analyst soon discovers that even an apparently simple relationship, such as a voter's party affiliation and loyalty, is more complicated than it seems. How often must one support the party's candidates to be classified as a loyal Democrat (or Republican)? Some persons who call themselves Democrats are active in their party's support, attend meetings, proselytize their friends and neighbors, wear campaign buttons, and contribute money, while others profess partisanship but scarcely bother to vote. Are both Democrats, and should both be classified in precisely the same way?

A more complicated illustration is presented by the notion of "conformity," a fashionable concept, widely discussed (and as widely deplored) by social theorists and lay commentators. One would, however, have difficulty

6. Kirkpatrick, E. M., *op. cit.,* p. 15.

finding in the outpouring of discursive writing on the subject a genuine operational definition that would permit one consistently to classify certain behavioral instances as conformist or deviant. Obviously, every one of us conforms to some standards and not to others, to some groups and sub-cultures and not to others. A member of the Communist party deviates from certain of the norms of American society but conforms rigidly to the norms of his party. A member of the radical right glorifies conformity to the "American way" but tends, in fact, to deviate sharply (as survey research has shown) from the explicit values contained in the Bill of Rights. One man's conformity may be another man's deviation, depending upon the reference groups and value systems to which they respectively respond. The point can further be illustrated by the differences in outlook between the political influentials and the general public. By the standards of the Constitution and the implicit "rules of the game," the political influentials are more conformist than the masses, for they embrace these standards with greater frequency, firmness, and understanding. The general public, though greatly outnumbering the influentials, are by these criteria more deviant. But which is the "true" norm—that which is described in the nation's offi-cial documents or that which is expressed by the majority? Clearly, the concepts of conformity and deviation are much too uncertain and potentially misleading to be allowed to stand as mere literary terms. A survey analyst who wishes to employ them cannot afford such vagueness. He must define the concepts so as to reveal precisely the forms of conformity and deviation he has in mind, who the criterion groups are, and what indicators he has devised for classifying individuals on these dimensions.

I am not suggesting that survey research will inevitably yield better definitions than other approaches will. A survey investigator, like any other scholar, may select a definition that is weak, confused, historically inaccu-rate, or biased. Nevertheless, once he has chosen a definition he must specify the objective and measurable criteria by which respondents may be classified or ranked with respect to it. If, for example, he is concerned with conservatism, he will first have to decide whether he is talking about classi-cal conservatism, economic and social welfare conservatism, conservatism in the matter of individual rights and duties, extreme conservatism of the radical right variety, or some combination of these. He will then have to select the questions or scale items or opinions that relate to his concept and that afford him an appropriate measure of it. He will further have to decide the form of his measure—whether it should be a scale, a single ques-tion, an index composed of several questions, an adjective check list, or a semantic differential. He will need to consider whether the measure should be based primarily on verbal responses or on actions, whether it should directly reflect the values embodied in the concept or utilize instead some secondary indicator such as liberal or conservative group membership. Although he may, despite these speculations, end up with a poor measure, he will have significantly reduced the risk. In addition, by operationalizing his terms, he will have made available to other scholars a clear description of what he has done so that they can check his work, repeat the study on other samples, confirm or refute the findings, and ascertain the limits to which the finding can be generalized.

The demands on a survey investigator are further increased if he elects to employ attitude or personality "scales" as his principal measures. If the items he has chosen reflect disparate elements or have been thrown together carelessly, his measure will not "scale," i.e., the items will not fall together in predictable ways and will not clearly differentiate persons who possess the trait in varying degrees. In constructing his scale, he may need to take account of how others perceive the dimension. He may do this by consulting authoritative works on the subjects, or by pooling the judgments of a panel of expert "raters." He may also wish to test the internal consistency or unidimensionality of the scale items or to ascertain how known populations actually respond to the items. All these are efforts to establish the validity of the scale. He may also introduce procedures to estimate the "reliability" of the scale, i.e., its ability to yield the same score on repeated trials and to present itself in the same way to different persons. These procedures are costly and time-consuming, but the results they make possible are likely to be more precise and accurate than are those produced by more intuitive methods.

Just as survey methods compel a student of politics to clarify and make operational his major constructs, so do they also encourage him to organize, arrange, and classify political phenomena according to their relative magnitude, their similarities and differences, and their statistical or analytic unities. The survey procedure promotes quantification and the statistical handling of data which in turn make possible the explicit formulation and testing of hypotheses. Thus, from the drawing of the sample to the analysis of the results, surveys are geared to the processing of research in a conscious, precise, systematic, quantitative, and objective manner.[7]

7. Merton, R. K., *Social Theory and Social Structure* (revised and enlarged edition). Free Press, Glencoe, Ill., 1957: introduction to Part III, "The Sociology of Knowledge and Mass Communications."

The survey method also promotes the scientific study of politics by offering unusual opportunities to acquire parallel sets of data. The systematic interview permits the same questions to be asked of people who function in different roles, contexts, or locations. Unlike comparisons in the more discursive forms of inquiry, which are often loose, impressionistic, and cast in metaphorical language, the comparisons made possible by surveys can be controlled and explicit, removing much doubt about what is being compared and what conclusions may properly be drawn. Through appropriate statistical tests, one can describe and assess precisely the magnitude of the differences turned up by the comparisons one has made, and one can further estimate the likelihood that these differences might have occurred by chance variation alone.[8]

The comparative analysis of survey data can also be extended to the weighing of variables across time, place, and situation. A given social force does not exert the same influence in all circumstances, but varies in its influence as conditions change or as the total configuration of forces change. This confronts social science with one of its most formidable difficulties, for one can never be certain that a given variable will beget the same results from one context to another. Surveys can assist by helping to correct the grand, reductivist theories which seek to explain all political events by reference to class, economics, religion, nationalism, geopolitics, ideology, or some other allegedly ineluctable force. By comparing survey results one can observe the varying impact of these factors as conditions change and as other influences vary. Surveys make it possible to estimate what part of an individual's voting preference can be ascribed to class, issues, religion, or party; to observe the differential influence of ideology on different classes of people; and to discern the shifting influence of social class from one political context to another. Given time, resources, and a sufficient number of research probes, we will eventually learn what to expect from each independent variable in each context, and we should be able to predict with considerable accuracy the consequences of putting together any given configuration of social forces.

The potential contribution of the survey method to the advancement of a science of politics has been greatly enhanced by the invention of the modern computer and the development of computer programs that are

8. Eulau, Heinz, "Segments of Political Science Most Susceptible to Behavioristic Treatment," in *The Limits of Behavioralism in Political Science*. Edited by J. C. Charlesworth. American Academy of Political and Social Science, Philadelphia, 1962, pp. 26–48, at pp. 39–40.

applicable to social science problems. With its astonishing capacity for storing and retrieving information on many variables at once, for performing numerous statistical calculations almost instantaneously, and for ordering, analyzing, and testing vast quantities of data, the computer is an ideal tool for the processing of survey data. The political scientist need no longer be overwhelmed by the formidable array of variables involved in explaining even the simplest act. The computer has made it feasible for him to relate each of these variables to its underlying dimension, to group variables into their appropriate clusters, to ascertain the precise contribution each of them makes to the total variance, and to discover uniformities and variations in large masses of data whose sheer bulk would previously have defeated him. Computer programs now permit him to carry out such statistical operations as factor analyses, cluster analyses, multiple regression analyses, and other procedures that were once too costly, time-consuming, and tedious to be practicable. Programs for partial and multiple correlations, multiple regressions and other statistical operations, permit the analyst to handle many different variables at once, to control for certain of them while permitting others to vary, to demonstrate the effects of combining them, and to rank them according to their contribution to the total variance. Computers also help to increase the sophistication of survey analysis by improving the quality of measures on which the political scientist can draw. Programs are being designed to construct indices and scales, to compute coefficients of reproducibility or other measures of validity, to produce item intercorrelations, and to provide tests for significance of differences. The formidable task of making survey data manageable, in short, is on the way to being solved.

The Substantive Contributions of Surveys

Although the survey has been a tool of political analysis for only three decades, it has become one of the most widely used research procedures in the field. The number and types of political surveys have multiplied so rapidly that we cannot possibly enumerate them all in a brief review. Even a summary, however, will illustrate the many ways in which surveys have been used in political studies and will document the value and richness of the findings yielded by this method.

The early political surveys were mainly concerned with public opinion and voting. As Angus Campbell has observed, they were dominated by concepts familiar to "aggregative analysis," such as age, residence, occupation, income, and other demographic characteristics on which official records were available.[9] Like any new tool, they tended at first to be focused on familiar questions and constructs. Political scientists still collect demographic information, of course, but the typical political survey has been broadened to include such dimensions as personality, role, motivation, attitude, cognition, reference groups, and status.[10] Surveys are still being used to study public opinion and voting, but they are also being turned to studies of political parties, ideology, political belief and affiliation, stability and change, political socialization, legislative processes, constituency representation, judicial behavior, comparative politics, foreign policy formation and opinion, and community power structure. These changes have been accompanied by an increase in the sophistication of the questions being asked. Whereas the early users of political surveys collected evidence on a variable like social class in order to observe its relation to, say, voting preference, a contemporary scholar is more likely to want to know whether a respondent shifts his political point of view as he moves downward or upward in social class; whether he suffers conflicts of status and hence is politically alienated; whether he holds or rejects the modal values of his class; and whether class and its concomitants affect his perceptions, motivations, values, and capacity for adopting the norms of the larger community. The contemporary scholar who uses survey methods often wants to go behind such concepts as class, age, education, residence, or religion in order to learn what they consist of and what gives them their power to influence political behavior. This tendency to translate crude categoric variables into more refined and dynamic ones, and to improve their explanatory power thereby, typifies the changes in intellectual posture that are taking place in almost every substantive area of political inquiry. The nature and scope of these changes will become more evident from the review that follows.

PUBLIC OPINION

The use of surveys to sound mass opinion remains one of their important functions, although they are not the only means by which public opinions can be divined. One may also consult journalistic and other published materials, private letters and diaries, the policies of public organizations, and the speeches of influential persons; but none of these can furnish an ade-

9. Campbell, Angus, "Recent Developments in Survey Studies of Political Behavior," in *Essays on the Behavioral Study of Politics*. Edited by Austin Ranney, *op. cit.*, pp. 31–46, at p. 32.
10. Alpert, Harry, *op. cit.*, p. 498.

quate portrait of the variety, range, and intensity of opinions held by the electorate. All are susceptible to the play of fortuitous factors, and are therefore bound to be distorted—biased by idiosyncracies in the selection procedure, by errors in reporting or self-representation, or by the preconceptions of the investigator. Often the opinions of those who are most visible or vociferous are mistakenly considered to be the opinions of all.

Public opinion studies are being carried out by commercial and government polls as well as by scholars. While polls are less concerned than academic surveys with explorations in depth and hypotheses-testing, the information they provide is important to scholars. Political scientists consult polls for information on party and candidate preferences, shifts in presidential popularity, public orientation toward issues, the level of public information on various political questions, popular responses to the behavior of the President, Congress, or the Supreme Court, the public's perception of impending legislation, and similar matters. Polls also enable scholars to relate public opinion to certain forms of overt political behavior, such as elections, organizational activities, congressional votes, and executive decisions. Some of these questions are being explored in comparative studies using data from commercial polls abroad.

The value of opinion polls to the political investigator, however, lies not only in the information they publish but also in the vast amounts of politically relevant data they collect but rarely bother to report. Almost every public opinion poll gathers information that may have been incidental to the initial survey but that is a potentially rich repository of materials for scholars. Until recently, most of this information was never used, but was simply stored on punch cards or left uncoded. The polling organizations, having skimmed off the relatively few items they were concerned to report, had little interest in the rest. Now, however, they are making their old data available to scholars for secondary analysis.

One or two examples will illustrate the opportunities for secondary analysis that have now been opened. The American Institute of Public Opinion (Gallup Poll) has for many years included in its national surveys questions that assess presidential popularity. As Gallup has reported in newspaper releases, the public's approval of the president rises and falls throughout his tenure. Poll information on the course of these shifts has proven invaluable to scholars who have wondered whether they are related to political events in some systematic, predictable way. They have asked, for example, whether presidential popularity rises rather than falls with the onset of international crises, and they have found that it does.[11] By exploring the poll archives, they can learn whether disaffection with the president occurs most frequently among the educated or non-educated; whether support for the president is related to presidential policies; whether and in what ways his popularity is affected by economic crises, personal style, congressional quarrels, shifts in opinion on issues, respondents' feelings of well-being, growing or declining affluence, and sense of economic opportunity. They can also investigate the relation between presidential popularity and subsequent voting behavior, and relate popular approval of the president to the support enjoyed by his party. Since these poll samples are characteristically miniatures of national or state electorates, the political scientist can explore these questions for every sub-stratum or "public" he thinks appropriate—Northerners or Southerners, young or old, rich or poor, urban or rural, Democratic or Republican, liberals or conservatives, or any combination of these. Secondary analysis of poll data has also been used with considerable benefit in studies of American political values,[12] foreign policy attitudes,[13] stratification and political orientation,[14] and popular responses to "McCarthyism."[15] Polls are proving useful even for cross-cultural political studies. Where they have asked parallel questions in more than one country, they have made possible comparative studies on such political subjects as voting preferences, response to leaders, the impact of left and right ideologies, the relation of mobility to political belief, and response to the party system.

The retrieval and analysis of commercial poll data is a relatively inexpensive way to conduct studies of mass political opinion. An investigator who can afford it, however, will usually prefer to design and execute a survey tailored to his own purposes, one that will yield answers to the exact questions he has in mind. A custom-made survey enables him to probe more deeply, to over-sample and investigate intensively the groups that especially

11. Polsby, N. W., *Congress and the Presidency.* Prentice-Hall, Englewood Cliffs, N. J., 1964, pp. 25–26.
12. Hyman, H. H. and P. B. Sheatsley, "The Current Status of American Public Opinion," in *Public Opinion and Propaganda.* Edited by Daniel Katz, *et al.* Ryerson Press, New York, 1954, pp. 33–48.
13. Almond, G. A., *The American People and Foreign Policy.* Harcourt, Brace, New York, 1950.
14. Lipset, S. M., *Political Man:* The Social Bases of Politics. Doubleday, Garden City, N.Y., 1960, pp. 97–130 and pp. 285–309.
15. Polsby, N. W., "Toward an Explanation of McCarthyism," *Political Studies,* Vol. 8, October, 1960, pp. 250–271.

interest him, and to explore the variables that seem on theoretical grounds to explain the political opinion he is studying. Since the political scientist is interested in the relation of opinions to certain political variables, he is often compelled to undertake his own survey in order to achieve the range and variety of responses required for his analysis.

So much is being learned about political opinions through the use of surveys that we can only illustrate their contribution. Surveys have confirmed that there is indeed more than one public and that political issues are often salient for one group and irrelevant for another. They have shown that popular opinions on political questions are frequently labile and that this instability especially characterizes the opinions expressed by the less informed members of the society.[16] They have made it increasingly clear that only a small proportion of the electorate can plausibly be described as "ideologically sophisticated," and that the number of persons who hold consistent and coherent political philosophies is very small.[17]

We have also begun to learn from surveys that not all persons holding the same manifest opinions mean the same thing by them. Unsophisticated voters, for example, often express opinions favoring political freedom largely because those opinions reflect familiar, honorific values. As a result, they frequently endorse these opinions in the abstract but reject them when they are applied to the concrete exercise of freedom. This discrepancy between the general and particular expressions of a principle is less likely to occur among the more articulate segments of the society. Their opinions are more firmly grounded in a coherent point of view and are applied with greater consistency. They are more likely to choose reference groups, candidates, and parties that are consonant with their underlying political beliefs. Articulate Republicans and Democrats, for example, differ more sharply on issues than do inarticulate Republicans and Democrats.[18]

Survey procedures have shown, however, that even educated people exhibit less consistency in their political views than one might suppose. It is not unusual, for example, to find well-informed people holding opinions that intermingle liberal and conservative values—conservatives who respond more favorably to left wing opinions than many liberals do, and persons who are liberal on economic issues but conservative on such matters as

16. Converse, Philip E., "The Nature of Belief Systems in Mass Publics," in *Ideology and Discontent.* Edited by D. E. Apter. Free Press, Glencoe, Ill., 1964, pp. 206–261.
17. Campbell, Angus, *et al., The American Voter, op. cit.,* chap. 10.
18. McClosky, Herbert, "Consensus and Ideology in American Politics," *American Political Science Review,* Vol. 58, June, 1964, pp. 361–382.

procedural rights, traditionalism, and social change. There is even a small, though predominantly inarticulate, segment of the population who simultaneously hold extreme right-wing and left-wing values. Such findings suggest that we may in the past have overstressed the role of ideas in the politics of modern democratic societies. A similar conclusion is suggested by the survey data bearing upon the presumed need for "consensus" as a precondition for democracy. The American electorate, for example, is found to be divided on some important political values and even on the so-called "rules of the game," yet the society remains viable.[19]

Survey evidence suggests that certain opinions deserve to be taken more seriously than others because more thought has gone into their adoption. Some opinions are embraced thoughtlessly and casually, while others are derived from strongly held political philosophies. Some merely reflect the current political mood, while others are deeply rooted in the value system. Some are stable and others are labile. Some express the innermost beliefs or interests of their holders, while others merely echo commonplace opinions or familiar phrases. Although *vox populi, vox Dei* has for centuries been proclaimed a literal truth, it is obvious from an enormous amount of survey data that the people often speak with more than one voice and that some of their opinions are misguided, contradictory, and repeated without reflection.

Surveys of public opinion have also shown that members of the same class may differ sharply in some opinions, and that class or other ecological categories are but crude classifications that often exert only a modest influence on the formation of political opinions. Being a Catholic or Protestant, for example, influences what one thinks about church-related questions such as support for parochial schools, but has little direct bearing on the opinions one holds about, say, government intervention in the economy, social welfare legislation, foreign policy, urban redevelopment, or civil rights.[20]

19. Prothro, J. W., and C. M. Grigg, "Fundamental Principles of Democracy: Bases of Agreement and Disagreement," *Journal of Politics,* Vol. 22, May, 1960, pp. 276–294; Key, V. O., Jr., *Public Opinion and American Democracy.* Knopf, New York, 1961, chap. 2; Dahl, R. A., *Who Governs?:* Democracy and Power in an American City. Yale University Press, New Haven, 1961, chap. 28; Stouffer, S. A., *Communism Conformity, and Civil Liberties:* A Cross Section of the Nation Speaks its Mind. Doubleday, New York, 1955; and McClosky, Herbert, "Consensus and Ideology . . . ," *op. cit.*

20. Allinsmith, Wesley and Beverly Allinsmith, "Religious Affiliation and Politico-Economic Attitude: A Study of Eight Major U.S. Religious Groups," *Public Opinion Quarterly,* Vol. 12, Fall, 1948, pp. 377–389.

In a modern, urban, pluralistic society—in which men are no longer confined to the company of a single group but mingle with persons from many groups and in which, despite differences in their origins, they often attend the same schools and receive the same communications from the same mass media—opinions on public questions are rarely controlled by a single categoric group.[21] Among the general electorate, and especially among the poorly educated, even party affiliation exerts only a modest influence on political opinions.[22] Although a voter's outlook on issues is sometimes correlated with his choice of candidates,[23] the *causal* connection between the electorate's opinions on these issues and their voting decision is by no means established. In the 1952 presidential election, in which Eisenhower voters favored his views on such issues as corruption in government more often than Stevenson voters did, there is reason to believe that many voters who had already decided to support Eisenhower embraced his views on these issues only after he began to stress them in his campaign.

Surveys are also helping us to understand the complex interplay between popular opinion and government decisions. We are, for example, now able to assess whether elected officials respond frequently to the opinions of the voters, whether they respond to some voters more than others, whether they listen to the "voice of the people" on some questions but not on others, and whether they relinquish their own strongly held convictions in favor of what they perceive to be voter sentiment.[24] Questions that have long been debated but never resolved—for example, whether popular opinion is heeded in matters of foreign policy—can now be examined with greater assurance that answers will be forthcoming.

In recent years, a few studies have tried to combine surveys of the electorate with surveys of political officials. Such studies enable us to compare the beliefs of the two samples, to estimate the response of political leaders to the wishes of the electorate, and to acquire vitally needed facts about the realities of representative government. They are helping us to discover when

21. Centers, Richard, "Attitude and Belief in Relation to Occupational Stratification," *Journal of Social Psychology,* Vol. 27, May, 1948, pp. 159–185.
22. McClosky, Herbert, *et al.,* "Issue Conflict and Consensus Among Party Leaders and Followers," *American Political Science Review,* Vol. 54, June, 1960, pp. 406–427.
23. Campbell, Angus, Gerald Gurin and W. E. Miller, *The Voter Decides.* Row, Peterson, Evanston, Ill., 1954, 145 ff.
24. Miller, W. E., and Donald Stokes, "Constituency Influence in Congress," *American Political Science Review,* Vol. 57, March, 1963, pp. 45–56.

a political leader can be expected to follow his own conscience, when he will respond to the opinions of the voters, and to what degree representation is affected by the intensity of party competition. They also make it possible to learn whether popular opinion prevails on domestic matters more than on foreign affairs, on bread and butter issues more than on symbolic or "style" issues, on simple, easily grasped issues more than on complex issues, on questions that touch the moral convictions of the people more than on questions that reflect practical considerations.

Survey methods are beginning to be used to investigate systematically the differences between the private convictions of political officials and their manifest conduct. Political ritual and necessity control so large a part of an officeholder's behavior that it is often difficult to know when he is following his own conscience and when he is concealing his beliefs in deference to political exigency. A properly designed survey that protects the anonymity of the leader-respondent may reveal what part of his behavior is backed by personal convicton and what part is political accommodation. By measuring the disparity between what is believed and what is manifestly said or done, one can assess the impact of other forces that play upon political actors and propel them in certain directions. Since private beliefs influence conduct even when their effects are not visible, ferreting them out is important to a full understanding of political behavior. It is also essential to a more adequate appreciation of the relation between attitudes and opinions on the one hand and overt behavior on the other. As yet, little is systematically known about this relation, or about the manner in which beliefs combine with various situational forces to evoke overt behavior. What part of our overt political behavior is a function of our values, and what part reflects group memberships, personal interest, and other external forces with which those beliefs interact? For the investigation of these matters, survey analysis is likely to be indispensable.

Although surveys have become vital to the efficient study of public opinion, their employment for this purpose is not without risk. There are, for example, problems associated with the interpretation of the answers that respondents give to survey questions. We have already observed that some people reply thoughtlessly or express contradictory opinions. Others give answers that do not accurately reflect the way they would behave if they were required to act on their beliefs. Much may depend on the way a question is put. For example, a review of survey opinions in the *Public Opinion Quarterly* reports that two-thirds of the respondents in a general population sample stated (in answer to a question put to them in 1950) that they believed people were "happier and more contented" thirty years ago than they are today.[25] But when asked if they would rather be living during the earlier period than the present one, approximately the same proportion acknowledged that they preferred the present one. An investigator who heeded only the first set of responses might be seriously misled about the public's feelings toward the present society, mistaking a superficial expression of nostalgia for a deeply felt conviction. Dangers of this type, however, can be minimized by using properly validated questions, skilled interviewing, or sophisticated attitude testing. With sufficient resources, care, and ingenuity, an investigator can in fact acquire a comprehensive, complex, and accurate portrait of the public mind on many of the questions that interest political scientists.

PARTICIPATION

While information on such matters as voting turnout and participation in party work has been available through official or organizational records, most of the interesting questions about political participation could not be effectively investigated prior to the development of the survey method. Surveys have proven invaluable in assessing the influence on participation of such factors as demography, sense of political effectiveness, party loyalty, partisanship, ideological conviction, and perception of candidates. They have also made it possible to explore systematically such matters as political recruitment and participation in party work.

A great deal has been learned through surveys about the demographic correlates of participation.[26] To what extent do demographic forces help to fashion individuals into participants or, alternatively, into non-voters? Although a given demographic factor may not register exactly the same im-

25. Erskine, H. G., "The Polls: Textbook Knowledge," *Public Opinion Quarterly*, Vol. 27, Spring, 1963, pp. 133–141.
26. Berelson, B. R., P. F. Lazarsfeld and W. W. McPhee, *Voting. op. cit.;* Campbell, Angus, *et al., The American Voter, op. cit.,* pp. 291–498; Lipset, S. M., *et al.,* "The Psychology of Voting: An Analysis of Political Behavior," in *Handbook of Social Psychology,* Vol. 2. Edited by Gardner Lindzey. Addison-Wesley, Reading, Mass., 1954, pp. 1124–1175; Almond, G. A. and Sidney Verba, *The Civic Culture.* Princeton University Press, Princeton, 1963, pp. 261–374; Lane, R. E., *Political Life.* Free Press, Glencoe, Ill., 1959, pp. 185–272; and Lipset, S. M., *Political Man, op. cit.,* chap. 6.

pact in every context, similar patterns of influence have been discerned from one country to another. Surveys have shown, for example, that voting and other forms of participation are more frequent among the better educated than the less educated, among men than women, the culturally advantaged than the disadvantaged, urban more than rural residents, the middle aged more than the very young or the very old, persons settled in the community more than transients, and individuals who participate in other forms of social and community activity more than those who do not. The underlying factors that govern these correlations appear to be social awareness, sophistication, and the ability to command one's environment. Political apathy, on the other hand, is in great measure a function of parochialism, ignorance, and feelings of political ineptitude and futility. Role perception may also contribute, as in the case of the lesser participation of women. In general, anything that exposes an individual to the political culture or enlarges his opportunity to learn about politics will stimulate him to acquire habits of political activity; apathy, in contrast, is induced by anything that separates him from the mainstreams of the society, isolates him from the articulate culture, removes him from the sources of political communication, or otherwise causes public events to seem remote, bewildering, or without consequence for his personal affairs.

Data collected from numerous surveys have shown that political participation is not a "natural" concomitant of citizenship, but has to be learned. A sense of civic duty tends to be correlated with participation, but is not its sufficient cause. It appears, rather, to be a concomitant or epiphenomenon of the same configuration of forces that induces participation itself. Hence, hortatory appeals to morality and conscience have little effect on voting turnout or active party involvement. Some people in the society are so far removed from the articulate culture that they never hear the appeals, while others, finding politics remote, impalpable, or irrelevant to their daily lives, turn a deaf ear. Interest in politics is subject to the same kinds of influence that govern interest and participation in other forms of human activity: one must be exposed, perceive politics as salient, understand in some measure what is going on, believe that one's participation matters (if only to oneself), and derive some type of reinforcement or "reward" from the activity. The reward may be the pleasure of competition, the approval and support of friends, the fulfillment of a sense of responsibility, the satisfaction of victory (realized or anticipated), or the promise of something concretely to be gained. A substantial proportion of the population fails, for one reason or another, to find such rewards in political activity, and hence do not bother to vote.

Participation is a function not so much of demographic influences as such but of the "dynamic" forces they embody and can unleash. The effect of a demographic factor, in other words, is not permanent, but is specific to time and circumstance. Thus, the less frequent participation of women will eventually be overcome as changes occur in their role and as they gain equality with men in such things as education. Similarly, the relatively greater apathy of Negroes in the United States will gradually be corrected as they achieve higher status and education, and become more accustomed to urban life. Farmers will doubtless vote as often as city dwellers when the impact of the mass media and the improvements in transportation further erase the communication distinctions between the city and the farm.

Survey methods have provided a far more accurate and comprehensive description than was previously available of the nature and incidence of political participation in various countries. Reliable information is being collected on voting, on the frequency of discussions and reading about politics, participation in election campaigns, attendance at meetings, and so forth. Surveys have documented with considerable accuracy what has long been suspected, namely, that the number of people who belong to the "political class" is fairly small (depending on how rigorously one defines the criteria, probably fewer than 10 per cent), while a larger group, but still a minority, participates to the extent of attending an occasional meeting, contributing money to a campaign, writing a letter to an elected official, or engaging in political discussions. By observing who does and does not engage in these activities, and by ascertaining their social, intellectual, and psychological characteristics, surveys have begun to shed much light on the sources and correlates of political activity.

Although few surveys have so far been conducted on "party actives," the American data indicate that, compared with other groups in the population, the actives are more ideological, more partisan, more responsive to their party's doctrine, and more inclined to hold a coherent and internally consistent set of political beliefs. This is not to say that they are "ideologically" oriented to the same degree that the active members of the small European parties have been, but only that they are far more developed in their political ideas than are most members of the American electorate. Survey data also show that the actives possess a firmer grasp of the constitutional principles and "rules of the game" on which the political system is founded. As a "class," they are among the most important repositories of the values that define the political culture. The survey evidence also suggests that the competition between parties takes place principally between their active members rather than between their rank-and-file supporters. Democratic and Republican actives, for example, are much further apart in their stands on issues than are their followers. Prior to the investigation of these matters through surveys, the contrary was often assumed.[27]

Until recently, most studies of political participation were confined to individual countries. Now, however, efforts are being made to investigate the subject across cultures. These studies aim to assess the influence of particular variables in different contexts and to determine how existing political institutions and the "political culture" itself affect political involvement. While some light has been thrown on this matter by comparing the results of surveys conducted separately in different countries, the new comparative studies use parallel surveys that ask similar questions and draw on comparable samples. The most notable example of this is the study of participation and civic involvement in five countries done by Gabriel Almond and Sidney Verba.[28] This study suggests that the sense and quality of civic competence varies according to the type of political culture, and this, in turn, is related to the level of education, industrialization, and urbanization. Political participation and sense of civic responsibility are more developed in the United States than in Italy or Mexico. Similarly, the sense of civic competence, i.e., the individual's feeling that he can affect the course of public policy, is significantly stronger in the United States and Great Britain than it is in Germany, Italy, and Mexico. In general, the forces that increase political involvement and participation in one country, e.g., education, also tend to increase them elsewhere.

Survey evidence shows that participation also varies with the "visibility" of the candidate, the character of the campaign, and the dramatic significance of the issues. Well-known candidates inspire a larger turnout than little-known candidates. Campaigns that feature a dramatic issue or highlight a national crisis bring some people to the polls who would otherwise not have turned out. Surveys, of course, are not the only means by which these facts might be learned, but they are needed in order to document in detail the degree to which candidates are "well-known," the sense of felt

27. McClosky, Herbert, *et al.,* "Issue Conflict. . . ," *op. cit.*
28. Almond, G. A. and Sidney Verba, *op. cit.*

crises among different groups of voters, the manner in which presumably dramatic issues are in fact perceived, and the attributes of the candidates that inspire (or discourage) voter participation. Surveys likewise may be used to assess the popular response to changing political situations and events. It is difficult at best to discover the impact of a given event on the behavior of citizens, but without some type of survey analysis, it is often impossible.

VOTING

No area of political inquiry has profited more bountifully from the development of the survey method than that of voting behavior. Whereas our knowledge of this phenomenon was formerly impressionistic and suffused with subjective and frequently erroneous beliefs, we now have available a large body of "hard" data of a type that has been repeatedly confirmed in studies of elections in various countries. We can, as a result, elaborate the explanatory model of voting well beyond what was once possible.

Before the development of survey methods, most systematic research on elections drew primarily on official aggregative data. By comparing the voting outcome with the social characteristics of the election district, one could make crude appraisals of the influence of ethnic, religious, economic, or other categoric group memberships. One could also identify voting trends in, say, rural and urban areas, certain districts and states, and even among particular ethnic groups. One could classify voting constituencies according to the closeness of the party vote, and one could relate this information to such other variables as the behavior of a constituency's representatives.

Aggregative data, however, not only reveal but conceal vital information for, while they make available gross figures about certain categories of voters, they do not tell us how individuals or subgroups in those categories actually behave or what influences them.[29] There are dangers in attributing to any individual the behavioral characteristics of the groups he belongs to —he may be a worker living in a working class district, but he is also Catholic or Protestant, white or Negro, white collar or blue collar, educated or uneducated, Republican or Democrat, participant or apathetic. He is also differentiated from others in the group by personality, attitudes, motivations, and habits of mind that diverge in subtle and complex ways from the modal

29. Robinson, W. S., *op. cit.*

pattern. Since similar variations mark all other individuals in the constituency, an investigator will miss much essential information about the configuration of forces that govern their respective voting decisions if he consults aggregative data alone. He would, for example, be unable to explain shifts in the voting preferences of a given constituency that has experienced no changes in its social composition.

The uncertainties surrounding the interpretation of aggregative election statistics are apparent in the widely divergent interpretations offered by politicians and commentators about the meaning of a given election. There is a long-standing myth that practicing politicians understand these matters better than other observers do. But one need only consult their post-election interpretations to have the myth quickly dispelled; like most other people, they tend to color their interpretations by their subjective readings and by their desires and fears. It is not uncommon for political opponents to claim that a given election outcome signifies support for or against the expansion of civil rights, for or against decentralization of national power, for or against a more militant foreign policy, for or against tax reform, for or against medical care for the aged—for or against, in short, whatever point of view they happen to value.[30] The interpretations of professional politicians are further warped by their almost unrelieved association with members of their own party and their overexposure to the party's communications. Partly for these reasons, they are notoriously inclined to predict victory for their party's candidate and to discover a popular mandate for its program.

Survey studies of elections make it possible to supply many needed details and to achieve a more realistic appraisal of the forces that decide the outcome. They have, for example, demonstrated that party affiliation—the single most compelling factor affecting the voting decision—is shaped and sustained by the family, and that some three-fourths of the adult voters retain the party preference of their parents. Party affiliation is further reinforced by congruent peer and other reference group attachments. Social or geographic mobility, however, including entrance into a "conflicting" economic or religious category, weakens the family's hold on the voter's party preference and leads him to waver in his party support or to switch parties entirely.

Election surveys have also documented the role played by such factors as religion and occupational status in fixing party preference. In the United States at least, the former is less important than the latter. Indeed when

---

30. Campbell, Angus, "Recent Developments in Survey Studies," *op. cit.,* p. 38.

socio-economic status is controlled, the influence of religious denomination over party preference tends to decline sharply. Occupational status remains among the most important of the demographic influences on party and voting preference, with the low status occupations tending to support the economically more liberal party, and the high status occupations leaning toward the more conservative party. Occupation, however, has only a modest effect on one's orientation toward the values that define the political culture; attitudes toward freedom, equality, private property, and the profit system, are in large measure shared by people in all socio-economic levels, especially if education is held constant.

Election surveys have also confirmed that occupational status and other "class" indicators do not exert a uniform influence on every election. In 1948, with neither presidential candidate able to register a strong personal appeal, the vote closely followed occupational status lines. But in the elections of 1952 and 1956, large numbers of lower income and working class voters shifted their support to Eisenhower, largely because of his popularity as a military figure. Again, in the 1964 election, the survey data so far available suggest that large defections from the Republican candidate occurred even among persons of upper economic status. These findings illustrate that surveys can enlighten us about a particular election, about the impact of the forces that affect election outcomes in general, and about the influence of any one of those forces in a particular election.[31]

As election survey techniques have developed, the handling of categoric factors has become more sophisticated. Investigators have sought to probe beyond the mere ecological categories into such matters as the strength of group identification, the cohesiveness of the groups to which voters belong, and the reference group configurations from which they derive their norms, opinions, and perceptions. They have explored the sources of conformity and deviation relative to a group's values and the location and role within the group of those who most fervently embrace its doctrines. They are no longer satisfied merely to discover that older voters tend to be more conservative and Republican than younger voters, but are now asking why this happens, and they are turning to surveys, in the main, to learn whether these

31. Converse, P. E., *et al.*, "Stability and Change in 1960: A Reinstating Election," *American Political Science Review*, Vol. 55, June, 1961, pp. 269–280; Lazarsfeld, P. F., *et al.*, *The People's Choice, op. cit.*; Wildavsky, Aaron, "The Intelligent Citizen's Guide to the Abuse of Statistics: The Kennedy Document and the Catholic Vote," in *Politics and Social Life*. Edited by N. W. Polsby, *et al.* Houghton-Mifflin, Boston, 1964, pp. 825–844.

correlations are generational in origin or a function of the aging process itself.

Numerous American and foreign surveys suggest that party affiliation is not only the single most powerful influence on voting, but that it may also be the most important force in inculcating and sustaining political beliefs. There is mounting evidence that parties are not merely the spokesmen of demographic or interest groups but are important reference groups in their own right, capable of inspiring, sustaining, and promoting the political doctrines to which voters respond. This observation holds especially for the active members and articulate supporters of the parties—the groups that are ideologically most highly developed and partisan. Inarticulate voters are more likely to refrain from voting or to shift their preferences from one election to another; articulate voters remain more strongly and consistently loyal to their party in both their beliefs and voting habits. While some articulate voters describe themselves as "independent," survey findings suggest that the classical portrait of the independent as a highly politicized, informed, objective, and conscientious voter is exaggerated; independency, in fact, is more likely to be associated with political indifference and a low level of political information.[32]

Although little systematic research has been done on the candidates' contributions to the outcome of elections, surveys have begun to make some inroads on this question also. We have observed, in the cases of Eisenhower and Goldwater, that a candidate may be so well-known and trusted— or, alternatively, so feared—that his candidacy will cause a large number of voters to shift from their habitual party preference. These instances, however, are atypical, for the candidates in a party election are often rather evenly matched in the degree to which they are known, and tend to be perceived by the voters as possessing similar qualities.[33] Most voters, in short, are unlikely to shift from the party they usually support unless there is a marked difference in the popularity and reputation of the candidates. Despite their protestation that they prefer to vote "for the man rather than for the party," they are likely in practice to reverse this order of preference.

32. Campbell, Angus, *et al.*, *The Voter Decides, op. cit.*, pp. 97–111; Berelson, B. R., *et al.*, *Voting, op. cit.*, pp. 25–28; for a contrary view, see Agger, R. E., "Independents and Party Identifiers: Characteristics and Behavior in 1952," in *American Voting Behavior*. Edited by E. L. Burdick and A. J. Brodbeck. Free Press, Glencoe, Ill., 1959, pp. 308–339.
33. Pool, I. de Sola, "TV: A New Dimension in Politics," in *American Voting Behavior*. Edited by E. L. Burdick and A. J. Brodbeck, *op. cit.*, pp. 236–261.

The survey procedure has also been invaluable for the study of the campaign—a feature of modern elections that has generated much mythology and many misperceptions. Prior to the studies inspired by Paul Lazarsfeld, little was known about the effects of the mass media, the contribution of the candidates, the influence of the campaign in shifting or stabilizing voter preferences, the effectiveness of various campaign techniques, and the processes by which campaign information is disseminated.[34] Our knowledge of these phenomena, regrettably, is still rather thin, but such hard data as we have managed to acquire has come largely through surveys.

The study of the campaign is best approached through the use of the panel survey. By reinterviewing respondents as the campaign progresses, an investigator can trace shifts in voter preferences, observe the process by which decisions are formed, and assess the impact on the voting decision of speeches, campaign activities, and political events. Unless the decision process is followed in this way, the observer of a campaign will find himself confronted by a bewildering assortment of simultaneously occurring forces and events that are difficult to distinguish from one another.

The data now available from surveys suggest that the influence attributed to campaigns by politicians, journalists and other "intuitive" observers is greatly exaggerated. Most voters have decided how they will vote even before the campaign begins—in fact, before the candidates are chosen. The campaign serves largely to reinforce this decision. Voters who at the beginning claim to be undecided soon decide in favor of the party they habitually support. The effect of the campaign, in short, is largely to polarize existing predispositions rather than to produce shifts from one party to the other. Issues may be stressed by the candidates, but, with rare exceptions, they play a much smaller role in forming voting preferences than is commonly supposed. Only a small proportion of voters take them seriously enough to reflect upon them deeply or to be moved by them to shift their voting intention. More likely, voters either ignore issues that conflict with their voting intention or adopt the stands taken by their party or candidate. Of course, if the competing parties are closely matched, any of a number of factors— issues, candidates, or style of campaigning—may shift a sufficient number of votes to win or lose the election.

The role of communication and the mass media in elections has also been explored through surveys. Most voters, it appears, consult the media largely to strengthen the voting intention they have already formed. They

34. Lazarsfeld, P. F., *et al., The People's Choice, op. cit.;* and Berelson, B. R., *et al., Voting, op. cit.*

tend to avoid communications that conflict with their voting decision, or to reinterpret them in a favorable light. They are, in the course of a campaign, bombarded by so many communications from so many sources on so many subjects that they can easily select whatever they wish to hear and reject whatever they wish to avoid. Since many of the events they are asked to judge are highly ambiguous, they are prone to accept the interpretations placed upon those events by their party's spokesmen. Many of the communications addressed to the voter during the campaign, therefore, either do not reach him at all, are reinterpreted by him to make them congruent with what he intends to do anyway, or are dismissed as inaccurate and biased. While this describes the typical pattern, there are of course exceptions. If a candidate is not well known, extensive newspaper or television coverage may increase his popularity sufficiently to put him over the mark; or a personally prepossessing candidate may succeed in using his television appearances to win over the conflicted voters or even to shift a few voters who initially supported his opponent. In unusual circumstances, the mass media may help to dramatize certain issues in a way that will benefit one candidate and harm the other.

Survey research by Lazarsfeld and others has also shown that communications via the mass media are more likely to be received by the educated and articulate segments of the population—by those voters who are already best informed about public affairs and most likely, therefore, to have arrived at a firm voting decision. The undecided voters, those whom the candidates most want to reach, are usually the most inaccessible. Similarly, the campaign more often engages the attention of the partisan than the uncommitted voters. A similar principle determines the selection of voters who are visited by party campaign workers, or who receive literature and phone calls from campaign headquarters. Obviously, these tendencies further diminish the impact that the campaign can register on the outcome of an election. The campaign does, however, bring out the party workers and inspire them to more enthusiastic efforts.

The politically informed also serve as intermediaries between the mass media and the ordinary voter. As survey research has shown, the media exert at least an indirect influence on the ordinary voter through a "two step flow of communication," in which the more informed members of the electorate receive information from the media and transmit it to ordinary voters.[35] Those who transmit information in this way have sometimes been

35. Katz, Elihu and P. F. Lazarsfeld, *Personal Influence.* Free Press, Glencoe, Ill., 1955.

described as "secondary leaders," whose role in conveying basic information from the campaign headquarters to the rank-and-file voters is an essential ingredient of the campaign.[36]

Surveys have enriched our understanding of the individual voting decision and have helped us to comprehend the nature and meaning of the election itself. From observing the motivations of individual voters, one survey research group has classified elections into three basic types—maintaining, deviating, and realigning—according to whether they closely reflect the prevailing party division, depart from it momentarily in response to some issue or candidate, or engender a lasting shift in the electorate's party preferences. A fourth type—in which the voters return to their traditional voting patterns after having "deviated" in the previous election—has been added to the classification and is known as a "reinstating election."[37] By making possible such classifications, surveys can help us to learn whether a given election foreshadows changes in the underlying patterns of party affiliation, whether certain questions or stands are likely to become an enduring source of party differentiation, whether the election signifies only a temporary deviation from the "normal" electoral division, and whether the majority's shift to a given candidate or party reflects changes in its doctrinal views.

By comparing the political opinions of voters with their actual voting habits, we can ascertain in what measure elections accurately convey the electorate's beliefs on various political questions. Surveys also enable us to inquire into the validity of such explanatory notions as the "band-

36. Berelson, B. R., *et al., Voting, op. cit.;* Lazarsfeld, P. F., *et al., The People's Choice, op. cit.;* Campbell, Angus, *et al., The American Voter, op. cit.,* p. 92, p. 271; Simon, H. A., and Frederick Stern, "Effect of Television upon Voting Behavior in Iowa in the 1952 Presidential Election," *American Political Science Review,* Vol. 49, June, 1955, pp. 470–477; Cutright, Phillips and P. H. Rossi, "Grass Roots Politicians and the Vote," *American Sociological Review,* Vol. 23, April, 1958, pp. 171–179; Rokkan, Stein and Henry Valen, "A Survey of the 1957 Norwegian Elections," *Revue Français de Science Politique,* Vol. 8, 1958, pp. 73–94; Matthews, D. R. and J. W. Prothro, "Social and Economic Factors and Negro Voter Registration in the South," *American Political Science Review,* Vol. 57, March, 1963, pp. 24–44; "Political Factors and Negro Voter Registration in the South," *American Political Science Review,* Vol. 57, June, 1963, pp. 355–367; and Eulau, Heinz, *Class and Party in the Eisenhower Years:* Class Roles and Perspectives in the 1952 and 1956 Elections. Free Press, Glencoe, Ill., 1962.
37. Key, V. O., Jr., "Theory of Critical Elections," *Journal of Politics,* Vol. 17, February, 1955, pp. 3–18.

wagon effect" and the "coattails effect," to learn whether they occur at all, and under what circumstances. The findings already available on these matters show that the correspondence between party preference and voter opinions on issues is frequently weak: Republican voters, for example, favor the opinions of Democratic leaders more than they do the opinions of Republican leaders. The large popular vote received by Eisenhower in 1952 and 1956 did not, as some have supposed, signify a trend toward economic conservatism or a renewed desire to reduce government intervention into social and economic affairs. Taking the election returns at their face value, therefore, would have been extremely misleading.

Election surveys have also proved exceedingly useful in studying the voting practices of particular groups or communities. Two of the most important pioneering election surveys, for example, were conducted in local communities, Sandusky, Ohio, and Elmira, New York.[38] Others have focused mainly on certain subgroups, such as Negroes[39] and Jews,[40] or on certain geographic regions, such as the South. As suggested earlier, the nature of the sample should be geared to the objectives of the inquiry. Much of the controversy over the appropriateness of a national versus a community sample for a study of voting is without point, for they serve somewhat different purposes, and each has advantages and disadvantages. A national voting study can accurately describe the motivations and voting decisions of the national electorate and of its major subgroups, divided geographically, ethnically, economically, and educationally. It is invaluable in helping to interpret the meaning of a particular election and makes possible comparisons of different regions and localities. A wide range of factors that affect the election outcome can be represented in appropriate frequency and strength. It is, of course, superior for predicting the election outcome or asesssing the influences that have determined the results.

Studies of a national election conducted in local communities, however, also offer advantages. They permit an investigator to take account of such factors as local party organization, the presence of certain local candidates on the ballot, the community's traditions and history, and the role of local influence groups such as trade unions and business associations. As these suggest, surveys of individual communities lend themselves especially to

38. Berelson, B. R., *et al., Voting, op. cit.*
39. Matthews, D. R. and J. W. Prothro, "Political Factors . . . ," *op. cit.*
40. Fuchs, L. H., *The Political Behavior of American Jews.* Free Press, Glencoe, Ill., 1956.

studies in depth. If one is primarily interested in discovering relationships between or among variables, rather than in describing the national election itself, a survey of a single "average" community can for many purposes be as useful as a national survey. One can use the local community, for example, to assess the correlation between education and level of political interest, the influence of personality on voting choice, or the degree to which party affiliation is rooted in family and other peer group memberships. To be sure, one has to use caution in deciding whether a local finding can or cannot be generalized to the nation as a whole; one would scarcely use data gathered on voters in Jackson, Mississippi to form generalizations about the role of civil rights issues for the rest of the nation. Many phenomena, however, are neither local nor idiosyncratic in nature, and one can safely assume that they yield a similar relationship in most or all communities within the same political culture. Ultimately, of course, all such assumptions—whether employed in a national or community survey—must be checked empirically.

Even this brief review suggests the considerable achievements and potentialities of survey methods for the study of elections. They have furnished solid information on the interaction of such socio-psychological factors as group membership, status, ideology, communication processes, personality, and demographic affiliations; and they have also supplied important information on "political" influences—e.g., party, issues, campaign techniques, partisanship, and candidates. There is, thus, little necessity for the fear, expressed by V. O. Key and others, that behavioral surveys of elections may focus so heavily on non-political variables as to neglect political influences. There is nothing inherent in the survey method to prevent one from taking account of party organization and activity, campaign propaganda, the role of the candidates, institutional influences on voter turnout, or dozens of other political factors. Furthermore, by knowing in a more exact way how much influence has been exerted by group memberships, personality, ideology, reference groups, or the mass media, one can more correctly assess the role played by the more strictly political influences.

POLITICAL ELITES AND LEADERSHIP

Although the survey method has so far been used chiefly for studies of mass responses, it is no less valuable for the investigation of political elites. Two difficulties, however, are likely to be encountered in elite studies. The first is that the universe is often more difficult to define, and the sampling procedures may, therefore, present special problems. It is, for example, difficult to decide precisely which groups comprise the universe of "party actives," or the "business elite," or the "foreign policy decision-makers." Second, certain elite groups such as Supreme Court judges or members of the White House staff are likely to be somewhat inaccessible to a survey interviewer. Neither of these difficulties is insurmountable, and they will be increasingly overcome as experience with elite studies is accumulated. Even now, the former of these difficulties does not apply to *all* political elites. There is little problem in defining the universe of state legislators, judges, or county committeemen. The members of these groups, furthermore, have been surprisingly willing to cooperate with survey investigators and, when properly approached, have submitted to lengthy and probing interviews on their political background, experience, and opinions.[41] Others, under the protection of anonymity, have cooperated in great numbers by completing lengthy, searching, self-administered attitude and personality questionnaires involving the most intimate opinions.

Studies of elites are of particular importance for political science. Politics, after all, is less the province of the electorate as a whole than of a small minority of office holders, party professionals, and amateur activists who contest for power, make decisions, and enforce policies. The central questions of political science concern are, "Who governs, how they gain power, how they exercise power, why men obey it, how they are controlled, to what ends they use power, and how its use relates to the values, aspirations, hopes, and fears of those who live under it. . . ."[42] We cannot hope to answer these questions without directly consulting the political elite, and for this the survey method is indispensable.[43] Obvious though this observation may seem, it has achieved currency only within the last decade or two, and only within certain quarters of the political science profession. Students of poli-

---

41. Marvick, Dwaine, ed., *Political Decision-Makers*. Free Press, Glencoe, Ill., 1961. Seligman, L. G., "Political Recruitment and Party Structure: A Case Study," *American Political Science Review,* Vol. 55, March, 1961, pp. 77–86; Wahlke, J. C., *et al., The Legislative System.* John Wiley & Sons, New York, 1962, especially pp. 69–143. For a documentary study, see Matthews, D. R., *The Social Background of Political Decision-Makers.* Doubleday, Garden City, N.Y., 1954. The most valuable summary of the research literature on political socialization is Hyman, H. H., *Political Socialization.* Free Press, Glencoe, Ill., 1959.

42. Kirkpatrick, E. M., *op. cit.,* p. 27.

43. Heard, Alexander, "Interviewing Southern Politicians," *American Political Science Review,* Vol. 44, December, 1950, pp. 886–896, at p. 894.

tics have traditionally observed political actors only from afar, studying them through their writings and speeches, or through such aggregative and anecdotal data as they could find. One may learn something about *individual* politicians through their autobiographies or biographies, their public statements, and their observed actions; but these sources cannot furnish the comprehensive portrait of motives, opinions, perceived interests, and ambitions needed for a scientific understanding of their behavior.

We have learned from surveys that political elites are disproportionately drawn from the more advantaged segments of the population—from those who enjoy higher ethnic, social, economic, or religious status. The typical member of the American political elite, for example, is a member of the middle or upper-middle class, college educated, a white Protestant from one of the "upper status" denominations, an urban resident, male, and above average age. He is likely to belong to a greater number of organizations than the average citizen and to participate more in community affairs generally. He has more opinions on public questions, and is ideologically more sophisticated. He displays greater consistency in his opinions, preferences, and political affiliations. He is more tolerant of those who express divergent opinions, and supports with greater understanding and conviction the procedural rights implicit in our democratic constitution.

Survey research has shown that, in the United States at least, the effect of political competition does not produce Tweedledee and Tweedledum parties: the forces that lead the parties to converge are counteracted by other forces that drive them apart. Nor does the support enjoyed by a party elite depend strongly on the particular opinions it expresses.[44] Nevertheless, party representatives and political office holders tend to respond to what they believe to be the desires of their constituents, although this tendency is not so strong as to exclude the expression of their own personal convictions.[45] Our present information also suggests that, contrary to the familiar opinion, the political class is less cynical about politics than are ordinary citizens, less willing to tolerate moral or political delinquency in other politicians, and more likely to embody the community conscience. The available data furnish little support for the widespread portrait of the politician as a callous, cynical, self-serving, purely opportunistic person who believes only in his own success, cares little for ideas, and would readily sacrifice the

44. McClosky, Herbert, *et al.*, "Issue Conflict . . . ," *op. cit.*
45. Miller, W. E. and Donald Stokes, "Constituency Influence . . . ," *op. cit.*

demands of conscience for the gains of political expediency. Obviously there are exceptions to these generalizations: survey research has identified political actors who are politically unaware, hold inconsistent opinions, or belong to a party but do not share its values. Some politicians have a poor grasp of the rules of the democratic game; some are cynical; and some are extremely confused ideologically. These sub-types have been identified, and something is being learned of their backgrounds, attitudes, personality traits, demographic characteristics, and group affiliations.

Surveys have also helped us to examine special classes of political actors, such as legislators and judges.[46] They have been used to investigate groups that bear a secondary or special relationship to politics, such as lawyers,[47] doctors,[48] military men,[49] business elites,[50] Negro elites,[51] and foreign policy elites.[52] They are also proving invaluable in the study of "community power" and community leaders. These studies have usually sought to identify the "political influentials" in particular communities—to discover the range of their powers and the subjects over which they have effective decision-making authority. Most of these studies have tried to assess the degree to which a community's political actors are the agents of interest groups or an independent force in their own right. Some surveys have identified and compared competing local elites, such as business elites, party elites, political office holders, and trade union elites. As more of these studies accumulate and comparison of their respective findings becomes possible, we will

46. Matthews, D. R., *U.S. Senators and Their World.* University of North Carolina Press, Chapel Hill, North Carolina, 1960; Wahlke, *et al., op. cit.,* pp. 29–39; Sorauf, F. J., *Party and Representation.* Atherton, New York, 1963; Patterson, S. C., "Patterns of Interpersonal Relations in a State Legislative Group: The Wisconsin Assembly," *Public Opinion Quarterly,* Vol. 23, Spring, 1959, pp. 101–109; Hirschfield, R. S., *et al.,* "Profile of Political Activists in Manhattan," *Western Political Quarterly,* Vol. 15, September, 1962, pp. 489–506; Truman, D. B., *The Congressional Party:* A Case Study. John Wiley & Sons, New York, 1959.
47. Eulau, Heinz, and J. D. Sprague, *Lawyers in Politics:* A Study in Professional Convergence. Bobbs-Merrill, Indianapolis, 1964.
48. Glaser, W. A., "Doctors and Politics," *American Journal of Sociology,* Vol. 66, November, 1960, pp. 230–245.
49. Janowitz, Morris, *The Professional Soldier,* Free Press, Glencoe, Ill., 1960.
50. Bauer, R. A., *et al., American Business and Public Policy.* Atherton, New York, 1963.
51. Wilson, James, *Negro Politics.* Free Press, Glencoe, Ill., 1960.
52. Rosenau, James, *Public Opinion and Foreign Policy.* Random House, New York, 1961.

have gained important new insights into the nature, source, and manifestations of elite power in the primary communities in which men live.[53]

POLITICAL IDEOLOGY AND EXTREME BELIEF

Although political scientists have long been interested in the study of liberalism-conservatism, isolationism, fascism, communism, pacifism, populism, and socialism, they have only recently begun to explore systematically the sources and correlates of such doctrines. What kinds of people embrace them, and how do they differ from those who reject them? What inspires and sustains such views? Are they related to economic status, social mobility, political change, personality characteristics, a sense of alienation? Are individuals of certain cognitive styles and capacities predisposed to accept or repudiate them? Do those who hold extremely deviant or conformist beliefs in one substantive area tend to deviate or conform in other areas as well?

Students of politics have increasingly turned to surveys to explore these questions. Surveys, for example, have confirmed the popular belief that liberalism—defined by reference to economic or social welfare attitudes—is most likely to prevail in the cities, among the young, the lower socioeconomic groups, minority ethnic groups, and Democrats. But the same pattern of correlations does not hold for other types of liberalism-conservatism —e.g., those expressing attitudes toward change, veneration of the past, or the right of individuals "to think and act for themselves." On these dimensions, the upper status and upper educated groups tend to be more liberal than the working class, the poor, and the uneducated. Young people and urban dwellers, however, are more liberal on these values as well. The articulate members of the society, it seems, have been more exposed to the liberal norms that prevail in the United States on non-economic matters; persons of lower education and status are often poorly situated to learn the value of procedural rights, tolerance of diversity, and social experimentation and change. Among the general population, therefore, the correlation is small between economic and non-economic liberalism-conservatism, whereas

53. Dahl, R. A., *Who Governs? op. cit.;* Agger, R. E. and Daniel Goldrich, "Community Power Structures and Partisanship," *American Sociological Review,* Vol. 23, August, 1958, pp. 383–392; Wildavsky, Aaron, *Leadership in a Small Town.* Bedminster Press, Totowa, N.J., 1964; Presthus, Robert, *Men at the Top.* Oxford University Press, New York, 1964; Hunter, Floyd, *Community Power Structure.* Doubleday, Garden City, N. Y., 1963; Vidich, A. J. and Joseph Bensman, *Small Town in Mass Society.* Princeton University Press, Princeton, 1958.

among the political influentials it is positive and significant. This reflects not only the greater exposure of political influentials to the prevailing norms, but also their greater ideological sophistication and inclination to adopt attitudes that are consistent with one another.

Surveys have also shown that liberalism-conservatism, especially of the classical or non-economic type, is markedly related to personality factors. Those psychological elements that lead to a pessimistic and suspicious view of human nature, to a punishing attitude toward human frailty, to misanthropy, or to inflexible and intolerant judgments about human diversity, are likely to be positively correlated with support for conservatism.[54] Similar personality characteristics turn up for those who hold extreme beliefs of either the right wing or left wing variety, or for those who score high on such measures as authoritarianism and totalitarianism. Such views are more frequently held by the inarticulate segments of the society (who are less able to discriminate them and to recognize their deviation from American democratic norms), and are also disproportionately expressed by individuals of misanthropic and inflexible personality dispositions who distrust mankind, who desire to control, regulate, and punish departures from approved standards, and who fear variety, contingency, and the "open" society. The embracing of these "radical" doctrines is associated with a tendency toward dogmatism and intolerance; and these traits, in turn, are related to intolerance of ambiguity and other marks of an inflexible personality.[55]

Comparable studies carried out on extreme isolationists show that they differ from non-isolationists in many of the ways that liberals differ from conservatives. They are intellectually less sophisticated, more parochial in outlook, and likely to lead more narrowly circumscribed lives. They are strongly given to dichotomous, and especially to we-they types of distinctions; and they are unusually intolerant of whatever is different or unfamiliar. The typical isolationist displays a strong element of misanthropy, a lack of sympathy for the misfortunes of others, and a fear and dislike of outsiders that amount almost to a ritualistic form of caste rejection. At the present stage of American history, isolationism is typically more xeno-

54. McClosky, Herbert, "Conservatism and Personality," *American Political Science Review,* Vol. 52, December, 1958, pp. 27–45; Lipset, S. M., *Political Man, op. cit.,* pp. 97–176, pp. 220–263; Campbell, Angus, *et al., The American Voter, op. cit.*
55. Rokeach, Milton, *et al., The Open and Closed Mind.* Basic Books, New York, 1960; Adorno, T. W., *et al., The Authoritarian Personality.* Harper & Bros., New York, 1950; Dicks, H. V., "Personality Traits and National Socialist Ideology," *Human Relations,* Vol. 3, August, 1950, pp. 111–154.

phobic and belligerent than pacific: its proponents appear to be less con-cerned with the well-being of other nations than with shutting them out and refusing responsibility for them.[56]

Survey methods have also been used to investigate particular kinds of extreme groups. Almond, for example, has employed a modified type of survey technique to interview former members of the Communist party from four different countries in an effort to discover, among other things, what motivated them to join the Communist party and what types of appeals were most effective in inducing individuals from different strata of the so-ciety to support the party. Something was also learned about the internal nature of the movement and about the intellectual differences between the members of the organization's *apparatus* and those who compose its rank and file.[57] Other surveys have probed the sources of support for various movements of the radical right, including the Christian Anti-Communist Crusade,[58] the Coughlin movement, and the John Birch Society.[59] Several studies of McCarthy supporters, drawing on survey materials, have shown that those who supported the senator did not disproportionately favor the reckless, bullying, and undemocratic policies with which he was identi-fied.[60]

56. McClosky, Herbert, "Attitude and Personality Correlates of Foreign Policy Orientation," in *Domestic Sources of Foreign Policy* (forthcoming). Edited by James Rosenau. Princeton University Press, Princeton.

57. Almond, G. A., *et al., The Appeals of Communism.* Princeton University Press, Princeton, 1954; Micaud, C. A., *Communism and the French Left.* Praeger, New York, 1963; Ernst, M. L. and D. G. Loth, *Report on the American Communist.* Henry Holt, New York, 1952; Cantril, Hadley, *The Politics of Despair.* Basic Books, New York, 1958.

58. Wolfinger, Raymond E., *et al.,* "America's Radical Right; Ideology and Politics," in *Ideology and Discontent:* The Concept of Ideology in the Light of Contemporary Social and Political Change. Edited by D. E. Apter. Free Press, Glencoe, Ill., 1964; and "The Clientele of the Christian Anti-Communism Crusade," paper delivered at American Political Science Association meeting, September, 1963.

59. Lipset, S. M., "Three Decades of the Radical Right: Coughlinites, McCarthyites, and Birchers," in *The Radical Right.* Edited by Daniel Bell. Anchor Edition. Double-day, Garden City, N.Y., 1964, pp. 313–377.

60. Trow, M. A., "Small Businessmen, Political Tolerance, and Support for McCar-thy," *American Journal of Sociology,* Vol. 64, November, 1958, pp. 270–281; Lipset, S. M., "Three Decades . . . ," *op. cit.,* pp. 313–377; Polsby, N. W., "Towards an Ex-planation . . . ," *op. cit.;* McClosky, Herbert, "McCarthyism: The Myth and the Reality," paper delivered at the American Psychological Association meeting, New York, September, 1957; Fenton, J. M., *In Your Opinion.* Little-Brown, Boston, 1960, pp. 135–144.

POLITICAL SOCIALIZATION, STABILITY, AND CHANGE

How are political beliefs and behavior patterns formed and maintained? Once established, how are they changed? Interest in such questions is currently strong and surveys are among the methods most frequently used to find the answers.

The research literature on political socialization prior to 1959 has been codified and reviewed by Herbert Hyman.[61] Merely to enumerate some of the topics covered by Hyman will suggest the range of survey (and other) research addressed to this subject. They include the sources of political participation, the ideals that inspire political involvement, the types of public heroes who serve as ego-ideals for youngsters, differences in political interest between boys and girls, the developmental stages at which voting preferences are firmly established, socio-economic influences on the formation of party preference, family sources of political belief, affiliation, and authoritarian or democratic tendencies, and the origins of tolerant and intolerant attitudes.[62] Survey research since 1959 has deepened and expanded the study of political socialization, examing such matters as children's images of political authority, the degree of political awareness at different ages and under different class conditions, the relation between stability of political preference and strength of family indoctrination, the recruitment of state legislators, and the effects of personality on the learning of political responses.[63] Some of these studies have directly surveyed young people, while

61. Hyman, H. H., *Political Socialization, op. cit.*
62. Hyman, H. H., *ibid.*, chap. 2.
63. Hess, R. D. and David Easton, "The Child's Changing Image of the President," *Public Opinion Quarterly*, Vol. 24, Winter, 1960, pp. 632–644; Easton, David and R. D. Hess, "The Child's Political World," *Midwestern Journal of Political Science*, Vol. 6, August, 1962, pp. 229–246: McClosky, Herbert and H. E. Dahlgren, "Primary Group Influence on Party Loyalty," *American Political Science Review*, Vol. 53, September, 1959, pp. 757–776; Eulau, Heinz, *et al.*, "The Political Socialization of American State Legislators," *Midwestern Journal of Political Science*, Vol. 3, May, 1959, pp. 188–206; Greenstein, F. I., "The Benevolent Leader—Children's Images of Political Authority," *American Political Science Review*, Vol. 54, December, 1960, pp. 934–943; "Sex-related Political Differences in Childhood," *Journal of Politics*, Vol. 23, May, 1961, pp. 353–371; "More on Children's Images of the President," *Public Opinion Quarterly*, Vol. 25, Winter, 1961, pp. 648–654; "Children and Politics," in *Yale Studies in Political Science*, Vol. 13. Yale University Press, New Haven, 1965; Maccoby, E. E., *et al.*, "Youth and Political Change," *Public Opinion Quarterly*, Vol. 18, No. 1, 1954, pp. 23–29; Verba, Sidney, *Small Groups and Political Behavior.* Princeton University Press, Princeton, 1961, pp. 17–60; Berelson, B. R., *et al.*, *Voting, op. cit.*, pp. 54–117.

others have interviewed adults about their early political experiences and development.

As already mentioned, surveys show that the habits of political participation and party preference are mainly implanted by the family and remain with the progeny long after they have left the family homestead. If the family's political interest is strong, and if no major changes in life-style are encountered, an individual is likely to retain these early habits throughout his lifetime. This prospect is reinforced by one's inclination to select friends and associates who share one's own political orientations, and by the tendency to remain in the life style inherited from one's parents. Shifts in political orientations and values do, of course, occur, in response to changing socio-economic status and peer group associations, new political experiences and standards, and the unfolding of political events. Conflicting primary group affiliations may prevent an individual from aligning himself strongly with any one political persuasion, and may lead him to political independency or to an unstable party attachment. The effectiveness of the competing influences will in part depend upon the strength of the family's initial indoctrination, the degree to which the family is attractive to him, and the frequency with which he continues to see them.

Even without "rebelling" against parents, each generation in a modern society is bound to differ somewhat from its predecessor; the offspring resemble the parents, but are not identical with them. Political change arises in part from the distance that invariably develops between generations. While their parents are transmitting one set of political values, the offspring are simultaneously acquiring a slightly different set from their peer culture and from the macro-society. Evidence from surveys conducted at different points in time, or on samples of different ages, plainly shows the extent of these shifts.

But the differences between parents and children on such doctrines as liberalism-conservatism do not result solely from generational changes; they are to some extent a function of the aging process itself, i.e., of experiences accumulated over time together with changes in physical and mental capacities. Generational differences, of course, may be further widened by the political experiences to which the youth have been exposed; war, depression, the election to the presidency of a powerful charismatic personality such as a Franklin Roosevelt, or the emergence of a compelling, overarching issue like civil rights may affect the lives of a generation so pervasively as to alter its views on many social questions. It appears, however, that shifts in political belief tend to be small and gradual rather than large and abrupt. We have sometimes been misled on this matter because of the drama that attends the conversion of an individual from one political extreme to another —from membership in the Communist party, for example, to affiliation with an extreme right-wing group. But such conversions are atypical; the more characteristic pattern is one in which the shifts are small, and proceed by slow stages and by gradual accommodation. Although no panel survey has so far addressed the issue of conversion directly, it would be an excellent device for observing political changes over time, and for uncovering the influences that induce those changes.

PSYCHOLOGY AND POLITICS

The most important spur to research on this subject was the publication in 1950 of *The Authoritarian Personality.*[64] This work and the many research efforts it inspired demonstrated that the adoption of certain political orientations—e.g., the extreme left orientations already discussed—is in part a function of personality characteristics. Hostile, paranoid, or "authoritarian" personality patterns are found with particular frequency among persons who are oriented toward fascism, communism, and other political doctrines that are intemperate, angry, and grandiose in their claims and ambitions. Persons who advocate "extreme" beliefs, whether of the left or right, are on the average more dogmatic, closed-minded, and psychologically inflexible than are those who hold moderate and democratic beliefs.[65] Similarly, those who strongly support doctrines that exclude certain groups or that magnify differences between themselves and others—e.g., isolationism, ethnocentrism, chauvinism, xenophobia—frequently also display the familiar symptoms of paranoia—excessive anxiety, the projection of hostility, grandiose self-inflation, unrealistic fear and depreciation of "outsiders" coupled with a tendency to ascribe mysterious and exaggerated powers to them, and so forth.[66] But while personality dispositions are most often engaged by "extreme" political doctrines, they may also, as we have seen,

64. Adorno, T. W., *et al., op. cit.;* Dicks, H. V., *op. cit.*
65. Rokeach, Milton, *et al., op. cit.,* pp. 109–131.
66. Adorno, T. W., *et al., op. cit.;* McClosky, Herbert, "Attitude and Personality Correlates . . . ," *op. cit.;* Perlmutter, H. V., "Correlates of Two Types of Xenophilic Orientation," *Journal of Abnormal Social Psychology,* Vol. 52, January, 1956, pp. 130–135; "Some Characteristics of the Xenophobic Personality," *Journal of Psychology,* Vol. 38, October, 1954, pp. 291–300.

affect the holding of more moderate beliefs, such as conservatism and liberalism.[67]

The relation of group membership to the establishment and retention of norms is another area of interest to political psychology. The research literature on this subject is so vast and well-known that there is no point in reviewing it here. Suffice it to say that the mechanisms by which primary and other reference groups succeed in indoctrinating their members are in great measure "psychological." Such groups not only set norms which serve their members as psychological anchoring points, but they also have the power to reward and punish, to give or withhold affection, to structure reality, and to determine the individual's self-image. Affiliation with a group, of course, may also be socially or economically instrumental. Whatever the reason for the attachment, survey and other data confirm that members of the same groups tend to hold similar political views, value similar objects and goals, affiliate with the same parties, and have common perspectives on the political process. The more palpable the group, the greater its influence: a peer group, for example, has more psychological weapons than a large and amorphous categoric group, and its capacity for instilling political habits and standards in its members will ordinarily be greater.[68]

Psychological approaches also figure prominently in the study of leadership. Though most of the work on the psychology of leadership has been done through laboratory studies of small groups, some beginnings have been made in applying survey methods to this subject. A few surveys have explored the relation of personality factors to one's choice of leaders and one's image of the qualities of leadership.[69] Several others have sought to learn whether political leaders are distinguished from non-leaders by their personality traits and whether leadership can in itself be considered a "trait" or combination of traits.[70]

Surveys are also beginning to be used to explore the psychological correlates of political conformity and deviation. This subject, too, has mainly

67. McClosky, "Conservatism and Personality," *op. cit.*
68. Verba, Sidney, *op. cit.*
69. Cantril, Hadley, *The Psychology of Social Movements.* John Wiley & Sons, New York, 1941, pp. 233–238; Sanford, F. H., *Authoritarianism and Leadership.* Stephenson Bros., Philadelphia, 1950.
70. McConaughy, J. B., "Certain Personality Factors of State Legislators in North Carolina," *American Political Science Review,* Vol. 44, December, 1950, pp. 897–903; Gibb, C. A., "Leadership" in *Handbook of Social Psychology.* Edited by Gardner Lindzey, *op. cit.,* pp. 233–238.

been studied through laboratory experiments. Surveys, however, can be useful in locating those who conform to or deviate from the modal political values of their sub-culture or of society. They can be used to observe the relationship between personality and the tendency to conform or deviate. Survey data now under analysis at the Survey Research Center, University of California, Berkeley, strongly suggest, for example, that certain forms of political "deviancy"—including deviancy from the norms of one's party and the embracing of extreme doctrines—are related to an individual's learning capacity and to the psychological needs and motivations that affect that capacity.

POLITICAL INSTITUTIONS AND SYSTEMS

The manner of applying surveys to the study of politics has been criticized in some quarters for an alleged tendency to ignore "politics" and political institutions in favor of social, psychological, and intellectual characteristics of individuals in the mass public. As Key observed, "Ultimately the concern of the student of politics must center on the operation of the state apparatus in one way or another. Both the characteristics of the survey instrument and the curiosities of those with a mastery of survey technique have tended to encourage a focus of attention on microscopic political phenomena more or less in isolation from the total political process."[71] Studies of primary groups, reference groups, or cross pressures, he complained, do not tell us much about the political order, and a bridge is needed "from observation of atoms of the political system to the system itself. . . ."

It must be admitted that political surveys have until now paid less attention to the institutional and systemic aspects of politics than to the forces which induce individual political behavior. This tendency can in part be traced to their ancestry. Having derived from the public opinion poll, academic political surveys continue to be regarded (even by many of their users) primarily as instruments for the assessment of opinion. There are, in addition, some inherent limitations on the utility of surveys for the study of political systems. Surveys, for example, would scarcely be the recommended procedure for observing rapidly changing behavior or institutional practices that involve many interactions occurring in different contexts over long periods of time. Some political processes can more appropriately be

71. Key, V. O., Jr. "The Politically Relevant in Surveys," *Public Opinion Quarterly*, Vol. 24, Spring, 1960, pp. 54–61, at p. 55.

observed through participant observation or through reports of journalists and other chroniclers of political events. The formal structure and procedures of a political system can more economically be ascertained by consulting its constitutional and statutory documents than by conducting elaborate surveys.

There are, nevertheless, many institutional and systemic questions that can usefully be approached through surveys. Studies of the actual organization and procedures of a legislature or party would be cases in point. Political institutions, after all, are more than the formal structures prescribed in constitutional documents, statutes, or executive orders. They are agencies or instrumentalities that discuss, respond, decide, and act—which means that they can for some purposes be conceptualized as aggregates of people standing in a certain relationship to each other. One way to understand an institution is to survey the people who occupy its roles and help to carry out its functions. Through appropriate sampling procedures and a well-designed questionnaire, one can learn much about the forces that play upon an institution, how it resolves its internal conflicts, how it arrives at decisions, what it does to put those decisions into practice, how it interacts with other institutions in the system, and how it perceives its constituency. Some of these questions cannot adequately be answered except by consulting the men and women who act for the organization.

Although gathered through interviews with individuals, survey findings have great potential value for the macroscopic understanding of political systems and institutions. For example, a survey of voters in a single election will tell us about that particular election or the individuals who participated in it; but a comparison of many election studies conducted in different places, at different times, under different circumstances, with different parties and issues can teach us something about competitive party systems, the role of ideas and consensus in the viability of democratic governments, and the realities of political representation under modern mass democracy. Election surveys have thrown light on the relation between political belief and party divergence, on the relative influence of two-party and multi-party systems in "balkanizing" the electorate,[72] and on the connection between sense of party responsibility and degree of ideological cleavage between parties. A survey of trade union members has

72. Campbell, Angus and Henry Valen, "Party Identification in Norway and the United States," *Public Opinion Quarterly,* Vol. 25, Winter, 1961, pp. 505–525.

furnished insights into the question of how oligarchical domination has been avoided and a competitive party system maintained in at least one trade union organization.[73] Voting surveys have shown how the form of the ballot affects straight or split-ticket voting, and which voters are most likely to be influenced.[74] They have also furnished new and better information on the ways in which voting laws affect turnout,[75] and on the forces that give rise to party realignment.[76] Similarly, comparative surveys have not only added to our knowledge of political participation, but have also told us something about political modernization and the impact of political cultures on a sense of civic competence.

Surveys are also being used to study "community power." By sampling political elites and voters, these surveys have significantly enlarged our understanding of local political institutions. They have supplied detailed information on the interplay between citizens, elected officials, administrative agencies, the business community, labor organizations, and other urban groups.[77]

The survey method has likewise increased the possibility of understanding the legislature as an institution. While furnishing information on individual legislators—e.g., their social backgrounds, training, motivations, self-images, opinions, partisanship—they simultaneously tell us something about the nature of the legislature itself. Recent surveys, moreover, have directly addressed the question of the legislature as an institution by examining lawmakers in their legislative roles. They have, for example, asked to what ex-

73. Lipset, S. M., M. A. Trow, and J. S. Coleman, *Union Democracy*. Free Press, Glencoe, Ill., 1956.
74. Campbell, Angus and W. E. Miller, "The Motivational Basis of Straight and Split-Ticket Voting," *American Political Science Review,* Vol. 51, June, 1957, pp. 293–312.
75. Campbell, Angus, "Recent Developments . . . ," *op. cit.,* p. 34.
76. Matthews, D. R. and J. W. Prothro, "Southern Images of Political Parties: An Analysis of White and Negro Attitudes," *Journal of Politics,* Vol. 26, February, 1964, pp. 82–111.
77. Dahl, R. A., *Who Governs? op. cit.;* Agger, R. E. and Daniel Goldrich, "Community Power Structures . . . ," *op. cit.,* pp. 383–392; Greer, S. A., "Mass Society and the Parapolitical Structure," *American Sociological Review,* Vol. 27, October, 1962, pp. 634–646; "Urbanism Reconsidered: A Comparative Study of Local Areas in a Metropolis," *American Sociological Review,* Vol. 21, February, 1956, pp. 19–25; *Metropolitics: A Study of Political Culture.* John Wiley & Sons, New York, 1963; *Governing the Metropolis.* John Wiley & Sons, New York, 1962; Banfield, E. C., *Political Influence.* Free Press, Glencoe, Ill., 1961; Presthus, Robert, *op. cit.*

tent a legislator's behavior is a response to his legislative party, to the intensity of interparty competition within his constituency, to pressures from the executive agencies, and to his own view of the "representative" function. They have asked how legislators perceive the norms of the institution, how they define their own role within the body, and what role they assign to the legislature in the political system as a whole. They have further sought to learn in what measure the legislative process depends upon its formal rules and organization and in what measure upon its informal structure—its cliques and factions, its party blocs and conflicts, and its response to lobbies and to reference groups outside the legislature. Some of these matters have been studied by consulting roll-call tabulations, official journals, aggregative data on constituency characteristics, and other documentary sources. Valuable as such sources are, they cannot furnish the detailed information on legislators' roles, perceptions, and responses needed for an adequate understanding of the legislature as an institution.[78]

Survey research on the executive and judicial branches of government has lagged behind the research on the representative bodies, although unsystematic interview studies of executive agencies have, of course, been attempted for some time. Behavioral research on the courts has for the most part drawn on documentary sources, such as biographies of judges or the official reports of their decisions. Various mathematical and scaling procedures have been developed to uncover the central tendency of a judge's decisions or to identify the colleagues with whom he habitually aligns himself. A few survey attempts have been made to relate the political attitudes of judges to their decisions and verdicts, but large-scale surveys of judges, comparable to those now available on legislators, party leaders, or voters, have not yet been undertaken. The empirical study of the judiciary, how-

78. Eulau, Heinz, *et al.*, "The Political Socialization of American State Legislators," *op. cit.*; Wahlke, J. C., *et al.*, *The Legislative System, op. cit.*; Sorauf, F. J., *op. cit.*; Miller, W. E. and Donald Stokes, *Congress and Constituency* (forthcoming); Silverman, Corrine, "The Legislators' View of the Legislative Process," *Public Opinion Quarterly,* Vol. 18, Summer, 1954, pp. 180–190; Patterson, S. C., *op. cit.*; Truman, D. B., *The Congressional Party, op. cit.*; MacRae, Duncan, Jr., *The Dimensions of Congressional Voting*. University of California Press, Berkeley, 1958. Reviews of the research on legislative bodies may be found in Meller, Norman, "Legislative Behavior Research," *Western Political Quarterly,* Vol. 13, March, 1960, pp. 131–153; and Wahlke, J. C., "Behavioral Analyses of Representative Bodies," in *Essays on the Behavioral Study of Politics.* Edited by Austin Ranney, *op. cit.*, pp. 173–190.

ever, is developing rapidly and surveys of greater scope and depth are bound to be forthcoming before long.[79]

Although interest in cross-cultural political surveys has been growing rapidly, the number of completed surveys that are genuinely comparative is still fairly small. Cross-cultural studies, of course, are likely to be expensive and to involve numerous technical problems arising out of the translation of terms, the framing of cognate concepts, and the validation of measures on different populations. Nor are there adequately trained field staffs in all countries or foreign communities in which one might wish to conduct a survey.

If these difficulties can be overcome, comparative surveys hold out many advantages. Employed, for example, in studies of modernization, surveys can be used to trace the actual changes in the values and behavior of individuals located at different points of the society. They can be used to supplement aggregate ecological data or to collect it when reliable ecological records are not available. By asking the same questions in different countries, an investigator can make precise comparisons, determine whether certain findings are unique or universal, observe variations in the political norms and practices, and assess the impact of different types of "political culture" on behavior. He might even be able to test the influence of certain institutional or systemic differences on behavior. How do different political settings affect political behavior and practices, such as voting, participation, political socialization, political recruitment, and intensity of party competition? Generalizations about so-called "national character" might also be checked out, e.g., are the French really more ideological than other people? Are the Germans authoritarian, the British politically pragmatic, the Italians politically romantic?

---

79. An excellent summary of the behavioral work on the judiciary is presented in Schubert, G. L., ed., *Judicial Decision-Making*. Free Press, Glencoe, Ill., 1963. See also Nagel, S. S., "Off-the-Bench Judicial Attitudes," in *ibid*, pp. 29–53; "Ethnic Affiliation and Judicial Propensities," *Journal of Politics*, Vol. 24, February, 1962, pp. 92–100; "Political Party Affiliation and Judges' Decisions," *American Political Science Review*, Vol. 55, December, 1961, pp. 843–850; Spaeth, H. J., "An Approach to the Study of Attitudinal Differences as an Aspect of Judicial Behavior," *Midwestern Journal of Political Science*, Vol. 5, 1961, pp. 165–180.

Although answers to such questions lie in the future, some beginnings have been made. Almond and Verba, as we noted, have carried out a five-nation comparative survey of political socialization, citizenship, and participation.[80] Almond has also conducted a four-nation study of former members of the Communist party, in an effort to compare the nature and effectiveness of the party's appeals.[81] This study has inspired similar studies in other parts of the world.[82] In an ambitious effort to assess the forces of modernization in underdeveloped countries, Columbia University's Bureau of Applied Social Research undertook a cross-cultural survey of seven Near-Eastern and Mediterranean nations.[83] This inquiry examined the effects of communication on the modernization process, and explored such variables as geographic mobility, exposure to media, the broadening of personal horizons, capacity for "empathy," demographic characteristics, sense of personal well-being and effectiveness, and the role of ideologies. Survey studies on a smaller scale have also been carried out by Campbell and Valen on party affiliation in Norway and the United States,[84] by Converse and Dupeux on political socialization in the United States and France,[85] and by Rokkan on comparative aspects of political participation and voting behavior.[86]

80. Almond, G. A. and Sidney Verba, *op. cit.*

81. Almond, *The Appeals . . . , op. cit.;* and Cantril, Hadley, *The Politics . . . , op. cit.*

82. Pye, L. W., *Guerilla Communism in Malaya:* Its Social and Political Meaning. Princeton University Press, Princeton, 1956.

83. Lerner, Daniel and Lucille Pevsner, *The Passing of Traditional Society:* Modernizing the Middle East. Free Press, Glencoe, Ill., 1958; Mosel, James, "Communication Patterns and Political Socialization in Traditional Thailand," in *Communications and Political Development.* Edited by L. W. Pye. Princeton University Press, Princeton, 1963, pp. 184–228.

84. Campbell, Angus and Henry Valen, *op. cit.*

85. Converse, P. E. and Georges Dupeux, "Politicalization of the Electorate in France and the United States," *Public Opinion Quarterly,* Vol. 26, Spring, 1962, pp. 1–33.

86. Rokkan, Stein, "Party Preferences and Opinion Patterns in Western Europe: A Comparative Analysis," *International Social Science Bulletin,* Vol. 7, 1955, pp. 575–576. For reviews of comparative research, particularly on voting and participation, see Rokkan, Stein and Henry Valen, "Parties, Elections and Political Behavior in the Northern Countries: A Review of Recent Research," in *Politsche Forschung.* Edited by Otto Stammer. Westdeutscher Verlag, Koeln-Opladen, 1960; and Rokkan, Stein, "The Comparative Study of Political Participation: Notes Toward a Perspective on Current Research," in *Essays on the Behavioral Study of Politics.* Edited by Austin Ranney, *op. cit.,* pp. 47–90; and other works by Rokkan.

New Applications for Survey Research

It is plain from the foregoing that survey research has penetrated many areas of political science and has become an indispensable tool of political inquiry. It is equally plain, however, that the potential of political surveys has only begun to be explored and that many important questions have not yet been addressed. We cannot list all the questions that might fruitfully be investigated by surveys but we can at least suggest their potential by considering their application to four areas of political study: leadership, internal party affairs, the relation of political belief to action, and the analysis of political events and trends.

POLITICAL LEADERSHIP

Although leadership is an everyday feature of political life, far less is scientifically known about it than is commonly supposed. Most of what is known has been learned from laboratory studies of small groups, with little having been done on political leadership as such.

Scholars interested in leadership have been unable to agree on its nature or source. Is it a "trait," a composite of traits, a relationship among people similar to other types of relationships (such as friendship), the product of a given environment and circumstance, or a combination of these? Although the trait theory presently enjoys little support among scholars, neither this nor any theory of leadership has been systematically explored and tested in the field of politics. This is, however, an area to which surveys could contribute immensely, especially if they were to be combined with procedures for assessing personality. By comparing political leaders with non-leaders, or with leaders from other elite groups, one might simultaneously test the trait theory of leadership, observe the influence of social background and "situation" on the recruitment and ascendancy of leaders, and learn something in the process about the relational-situational type of explanation.

Surveys might help us to answer some elementary questions about which, at present, we can only conjecture. To what extent does leadership depend upon a correspondence of views between leader and followers? Are would-be leaders who possess certain outlooks, temperaments, or capacities more likely to be selected under one set of circumstances (say, for example, military exigency) than others? By what criteria or signs do the active members of a political party "select" certain individuals as party leaders or candidates? Do the leaders selected differ in appearance, background, style, personality, or other traits from other party members or from the members of other elites? Are the attributes actually possessed by leaders discernible to the voters or even to the active party members who helped to choose them? Although surveys are now being addressed to some of these questions, we are a long way from having the hard data we need to deal with them adequately.

The nature of the politician, as distinguished from other social types, has long fascinated political observers, and has inspired numerous discursive essays.[87] Few systematic research efforts, however, have been addressed to this question, and we have little established knowledge on which to draw. It has often been thought, for example, that politicians differ markedly from, say, bureaucrats in their adaptability to change, their willingness to indulge human frailty and variety, their empathy and capacity for warm personal relations, and their flexibility in the enforcement of rules. The vocational politician is considered by some observers to have a dislike of theory and idealism, and to embrace a pragmatic, hard-headed realism bordering on cynicism. Surveys are among the principal devices by which these and related claims can be tested. Carried out in more than one country, they can tell us whether there is a universal political vocation or whether the dominant type varies, in predictable ways, from one political system to another, and from one era to another. Such surveys would also furnish essential information on the leaders' educational, occupational, or religious backgrounds, their previous political experience, their reference groups, and so forth. Comparison of vocational politicians in and out of office, or those serving at different levels or in different branches of government, would also be possible.

INTERNAL PARTY AFFAIRS

Political scientists have devoted considerable attention to the study of political parties, but systematic information is still lacking on many important questions that bear upon the internal life of the party. Little is known, for example, about the nature and sources of party loyalty and partisanship, and about the relation of these to attitudes toward party discipline and responsibility. Our own inquiries suggest that the correlation is imperfect

87. Probably the most brilliant of these is Weber, Max, "Politics as a Vocation," in *From Max Weber:* Essays in Sociology. Edited by H. H. Gerth and C. W. Mills. Oxford University Press, New York, 1946, pp. 77–128.

and that many loyal party participants are unwilling to impose strong party discipline upon other members. Our evidence also suggests that those with the strongest party loyalty do not always conform to the party's modal outlook, a disparity that is especially apparent among the less informed members of the organization. We know much less than we should about the reasons for defection from traditional membership, or withdrawal from active participation. To what extent, for example, do shifts result from changes in party programs, from the impact of significant events (such as depression or war), or from changes in the style and tone imprinted upon a party by its leaders?

We still know little about the nature and sources of factionalism within parties. Do cleavages in the American parties tend to be ideological or personal? Do they characteristically develop around geographic or economic interests, contending leaders, differences on issues, responses to oligarchical domination, or conflicting tactical orientations? Are the members of minority factions more militant or "radical" than those in the dominant faction? How does factionalism in mass parties of the American type differ from factionalism in the smaller, more stringently ideological parties of Europe?

These and dozens of other questions about internal party affairs can be approached with considerable profit through survey procedures. By directly consulting party members, one could ascertain which factions or leaders they identify with, where they stand on party issues, how partisan and loyal they are, how they feel about the organization and management of their party, and, most important, whether they respond to these questions in a patterned way. By surveying members at different levels of the party, one could also test current hypotheses concerning the role of leaders in formulating and transmitting the organization's norms. One might also learn whether the distinction Almond finds between the esoteric and exoteric doctrines of an organization like the Communist party holds to any degree among moderate, non-revolutionary parties. Through repeated surveys, one might also determine whether members change their outlook on certain questions as their party moves in and out of power.

Surveys, of course, are not the only research procedures by which the internal affairs of political parties can be studied. For best results, they should be combined with macro-studies of the parties. Survey findings become far more meaningful if one takes account of the party's official activities, its public stand on issues, its choice of candidates, the pronouncements of its spokesmen, and other marks of the party in action.

RELATION OF BELIEF TO ACTION

Surveys are repeatedly used to measure beliefs (political and others), but the relation of those beliefs to action has received little attention. Although beliefs are unquestionably important clues to how people act, they are not perfect indicators of action, and the exact connection between the two must therefore be explored if we are to achieve a more scientific understanding of politics. What, for example, are the "behavioral" consequences of changing people's attitudes? Is the correspondence between belief and action greater among articulates or inarticulates, among persons who hold conventional beliefs or those who hold unconventional ones, among those who lead or those who follow? Under what conditions will persons who embrace totalitarian beliefs act on them in a way that endangers democracy? How far can political loyalties be strained without breaking? At present, we lack basic information on most questions of this kind.

Surveys can help in several ways to assess the relation between political belief and action. They can be used, for example, to select for closer observation under laboratory conditions people who express certain political beliefs. Experiments might be aimed at testing the relation between their beliefs as reported in a survey and their overt behavior in response to certain stimuli. Using a measure like the California F Scale, one might employ a survey to select samples of "authoritarians" and "equalitarians," who might then be compared in their responses to "democratic" and "authoritarian" situations as simulated in the laboratory. Would the low and high scorers differ significantly in the way they behave toward power figures, peers, and subordinates? Would they be rigid in the enforcement of the rules of the game, or tolerant and flexible? How would they behave toward members of minority groups?

Surveys might similarly be used to compare conformity "attitudes" with conformity "behavior." By utilizing a conformity scale in a survey questionnaire, one might easily identify respondents who prize conventionality, demand conformity from others or, alternatively, who express independence and applaud "deviation." If these groups were then subjected to conformity pressures of the type employed by Asch and Crutchfield in their laboratory studies of conformity,[88] how would they behave? Would they succumb to

88. Asch, S. E., "Effects of Group Pressure upon the Modification and Distortion of Judgment," in *Groups, Leadership, and Men.* Edited by H. S. Guetzkow. Carnegie Press, Pittsburgh, 1951; Crutchfield, R. S., "Personal and Situational Factors in Conformity to Group Pressure," *Acta Psychologica,* Vol. 15, 1959, pp. 386–388.

group judgments even when those judgments are patently absurd, or would they stand up to the group in defense of their own judgments? From the interplay of their verbal responses, as elicited in the survey, and their overt responses, as evoked by the experiment, an investigator might learn a great deal about the relation between thought and action in this domain. He might add dimension to the inquiry by simulating in the laboratory a council or legislative body or jury, and by observing the effects of communication and persuasion on persons holding different attitudes. This combination of research methods might also be employed to see whether a respondent who presents himself on a questionnaire as politically responsible, flexible, and open to negotiation actually behaves this way in an experimental group. One might also compare a respondent's professed belief in civil liberties and procedural rights with his tendency to behave tolerantly or repressively in political or judicial situations simulated in the laboratory. The effect of beliefs on overt behavior can in some instances also be examined in "real-life" situations outside the laboratory; here, the respondents selected by survey procedures might be observed as they participate politically, make choices, respond to political communications, engage in political discussions, and align themselves with one political group or another.

It is also possible to compare political beliefs and actions without going outside the survey method itself. One can, for example, reinterview respondents to see whether they have acted consistently with the opinions they expressed in earlier interviews. Even a one-shot survey may permit the investigators to compare the beliefs a respondent expresses in the interview and the overt behavior he reports about himself. One may find respondents who claim to be politically independent but invariably vote for the same party; others who assert beliefs about democracy, tolerance and party loyalty to which, as their responses show, they fail to adhere in practice. A survey investigator can also make use of the case method, presenting respondents with problem cases to see whether their responses are consistent with the principles they have previously stated. How, for example, would the respondent vote if he were on a jury hearing a case of high treason? Would he intercede with the police to gain protection for a group of civil rights workers threatened by segregationists? A respondent's answers to such questions will not predict perfectly how he would actually behave under the circumstances stated, but they do introduce an action dimension that goes beyond the mere expression of opinions. It is, in any event, clear from these and the foregoing examples that the survey method does not restrict the political scientist to the study of opinions and attitudes. Used imaginatively, it permits him to learn something about overt political behavior as well.

HISTORICAL AND TREND ANALYSIS

Key, among others, has criticized surveys for being "static," and for providing us "with a reading at one point in time." Even panel studies, he maintains, cover too brief a period to make a correct reading of the "great and really significant political actions . . . [that] take place over comparatively long periods of time."[89]

Although there is some merit in this criticism, the survey method does not need to be time-bound to the degree that Key's comment implies. Since the method is new, we have not yet had an adequate test of its capacity to furnish parallel data collected over long periods of time. It is not necessary to conduct panel studies in order to document trends, for this can also be done by surveys repeated on different samples of the same universe. Surveys conducted in series can reveal important changes in beliefs, practices, life styles, social characteristics, and patterns of response to given stimuli. By accumulating parallel data collected at different points in time, surveys make it possible both to trace changes in the political culture and to ascertain the events that have produced those changes. As survey data accumulate, there will be less need to rely on the familiar secondary indicators upon which historians have had primarily to depend—newspapers, diaries, business invoices, published speeches, etc. These sources should not be depreciated, of course, but they rarely furnish hard and reliable data in as useful a form as can be obtained through parallel surveys conducted over time. Deriving cumulative data from surveys diminishes the selection bias that plagues the historian's efforts, and he is less likely, therefore, to be misled by the writings, speeches, or documents that happen to fall into his hands or that his leanings have led him to search out.

Surveys conducted at different historical stages will help us to ascertain something about changes in the value system and mood of a nation, the people's sense of well-being or malaise, their satisfaction with political institutions, and their attitudes toward government policies. We will be able to learn which aspects of political culture are stable and universal, and which are labile, transitional, or unique to a given time and place. We will also be able to discover which policies increase or diminish political morale, awaken

89. Key, V. O., Jr., "The Politically Relevant . . . ," *op. cit.*

or dampen one's sense of civic responsibility, and incite certain segments of the population to protest and disaffection. Thus, while a single survey may furnish a portrait of political life at a given moment in time, successive surveys on parallel questions become the equivalent of a moving portrait.

Hence, if one is interested in such phenomena as "modernization," one can trace in considerable detail the process by which a political system or nation unfolds, opens itself to experience, casts off old forms, and integrates new ones. One can also discern which influences and events retard or speed up the diffusion of political values.

The quality of trend analyses can be significantly improved through the use of computers to process the mountains of data that are bound to be generated by a series of surveys. Computers can be set to divine trends, to reveal discontinuities, to take notice of deviations from modal patterns, and to search out configurations that have held for a long time. They can show which influences remain constant, despite changing institutions and events, and which vary as conditions change. Their extraordinary capacity for retrieving and processing data will permit us to test numerous hypotheses that until now have been difficult or impossible to test. If, for example, one is interested in the effects of certain types of international events on a nation's attitudes, one can "ask" the computer to select all instances of such events on which survey data are available, tabulate the responses, and compute the statistics needed by the investigator to test his hypotheses.

It is also possible to use surveys—or, more accurately, the findings drawn from surveys—to reanalyze past historical events. By applying survey results retroactively, for example, one can analyze past elections with the more sophisticated concepts and knowledge learned from survey studies of recent elections. A few historians have already begun to conduct such studies, and their efforts have thrown considerable doubt on the standard interpretations of these events.[90] Equally important, an investigator's awareness of survey results may impel him to search out new, systematic, and more trustworthy data on which to test his explanations. An historian who works in this way will no longer be satisfied with impressionistic observations and *ad hoc* explanations, but will attempt to force the historical repositories to relinquish their secrets in more quantifiable and systematic form. He will also be able to avoid assumptions he has reason to believe are unfounded:

90. Benson, Lee, "Research Problems in American Political Historiography," in *Common Frontiers of the Social Sciences*. Edited by Mirra Komarovsky. Free Press, Glencoe, Ill., 1957, pp. 118–183.

he is unlikely, considering what is known about the contemporary electorate, to attribute a high level of political awareness and ideological sophistication to the voters of the past, especially when one considers their lower average education and greater removal from the sources of political communication.

The Contribution of Surveys to Theory

Surveys are normally thought of as fact-gathering procedures, and their ability to perform this function, as the foregoing attests, is formidable. Less often appreciated, however, is their potential contribution to the construction and testing of theory.

The value of surveys for political theory lies, to begin with, in the intellectual rigor demanded by their methodology. A survey user must clarify the meaning of his principal terms and decide precisely how they are to be measured. He must try to state his theory in an orderly, coherent form and to derive from it the hypotheses he wishes to examine. He must decide by what evidence and by what logic these hypotheses are to be tested. When his results are in, he must analyze and reason about them, deciding in what measure his theory has been supported and in what ways it must be qualified or changed.

A theory need not be tested to survive, but it is more likely to retain its vitality if its claims can be validated. In the absence of an empirical confrontation, it may be passed on, without challenge, from one generation to another, but it will probably grow limp and cease to have force. Theoretical advances depend not only on the theorist's intuitive brilliance, but on his ability to face facts and to furnish meaningful explanations for them. As facts emerge from surveys and other types of empirical inquiry, they compel the investigator to reconsider and adjust his theories so as to account more adequately for the new data. The influence of surveys on political theory can be discerned in virtually every branch of the subject in which they have been employed. We have space, however, only to point to a few examples.

One area that has felt the impact of survey findings most sharply is that of democratic theory. Findings from survey research have forced scholars to revise their views about the nature and practice of democratic government. Although no single or standard definition of democracy has been accepted everywhere and at all times, the model most frequently presented in the textbooks portrays democracy as a system based on the active consent of an alert popular electorate which chooses its rulers only after a careful appraisal of alternatives. The electorate is represented, in effect, as enjoying perfect communication and full knowledge of all competing parties, candidates, and programs. They are presumed to exercise their choice in a perfectly rational manner after having weighed their own best interests and the interests of the nation. Upon observing their would-be rulers, a majority forms, achieves consensus, and selects the men who will represent the people for the period prescribed in the constitution. The majority choice is usually the "correct" one, for the people are supreme not only in law but in wisdom.

Our concern here is not with the utility of this or any other "rational" model of democracy, for such models unquestionably have their usés (much as a rational model of a perfectly competitive economy is useful to the economist). We are obliged, nevertheless, to observe that survey research on voting and other democratic processes shows various elements in the textbook theory to be empirically indefensible and to misrepresent the process by which democratic systems actually function and manage to survive. Moved by this realization, students of democratic politics have begun, here and there, to modify the theory in order to take account of the part actually played by the electorate in the exercise of consent, and to reconsider the role of the parties, candidates, issues, communication processes, etc., in the conduct of elections.[91] They have likewise begun to reconsider the meaning of such concepts as public, public opinion, and majority rule, redefining these terms to reflect their nature and complexity, as revealed by survey research. The role of elites in democracy is being re-evaluated, and their value as repositories of democratic beliefs and as the agencies that enforce the democratic rules of the game is being stressed.[92] Also being questioned are the traditional assumptions about the "natural" democracy of the poor, the ignorant, and the unsophisticated. As a result of survey findings on the divided political beliefs of the American electorate, suggestions are being made to modify the long-standing assumptions about consensus, i.e., about the alleged need for agreement on constitutional norms as a precondition for democracy.[93]

Survey results are also inspiring changes in our theories about political parties and their role in the political process. The familiar portrait of the

91. Berelson, B. R., *et al., Voting, op. cit.,* chap. 14.
92. Dahl, R. A., *Who Governs? op. cit.,* chap. 28.
93. Key, V. O., Jr., *Public Opinion and American Democracy, op. cit.,* chap. 2; McClosky, Herbert, "Consensus and Ideology . . . ," *op. cit.*

parties as mere agencies of interest groups is being reconsidered. The parties, it seems, are principals as well as agents, reference groups in their own right, that formulate policy out of intellectual conviction as well as political accommodation. The data also show that loyalty to a party (in the United States, at least) depends less on agreement with its doctrines than on various non-rational factors, such as primary group attachments. These and numerous other observations derived from surveys are forcing political scientists to re-examine such questions as the nature and role of so-called "brokerage" parties in a two-party system, the alleged differences between these parties and the presumably more ideological parties of multi-party systems, the place of parties in the democratic process, their function in helping to achieve a balance between cleavage and consensus, and so forth.

Survey research is also forcing modifications in our theories about extreme political belief and affiliation. Among other changes, the introduction of social-psychological constructs in the survey analysis of these phenomena has altered and added new theoretical dimensions to our understanding. We now appreciate, for example, that we cannot understand the adoption of extreme right-wing or left-wing beliefs by reference to political or socioeconomic factors alone, but must also take account of such personality predispositions as paranoia, psychological inflexibility, dogmatism, and "authoritarian" tendencies.[94] Persons attracted to the radical right and other extreme doctrines can be found in all occupations, educational categories, and communities; what they often have in common are the same personality needs, the same ways of meeting the disappointments and frustrations of the world, the same rages and anxieties.

Similar observations leading to appropriate theoretical adjustments are also being suggested for the explanation of such phenomena as alienation and anomy. The standard theories that relate these responses to industrialism, urbanization, mass society, status frustration, or the decline of ideology appear from survey evidence to be inadequate or questionable; theoretical revisions are required that will take account of the role of personality factors in inducing "anomic" responses, and of the learning and socialization processes which affect the internalization of norms.

We are also discovering from survey data that the *a priori* political categories set out by theorists and publicists frequently do not hold up in practice. The political left and the political right, for example, are not in all

94. Rokeach, Milton, *et al., op. cit.;* Adorno, T. W., *et al., op. cit.*

respects the polarities they are made out to be; often, indeed, the values of both are embraced by the same individuals. Respondents are turned up by surveys who score high on both left wing and right wing scales, or who are, by different measures, liberal and conservative at the same time, or who favor the same leaders but diverge in their beliefs. Traditional political theories have tended to oversimplify political attachments and to attribute more order to political thought than is usually manifested in behavior. The research findings, however, are compelling scholars to reconsider the standard assumptions about these matters and to arrive at explanations that more plausibly account for such facts as these: both the radical right and radical left reject existing political institutions, especially parliamentary government, liberal democracy, the open society, freedom of speech and press, and the right of individuals to think and act for themselves; both exhibit strong underlying elements of paranoia, such as conspiratorialism, megalomania, and unfounded fears; both are intemperate and angry, righteous, inflexible, intolerant, dogmatic, and contemptuous of human frailty. These qualities, which show up in survey analyses of extreme groups, can also be observed in the macro-analyses of extreme left or right movements (Nazism, Communism, etc.). The shift that is beginning to take place in our theoretical understanding of these phenomena cannot, of course, be credited to surveys alone; but survey research has added important documentation and thereby reinforced what some scholars working in other ways have long suspected.

Limitations and Problems in the Use of Political Surveys

To recognize that surveys have extraordinary utility for the study of politics is not to deny that there are problems associated with their use. Surveys are not a methodological panacea. They have limitations, some of which are inherent and some of which are by-products of their present stage of development.

One inherent limitation is their high cost for, while they are addressed to only a small proportion of the universe being studied, the expense of questioning even this number is usually fairly large. Another limitation arises from the inaccessibility of certain respondents, either because they occupy eminent and unapproachable roles (e.g. Supreme Court justices), or because they are uneducated, poor, geographically isolated, or for some other reason difficult to communicate with. Some potential respondents simply refuse to be interviewed. Other limitations grow out of the fact that certain problems cannot be studied unless the investigator can manipulate public events to meet the conditions of his hypothesis—a requirement that can rarely be fulfilled. An investigator, for example, has little chance of persuading public officials to adopt certain policies, even temporarily, in order to test their impact on the mass public.

Like other rigorous empirical procedures, surveys may have little value if the constructs one deals with cannot be operationalized, or cannot be presented in a form appropriate to a questionnaire. The attempt to operationalize concepts sometimes leads to their oversimplification; the conversion of a rich, complex, subtle, or multifaceted concept into a measure that can be used on a questionnaire may reduce it to a bloodless, uninteresting, or oversimplified version of the original. Even notions that appear simple are often complex and difficult to capture adequately in a brief interview. Take, for example, party loyalty, which is often measured by asking the respondent how strongly he feels about his party, and by giving him an opportunity to say "very strongly" or "strongly" or "not so strongly." Unfortunately, however, not all groups perceive or respond to party loyalty in the same way. Uneducated people are far more willing to proclaim undying love for their party, though they do not necessarily practice it. Some groups, no matter how attached to a party, like to think of themselves as independent and free of any affiliation that blinds their judgment. Some are intensely loyal to their party so long as it takes political stands they approve of, while others are emotionally or symbolically attached in a way that has nothing to do with the party's program. Some believe themselves to be loyal to a party but defect from it for casual reasons, while others call themselves independent but invariably vote a straight ticket. Party attachment, in short, is not the simple one-dimensional response it seems. To get at it properly, one may need more and subtler questions than one can ordinarily assign to it.

It is also a limitation of the survey method that it cannot easily observe aggregates or institutions. Something can be learned about an institution by studying the individuals who occupy various roles within it, but this will not necessarily provide an overview of the institution as a functioning entity. To achieve the latter, one needs to take account of the formal rules that govern the institution, its power and structure, its relation to other institutions in the system, and so on. One can, in short, learn a great deal about the nature and conduct of the British parliament without interviewing a single member. All this merely underscores what we have intimated earlier, that surveys are not equally appropriate to all forms of social science inquiry, that they have limits, but that they also have great utility—either in their own right or as supplements to other methods.

We have cited the complaint that surveys are in the nature of still photographs that capture responses at a single instant in time, and we have observed, in rejoinder, that by conducting surveys in serial fashion we may achieve something akin to a motion picture. Nevertheless, it must be admitted that surveys are not the optimal procedure for observing change, process, or action. They can enlighten us to some degree about these phenomena and, when used in conjunction with other approaches, they can enhance what is learned. One would not use a survey to follow a bill through the legislature, but one might augment the study of that process by interviewing legislators, lobbyists, interest groups, and citizens who are involved in the passage of the bill. Similarly, surveys would not be the prescribed procedure for studying certain kinds of political *relationships*—for example, the relationship between a leader and his supporters. But one might be wise to employ survey methods in an auxiliary role to gain a fuller understanding of how the governed perceive their leaders, and what forces strengthen or weaken their support. Surveys, in short, are not primarily designed to observe interaction among individuals or groups, for that requires the simultaneous observation of two or more people. This can best be done through laboratory experiment, participant observation, or on-the-scene observation of the type practiced by anthropologists. Each of these, however, can beneficially be combined with the survey method.

While the complaint that surveys characteristically measure political beliefs rather than actions is exaggerated and even a bit "tired," it must, nevertheless, be conceded that surveys have most often centered on verbal behavior, and that they have paid insufficient attention to the institutional forces and political contexts from which verbal responses spring. Few political surveys (except those concerned with voting) have tried to predict the future behavior of respondents or taken into account the consequences of holding certain opinions. One reason for neglecting this task is the obvious difficulty of fulfilling it. The difficulties, however, are not insurmountable and can, with imagination, be overcome, as they eventually will be.

The investigation of beliefs and attitudes is an integral feature of the study of overt "behavior." Beliefs and attitudes represent facets of behavior and both must be assessed if political life is to be understood adequately. The difficulty of assessing them, however, has to do not only with the limitations of the survey method but with the imponderables and contingencies in complex human situations. A person holding a given attitude may be unable to act on it because the conditions in which he finds himself are uncongenial. Conditions may even force him to act in ways that violate his private convictions. A man holding race prejudices may act on them in the South but conceal them in the North, while a man free of such prejudices may in the South be led to discriminate in order to survive in business or be accepted by the community. How a person behaves in an actual situation depends, in short, upon the content and intensity of his attitudes, the strength of the external forces that play upon him, and the conditions in which he must act. Surveys cannot always predict overt behavior because it is difficult to ascertain all these factors in any given case. Similar restrictions hold, however, for other research procedures, and the need to find ways to overcome them is common to all types of inquiry.

There are also a number of technical limitations associated with political surveys. Some have to do with sampling, e.g., the characteristics of the universe are not always known, some persons cannot be reached or refuse to participate, or a carefully designed probability sample may be physically or financially unfeasible. Other limitations have to do with the nature of the questionnaire and the quality and interpretation of the responses. Not only must one's measures be valid and reliable, but they must be appropriate to the groups on which they are being used. A measure useful in surveying, say, intellectuals may be extremely misleading if used on the uneducated. Nor can a respondent's answers always be taken at face value. His responses may be uninformed and even capricious, they may vary with time, or be inconsistent with other beliefs he holds. He may, for reasons of his own, furnish answers that he knows to be false or, if intimidated or "led" by the interviewer, give answers he thinks the interviewer wants. Since politics is for many people a taboo or threatening subject, not to be discussed with strangers, the possibility of such misrepresentation can be serious. Some reporting errors are made innocently, as when a respondent is too uninformed to classify his own political views correctly or cannot accurately recall the candidates he supported in earlier elections. Difficulties of this type can be mitigated somewhat by employing attitude scales and complex measures that do not depend on answers to one or a few questions but contain numerous items that have been carefully tested and validated. Even these, however, may be subject to "response set" and other biases associated with their wording, content, or form. Some respondents, for example, are inclined to agree with statements presented to them, regardless of content; others tend to disagree. Some dissemble, either because they prefer to present themselves in a certain light, or because they are too defensive to perceive realistically their own motivations and behavior. Some respondents do not take the research task seriously and make frivolous responses, while others take it so seriously that they are crippled and unable to answer honestly. We have alluded to other difficulties that arise in cross-cultural surveys where, in addition to the problems just recited, there are difficulties arising from the translation of terms, the posing of cognate questions, and the interpretation of responses elicited in different cultures. All these difficulties are potentially serious but not insurmountable—particularly as the measuring methods and the techniques for assessing opinions, attitudes, personality, and actions are continually being improved.

I have left for last a class of criticisms leveled against survey research—and, for that matter, against all types of behavioral studies—by critics whose persuasion is predominantly humanistic. Survey research, they allege, deprives the study of politics of its "vitality." By collecting verbal responses at a single moment in time, by dealing with component variables rather than with the individual as a whole, by focusing upon isolated instances of behavior rather than upon the total configuration of responses, by seeking to convert man's flesh-and-blood characteristics into quantities that can be dealt with abstractly and statistically, and by neglecting normative and moral questions in favor of empirical ones, the survey analyst (they claim) both outrages and misrepresents man's nature. He debases man's character and motives by reducing him to dimensions that can be measured; and he diminishes man as a political animal by regarding him as a bundle of needs, motives, group memberships, roles, and statuses.

It is difficult to decide how much of this criticism to take seriously, for much of it is vague and represents feeling rather than reason. To a student of behavioral science, it seems plain that the quantification made possible by surveys adds to rather than detracts from our understanding of political phenomena. The difference between the measurements used in surveys and the observations made by earlier methods lies not in their reliance upon quantification but in the rigor and precision of the quantitative methods employed. Even traditional political studies can scarcely avoid such terms as "many," "most," "usually," "as a rule," a "minority," "more than," and so forth. They describe "the farmers" as resentful, "the workers" as Democrats, or "the businessmen" as opposing social legislation. But how many farmers, or workers, or businessmen, how frequently and with what degree of intensity are they resentful or Democrats or opposed to social legislation? It is impossible, in short, to record meaningful political observations without resorting to statements of magnitude or proportion; one can strive for statements that are either precise and based on careful measurement, or that are vague and based on crude impressions. By electing the former, survey users have enriched rather than narrowed the range and variety of questions on which they can make useful observations.

What of the argument that survey research deprives the study of politics of its vitality by dealing with political man as a conglomeration of abstract "variables" that are examined independently of the individuals who possess them? This claim (it will be recognized) is essentially the "whole man" argument so frequently advanced by humanistic critics of the social sciences. The response to the argument, of course, is that it is impossible to understand any man, much less a group of men, all at once and in his (or their) entirety. Since every man is potentially many things, plays many roles, behaves differently in different contexts, and holds various and often conflicting beliefs, he cannot possibly be understood as a "totality." His behavior cannot be explained by describing everything about him at once, even if it were physically possible to do so. When one asks what "causes" a political actor to behave in a certain way, one expects an answer in terms of some specific force that one has reason to believe is relevant to that particular type of behavior.

When we say that a man is a union member, a Republican, educated, a Southerner, hostile in personality, politically apathetic, or a leader of his party, we neither violate him as a person nor diminish our capacity for understanding him. On the contrary, only by observing him in the ways he can be classified can we hope to understand his behavior. Thus, we observe him as an economic actor, as a member of a social class, as a voter, or as a consumer of mass communications. By the statistical manipulation of these observations, we can learn much about the ways in which these categories affect each other, and our understanding of human behavior will, thereby, be enhanced rather than diminished. A science strives to achieve a set of generalizations, preferably of a highly abstract order, in the hope of being able to explain complex phenomena with the fewest possible number of assumptions and a small number of observations. It is difficult to see why this aim is less defensible when applied to man's behavior than when applied to other natural phenomena.

The argument that politics is a unique domain that cannot be understood except in "political" terms is similar in some ways to the arguments about the "whole man." Politics is hereby invested with a mystique that places it beyond ordinary understanding. But to observe individuals in their group, class, or personality characteristics does not violate what is "political" about man; on the contrary, it adds new and important dimensions to our knowledge of his political behavior.

We come, finally, to the relation of surveys to normative questions. It must, of course, be conceded that surveys cannot be employed to confirm normative statements, for no form of empirical inquiry can do this. Surveys can, however, throw light upon the factual status of many of the empirical claims implicit in normative systems of thought. Although they cannot, for example, decide where sovereignty ought to lie, they can tell us much about the limits of popular participation in government, the ability of the electorate to exercise consent effectively, the extent to which people can be expected to obey certain kinds of laws, the questions that citizens of low education can be expected to understand and judge, and the degree to which voters correctly perceive the beliefs and actions of their leaders. Surveys can, in short, teach us a great deal about how popular sovereignty *works* or can be expected to work under various conditions, and this may help us to decide what types of power ought to be exercised by the people.

For those interested exclusively in normative questions, the empirical findings yielded by surveys are sometimes regarded as trivial. But for those who are also empirically oriented, the question of what is significant and what is trivial becomes difficult to decide. All questions, of course, are not equally significant, but many questions, seemingly inconsequential in themselves, take on significance by their relationship to other, obviously important questions. The topics to which surveys have been addressed, and which we have reviewed, can scarcely be described as inconsequential. They deal with voting, loyalty, conformity, leadership, communication, role perceptions, representation, decision-making, and numerous other topics of major interest to political science. That some survey analysts ask trivial questions and compile insignificant data cannot be denied; survey users are in this respect no different from scholars who use other methods. Every discipline has its share of men who are preoccupied with trivial questions and who turn up insignificant results. It is not the method that determines the significance of the product but the intellectual force that lies behind the use of the method. A scholar with serious intellectual concerns, a sense of what is important in his field, and a technical mastery of research procedures stands a chance of doing useful work no matter which research technique he employs. A man lacking these traits will probably contribute little even if his methods are the best available.

Bibliography

Adorno, T. W., *et al.*, *The Authoritarian Personality*. Harper & Bros., New York, 1950.

Agger, R. E., "Independents and Party Identifiers: Characteristics and Behavior in 1952," in *American Voting Behavior*. Edited by E. L. Burdick and A. J. Brodbeck. Free Press, Glencoe, Ill., 1959, pp. 308–339.

Agger, R. E. and Daniel Goldrich, "Community Power Structures and Partisanship," *American Sociological Review*, Vol. 23, August, 1958, pp. 383–392.

Allinsmith, Wesley and Beverly Allinsmith, "Religious Affiliation and Politico-Economic Attitude: A Study of Eight Major U.S. Religious Groups," *Public Opinion Quarterly*, Vol. 12, Fall, 1948, pp. 377–389.

Almond, G. A., *The American People and Foreign Policy*. Harcourt, Brace, New York, 1950.

Almond, G. A., *et al.*, *The Appeals of Communism*. Princeton University Press, Princeton, 1954.

Almond, G. A. and Sidney Verba, *The Civic Culture*. Princeton University Press, Princeton, 1963, pp. 261–374.

Alpert, Harry, "Public Opinion Research as Science," *Public Opinion Quarterly*, Vol. 20, Fall, 1956, pp. 493–500.

Asch, S. E., "Effects of Group Pressure Upon the Modification and Distortion of Judgment," in *Groups, Leadership, and Men*. Edited by H. S. Guetzkow. Carnegie Press, Pittsburgh, 1951.

Banfield, E. C., *Political Influence*. Free Press, Glencoe, Ill., 1961.

Bauer, R. A., *et al.*, *American Business and Public Policy*. Atherton, New York, 1963.

Benson, Lee, "Research Problems in American Political Historiography," in *Common Frontiers of the Social Sciences*. Edited by Mirra Komarovsky. Free Press, Glencoe, Ill., 1957, pp. 113–183.

Berelson, B. R., P. F. Lazarsfeld and W. W. McPhee, *Voting:* A Study of Opinion Formation in a Presidential Campaign. University of Chicago Press, Chicago, 1954, pp. 24–33; pp. 54–117; chap. 14.

Campbell, Angus, "Recent Developments in Survey Studies of Political Behavior," in *Essays on the Behavioral Study of Politics*. Edited by Austin Ranney. University of Illinois, Urbana, 1962, pp. 31–46.

Campbell, Angus, Gerald Gurin, and W. E. Miller, *The Voter Decides*. Row, Peterson, Evanston, Ill., 1954.

Campbell, Angus and George Katona, "The Sample Survey: A Technique for Social Science Research," in *Research Methods in the Behavioral Sciences*. Edited by Leon Festinger and Daniel Katz. Dryden Press, New York, 1953.

Campbell, Angus and W. E. Miller, "The Motivational Basis of Straight and Split-Ticket Voting," *American Political Science Review*, Vol. 51, June, 1957, pp. 293–312.

Campbell, Angus and Henry Valen, "Party Identification in Norway and the United States," *Public Opinion Quarterly,* Vol. 25, Winter, 1961, pp. 505–525.

Campbell, Angus, *et al., The American Voter.* John Wiley & Sons, New York, 1960.

Cantril, Hadley, *The Psychology of Social Movements.* John Wiley & Sons, New York, 1941, pp. 233–238.

Cantril, Hadley, *The Politics of Despair.* Basic Books, New York, 1958.

Centers, Richard, "Attitude and Belief in Relation to Occupational Stratification," *Journal of Social Psychology,* Vol. 27, May, 1948, pp. 159–185.

Converse, P. E., "The Nature of Belief Systems in Mass Publics," in *Ideology and Discontent.* Edited by D. E. Apter. Free Press, Glencoe, Ill., 1964, pp. 206–261.

Converse, P. E. and Georges Dupeux, "Politicalization of the Electorate in France and the United States," *Public Opinion Quarterly,* Vol. 26, Spring, 1962, pp. 1–23.

Converse, P. E., *et al.,* "Stability and Change in 1960: A Reinstating Election," *American Political Science Review,* Vol. 55, June, 1961, pp. 269–280.

Crutchfield, R. S., "Personal and Situational Factors in Conformity to Group Pressure," *Acta Psychologica,* Vol. 15, 1959, pp. 386–388.

Cutright, Phillips and P. H. Rossi, "Grass Roots Politicians and the Vote," *American Sociological Review,* Vol. 23, April, 1958, pp. 171–179.

Dahl, R. A., "The Behavioral Approach in Political Science: Epitaph for a Monument to a Successful Protest," *American Political Science Review,* Vol. 55, December, 1961, pp. 763–772.

Dahl, R. A., *Who Governs?:* Democracy and Power in an American City. Yale University Press, New Haven, 1961, chap. 28.

Dicks, H. V., "Personality Traits and National Socialist Ideology," *Human Relations,* Vol. 3, August, 1950, pp. 111–154.

Easton, David and R. D. Hess, "The Child's Political World," *Midwestern Journal of Political Science,* Vol. 6, August, 1962, pp. 229–246.

Ernst, M. L. and D. G. Loth, *Report on the American Communist.* Henry Holt, New York, 1952.

Erskine, H. G., "The Polls: Textbook Knowledge," *Public Opinion Quarterly,* Vol. 27, Spring, 1963, pp. 133–141.

Eulau, Heinz, *The Behavioral Persuasion in Politics.* Random House, New York, 1963.

Eulau, Heinz, "Segments of Political Science Most Susceptible to Behavioristic Treatment," in *The Limits of Behavioralism in Political Science.* Edited by J. C. Charlesworth. American Academy of Political and Social Science, Philadelphia, 1962, pp. 26–48.

Eulau, Heinz, *Class and Party in the Eisenhower Years:* Class Roles and Perspectives in the 1952 and 1956 Elections. Free Press, Glencoe, Ill., 1962.

Eulau, Heinz and J. D. Sprague, *Lawyers in Politics:* A Study in Professional Convergence. Bobbs-Merrill, Indianapolis, 1964.

Eulau, Heinz, *et al.,* "The Political Socialization of American State Legislators," *Midwestern Journal of Political Science,* Vol. 3, May, 1959, pp. 188–206.

Fenton, J. M., *In Your Opinion.* Little-Brown, Boston, 1960, pp. 135–144.

Fuchs, L. H., *The Political Behavior of American Jews.* Free Press, Glencoe, Ill., 1956.

Gibb, C. A., "Leadership," in *Handbook of Social Psychology,* Vol. 1. Edited by Gardner Lindzey. Addison-Wesley, Reading, Mass., 1954, pp. 233–238.

Glaser, W. A., "Doctors and Politics," *American Journal of Sociology,* Vol. 66, November, 1960, pp. 230–245.

Greenstein, F. I., "The Benevolent Leader—Children's Images of Political Authority," *American Political Science Review,* Vol. 54, December, 1960, pp. 934–943.

Greenstein, F. I., "Sex-Related Political Differences in Childhood," *Journal of Politics,* Vol. 23, May, 1961, pp. 353–371.

Greenstein, F. I., "More on Children's Images of the President," *Public Opinion Quarterly,* Vol. 25, Winter, 1961, pp. 648–654.

Greenstein, F. I., "Children and Politics," in *Yale Studies in Political Science,* Vol. 13. Yale University Press, New Haven, 1965.

Greer, S. A., "Urbanism Reconsidered: A Comparative Study of Local Areas in a Metropolis," *American Sociological Review,* Vol. 21, February, 1956, pp. 19–25.

Greer, S. A., "The Mass Society and the Parapolitical Structure," *American Sociological Review.* Vol. 27, October, 1962, pp. 634–646.

Greer, S. A., *Governing the Metropolis.* John Wiley & Sons, New York, 1962.

Greer, S. A., *Metropolitics:* A Study of Political Culture. John Wiley & Sons, New York, 1963.

Heard, Alexander, "Interviewing Southern Politicians," *American Political Science Review,* Vol. 44, December, 1950, pp. 886–896.

Hess, R. D. and David Easton, "The Child's Changing Image of the President," *Public Opinion Quarterly,* Vol. 24, Winter, 1960, pp. 632–644.

Hirschfield, R. S., *et al.,* "Profile of Political Activists in Manhattan," *Western Political Quarterly,* Vol. 15, September, 1962, pp. 489–506.

Hunter, Floyd, *Community Power Structure.* Doubleday, Garden City, N.Y., 1963.

Hyman, H. H., *Political Socialization.* Free Press, Glencoe, Ill., 1959.

Hyman, H. H. and P. B. Sheatsley, "The Current Status of American Public Opinion," in *Public Opinion and Propaganda.* Edited by Daniel Katz, *et al.,* Ryerson Press, New York, 1954, pp. 33–48.

Janowitz, Morris, *The Professional Soldier.* Free Press, Glencoe, Ill., 1960.

Katz, Elihu and P. F. Lazarsfeld, *Personal Influence.* Free Press, Glencoe, Ill., 1955.

Key, V. O., Jr., "Theory of Critical Elections," *Journal of Politics,* Vol. 17, February, 1955, pp. 3–18.

Key, V. O., Jr., "The Politically Relevant in Surveys," *Public Opinion Quarterly,* Vol. 24, Spring, 1960, pp. 54–61.

Key, V. O., Jr., *Public Opinion and American Democracy.* Knopf, New York, 1961, chap. 2.

Kirkpatrick, E. M., "The Impact of the Behavioral Approach on Traditional Political Science," in *Essays on the Behavioral Study of Politics.* Edited by Austin Ranney. University of Illinois Press, Urbana, 1962, pp. 24–25.

Lane, R. E., *Political Life.* Free Press, Glencoe, Ill., 1959, pp. 185–272.

Lazarsfeld, P. F., B. R. Berelson, and Hazel Gaudet, *The People's Choice:* How the Voter Makes up his Mind in a Presidential Campaign. Duell, Sloan and Pearce, New York, 1944.

Lerner, Daniel and Lucille Pevsner, *The Passing of Traditional Society:* Modernizing the Middle East. Free Press, Glencoe, Ill., 1958.

Lipset, S. M., *et al.,* "The Psychology of Voting: An Analysis of Political Behavior," in *Handbook of Social Psychology,* Vol. 2. Edited by Gardner Lindzey. Addison-Wesley, Reading, Mass., 1954, pp. 1124–1175.

Lipset, S. M., *Political Man:* The Social Bases of Politics. Doubleday, Garden City, N.Y., 1960.

Lipset, S. M., "Three Decades of the Radical Right: Coughlinites, McCarthyites, and Birchers," in *The Radical Right,* Anchor Edition. Edited by Daniel Bell. Doubleday, Garden City, N.Y. 1964.

Lipset, S. M., M. A. Trow and J. S. Coleman, *Union Democracy.* Free Press, Glencoe, Ill., 1956.

McClosky, Herbert, "McCarthyism: The Myth and the Reality." Paper delivered at the American Psychological Association meeting, New York, September, 1957.

McClosky, Herbert, "Conservatism and Personality," *American Political Science Review,* Vol. 52, December, 1958, pp. 27–45.

McClosky, Herbert, "Consensus and Ideology in American Politics," *American Political Science Review,* Vol. 58, June, 1964, pp. 361–382.

McClosky, Herbert, "Attitude and Personality Correlates of Foreign Policy Orientation," in *Domestic Sources of Foreign Policy,* (forthcoming). Edited by James Rosenau. Princeton University Press, Princeton.

McClosky, Herbert and H. E. Dahlgren, "Primary Group Influence on Party Loyalty," *American Political Science Review,* Vol. 53, September, 1959, pp. 757–776.

McClosky, Herbert, *et al.,* "Issue Conflict and Consensus Among Party Leaders and Followers," *American Political Science Review,* Vol. 54, June, 1960, pp. 406–427.

McConaughy, J. B., "Certain Personality Factors of State Legislators in North Carolina," *American Political Science Review,* Vol. 44, December, 1950, pp. 897–903.

MacRae, Duncan, Jr., *The Dimensions of Congressional Voting.* University of California Press, Berkeley, 1958.

Maccoby, E. E., *et al.,* "Youth and Political Change," *Public Opinion Quarterly,* Vol. 18, No. 1, 1954, pp. 23–29.

Marvick, Dwaine, ed., *Political Decision-Makers.* Free Press, Glencoe, Ill., 1961.

Matthews, D. R., *The Social Background of Political Decision-Makers.* Doubleday, Garden City, N.Y., 1954.

Matthews, D. R., *U.S. Senators and Their World.* University of North Carolina Press, Chapel Hill, 1960.

Matthews, D. R. and J. W. Prothro, "Political Factors and Negro Voter Registration in the South," *American Political Science Review,* Vol. 57, June, 1963, pp. 355–367.

Matthews, D. R. and J. W. Prothro, "Social and Economic Factors and Negro Voter Registration in the South," *American Political Science Review,* Vol. 57, March, 1963, pp. 24–44.

Matthews, D. R. and J. W. Prothro, "Southern Images of Political Parties: An Analysis of White and Negro Attitudes," *Journal of Politics,* Vol. 26, February, 1964, pp. 82–111.

Matthews, D. R. and J. W. Prothro, *Negroes and the New Southern Politics.* Harcourt Brace and World, New York, 1966.

Meller, Norman, "Legislative Behavior Research," *Western Political Quarterly,* Vol. 13, March, 1960, pp. 131–153.

Merton, R. K., *Social Theory and Social Structure,* Free Press, Glencoe, Ill., 1957.

Micaud, C. A., *Communism and the French Left.* Praeger, New York, 1963.

Miller, W. E. and Donald Stokes, "Constituency Influence in Congress," *American Political Science Review,* Vol. 57, March, 1963, pp. 45–56.

Miller, W. E. and Donald Stokes, *Congress and Constituency*, (forthcoming).

Mosel, James, "Communication Patterns and Political Socialization in Traditional Thailand," in *Communications and Political Development*. Edited by L. W. Pye, Princeton University Press, Princeton, 1963, pp. 184–228.

Nagel, S. S., "Political Party Affiliation and Judges' Decisions," *American Political Science Review*, Vol. 55, December, 1961, pp. 843–850.

Nagel, S. S., "Ethnic Affiliation and Judicial Propensities," *Journal of Politics*, Vol. 24, February, 1962, pp. 92–100.

Nagel, S. S., "Off-the-Bench Judicial Attitudes," in *Judicial Decision-Making*. Edited by G. L. Schubert. Free Press, Glencoe, Ill., 1963, pp. 29–53.

Patterson, S. C., "Patterns of Interpersonal Relations in a State Legislative Group: The Wisconsin Assembly," *Public Opinion Quarterly*, Vol. 23, Spring, 1959, pp. 101–109.

Perlmutter, H. V., "Some Characteristics of the Xenophobic Personality," *Journal of Psychology*, Vol. 38, October, 1954, pp. 291–300.

Perlmutter, H. V., "Correlates of Two Types of Xenophilic Orientation," *Journal of Abnormal and Social Psychology*, Vol. 52, January, 1956, pp. 130–135.

Polsby, N. W., "Toward an Explanation of McCarthyism," *Political Studies*, Vol. 8, October, 1960, pp. 250–271.

Polsby, N. W., *Congress and the Presidency*. Prentice-Hall, Englewood Cliffs, N.J. 1964, pp. 25–26.

Pool, I. de Sola, "TV: A New Dimension in Politics," in *American Voting Behavior*. Edited by E. L. Burdick and A. J. Broadbeck. Free Press, Glencoe, Ill., 1959, pp. 236–261.

Presthus, Robert, *Men at the Top*. Oxford University Press, New York, 1964.

Prothro, J. W. and C. M. Grigg, "Fundamental Principles of Democracy: Bases of Agreement and Disagreement," *Journal of Politics*, Vol. 22, May, 1960, pp. 276–294.

Pye, L. W., *Guerilla Communism in Malaya*: Its Social and Political Meaning. Princeton University Press, Princeton, 1956.

Ranney, Austin, ed., *Essays on the Behavioral Study of Politics*. University of Illinois Press, Urbana, 1962.

Ranney, Austin, "The Utility and Limitations of Aggregate Data in the Study of Electoral Data," in *Essays on the Behavioral Study of Politics*. Edited by Austin Ranney. University of Illinois Press, Urbana, 1962.

Robinson, W. S., "Ecological Correlation and the Behavior of Individuals," *American Sociological Review*, Vol. 15, June, 1950, pp. 351–357.

Rokeach, Milton, *et al.*, *The Open and Closed Mind*. Basic Books, New York, 1960.

Rokkan, Stein, "Party Preferences and Opinion Patterns in Western Europe: A Comparative Analysis," *International Social Science Bulletin*, Vol. 7, 1955, pp. 575–576.

Rokkan, Stein, "The Comparative Study of Political Participation: Notes Toward a Perspective on Current Research," in *Essays on the Behavioral Study of Politics*. Edited by Austin Ranney. University of Illinois Press, Urbana, 1962, pp. 47–90.

Rokkan, Stein and Henry Valen, "A Survey of the 1957 Norwegian Elections," *Revue Français de Science Politique*, Vol. 8, 1958, pp. 73–94.

Rokkan, Stein and Henry Valen, "Parties, Elections and Political Behavior in the Northern Countries: A Review of Recent Research," in *Politsche Forschung*. Edited by Otto Stammer. Westdeutscher Verlag, Koeln-Opladen, 1960.

Rosenau, James, *Public Opinion and Foreign Policy.* Random House, New York, 1961.

Sanford, F. H., *Authoritarianism and Leadership.* Stephenson Brothers, Philadelphia, 1950.

Schubert, G. L., ed., *Judicial Decision-Making.* Free Press, Glencoe, Ill., 1963.

Seligman, L. G., "Political Recruitment and Party Structure: A Case Study," *American Political Science Review,* Vol. 55, March, 1961, pp. 77–86.

Silverman, Corrine, "The Legislators' View of the Legislative Process," *Public Opinion Quarterly,* Vol. 18, Summer, 1954, pp. 180–190.

Simon, H. A. and Frederick Stern, "Effect of Television Upon Voting Behavior in Iowa in the 1952 Presidential Election," *American Political Science Review,* Vol. 49, June, 1955, pp. 470–477.

Sorauf, F. J., *Party and Representation.* Atherton, New York, 1963.

Spaeth, H. J., "An Approach to the Study of Attitudinal Differences as an Aspect of Judicial Behavior," *Midwestern Journal of Political Science,* Vol. 5, 1961, pp. 165–180.

Stouffer, S. A., *Communism, Conformity, and Civil Liberties:* A Cross Section of the Nation Speaks Its Mind. Doubleday, New York, 1955.

Trow, M. A., "Small Businessmen, Political Tolerance, and Support for McCarthy," *American Journal of Sociology,* Vol. 64, November, 1958, pp. 270–281.

Truman, D. B., "Research in Political Behavior," *American Political Science Review,* Vol. 46, December, 1952, pp. 1003–1006.

Truman, D. B., *The Congressional Party:* A Case Study. John Wiley & Sons, New York, 1959.

Verba, Sidney, *Small Groups and Political Behavior.* Princeton University Press, Princeton, 1961, pp. 17–60.

Vidich, A. J. and Joseph Bensman, *Small Town in Mass Society.* Princeton University Press, Princeton, 1958.

Wahlke, J. C., "Behavioral Analyses of Representative Bodies," in *Essays on the Behavioral Study of Politics.* Edited by Austin Ranney. University of Illinois Press, Urbana, 1962, pp. 173–190.

Wahlke, J. C., *et al., The Legislative System.* John Wiley & Sons, New York, 1962.

Weber, Max, "Politics as a Vocation," in *From Max Weber:* Essays in Sociology. Edited by H. H. Gerth and C. W. Mills. Oxford University Press, New York, 1946, pp. 77–128.

Wildavsky, Aaron, *Dixon-Yates:* A Study in Power Politics. Yale University Press, New Haven, 1962.

Wildavsky, Aaron, "The Intelligent Citizen's Guide to the Abuse of Statistics: The Kennedy Document and The Catholic Vote," in *Politics and Social Life.* Edited by N. W. Polsby, *et al.* Houghton-Mifflin, Boston, 1964, pp. 825–844.

Wildavsky, Aaron, *Leadership in a Small Town.* Bedminster Press, Totowa, N.J., 1964.

Wilson, James, *Negro Politics.* Free Press, Glencoe, Ill., 1960.

Wolfinger, R. E., "The Clientele of the Christian Anti-Communism Crusade," paper delivered at the American Political Science Association meeting, September, 1963.

Wolfinger, R. E., *et al.,* "America's Radical Right: Ideology and Politics," in *Ideology and Discontent:* The Concept of Ideology in the Light of Contemporary Social and Political Change. Edited by D. E. Apter. Free Press, Glencoe, Ill., 1964.

The Practice and Potential of Survey Methods in

Psychological Research

by Daniel Katz
Survey Research Center
University of Michigan

A Social Psychological Taxonomy

Group Involvement and Social Interaction
Population Statistics of Personality Types
Descriptive Statistics of Deviancy from Social Norms
Descriptive Accounts of Beliefs, Attitudes and Values
> A basis for interpretation. Test of cognitive theory. Knowledge of social change.

The Study of Complex Social Psychological Problems

Socialization and the Development of Personality
The Adult Socialization Process
The Nature and Determinants of Mental Disorder
Psychological Basis of Groups and Organizations
Individual Involvement and Organizational Norms
Predictable Behavior as a Basic Organizational Objective
> System rewards and motivational patterns. Organizational typology.

The Practice and Potential of Survey
Methods in Psychological Research

PSYCHOLOGY, as the basic discipline which integrates knowledge of man as a biological organism and as a social agent, enjoys tremendous advantages from this central position. It also suffers from its failures to integrate the two logics of research and the two theoretical approaches of the biological laboratory and the social world. Methods are often used inappropriately and the mixture of theoretical concepts is a continuing source of confusion.

The one logic of research stems from the laboratory. In laboratory experimentation the controls come from the exclusion of some variables, the holding constant of others, and the measurable manipulation of the independent variable. The attempt is made to reduce the complexities of events to the basic processes singled out for the experimental study. There is no concern with the representativeness of the subjects employed with respect to the universes from which they are selected. A rat is a rat, is a rat, or a college sophomore is a human being, is a human being. The random assignment of subjects to control and experimental conditions avoids selective bias within the experimental population used. The basic psychological processes under investigation are so close to the biology of the species that representativeness with respect to social variables is considered irrelevant. For example, the aftereffects of the visual perception of curved lines which make straight lines appear curved in the opposite direction are not dependent upon the social class or ethnic origin of the subject.[1]

The second fundamental method, the one with which this volume is concerned, the survey or field method, studies the effects of manipulations of social forces not under the control of the investigator. The major controls are statistical rather than experimental. In this approach, sample design is a crucial factor; otherwise there is little basis for the interpretation of the statistical evidence. Moreover, the measurement of many more factors is necessary than in laboratory experimentation. The laboratory can exclude

1. Sagara, Moriji and Tadasu Oyama, "Experimental Studies on Figural Aftereffects in Japan," *Psychological Bulletin,* Vol. 54, 1957, pp. 327–338.

or hold factors constant by direct manipulation. The field study cannot and so must be able to factor out the effect of a large number of potentially relevant variables. The field method is not restricted to national sampling designs, but it does involve design concerned with the segment of the universe with which it deals. The survey method may utilize behavioral observation, or verbal or written questioning, and trend studies on comparable samples over time or panel studies of the same sample. Thus, survey methodology includes any set of quantitative measurements taken of people in their natural habitat, utilizing sampling procedures; this is true whether the investigation is confined to a sample of role incumbents in a single organization, or a representative group of executives from large scale organizations, or a national sample of the electorate.

A common failing of psychologists in dealing with problems of a non-laboratory character is to neglect the appropriate tools of survey research and become preoccupied with the specific techniques of laboratory experimentation. The greater prestige of the experimental laboratory, representing hard science, has resulted in the curious development of studies which attempt a direct transplanting of laboratory technology into many areas of abnormal and social psychology. The psychological journals abound with small studies in which the character of complex psychological processes is examined by comparisons of groups which vary in some psychological attributes. A typical example is the investigation in which the available schizophrenics or otherwise disordered personalities in a hospital are subjected to some experimental manipulation such as verbal conditioning. The control group of normals will either be the hospital attendants and/or non-psychiatric hospitalized volunteers. The experiment itself will be carefully run with nice balancing of the order of presentation and careful before-and-after measures. The literature in this field adds up to very little, however, because the generalizations the investigators seek cannot be made without adequate sampling design. The assumption is implicitly made in these studies that a schizophrenic or alcoholic or neurotic state, or normal condition, is equivalent to the presence or absence of some drug in an experimental study. All subjects in this condition are like all other subjects and so any few can be selected to represent the rest.

A minor theme with which we shall be concerned in this chapter is the appropriateness of the experimental and the field approaches to the study of psychological problems. The psychological laboratory is addicted to a narrow type of scientism which pushes for highly formal models that lack empirical content. The variables are described so genotypically that they contain no specifications at the theoretical level about their operational identification, or else they are described in terms of their effects so that prediction becomes circular. For example, in learning theory, reward is not defined theoretically save in terms of its reinforcing effects. In the laboratory the predictions from theory can be tested because of agreement about the meaning of the variables manipulated; but, outside the laboratory, the emptiness of the theory for making predictions before the fact is soon apparent. There is no way of specifying what a reward is before it becomes rewarding. One reason why psychologists employing rigorous models from the laboratory can say so little about human behavior is that their theoretical concepts contain little in the way of definition of relevant variables and parameters. Research in the social field tends to generate such substantive concepts as leadership, anomie, legitimacy, status relationships, the two-step process of social influence, racial prejudice, the projection of hostility, perception of threat to the group, role conflict, potency of group involvement, multiple group membership. Some of these may prove to be too phenotypical to be very useful in theory building but they indicate the need for a psychology which is not devoid of content. It is the thesis of the writer that survey and field research can contribute heavily to the development of a more adequate psychology by adding specifications to present theory and by encouraging new theoretical developments.

To state this thesis another way is to say that science develops through a continuous interaction between theoretical hypotheses and empirical findings of research. If this interaction is based solely upon the contact with the narrow social realities of the laboratory, it will greatly limit the development of psychological theory. The use of field methods in psychology thus is not merely the application of principles developed in the laboratory but the revision and addition to these general concepts resulting from dealing with a larger and more diverse universe of psychological fact.

We shall attempt to develop the potentialities of survey methodology with respect to two areas in which the field method can contribute to psychology as a behavioral science. (1) *A social psychological taxonomy of human behavior*. A naturalistic description of the behavior of human beings in various social contexts is a prerequisite for the understanding of man, for the development of theory, and for the formulation of significant verifiable hypotheses. The anthropologists have attempted this for primitive cultures utilizing the primitive methods of uncontrolled observation and gathering of information from key informants. (2) *The study of complex social psychological problems.* Many psychological problems do not lend themselves to laboratory manipulation either because of the time dimension, the complexity of variables, or the power of the social manipulation. The childhood socialization process, admittedly a critical determinant of personality and character, cannot be studied within the laboratory for all of these reasons: the temporal dimension, the many variables affecting the child including the sibling pattern, family structure and other early social influences, and the continuing power of these influences which the laboratory in a humanitarian society could not attempt to duplicate.

A Social Psychological Taxonomy

The factual materials available for a description of social behavior consist for the most part of statistics gathered by some governmental or private agency for some practical purpose and are generally in the form of aggregate statistics. Such aggregate figures are very limited if an investigator attempts to establish relationships between characteristics of individuals. Moreover, they have been restricted in scope to relatively few topics. In an age of science where knowledge has been pushed to open up new vistas of information about outer space, we still know surprisingly little about our own society. The Kinsey studies of sexual behavior, in spite of their weak sampling and poor methodology, were widely acclaimed and perhaps justly so, for they undoubtedly gave a more accurate account of sexual practices than the conventional interpretations of moralists.[2]

In two areas, however, survey research has been utilized to supplement the aggregate statistics already available, namely, in economic behavior (see chap. 4) and political behavior (see chap. 2). The continuing studies in these fields by the Michigan Survey Research Center and other organizations have given us a wealth of precise data which have permitted behavioral scientists to check their theories of economic and political events. To the established areas may soon be added the public health field in which both physical and mental disease, as well as the conceptions people hold about health problems, are receiving attention (see chap. 8). Of special interest in this connection is the nationwide survey conducted by Gurin,

---

2. Kinsey, A. C., W. B. Pomeroy, and C. E. Martin, *Sexual Behavior in the Human Male.* W. B. Saunders, Philadelphia, 1948; Kinsey, A. C., *et al., Sexual Behavior in the Human Female.* W. B. Saunders, Philadelphia, 1953.

Veroff and Feld in which the respondents themselves evaluated their own personal problems and reported on their worries and sources of unhappiness.[3]

Most knowledge about the psychological characteristics of our society, however, comes from journalistic accounts, the non-quantitative observations of scholars, statistics gathered for limited purposes as already noted, and fragmented studies of a field character which generally lack any sampling design. The gathering of descriptive data about the people of a society on a systematic basis is not only costly but has a low priority for most behavioral scientists, since it represents spade work rather than the development of exciting theory. Yet a naturalistic study of a population, its daily habits and activities, is an indispensable basis for an adequate and valid social psychology. How people earn their living, how they spend their leisure time, what groups they belong to, how they order their lives, what norms they accept as legitimate and what norms they follow in practice (the extent of various types of deviancy), the distribution of personality characteristics in the nation and among its subgroupings, the kinds and frequencies of various value patterns and attitudinal constellations, the acceptance of various sources of social influence such as mass media, and types of leaders, are all subjects on which quantitative information geared to a known population base would be helpful for psychological science. Trend studies in all these areas are also vital to reveal the constancies and the variations in the same culture over time and to pinpoint significant problems.

We will consider briefly four areas in which a descriptive psychological taxonomy would be helpful: (1) the incidence and nature of the involvement and participation of people in the groupings of their society (2) the types of personality characteristics found in a society and their distribution in the nation and its various sub-structures (3) the incidence of various forms of deviant behavior from social norms, and (4) the distribution of types of value patterns in the culture, i.e. the cherished belief systems, the attitudes, and aspirations.

GROUP INVOLVEMENT AND SOCIAL INTERACTION

Statistics are available on the numbers of people in some social categories, such as occupation, and on the formal membership of certain major group-

3. Gurin, Gerald, Joseph Veroff and Sheila Feld, *Americans View Their Mental Health*. Basic Books, New York, 1960.

ings in our society, such as church and labor unions. We know little, however, about membership in the many associations in which people are involved. In a mid-western community of only 60,000 people, a count of the organized groups showed over 400 different organizations.

The significant psychological information we need, however, is not the sheer count of people in various organizations, useful though such statistics may be. We need to know what the reference groups are for people throughout the society and in various subdivisions of it. What groups do people identify with, what groups furnish cognitive frames of reference, what groups are influential because of their sanctions and rewards? In other words, what is the psychological meaning of group involvement whether it be in an occupational grouping or a formal organization? For example, in addition to knowing how many people belong to various churches, we also need to know the strength of identification with a particular church, the nature of the tie of the individual to it, whether theological, moral, or social, the extent of his religious behavior, i.e. church-going and other religious actions, and the relevance of the perceived norms of the church for other than church affairs.

A pioneering survey by Lenski explored the religious views and practices, the involvement in church organizations, and the role of religion in the lives of a representative sample of people in the Detroit area.[4] This was followed up by interviews with a small number of the clergy in the community. Lenski concluded "that religion in various ways is constantly influencing the daily lives of the masses of men and women in the modern American metropolis. More than that; through its impact on individuals, religion makes an impact on all other institutional systems of the community in which these individuals participate."[5] Membership in a socio-religious group affects a host of attitudes such as political preference, school integration, freedom of speech, welfare state, and also such actions as instalment buying, saving for the future, migrating to another community, maintaining close ties to one's family, and rising in the class system. In short, *"socio-religious group membership is a variable comparable in importance to class, both with respect to its potency and with respect to the range, or extent, of its influence."*[6] A fairly clear distinction is drawn between an orthodox and a devotional orientation

4. Lenski, G. E., *The Religious Factor:* A Sociological Study of Religion's Impact on Political and Family Life. Doubleday, New York, 1961.
5. *Ibid.,* p. 289.
6. *Ibid.,* p. 295.

to religion. The orthodox orientation is related to a compartmentalized religious attitude, whereas the devotional is more integrative and is tied to a humanitarian approach to the problems of life.

Years ago, Centers established the fact that psychological identification of the individual with social class gives additional predictive power to the demographic variable of occupation in anticipating social, political and economic attitudes.[7] Studies of political behavior indicate that, with the shift of workers from the secondary occupations of manufacture to the tertiary occupations of service and communication, the occupational grouping of the individual alone is an inadequate indicator of his political orientation. Some occupationally mobile people hold to the political faith of their fathers; others take on the political views dominant in their present occupational calling.[8] Again, psychological measures of the strength of identification with family, occupation, and other group structures are necessary.

The nature of group membership requires even more specification than measures of identification. The study of labor unions by Kahn and Tannenbaum indicates that the commitment of members to their unions does not involve active participation at many meetings or in many union activities.[9] Nevertheless, there is heavy cathexis upon the union as their organization, and this involvement is readily mobilized when the group is threatened or when critical issues such as a strike vote are to be considered. This may be the pattern of involvement of people in almost all voluntary organizations, namely, membership involvement at critical points rather than a continuing active participation.

It has been hypothesized that people are tied into the social structure through their role in occupational groups and that this occupational role is primary as a determinant of their social values and political behavior. The studies of Converse and others have demonstrated the oversimplification in this theory, but we still need studies of the potency of involvement of people in social groupings and the relevance of this involvement for various types of behavior.

The need for a taxonomy of group membership is illustrated by the wel-

7. Centers, Richard, *The Psychology of Social Class:* A Study of Class Consciousness. Princeton University Press, Princeton, 1949.
8. Valen, H. and D. Katz, *Political Parties in Norway*. Tavistock Publications, London, 1964.
9. Tannenbaum, A. S. and R. L. Kahn, *Participation in Union Locals*. Row, Peterson, Evanston, Ill., 1958.

come reception of the local survey by Axelrod in Detroit.[10] In his probability sample of this urban area, Axelrod found little support for the characterization of America as a nation of joiners. Even when union membership was included, over one-third of the sample did not belong to any organization, another third belonged to only a single organization, and only one-fifth of the sample could be considered activists. Both extent of membership and degree of activity were positively related to socio-economic status, with people higher in education and income showing greater membership and participation than people lower in the social scale. For the great majority of people, however, informal associations with relatives, friends, neighbors, and co-workers were the most frequent forms of contact. Of these groups, the extended family was the most important. Half of the people saw their relatives at least once a week. The network of informal association in the community remains a significant influence, in spite of the pervasive penetration of mass media and the growth of bureaucratic structures.

The findings of the Axelrod study have been confirmed at the national level by the work of Wright and Hyman, who have extended our information about the group memberships in our society through a secondary analysis of materials from two national surveys.[11] These investigators found that the majority of Americans do not belong to any voluntary organizations, that degree of membership is directly related to socio-economic status, that three-fourths of blue collar workers belong to no organizations apart from unions, that length of residence in a community bears no relation to degree of voluntary membership, and that membership in organizations is correlated with interest in public and civic affairs.

An area closely related to group involvement is that of social contact and interaction. We know little about the nature, types, and extent of interpersonal communication in our society. What are the types of contact of people in our society within their own informal and formal groups? To whom do people turn for help and leadership? How much interpersonal communication is there between people of differing group involvements? On the international scale, what is the nature of personal contact with the nationals of

10. Axelrod, Morris, "Urban Structure and Social Participation," *American Sociological Review,* Vol. 21, February, 1956, pp. 13–18.
11. Wright, C. R. and H. H. Hyman, "Voluntary Association Memberships of American Adults: Evidence from National Sample Surveys," *American Sociological Review,* Vol. 23, June, 1958, pp. 284–294.

other countries? The focus here is not on the relationships of groups but upon the individual as a matrix of group identifications and of relations with individuals of other groupings.

The Axelrod study indicated that the social environment of the city dweller outside his working hours is made up of primary groups of relatives, friends, and neighbors, and not of formal organizations. Lenski believes that interaction networks develop among the members of any religious association and that socio-religious groups are among the most important primary groups in the modern American community.[12] This interpersonal environment nonetheless tends to be very homogeneous both because like-minded people flock together and because association produces like-mindedness. Berelson, Lazarsfeld, and McPhee report in their Elmira study that most people move in a circle of associates of the same political views.[13] Eighty per cent of the Republicans in their sample had no Democrats among their immediate associates, and sixty per cent of the Democrats had no Republicans among their immediate associates. Whatever the diversity of the larger society, the individual preserves a personal world that is congenial and consistent.

One survey in an urban area found that the majority of people named some local political figure as the recognized leader in their neighborhood (the city in question has one of the strongest political organizations in the country) and a lawyer as the person to whom they turn when they have problems.[14] The reliance upon political leadership in the neighborhood was characteristic of the poorer economic areas rather than the upper income localities. These findings may reflect a survival of the older political structure of big eastern cities. Here again trend studies would be useful.

The patterns of personal influence in an American community have been studied by Katz and Lazarsfeld in a probability sample of women in Decatur, Illinois.[15] In the earlier study of voting behavior in Erie County, Ohio, Lazarsfeld and his colleagues had found evidence for a two-step flow of

12. Lenski, G. E., *op. cit.*
13. Berelson, B. R., P. F. Lazarsfeld, and W. W. McPhee, *Voting:* A Study of Opinion Formation in a Presidential Campaign. University of Chicago Press, 1954.
14. Reid, I. de A. and E. L. Ehle, "Leadership Selection in Urban Locality Areas," *Public Opinion Quarterly,* Vol. 14, No. 2, 1950, pp. 262–284.
15. Katz, Elihu and P. F. Lazarsfeld, *Personal Influence:* The Part Played by People in the Flow of Mass Communications. Free Press, Glencoe, Ill., 1955.

ideas: political information reached opinion leaders through mass media and in turn was communicated to less active members of the community.[16] In the Decatur study, this hypothesis was tested in other than political areas. Influentials were identified by members of the sample who named the people whom they regarded as knowledgeable and trustworthy (the "general influentials"), the people who had in fact influenced them on specific decisions (the "specific influentials"), and the people with whom they interacted most frequently with respect to information reaching them from the mass media. The first category of general influentials were often outside the family circle, whereas the specific influentials and the frequent interactors were within the family in the majority of instances. These opinion leaders were also interviewed, and it was found that they read and listened more to mass media than non-leaders, and this held true for the specific areas of influence under consideration. Factors related to opinion leadership were gregariousness, social status, and position in the life cycle. Unmarried women under 35 were more likely to be opinion leaders in the field of fashion, whereas influence in public affairs was more related to gregariousness and social status.

An earlier study by Merton had made the interesting disclosure of two types of opinion leadership in public affairs at the community level: the "cosmopolitan" leader and the "local" leader.[17] The cosmopolitans exerted influence in the area of national and international problems and typically had access to news media which originated outside the community. The local influentials, on the other hand, had special communication advantage with respect to events within the community. The mode of influence of the two leadership types differed. The cosmopolitan led because of the expertness attributed to him, whereas the local influential was seen as having a sympathetic understanding of others. In other words, the latter's leadership was more personal than institutional in character. This study suggests that the process of opinion formation in a community consists of a complex pattern in which persons at the boundary of one sub-system with membership in other systems (the cosmopolitans) are key communicators, but that overall acceptance of ideas requires considerable activity of the interpersonal leaders.

16. Lazarsfeld, P. F., B. R. Berelson, and Hazel Gaudet, *The People's Choice,* 2nd ed. Columbia University Press, New York, 1948, chap. 2.
17. Merton, R. K., *Social Theory and Social Structure:* Toward the Codification of Theory and Research. Free Press, Glencoe, Ill., 1949.

POPULATION STATISTICS OF PERSONALITY TYPES

In addition to knowing how people are tied into the complex social structures of a society, it is also of importance to know what they are like. The basic psychological characteristics of given populations have been the subject of countless volumes of assertion, speculation, and interpretation. Interpretations range from the extreme of belief in the innate determination of racial differences, currently experiencing a revival in some quarters, to the doctrine that perceived differences between national groups are predominantly a function of the stereotypes of the perceiver. Intermediate would be the position that genuine differences between groups may exist in basic personality structure as a result of socialization practices and social inheritance rather than of biological inheritance. Nonetheless, the evidence for types of differences in personality traits between nations or between subgroups of a national population is fragmentary. For instance, the voluminous literature on the authoritarian character structure of the German people does not include a single quantitative study of representative samples of Germans and non-Germans. The problem of national character which has been with us for so long is made to order for an attack through survey methods. The future historian of the social sciences will speculate on why it took so long to use appropriate and available tools to find answers to age-old questions.

Within nations, the attempt to furnish descriptive statistics of sub-populations at the personality level has been limited to measures of ability and intelligence. Though scales of intelligence were originally standardized on the more educated segments of the public, non-verbal techniques and other devices to overcome the shortcomings of these instruments have seen considerable development. And though intelligence tests are so closely tied to scholastic training that their results cannot be interpreted as pure measures of innate ability, they are still useful in indicating fairly stable characteristics of a group. Their results can be utilized to direct more resources to given segments of the population who suffer educational deprivation. Moreover, the use of the Wechsler Adult Intelligence Scale in surveys of attitudes and behavior can furnish a control on scholastic aptitude which may be contributing a considerable part of the variance to the results of a given study.

Measures of personality traits have been expanded to cover many of the concepts elaborated in modern theorizing about personality structures. Tests of ego strength, of self-acceptance, of self-disclosure, of impulse control, of manifest anxiety, of intropunitiveness-extrapunitiveness, of authoritarianism, of defense mechanisms, and of motive patterns have been devised for college and clinical populations. With ingenuity they can be applied to non-academic groups. Whether ours is an achieving society or a conforming society or in some degree a combination of both motive patterns no longer has to remain a speculative problem. Representative sample studies of the incidence of motive patterns in our nation would not solve all the issues at stake, but they would provide a genuine empirical basis for the discussion. In general we have had few nation-wide studies utilizing available personality measures. There have been many studies in which comparisons have been made of subgroups in the population on given personality characteristics, but little if any attention has been paid to a sampling design that permits generalization of the findings. Most studies are in agreement, however, in finding an inverse correlation between authoritarianism as measured by the F scale and educational level, but these findings may well be due to differences in ideology rather than to differences in basic personality.[18] The lower the education, the more likely it is that the person's ideas are reflections of the more traditional ideology of the culture.

One breakthrough has been achieved in the extension of measures of motive patterns from the laboratory to the field situation. Veroff, Atkinson, Feld, and Gurin adapted the projective picture tests, designed to measure need for achievement, need for affiliation and need for power, to a national sample of respondents interviewed in determining attitudes toward mental health.[19] A decade of laboratory experimentation had shown "that experimentally induced motivational states influence the content of imaginative thought in ways that can be reliably coded to yield measures of important social motives. . . ."[20] Separate sets of six pictures for men and women were pre-tested, then presented to respondents with these instructions:

> Another thing we want to find out is what people think of situations that may come up in life. I'm going to show you some pictures of these situations and ask you to think of stories that go with them. . . . For example, here is the first picture. I'd like you to spend a few minutes thinking of a story to go with it. To get at the story you're thinking of I'll ask questions like: Who are these people? What do they want, and so on. Just answer with anything that comes to mind. . . .[21]

18. Titus, H. E. and E. P. Hollander, "The California F Scale in Psychological Research: 1950–1955," *Psychological Bulletin,* Vol. 54, 1957, pp. 47–64.
19. Veroff, Joseph, *et al.,* "The Use of Thematic Apperception to Assess Motivation in a Nationwide Interview Study," *Psychological Monographs,* Vol. 74, No. 12, 1960.
20. *Ibid.,* p. 1.
21. *Ibid.,* p. 7.

The stories were recorded verbatim by the interviewers, and later coded by a number of independent judges according to a detailed set of categories. Though the coding reliability was not as high as in previous laboratory studies, the median coefficient was .77. A correction was introduced for verbal fluency to take account of educational differences in respondents and this correction reduced considerably the variation in motivation scores attributable to interviewer differences. The greatest apparent weakness in the method was the fact that the protocols of some respondents were inadequate for coding. Some 17 per cent of the men in the sample and some 14 per cent of the women, mostly from the least educated groups, were lost for the motivational analysis. Though this was a serious loss, it is less than might have been anticipated and may well be reduced in future studies after further methodological research.

Though the projective measures had laboratory validation, their meaning for an adult nation-wide sample remains to be established, i.e., do they really reflect consistent patterns of motivation to achieve, to seek social support, to attain power. Occupational groups did respond as might be expected with respect to the need for achievement. Unskilled workers and farmers were lowest in this motivational pattern and professional and managerial groups were highest. And professional and managerial groups differed in need for power, with professional people lower than managerial.

Moreover, a subsequent analysis of these projective data by Crockett revealed significant relationships between strength of achievement motivation and upward social mobility.[22] Crockett compared the prestige of the occupation of the respondent with that of his father, utilizing the NORC scale. Those who had moved up the occupational ladder were higher in the need to achieve than those who had not. Thus the measure of the intervening psychological variable can give additional information for theorizing about social mobility.

All in all, this investigation demonstrated that projective methods are feasible on a nation-wide sample and that the results they obtain can be satisfactorily quantified. Thus a new avenue opens up for the use of more sophisticated measurements of psychological variables outside the laboratory. The authors conclude:

> Careful inquiries into the relationship of these measures to other psychological variables and to demographic indices in this survey, and in

22. Crockett, H. J., Jr., "The Achievement Motive and Differential Occupational Mobility in the U.S.," *American Sociological Review,* Vol. 27, April, 1962, pp. 191–204.

subsequent national studies, should greatly enhance our understanding of the social origins and consequences of motivation. . . . The use of thematic apperception to assess motivation in survey studies of national character will mean that factual evidence concerning personality configurations within American society can be integrated with the fund of factual evidence concerning the dynamics of motivation already derived from experimental and clinical use of these same measures.[23]

In a provocative analysis of problems in the study of national character, Inkeles and Levinson suggest that research be directed at these issues: the relation of the individual to authority, the conception of the self, the basis for maintaining inner equilibrium, the major forms of anxiety, ways of dealing with primary conflicts or dilemmas, modes of cognitive functioning, styles of expressive behavior, and the handling of major dispositions such as aggression and dependency.[24] In an investigation of various societies, it would be necessary to develop specifications in terms of descriptive categories for these areas. These authors would thus accept authoritarian personality theory as a starting point but would urge the development of more specific and adequate categories to insure comparability and enable investigators to provide information both about similarities and differences in modal personality across cultures. Though the theoretical spade work for the exploration in depth of national differences has been going on for some time through the efforts of Erikson, Fromm, Frenkel-Brunswick, and Inkeles and Levinson, the follow-through in terms of research operations has made little progress.[25]

Another type of psychological information which is now uneven and very incomplete has to do with the problem of personality stability and change in the various life stages from birth to old age. Childhood, adolescence, marriage, parenthood, advanced middle age, and retirement are common experiences but we do not know with any degree of precision what these patterns mean for the individual, what in fact can be assumed as uniform behavior associated with these periods, and what variations are found because of personality determinants.

23. Veroff, Joseph, *et al.,* "The Use of Thematic . . . ," *op. cit.,* p. 30.
24. Inkeles, A. and D. J. Levinson, "National Character," in *Handbook of Social Psychology,* Vol. 2. Edited by Gardner Lindzey. Addison-Wesley, Reading, Mass., 1954, pp. 977–1020.
25. Adorno, T. W., *et al., The Authoritarian Personality,* Harper & Bros., New York, 1950, chap. 2.

An interesting field study of retired men suggests that common-sense interpretations of adjustment to aging and retirement are far from adequate accounts of the problem. Considerable variation was found by Reichard, Livson, and Petersen in their study of 87 older men.[26] These investigators report that retirement was not a traumatic experience for many of their subjects who found greater self-acceptance in their declining years than in their younger years. Five patterns of adjustment appeared in this small sample. There were those who maintained a mature and realistic orientation and found genuine gratification from their relationship with others and their activities. There were those who adjusted successfully through a passive attitude in which they gladly threw off responsibilities. Still another successful type of adjustment was shown by the group who remained active and maintained their strong defenses. A fourth pattern was less adjustive, namely the extra-punitive reactions of the bitter and frustrated. Finally, another group blamed themselves for their failures in life and were marked by feelings of self-hatred. These same patterns had characterized many of the subjects throughout their lives. The poorly adjusted had had the same basic problems before retirement.

Again, these findings are not so much generalizations about the last stage in the life cycle as hypotheses for further research.

DESCRIPTIVE STATISTICS OF DEVIANCY FROM SOCIAL NORMS

Information on how people are tied into the social structure needs to be supplemented with quantitative studies of the kind and extent of deviancy from personality norms, group standards, and legal norms. Who are people who do not fit into social systems? The incidence of mental disorder, alcoholism, abnormal sex practices, delinquency, and of suicide in a given society and its subgroupings would often furnish psychological as well as social statistics. The report of Goldhamer and Marshall on the constant rate of admission to our mental hospitals for people under fifty years of age over the past one hundred years in this country has implications for psychogenetic theories of psychosis.[27]

The extent of juvenile delinquency in a given teenage population may indicate that we are dealing with the normative behavior of that subgroup

26. Reichard, S. K., Florine Livson, and P. G. Petersen, *Aging and Personality*. John Wiley & Sons, New York, 1962.
27. Goldhamer, H. H., and A. W. Marshall, *Psychosis and Civilization:* Two Studies in the Frequency of Mental Disease. Free Press, Glencoe, Ill., 1953.

rather than with youngsters lacking in impulse control or characterized by psychopathology. This has in fact been the thesis of Cohen who argues that the bulk of juvenile delinquency is the result of participation in a delinquent sub-culture.[28] With Short, Cohen has further elaborated his position in describing five types of male delinquent sub-cultures: (1) the parent male or garden variety in which fathers are characterized by negativeness, short-run hedonism, and maliciousness; (2) the conflict-oriented sub-culture or the culture of large gangs; (3) the drug addict sub-culture of the most deprived elements in a community; (4) semi-professional theft where crime takes on a more utilitarian and occupational way of life; and (5) middle class delinquent sub-culture.[29] The description of these five patterns is still at the speculative level and the actual identification of such delinquent sub-cultures is a matter for field research. In one of the most careful survey studies of delinquency and class structure, Riess and Rhodes were not able to isolate the common sub-type described by Cohen and Short as the parent male delinquent sub-culture even though they operationalized all of the criteria for this pattern.[30] The Riess-Rhodes study was confined to white boys in one county in Tennessee and some of its findings were:

There is more frequent and serious delinquent deviation in the lower and middle stratum. . . .
The career oriented delinquent is found only among lower class boys. . . .
Peer oriented delinquency is the most common form of delinquent organization at both status levels. . . .
The major type of lower status boy is a conforming nonachiever while the conforming achiever is the major type in the middle class. . . .[31]

Another interesting example of the use of the survey method in the investigation of delinquency is the study by Maccoby, Johnson, and

28. Cohen, A. K., *Delinquent Boys:* The Culture of the Gang. Free Press, Glencoe, Ill., 1955.
29. Cohen, A. K. and J. F. Short, "Research in Delinquent Subcultures," *Journal of Social Issues,* Vol. 14, No. 3, 1958, pp. 20–37.
30. Reiss, A. J. and A. L. Rhodes, "Distribution of Juvenile Delinquency in the Social Class Structure," *American Sociological Review,* Vol. 26, October, 1961, pp. 720–732.
31. *Ibid.,* p. 732.

Church.[32] The hypothesis tested concerned community integration rather than social class. Two neighborhoods were selected which were as close as possible in socio-economic status but which differed widely in juvenile delinquency. Samples of residents from both neighborhoods were interviewed and the hypothesis was supported, in that the residents in the high delinquency area compared to those in the low area were less attached to their neighborhood, did not know their neighbors as well, and did not feel that they shared the same values and attitudes. Yet there were no significant differences in the two areas in length of residence. Moreover, no evidence was found to suggest a delinquent sub-culture, though this was not the main objective of the study.

These findings are consistent with the old doctrine of *anomie* or normlessness as a central factor in deviancy. In recent years, Durkheim's concept has been revived and scales have been developed for its study. Dean, for example, devised items and adapted others from previous instruments to measure three components of alienation: (1) powerlessness or helplessness of people to control their social destiny, (2) normlessness referring either to the absence of standards or the conflict of standards, and (3) social isolation or separation from the group.[33] These three components were significantly interrelated; in fact, powerlessness and normlessness were as highly intercorrelated as one could predict from the reliabilities of the two subscales. Significant but very low correlations were found in the expected direction with occupation, education, and income. The use of these scales for more appropriate targets such as various types of deviant groups on some more adequate sampling basis is indicated.

Because deviant behavior constitutes an immediate problem, we have official statistics about various forms of deviancy, especially in those areas where the deviancy receives social treatment. Generally, however, these statistics are a by-product of such treatment and leave a great deal to be desired from the point of view of behavioral science. They often do not give adequate information about the individual case, and they are restricted to people who get caught or are involved in institutional treatment. Hence, our

---

32. Maccoby, E. E., J. P. Johnson, and R. M. Church, "Community Integration and the Social Control of Juvenile Delinquency," *Journal of Social Issues,* Vol. 14, No. 3, 1958, pp. 38–51.
33. Dean, D. G., "Alienation: Its Meaning and Measurement," *American Sociological Review,* Vol. 26, October, 1961, 753–758.

social statistics on deviancy need to be supplemented by periodic sample studies which would not only be useful in assessing social trends and in identifying the exact social location of the problem, but would also furnish basic data about the psychological correlates of various types of deviancy.

DESCRIPTIVE ACCOUNTS OF BELIEFS, ATTITUDES AND VALUES

In addition to inventories of individual behavior and of basic personality characteristics, there is also the need for continuing studies of the beliefs and value structures of the national population and of its many subgroupings. Thus far, the public opinion polls are the best source of information about the distribution of various types of beliefs and attitudes of the nation. But there are great limitations both in the breadth and depth of this information. The questions commonly posed in the opinion poll deal with some newsworthy event or some item that will have news value. Hence the findings are very selective and fragmentary. Moreover, there is no systematic exploration by the polls of the structure of given beliefs and attitudes, so that our knowledge of what people think and believe is not only fragmentary but is also fragmented.

Systematic studies of attitudes are immediately recognized as of great practical value. Government officials and leaders of all types are constantly in need of information about how policies can be effectively implemented through public understanding and acceptance. Political parties are increasingly utilizing survey information for the conduct of campaigns. But the value to science of descriptive studies of the values of people has received practically no recognition. Since science in its advanced stages is concerned with explanation and is heavily theoretical, we often forget that in its beginning stages it must also be descriptive. We need to know a great deal about the units of our science before we can make much progress. In psychology our units are people, and we need a great deal of knowledge about what they think and how they think to check our theories and to give us a basis for further theorizing.

Trend studies of the attitudes and values geared to a known population have at least three advantages for behavioral science: (1) they would afford a good control for the interpretation of other psychological findings, (2) they would provide a test of the conditions and limitations of theories about cognitive functioning, and (3) they would contribute to psychological knowledge of social change.

A basis for interpretation. The importance of measures of an individual's personality must be judged against the attitudes and values prevailing in his groups. Hyman and Sheatsley, in their critique of *The Authoritarian Personality,* have pointed out that aggression and prejudice toward outgroups may not reflect deep-lying authoritarian trends in the personality but the normative values of the group to which the person belongs.[34] If we know, for example, that an individual has grown up in a rural southern community, then his high score on the F scale may represent the accepted values of his group rather than the repression of hostility toward his parents. Nor can we accept the fictions people subscribe to as evidence of the delusional system of a paranoid unless we know what the common patterns of beliefs and values are among their kind. Knowledge, then, of prevailing attitudes and cognitions is necessary for the interpretation of many psychological measures.

Test of cognitive theory. Current psychological theory about belief systems is reminiscent of the old model of rational man. The modern formulation is organized around the theme of self-consistency, of a strain toward congruence in belief system, and of consonance between attitudes and behavior. Many of the concepts of consistency stem from the balance theory of Heider who postulated a symmetry in belief systems.[35] Heider maintains that two related but opposed beliefs will create imbalance which will be resolved by changes in the contradictory beliefs to achieve symmetry. Newcomb has developed balance theory with respect to attitudes toward objects and people in his A-B-X system.[36] If individual A has a favorable attitude toward individual B, he will also tend to have favorable attitudes toward an object x, if B also has such a favorable attitude. In similar fashion, Osgood has formulated a congruity hypothesis which states that if one has a high opinion of a prestige person, one will also tend to have a high opinion of

34. Hyman, H. H. and P. B. Sheatsley, "The Authoritarian Personality—A Methodological Critique," in *Studies in the Scope and Method of 'The Authoritarian Personality.'* Edited by Richard Christie and Marie Jahoda. Free Press, Glencoe, Ill., 1954, pp. 50–122.
35. Heider, Fritz, *The Psychology of Interpersonal Relations.* John Wiley & Sons, New York, 1958.
36. Newcomb, T. M., *The Acquaintance Process.* Holt, Rinehart & Winston, New York, 1961.

those events and objects of which the prestigeful person approves.[37] The most ingenious experiments on the problem of consistency are those of Festinger, who uses the term "cognitive dissonance" to refer to the situation in which an individual is confronted by information contradictory to his own beliefs.[38] Festinger argues that people will change their attitudes or their behavior in such a manner as to reduce the cognitive dissonance. If, for example, people must exert effort or experience deprivation to achieve certain goals, they will value these goals more highly since this will justify the unpleasant experiences and undue effort.[39]

Though there undoubtedly are forces within the individual pushing him toward self-consistency, this type of psychological theorizing needs much more elaboration before it fits the complexities of people behaving in the real social world. Surveys and field studies commonly encounter gross contradictions in people's belief systems and gross discrepancies between people's beliefs and actions. Rationalization is as common as rational resolution, compartmentalization as frequent as unification, and distortion and selection of incoming information as universal as accurate assessment. It is possible, of course, to regard these devices of rationalizing, compartmentalizing, and distorting as indications of the individual's need for self-consistency. The point is, however, that it may be easier to predict belief systems and behavior from underlying motivations rather than from a need for consistency. If some people achieve consistency through a rational resolution and others through compartmentalizing inconsistent notions, then we have no purchase on the task of predicting attitudes, values, and actions.

The starting point for studying the structure of the value systems in the individual is his conception of the group or situational appropriateness of his beliefs. Most people experience little difficulty in showing logically inconsistent patterns of ideas and behavior, because they accept the different demands of varying social situations or group settings. Since the world is a complex one, double and multiple standards are seen as a natural and appropriate way of dealing with it. A political leader plays the game of politics

37. Osgood, C. E., "Cognitive Dynamics in the Conduct of Human Affairs," *Public Opinion Quarterly,* Vol. 24, Summer, 1960, pp. 341–365.
38. Festinger, L., *A Theory of Cognitive Dissonance*. Row, Peterson, Evanston, Ill., 1957.
39. Cohen, A. R., "Attitudinal Consequences of Induced Discrepancies Between Cognitions and Behavior," *Public Opinion Quarterly,* Vol. 24, Summer, 1960, pp. 297–318.

according to its rules of compromise, trading, and even deception; but in his family circle may follow a different code of conduct.

Over thirty years ago, Schanck, on the basis of his field study of a community, described the major discrepancies between the attitudes of people on religious and moral issues in terms of the concept of public and private attitudes.[40] It has been customary to think of the private opinions of people as the true or valid attitudes and the public responses as due to what today would be termed the acquiescence or social desirability factor. The basic truth in the Schanck finding, however, is that people will hold contradictory beliefs in different social settings and that the publicly expressed beliefs can be more effective than the privately expressed beliefs for the determination of social behavior.

Even within the demands of a given group, people do not necessarily follow the logical requirements of organizational allegiance. They define the area of compliance to group norms in their own terms. Within the political domain, attitudes toward the political parties and their representatives, though correlated, are far from being perfectly associated. The same voters who returned President Eisenhower to office in 1956 also gave him a Democratic congress. The study by Campbell, Gurin, and Miller of the 1952 election showed that many Democrats in almost all subgroups, including labor union members, defected to the Republican side.[41] The subsequent study of Campbell, Stokes, Miller, and Converse of the 1956 election, together with the earlier study, documented the observation that Eisenhower was perceived by many people as standing above the political arena.[42] Democrats felt no psychological inconsistency in voting for him because they did not see him as a partisan political figure.

Account has to be taken not only of the individual's ability to accept differing group demands, but also of how he organizes his beliefs on issue areas. Prejudices toward outgroups, for example, should reveal a high degree of consistency in that they are concerned with basic emotional and cognitive functioning related to the same problem. Studies do in fact indicate general-

40. Schanck, R. L., "A Study of a Community and Its Groups and Institutions Conceived of as Behaviors of Individuals," *Psychological Monographs,* Vol. 43, No. 2, 1932.
41. Campbell, Angus, G. Gurin, and W. E. Miller, *The Voter Decides.* Row, Peterson, Evanston, Ill., 1954.
42. Campbell, A. *et al., The American Voter.* John Wiley & Sons, New York, 1960.

ization of bias toward minority outgroups. Yet the correlation is not striking. Prothro, in a study of 383 middle-class adults, found a correlation of .49 between anti-Negro and anti-Jewish prejudice, which would account for only 25 per cent of the variance in his sample.[43] Apparently there are other organizing principles at work in the minds of people besides the ingroup-outgroup dichotomy, as Rokeach has pointed out.[44]

A third point to bear in mind is that we may impute too high a level of abstraction to the philosophical integration of the beliefs sytems of most people. The academic social scientist may be impressed by the ability of some of his colleagues to be consistent on every issue which arises, whether it be socialized medicine, the U.S. position in Viet Nam, a special loyalty oath for teachers, desegregation, nuclear testing, or the role of the House Committee on Un-American Activities. With the exception, however, of the small minorities comprising the radical right and the radical left, the American people lack consistent integration of beliefs about social, economic, and political matters.

One interesting outcome of survey research has been the finding of two opposing cleavages on the liberalism-conservative dimension. Though the two factors account for only a small amount of the variance, they are significant trends in the American population. One has to do with economic and political conservatism, the other with civil liberties, humanitarian values, and tolerance. On the one hand, attitudes toward New Deal and Fair Deal legislation (e.g. social security, medicare, governmental regulation and control of business, minimum wages) would classify the lower socio-economic groups as liberal and the upper groups as conservative. On the other hand, attitudes toward non-conformers, civil liberties, and non-authoritarian practices with respect to child rearing, would classify the lower socio-economic groups as conservative and the upper groups as liberal. Lipset has noted this bifurcation in the liberalism-conservatism syndrome and has distinguished between economic and non-economic liberalism.[45] In some European countries there is indication of another basic set of dimensions cutting across conservative or liberal beliefs, namely, whether attitudes are

43. Prothro, E. T., "Ethnocentrism and Anti-Negro Attitudes in the Deep South," *Journal of Abnormal and Social Psychology,* Vol. 47, January, 1952, pp. 105–108.
44. Rokeach, Milton, "On the Unity of Thought and Belief," *Journal of Personality,* Vol. 25, 1956, pp. 224–250.
45. Lipset, S. M., "Democracy and Working-Class Authoritarianism," *American Sociological Review,* Vol. 24, August, 1959, pp. 482–501.

focused on foreign or on domestic issues. In the United States, these dimensions can also be observed at the leadership level.

Economic or social welfare liberalism as a differential for social strata reflects an overall tendency and not a clear-cut organizing principle. It varies considerably with the specific issues and with the circumstances of the time, as Key has observed.[46] Centers, for example, found very clear relationships in his nation-wide study conducted in 1945.[47] The correlation between conservatism-radicalism and occupational stratification was .61. The questions furnishing the index of conservatism-radicalism concerned America as the land of opportunity, public vs. private ownership of industries, the power position of the workers, individualism vs. collectivism, identification with employers or workers in strikes, and treatment of workers by employers. These findings are very similar to other investigations in the 1930's and the 1940's by Kornhauser,[48] Cantril, and Jones.[49] A sharp decline in this relationship between occupation and conservatism is reported in the 1956 nationwide study of *The American Voter,* by Campbell *et al.,* analyzed by Converse.[50] Using three questions comparable to those employed by Centers, Converse found relationships of a much lower order of magnitude. In general, radical changes in governmental structure no longer find support in the lower income groups, but they continue to support social welfare and security measures. Thus, though the memory of the depression years had faded in the 1950's, some issues still divided people according to socio-economic status. The same 1956 study of Campbell and his colleagues found 65 per cent of unskilled workers in favor of government intervention for low-cost medical and hospital care in contrast to 45 per cent of the business people.

On the dimension of liberalism as an expression of individual rights and civil liberties, the relationship with socio-economic status runs the other

46. Key, V. O., Jr., *Public Opinion and American Democracy*. Knopf, New York, 1961.

47. Centers, Richard, *op. cit.*

48. Kornhauser, A. W., "Analysis of Class Structure of Contemporary American Society," in *Industrial Conflict:* A Psychological Interpretation. Edited by G. W. Hartman and T. M. Newcomb. Dryden Press, New York, 1939, pp. 199–264.

49. Jones, A. W., *Life, Liberty and Property:* A Story of Conflict and a Measurement of Conflicting Rights. J. B. Lippincott, Philadelphia, 1941.

50. Converse, P. E., "The Shifting Role of Class in Political Attitudes and Behavior," in *Readings in Social Psychology,* 3d ed. Edited by E. E. Maccoby, T. M. Newcomb, and E. L. Hartley. Henry Holt, New York, 1958, pp. 388–399.

way. Stouffer's nationwide survey measured the tolerance of people for various types of non-conformity and found the following percentages of tolerant respondents in the various occupational groups:[51]

Professional and semi-professional	66%
Proprietors, managers and officials	51
Clerical and sales	49
Manual workers	30
Farmers and farm workers	20

The Michigan Survey Research Center's 1956 political study (Campbell *et al.*) asked about federal governmental intervention in school integration.[52] Again wage workers were more conservative than the business and professional groups. Authoritarian ideology has also been found to be more prevalent in the lower income groups, but there have not been adequate controls on response acquiescence to warrant firm conclusions about these results. The consistency of the findings and their support from related measures, however, lends plausibility to the validity of correlations between educational level and authoritarian values.

A systematic attempt to discover the degree of ideology in the attitudes of the public is the analysis of the 1956 nation-wide political survey by Campbell and his colleagues. They found that, of ten domestic issues to which people were asked to respond, only five constituted a scale according to the Guttman criterion of scaling for unidimensionality. These items concerned aid to education, medical care, employment guarantees, FEPC and Negro housing, and public vs. private control of electricity and housing. But the issues of the role of big business in government, the influence of unions in government, desegregation in schools, taxation, and the firing of suspected communists could not be fitted into the same scale, nor did they comprise a scale of their own. Four of the six foreign policy items showed sufficient relationships to comprise a Guttman scale. There is some evidence of attitude structures for domestic and foreign questions, but they are not highly elaborated structures and do not encompass many relevant issues. The authors state, "The data evince a rather slight degree of structure in the attitudes of the mass electorate."[53] It should also be noted that there

51. Stouffer, S. A., *Communism, Conformity and Civil Liberties:* A Cross-Section of the Nation Speaks its Mind. Doubleday, New York, 1955.
52. Campbell, Angus, *et al., The American Voter, op. cit.*
53. *Ibid.*, p. 195.

was no relationship between the two scale dimensions of social welfare and an internationalist position of the public as a whole.

An examination of the correlates of positions on the domestic issues led the authors to the conclusion that they represent expressions of primitive self-interest rather than integrated ideological structures. Thus they say:

> We have no quarrel with the view that ideological position is largely determined by self-interest. But we do maintain that it matters whether self-interest proceeds in a simple and naked sense, or has indeed become imbedded in some broader ideological structure. We have suggested, for example, that the possession of ideology equips the individual to perceive the connectedness of many superficially diverse events and relate them to one another coherently.[54]

They proceed to examine the attitudes of low income people who vote Republican to see if they follow the ideology of the party position. On the social welfare scale, however, these Republican voters took the same position as low-income Democrats. They voted Republican because of the attractiveness of its candidate or long-standing loyalty to the party and not for ideological reasons.

Campbell and his colleagues also compared the McClosky scale of conservatism with attitudes on domestic issues. The McClosky scale measures orientations toward change with respect to a broad variety of types of innovation. No consistent pattern of correlations appeared between this measure of conservatism and responses of the public to questions of social welfare and other domestic issues. In fact, the negative relationships were greater in magnitude than the positive relationships. McClosky himself reports as the result of his research that liberalism and conservatism seem to have little relationship to party preferences, economic views, and public issues.[55]

One very interesting analysis in the Campbell study was a four-fold classification of people based upon their levels of conceptualization of the parties and the candidates in the 1956 campaign. The free answers to open-ended questions were used for this categorization. The first level consisted of respondents who showed some organization of belief which might be considered ideological in the type of abstraction employed, whether the

54. *Ibid.,* p. 204.
55. McClosky, Herbert, "Conservatism and Personality," *American Political Science Review,* Vol. 52, December, 1958, pp. 27–45.

organizing principle was liberalism-conservatism or some other dimension. The second level was made up of those whose comments were limited to short-term group interest or fairly concrete issues. Respondents who talked only in terms of the goodness or badness of the times and the party in power, or who talked of some single isolated issue, were assigned to the third category. Finally, the fourth level was for those whose comments made reference to issues but were concerned with liking for candidate or for party. As is clear in the following table, a clear ideological orientation toward politics characterized a negligible proportion of the population—only 2.5 per cent.

SUMMARY OF THE DISTRIBUTION OF THE TOTAL SAMPLE IN
LEVELS OF CONCEPTUALIZATION*

A.	Ideology	
	1. Ideology	2.5%
	2. Near-ideology	9
B.	Group Benefits	
	1. Perception of conflict	14
	2. Single-group interest	17
	3. Shallow group benefit responses	11
C.	Nature of the times	24
D.	No issue content	
	1. Party orientation	4
	2. Candidate orientation	9
	3. No content	5
	4. Unclassified	4.5
		100%

* From *The American Voter* by Angus Campbell, P. E. Converse, W. E. Miller, and D. E. Stokes. John Wiley & Sons, New York, 1960, p. 249.

From the many studies of attitudes involving samples of the population, it is clear that doctrines of consistency and congruence can be very misleading in understanding and predicting beliefs and behavior. The level of abstraction necessary to encompass a variety of cognitions on related topics in a coherent unifying philosophy is found among few people. Differing group forces may affect the individual, but the effect is not one in which the ideology of the group is internalized as a cognitive structure by the individual. What is internalized is the readiness to accept and take on those ideas and those actions which are necessary to continued involvement in the group structure. Ideology is thus more of a system than an individual property, and the individual need absorb only as much of it as is necessary to be a good member of the system.

Knowledge of social change. Trend studies of cognitive structures would afford an interesting index of social change. They could also show the types of beliefs which fluctuate with circumstance, the types which are amenable to gradual change in a consistent direction and the types which are inherently stable and resistant to change. Such discoveries of volatile, growing, and stable values would be of profound interest if they could be demonstrated across cultures. Some writers have speculated about the consistent trends over the years toward the acceptance of a democratic ideology. Within the United States, they point to the spread of democratic ideas from the political sphere to the family, to the upbringing of children, to the school, and even to such authoritarian systems as industry and the military services. Many of these changes go unnoticed because of their gradual character. In industry, for example, one would find a marked contrast in the foreman's handling of his workers and in management philosophy toward employees between 1910 and 1960. The same line of argument would emphasize the changes in Negro-white relations over the past thirty years. Though discrimination and prejudice are still rampant, they can no longer be supported by appeals to a non-democratic ideology. The present generation of Negroes themselves have given up a passive attitude. Identification with the aggressor has been replaced by a militant leadership demanding equal rights. Parenthetically, social science suffered a major setback in its failure to launch a research program in communities throughout the land following the first Supreme Court decision that separate school facilities were not psychologically equal opportunities.

The same type of argument could be applied to the peoples around the world who are going through the throes of national self-determination after generations of colonialism. The assumption in this thesis is that human beings are sufficiently alike the world over to prefer freedom to bondage, equality to privilege, and self-development to subservient roles. Unfortunately, evidence can also be assembled to show that people are easily misled and not as willing to make the commitment in personal thought and effort that would insure democratic institutions and hence they become a prey to totalitarian regimes.

Trend studies could furnish a baseline for studying the forces related to change. The laboratory has isolated such factors in changing opinions and actions as the power of the immediate group, the influence of prestige sources, and the effectiveness of reward and punishment. The interaction of these variables and of other motivational forces in the social world are also deserving of study. The cumulative impact of a number of forces over time can be investigated in no other way than through longitudinal field studies. The hypothesis was suggested by wartime opinion studies that people are resistant to changes in their attitudes unless there are multiple forces brought to bear upon them. The assumptions are that, in the real world, the individual is constantly subject to a barrage of influences reinforcing his value systems and that, for change to take place, there must not only be repetition of a stimulus but variety in stimuli to engage as many interests of the individual as possible.

Theories of social change vary from those which give priority to the objective conditions controlling behavior to those which emphasize the psychological or personality determinants of change. For example, the McClelland thesis, presently to be described, sees the achievement motive as prior to economic development, whereas many economists and sociologists would give the objective development the heavier weighting. Available evidence on changes in values and attitudes over time is not definitive. Nor does it help much for those who take an interaction position and stress the interplay of both sets of forces, because we still need specifications of how the interaction takes place. Katona has pointed to the significant increases in optimism toward economic affairs among the American people since the depression years, which may account in part for the spectacular change in rate of children born during the first year of marriage.[56] In 1937, 28 per cent of married couples had a child in the first year of marriage and in 1960 the percentage had jumped to 46 per cent. The increased optimism and the resulting shifts in various economic attitudes can be attributed to the shift from an entrepreneurial to a bureaucratic society but also, as Katona suggests, to the fact that with a shift from blue collar to white collar occupations the peak earning years come later and are more sustained. Thus the young people who are a large component of our society can look forward to increasing incomes whereas formerly their peak earning came early in life and then declined. Economic conditions may have created a new psychological world for generations entering adult occupational roles.

---

56. Katona, George, personal communication to the author.

Research on desegregation has also shown the importance of conditions which control behavior. Where the legal norms can be clearly defined and implemented, desegregation practices receive more acceptance.[57] There is no clear immediate change in attitudes shown by the measurements so far attempted. Over time, however, the expectation would be that people would change their feelings and evaluations in line with their behavioral change.

A trend survey was able to measure the impact of changes in role behavior upon attitudes in a natural field experiment in a large industrial plant. Lieberman measured the beliefs and values of all factory workers in a machine-producing enterprise and returned a year later to repeat his measurements.[58] At the time of second testing some of the workers had been promoted to foremen, others had been elected union stewards, but the majority were still workers. The before-and-after comparisons and the group comparisons gave a nice check on the causal factors at work. There was nothing to differentiate the foremen from the stewards when they were workers, though they differed from other workers. Both foremen-to-be and stewards-to-be were more critical of company policy and practice, more knowledgeable about the plant situation, and more supportive of union ideology than their fellow workers. A year later, however, the men who had become foremen had shifted markedly to company ideology and the stewards had moved further toward union values. In other words, assuming a given social role had produced predictable changes in attitudes and values.

The Study of Complex Social Psychological Problems

Some of the most significant psychological problems are not amenable to laboratory study. Their full expression and their determinants cannot be set up within the laboratory, either because of their complexity or their temporal duration. Some of these problems which can be most appropriately studied through a field approach are: (1) the childhood socialization process or the genetic development of personality, (2) the adult socialization process, i.e., the induction of people into groups and organizations, (3) the nature and determinants of mental disorder, (4) the psychological aspects of the nature and functioning of organizations and formal social

57. Cook, S. W., "Desegregation: A Psychological Analysis," *The American Psychologist,* Vol. 12, 1957, pp. 1–13; Pettigrew, T. F., ed., "Desegregation Research in the North and South," *Journal of Social Issues,* Vol. 15, No. 4, 1959, pp. 1–71.
58. Lieberman, Seymour, "The Effects of Changes in Roles on the Attitudes of Role Occupants," *Human Relations,* Vol. 9, No. 4, 1956, pp. 385–402.

structures, (5) particular influences on the behavior of individuals in organizations, and (6) predictability of behavior as an organizational objective.

SOCIALIZATION AND THE DEVELOPMENT OF PERSONALITY

The bulk of the theoretical knowledge about personality development stems from the work of Freud, his immediate followers, and the neo-Freudians. Freudian theory originally had no relation to the psychology laboratory and hence academic psychology for a long period rejected its concepts about motivation, conflict, developmental processes, defense mechanisms, and psychological functioning. Even today academic psychology has not been able to absorb, let alone integrate, these theoretical notions into more traditional theory. The first concepts to gain acceptance and still the most prevalent in general psychological use pertain to the defense mechanisms such as identification, projection, and displacement and repression. The interesting point to bear in mind in this connection is that these theoretical contributions grew out of observation of people outside the laboratory who were coping and failing to cope with the social realities of their world. The testing of derivations from Freudian concepts in social behavior remains, however, as a major task for the social psychology of the future.

Central as the socialization process is to understanding of human behavior, its systematic study is still not far advanced. Field methods—with their advantages of adequate and representative samples, of measurement of the many related variables, of interviews and observations in the family setting, and of panel and trend studies—have in general not been utilized to exploit the strength of the methodology. There has been, for example, only one study on a nationwide sample designed to describe child rearing practices and their consequences for personality development; this was the 1932 Anderson study.[59]

In his review of studies on child rearing, Sewell has written:

> With our present knowledge of sampling procedures, data-gathering methods, and analysis techniques, a carefully designed large-scale study using a sample of sufficient size to permit social and ethnic breakdowns and other needed controls and concentrating on various aspects of child rearing ranging over the whole period of childhood is the indi-

59. Anderson, H. E., *The Young Child in the Home.* Appleton-Century-Crofts, New York, 1936.

cated next step. Additional studies of small local communities with relatively narrow stratification systems or studies in larger communities with samples that are inadequate to represent the full range of the stratification system are not likely to add much to the knowledge already available from existing studies and could well be dispensed with.[60]

Sears, Maccoby, and Levin point out the diversity of practices within the United States on the basis of information from three communities: a small village in New Mexico, a nearby town with a different ethnic composition, and a suburban metropolitan area in New England.[61] In the first community, 50 per cent of the mothers had completed the weaning process before the child was eight months old, in the second none had, and in the third 37 per cent had. The communities also differed on the reliance on physical punishment as the major method of discipline, with 39 per cent of the families in the village, 5 per cent in the second community, and 20 per cent in the New England area falling into this category.

Social theorists have acknowledged the variations in child rearing practices for American society as a whole, but have reduced the amount of diversity by postulating major differences between social classes with fairly homogeneous methods of socialization prevailing within the different social strata. Davis, for example, developed the interesting theory that middle-class culture penalizes aggression and sexual behavior in children, that it resorts to internalization of guilt feelings rather than physical punishment, that it emphasizes the renunciation of immediate satisfactions, and that it places a premium on the early attainment of norms with respect to cleanliness and other goals of training.[62] These middle-class practices create a socialized anxiety among growing youngsters which is expressed in striving for success. An achievement-orientated personality is the result. Thus the insecurity of middle-class status which requires new validation of position in each new generation develops appropriate socialization procedures to meet this need. In contrast, the working classes, though using more physical punishment,

60. Sewell, W. H., "Social Class and Childhood Personality," *Sociometry,* Vol. 24, December, 1961, p. 351.

61. Sears, R. R., E. E. Maccoby, and H. Levin, *Patterns of Child Rearing.* Row, Peterson, Evanston, Ill., 1957.

62. Davis, Allison, "Socialization and Adolescent Society," in *Adolescence Forty-Third Yearbook, Part I.* Edited by N. B. Henry. University of Chicago Press, Chicago, 1944, chap. 11.

are more permissive, less concerned about the early attainment of norms, and not as punitive in dealing with aggressive and sexual behavior.

This type of theory was attractive in the behavioral sciences because it had significance not only for the understanding of personality but for the motivational dynamic of social classes. The Marxian theory implied a class dynamic based upon the direct expression of economic group interest. Workers sharing a common economic fate were driven toward collective actions in their own interest; the owning classes moved to increase their holdings and to keep workers in subjection and the middle classes, with their bourgeois aspirations (now labeled achievement-striving), were caught between two polarized groups. The socialized anxiety postulated by Davis, however, calls for a more complex set of forces in the middle classes. The Marxian theory, for example, would see a dispossessed middle class, reduced to the status of workers, receptive to the same socialistic notions as workers find attractive. The personality mechanisms developed through middle-class socialization, however, would predict a different outcome.

Empirical support for the intriguing theory of Davis is, however, very weak. Though Davis and Havighurst found differences in child rearing between middle-class and lower-class families in the predicted direction and though these results were confirmed by the investigation of Ericson, subsequent studies have reported opposed findings.[63] Specifically, in Davis' Chicago studies, middle-class mothers followed a more restrictive pattern than working-class mothers. They weaned their children earlier, introduced toilet training earlier, and in general followed a stricter and more ordered regime of child training. But the Harvard study of Sears, Maccoby, and Levin, based upon interviews with 379 New England middle-class and lower-class mothers, not only failed to substantiate the earlier results but on many counts offered contradictory evidence.[64] There were no differences between the classes in infant-feeding practices and, in other areas of training, the lower-class mothers were in general less permissive than middle-class mothers. The former were more severe and restrictive with respect to toilet training, the expression of aggression, and sex training. The majority of the studies conducted since the Davis-Havighurst investigation have found fewer class-related differences and those differences which have been re-

63. Ericson, M. C., "Social Status and Child-Rearing Practices," in *Readings in Social Psychology,* 1st ed. Edited by T. M. Newcomb and E. L. Hartley. Henry Holt, New York, 1947, pp. 494–501.
64. Sears, R. R., E. E. Maccoby, and H. Levin, *op. cit.*

ported are consistently in the direction of the Sears-Maccoby-Levin findings.

To a minor extent, the contradictions between the earlier and later studies can reflect methodological weaknesses in the design of the research. In the Davis-Havighurst study of Chicago school children there was no adequate sampling design: the 48 middle-class children all came from nursery schools and selective biases also entered into the sample of 52 working-class children.[65] In fact, many of the studies which generalize about class differences in socialization are based upon subjects selected not according to sampling design but according to the convenience of the researcher or for practical purposes extraneous to the research objectives. Thus Klatskin's sample of New Haven mothers consisted of the women enrolled in the Yale Rooming-in Project who brought their babies back for a check-up a year after they had left the hospital.[66]

The major reason for the discrepant results of studies on class differences, however, is probably found in the explanation of Bronfenbrenner of time changes in patterns of child rearing among the social classes.[67] In an ingenious analysis of the investigations in this field, Bronfenbrenner re-examined the data to achieve as much comparability as possible and to take account of the time period to which the information on child rearing practices referred. This re-analysis suggests that the Davis theory may have had some basis in the period between 1930 and 1945 but that since World War II, middle-class mothers have become more permissive in weaning and toilet training and demand feeding than working-class mothers. Bronfenbrenner relates these changes to the changes in the literature on child care reported by Wolfenstein, whose content analysis of successive editions of the United States Children's Bureau bulletin on *Infant Care* shows that the earlier emphasis upon regularity and firm following of schedules has been replaced by the doctrine of permissiveness and gentle guidance.[68] This

---

65. Davis, Allison and R. J. Havighurst, "Social Class and Color Differences in Child Rearing." *American Sociological Review,* Vol. 11, December, 1946, pp. 698–710.
66. Klatskin, E. H., "Shifts in Child Care Practices in Three Social Classes Under an Infant Care Program of Flexible Methodology," *American Journal of Orthopsychiatry,* Vol. 22, 1952, pp. 52–61.
67. Bronfenbrenner, U., "Socialization and Social Class Through Time and Space," in *Readings in Social Psychology,* 3rd ed. Edited by E. E. Maccoby, T. M. Newcomb, and E. L. Hartley. Henry Holt, New York, 1958, pp. 400–425.
68. Wolfenstein, Martha, "Trends in Infant Care," *American Journal of Orthopsychiatry,* Vol. 23, 1953, pp. 120–130.

trend in governmental periodicals has been paralleled by similar changes in the general literature on child training. Middle-class mothers are reached more easily by these media than are working-class mothers. In defense of the Davis hypothesis, however, the studies still show techniques of training among the middle classes oriented toward the internalization of social controls, and the working-class parents more given to the use of physical punishment. But as Bronfenbrenner points out, we are still in a process of flux and the chances are that the approved middle-class practices are gaining acceptance among the lower-income groups. There are some indications that the extreme permissiveness in some middle-class groups is being replaced by the use of physical punishment so that the past reports on class differences with respect to punishment techniques may be reversed in the future.

In conclusion, then, the differential dynamics in socialization for the various social classes may turn out to be generational differences within social classes. It is clear, moreover, that to make any firm generalizations even for given generations will require more thorough study than we have as yet seen in this area of investigation. Prior questions will also have to be answered by field studies, namely, how great is social mobility for different subgroups within the population and what are the lines of cleavage in our society both with respect to the values and goals of subgroups and the major informational sources to which they react? Is the major difference, for example, between working and middle classes in the impact of cultural change merely one of time taken to absorb information?

Miller and Swanson, in their interesting study in the Detroit area, inquired into child rearing practices in terms of a different conception of the nature of social structure.[69] In place of the middle class-working class dichotomy, they felt that a more appropriate analysis could be based upon their theory of an historical shift in the United States from an entrepreneurial society to a bureaucratic society. This shift is seen most strikingly in the middle classes, but it also has reverberations among the working classes. The change in American society is marked by the growth of organizations and of specialization, so that more and more people are involved in bureaucratic structures and more and more of their lives are encompassed within a bureaucratic setting. The independent craftsman, the shop owner, and the

69. Miller, D. R. and G. E. Swanson, *The Changing American Parent:* A Study in the Detroit Area. John Wiley & Sons, New York, 1958; Miller, D. R. *et al., Inner Conflict and Defense.* Henry Holt, New York, 1960.

owner of a small enterprise, mill, or factory have declined in number relatively speaking and even where nominal independence of the small businessman remains, he is often in fact an extension of the larger enterprise. Entrepreneurial society makes different skill and value demands than does large-scale bureaucracy. The former demands a high degree of individual ambition or internalized motivation, a high degree of self control and self denial, and active manipulative skills. The latter requires organizational loyalty, steadiness and stability, and a high degree of teamwork and accommodation to other group members.

The Miller-Swanson hypothesis is that significant differences between families will derive from their belonging to the older declining type of entrepreneurial setting or to the newer bureaucratic setting. The entrepreneurial orientation should be found in families in which the husband owns his own small business or works for an organization with a simple division of labor and small capitalization. Competition and risk taking are still the order of the day in this setting. In contrast, the family with a bureaucratic orientation is one in which the husband works in a large, complex organization where security and financial returns are more system rewards than individual rewards. In other words, there may be greater differences between the integrative setting of the family than between working and middle classes and, at the very least, both social classes should be broken down into these two different types.

The Miller-Swanson findings from the Detroit area sample were not particularly encouraging in supporting their hypothesis. There was some indication that the bureaucratic middle-class mothers were more permissive and did less to internalize controls than did the entrepreneurial middle-class mothers. Overall, however, there was little support for the proposition that entrepreneurial more than bureaucratic mothers trained their children in the direction of an active manipulative orientation toward the world. This failure to confirm the hypothesis may well have been due to inadequate measures, controls, and number of cases.

In spite of the diversity of child rearing practices within a single nation, it has long been popular for some social scientists to talk of national character as reflecting a basic modal personality of a society. In the theorizing of Kardiner, the primary institution of a society is the familial pattern of child rearing.[70] Basic personality is the outcome of the socialization process and,

70. Kardiner, Abram, *et al., The Psychological Frontiers of Society.* Columbia University Press, New York, 1945.

in turn, is the dominant determinant of secondary institutions of religion, folklore, and magic. Kardiner and Linton have analyzed small, primitive societies according to this model. It has remained for McClelland to apply this type of thinking on a grand scale in that he makes variations in achievement motivation his basic personality syndrome, an important determinant of reality systems such as economic institutions, as well as of projective systems.

In his imaginative work, *The Achieving Society,* McClelland relates economic growth and the rise of industrialism to the strength of the need for achievement.[71] Achievement motivation is an internalized drive in which the individual competes both against others and to meet his own standards of excellence. It is a psychological counterpart of Max Weber's doctrine that the Protestant ethic, with its emphasis upon individual responsibility, fostered the capitalistic spirit and capitalistic society. The Weber and the Mc-Clelland thesis stands on its head the Marxian theory that the free market for goods led to the free market in religion and in ideas. McClelland traces the achievement motive to the socialization process. Parents who set high standards for their children and expect self reliance and mastery at an early age will tend to have children with high achievement motivation. Thus the Jewish family expects its sons to get top grades in school from the first grade on. Empirical support for the importance of socialization in inducing the need for striving comes from a small study by Winterbottom.[72] In this investigation the mothers of eight-year old boys were interviewed about their child rearing attitudes and practices, and these results were compared with the scores the boys themselves made in an experimental test of achievement motivation. The evidence supported the hypothesis. McClelland and his colleagues have used this hypothesis to interpret ancient societies by analyzing their folklore and literature, to explain certain aspects of primitive societies by examining the Yale cross-cultural index, to account for entrepreneurial behavior and economic advancement, and to suggest methods for accelerating economic growth in underdeveloped countries.

Typical of the McClelland approach is his study of characteristics of managers and professionals in the United States, Italy, Turkey, and Poland. In the United States a comparison was made of business executives and male college graduates as well as of managers and professional people. Both sets

71. McClelland, D. C., *The Achieving Society.* D. Van Nostrand, Princeton, 1961.
72. Winterbottom, M. R., *The Relation of Childhood Training in Independence to Achievement Motivation.* Doctoral thesis, University of Michigan, 1953.

of comparisons showed higher need for achievement among the entrepreneurs than among the non-entrepreneurs. The four-country comparison again showed the managers scoring higher in achievement motivation in
all countries save Turkey. And American managers had stronger need for
achievement than did the managers in the less developed countries. McClelland concludes that the "need achievement levels reflect the determination
to move ahead economically among those elite groups most responsible for
managing a nation's economy."[73]

Intriguing as the many ramifications are of the achievement hypothesis,
the studies cry for replication and extension with adequate field methodology.
There is almost a complete disregard of sampling design in these pilot investigations. The handful of managers studied (31 in the United States, 68 in
Italy, 17 in Turkey, and 31 in Poland) were not selected on any other basis
than that of practical convenience. In Italy and Turkey they happened to
be the managers in attendance at a management training course. The professionals in Italy were students of law, medicine, and theology from Torino
and students of law and medicine in Palermo. The professionals in Turkey
were from the pedagogy program at a teacher training college, and those
in Poland were priests and educators. The experimentalist bias of the psychologist—that a subject is a subject, is a subject—is still the dominant tradition even when the experimentalists leave their laboratories. A final, fee-
ble gesture toward sampling design was attempted, however, by trying to
get a comparable sample of U.S. managers and professionals matched on age,
position level, and educational background. But they were all from the General Electric Company.

The importance of sampling bias in generalizing about motivational
characteristics of a population is dramatically demonstrated in the work of
Veroff, Feld, and Gurin in checking on achievement motivation of religious
groups.[74] Though McClelland and his colleagues had found that Protestants had higher achievement standards for their children than Catholics,
the nation-wide survey revealed that for the United States as a whole, the
opposite is true: Catholic men tend to have higher need of achievement
scores than do Protestant men. The McClelland studies were probably dealing with a restricted group of prosperous, upper-status people in the North-
east, and a breakdown of the national sample indicated a similar finding for

73. McClelland, D. C., *op. cit.*, p. 266.
74. Veroff, J., S. Feld, and G. Gurin, "Achievement Motivation . . . ," *op. cit.*

this fragment of the population. Moreover, in the nation as a whole, achievement motivation was associated with higher income among Protestants, but was associated with low incomes and large families among Catholics.

The fragmentary and inadequate evidence in the McClelland studies does not mean that his hypothesis is wrong but that it is unproved. An interesting set of findings on a national sample in the United States is reported by Hyman—findings which are consistent with the McClelland theory.[75] When people were asked to choose between risk and security in a job, 60 per cent of factory workers preferred a secure job, even though the income was low, to a risky position with a promising career, whereas only 26 per cent of the professional and executive individuals chose the safer alternative.

Apart from the question of what in fact are the socialization practices in a given culture, or a sub-culture, we still lack compelling evidence on two major issues. (1) How much is the adult personality a product of early socialization practices? (2) To the extent that childhood socialization affects the adult personality, what types of early influences determine given types of adult personality syndromes? The Freudian and neo-Freudian theory that the adult is essentially working out his childhood conflicts is plausible but unproved. The opposed notion that adults have put away their childhood problems and are reacting in terms of present needs and present pressures also has its plausible features. Question (1) will not be answered, however, until we deal with the specifics of Question (2). There are a number of steps which are passed over too quickly in many developmental theories. In the first place, parents in a given type of life, whether working-class, bureaucratic, or agrarian, may not possess in full measure the values which theoretically should go with that way of life. In the second place, they may vary considerably in the skill and thoroughness of their child rearing practices. In the third place, children may react quite differentially to familial socialization. In the fourth place, the effects that are achieved may be trivial for their adult personalities.

In other words, parents may not behave toward their children as theory would have it according to their social roles; or they may so behave but it may have negligible effect upon the immediate personalities of their children; or parents may behave as they are supposed to and children may respond as they are supposed to but, by the time the child becomes an adult, other variables have washed out the childhood effects.

75. Hyman, H. H., "The Value Systems of Different Classes," in *Class, Status, and Power: A Reader in Social Stratification*. Edited by Reinhard Bendix and S. M. Lipset. Free Press, Glencoe, Ill., 1953, pp. 426–441.

Sewell's interesting study some fifteen years ago should have sounded a note of caution over the common assumption that a given pattern of child rearing practices can be used as an indication of personality syndromes.[76] Psychoanalytic theory was utilized to predict that child rearing practices concerning feeding, weaning, bowel and bladder training, and punishment would be significantly related to the personality characteristics of children. Some 165 rural Wisconsin mothers were interviewed at length, and the personality characteristics of their children were measured by projective tests, paper-and-pencil tests, and ratings of behavior by teachers and mothers. The search for significant relationships, however, was spectacularly unsuccessful. The number of significant results were even less than would have been expected by chance. A replication of this investigation by Straus in Ceylon and India was also unsuccessful in predicting from child rearing practices to the personality characteristics of children.[77] If socialization effects are so difficult to detect in the personalities of children, how much more difficult will it be to predict to adult outcomes?

It should be easier to establish relationships between generations in personal values and orientations than to predict the personality syndrome of a generation from the complex dynamics involved in the internalized reactions of children to their experiences in the socialization process. It is possible for one generation to reflect the attitudes of their fathers because these ready-made values in the home are the most easily available frames of reference. No anchoring in complex personality mechanisms is necessary. As we have previously noted, the child growing up in an authoritarian, prejudiced subculture may absorb its ideology without repressing his hatred for his authoritarian father and releasing his aggression against people below him in the social scale.

Thus an explanation in terms of personality is not necessary to account for the social inheritance of attitudes and values from one generation to the next. A simpler explanation can be found in learning theory with its emphasis upon punishment and reward. A large problem for social psychology is to assess the relative weighting of both adaptive learning and of Freudian defense mechanisms in such outcomes of socialization as prejudice, delinquency, jingoism, authoritarianism, and anomie. In general, when attitude and value systems remain stable over generations in spite of new problems

76. Sewell, W. H., "Infant Training and the Personality of the Child," *American Journal of Sociology,* Vol. 58, September, 1952, pp. 150–159.
77. Straus, M. A., "Anal and Oral Frustration in Relation to Sinhalese Personality," *Sociometry,* Vol. 20, March, 1957, pp. 21–31.

and new needs and new information, one suspects that there is a deeper explanation of the Freudian type. In fact, the neo-Freudian analysis of socialization has furnished the best psychological explanation of social stability. Each generation reflects the same values as its predecessors because it has developed the same projective systems out of its frustrations and internal conflict and, in turn, frustrates and socializes its children in the same manner. When, however, values change as if they represented a new adaptation to a changing world, the Freudian explanation is not only parsimonious but downright inadequate. The pessimistic philosopher of society observing people caught up in their old ways, following the same myths of national sovereignty as their forebears, meeting threats at the national level in a reactive manner, will conclude that Freud was right even to his postulation of a death instinct. The behavioral scientist will insist on a scientific study of the matter to see to what extent the irrationality of projective systems and ego defenses is at work and where and how the rifts occur in which adaptive learning takes over.

THE ADULT SOCIALIZATION PROCESS

Though interest in socialization has concentrated on childhood development, an important determinant of adult social behavior is the socialization that takes place when an individual enters a group. This adult molding consists both of the formal orientation, training and indoctrination programs and of the many systems of informal communication which convey the customary group standards and practices of the various sub-systems of the organization. There is often a period of mutual testing by the newcomer and established group members, with the power on the side of the established group members. The natural field experiment of Lieberman demonstrated this power in that workers critical of management and pro-union in orientation became indistinguishable from other supervisors after a year in the role of foremen.[78] Even as adults we are molded into the pattern of the social structure by the forces existing as we take our places in that structure. Field studies could of course investigate the continuity of early and late socialization forces and their consequences. Anthropologists have observed differences in socialization between primitive and complex cultures and report more discontinuity in our total socialization pattern than in primitive cultures.

78. Lieberman, Seymour, *op. cit.*

A central factor in organizational socialization is the commitment to the legitimate sources and symbols of authority. In the feudal period, oaths of allegiance were a major device in securing such commitment. They have survived in our bureaucratic structures, sometimes in fairly literal form, but often in translated version. Even in their old form, they are still effective as is attested by the use Hitler made of them in holding the allegiance of his military forces. Many organizations still require formal pledges, but the most common translation is some action which certifies to the membership-character of the individual in the group. The neophyte, to become a gang member, must often perform some act attesting to his courage. The new worker in a factory gains membership in the informal group of his fellows by immediately accepting in deed as well as in word its standards for productivity. The act of allegiance means psychologically that the new member is adopting a generalized attitude of acceptance of the group norms and that he will govern his specific actions in accordance with their dictates. In the past there has often been a special period of indoctrination in penal institutions to impress upon prisoners the formal authority structure of the institution. On the informal side the older prisoners also set up their own procedures to keep the newcomers loyal to their own kind.

An outstanding example of a field study of adult socialization is the early investigation by Newcomb at Bennington College.[79] The girls entering Bennington came from upper-class homes where the values were much more conservative than those of the college. Most of the girls developed more liberal attitudes in the Bennington climate and obtained more information on public issues to support these attitudes. The average student showed these changes to a moderate degree, but the leaders on campus showed them to a considerable degree. Prestige in the group and movement toward positions of influence were thus associated with the acceptance and internalization of the values of the college community. Some girls, however, were never assimilated into the college pattern of social values, either because of their lack of social skills or their greater attachment to their families and the values dominant in the home. The process of socialization into the adult group is thus not automatic but is related to the personal mode of adaptation of the individual.

The assimilation of the person to a new social structure generally means

79. Newcomb, T. M., *Personality and Social Change:* Attitude Formation in a Student Community. Dryden Press, New York, 1943.

that he will move toward the values of the prestigeful sector of that structure. Merton and Kitt formulated this hypothesis and tested it with respect to soldiers in the American army in World War II.[80] They found confirmation of it in that replacement troops took on the values of the combat veterans rather than those of other military groups.

Research has recently been directed at the problem of socialization into the professions, especially the medical profession. One factor in the cohesion of the medical group may be the long period of apprenticeship of the initiate covering years of training as a medical student and intern. Seeman and Evans tested the attitudes of 42 interns, on the day of their arrival in the hospital and a year later, on items dealing with power differences, social distance, and prestige distinction of the status groups within the hospital.[81] Over the year the interns had changed so that they were more egalitarian with respect to status differences between themselves and the established physicians but less egalitarian with respect to nurses and other subordinate groups. They had taken over the status commitment of the profession and saw themselves as integral members of the ingroup.

THE NATURE AND DETERMINANTS OF MENTAL DISORDER

Psychotic breakdown is a complex process to which biological factors, personality structure, and situational pressures all contribute. The interaction of the precise variables which results in a given psychotic condition is far from understood. The problem is not only one of the gravest practical import, but the study of psychological malfunctioning has significant theoretical implications for the understanding of the nature of basic psychological processes in general.

The pendulum has swung widely over the years from one theory of the etiology of disorder to another. Sometimes the emphasis has been upon heredity, sometimes upon organic lesions, sometimes upon psychogenetic factors, sometimes upon social-psychological causes, and sometimes upon faulty biochemical functionings. Treatment has also varied and has covered a number of practices such as occupational therapy, hypnosis, chemical or

80. Merton, R. K. and A. S. Kitt, "Contributions to the Theory of Reference Group Behavior," in *Continuities in Social Research:* Studies in the Scope and Method of "The American Soldier." Edited by R. K. Merton and P. F. Lazarsfeld. Free Press, Glencoe, Ill., 1950, pp. 40–105.
81. Seeman, Melvin and J. W. Evans, "Apprenticeship and Attitude Change," *American Journal of Sociology,* Vol. 67, January, 1962, pp. 365–378.

electrical shock, psychoanalysis, group therapy, tranquillizers, the manipulation of social roles in the open ward, transitional community living, and the therapeutic community.

In spite of the resources devoted to the problem of mental disorder and in spite of the proliferating research in this area, there has been an incredible backwardness in exploiting survey methodology in investigation of causal factors and of the efficacy of various types of therapies. Before we can understand the etiology of breakdown we need systematic knowledge for five fundamental purposes:

(1) to establish a baseline for the evaluation of causal factors,
(2) to give primary rather than secondary data on the life history,
(3) to give adequate information about social-psychological context,
(4) to extend our knowledge of non-institutionalized psychotics and
(5) to explore the factors conducive to recovery in discharged patients.

(1) We need to know how people suffering from mental illness are similar to and how they differ from those not affected, in psychological attributes, life experiences, social environmental background, and situational stress. At the present time there is no baseline for such a comparison. A given psychogenetic factor such as maternal rejection or faulty role identification will be seized upon as an explanation without an adequate knowledge of how frequent these psychological processes are in the normal population, or how they operate in differing types of personalities. The institutionalized population when studied by itself furnishes an inadequate baseline for evaluating causal processes. Such studies are like running experiments without control groups or control conditions.

(2) In addition to a control baseline, we need to have valid data about the life histories of psychotics. At the present time these are supplied by an historical-clinical method in which an attempt is made to reconstruct from the patients' own account, from the social workers' reports, and from available records, the life story of the patient. This information is fragmentary; it consists not of direct observation but of secondary materials. It obviously suffers from omission and distortion and from a lack of knowledge of the types of omission and distortion. We need studies before breakdown occurs and hence a trend study is required on a panel of individuals of sufficient size to give some cases of mental disturbance over time. This

seems like an extremely ambitious undertaking but the probabilities of break-down are of such a magnitude that a panel study of 10,000 cases should yield valuable information. A beginning has been made in this direction by Hollingshead in an intensive field study of schizophrenia in Puerto Rico. He writes: "Our Puerto Rican study requires that each person drawn in the sample be given a two-and-one-half to three hour psychiatric examination. Whether the examining psychiatrist diagnoses the person as schizophrenic or as having no mental illness, we study him in elaborate detail. The schizo-phrenic person, as well as the one with 'no mental illness'—and other adult members of their households—are interviewed by psychiatric social workers and social scientists in the home, from 110 to 125 hours."[82]

(3) Another objective of systematic studies would be more adequate information about the patterns of social interaction and role interrelation-ships in which breakdown occurs. The contribution of the social pattern to breakdown is difficult to ascertain when the focus of information-getting is on the single individual as the major actor. The psychiatrist generally has no direct knowledge of the family, the friends, the work mates, or the boss of the patient he is treating in his private practice. He has to interpret what these patterns of social relationship are. No wonder, then, that his most in-telligent guesses may be in error. There is usually more information about the hospitalized patient, but again we need to know more of the social pat-ternings and what takes place in them before breakdown occurs. The Hollingshead suggestion for interviews with other members of the household as well as members of the individual's social groupings should be heeded.

We are not attempting to prejudge the significance of social factors in the etiology of mental breakdown. The plausible, commonly accepted belief that the strains of modern urbanized life have led to an increase in psychotic disorder, has received no confirmation from one careful investigation of the problem. In a study of the statistics of admission to mental institutions over the past hundred years, Goldhamer and Marshall found the proportion of people admitted is no greater today than one hundred years ago, save for people over fifty.[83] This higher rate for older people is easily explained by the failure of the modern family to accommodate its aging, afflicted members and the greater institutional facilities available. It is puzzling, moreover, that with less stigma attached to mental disorder, more recognition of psychotic

82. Hollingshead, A. de B., "Some Issues in the Epidemiology of Schizophrenia," *American Sociological Review*, Vol. 26, February, 1961, pp. 5–13.
83. Goldhamer, H. H. and A. W. Marshall, *op. cit.*

symptoms and increased hospital care, there has been no increase in admission rate for people under fifty. One interpretation would be that mental disorder is more biological than social in origin. Research, however, must provide the final answer.

(4) Studies of institutionalized neurotics and psychotics need to be supplemented with studies of people suffering from similar disturbances who are not institutionalized. The commitment to an institution probably selects out certain types of cases and their institutionalization affects the progress of the disease and the recovery, sometimes for the better and sometimes possibly for the worse. The convenience of the institutionalized group for study should not be a decisive reason for limiting investigation of the mentally disturbed to hospitalized patients.

(5) Field methods should be used in follow-up studies of patients released from hospitals and individuals formerly under treatment by psychiatrists in private practice. We need to know more about the differences among discharged patients who are recommitted very soon, patients who make some adjustment but require some further hospitalization, and patients who make a permanent recovery. Studies of this sort are in their infancy and generally suffer from a lack of thorough exploration of the social setting to which the patient returns and of direct information from his new and old role associates.

The need for more study of the outcome of therapy and of factors associated with recovery and recidivism is indicated by the research of Marks, Stauffacher, and Lyle.[84] These investigators utilized 144 measures in trying to predict which of 78 discharged patients would have to return to the hospital within a year. The predictive measures included a battery of psychological tests, interview and behavior ratings by the hospital staff, follow-up observations a month after discharge, and demographic variables. Although about half of the patients did return to the hospital within a year, only one of the 144 predictors showed a significantly correct prognosis—a purely chance result. In other words, all the therapists' judgments, all the psychological tests, and all the staff observations, were useless in predicting recovery.

The current trend in therapy is toward the open ward, the conversion of the whole hospital into a therapeutic community, the open hospital and half-

84. Marks, J., J. C. Stauffacher, and C. Lyle, "Predicting Outcome in Schizophrenia," *Journal of Abnormal and Social Psychology,* Vol. 66, February, 1963, pp. 117–127.

way houses between the hospital and the community.[85] The high rate of recidivism, and studies of the hospital as a social structure not necessarily conducive to recovery, have been influential in reviving the old Tavistock concept of transitional social systems in rehabilitation. The patient is not sent back directly to the stressful world in which he experienced breakdown but to a more protected environment. The sheltered workshop has a long history in the rehabilitation of the physically disabled and is now receiving more attention for the psychologically handicapped. Research evaluation of transitional communities is one of the urgent needs in this field, both for practical and theoretical purposes. An interesting inquiry into the success of the half-way house in rehabilitation was carried out by Meyer and Borgatta.[86] Patients who had the benefit of the program of the Altro Work Shops, where amount of time worked in gainful employment is regulated by the supervising psychiatrist, were compared with patients returned directly to the community. Fewer of the Altro alumni had to be rehospitalized than of the comparison group, but the total numbers were too small to yield statistically significant differences. An examination of the experimental cases revealed that greater exposure to the rehabilitation program was accompanied by greater success, but again the numbers were not large enough to permit generalization.

Field studies can also be helpful in furnishing information about the therapeutic efficacy of the hospital as a social system. Stanton and Schwartz investigated a small mental hospital and focused upon the role systems and their relationship to the behavior of patients.[87] Therapeutic progress of patients was related to the communication system of the institution. The filtering of information through the coding categories of various roles and the subsequent distortions and omissions was a significant variable. At the present time the mental hospital is the subject for similar field investigations, and experimental changes in its structure are being evaluated with respect to the effects upon patients. One interesting departure is the concept of the open hospital, in which patients are given maximum freedom in the development of therapeutic community. These studies not only have prac-

85. Wechsler, Henry and David Landy, eds., "New Pathways from the Mental Hospital," *Journal of Social Issues,* Vol. 16, No. 2, 1960, pp. 1–78.
86. Meyer, H. J. and E. F. Borgatta, *An Experiment in Mental Patient Rehabilitation:* Evaluating a Social Agency Program. Russell Sage Foundation, New York, 1959.
87. Stanton, A. H. and M. S. Schwartz, *The Mental Hospital:* A Study of Institutional Participation in Psychiatric Illness and Treatment. Basic Books, New York, 1954.

tical import but they can contribute to a theoretical understanding of the processes critical to mental disorder.

An effective plea for the use of survey methodology in the study of schizophrenia has been made by Hollingshead, who writes:

> The fact is, we do not know what causes the disease, disorder, or reaction the psychiatrist labels schizophrenia. Epidemiological study may furnish the answer. . . . When we study persons and groups in the socio-cultural environments which enmesh them, we gain new knowledge about their motivations, frustrations, conflicts, joys and sorrows. Systematic and sophisticated study of the ecology of human life may unravel the etiological threads that lead to schizophrenia.[88]

He continues:

> Systematic field study of the processes which give rise to schizophrenia, as well as non-schizophrenic behavior, is indicated at the present time. When this is done, and I think it will be done eventually, socio-cultural factors should be studied along with heredity, biochemical processes, organic results, and psychological mechanisms. The possible etiological effects of each of these factors can be understood only in their concomitant interdependence.[89]

In a pioneering study, Hollingshead and Redlich have taken one step in obtaining field information on mental illness in their attack upon the questions of incidence and treatment.[90] They attempted to achieve a complete psychiatric census of the New Haven metropolitan area by systematic inquiries at psychiatric facilities in New England and New York City, including clinics, hospitals, and private practitioners. Their census is thus of cases of mental illness which had been treated rather than of all mental illnesses. Types of mental illness were then related to the background variable of social class. Five social classes were distinguished on the basis of occupation, education, and residence on the theory that this combined index would reflect different styles of life. Though the investigators reported an inverse relationship between social class and incidence of mental illness, i.e., the higher the class the less the illness, their data, as Miller and Mishler point

88. Hollingshead, A. de B., "Some Issues . . . ," *op. cit.,* p. 9.
89. *Ibid.,* pp. 12–13.
90. Hollingshead, A. de B. and F. C. Redlich, *Social Class and Mental Illness:* A Community Study. John Wiley & Sons, New York, 1958.

out in their excellent review of this Hollingshead-Redlich study, are conclusive on only one point: there is a disproportionate incidence and prevalence of mental illness within the lowest class as compared to the four classes above it.[91] There is no clear and consistent pattern of findings among the upper four classes in terms of their hierarchical arrangement. The major finding is of interest, however, in that it suggests that social influences play a significant role in the etiology of mental disturbances. The lowest social class, constituting a little under one-fifth of the New Haven population, is made up of unskilled and semi-skilled workers of low education—the most deprived group and the most apathetic in organizational and community involvement—in other words, the *lumpen proletariat*.

It is still true that social deprivation was not shown to be a causal factor in the Hollingshead-Redlich study. The simplest explanation is that members of the lowest class are most likely to be institutionalized and publicly listed as mental cases. Myers and Roberts, however, followed the first study and selected 25 cases of mental disorder from the lowest class (Class V) and 25 cases from the lower middle class of salaried white collar, small business men, and skilled workers (Class III).[92] These fifty people were interviewed intensively by a psychiatrist on the research team on at least three occasions, and at least two members of their families were interviewed in their homes. Finally, the therapists of the patients were also interviewed. The external social pressures differed in the two social classes. "Social mobility was associated strongly with the development of psychiatric illnesses in Class III but not in Class V whose adverse economic conditions and isolation from community institutions permeated all aspects of their culture."[93] It was much more difficult for Class V patients to establish childhood identifications or to identify with socially acceptable models than it was for patients in Class III. Those in the latter class had their problems in identification during adolescence. The patients from the lowest class felt neglected, rejected and victimized by circumstances beyond their control. The Class III group was more likely to suffer from guilt and other internal tensions. Myers and Roberts conclude, in part: "Our data suggest that certain life conditions in Class V might be more conducive than those in Class III to the

91. Miller, S. M. and E. G. Mishler, "Social Class, Mental Illness, and American Psychiatry," *Milbank Memorial Fund Quarterly*, Vol. 37, 1959, pp. 174–199.
92. Myers, J. K. and B. H. Roberts, *Family and Class Dynamics in Mental Illnesses*. John Wiley and Sons, New York, 1959.
93. *Ibid.*, p. 265.

isolation and withdrawal of the frustrated patient who develops schizo-phrenia."[94] This is appropriately presented, however, as a hypothesis for future research, in view of the exploratory nature of the study.

Many experimental studies have been carried out on schizophrenic sub-jects to furnish information about their perceptual, intellectual and personal-ity functioning compared to normals. The findings indicate, for example, that schizophrenics condition more readily than normals, they are less stable in their use of concepts, and they utilize concepts in a less contextual fashion and less autonomous manner than normals.[95] In many of these studies, however, there has been an inadequate baseline for comparing mental pa-tients and normals. Sampling design is often neglected and the control group of normals is likely to consist of hospital attendants, nurses, or a hospitalized non-psychiatric group—in short, any set of subjects who can be conven-iently enlisted in the experiment. Matching is sometimes attempted on one or two characteristics. What is clearly needed is a combination of field and experimental methods in which field research builds up more adequate information about the nature of the two universes. Then samples can be drawn and the subjects assigned to experimental conditions as representa-tive of some known population dimension.

PSYCHOLOGICAL BASIS OF GROUPS AND ORGANIZATIONS

The most neglected area of study by psychologists is the behavior of people in organizations and formal group structures. It has been legitimate for psychology to be concerned with the impact of culture upon the individ-ual. At the other end of the scale, there has been rich development of research on the individual in the small informal group. The facts are, how-ever, that most people in complex societies spend most of their waking hours in formal groups and organizations. Field research can give us a tre-mendously expanded conception of human behavior by examining the func-tioning of people in the social systems and sub-systems which their own patterned interdependence creates.

Sociology deals with the abstractions of this patterned interdependence and with the global outcomes of formalized collective behavior. Individual psychology deals with generalized mechanisms of behavior and with their

---

94. *Ibid.*, p. 266.
95. For a review of some of this literature, see Goldman, A. E., "A Comparative-Developmental Approach to Schizophrenia," *Psychological Bulletin*, Vol. 59, No. 1, 1962, pp. 57–69.

integration within the individual, i.e., with his personality. It remains for social psychology to deal with the gap in our knowledge of social behavior. Two approaches have attempted to meet this problem in the past. One studies the fit between organizational functioning and personality structure, e.g., does the bureaucratic structure attract or create bureaucratic personality? This approach is too much of an oversimplification, and there is confusion between the concepts of the social system and the personality system. The functioning of the larger structure is not a matter of the additive functioning of similar personalities. Neither can the organization be regarded as a blown-up representation of the modal personalities of its members, nor can the personal functioning of the individual within it be seen as a miniature picture of the total organizational pattern.

The second approach to bridging the gap between the individual and the social system is through the concept of role. This concept has been of considerable utility, but it has emphasized the common prescriptions for behavior in the social system and has suffered on two counts. First, it does not deal adequately with the meaning of the role in the functioning of the system or of the individual; and second, it abstracts certain behaviors as requirements for the role without dealing with the problem of the actual functional units of behavior in the organization. We need to study the individual in the organization as a sub-system producing various types of role behavior in relation to other organizational members as sub-systems. A fairly similar position to the one here advocated has been formulated by Gross, Mason, and McEachern, whose empirical studies in this area are significant landmarks.[96] They urge that the role concept be developed in terms of individuals to take account of the actual functioning of people placed in specific social structures. They write:

> Another possible reason for the paucity of theoretical hypotheses capable of empirical examination deriving from existing role conceptions is the holistic manner in which the role concept has been defined. Our research experience suggests that when a more differentiated set of concepts are developed to denote subsidiary notions involved in the general conception of role, these microscopic terms may be fruitfully used in theoretical propositions.[97]

96. Gross, N. C., W. S. Mason, and A. W. McEachern, *Explorations in Role Analysis.* John Wiley & Sons, New York, 1958.
97. *Ibid.,* p. 324.

Our proposal, then, is that we regard the behavior of the individual in the organization not as his degree of conformity to role requirements, nor as an expression of his personality, but as one pattern of his functioning. William James once proposed the concept of social *selves* to emphasize the fact that individuals have different patterns of behavior characteristic of their adaptation to different sets of social influences. We are, in effect, applying this notion to the behavior of people in organizations and will refer to the individual's activities when an organizational member as the "organizational self." The organizational self of the person is the meaningful psychological unit or sub-system of the organization. It does not refer to total personality, though it is to some degree affected by personality determinants. Nor does it refer to organizational role as set by formal requirements or expectations from above. It is the characteristic way in which the individual handles his role in the organization. As such, it is affected not only by his personality and the formally set requirements but also by the organizational selves of those around him and by the actual functioning of the immediate parts of the organization with which he is in contact. The notion of informal group structure is not necessarily the equivalent of this concept at the group level, since *informal* requirements are often set in opposition to *formal* ones. The organizational self refers to whatever compromises or integrations are achieved between formal and informal demands.[98]

The work of Elton Mayo and his followers took a long step forward in discovering the small group and its informal standards. The interpretation of this discovery is often, however, a picture of organizations as dichotomous with a basic opposition between the requirements as set by the top echelons and the informal patterns developed by the underlings, with the informal patterns being the stronger. This interpretation has led to a neglect of organizational structure by some who attempt to solve organizational problems by improving interpersonal relations. Similarly, some advocates of group dynamics see the solution in improving group processes at the small group level, ignoring the structures in which such small groups must operate.

The facts of the matter are that the opposition between informal standards and organizational requirements is met by a viable compromise which both the rank and file and the executive of the organization accept and maintain.

98. See also Miller, D. R., "The Study of Social Relations: Situation, Identity and Social Interaction" in *Psychology:* A Study of a Science, Vol. 5. Edited by S. Koch, McGraw-Hill, New York, 1963.

The outside consultant, as a representative of some staff group of an enterprise, is often surprised by the resistance his proposed changes encounter
from various levels of management as well as from the rank and file. He
expects that the men down the line may object to his desires for increasing
productivity but is not prepared for the resistance from operational management. The point is that the foreman and the officers above him have just as
much of a problem with the upsetting of the working arrangements as do
the men. The existing accommodation between the foreman and his men
which keeps the "eager beavers" in check and makes for predictable performance has real advantages for the line management.

Kaye has developed the concept of *interaction modality*—a very similar
formulation to that of the organizational self—from an analysis of a field
study of a large department in an insurance company.[99] In the Kaye analysis,
the key method was intensive interviewing of division managers and their
subordinate supervisors; supplementary information was provided by interviews with all rank-and-file personnel. Kaye found four patterns of interaction modality for division managers: *control, manipulative identification,
withdrawal,* and *projective gratification.*

The *control* pattern was one in which the manager fell back upon rigid
external controls, both in directing his own organizational behavior and in
directing the behavior of others. Any manifestation of impulsivity in his
environment would immediately elicit this pattern. In dealing with his employees, he attempted to help them control themselves. He utilized fully
all the formal organizational devices to get the job done. Though he was
disliked by his employees, he was able to run a tight shop and maintain
productivity.

Manipulative identification, as used by another manager, involved
understanding the feelings and motives of others and attempting to handle
them so as to achieve organizational objectives. He was not primarily concerned with keeping employees happy but with keeping them positively
motivated toward productivity. Nevertheless, his identification with their
needs was sufficiently strong to provide some interpersonal gratification for
them. He gave as well as took. The productivity of his division was high
and he was well liked by rank-and-file workers, though his supervisors were
less positive in their feelings toward him.

---

99. Kaye, C., "Some Effects Upon Organizational Change of the Personality Characteristics of Key Role Occupants." Doctoral thesis, University of Michigan, 1958.

A third type of interaction, *withdrawal,* consisted of reducing the amount of interaction with other organizational members and delineating carefully the restricted areas of interaction. This pattern was evidenced both toward superiors and subordinates, a rejection of authority from above and a projection of anti-authority feelings on those below. It was almost as if this manager were saying: "I hate my boss and my employees must hate me." His refuge was in the technical aspects of his job, so that he was not a political leader but a technical expert. Both the morale and productivity of his division were low.

Finally, the manager following the modality of *projective gratification* utilized his employees to satisfy his own needs for security and approval. He attempted a close, supportive relationship with his people and sought to maximize these interactions. Though he did succeed in establishing warm personal relations with those under him, he was unable to relate effectively to those above him. He was well liked both by his supervisors and workers but his division was low in productivity.

These descriptions of modal patterns of interaction are helpful for the understanding of organizational functioning. Such a wide range of behavior in people supposedly carrying out identical roles is not found at the lowest management level of a business organization. The managers studied by Kaye represented the second level of supervision. Nonetheless, the organization ranked as a tightly structured bureaucracy, and the second level of supervision was fairly low in the organizational hierarchy, with not much freedom for decision-making.

Another study indicating the need for a more detailed and precise description of how role incumbents react in an organizational setting is that of Gross, Mason, and McEachern.[100] This study was based upon a 48 per cent stratified sample of all school superintendents in Massachusetts in 1952–1953. In addition, the investigators interviewed members of the corresponding school boards, so that their total sample consisted of 105 school superintendents and 508 members of school boards. On the majority of items used to describe the roles of the two groups, there were significant differences between the two samples. One part of the investigation concerned role conflict. Superintendents were presented with four situations in which they often encounter incompatible expectations from teachers, school boards, and various relevant groups in the community. These situations had to do

100. Gross, N. C., W. S. Mason, and A. W. McEachern, *op. cit.*

with (1) the hiring and promotion of teachers, (2) salary increases for teachers, (3) the priority given by the superintendent in drawing up the budget for educational needs, and (4) the superintendent's allocation of after-office duties.

The superintendent was asked to indicate one of three possible types of expectations that he perceived each of the 18 relevant groups of individuals would be likely to have toward his own behavior in each of the four situations. He was also asked to indicate which of these expectations were "legitimate" and which were not, and whether sanctions might be employed by the people holding these expectations. For every situation the majority of superintendents perceived conflicting expectations, ranging from 53 per cent on time allocation to 91 per cent on budget recommendations. The investigators then attempted to predict how the various superintendents would resolve these conflicts, i.e., by accepting one set of expectations, by a compromise, or by a position which avoided conforming to either set of conflicting expectations. In addition to the information from the superintendents about the legitimacy of the expectations and the possible sanctions, there was also data for describing the decisions as basically moral in orientation, expedient in orientation, or moral-expedient. In other words, some of the respondents gave great weight to doing what was right as a school superintendent, others were more realistic or interested in keeping the support of people or groups that mattered, and some combined both approaches. Thus, if the moralist saw a set of expectations as legitimate, it was predicted that he would conform to it no matter what the negative sanctions might be. On the other hand, if the respondent had a moral-expedient orientation and one set of expectations was seen as legitimate, whereas its alternative had more sanctions behind it, the prediction was that a compromise solution would be reached. The theory predicted 264 out of 291 conflict solutions. This study is of great interest in that it indicates the many dimensions of the behavioral setting so casually covered by the concept of role. Though the authors introduced considerable simplification in testing their theory, they still had to include the perceived legitimacy of differing sets of expectations, the perceived sanctions which could be invoked, the value orientation of the role incumbent, and various types of resolutions —from avoidance to compromise.

This investigation is of theoretical import in that it attempts to relate the social unit of behavior in a social system to the underlying personality structure. In other words, the behavior of an individual occupying a role is seen as the interaction of his perceptions of the demands of the situation and his basic value orientation—a personality dimension. There was no systematic attempt, however, to link the social unit of behavior to the larger system of which it is a part. Perception of the legitimacy of demands is the only tie to the larger structure. Gross and his colleagues are on sound ground, however, in their plea that the general concept of role be replaced with a family of differentiated concepts. They suggest the concept of "role sector" to give specification to the aspect of the role under consideration—the concept of expectation as an evaluative standard, the concept of role behavior as the actual behavior as distinct from the evaluative standard, the legitimacy of role expectations, and the differentiation between intra- and inter-role conflict. Finally, they inquire into the differences in role expectation of different role definers; for example, the definition by an incumbent of a focal position and by the incumbent of a counter position.

INDIVIDUAL INVOLVEMENT AND ORGANIZATIONAL NORMS

In studying the behavior of individuals in organizations, three basic variables need to be identified and measured. Allport has conceptualized two of them as "potency of involvement" and "relevance of system norms."[101] Potency of involvement has to do with the total psychological investment of the individual in the system. A large number of factors can contribute to this involvement, such as internalization of organizational goals, the fit between the individual's objectives and organizational goals, specific rewards from participation, and the lack of alternatives for need satisfactions. Allport and his students have measured potency of involvement through the principle of negative causation. They confronted the individual with the possibility of the collapse of the system, or the situation he would be in if he had to leave it, and asked him about the amount of effort he would exert to maintain the system. In other words, they tried to get at the degree to which the individual's own way of life is tied to the existence of a given social structure. Relevance is the perceived appropriateness of a given belief to action for the maintenance of the system.

"Legitimacy" can be discussed in relation to involvement and relevance if we define legitimacy as the extent to which the individual accepts the norms of the subgroup or the directives of the organizational leaders as

---

101. Allport, F. H., "A Structuronomic Conception of Behavior: Individual and Collective," *Journal of Abnormal and Social Psychology,* Vol. 64, No. 1, 1962, pp. 3–30.

rightful injunctions which people should obey. Thus, legitimacy cuts across organizations and groups and is the recognition by the individual that there are rules of the game which everyone should observe. This generalized recognition of normative rules is then tied to any system in which the individual sees himself as a participant. As long as there is a minimum of involvement, the individual accepts the directives of properly constituted authority. As his potency of involvement increases, he will be more likely to follow such directives consistently and enthusiastically. Relevance has to do with the limits within which legitimacy holds. The foreman is within his constituted authority when he asks his workers to give priority to one task assignment rather than another, but his directions to them about reporting to work an hour earlier in the morning are usually not relevant to his authority and will probably not be considered legitimate orders.

Perceptions of legitimacy will vary especially as to the appropriateness of organizational directives outside the confines of the organization. For example, in a study of political behavior in the Detroit area, Katz and Eldersveld found that even in unions heavily oriented toward political action, the members were fairly equally divided about whether the position of the union and its leaders had any relevance to the way they should vote.[102] Hence, it is important for an understanding of the behavior of people as members of an organization to have data both on their potency of involvement and their conceptions of the relevance and legitimacy of organizational norms and directives to given areas of belief and action.

The concepts of legitimacy and relevance have another important implication for the behavior of people within systems. They are linked to the individual's sense of responsibility for organizational behavior. Since most of the decisions are made at the executive level, people feel a very limited sense of responsibility both with respect to organizational outcomes and to their own actions. The legitimate authorities are to blame. This shifting of responsibility can be pushed even further, as in the case of individual officials who say that we are only individuals and the whole authority structure or "system" itself is to blame. Here we face a social determinism in which the many individual acts contributing to an organizational outcome are heavily influenced by the structure and functioning of the system. The

---

102. Katz, Daniel and Samuel Eldersveld, "Political Behavior in the Detroit Area" (unpublished Detroit Area report).

responsibility is that of the system and it is difficult in many instances to assess individual responsibility.

Our purpose is not to deal with the ethical problem involved but to point out that the limited sense of responsibility associated with legitimacy can have results not desired by the overwhelming majority of an organization's members. Many wars have this character. Because of its power, legitimacy is often exploited in immoral ways by the few to control the many. The extreme example is the Nazi leadership in Germany, which tried to throw a legal cloak over its most anti-social actions to secure acceptance by a nation of people whose organizational selves dominated their personal values.

PREDICTABLE BEHAVIOR AS A BASIC ORGANIZATIONAL OBJECTIVE

To insure coordinated collective action, social systems employ many devices to produce stable and predictable behavior among their members. The variability of the performance of an individual in assuming his role must be reduced, and the variability between people in similar roles must also be reduced. Sustained and consistent effort is the basic requirement. The three factors contributing to predictable performance derive from the task requirements themselves, the shared values of the work group, and the rule enforcements of the legitimate authority structure. The differential weighting of these factors will account for the consistency, the level and the quality of performance, and the satisfactions accruing to system members. The more the requirements grow out of the task itself and the shared values of the immediate group, the greater the quality of individual performance and the higher the level of motivation and satisfaction. On the other hand, these two factors alone do not insure the consistent coordinated activity necessary for overall organizational effectiveness. The quality of one man's performance may be greater than needed, or the time taken to produce quality may slow the overall effort. Hence, there is always a resort to rules and their enforcement in large organizations.

For over fifteen years the Michigan Survey Research Center has been engaged in a program of research on the behavior of people in organizations. It has made a beginning in analyzing the types of motivation operative in organizations, their determinants and outcomes. It has also addressed itself to the problem of organizational effectiveness and has gathered some material bearing on the problem of the effects of the differential weighting of the three conditions for collective effort: the task requirements, shared values of the work group, and rule enforcement. The early results of this program have been summarized in good part in Likert's *New Patterns of Management*.[103]

System rewards and motivational patterns. Just as the assessment of individual responsibility for organizational behavior is difficult in a complex social system, so too is the allocation of rewards on an individual basis. The return to people in perquisites, income, and intangible satisfactions is tied to their membership in the system or sub-system more than to their individual differential performances. To maintain membership, some minimum level of performance is necessary but in complex organizations, system rewards for membership are the operating practice for the majority of the members. For example, the conditions of work are dependent upon where and how a sub-system is housed. If there is a new building for a unit of the organization, any member of that unit enjoys the advantages of the building. Air conditioning of the plant is not apportioned on the basis of individual performance. Recreational facilities for the organization are also system advantages and are not allocated on the basis of individual achievement. Perquisites and fringe benefits follow the same principle; a group insurance rate is neither raised for the less productive member nor lowered for the more productive member. In the very nature of the case, many rewards have to apply to all members of the system or of some functional sub-system. This is even true of wages and salaries. For rank-and-file workers, the major differential in income is not how productive and efficient the individual is but what sub-system he belongs to. The differentials between automobile workers in Detroit and railroad workers in the Midwest are greater than the differentials within the ranks of either group. Moreover, differentials within groups according to individual contribution have been difficult to work out, so that the dominant picture is one of a standard rate for a given classification of workers, i.e., for membership in a sub-system. Work requiring more responsibility, more training, more individual resourcefulness, intellect, or other capacity, is more subject to variation in reward on an individual basis. Again, however, the differentials within a sub-system for individuals are less than the differentials across sub-systems. The salary differences among professors of the same seniority category in a university

103. Likert, Rensis, *New Patterns of Management*. McGraw-Hill, New York, 1961.

are much smaller than the differences between professors and scientists in industry.

Because common system rewards accord with the nature of bureaucratic structure more than do differentiated individual rewards, incentive wage systems have been difficult to apply in modern industrial organizations. Payne surveyed 316 companies over a fifteen-year period and found that 78 per cent of the incentive wage systems failed or encountered serious difficulties.[104] Stogdill, in his review of the literature, reports that most of the studies on pay incentives reach similar conclusions.[105]

In any serious study of the morale and motivation of individuals in large organizations, a distinction must be made between *motivation to stay in the system* and motivation to perform at a high level of one's capacity in that system. Moreover, the motivation to perform must further be broken down into the *willingness to meet organizational requirements* and the *desire to go beyond the line of duty* and contribute to organizational goals. For example, a nurse in the hospital may perform her assigned duties perfectly and thus meet organizational requirements. Another nurse may go beyond this role designation to save a patient's life. The nurses and the other personnel in the eastern hospital who for several days fed the vomiting infants milk containing salt instead of sugar, were following their organizational assignments. None of them tasted the milk or did anything to find out what was going on. Though nurses, like soldiers, are trained to stick to their roles, organizations which divorce their objectives from the motivations of their members court disaster. Soldiers are singled out for the highest awards when they have performed beyond the call of duty.

These three patterns of motivated activity—to stay in the system, to meet requirements, and to go beyond requirements—are not necessarily activated by the same set of organizational conditions and rewards. As already indicated, system rewards hold the individual in the organization to some acceptable minimal level of performance. Exceptional performance at the prescribed job is facilitated by the challenging nature of the job itself, favorable norms of the work group, and effective leadership. The spontaneous and innovative acts beyond the call of duty, and the many cooperative behaviors

104. Ross, R. B., ed., *Proceedings:* Annual Fall Conference on Principles, Methods and Techniques for Increasing Productivity and Improving Human Relations. Society for the Advancement of Management (for Payne Report), New York, 1951.
105. Stogdill, R. M., *Individual Behavior and Group Achievement:* A Theory, The Experimental Evidence. Oxford University Press, Fair Lawn, N.J., 1959.

with one's fellows not prescribed by the organization, are more a matter of the internalization of organizational goals or the goals of the relevant substructures. Such internalization comes about through group participation in decisions and rewards and the appeal of the organizational mission to the individual's own values and self-concept.

This, in brief, is a differential theory of types of motivation necessary for effective organizational functioning. The research evidence for its support is limited, but it indicates the role of field studies in the development of our knowledge. Reference has been made to the difficulty of utilizing pay incentives to increase performance, but there is little empirical evidence to support the plausible hypothesis that good wage scales and system benefits decrease turnover and absenteeism. One suggestive piece of evidence did appear in a study of clerical employees in a large insurance company.[106] The most productive workers were not those who placed a high premium on system benefits but those who found their jobs more challenging. In a study of a manufacturing plant, the workers placed more emphasis upon job security than upon pay as an important factor in their working at that plant.[107] Security came first and good treatment by the company second, whereas earnings were eighth in ranking. Employees apparently were thinking of system advantages when asked about working for the particular company, but unfortunately it was not possible to relate these responses to individual productivity, absenteeism, or turnover.

Most studies of worker morale show a high relationship between the complexity and variety of the job and intrinsic job satisfaction. Generally, complexity and variety go with higher pay and privilege so it is difficult to interpret these findings according to our more differentiated motivational analysis. In a study by Morse, however, it was possible to hold the factor of earnings constant; the relationship between the challenge of varied work and intrinsic job satisfaction still held for a sample of 580 clerical employees.[108]

106. Katz, Daniel, Nathan Maccoby, and N. C. Morse, *Productivity, Supervision and Morale in an Office Situation.* Survey Research Center, University of Michigan, Ann Arbor, 1950.
107. Katz, Daniel and R. L. Kahn, "Some Recent Findings in Human Relations Research," in *Readings in Social Psychology.* 2nd ed. Edited by G. E. Swanson, T. M. Newcomb, and E. L. Hartley. Henry Holt, New York, 1952, pp. 650–655.
108. Morse, N. C., *Satisfactions in the White-Collar Job.* Institute for Social Research, University of Michigan, Ann Arbor, 1953.

The implications of these findings in industry with respect to the validity of the ego motivations of self-determination and self-expression are clear. People find a great deal of gratification in the expression of their skills, in the sense of accomplishment from successful performance, and in the feeling of autonomy in making decisions of their own. Moreover, this occurs in spite of the deadening of expectations about participation in the work process in large-scale mechanized production.

Corroborative findings have been reported from a national sample in a study in which the focus was upon mental health. Employed males were asked about their satisfactions and dissatisfactions with their jobs and their responses were coded in terms of intrinsic gratifications and extrinsic attractions. The intrinsic category included the interest, variety, and the skills involved; the opportunities for the expression of responsibility, independence, and competence; and the potential the job afforded for the gratification of interpersonal and friendship needs. The extrinsic reasons included earnings, job security, and working conditions. The results showed that the degree of satisfaction with a job was associated with the fulfillment of ego needs. "Gratification in the job only in extrinsic terms occurs disproportionately among those who are generally dissatisfied with the job."[109]

Other determinants of the level of job performance have been suggested by research as centering in leadership practices and group norms. In the famous Hawthorne experiment, both of these factors were operative as well as a host of others. Group norms have been the target of the successful efforts to raise productivity, as reported by Bavelas[110] and Koch and French.[111] Seashore has demonstrated that a cohesive group can either raise or lower productivity depending upon the group norms.[112] Utilizing survey data involving several thousand workers in a large factory, Seashore found that work groups highly attractive to their members tended to be either above or below production standards, whereas less cohesive groups clustered around the average standard.

---

109. Gurin, Gerald, Joseph Veroff, and Sheila Feld, *op. cit.,* p. 151.
110. Maier, N. R. F., *Psychology in Industry:* A Psychological Approach to Industrial Problems. Houghton Mifflin, Boston, 1946 (Bavelas experiment reported, pp. 264–266).
111. Koch, L. and J. R. P. French, "Overcoming Resistance to Change," *Human Relations,* Vol. 1, No. 4, 1948, pp. 512–532.
112. Seashore, S. E., *Group Cohesiveness in an Industrial Work Group.* Institute for Social Research, University of Michigan, Ann Arbor, 1954.

The facets of leadership making for higher group performance have seen some study. Two dimensions of supervision—task orientation and socio-emotional orientation—have both shown positive relationships with productivity, depending upon the area of freedom for the leader in exercising these functions. In a company in which the first-line supervisor had little opportunity to give technical direction because of the tightness of structure, Katz, Maccoby, and Morse found that the leaders stressing the socio-emotional aspects of their roles had the higher producing work groups.[113] In this instance, a genuine concern with worker needs and a general rather than a close pattern of supervision were effective. Among railroad section gangs, however, where there was considerable freedom for task direction by foremen not constrained by a methods department, the effective leaders were those who had superior technical skills.[114]

The leadership dimension in organizational structures is more complicated than these two dimensions, in that the leader of a group must not only deal with his own subordinates but must be able to relate well to his superiors. Standing at the boundary of a sub-system, he is in effect the integrating tie with other sub-systems. Pelz, in a study of a large utility, has shown that the effective leader at lower levels is the man who is not only able to understand his subordinates but can also represent their needs effectively to the echelon to which he reports.[115] Likert has developed a related concept of management, in which each officer in the hierarchy is regarded as a linking pin in the organization.[116] He belongs to two organizational families—he and his men are one and he and his coordinate officers and their superior another. Full utilization of group process in these organizational families can maximize a two-way flow of communication in the organization and can integrate its many sub-units.

Research data concerning the methods for producing internalization of organizational objectives and sub-goals are scarce. McGregor reports that the Scanlon Plan, involving profit-sharing and participation in decision-making, has had the results of motivating employees to activities far beyond

113. Katz, Daniel, Nathan Maccoby, and N. C. Morse, *op. cit.*

114. Katz, Daniel, *et al., Productivity, Supervision and Morale Among Railroad Workers.* Survey Research Center, University of Michigan, Ann Arbor, 1951.

115. Pelz, D., "Influence, a Key to Effective Leadership in the First-Line Supervisor." *Personnel,* Vol. 29, 1952, pp. 209–217.

116. Likert, Rensis, *op. cit.*

organizational requirements because the company is, in reality, theirs.[117] Though controlled studies of the Scanlon Plan have not been reported, the work of the Tavistock group in a textile mill in India and coal mines in Great Britain does supply some relevant evidence. Rice reorganized the work in an Indian mill, following the unsuccessful introduction of new weaving looms, so that the group had a meaningful cycle of work and a group life centering about its work objective.[118] The outcome was increased productivity as well as increased spontaneous behavior beyond the call of duty. Trist and his colleagues have had the same experience in a reorganization of the work process in some British coal fields.[119] By giving the miners a sense of participation in their own work activity and a sense of responsibility for group performance, the output was markedly improved and, in addition, the men went out of their way to keep the working place clean and orderly for the next shift.

Organizational typology. We know that organizations differ in many aspects: in size, in degree of role differentiation, in the locus and exercise of power, in separation or consolidation of executive and legislative sub-systems, in more vs. less inclusion of the personalities of staff, in communication systems, in degree of openness of boundaries to the external world, in dependence upon external structures, in type of input and output, and in type of export. But we have not done enough in empirical, quantitative descriptions of what these concepts mean with respect to the behavior of people in specific organizations. Organizational theory will profit if the intervening variables represented by human beings in interaction are systematically studied. It is possible to conceptualize organizations and social systems with respect to environmental conditions and system outputs. But it is also possible to study people as they function in organization settings. The micro-approach is not obviated because of the advances in the macro-approach. In fact, we may have pushed the division of the disciplines of sociology and social psychology too far in holding that what is studied by one science is its own private subject matter. The social world is not that neatly divided and

117. McGregor, Douglas, *The Human Side of Enterprise.* McGraw-Hill, New York, 1960.
118. Rice, A. K., *Productivity and Social Organization:* The Ahmedabad Experiment. Tavistock Publications, London, 1958.
119. Trist, E., *et al., Organizational Choice.* Tavistock Publications, London, 1963.

science should not waste energy on jurisdictional disputes. The study of people outside the laboratory is the proper subject matter of all behavioral science. In his excellent review of recent developments in social psychology, Brewster Smith tellingly makes the point that, in spite of some persisting disciplinary parochialism, both psychologists and sociologists have contributed to a growing area of research implementing the body of theory in social psychology which began with G. H. Mead and C. H. Cooley.[120] This theory is directed at "the processes of symbolic interaction through which the raw biological stuff of human potentiality is transmitted into human nature to provide the psychological basis for organized society." The focal problems of social psychology remain those of socialization and those "that have to do with the interrelations of already socialized persons in social contexts."[121]

120. Smith, M. B., "Recent Developments in the Field of Social Psychology," *Annals of the American Academy of Political and Social Science,* Vol. 338, November, 1961, pp. 137–143.
121. *Ibid.,* p. 137.

Bibliography

Adorno, T. W., *et al., The Authoritarian Personality.* Harper & Bros., New York, 1950, chap. 2.

Allport, F. H., "A Structuronomic Conception of Behavior: Individual and Collective," *Journal of Abnormal and Social Psychology,* Vol. 64, No. 1, 1962, pp. 3–30.

Anderson, H. E., *The Young Child at Home.* Appleton-Century-Crofts, New York, 1936.

Axelrod, Morris, "Urban Structure and Social Participation," *American Sociological Review,* Vol. 21, February, 1956, pp. 13–18.

Berelson, B. R., P. F. Lazarsfeld, and W. W. McPhee, *Voting:* A Study of Opinion Formation in a Presidential Campaign. University of Chicago Press, Chicago, 1954.

Bronfenbrenner, Urie, "Socialization and Social Class Through Time and Space," in *Readings in Social Psychology,* 3rd ed. Edited by E. E. Maccoby, T. M. Newcomb, and E. L. Hartley. Henry Holt, New York, 1958, pp. 400–425.

Campbell, Angus, *et al., The American Voter.* John Wiley & Sons, New York, 1960.

Campbell, Angus, Gerald Gurin, and W. E. Miller, *The Voter Decides.* Row, Peterson, Evanston, Ill, 1954.

Centers, Richard, *The Psychology of Social Class:* A Study of Class Consciousness. Princeton University Press, Princeton, 1949, chap. 2.

Cohen, A. K., *Delinquent Boys:* The Culture of the Gang. Free Press, Glencoe, Ill., 1955.

Cohen, A. K. and J. F. Short, "Research in Delinquent Subcultures," *Journal of Social Issues,* Vol. 14, No. 3, 1958, pp. 20–37.

Cohen, A. R., "Attitudinal Consequences of Induced Discrepancies Between Cognitions and Behavior," *Public Opinion Quarterly,* Vol. 24, Summer, 1960, pp. 297–318.

Converse, Phillip E., "The Shifting Role of Class in Political Attitudes and Behavior," in *Readings in Social Psychology,* 3rd ed. Edited by E. E. Maccoby, T. M. Newcomb, and E. L. Hartley. Henry Holt, New York, 1958, pp. 388–399.

Cook, S. W., "Desegregation: A Psychological Analysis," *The American Psychologist,* Vol. 12, 1957, pp. 1–13.

Crockett, H. J., Jr., "The Achievement Motive and Differential Occupational Mobility in the United States," *American Sociological Review,* Vol. 27, April, 1962, pp. 191–204.

Davis, Allison, "Socialization and Adolescent Society," in *Adolescence Forty-Third Yearbook, Part I.* Edited by Nelson B. Henry. University of Chicago Press, Chicago, 1944, chap. 11.

Davis, Allison and R. J. Havighurst, "Social Class and Color Differences in Child-Rearing," *American Sociological Review,* Vol. 11, December, 1946, pp. 698–710.

Dean, D. G., "Alienation: Its Meaning and Measurement," *American Sociological Review,* Vol. 26, October, 1961, pp. 753–758.

Ericson, M. C., 'Social Status and Child-Rearing Practices," in *Readings in Social Psychology,* 1st ed. Edited by T. M. Newcomb and E. L. Hartley. Henry Holt, New York, 1947, pp. 494–501.

Festinger, L., *A Theory of Cognitive Dissonance.* Row, Peterson, Evanston, Ill., 1957.

Goldhamer, H. H. and A. W. Marshall, *Psychosis and Civilization:* Two Studies in the Frequency of Mental Disease. Free Press, Glencoe, Ill., 1953.

Goldman, A. E., "A Comparative-Developmental Approach to Schizophrenia," *Psychological Bulletin,* Vol. 59, No. 1, 1962, pp. 57–69.

Gross, N. C., W. S. Mason and A. W. McEachern, *Explorations in Role Analysis:* Studies of the School Superintendent's Role. John Wiley & Sons, New York, 1958.

Gurin, Gerald, Joseph Veroff, and Sheila Feld, *Americans View Their Mental Health.* Basic Books, New York, 1960.

Heider, Fritz, *The Psychology of Interpersonal Relations.* John Wiley & Sons, New York, 1958.

Hollingshead, A. de B., "Some Issues in the Epidemiology of Schizophrenia," *American Sociological Review,* Vol. 26, February, 1961, pp. 5–13.

Hollingshead, A. de B. and F. C. Redlich, *Social Class and Mental Illness:* A Community Study. John Wiley & Sons, New York, 1958.

Hyman, H. H., "The Value Systems of Different Classes," in *Class, Status, and Power:* A Reader in Social Stratification. Edited by Reinhard Bendix and S. M. Lipset. Free Press, Glencoe, Ill., 1953, pp. 426–441.

Hyman, H. H. and P. B. Sheatsley, "The Authoritarian Personality—A Methodological Critique," in *Studies in the Scope and Method of 'The Authoritarian Personality.'* Edited by Richard Christie and Marie Jahoda. Free Press, Glencoe, Ill., 1954, pp. 50–122.

Inkeles, A. and D. J. Levinson, "National Character," in *Handbook of Social Psychology,* Vol. 2. Edited by Gardner Lindzey. Addison-Wesley, Reading, Mass., 1954, pp. 977–1020.

Jones, A. W., *Life, Liberty and Property:* A Story of Conflict and a Measurement of Conflicting Rights. J. B. Lippincott, Philadelphia, 1941.

Kardiner, Abram, *et al., The Psychological Frontiers of Society.* Columbia University Press. New York, 1945.

Katz, Daniel and R. L. Kahn, "Some Recent Findings in Human Relations Research," in *Readings in Social Psychology,* 2nd ed. Edited by G. E. Swanson, T. M. Newcomb, and E. L. Hartley. Henry Holt, New York, 1952.

Katz, Daniel, Nathan Maccoby, and N. C. Morse, *Productivity, Supervision and Morale in an Office Situation.* Survey Research Center, University of Michigan, Ann Arbor, 1950.

Katz, Daniel, *et al., Productivity, Supervision and Morale Among Railroad Workers.* Survey Research Center, University of Michigan, Ann Arbor, 1951.

Katz, Daniel and Samuel Eldersveld, "Political Behavior in the Detroit Area," (unpublished Detroit Area report).

Katz, Elihu and P. F. Lazarsfeld, *Personal Influence:* The Part Played by People in the Flow of Mass Communications. Free Press, Glencoe, Ill., 1955, chap. 2.

Kaye, C., "Some Effects Upon Organizational Change of the Personality Characteristics of Key Role Occupants." Doctoral thesis, University of Michigan, 1958.

Key, V. O., Jr., *Public Opinion and American Democracy*. Knopf, New York, 1961.

Kinsey, A. C., W. B. Pomeroy, and C. E. Martin, *Sexual Behavior in the Human Male*. W. B. Saunders, Philadelphia, 1948.

Kinsey, A. C., *et al.*, *Sexual Behavior in the Human Female*. W. B. Saunders, Philadelphia, 1953.

Klatskin, E. H., "Shifts in Child Care Practices in Three School Classes Under an Infant Care Program of Flexible Methodology," *American Journal of Orthopsychiatry*, Vol. 22, 1952, pp. 52–61.

Koch, L. and J. R. P. French, "Overcoming Resistance to Change," *Human Relations*, Vol. 1, No. 4, 1948, pp. 512–532.

Kornhauser, A. W., "Analysis of Class Structure of Contemporary American Society," in *Industrial Conflict:* A Psychological Interpretation. Edited by G. W. Hartmann and T. M. Newcomb. Dryden Press, New York, 1939, pp. 199–264.

Lazarsfeld, P. F., Bernard Berelson, and Hazel Gaudet, *The People's Choice:* How the Voter Makes up His Mind in a Presidential Campaign, 2nd ed. Columbia University Press, New York, 1948.

Lenski, G. E., *The Religious Factor:* A Sociological Study of Religion's Impact on Political and Family Life. Doubleday, New York, 1961.

Lieberman, Seymour, "The Effects of Changes in Roles on the Attitudes of Role Occupants," *Human Relations*, Vol. 9, No. 4, 1956, pp. 385–402.

Likert, Rensis, *New Patterns of Management*. McGraw-Hill, New York, 1961.

Lipset, S. M., "Democracy and Working-Class Authoritarianism," *American Sociological Review*, Vol. 24, August, 1959, pp. 482–501.

McClelland, D. C., *The Achieving Society*. D. Van Nostrand, Princeton, 1961.

McClosky, Herbert, "Conservatism and Personality," *American Political Science Review*, Vol. 52, December, 1958, pp. 27–45.

McGregor, Douglas, *The Human Side of Enterprise*. McGraw-Hill, New York, 1960.

Maccoby, E. E., J. P. Johnson, and R. M. Church, "Community Integration and the Social Control of Juvenile Delinquency," *Journal of Social Issues*, Vol. 14, No. 3, 1958, pp. 38–51.

Maier, N. R. F., *Psychology in Industry:* A Psychological Approach to Industrial Problems. Houghton Mifflin, Boston, 1946.

Marks, J., J. C. Stauffacher, and C. Lyle, "Predicting Outcome in Schizophrenia," *Journal of Abnormal and Social Psychology*, Vol. 66, February 1963, pp. 117–127.

Merton, R. K., *Social Theory and Social Structure:* Toward the Codification of Theory and Research. Free Press, Glencoe, Ill., 1949.

Merton, R. K. and A. S. Kitt, "Contributions to the Theory of Reference Group Behavior," in *Continuities in Social Research:* Studies in the Scope and Method of "The American Soldier." Edited by R. K. Merton and P. F. Lazarsfeld. Free Press, Glencoe, Ill., 1950, pp. 40–105.

Meyer, H. J. and E. F. Borgatta, *An Experiment in Mental Patient Rehabilitation:* Evaluating a Social Agency Program. Russell Sage Foundation, New York, 1959.

Miller, D. R., "The Study of Social Relations: Situation, Identity, and Social Interaction" in *Psychology:* A Study of a Science, Vol. 5. Edited by S. Koch. McGraw-Hill, New York, 1963.

Miller, D. R. and G. E. Swanson, *The Changing American Parent:* A Study in the Detroit Area. John Wiley & Sons, New York, 1958.

Miller, D. R., *et al., Inner Conflict and Defense*. Henry Holt, New York, 1960.

Miller, S. M. and E. G. Mishler, "Social Class, Mental Illness, and American Psychiatry," *Milbank Memorial Fund Quarterly,* Vol. 37, 1959, pp. 174–199.

Morse, N. C., *Satisfactions in the White-Collar Job*. Institute for Social Research, University of Michigan, Ann Arbor, 1953.

Myers, J. K. and B. H. Roberts, *Family and Class Dynamics in Mental Illness*. John Wiley & Sons, New York, 1959.

Newcomb, T. M., *Personality and Social Change:* Attitude Formation in a Student Community. Dryden Press, New York, 1943.

Newcomb, T. M., *The Acquaintance Process*. Holt, Rinehart & Winston, New York, 1961.

Osgood, C. E., "Cognitive Dynamics in the Conduct of Human Affairs," *Public Opinion Quarterly,* Vol. 24, Summer, 1960, pp. 341–365.

Pelz, D., "Influence, a Key to Effective Leadership in the First-Line Supervisor," *Personnel,* Vol. 29, 1952, pp. 209–217.

Pettigrew, T. F., ed., "Desegregation Research in the North and South," *Journal of Social Issues,* Vol. 15, No. 4, 1959, pp. 1–71.

Prothro, E. T., "Ethnocentrism and Anti-Negro Attitudes in the Deep South," *Journal of Abnormal and Social Psychology,* Vol. 47, January, 1952, pp. 105–108.

Reichard, S. K., Florine Livson, and P. G. Petersen, *Aging and Personality:* A Study of 87 Older Men. John Wiley & Sons, New York, 1962.

Reid, I. de A. and E. L. Ehle, "Leadership Selection in Urban Locality Areas," *Public Opinion Quarterly,* Vol. 14, No. 2, 1950, pp. 262–284.

Reiss, A. J. and A. L. Rhodes, "Distribution of Juvenile Delinquency in the Social Class Structure," *American Sociological Review,* Vol. 26, October, 1961, pp. 720–732.

Rice, A. K., *Productivity and Social Organization:* The Ahmedabad Experiment. Tavistock Publications, London, 1958.

Rokeach, Milton, "On the Unity of Thought and Belief," *Journal of Personality,* Vol. 25, 1956, pp. 224–250.

Ross, R. B., ed., *Proceedings:* Annual Fall Conference on Principles, Methods and Techniques for Increasing Productivity, Reducing Costs and Improving Human Relations. Society for the Advancement of Management (for Payne Report), New York, 1951.

Sagara, Moriji and Tadasu Oyama, "Experimental Studies on Figural Aftereffects in Japan," *Psychological Bulletin,* Vol. 54, 1957, pp. 327–338.

Schanck, R. L., "A Study of a Community and Its Groups and Institutions Conceived of as Behaviors of Individuals," *Psychological Monographs,* Vol. 43, No. 2, 1932.

Sears, R. R., E. E. Maccoby, and H. Levin, *Patterns of Child Rearing*. Row, Peterson,

Evanston, Ill., 1957.

Seashore, S. E., *Group Cohesiveness in an Industrial Work Group*. Institute for Social Research, University of Michigan, Ann Arbor, 1954.

Seeman, Melvin and J. W. Evans, "Apprenticeship and Attitude Change," *American Journal of Sociology*, Vol. 67, January, 1962, pp. 365–378.

Sewell, W. H., "Infant Training and the Personality of the Child," *American Journal of Sociology*, Vol. 58, September, 1952, pp. 150–159.

Sewell, W. H., "Social Class and Childhood Personality," *Sociometry*, Vol. 24, December, 1961, pp. 340–356.

Smith, M. B., "Recent Developments in the Field of Social Psychology," *Annals of the American Academy of Political and Social Science*, Vol. 338, November, 1961, pp. 137–143.

Stanton, A. H. and M. S. Schwartz, *The Mental Hospital:* A Study of Institutional Participation in Psychiatric Illness and Treatment. Basic Books, New York, 1954.

Stogdill, R. M., *Individual Behavior and Group Achievement:* A Theory, The Experimental Evidence. Oxford University Press, Fair Lawn, N.J., 1959.

Stouffer, S. A., *Communism, Conformity and Civil Liberties:* A Cross-Section of the Nation Speaks Its Mind. Doubleday, New York, 1955.

Straus, M. A., "Anal and Oral Frustration in Relation to Sinhalese Personality," *Sociometry*, Vol. 20, March, 1957, pp. 21–31.

Tannenbaum, A. S. and R. L. Kahn, *Participation in Union Locals*. Row, Peterson, Evanston, Ill., 1958.

Titus, H. E. and E. P. Hollander, "The California F Scale in Psychological Research: 1950–1955," *Psychological Bulletin*, Vol. 54, 1957, pp. 47–64.

Trist, E., *et al.*, *Organizational Choice*. Tavistock Publications, London, 1963.

Valen, H. and D. Katz, *Political Parties in Norway*. Tavistock Publications, London, 1964.

Veroff, Joseph, S. Feld and G. Gurin, "Achievement Motivation and Religious Background," *American Sociological Review*, Vol. 27, April, 1962, pp. 205–217.

Veroff, Joseph, *et al.*, "The Use of Thematic Apperception to Assess Motivation in a Nationwide Study," *Psychological Monographs*, Vol. 74, No. 12, 1960.

Wechsler, Henry and David Landy, eds., "New Pathways from the Mental Hospital," *Journal of Social Issues*, Vol. 16, No. 2, 1960, pp. 1–78.

White House Conference on Child Health and Protection, 1930 (Committee on the Infant and Pre-School Child), *Young Child in the Home:* A Survey of Three Thousand American Families. Appleton-Century, Chicago, 1936.

Winterbottom, M. R., "The Relation of Childhood Training in Independence to Achievement Motivation." Doctoral thesis, University of Michigan, Ann Arbor, 1953.

Wolfenstein, Martha, "Trends in Infant Care," *American Journal of Orthopsychiatry*, Vol. 23, 1953, pp. 120–130.

Wright, C. R. and H. H. Hyman, "Voluntary Association Memberships of American Adults; Evidence from National Sample Surveys," *American Sociological Review*, Vol. 23, June, 1958, pp. 284–294.

Contributions of
Survey Research to

Economics

by James N. Morgan
Survey Research Center
University of Michigan

What Has Already Been Done?
Household Surveys
Other Economic Activities of Households
Business Behavior

How Survey Data Are Used in Economics
Behavioral Theory in Economics
Short-run Changes in Behavior
Middle-range Changes in Behavior
Use of Survey Data in Structural Models
Long-term Changes
Testing Economic Hypotheses

Some Methodological Developments, Problems and Prospects
Accuracy and Validity of Data
Methods of Analysis
The Economic Problems of Survey Research
New Sources and Types of Survey Data
Other Areas for Further Study

Summary

Contributions of Survey Research to Economics

THE FIRST and simplest contribution of surveys to economics is in estimating economic magnitudes which for some reason cannot be estimated from the available records. Estimates of the overall proportions of
income spent by the average workingman's family on various things are
essential if one is to assign weights to the different prices in a cost of living
index, yet they cannot be estimated from aggregate consumption figures.
The proportion of families with life insurance cannot be estimated from the
known number of policies outstanding since some families have many policies. The current incomes of the insured cannot be known from the incomes
declared when the policies were issued because they have changed. The
extent of poverty cannot be measured by the number of applications for
relief or welfare, since some proud people starve in silence.

The next stage comes when we remember that economists are more
interested in how things change than in how they are. In particular, how
will they change if people's incomes, or relative prices, change? So survey
data, originally collected to provide weights for the cost of living index or
to describe differences in the population, were turned to the purpose of
looking at differences between families at different income levels, as a clue
to what other families might do if they achieved the same levels.

Business firms might be interested in particular commodities or brands,
but the economist is most concerned with the allocation of the family income among broad categories such as immediate consumption expenditures, purchase of houses or durable goods, and saving in bonds, bank
accounts, or other investments (e.g. real estate, stock). For this purpose,
single cross-sections are useful but a series of such studies over time provide more promise, particularly if they incorporate periodic reinterviews
with the same families.

The effects of price changes are, of course, difficult to study since prices
neither change rapidly nor differ much between areas within a sample, and
in neither case are other things constant. Incomes vary a great deal from
family to family, of course, but so do many other things, and it is always
possible that the *effects* of income depend on things other than its size.

Hence, more elaborate analyses of saving or of spending on durables take account of other variables, partly as unwanted "noise" in the estimating of the effects of income, but partly in their own right. A particular case in point was the concern with the effects of assets on saving. Would the wartime accumulation of savings discourage future saving, people feeling that they could now spend most of their incomes? The issue was important in economics for a second reason, namely, a theory attributed to Pigou, that general price declines would make people's savings worth more in terms of goods, encourage them to spend more of their incomes, and thus stop a recession.[1]

A more promising development for both understanding and predicting behavior was initiated by Katona.[2] Starting with a concern with the dynamics of aggregate spending-saving behavior, he asked what could cause many consumers to change their behavior at the same time. It seemed logical to suggest that anything which made people uncertain, fearful of their own or the country's economic future, would keep them from spending their money and make the flexibility of holding liquid assets attractive. Since it was not possible to be sure how people would interpret events, it was necessary to conduct surveys over many years under changing circumstances in order to discover how social learning and social reactions to events operated.

In addition to these concerns at the aggregative level, and the associated studies of individual behavior, there have been many studies of particular kinds of economic behavior where some issue of economics or of public policy was involved.

Sometimes these studies required only analysis of data collected in a survey with other purposes, sometimes they required special surveys. The topics included consumer debts and attitudes toward instalment credit, life insurance, housing, cars, durable goods, education of children, mobility, philanthropy, medical care, sources of income, labor force participation of wives, family planning, rehabilitation and the receipt of compensation for injury, travel and tourism, financial investments and attitudes, the situation of the disabled, of the aged, and of the non-whites. More recently the studies have been on the economic use of time, receptivity to new things, planning ahead, attitudes toward public expenditure programs, financial investments,

---

1. Pigou, A. C., "The Classical Stationary State," *Economic Journal,* Vol. 53, December, 1943, pp. 343–350.
2. Katona, George, *Psychological Analysis of Economic Behavior*. McGraw-Hill, New York, 1951. The thesis is further developed in Katona's *The Powerful Consumer* and *The Mass Consumption Society*.

and the impact of the tax cut. There have also been a few studies of business-men's behavior and their economic attitudes.

What Has Already Been Done?

HOUSEHOLD SURVEYS

It is manifestly impossible in this chapter to provide a history of the long development of survey studies of consumers. A comprehensive bibliography of family living studies up to the time of World War II exists, and the author previously attempted to review post-war research on consumer be-havior up to 1955.[3] A series of case studies of surveys in different countries has been published by the International Labour Office (1961).[4] A bibliog-raphy of the studies conducted at the Survey Research Center, University of Michigan, over the past twenty years is available.[5]

Early studies were concerned with poverty and with how the poor got along, starting with the monographs of Frederic Le Play in the middle of the nineteenth century, through the work of Quetelet, Engel, Wright, and Mayhew, and culminating in the monumental study of living conditions of the working class in London by Charles Booth, published in 1902 in 17 volumes.

Neither the sampling nor the methods of eliciting information were very scientific in early studies, but the interest they stirred led to demand for more widespread and extensive studies, the largest of which was the 1935–1936 consumer expenditure study in the United States.[6]

World War II resulted not only in price changes and controversy about

3. Williams, Faith, and C. C. Zimmerman, *Studies of Family Living in the United States and Other Countries:* An Analysis of Material and Method. U.S. Department of Agriculture, Miscellaneous Publication No. 223, Washington, December, 1935; Morgan, James, "A Review of Recent Research on Consumer Behavior," (with bibli-ography), in *Consumer Behavior,* Vol. 3. Edited by L. Clark. Harper & Bros., New York, 1958; Houthakker, H. S., "The Present State of Consumption Theory," *Econometrica,* Vol. 29, October, 1961, pp. 704–740; Ferber, Robert, "Research on Household Behavior," *American Economic Review,* Vol. 52, March, 1962, pp. 19–63.
4. International Labour Office, *Family Living Studies:* A Symposium, I.L.O., Geneva, 1961. The International Labour Office symposium focuses on methodology and pur-poses, not on the findings of the surveys.
5. Except where otherwise noted, subsequent references in this chapter to the Survey Research Center refer to the Center at the University of Michigan.
6. U.S. Bureau of Labor Statistics, *1935–36 Consumer Expenditure Study,* in various Bulletins of the Bureau of Labor Statistics, the W.P.A., and the Dept. of Agriculture.

the cost of living but also in shortages and changes in consumption patterns, which required new expenditure studies in order to provide the proper weights in cost of living indices. The war also focused attention on health and nutrition and housing, and aroused the underdeveloped countries to the need for information on which to base their programs for advancement. Even in advanced countries with statistical collection systems, many distributional facts were available only through surveys. Such simple things as the proportion of people with life insurance or health insurance, or the distribution of holdings of War Bonds and United States Savings Bonds, could only be determined by surveys, and at the same time it was possible to secure information about what people were intending to do with their wartime accumulated savings.[7]

Even before World War II, controversy raged about the extent of unemployment and the impact of unemployment on the family. The United States Census and the Bureau of Labor Statistics, starting in 1940, have developed a continuing series of surveys of the labor force and population in the United States.[8] Incorporated into these studies have been studies of migration, family composition, income, stocks of durables, and even short-run buying plans.[9] The focus on precision of estimates led to a rapid development of scientific sampling techniques, and a series of experiences with response variations has led to even more attention to training of interviewers and control of the interviewing process.[10]

The 1950 Bureau of Labor Statistics study of consumer expenditures was focused on urban wage earners and on securing expenditure patterns neces-

7. The Surveys of Consumer Finances from 1946 through 1959 are reported in the *Federal Reserve Bulletin,* various issues each year; since then in annual publications of the Survey Research Center.
8. See Eckler, A. R., "The Continuous Population and Labour Force Survey in the United States," in *Family Living Studies,* I.L.O., *op. cit.;* for current data, see the *Monthly Labor Review.*
9. See the various series of *Current Population Reports* issued by the U.S. Census. For some buying plans, see the *Federal Reserve Bulletin,* Aug., 1946; Aug., 1947; July, 1948; June, 1949; April, 1950; June, 1951; July, 1952; June, 1953; March issues 1954–1959; and the annual volumes entitled *Survey of Consumer Finances,* from the Survey Research Center.
10. A changed Current Population Survey sample led to a jump in the estimate of the number of unemployed, which proved to be largely the result of superior training of the new interviewers, not of any changes in the sample. See discussion by Hansen, Morris, in "Questions and Answers," *American Statistician,* Vol. 8, October, 1954, pp. 33–34; see also *Report of the Special Advisory Committee on Employment Statistics,* U.S. Bureau of the Census, 1954.

sary for reweighting the cost of living index. The techniques and sample were better and more representative than in the 1935–1936 study, but the sample was still not genuinely representative even of all urban places, and some bias was introduced by interviewing people next door when the designated respondents were not at home. The 1960–1961 BLS study is based on a representative sample and improved techniques.

The major purpose of all these studies was descriptive rather than explanatory. Though they had swung from detailed studies of non-representative sub-populations to large-scale representative descriptive studies, they were not focused on explaining behavior but on measuring and describing conditions, behavior, and levels of living. The same can be said of the 1955 Food Consumption Surveys of the Department of Agriculture, of the National Health Surveys—a continuing series—and of a number of other special-purpose surveys. Even data collected largely for descriptive purposes can, however, be analyzed with more attention to the explanation of the behavior of the individuals involved and with more elaborate description than is provided in simple two-way tables. The basic data from that 1935–1936 study were never made available for this purpose, but the 1950 Bureau of Labor Statistics study was analyzed with the aid of a grant from the Ford Foundation. A number of economists used a wide variety of techniques and a variety of research strategies varying from attempts to test a single relatively narrow (permanent income) hypothesis to assessment of a variety of complex main effects and interactions.[11] The 1960–1961 BLS survey's main data have been made available on computer tape at moderate cost.[12]

Elaborate analyses were also provided of two national studies of medical care and medical debt by the National Opinion Research Center, and of a special census study of the economic problems of the aged by Steiner and Dorfman.[13]

11. See *Study of Consumer Expenditures, Incomes and Savings,* 18 vols. University of Pennsylvania Press, Philadelphia, 959; see also Lamale, Helen, *Methodology of the 1950 Consumer Expenditure Survey,* University of Pennsylvania Press, Philadelphia, 1959; and Friend, Irwin and Robert Jones, *Conference on Consumption and Savings,* 2 vols. University of Pennsylvania Press, Philadelphia, 1960.

12. The main findings are available in a series of U.S. Bureau of Labor Statistics reports entitled *Consumer Expenditures and Income.* B.L.S. Report 237-xx or U.S. Dept. of Agriculture Report CES-xx, U.S. Government Printing Office, 1964–1966.

13. Anderson, Odin and Jacob Feldman, *Family Medical Costs and Voluntary Health Insurance:* A Nationwide Survey. McGraw-Hill, New York, 1956; Anderson, Odin, Patricia Collette, and Jacob Feldman, *Changes in Family Medical Costs and Voluntary Health Insurance.* Harvard University Press, Cambridge, 1963; Steiner, P. O. and

The Surveys of Consumer Finances were conducted for thirteen years (1947 through 1959) jointly by the Board of Governors of the Federal Reserve System and the Survey Research Center, and since then by the latter with support from the Ford Foundation and private business. They were sponsored originally because of a (largely descriptive) interest in ownership of assets and debts.[14] Questions on buying plans and expectations and attitudes, urged by the Survey Research Center on theoretical grounds, were accepted only because they were necessary to keep a financial survey from being too dull and uninteresting to the respondent. The reports in the *Federal Reserve Bulletins* during the period from 1947 through 1959, and as published by the Center since then, have focused on basic descriptive data on the distribution of consumer assets, debts, housing, incomes, major purchases, and plans to buy major items. The samples were small but the variety of data available for the same units allowed a number of complex analytical studies to be done. More remains to be done with these studies.[15]

Indeed, the variety of special studies already published from the various Surveys of Consumer Finances is too large to detail here, but it is important to provide the flavor of the findings.[16] The fact that only a small fraction of the people own common stock, most of them in the higher income groups, had a bearing on interpretations of the possible impact of a dramatic fall in stock prices—the capital losses were deemed unlikely to affect consumer spending much. The fact that most users of instalment credit were in the middle income groups, that few of them saw anything wrong with it, and

Robert Dorfman, *The Economic Status of the Aged*. University of California Press, Berkeley, 1957.

14. For the major trend data see *Federal Reserve Bulletins* 1946–1959; Survey Research Center, *1960 Survey of Consumer Finances,* Survey Research Center, *op. cit.,* which contains a bibliography of analytical studies using Survey Research Center data; and subsequent annual monographs entitled *19— Survey of Consumer Finances*. See also Klein, L. R., ed., *Contributions of Survey Methods to Economics*. Columbia University Press, New York, 1954; Institute for Social Research, *Economic Survey Data* (basic data available to academic researchers), University of Michigan, Ann Arbor, 1960; Morgan, James, "Repeated Surveys of Consumer Finances in the United States," in *Family Living Studies,* I.L.O., *op. cit.*

15. These data are generally available to academic researchers from the Survey Research Center or, as a consistent but limited trend series, from the University of Wisconsin's Social Systems Research Institute.

16. A list is available from the Survey Research Center, University of Michigan, Ann Arbor.

that many of them had money in the bank too, kept informed economists from thinking of credit as only the desperate resource of the poor. When a large increase in aggregate instalment credit outstanding appeared, even relative to aggregate income, it was extremely useful to know that the increase resulted largely from the increased proportion of middle and upper income people using credit, so that the proportion with debt more than, say, 20 per cent of income, had hardly changed. Expenditures on cars, durables and additions and repairs, proved to be proportional to income, and thus could be considered neither luxury nor necessity. And in the resistance to high prices in 1951, the recently married hardly reduced their expenditures on durables at all, indicating that for some people who were just stocking up, durables were seen as necessities.

This kind of study revealed the great advantage of a series of comparable surveys over time. Trends in the position of various subgroups in the population could be observed and interpreted. At the same time, special topics could be emphasized if they were currently crucial. For example, when recessions and unemployment became important in the 1950's, it was useful to know the impact of unemployment on the whole family and during the previous year, to supplement the official statistics on current unemployment. Special emphasis has been given in some years to debt, housing, retirement plans, and travel.

There have been expenditure or saving surveys in a number of other countries, including Great Britain, Israel, Puerto Rico, Sweden, Ceylon, India, Japan, Mexico and Canada; but only the Surveys of Consumer Finances in this country provide a continuing annual survey of consumer finances and of major expenditures which allows analysis of changes over time both in consumer situations and in the relationships found in a single cross section.[17]

17. Lydall, Harold, *British Incomes and Savings.* Basil Blackwell, Oxford, 1955; Vandome, Peter, "Aspects of the Dynamics of Consumer Behavior," *Bulletin of the Oxford University Institute of Statistics,* Vol. 20, February, 1958, pp. 65–105; Prais, S. J. and H. S. Houthakker, *The Analysis of Family Budgets.* Cambridge University Press, Cambridge, 1955; Bank of Israel, *Survey of Family Savings, 1957–58* (preliminary report), Jerusalem, October, 1959; Yang, C. Y., "An International Comparison of Consumption Functions," *Review of Economics and Statistics,* Vol. 56, August, 1964, pp. 279–286; Japan: Bureau of Statistics, Office of the Prime Minister, *Family Income and Expenditure Survey,* Tokyo (for analysis, see Tsumimura, Kotaro and Tamotsu Sato, "Irreversibility of Consumer Behavior in Terms of Numerical Preference Fields," *Review of Economics and Statistics,* Vol. 46, August, 1964, pp.

However, even in the United States, the most recent survey which actually collected all the components of savings for each family was the 1951 Survey of Consumer Finances. Various of the Surveys of Consumer Finances, particularly the reinterview surveys, have collected data on major components of saving. The 1960–1962 Survey involved a panel of respondents interviewed three times and provided a great deal of ancillary data as well as estimates of saving over a two-year period for those who did not move.[18] The 1960–1961 Bureau of Labor Statistics consumer expenditure surveys provide some data on saving as a by-product of their system of checking on the reliability of expenditure reports, but without the important ancillary data on assets, debts, attitudes, and plans.

A variety of other surveys conducted by the Survey Research Center in the twenty years of its existence have focused on selected aspects of consumer behavior, always with the hope not only of describing and inferring causation, but also of being able more directly to understand and predict consumer behavior. Of major importance has been a series of surveys devoted to periodic assessment of consumer attitudes, intentions, and expectations. Based upon a theoretical model which implies that major events can change consumer attitudes in the same direction for many consumers, and that these attitudes affect their subsequent spending-saving behavior, these studies have served for short-run forecasting and for the more basic purpose of investigating the effects of events on attitudes, and the effects of attitudes on behavior.[19] It can be seen that such a program of research fitted neatly into the needs of economists for both theory and measurement

---

305–319); Thore, Sten, *Household Saving and the Price Level.* National Institute of Economic Research (Konjunctur Institutet), Stockholm, 1961 analyzes the data from the first of two Swedish savings surveys; Canada: Royal Commission on Banking and Finance, *Consumer Survey* (conducted by McDonald Research Ltd.), Ottawa, no date (survey done in 1962); Due, J. M., "Postwar Family Expenditure Studies in Western Europe," *Journal of Farm Economics,* Vol. 38, August, 1956, pp. 846–856; Asimakopulos, Athenasios, "Analysis of Canadian Consumer Expenditure Surveys," *Canadian Journal of Economics and Political Science,* Vol. 31, May, 1965, pp. 222–241, which contains references to the original Dominion Bureau of Statistics publications and to other, secondary analyses. A savings survey is planned for France by the Centre de Recherche Economique sur L'Epargne.

18. See Kosobud, Richard, and James Morgan, eds., *Consumer Behavior of Individual Families over Two and Three Years.* Monograph 36, Institute for Social Research, University of Michigan, Ann Arbor, 1964.

19. Mueller, Eva, "Ten Years of Consumer Attitude Surveys: Their Forecasting Record," *Journal of the American Statistical Association,* Vol. 58, December, 1963, pp. 899–917; Mueller, Eva, "Effects of Consumer Attitudes on Purchases," *American*

which was useful for the aggregate dynamic analysis of the economic system. Many economists have accepted the use of consumer buying-plans data, without being convinced that attitudes mattered or that events would affect attitudes in an understandable or uniform way. Indeed, the focus on buying plans led to the development of a private commercial telephone survey of buying intentions; and, in the pursuit of larger samples, led the Federal Reserve Board to engage the Census to conduct a series of buying-plans surveys. That series has been continued by the Census. Much more research needs to be done but the promise is great, and the potential importance of the findings for economic analysis and forecasting clearly justifies intensified work in this area.

The continuing series of surveys by the Michigan Survey Research Center combines the repetition necessary for investigating the effect of events on attitudes and of attitudes on consumer behavior, with experimentation in questions and special areas of interest such as the effects of retirement plans on saving and, more recently, the effects of a tax cut on the attitudes and reported behavior of individuals. In addition to articles and the data reported in the annual books which also report the Surveys of Consumer Finances, there is an occasional summarization such as Katona's *The Powerful Consumer* and his *The Mass Consumption Society.*

The advantages of programmatic survey research utilizing a series of surveys in an area of consumer behavior are also illustrated by sequences of studies at the Center in such fields as travel and recreation, unemployment and its impact on the whole family, attitudes toward and use of instalment credit.

The advantages of multipurpose surveys which investigate simultaneously different but interrelated facets of consumer behavior, are illustrated in a study of the backgrounds of low income families, and the extent to which

---

Economic Review, Vol. 47, December, 1957, pp. 946–965; Katona, George and Eva Mueller, *Consumer Expectations 1953–1956.* Institute for Social Research, University of Michigan, Ann Arbor, 1956; Katona, George, *Psychological Analysis of Economic Behavior,* McGraw-Hill, New York, 1951; Katona, George, *The Powerful Consumer.* McGraw-Hill, New York, 1960; various articles in two National Bureau of Economic Research volumes: *Short Term Economic Forecasting,* Princeton University Press, Princeton, 1955, and *The Quality and Economic Significance of Anticipations Data.* Princeton University Press, Princeton, 1960; Katona, George, *The Mass Consumption Society.* McGraw-Hill, New York, 1964; see also Mueller, Eva, "The Impact of Unemployment on Consumer Confidence," *Public Opinion Quarterly,* Vol. 30, Spring, 1966, pp. 19–32.

low incomes are transmitted from one generation to the next.[20] The same study provides an analysis of the forces and decisions affecting the components and total of family income, and of the redistribution of income through public transfer systems, private philanthropy, and interfamily aid. The explanatory variables include the usual demographic and economic facts, plus family history, past mobility, local area factors such as the extent of unemployment, attitudes, and even a personality measure of achievement motivation.[21] It is this combination of explanatory factors from several disciplines which makes survey research interdisciplinary, and the attempt to predict some actual behavior which makes it scientific.

Growing out of that study is one just finished which focuses on such basic economic behaviors as the productive use of time, receptivity to new ways of producing and consuming, and deliberate planning for the future.[22] Such behaviors are crucial not only to a family's economic status but to the economic growth of a nation, and hence need to be studied in many countries, both for their own economic development programs and for the insights that comparisons between countries provide. These comparisons have the advantage of the rich micro-analysis in each country, and do not require the impossible, i.e., deciding which of many things that differ between two countries really accounts for their overall differences in the average behavior of consumers and workers.

As the interdisciplinary nature of studies of behavior becomes more obvious, relevant information for economists sometimes comes from surveys whose main purpose was sociological or psychological or political. For instance, recent studies of family planning and ideal family size have shown some economic forces to be important (income) and others surprisingly unimportant (desire for advanced education for children).[23]

There have been a very few experiments involving interviews, too, such

20. Morgan, James, *et al.*, *Income and Welfare in the United States.* McGraw-Hill, New York, 1962.

21. Morgan, James, "The Achievement Motive and Economic Behavior," *Economic Development and Cultural Change*, Vol. 12, April, 1964, pp. 243–267 (reprinted in *A Theory of Achievement Motivation.* Edited by J. W. Atkinson and N. T. Feather. John Wiley & Sons, New York, 1966).

22. Morgan, James, Ismail Sirageldin, and Nancy Baerwaldt, *Productive Americans.* Survey Research Center, University of Michigan, Ann Arbor, 1966.

23. See Goldberg, David, "Some Recent Developments in American Fertility Research," in *Demographic and Economic Change in Developed Countries.* Princeton University Press, Princeton, 1960; see also Westoff, Charles, *et al.*, *Family Growth in Metropolitan America.* Princeton University Press, Princeton, 1961; Freedman, Ron-

as one on milk consumption, and another on satisfaction with different grades of meat (all of which had been purchased at the same price).[24] There have been laboratory experiments, not reviewed here, which have provided hypotheses but rarely adequate methods of measuring theoretical concepts that could be used in surveys. And there is market research which we have omitted because only a small fraction of it is available, except by hearsay.

A rapidly developing field of interest has been surveys devoted specifically to providing crucial information in fields where public policy decisions must be based on knowledge of actual and potential reactions of individuals. Studies of those who exhaust their unemployment compensation, of people on relief, of bankruptcies or garnishments, of injured workers, of auto accident victims, all fall into this category. For instance, it has long been argued that if an injured worker who had been receiving weekly workmen's compensation payments had it all paid to him in a lump sum, he would be more likely to return to work. A study in Michigan of people who had accepted such "lump sum redemption settlements" indicated that more than a year and a half later, a majority of them were still not back at work.[25] The study also made clear that there were other problems with the whole system, and that going into business for oneself was a rare and not to be expected outcome of such settlements.

A study by the Survey Research Center and the Bureau of Hospital Ad-

ald, Pascal Whelpton, and Arthur Campbell, *Family Planning, Sterility, and Population Growth.* McGraw-Hill, New York, 1959; Berelson, B. R. and Ronald Freedman, "A Study in Fertility Control." *Scientific American,* Vol. 210, May, 1964, pp. 29–37; Freedman, Ronald, "Sample Surveys for Family Planning Research in Taiwan." *Public Opinion Quarterly,* Vol. 28, Fall, 1964, pp. 373–382; Corsa, Leslie, Jr., "The Sample Survey in a National Population Program." *Public Opinion Quarterly,* Vol. 28, Fall, 1964, pp. 383–388; Stycos, J. M., "Survey Research and Population Control in Latin America." *Public Opinion Quarterly,* Vol. 28, Fall, 1964, pp. 367–372; Freedman, Deborah, "The Relation of Economic Status to Fertility," *American Economic Review,* Vol. 53, June, 1963, pp. 414–426.

24. Baker, D. J. and C. H. Berry, "The Price Elasticity of Demand for Fluid Skim Milk," *Journal of Farm Economics,* Vol. 35, February, 1953, pp. 124–129; Lasley, F. G., E. R. Kiehl, and D. E. Brady, *Consumer Preference for Beef in Relation to Finish.* (Finish is the fat of animals ready for market.) Missouri Agricultural Experiment Station Research Bulletin 580, University of Missouri, Columbia, March, 1955.

25. Morgan, James, Marvin Snider and Marion Sobol, *Lump Sum Redemption Settlements and Rehabilitation.* Institute for Social Research, University of Michigan, Ann Arbor, 1959; see also Cheit, E. F., *Injury and Recovery in the Course of Employment.* John Wiley & Sons, New York, 1961.

ministration of the University of Michigan showed how attitudes and insurance coverage and age, sex and income were related to utilization of medical services in Michigan.[26] It also indicated that better insurance coverage was associated with reporting fewer unmet medical needs, so that part of the correlation of insurance coverage with utilization of medical services resulted from inadequate care for the uninsured rather than overuse by the insured.

A study by Columbia University's Bureau of Applied Social Research focused on the economic problems of Puerto Rican migrants into New York, and the high costs of their lack of information and consequent reliance on the door-to-door easy-credit merchants.[27]

A number of studies of auto accident victims have been done, some primarily to estimate the economic cost of auto accidents or the motives behind suing.[28] The study by Conard and others in Michigan involved interviewing not only victims but also their lawyers and some defendants; information was also secured from defense attorneys and from hospitals on some of the same cases. The undercompensation of the more serious accidents and the tendency for some smaller accidents to involve compensation larger than the *economic* costs, were apparent. Even more striking was the fact that, in a system justified in part as placing upon the negligent driver the costs of the accident, many defendants in suits did not even know whether their victims had ever received any compensation.

A series of studies of travel conducted between 1955 and 1962 were summarized in a recent book; and studies have appeared of labor mobility, how people pay for college, and of persistent unemployment.[29] A number of

26. McNerney, W. J., *et al.*, *Hospital and Medical Economics,* 2 vols. Hospital Research and Educational Trust, Chicago, 1962, Vol. 1, pp. 61–357; see also Wirick, Grover and Robin Barlow, "The Economic and Social Determinants of the Demand for Health Services," in *The Economics of Health and Medical Care.* Proceedings of a conference sponsored by the Bureau of Public Health Economics and the Department of Economics, University of Michigan, Ann Arbor, 1964.
27. Caplovitz, David, *The Poor Pay More:* Consumer Practices of Low Income Families. Free Press, Glencoe, Ill., 1963.
28. Conard, Alfred, *et al., Automobile Accident Costs and Payments:* Studies in the Economics of Injury Reparation. University of Michigan Press, Ann Arbor, 1964; Adams, J. F., "Economic-Financial Consequences of Personal Injuries Sustained in 1953 Philadelphia Auto Accidents," *Economics and Business Bulletin,* Temple University, Philadelphia, 1955; Hunting, R. B. and G. S. Neuwirth, *Who Sues in New York City?* Columbia University Press, New York, 1962.
29. Lansing, John B. and Dwight M. Blood, *The Changing Travel Market.* Survey Research Center, University of Michigan, Ann Arbor, 1964. See also Mueller,

small studies of recreation or tourism have been done in single states or localities, frequently by state university bureaus of business research. And in a society where popular acceptance of both public programs and new products of private industry is important, studies have been done of attitudes toward innovation and toward public expenditure programs.[30]

In the midst of a period of rapid expansion of private pension plans, mostly provided without choice to workers and added to their social security programs, two studies of the effects of the expectation of added retirement benefits on current saving behavior indicated that psychological theories of rising aspiration and of the motivational power of realizable goals were more useful than economic theories of diminishing utility—those with private pension plans, other things equal, saved *more* in addition, not less.[31]

In matters of monetary policy, fiscal policy, and tax policy, it is the behavior of the upper-income, high-asset people which matters most. The early Surveys of Consumer Finances were over-sampled in high rent dwellings and weighted to preserve representativeness. Such sampling is not efficient—some low-income people live in expensive dwellings and the reverse. No better method of sampling was available until recently, when studies were done first in one Midwest city and then on a national sample.[32]

Eva and Gerald Gurin, *Participation in Outdoor Recreation:* Factors Affecting Demand Among American Adults. U.S. Government Printing Office, Washington, 1962; Lansing, J. B., *et al., The Geographic Mobility of Labor:* A First Report. Survey Research Center, University of Michigan, Ann Arbor, 1963; Lansing, J. B., Thomas Lorimer and Chikashi Moriguchi, *How People Pay for College.* Survey Research Center, University of Michigan, Ann Arbor, 1963; Mueller, Eva and Jay Schmiedeskamp, *Persistent Unemployment 1957–1961.* Upjohn Institute for Employment Research, Kalamazoo, Mich., 1962. For studies based on Survey of Consumer Finances data, see the bibliographies in the annual volumes.
30. Mueller, Eva, "The Desire for Innovations in Household Goods," in *Consumer Behavior.* Edited by Lincoln Clark. Harper & Bros., New York, 1958. Mueller, Eva, "Public Attitudes Toward Fiscal Programs," *Quarterly Journal of Economics,* Vol. 78, May, 1963, pp. 210–235.
31. Katona, George, *Private Pensions and Individual Saving.* Survey Research Center Monograph 40, Institute for Social Research, University of Michigan, Ann Arbor, 1965; Cagan, Philip, *The Effect of Pension Plans on Aggregate Saving.* Occasional Paper 95, National Bureau of Economic Research, Columbia University Press, New York, 1965.
32. Katona, George and John Lansing, "The Wealth of the Wealthy," *Review of Economics and Statistics,* Vol. 46, February, 1964, pp. 1–13; Morgan, James, Robin Barlow, and Harvey Brazer, "A Survey of Investment Management and Working Behavior among High-Income Individuals," *American Economic Review,* Vol. 55,

These studies showed not only a wide variety of levels of sophistication and information on the part of people about investment of savings, but much less concern with taxes in making investment decisions than had been thought. The national study also showed that the impact of marginal tax rates on willingness to work was also far smaller than had been thought.

Studies focused on low-income families have been intended largely to estimate their numbers and describe their problems.[33]

The reduction in federal income tax rates in 1964–1965 raised questions about what people would do with the money, and with what speed. A panel study was designed, interviewing the same people five times over a period of a year and a half, to study the dynamics of changes in income and spending. The results will be made available in a book by Eva Mueller and George Katona, to be published by the Brookings Institution.

The rapidly changing interest rates on savings accounts revived interest in the way people view liquidity and use various forms of savings, and led to a series of cooperative studies between the Federal Reserve Board and the Survey Research Center, early findings of which have been published.[34]

OTHER ECONOMIC ACTIVITIES OF HOUSEHOLDS

As a society becomes more affluent, people have more freedom to decide how much they will work. A household no longer merely decides what to do with the income it can earn, but decides what it wants, and how much it must work to get the income to buy it. Hence, studies of labor force and labor mobility expand to encompass the hours of work of both family heads

May, 1965, pp. 252–264; Barlow, Robin, Harvey Brazer, and James Morgan, *The Economic Behavior of the Affluent,* Brookings Institution, Washington, 1966; see also Break, George, "Income Taxes and Incentives to Work: An Empirical Study," *American Economic Review,* Vol. 47, September, 1957, pp. 529–549 (a study of self-employed professional people in Great Britain); and Projector, Dorothy and Gertrude Weiss, *Survey of Financial Characteristics of Consumers.* Board of Governors of the Federal Reserve System, Washington, 1966.

33. For a recent example, see Greenleigh Associates, *Home Interview Study of Low-Income Households in Detroit, Michigan.* Greenleigh Associates, New York, February, 1965. The U.S. Census is currently conducting a special survey with a very large sample in order to provide a more precise estimate of the number of poor as a basis for allocating funds under the Economic Opportunity (Poverty) Act.

34. Mueller, Eva and Harlow Osborne, "Consumer Time and Savings Balances: Their Role in Family Liquidity," *American Economic Review,* Vol. 55, May, 1965, pp. 265–275.

and wives, and include non-money work which may be an alternative to earning money. A recent summary of scattered data on historical trends argues that increasing affluence has not brought increased leisure.[35] Rapid increases in labor force participation of women have led to a number of studies of that phenomenon.[36]

Forms of economic behavior other than working and consuming are also important; these include the use of instalment credit, philanthropy (with time or money), risk avoidance such as use of seat belts, and planning ahead. They appear as parts of a number of recent past and current studies of the Survey Research Center. In one study, for instance, evidence is assembled to show that past economic success or failure affects the attitudes and related behaviors of individuals in such a way as to reinforce the very propensities which led to success or failure in the past. Hence there is evidence of a cumulative process by which success leads to enhanced ambition, planning, receptivity to change, and concern for progress which are likely to lead to further success, while past failure and difficulty have a reverse effect.

BUSINESS BEHAVIOR

In the field of business behavior, there has been much emphasis on assessing short-range business plans and expectations. Dun and Bradstreet, the Securities and Exchange Commission in conjunction with the Commerce Department, and McGraw-Hill, have all conducted for a number of years surveys of business plans and expectations. While these are largely for the purposes of short-run forecasting, their changes over time and realization in

---

35. deGrazia, Sebastian, *Of Time, Work and Leisure.* Twentieth Century Fund, New York, 1962.
36. Rosett, R. N., "Working Wives: An Economic Study," in *Studies in Household Economic Behavior.* Yale University Press, New Haven, 1958; Sobol, M. G., "Correlates of Present and Expected Future Work Status of Married Women," doctoral thesis, University of Michigan, Ann Arbor, 1960; Mahoney, T. A., "Factors That Determine the Labor-Force Participation of Married Women," *Industrial and Labor Relations Review,* Vol. 14, July, 1961, pp. 563–577; Morgan, James, *et al., Income and Welfare in the United States, op. cit.,* chap. 9; Mincer, Jacob, "Labor Force Participation of Married Women: A Study of Labor Supply," *Aspects of Labor Economics,* National Bureau of Economic Research, New York, 1962; Morgan, James, "Time, Work and Welfare," in *Patterns of Market Behavior.* Edited by M. J. Brennan. Brown University Press, Providence, R.I., 1965; Morgan, James, Ismail Sirageldin, and Nancy Baerwaldt, *op. cit.;* Cain, Glen, *Labor Force Participation of Married Women.* University of Chicago Press, Chicago, 1966.

each subsequent period have been used for analysis of what affects business behavior.[37]

A controversial beginning in studies of business decisions was made in the late 1930's by Richard Lester. He tried to see whether the economic theories of marginal revenue and marginal cost were correct by asking manufacturers questions about the effects of changing wage rates on the substitution of capital for labor. A great controversy ensued in which the final word, from the point of view of many economists, was that of Machlup, who pointed out that regardless of what businessmen said, only those who behave as the economists said they should would stay in business; consequently, we should not trust their answers.[38] There was also a great deal of controversy about the methods used in the early Lester study.

Some years later McLaughlin and Robock interviewed a number of plant executives who had moved to the South.[39] Katona, Morgan, and Guthrie did a study of factors influencing expansion and plant location in Michigan, followed by a similar study eleven years later which provided comparisons over time and with neighboring Ohio.[40] A study in New England of plants that had moved there was done by Ellis.[41]

Two small studies were done in Great Britain. One by Harold Lydall was

37. Morrissett, Irving, "Psychological Surveys in Business Forecasting," in *Some Applications of Behavioral Research,* UNESCO, Paris, 1957; Friend, Irwin and Jean Bronfenbrenner, "Plant and Equipment Programs and Their Realization," in *Short Term Economic Forecasting,* Princeton University Press, Princeton, 1955.
38. Machlup, Fritz, "Marginal Analysis and Empirical Research," *American Economic Review,* Vol. 36, September, 1946, pp. 519–554; the whole series of articles and rejoinders is reprinted in *Readings in Economic Analysis,* Vol. 2. Edited by Richard Clemence. Addison-Wesley, Cambridge, 1950.
39. McLaughlin, G. E. and Stefan Robock, *Why Industry Moves South.* Committee of the South, National Planning Association, Washington, 1949.
40. Katona, George and James Morgan, "The Quantitative Study of Factors Determining Business Decisions," *Quarterly Journal of Economics,* Vol. 66, January, 1954, pp. 69–90; see also *Industrial Mobility in Michigan.* Institute for Social Research, University of Michigan, Ann Arbor, 1950; Mueller, Eva, Arnold Wilken and Margaret Wood, *Location Decisions and Industrial Mobility in Michigan,* 1961. Survey Research Center, University of Michigan, Ann Arbor, 1962; Mueller, Eva and James Morgan, "Location Decisions of Manufacturers," *American Economic Review,* Vol. 52, May 1962, pp. 204–217; see also Heller, W. M., "The Anatomy of Investment Decisions," *Harvard Business Review,* Vol. 29, March, 1951, pp. 95–103.
41. Ellis, George, "Postwar Industrial Location in New England," doctoral thesis, Harvard University, Cambridge, 1950.

on the effects of a credit squeeze on businessmen's behavior. He discovered that almost no one had found it difficult to get credit, or even expected to find it difficult, but some had restricted their output on the assumption that customers might find it difficult to get credit.[42] Another study, of solicitors and accountants, found very little evidence that they were restricting their work effort because of income taxes.[43]

In an American study, Katona *et al.* have considered the attitudes and experience of large-scale business in the use of bank financing.[44] Eisner and Modigliani have done a personal interview study of business investment decisions and factors affecting them.[45]

More effort has gone into statistical studies of business investment based on available data from records. As these become more sophisticated, the need to combine them with personal interview data from the decision-makers becomes more obvious.[46]

Finally, a growing body of research on the acceptance of innovations, most of it done on farmers by rural sociologists and agricultural economists, bids fair to extend beyond farmers (and doctors) to other economic units.[47]

How Survey Data Are Used in Economics

With this brief look at some of the survey research that has been done, it is time to turn to the question: what is the relation of all this to economics? Is

42. Lydall, Harold, "The Impact of the Credit Squeeze on Small and Medium Sized Firms." *Economic Journal,* Vol. 67, September, 1957, pp. 415–431.

43. Break, George, "Income Taxes and Incentives to Work," *op. cit.*

44. Katona, George *et al., Business Looks at Banks.* University of Michigan Press, Ann Arbor, 1957.

45. Eisner, Robert, *Determinants of Capital Expenditure—An Interview Study.* Bureau of Economic and Business Research, University of Illinois, Urbana, 1956; see also Eisner, Robert, "Interview and Other Survey Techniques in the Study of Investment," in *Problems of Capital Formation,* Princeton University Press, Princeton, 1961.

46. For good examples see Meyer, John and Edwin Kuh, *The Investment Decision: An Empirical Study.* Harvard University Press, Cambridge, 1957; and Mansfield, Edwin, "Industrial Research and Development Expenditures: Determinants, Prospects, and Relation to Size of Firm and Inventive Output," *Journal of Political Economy,* Vol. 72, August, 1964, pp. 319–340; Mansfield, Edwin, "Size of Firm, Market Structure, and Innovation," *Journal of Political Economy,* Vol. 71, December, 1963, pp. 556–576.

47. For an excellent and critical summary, see Rogers, E. M., *Diffusion of Innovations.* Free Press, Glencoe, Ill., 1962. It contains a 41-page bibliography.

it more than descriptive background knowledge? And if economists need survey results, in what directions must surveys go to satisfy them?

Economics is the study of how economic systems work, or ought to work, in the allocation of resources to serve the various ends of society. In the process, economists study how buyers and sellers meet in markets and how markets determine prices and quantities. Then they study how the sub-parts of the economic system fit together into a dynamic interlocked system. Whatever the relative emphasis on three main policy goals of the economy —price stability, economic growth, and full employment—the *analysis* tends to focus on aggregate dynamics. In other words, economists study the forces that affect the aggregate flows in the system and the way the aggregates influence one another and fit together in a complete structural system.

It is a complex task to spell out the implications of whatever assumptions are made about the structure of the economic system. Two kinds of assumptions are made in structural dynamic models of economics. One set consists largely of identities and definitions. For instance, consumption plus investment plus net exports plus government expenditures add up to the gross national product. The other assumptions are essentially behavioral relations commonly at the aggregate level. In other words, they are relations between aggregate investments and interest rates, or between aggregate consumption and aggregate income. Behind these aggregate assumptions are assumptions, often implicit, about the behavior of individual actors— consumers, workers, or investors.

Progress in economics requires both a theory of behavior of these individuals and a method of going from behavior of individuals to the behavior of aggregates. It also requires estimates of the actual strength of the relationships, i.e., measures of the strength with which different factors actually affect the behavior of individuals—consumers, workers, or businessmen. Without such quantification, the most elaborate models can tell us little about the real world. By fitting an econometric model to time-series data of the aggregate flows, however, there is a way of estimating the relation among the aggregates without worrying about individuals. As our aggregate time-series data have improved and been available for the calculation of sub-aggregates such as major components of consumer expenditure, and as the number of years for which we have data has grown, this work has continued. The latest such model even builds in as one of its variables the results of the McGraw-Hill survey of business investment plans, using the latest survey results, along with other initial conditions such as expected government budgets and tax laws, to develop a forecast for the economy for the next year.[48] Such models may yet incorporate average or summary measures from *consumer* surveys which are also available, for similarly long periods on a comparable basis, in the Surveys of Consumer Finances.

There are serious limits to the possible results of models based on time-series data, because there will never be enough years to provide the necessary degrees of freedom for the statistical analysis, and because the behavioral assumptions in dealing with aggregates are necessarily crude and not strictly derivable from data on individual behavior. Using months or quarter years does not really add that much more information or "degrees of freedom." Some combination of the rich cross-section survey data with time-period changes is essential.

BEHAVIORAL THEORY IN ECONOMICS

The development of behavioral theory by economists has been affected by the purposes to which the theory was to be put. Economists needed a theory of the response of individuals or firms to changes, and primarily to changes in economic forces such as income (or profits), interest rates, prices, or to government policies such as tax laws.

Many of the variables interesting to a clinical psychologist in interpreting behavior are of no interest to the economist. There are two reasons for this. Some variables useful in explaining individual differences do not change over time. The fact that Catholics have more children than Protestants do is far less important to the economist than the possibility of fewer people having children this year than last if unemployment is high. The religious difference might be important in longer-run analysis *if* one expected the proportion of Catholics in the population to change. The fact that some people are more frugal than others because of their early training is only useful for economists to know if the proportions of frugal people in the population are changing. The second reason is that some factors which affect behavior and also change over time, change in different directions for different people, in a kind of random fashion which cancels out in the aggregate. A man's moods may change from day to day and even affect his economic behavior, but unless everyone's mood changes in the same direction in response to identifiable forces, this fact is not particularly useful. So

48. Evans, M. K. and E. W. Green, "The Relative Efficacy of Investment Anticipations," *Journal of the American Statistical Association,* Vol. 61, March, 1966, pp. 104–116.

the economist needs a theory that is dynamic, explaining changes in behavior, and one that is general, explaining changes of whole groups—changes that do not cancel one another out and average to zero.

Theories of behavior of households or businessmen, developed with these purposes in mind and before surveys offered a way to test them or assess the strength of relations, probably went too far in restricting the number of variables. Classical economics developed a theory of the consumer maximizing a one-dimensional utility by spending a fixed income, and a theory of the businessmen maximizing profit under changing prices, costs, and technology, with some risk discounts for uncertainty. This oversimplification led to elegant theories where prices became nothing but LaGrange multipliers, and Euler's Theorem proved that it all worked out if everyone were paid according to his marginal productivity.

But when it became necessary to implement the theory and use it to talk about public policy, or to make projections of the future, it became important to know at least how the consumer or businessman reacted to the few forces which had been considered and which were a part of a structural system—such as prices, incomes, and interest rates. In order to do this, account had to be taken of other motives people might have, if only to improve our measures of income elasticities or price elasticities in behavior.

Other factors were not all "noise." It is becoming clear that we need a better theory both about what is being maximized, and subject to what constraints. People have more than one goal called "utility." They have physical needs, and future needs, and a need for some financial security from risk. But they may also have needs for a sense of achievement or affiliation with their fellow man, or power over other people, or independence from their power. How else can we explain the taking of calculated risks with actually lower expected values, or output restrictions among workers on piece rates, or contributions to the Community Chest, or insistence on self-employment by farmers and artisans, even at a lower income and more risk?

Indeed, a field of great interest today is education, and a major force in education is the willingness of parents to "invest" in the education of their children. An explanation of that behavior as maximizing something would have to include in the "something" the vicarious satisfaction in the success and happiness of one's children. Certainly few parents expect to "get it back" in any concrete monetary help from their children.

A great deal can be done to improve the quality of economic analysis by simply having better background data about what our society is really like.

Still more can be done with simple relations of various forms of spending-saving behavior to income and with trends over time in distributions of income and assets. Ultimately, economists need to use information about consumers to explain and predict changes in their behavior. Of course, optimal prediction also requires explanation. It will simplify matters if we discuss separately short-range predictions, middle-range predictions, and long-range intergenerational predictions. In all three it becomes necessary to combine survey data with other data in a fairly sophisticated manner in order to do anything useful. Let us take a look, first, at the short-run forecasting problem.

SHORT-RUN CHANGES IN BEHAVIOR

If we really had a completely worked out theory of consumer behavior, we could take an event like an international crisis, guess how it would affect consumer attitudes, plans, and behavior, and then make a direct estimate of the future of consumer spending under the impact of each major event that comes along. The fact is that we commonly do not know how events will affect consumers. We know from hindsight that the outbreak of a steel strike a few years ago led to serious misgivings by consumers, who felt that the outcome would be either no wage increase, or an inflationary increase in steel prices as well as wages, and that the strike's settlement encouraged consumers to spend. But we also know from hindsight that the breakdown of the Paris peace conference after the U-2 incident had almost no effect on American consumers. Consequently, short-run survey data on consumer attitudes and expectations are still crucial in short-run forecasting. Furthermore, they are even more useful if collected over a period of changing events, for the development of a better theory of what changes consumer attitudes and how attitudes, in turn, motivate and affect consumer behavior. Consequently, we need a periodic assessment of what the consumer's situation is and how he is reacting to the state of the world.

To do this properly is an expensive operation for two reasons. First, it is necessary to have accurate measurements of the consumer's state of mind and occasionally of the state of his pocketbook for a representative sample. Second, and perhaps more important, we are still in the development stage of knowing what to ask and how to use the answers. Hence, there is still a great need for research, experimentation, and development. At this stage it is useful to have the large-scale samples of buying plans collected by the Census. At the same time it would be a tragedy if this stopped the kind of development work that is necessary to improve the measures and to increase our knowledge of how the consumer reacts to events and how events shape his attitudes and his spending behavior. In addition to consumer attitudes and plans, of course, it is essential also to have periodic assessments of consumers' financial conditions—their assets, debts, and the distributions of their incomes—in order to assess changes in the distribution of *ability* to buy. Whenever *average* incomes and assets are changing, it becomes important to know whether the *distributions* are also changing.

In both the consumer and business area, it has been tempting to shortcut theoretical development and focus on the more immediately practical aspects of surveys. Hence, there have been surveys devoted almost entirely to the mechanical collection of data about buying plans. Perhaps the extreme case is the business-expectation data which rely upon reported expectations only about directions of change, not amounts, and have developed an elaborate mathematics to show how under many circumstances "diffusion indexes" created from such data have a quantitative aspect too.[49] The fact that so little is asked of the respondent, and that a feedback of average results is valued by business firms, has made it possible to develop such series in many countries where personal interview surveys could not have been afforded. The disadvantage is that such data provide little understanding of why the forecasts work, how the expectations are formed, or how they affect behavior. The relatively mechanical focusing on purchase plans in this country leads naturally to investigations of the extent to which such plans are fulfilled, and hence predict behavior.[50] The real complexity of human

49. Marquardt, Wilhelm and Werner Strigel, *The Konjunkturtest:* A New Method of Economic Research. IFO-Institute for Wirtschaftsforschung, Munich, 1960.
50. Klein, L. R. and J. B. Lansing, "Decisions to Purchase Consumer Durable Goods," *Journal of Marketing,* Vol. 2, October, 1955, pp. 109–132. Lansing, J. B. and Stephen Withey, "Consumer Anticipations, Their Use in Forecasting Consumer Behavior," in *Short Term Economic Forecasting,* Princeton University Press, Princeton, 1955; Tobin, James, "On the Predictive Value of Consumer Intentions and Attitudes." *Review of Economics and Statistics,* Vol. 41, February, 1959, pp. 1–11, and "Comments by George Katona," *Review of Economics and Statistics,* Vol. 41, August, 1959, p. 317; Mueller, Eva, "Effects of Consumer Attitudes on Purchases," *op. cit.;* Mueller, Eva, "Consumer Attitudes: Their Influence and Forecasting Value," in *The Quality and Economic Significance of Anticipations Data,* Princeton University Press, Princeton, 1960; Lininger, Charles, Eva Mueller, and Hans Wyss, "Some Uses of Panel Studies in Forecasting the Automobile Market," *Proceedings of the Business and Economic Statistics Section,* American Statistics Association, September, 1957, pp. 409–421; Juster, F. T., *Anticipations and Purchases.* Princeton University Press, Princeton, 1964; Mueller, Eva, "Ten Years of Consumer Attitude Surveys, *op. cit.*

motivation and the need for a better theoretical treatment of plans is revealed by the large proportion who do not carry out their plans, and the substantial number (though a small proportion) who buy without having expressed a plan. There have also been attempts to assess data on business plans and anticipations data by seeing how well they help forecast the level of national product.[51]

MIDDLE-RANGE CHANGES IN BEHAVIOR

Turning now to middle-range predictions—predictions of what the consumer or businessman might do over the next year or two or three—it becomes even more obvious that we must take account of not only their own expectations, situations, and plans, but of the economy and changes in the situations they face. Simple descriptive background information is useful even here. If it is known that people react adversely to an inflation, or that an expectation of an income increase stimulates them to buy durables, or that they dislike living with their relatives, or that more and more of them are getting into the stock market (so that a fall in the price of stocks would affect a larger number of people), this helps the economist in thinking about how people may react to events which have not yet happened.

It is also possible to combine information from surveys with demographic knowledge of the structure of the population. It is always easy to predict the age distribution of the population a few years hence. People have a neat habit of getting one year older each year. A few years hence the teenagers will be college students, and the college students of today will be young married couples buying furniture. One can extrapolate trends in such things as the proportion who own their homes or the proportion of wives at various ages who will be working. Knowing the different patterns of behavior of different age groups of the population, particularly if we have surveys at different points in time, one can then look at the implications of assuming that this behavior is a result of their chronological age or the period in which they grew up. In the case of air travel, for instance, the younger generation took their first air trips at a much earlier age than did the older generation. By the time our present twenty-five-year olds are forty-five, many more of

---

51. Okun, Arthur, "The Value of Anticipations Data in Forecasting National Product," and "Comments by George Katona," in *The Quality and Economic Significance* . . . , *op. cit.;* Eisner, Robert and Robert Strotz, "Determinants of Business Investment," in *Impacts of Monetary Policy*. Commission on Money and Credit, Prentice-Hall, Englewood Cliffs, N.J., 1963.

them will have had experience with air travel than our present forty-five-year olds. Hence, we can use data from surveys about relationships of economic behavior to demographic facts or income, or changes in income combined with forecasts of basic shifts in the distribution of the population by age, income, and so forth, to make intelligent estimates about what the situation might be like in the future.

USE OF SURVEY DATA IN STRUCTURAL MODELS

A new possibility is now on the horizon—the possibility of building survey data into structural models of the economic system. There are two basic types of models. First, there are the traditional macro-models of the Klein-Goldberger sort.[52] The Surveys of Consumer Finances and the interim surveys of the Survey Research Center will soon cover enough years so that data from them can be built into time series to be combined with aggregate time-series data. For instance, from a series of surveys running over twenty years, one can get measures each year of the inequality of income, the proportion whose debt is more than a given per cent of their income, the proportion with debt payments which will continue for a given time, the proportion whose income has increased, the proportion with no liquid assets, the proportion who have buying plans or are optimistic about their financial future, and so forth. These variables can then be built into an ordinary structural equation model of the economy along with the national income data. Not much has been done along these lines until recently, except for the use of McGraw-Hill business surveys in the Klein model, simply because there were only 10 or 15 years of data.[53] The time is at hand when it is feasible and useful to try including survey data in such models. The process of disaggregating structural equation models is going on apace, using finer parts of the national income statistics and sometimes state data. The next step is to incorporate data from cross-section surveys of consumers and of

52. Klein, L. R. and A. S. Goldberger, *Econometric Model of the U.S., 1929–1952:* Contributions to Economic Analysis, Vol. 9. North Holland Publishing, Amsterdam, 1955; Suits, Daniel, "Forecasting and Analysis with an Econometric Model," *American Economic Review,* Vol. 52, March, 1962, pp. 104–132.

53. Instead, attempts had been made to estimate behavioral *relations* from surveys and then incorporate them into time-series studies, but this raised serious problems. The survey relations were long-run effects but time series deal with short-run effects. See: Kuh, Edwin and J. R. Meyer, "How Extraneous are Extraneous Estimates?" *Review of Economics and Statistics,* Vol. 39, November, 1957, pp. 380–393. For the Klein use of business plans, see Evans, M. K. and E. W. Green, *op. cit.*

businessmen. For this reason, it is extremely important to continue a basic series of cross-section surveys like the Surveys of Consumer Finances—surveys which collect on a comparable basis data on incomes, assets, debts, as well as attitudes and plans of consumers.

An even more enticing method of using survey data along with other data in large-scale models is in the new iterative micro-analysis models. These models use survey data of a conditional probability sort—relation between initial assets and spending, between income change and spending, and so forth. These models require a very large amount of detailed information to simulate the dynamics of an economic system. They allow much more use of what we know about the behavior of people and they provide information on the implications of assumptions about interactions. They dodge the troublesome and basically insoluble problems of getting from individual behavior to aggregate behavior assumptions, since it is the computer that does the aggregation: the data are added, not the relationships. Most of the path-breaking work in this area has been done by Guy Orcutt and his colleagues at the University of Wisconsin.[54] Those who have studied the mathematics of such models have been impressed with the tremendous need for empirical data:

> Because computer models have such a large capacity for utilizing empirical data, a burden may be placed upon the actual collection of empirical information. We know of no obviously optimal procedure for gathering information that exists inside firms or inside consumer's heads. Nevertheless this is the kind of information which economists desire and which computer models can readily handle. Once the reduction of a system to its individual decision-making units has been accomplished, there is great hope for a solution to the aggregation problem. Thus through computer models we see the possibility of developing working models of the economy that will have a solid empirical basis.[55]

54. Orcutt, Guy *et al., Microanalysis of Socioeconomic Systems.* Harper & Bros., New York, 1961; Orcutt, Guy, "Simulation of Economic Systems," *American Economic Review,* Vol. 50, December, 1960.
55. Cohen, K. J., and R. M. Cyert, "Computer Models and Dynamic Economics," *Quarterly Journal of Economics,* Vol. 75, February, 1961, pp. 112–127. See also Cyert, R. M., E. A. Feigenbaum, and J. G. March, "Models in a Behavioral Theory of the Firm," *Behavioral Science,* Vol. 55, April, 1959, pp. 81–95.

It may not be obvious why it is so difficult to derive a relationship between aggregate income and aggregate spending, for example, from relationships between income and spending for individuals. To take a simple but extreme example: suppose that no one with an income under $3,000 buys a suit of clothes, and that everyone with an income of $3,000 or more buys just one suit per year. In this situation, relations between aggregate income (or average income for the population) and aggregate numbers of suits purchased, would not only produce a misleading relationship but one that would not be stable as incomes rose. At the point where everyone had an income of $3,000 or more, additional increases in income would have no effect on suit sales!

A great deal of mathematical analysis of the problem of aggregation has been done, but it turns out upon closer examination that one can derive aggregate relationships from micro-relationships only if one is willing to make enough restrictive assumptions. The difficulty is that the assumptions must be so restrictive as to make the conclusions useful largely as exercises in mathematics.

By using many household and business units, each representing a highly homogeneous set of similar units in the population, it is possible to make use of detailed and realistic relationships—derived largely from survey data—between initial conditions and subsequent behavior in a short period. As the iterative process proceeds, the computer takes account of the demands and supplies in markets to adjust prices, and can force other aggregate relationships to come out right. The effects on the behavior of an individual of what others have been doing can be built into the system, as well as probabilistic factors such as mortality and fecundity. The details of the model, and of the way in which a large-scale computer is used to simulate the real world, need not detain us here. The crucial thing is that the model can make use of an almost limitless amount of information about human behavior, yet can get along without some of it by making cruder, less differentiated assumptions. It deals with the behavior of representative individuals, yet can always show what happens to the aggregates. It can show us ultimately the results of changed behavior patterns, or possible results of changed government policies or laws.

For the first time, instead of having a great deal of detailed information about consumer behavior on the one hand, and aggregate models which could not make use of it on the other, economists now have the possibility of converting data about the behavior of individuals directly into a system which tells them about the aggregate dynamics of the system as a whole. This approach is a major scientific breakthrough.

New possibilities for using complex behavioral relations make even more pressing the need for better methods of discovering such relationships. Survey data must be analyzed in such a way as to discover such relations and quantify them properly. If one only wants an effect of income on spending, as free as possible from the effects of other ("noise") variables, then a multiple correlation may be satisfactory. But if the effects of income changes are different for different kinds of people—something we can find out in a survey—and if there is a micro-analysis method which can make use of the information, then methods of analysis are needed which can discover such interaction effects.

Sociologists, starting with purposes of finding interactions and patterns, and weaned on the analysis of variance, have no difficulty appreciating this. Economists, used to assuming that everything is linear to a first approximation, do not always realize that the "multivariate analysis" using regression really throws away everything except all the possible two-way tables. They fail to use the rich detail available in survey data. We shall return to this problem later in the chapter.

Any model of the whole economic system requires information also about factors affecting business decisions. While there have been a number of studies, using only published data, of business decisions inferring causation from the differences between firms, the necessity for more detailed information available only through surveys frequently becomes apparent:

> The only way to avoid this difficulty is to have a detailed approach to individual firms involving the study and collection of basic data on such matters as the planning horizon, length of the production period, revision of plans within periods, sales forecasting methods, price forecasts, etc. The collection of actual data on expectational and planned variables would then enable various parts of the model to be tested separately and might hopefully lead to the development of a more realistic theory of output determination.[56]

LONG-TERM CHANGES

Turning to the analysis of changes in consumer behavior over longer periods of time, our conditional probabilities tend to become intergenera-

56. Johnston, J., "An Econometric Study of the Production Decision." *Quarterly Journal of Economics*, Vol. 71, May, 1961, pp. 234–261, especially, p. 261.

tional. Theories deal less with the effects of events on attitudes and the effects of these attitudes on behavior, and more with the way in which parents influence the personality characteristics of their children, or invest in their children's education.

In some recent work on change in the level of completed education between one generation and the next, we have looked at the possibility of extrapolating by using a distribution of transition probabilities between father and son over several generations of the future, to see what the distribution of education would look like three generations hence if the same pattern continued. Examination of this so-called Markov process shows that the average levels of education in the country will increase, but probably at a decreasing rate.[57] Converting transition probabilities into a Markov process is tricky, of course, because people have different numbers of children, and the number of children may affect the transmission itself. Children of large families tend to get less education. By starting with a population of heads of spending units (most of the men in the population) and using the relation of their education to that of their fathers, one weighs the conditional probabilities by the number of sons to which they apply.

Such analyses are crucial because estimates of the future labor force, the demand for public support for education, and the possible shortage of teachers, all depend on the results of such projections. Similar long-term analyses of the participation of wives in the labor force can be devised using several alternative approaches. The more we know about the details of the present situation and its trends, the more intelligent these projections can be. Better theories of the causes and effects of stable motivational dispositions will also help. Indeed, for analyzing long-run problems of economic development as a whole, the field has been invaded by a path-breaking new theory of motivational determinants plus some scattered, but exciting empirical evidence.[58] The theory, in brief summary, is that early independence training in childhood tends to develop a stable personality disposition oriented toward achievement—overcoming obstacles by one's own effort in situations where there is a clear standard of excellence. The economist's picture of the entrepreneur fits the definition of a person with a high need for achievement. Evidence is accumulating both from laboratory experi-

57. See Morgan, James *et al., Income and Welfare in the United States, op. cit.*
58. McClelland, David, *The Achieving Society.* D. Van Nostrand, Princeton, N.J., 1961; Atkinson, John, *Motives in Fantasy, Action and Society.* D. Van Nostrand, Princeton, N.J., 1958.

ments and survey data that there are such differences between people and that they help explain differences in behavior.[59]

TESTING ECONOMIC HYPOTHESES

The use of survey data in testing specific hypotheses derived from economic theory has been infrequent, largely because the very simple assumptions of economic theory do not lend themselves to many testable propositions. Kuenne found, "The number of general systems from which we can derive any operational theorems is relatively small, and the empirical content of these hypotheses quite disappointing in scope and restrictiveness."[60]

Perhaps the closest thing to testing hypotheses are tests of the consistency of preferences as revealed in actual behavior, which are generally done in the laboratory but occasionally by ingenious use of survey data.[61] A vast amount of secondary analysis of survey data was precipitated by Friedman's "permanent income theory," but the more recent and sophisticated writers have concluded that its contribution is more one of statistical estimation (a problem of errors in variables) than of testing a proposition about human behavior.[62] And insofar as one did estimate the relation between "permanent income" and "permanent consumption," the results are of little use in predicting consumer responses to short-run changes in income.

More recently, some interesting uses of data from a series of labor force surveys to test hypotheses about the effects of unemployment in discouraging workers from staying in the labor force, or encouraging their wives to

59. Atkinson, John, *A Theory of Achievement Motivation.* John Wiley & Sons, New York, 1966.
60. Kuenne, R. E., *The Theory of General Economic Equilibrium.* Princeton University Press, Princeton, N.J., 1963, p. 37.
61. Koo, A. Y. C., "An Empirical Test of Revealed Preference Theory," *Econometrica,* Vol. 31, October, 1963, pp. 646–664.
62. Friedman, Milton, *A Theory of the Consumption Function.* Princeton University Press, Princeton, 1957. For an example of the discussion, see Houthakker, H. S., "The Permanent Income Hypothesis," *American Economic Review,* Vol. 48, June, 1958, pp. 396–404; Eisner, Robert, "The Permanent Income Hypothesis: Comment" *American Economic Review,* Vol. 48, December, 1958, pp. 972–991; and Houthakker, H. S., "The Permanent Income Hypothesis: Reply," *American Economic Review,* Vol. 48, December, 1958, pp. 991–993. For the present state, see Liviatan, Nissan, "Tests of the Permanent-Income Hypothesis Based on a Reinterview Savings Survey," (with comment by Milton Friedman and a reply), in *Measurement in Economics.* Stanford University Press, Stanford, 1963.

enter it, have appeared.[63] They deal with a real immediate problem, since attempts to abolish unemployment are complicated by the tendency for more people to enter the labor force when employment conditions are better—the goal of full employment tends to recede as one approaches it.

Some Methodological Developments, Problems and Prospects

ACCURACY AND VALIDITY OF DATA

Economists coming from a long tradition of dealing with records which are generally assumed to be accurate, have oscillated between the view that survey data are no good at all and a desire to use them for purposes for which they are not adequate, such as estimating aggregates. Many economic quantities are distributed in a skewed fashion with a few large holders, so that means estimated from small samples are unstable, and their sampling errors not even normally distributed.

In addition, the largest items are subject to conceptual difficulties—such as joint ownership, trust arrangements and valuation estimates—and errors from non-response or biased response. A good deal of information is being accumulated about the reliability of factual information that is col-lected from consumers. Of course, respondents are sometimes wrong in what they report, or unwilling to report at all. If, however, one regards the data as rough indicators of order of magnitude they are still useful for test-ing hypotheses. Indeed, unless the errors are biased in some particular way, they can only keep us from finding a significant relation if one exists. They are quite unlikely to lead us to accept hypotheses which are, in fact, erro-neous. They can, however, distort our impressions as to which factors would be most meaningful if only they were all measured equally well.

There is an unfortunate tendency to believe that if survey estimates, when "blown up," do not agree with aggregate statistics based on records, then survey data are not good for analyses of relationships, or rough differentiation. A good deal of methodological work has been done since 1950 to uncover possible sources of error and develop improved techniques, but the justification of, for example, a new national survey of saving, should never be as a method of estimating aggregates. After ten years, with the new higher prices and higher incomes, even relatively crude estimates of changes in the patterns of savings behavior would be revealing.

63. Dernberg, Thomas and Kenneth Strand, "Hidden Unemployment 1953–62: A Quantitative Analysis by Age and Sex," *American Economic Review,* Vol. 56, March, 1966, pp. 71–75.

There have been a number of validity studies, reporting various levels of accuracy, and making various suggestions for improvement.[64] One difficulty is that there is enough sensitivity of response error to the details of the subject matter, the method, etc., so that it is difficult to generalize. Secondly, not enough is known about the *reasons* behind the response errors.

It is also an interesting question, if a man erroneously thinks his liquid assets are higher than they were a year ago, whether it is his impression of the facts, or the facts, which will influence his behavior. Studies of what is behind many aggregate statistics might well show difficulties in *their* interpretation, and inaccuracies, not now dreamed of.

There will always be limitations on what kind of data one can expect to collect in surveys. Recent validity studies indicate that, particularly among people with complex affairs, precise estimates of asset holdings and even of incomes may well be impossible.

There is reason to believe that people's memory of the dating of events and of the amount of time devoted to tasks is also subject to error. In a recent study of productive use of time, the Survey Research Center has not relied entirely on estimates of the time taken in regular housework, but is also focusing on how much of that time is "bought back" by hiring someone else to do the work around the house, or by eating in restaurants or sending

64. Kish, Leslie and J. B. Lansing, "Response Errors in Estimating the Value of Homes," *Journal of the American Statistical Association,* Vol. 49, September, 1954, pp. 520–538; Sirkin, Monroe, E. S. Maynes and John Frechtling, "The Survey of Consumer Finances and The Census Quality Check," in *An Appraisal of the 1950 Census Income Data.* Princeton University Press, Princeton, 1958; Ferber, Robert, *Collecting Financial Data by Consumer Panel Techniques.* Bureau of Economic and Business Research, University of Illinois, Urbana, 1959; Lansing, J. B., Gerald Ginsburg, and Kaisa Braaten, *An Investigation of Response Error.* Bureau of Economic and Business Research, University of Illinois, Urbana, 1961; Barlow, Robin, James Morgan, and Grover Wirick, "A Study of Validity in Reporting Medical Care in Michigan," *Proceedings of the Social Statistics Section,* American Statistical Association, 1960; Neter, John and Joseph Waksberg, "A Study of Response Errors in Expenditure Data from Household Surveys," *Journal of the American Statistical Association,* Vol. 54, March, 1964, pp. 18–55; Neter, John and Joseph Waksberg, "Conditioning Effects from Repeated Household Interviews," *Journal of Marketing,* Vol. 18, April, 1964, pp. 51–56; Maynes, E. S., "The Anatomy of Response Errors: Consumer Saving," *Journal of Marketing Research,* Vol. 2, November, 1965, pp. 378–387; Ferber, Robert, "The Reliability of Consumers Surveys of Financial Holdings: Demand Deposits," *Journal of the American Statistical Association,* Vol. 61, March, 1966, pp. 91–103.

the laundry out. There will also be an attempt to estimate how much *extra* work is devoted to dressmaking or preserving food. Even with some error, it will be important to understand the large differences in patterns of time use.

We have already noted that for understanding and predicting the behavior of consumers and businessmen, a complex and relevant theory of behavior is needed. It may even be necessary to use variables that are not of much interest to economists in order to eliminate their effects and see what variables are important among those that will remain when we aggregate across a group of consumers. Economists may find themselves contributing to the fields of sociology or psychology, a by-product of their main concern with isolating the effects of variables which are important in models of an economic system. What many economists do not realize, however, is that the development of techniques of interviewing and content analysis make it possible to quantify things which economists say are non-measurable. It is, of course, quite true that it is impossible really to compare the level of satisfaction or happiness of two individuals. On the other hand, it is possible to develop an arbitrary scale of expressed satisfaction and see how differences in this scale are correlated with other variables, on the assumption that the random process of selecting individuals would still leave a visible effect of the factor we are investigating *if* it indeed does affect consumer satisfaction. Indeed, it is even possible that some apparently "soft" information, such as people's expectations, may be quantifiable with more accuracy than such "hard facts" as the value of their assets or the size of the last hospital bill.

In summary, there are many levels at which survey data can be used to explain and predict consumer and business behavior, and ultimately these data will have to be combined with other more traditional forms of aggregate data and data from other sources. But the critical fact is that the data from other sources have been plentiful and are becoming more plentiful all the time, while good information about consumers and businessmen—how they behave and some of the reasons for their behavior—is extremely scarce and threatens to be the bottleneck in the development of economics as a science.

METHODS OF ANALYSIS

The use by economists of the new cross-section survey data containing rich details about individuals, in an attempt to find out what influences consumer and business behavior, has led to a whole new series of statistical problems in the analysis of data. First, there is not one simple hypothesis to test but there are a number of alternative hypotheses to choose among. Consequently, statistical significance is less crucial than reduction in errors of prediction. How much can one reduce the error in predicting the behavior of a group of people if a particular fact is known about each one of them?

Second, there are not only the usual multi-collinearity problems that have plagued the analysis of time series, but problems associated with non-linearity in the relationships and with explanatory factors which are not variables but classifications. There is a rapidly growing tendency to deal with the problem of "classification variables" and at the same time with the problem of non-linearity in the effects of these factors by the use of dummy variables in a multiple regression.[65] The problem of non-linearity in the *relations* (interaction effects) is a far more serious problem and not so easy to deal with. One can put cross-product variables into a regression analysis, but certainly not all possible ones, particularly where dummy variables are used for each class of each characteristic. When these interaction effects are so included, it becomes difficult to say anything about the effects of any one component factor, though that is to be expected whenever interactions exist. Sometimes an additive approximation is close, particularly where the group which reacts differently is only a small subgroup of the main population.

However, substantial evidence of interaction effects already exists. For instance, age and education jointly affect earnings, just as age and sex jointly affect the need for medical care—the young women have babies and the men collapse when they retire. A particularly useful example is the combination of age, marital status, and age of the youngest child which defines stages in the life cycle of the family.[66]

A third problem arises from the fact that we have measured classifications or variables which are only remotely connected to the theoretical

65. See Suits, Daniel, "Use of Dummy Variables in Regression Equations," *Journal of American Statistical Association,* Vol. 52, December, 1957, pp. 548–551. See also Hill, T. P., "Analysis of the Distribution of Wages and Salaries in Great Britain," *Econometrica,* Vol. 27, July, 1959, pp. 355–381.
66. Lansing, J. B. and James Morgan, "Consumer Finances Over the Life Cycle," in *Consumer Behavior,* Vol. 2. Edited by Lincoln Clark. New York University Press, New York, 1955; Kish, Leslie and J. B. Lansing, "Family Life Cycle as an Independent Variable," *American Sociological Review,* Vol. 22, October, 1957, pp. 512–519.

constructs, the effects of which we should like to test. We treat the things we can measure as proxy variables for the concepts we cannot. Frequently a single thing like age or education or liquid asset holdings is a proxy for more than one concept. Race may represent differences in family background, in education, the effects of discrimination, and perhaps differences in motivation resulting from everything else (but not easily changeable). Age may represent a chronological age or a difference in the period of history in which the individual grew up. In looking at the demand for housing, family size represents both the need for more housing space and pressures to use the income for food and clothing instead. A high level of initial liquid assets represents both a capacity to spend more than one's income and the probability that this is a family that has resisted the temptation to spend as much as their income over periods in the past while they were accumulating these liquid assets. Actually, the attitudinal questions which seem too imprecise at first, may be a closer approximation to an operationally defined variable than the demographic facts which are only proxies for something else.

This third problem affects our ability to determine which factors are most important. It may be that if we could only measure it correctly, a particular factor would prove to be most important of all. For immediate practical purposes, like forecasting, this may not be important, but for longer-run development of the science, it is crucial. Also, a variable which proves unimportant because it relates only to a small subgroup in the population may become important if that group becomes larger, e.g., owners of common stock. Hence, interpretation remains something of an art requiring judgment, and the bringing to bear of other information.

A final problem in analysis and interpretation arises because causation generally operates in time, and in sequential chains. We do not really have a large number of independent or even simultaneously interacting factors affecting behavior. Some forces are logically prior to others in the sense that they can affect the others but cannot be affected by them. For instance, early childhood (rural schools, parental religion, etc.) can affect the amount and quality of education a man gets, but not the reverse.

To place all these factors on the same level in a simultaneous determination of some dependent variables is clearly a violation of reality. To take only residuals from the analysis of the first-stage early variables to analyze the effects of the second set, assumes that there are no interaction effects between them. (The effects of education may depend on the individual's parental background.)

We have multivariate techniques, which can handle classifications (in place of variables) using dummy variables, and some interaction effects (assuming that they are universal) using interaction dummies. We can take account of sequences in the causal chain by analyzing the residuals from one analysis against a new set of variables, even building in some possible interaction effects with variables whose main effects have been removed. But the process is cumbersome and requires a great deal of selection of hypotheses and variables at the beginning.

More recently, a computer technique has been developed for searching for interaction effects—a simulation which applies the specific tests of a good researcher but with endless patience—in examining a body of survey data.[67] With it, new patterns of influences have been uncovered that even dummy-variable multiple regression had failed to find. For example, in the analysis of saving, it turned out that initial assets were positively associated with saving for home owners, and negatively associated with the subsequent saving of non-owners. Thus, two conflicting hypotheses of economists both turned out to be true, but for different segments of the population.[68]

An important methodological problem has to do with three explanatory factors which are so related that it is impossible to untangle them completely: the age of the individual, the generation to which he belongs (his date of birth), and the year when the action takes place. There is no way to hold two of these constant and vary the third, and that is what is required if we are to determine the effect of that third one. In any one year, there is a perfect correlation between a man's age and the year when he was born. In a series of reports on the actions of individuals born in a given era, there is a perfect correlation between the year of the action and their ages. If we take data from a number of years about the behavior of a particular age group, there is a perfect correlation between their year of birth and the year of

67. See Morgan, James and John Sonquist, "Problems in the Analysis of Survey Data, and a Proposal," *Journal of the American Statistical Association*, Vol. 58, June, 1963, pp. 415–434; Sonquist, John and James Morgan, *The Detection of Interaction Effects*. Monograph 35, Survey Research Center, Institute for Social Research, University of Michigan, Ann Arbor, 1964.
68. Kosobud, Richard and James Morgan, eds., *Consumer Behavior of Individual Families . . . , op. cit.*

the action. Hence, if there are actually three separate effects—the effect of the year of birth and the era when one grew up, the effect of actual age, and the effect of a general trend indicated by the year—then we can never separate them. Only if we can assume that one of the three is negligible, can we separate the influence of the other two. For instance, if chronological age does not matter, we can look at the time trends in the behavior of different generations, to see whether they are separate, or interacting. If the generation of birth does not matter, we can look at trends over time in the differences between age groups. And if there is no time trend, we can use information on the behavior of the same individuals at different points in time to separate the effects of their age and the date of their birth.

There is, however, much to be learned from series of surveys over time, which at least allow one to observe trends in the behavior of each generation, not only in their economic behavior but in the attitudes and the reasons they give for their behavior.

There is also much to be learned from comparative surveys in different countries or areas. With these, as with comparisons over time, analysis problems arise. The optimal procedure seems to be a within-country-between-country design or, in the case of repeated surveys in one place, a within-year-between-years design. By applying the same multivariate analysis to survey data from different places or different years, one can ask whether:

1. The same explanatory variables operate in the same way, but their distribution in the population is different.[69] For instance, education has the same powerful effects, but more people are educated in one time or place than the other.
2. The estimated effects of some of the predictors are different. For instance, religious preference may matter in this country, and not in Europe.
3. Neither of these is true, and only the constant term in the equation differs.

In the last case, we are reduced to speculation unless there are enough different countries or times to provide a few degrees of freedom. Fortu-

69. An international comparison of income elasticities is: Houthakker, H. S., "An International Comparison of Household Expenditure Patterns Commemorating the Centenary of Engel's Law," *Econometrica*, Vol. 25, October, 1957, pp. 532–551.

nately, there is so much variation within populations, between different sub-groups, that it seems likely that at least some of the differences between times or places can be attributed more precisely.

THE ECONOMIC PROBLEMS OF SURVEY RESEARCH

We turn briefly from discussing survey research on economic problems to discussing some economic problems of survey research. They are common to survey research in other fields, of course, but are discussed here because the author is an economist.

One of the reasons there has been so little survey research when so many economic problems cry for better information, is that it is expensive. It is expensive both because it requires the combining of a number of scarce skills, and because it involves heavy tooling-up costs. Survey research is a high overhead cost industry, involving expenses in hiring and training inter-viewers, designing samples and developing lists of addresses, maintaining a staff of specialists in sampling, questionnaire design, content analysis, and data processing. Once an organization is tooled up to do national sample surveys, its efficiency in conducting a series is much greater because the overhead costs can be spread over a number of surveys.

Even with sequences of surveys, the costs of designing and conducting each survey are still so great that small-scale pilot studies are needed to test out hypotheses and procedures, and to select those worth testing and quantifying on a national probability sample. The development of a number of survey centers in major universities is a hopeful sign.

It is still a major problem that there is not enough support for survey re-search on economic behavior to keep even one major center operating at capacity. If there is such a crying need for such research, why is so little being done and most of that paid for by foundations? The reason is, sim-ply, that no one wants to pay for something if someone else will. Since one does not lose information by giving it away, it is not a commodity of finite quantity which can be distributed to those willing to pay for it.

There are certain kinds of goods and services which are not adequately provided by a free private enterprise system. This is particularly true of goods and services where one's enjoyment of these services is not decreased if another person also enjoys them. A classic textbook case is a fireworks display, whose total social value depends on the number of people who watch it and enjoy it. It does not have a fixed total utility value that is divided among people. Particularly in the economic survey data field, a strong case can be made that such data are social goods, not marketable in the usual sense. The marginal cost of giving the information to other people is negligible once it is collected. Hence, there are strong reasons why society should pay for the collection of broadly useful background information including survey data.

Someone, of course, has to decide what kinds of data and how much of each are needed. It is possible to argue that economic survey data deserve a very large amount of public support because of their crucial importance in understanding and guiding our economic system. Our legislatures are making decisions involving millions of dollars every day on the basis of assumptions about how people will behave. When the social security system is changed, assumptions are made about the incentive to work, about when people want to retire, about the importance of economic security. When the tax laws are changed, assumptions are made about what people will do with any tax cuts, and about the extent to which people's other decisions are being influenced by tax considerations. When legislators decide that it is all right to have an unbalanced federal budget, or that some other fiscal policy is needed, they are making assumptions both about the levels of planned expenditures of consumers and businessmen, and also about the way people may react to the coming changes in the economy, and indeed to the fiscal policy itself. When states change their workmen's compensation laws, they too are making assumptions about human behavior. When the welfare department attempts to crack down on people on welfare, they too are making assumptions about such things as the effects of monetary payments on the tendency to have an illegitimate child.

Ultimately, someone has to make a decision as to how much survey data can be collected and analyzed, but it seems clear that the amount of financial support for research in the area of consumer and business behavior is grossly inadequate to the problems, the best solution of which require this information. A final problem arises whenever it becomes necessary for the government to support research in this or any other area. Government agencies are ideally suited for standard collection of well-agreed-upon information. But when it comes to more basic developmental work, there is a lot to be said for farming research out to a number of independent agencies. This is already being done in other fields by such organizations as the Rand Corporation. But it needs to be extended to the fields of survey research in a much broader way than it is or has been in the past. The creation of a

Center for Studies of Poverty at the University of Wisconsin may be a step in this direction.

Survey data are cross-section snapshots. How does one get from such static information to dynamic relationships? There are a number of ways. The simplest is to infer them from differences in the cross section, on the assumption that if people move to a different subgroup, they are likely to change their behavior in the direction of that group's behavior—not necessarily because the group influences them, but largely because they are facing the same set of circumstances. But one can do more than this. Survey data cover both conditions at the beginning of a period and behavior during that period. This produces dynamic relations of the conditional-probability sort that are used in the Orcutt simulation system. While memory errors surely increase as one asks for events more distant in time, more can be done with family history. Indeed, the 1961 Survey of Consumer Finances attempted in a national cross section to elicit information about the earnings of the head of the spending unit at various times in the past. While there is some distortion, the overall results look good enough for analysis to help, for instance, explain differences in the accumulation of assets.

Reinterviews and panel studies provide still more dynamic data, and are the only way one can relate initial attitudes, plans, and other things difficult to remember, to subsequent behavior. Since there are so many idiosyncratic forces affecting attitudes and behavior, however, the real payoff only comes with a sequence of three interviews with the same people, where *changes* in initial conditions between the first two waves can be related to *changes* in the behavior reported subsequently, in the second and third interviews. It may thus be possible, in spite of past disappointments, to derive from panel surveys more appropriate short-run functional relationships—particularly income elasticities of expenditures on major items—and incorporate them into time-series models. This reduces the number of things that must be estimated from the time-series data. It is true, however, that a panel rapidly ceases to be representative of the whole population, not only because of "mortality" through moving, refusal, death, etc., but also because of possible effects of the interviewing itself.

Additional insights can be gained by repeated surveys with different but representative cross sections, during periods when economic conditions change. Changed behavior of identifiable subgroups can then be interpreted.

Survey methods are now developed to the point where such comparisons can be made with some confidence even for attitudes.

A number of people have suggested variants of a procedure involving the sampling of records. Interviewing people known to have a particular asset or to have engaged in one particular transaction provides evidence of biases and under-reporting and over-reporting which can be used to make adjustments to survey data. If enough different sources were available and could be put together, one could even make estimates of distributions that way.

One can also interview people known to have some asset, or to have engaged in some transaction, to ascertain other relevant explanatory facts about those same individuals. A study of stockholders now being made by Friend and Crockett is an example.

Even more exciting is the possibility of mass merging of different data sources. It should be possible to develop a central data bank where information about the same individuals from various sources can be cross-analyzed without any violation of confidential interviews. Of particularly great potential would be a national data bank containing basic information from censuses and the Internal Revenue Service, covering the whole country. Small samples from surveys could then be merged and analyses made using the combined data, with no identification of individuals outside the computer. A prerequisite for such a development might be a constitutional amendment guaranteeing the privacy of such individual records.

There are, of course, problems, particularly with changing compositions of families, and the basic unit might well have to be the individual and his social security number. But the development both of computers and of multivariate analysis procedures is far ahead of the organization required to maximize their utility.

Another exciting prospect is the possibility of putting meaning into aggregate statistics by knowing something about what is behind them. Suppose, for instance, that by sampling recent withdrawals from some type of asset, it is discovered that a large proportion of the individuals responsible have shifted to another asset for some particular reason, or that they are mostly small businessmen with losses. This is very useful in interpreting the aggregate statistics. Such information would reduce the tendency to assume the motive from the institutional source of the data.

Finally, it is possible to throw light on consumer or business behavior by comparable studies done in different countries, at different stages in their development, or with different systems of taxes or social security, etc.

There has been inadequate communication and few surveys in other countries using modern, reliable, and comparable methods. One notable exception was the British saving surveys which were modeled after the Surveys of Consumer Finances. They allowed some comparisons.[70] It turned out, for instance, that the distribution of income is considerably more unequal in this country, largely because we have so many poor farmers.

OTHER AREAS FOR FURTHER STUDY

In addition to the many areas of economic behavior in which continued study is needed, there are some ancillary areas where we need to know more. For instance, we may understand decisions better if we study the decision-making *process,* not just its outcome. How much information seeking and deliberation takes place?[71] What happens within a family when several different sets of desires and preferences are involved?[72] How much communication and how much consensus is there between husband and wife? Even apart from the substantive interest, the answer to the last question will help decide whom to interview, and whether to ask respondents how others in the family feel, and how to interpret such information.

People's levels of information and of economic insight affect their decisions, hence we need to know more about how people get such information and insights. Modern national policies require citizen support, but that support needs to be informed and intelligent. Studies of what people understand about economic policy and problems and how they react to new information and insight are sorely needed.

Finally, there are areas of social decision where it is becoming increasingly important to know what people really want. As more "collective consumption" in the form of public recreational facilities and similar things is proposed, some method more effective and less subject to distortion than the ballot box needs to be developed to guide congressmen. Indeed, a new

70. Lyndall, Harold and J. B. Lansing, "A Comparison of Distribution of Personal Income and Wealth in the United States and Great Britain," *American Economic Review,* Vol. 49, March, 1959, pp. 43–67; Lyndall, Harold and J. B. Lansing, "An Anglo-American Comparison of Personal Saving," *Bulletin of the Oxford University Institute of Statistics,* Vol. 22, 1960, pp. 225–258.
71. Mueller, Eva, "A Study of Purchase Decisions," in *Consumer Behavior.* Edited by Lincoln Clark. New York University Press, New York, 1955.
72. Morgan, James, "Decision-Making in the Family," in *Household Decision Making, Consumer Behavior,* Vol. 4. Edited by Nelson Foote. New York University Press, New York, 1960.

law providing congressmen with free mailing to every household in their districts has started members of the national congress on a spree of polling of their constituents. But policy should not be made by polls. There need to be sophisticated assessments of people's concerns and problems which the legislators then interpret into policy.

Summary

New techniques of sampling human populations, eliciting information from them, and analyzing the rich data which result, provide the economist today with information about consumers and businessmen and about the forces that affect their economic decisions. Even if such information is used only in the interpreting of aggregate statistics or in the building of more realistic aggregative models, it will be useful. It promises to be even more useful when built directly into economic models. In particular, the new micro-models which simulate the behavior of the economic system make it possible to use almost anything that can be found out about human behavior, and to derive from them answers about the working of the whole economic system, which are what the economist seeks.

Assessment of the efficiency and equity of an economic system in allocating productive resources and in distributing the fruits of production to people, also requires knowing more about the individual decisions that affect such processes. Why don't workers move where the jobs are? Are consumers really being deceived by advertising and packaging and the hidden costs of credit? How seriously is ignorance or lack of understanding hampering the effectiveness of our relatively free enterprise system?

Faced with a growing need for better information about human behavior, both for economic research and for more immediate policy decisions such as those in social welfare and tax legislation, economists must deal with the social nature of information and of research findings. The problem of adequate, stable, and properly allocated financing of survey research is itself a problem in economic analysis and policy which requires an early answer.

Bibliography:

Adams, J. F., "Economic-Financial Consequences of Personal Injuries Sustained in 1953 Philadelphia Auto Accidents," *Economics and Business Bulletin,* Temple University, Philadelphia, 1955.

Anderson, Odin and Jacob Feldman, *Family Medical Costs and Voluntary Health Insurance:* A Nationwide Survey. McGraw-Hill, New York, 1956.

Anderson, Odin, Patricia Collette, and Jacob Feldman, *Changes in Family Medical Care and Voluntary Health Insurance.* Harvard University Press, 1963.

Asimakopulos, Athanasios, "Analysis of Canadian Consumer Expenditure Surveys," *Canadian Journal of Economics and Political Science,* Vol. 31, May, 1965, pp. 222–241.

Atkinson, John, *Motives in Fantasy, Action and Society.* D. Van Nostrand, Princeton, N.J., 1958.

Atkinson, John, *A Theory of Achievement Motivation.* John Wiley & Sons, New York, 1966.

Baker, D. J. and C. H. Berry, "The Price Elasticity of Demand for Fluid Skim Milk," *Journal of Farm Economics,* Vol. 35, February, 1953, pp. 124–129.

Bank of Israel, *Survey of Family Savings, 1957–58,* (Preliminary Report). Jerusalem, October, 1959.

Barlow, Robin, Harvey Brazer, and James Morgan, *The Economic Behavior of the Affluent.* Brookings Institution, Washington, 1966.

Barlow, Robin, James Morgan, and Grover Wirick, "A Study of Validity in Reporting Medical Care in Michigan," *Proceedings of the Social Statistics Section,* American Statistical Association, 1960, pp. 54–65.

Berelson, B. R. and Ronald Freedman, "A Study in Fertility Control," *Scientific American,* Vol. 210, May, 1964, pp. 29–37.

Break, George, "Income Taxes and Incentives to Work: An Empirical Study," *American Economic Review,* Vol. 47, September, 1957, pp. 529–549.

Cagan, Philip, *The Effect of Pension Plans on Aggregate Saving.* Occasional Paper 95, National Bureau of Economic Research, Columbia University Press, New York, 1965.

Cain, Glen, *Labor Force Participation of Married Women.* University of Chicago Press, Chicago, 1966.

Canada: Royal Commission on Banking and Finance, *Consumer Survey* (conducted by McDonald Research Ltd.), Ottawa, no date (survey done in 1962).

Caplovitz, David, *The Poor Pay More:* Consumer Practices of Low Income Families. Free Press, Glencoe, Ill., 1963.

Cheit, E. F., *Injury and Recovery in the Course of Employment.* John Wiley & Sons, New York, 1961.

Clemence, Richard, ed., *Readings in Economic Analysis,* Vol. 2. Addison-Wesley, Cambridge, Mass., 1950.

Cohen, K. J. and R. M. Cyert, "Computer Models and Dynamic Economics, " *Quarterly Journal of Economics,* Vol. 75, February, 1961, pp. 112–127.

Conard, Alfred, *et al., Automobile Accident Costs and Payments:* Studies in the Economics of Injury Reparation. University of Michigan Press, Ann Arbor, 1964.

Corsa, Leslie, Jr., "The Sample Survey in a National Population Program," *Public Opinion Quarterly,* Vol. 28, Fall, 1964, pp. 383–388.

Cyert, R. M., E. A. Feigenbaum, and J. G. March, "Models in a Behavioral Theory of the Firm," *Behavioral Science,* Vol. 55, April, 1959, pp. 81–95.

deGrazia, Sebastian, *Of Time, Work and Leisure.* Twentieth Century Fund, New York, 1962.

Dernberg, Thomas and Kenneth Strand, "Hidden Unemployment 1953–62: A Quantitative Analysis by Age and Sex," *American Economic Review,* Vol. 56, March, 1966, pp. 71–75.

Due, J. M., "Postwar Family Expenditure Studies in Western Europe," *Journal of Farm Economics,* Vol. 38, August, 1956, pp. 846–856.

Eckler, A. R., "The Continuous Population and Labour Force Survey in the United States," in *Family Living Studies:* A Symposium. International Labour Office, Geneva, 1961.

Eisner, Robert, *Determinants of Capital Expenditures—An Interview Study.* Bureau of Economic and Business Research, University of Illinois, Urbana, 1956.

Eisner, Robert, "The Permanent Income Hypothesis: Comment," *American Economic Review,* Vol. 48, December, 1958, pp. 972–991.

Eisner, Robert, "Interview and Other Survey Techniques in the Study of Investment," in *Problems of Capital Formation,* Princeton University Press, Princeton, 1961.

Eisner, Robert and Robert Strotz, "Determinants of Business Investment," in *Impacts of Monetary Policy,* Commission on Money and Credit, Prentice-Hall, Englewood Cliffs, N.J., 1963.

Ellis, George, "Postwar Industrial Location in New England," doctoral thesis, Harvard University, Cambridge, 1950.

Evans, M. K. and E. W. Green, "The Relative Efficacy of Investment Anticipations," *Journal of the American Statistical Association,* Vol. 61, March, 1966, pp. 104–116.

Ferber, Robert, "Research on Household Behavior," *American Economic Review,* Vol. 52, March, 1962, pp. 19–63.

Ferber, Robert, *Collecting Financial Data by Consumer Panel Techniques.* Bureau of Economic and Business Research, University of Illinois, Urbana, 1959.

Ferber, Robert, "The Reliability of Consumers Surveys of Financial Holdings: Demand Deposits," *Journal of the American Statistical Association,* Vol. 61, March, 1966, pp. 91–103.

Freedman, Deborah, "The Relation of Economic Status to Fertility," *American Economic Review,* Vol. 53, June, 1963, pp. 414–426.

Freedman, Ronald, "Sample Surveys for Family Planning Research in Taiwan," *Public Opinion Quarterly,* Vol. 28, Fall, 1964, pp. 373–382.

Freedman, Ronald, Pascal Whelpton and Arthur Campbell, *Family Planning, Sterility, and Population Growth.* McGraw-Hill, New York, 1959.

Friedman, Milton, *A Theory of the Consumption Function.* Princeton University Press, Princeton, 1957.

Friend, Irwin and Jean Bronfenbrenner, "Plant and Equipment Programs and Their Realization," in *Short Term Economic Forecasting*. Princeton University Press, Princeton, 1955.

Friend, Irwin and Robert Jones, *Conference on Consumption and Saving*. 2 vols. University of Pennsylvania Press, Philadelphia, 1960.

Goldberg, David, "Some Recent Developments in American Fertility Research," in *Demographic and Economic Change in Developed Countries*. Princeton University Press, Princeton, 1960.

Greenleigh Associates, *Home Interview Study of Low-Income Households in Detroit, Michigan*. Greenleigh Associates, New York, February, 1965.

Hansen, Morris, "Questions and Answers," *American Statistician,* Vol. 8, October, 1954, pp. 33–34.

Heller, W. M., "The Anatomy of Investment Decisions," *Harvard Business Review,* Vol. 29, March, 1951, pp. 95–103.

Hill, T. P., "Analysis of the Distribution of Wages and Salaries in Great Britain," *Econometrica,* Vol. 27, July, 1959, pp. 355–381.

Houthakker, H. S., "An International Comparison of Household Expenditure Patterns Commemorating the Centenary of Engel's Law," *Econometrica,* Vol. 25, October, 1957, pp. 532–551.

Houthakker, H. S., "The Permanent Income Hypothesis," *American Economic Review,* Vol. 48, June, 1958, pp. 396–404.

Houthakker, H. S., "The Permanent Income Hypothesis: Reply," *American Economic Review,* Vol. 48, December, 1958, pp. 991–993.

Houthakker, H. S., "The Present State of Consumption Theory," *Econometrica,* Vol. 29, October, 1961, pp. 704–740.

Hunting, R. B. and G. S. Neuwirth, *Who Sues in New York City?* Columbia University Press, New York, 1962.

Institute for Social Research, *Economic Survey Data*. University of Michigan, Ann Arbor, 1960.

Institute for Social Research, *Industrial Mobility in Michigan*. University of Michigan, Ann Arbor, 1950.

International Labour Office, *Family Living Studies: A Symposium*. I.L.O., Geneva, 1961.

Japan: Bureau of Statistics, Office of the Prime Minister, *Family Income and Expenditure Survey*. Tokyo.

Johnston, J., "An Econometric Study of the Production Decision," *Quarterly Journal of Economics,* Vol. 71, May, 1961, pp. 234–261.

Juster, F. T., *Anticipations and Purchases*. Princeton University Press, Princeton, 1964.

Katona, George, *Psychological Analysis of Economic Behavior*. McGraw-Hill, New York, 1951.

Katona, George, "Comments by George Katona," *Review of Economics and Statistics,* Vol. 41, August, 1959, p. 317.

Katona, George, *The Powerful Consumer*. McGraw-Hill, New York, 1960.

Katona, George, *The Mass Consumption Society*. McGraw-Hill, New York, 1964.

Katona, George, *Private Pensions and Individual Saving*. Survey Research Center

Monograph 40, Institute for Social Research, University of Michigan, Ann Arbor, 1965.

Katona, George and John Lansing, "The Wealth of the Wealthy," *Review of Economics and Statistics,* Vol. 46, February, 1964, pp. 1–13.

Katona, George and James Morgan, "The Quantitative Study of Factors Determining Business Decisions," *Quarterly Journal of Economics,* Vol. 66, January, 1954, pp. 69–90.

Katona, George and Eva Mueller, *Consumer Attitudes and Demand, 1950–52.* Institute for Social Research, University of Michigan, Ann Arbor, 1953.

Katona, George and Eva Mueller, *Consumer Expectations 1953–1956.* Institute for Social Research, University of Michigan, Ann Arbor, 1956.

Katona, George, *et al., Business Looks at Banks.* University of Michigan Press, Ann Arbor, 1957.

Kish, Leslie and J. B. Lansing, "Response Errors in Estimating the Value of Homes," *Journal of the American Statistical Association,* Vol. 49, September, 1954, pp. 520–538.

Kish, Leslie and J. B. Lansing, "Family Life Cycle as an Independent Variable," *American Sociological Review,* Vol. 22, October, 1957, pp. 512–519.

Klein, L. R., ed., *Contributions of Survey Methods to Economics.* Columbia University Press, New York, 1954.

Klein, L. R. and A. S. Goldberger, *Econometric Model of the U.S., 1929–1952:* Contributions to Economic Analysis, Vol. 9. North Holland Publishing, Amsterdam, 1955.

Klein, L. R. and J. B. Lansing, "Decisions to Purchase Consumer Durable Goods," *Journal of Marketing,* Vol. 2, October, 1955, pp. 109–132.

Koo, A. Y. C., "An Empirical Test of Revealed Preference Theory," *Econometrica,* Vol. 31, October, 1963, pp. 646–664.

Kosobud, Richard and James Morgan, eds., *Consumer Behavior of Individual Families Over Two and Three Years.* Monograph 36, Institute for Social Research, University of Michigan, Ann Arbor, 1964.

Kuenne, R. E., *The Theory of General Economic Equilibrium.* Princeton University Press, Princeton, 1963.

Kuh, Edwin and J. R. Meyer, "How Extraneous are Extraneous Estimates?" *Review of Economics and Statistics,* Vol. 39, November, 1957, pp. 380–393.

Lamale, Helen, *Methodology of the 1950 Consumer Expenditure Survey.* University of Pennsylvania Press, Philadelphia, 1959.

Lansing, J. B. and D. M. Blood, *The Changing Travel Market.* Survey Research Center, University of Michigan, Ann Arbor, 1964.

Lansing, J. B., Gerald Ginsburg, and Kaisa Braaten, *An Investigation of Response Error.* Bureau of Economic and Business Research, University of Illinois, Urbana, 1961.

Lansing, J. B., Thomas Lorimer, and Chikashi Moriguchi, *How People Pay for College.* Survey Research Center, University of Michigan, Ann Arbor, 1963.

Lansing, J. B. and James Morgan, "Consumer Finances Over the Life Cycle," in *Consumer Behavior,* Vol. 2. Edited by Lincoln Clark, New York University Press, New York, 1955.

Lansing, J. B. and Stephen Withey, "Consumer Anticipations, Their Use in Forecasting Consumer Behavior," in *Short Term Economic Forecasting*. Princeton University Press, Princeton, 1955.

Lansing, J. B., *et al., The Geographic Mobility of Labor:* A First Report. Survey Research Center, University of Michigan, Ann Arbor, 1963.

Lasley, F. G., E. R. Kiehl and D. E. Brady, *Consumer Preference for Beef in Relation to Finish.* (Finish is the fat of animals ready for market.) Missouri Agricultural Experiment Station Research Bulletin 580, University of Missouri, Columbia, March, 1955.

Lininger, Charles, Eva Mueller, and Hans Wyss, "Some Uses of Panel Studies in Forecasting the Automobile Market," *Proceedings of the Business and Economic Statistics Section,* American Statistics Association, September, 1957, pp. 409–421.

Liviatan, Nissan, "Test of the Permanent-Income Hypothesis Based on a Reinterview Savings Survey," (with comment by Milton Friedman and a reply) in *Measurement in Economics*. Stanford University Press, Stanford, 1963.

Lydall, Harold, *British Incomes and Savings*. Basil Blackwell, Oxford, 1955.

Lydall, Harold, "The Impact of the Credit Squeeze on Small and Medium Sized Firms," *Economic Journal,* Vol. 67, September, 1957, pp. 415–431.

Lydall, Harold and J. B. Lansing, "A Comparison of Distribution of Personal Income and Wealth in the United States and Great Britain," *American Economic Review,* Vol. 49, March, 1959, pp. 43–67.

Lydall, Harold and J. B. Lansing, "An Anglo-American Comparison of Personal Saving," *Bulletin of the Oxford University Institute of Statistics,* Vol. 22, 1960, pp. 225–258.

McClelland, David, *The Achieving Society*. D. Van Nostrand, Princeton, N.J., 1961.

McLaughlin, G. E. and Stefan Robock, *Why Industry Moves South*. Committee of the South, National Planning Association, Washington, D.C., 1949.

McNerney, W. J., *et al., Hospital and Medical Economics,* 2 vols. Hospital Research and Educational Trust, Chicago, 1962, Vol. 1, pp. 61–357.

Machlup, Fritz, "Marginal Analysis and Empirical Research," *American Economic Review,* Vol. 36, September, 1946, pp. 519–554.

Mahoney, T. A., "Factors That Determine the Labor-Force Participation of Married Women," *Industrial and Labor Relations Review,* Vol. 14, July, 1961, pp. 563–577.

Mansfield, Edwin, "Size of Firm, Market Structure, and Innovation," *Journal of Political Economy,* Vol. 71, December, 1963, pp. 556–576.

Mansfield, Edwin, "Industrial Research and Development Expenditures: Determinants, Prospects, and Relation to Size of Firm and Inventive Output," *Journal of Political Economy,* Vol. 72, August, 1964, pp. 319–340.

Marquardt, Wilhelm and Werner Strigel, *The Konjunkturtest:* A New Method of Economic Research. I.F.O.—Institut für Wirtschaftsforschung, Munich, 1960.

Maynes, E. S., "The Anatomy of Response Errors: Consumer Saving," *Journal of Marketing Research,* Vol. 2, November, 1965, pp. 378–387.

Meyer, John and Edwin Kuh, *The Investment Decision:* An Empirical Study. Harvard University Press, Cambridge, 1957.

Mincer, Jacob, "Labor Force Participation of Married Women: A Study of Labor Supply," *Aspects of Labor Economics,* National Bureau of Economic Research, New York, 1962.

Morgan, James, "A Review of Recent Research on Consumer Behavior," (with Bibliography), in *Consumer Behavior,* Vol. 3. Edited by Lincoln Clark. Harper & Bros., New York, 1958.

Morgan, James, "Decision-Making in the Family," *Household Decision Making, Consumer Behavior,* Vol. 4. Edited by Nelson Foote. New York University, New York, 1960.

Morgan, James, "Repeated Surveys of Consumer Finances in the United States," in *Family Living Studies:* A Symposium. International Labour Office, Geneva, 1961.

Morgan, James, "Time, Work and Welfare," in *Patterns of Market Behavior.* Edited by M. J. Brennan, Brown University Press, Providence, R.I., 1965.

Morgan, James, "The Achievement Motive and Economic Behavior," *Economic Development and Cultural Change,* Vol. 12, April, 1964, pp. 243–267. Reprinted in *A Theory of Achievement Motivation.* Edited by J. W. Atkinson and N. T. Feather, John Wiley & Sons, New York, 1966.

Morgan, James, Robin Barlow, and Harvey Brazer, "A Survey of Investment Management and Working Behavior among High-Income Individuals," *American Economic Review,* Vol. 55, May, 1965, pp. 252–264.

Morgan, James, Marvin Snider, and Marion Sobol, *Lump Sum Redemption Settlements and Rehabilitation.* Institute for Social Research, University of Michigan, Ann Arbor, 1959.

Morgan, James, Ismail Sirageldin, and Nancy Baerwaldt, *Productive Americans.* Survey Research Center, University of Michigan, Ann Arbor, 1966.

Morgan, James and John Sonquist, "Problems in the Analysis of Survey Data, and a Proposal," *Journal of the American Statistical Association,* Vol. 58, June, 1963, pp. 415–434.

Morgan, James, *et al., Income and Welfare in the United States.* McGraw-Hill, New York, 1962.

Morrissett, Irving, "Psychological Surveys in Business Forecasting," in *Some Applications of Behavioral Research.* UNESCO, Paris, 1957.

Mueller, Eva, "A Study of Purchase Decisions," in *Consumer Behavior.* Edited by Lincoln Clark, New York University Press, New York, 1955.

Mueller, Eva, "Effects of Consumer Attitudes on Purchases," *American Economic Review,* Vol. 47, December, 1957, pp. 946–965.

Mueller, Eva, "The Desire for Innovations in Household Goods," in *Consumer Behavior.* Edited by Lincoln Clark. Harper & Bros., New York, 1958.

Mueller, Eva, "Consumer Attitudes: Their Influence and Forecasting Value," in *The Quality and Economic Significance of Anticipations Data.* Princeton University Press, Princeton, 1960.

Mueller, Eva, "Public Attitudes Toward Fiscal Programs," *Quarterly Journal of Economics,* Vol. 78, May, 1963, pp. 210–235.

Mueller, Eva, "Ten Years of Consumer Attitude Surveys: Their Forecasting Record," *Journal of the American Statistical Association,* Vol. 58, December, 1963, pp. 899–917.

Mueller, Eva, "The Impact of Unemployment on Consumer Confidence," *Public Opinion Quarterly,* Vol. 30, Spring, 1966, pp. 19–32.

Mueller, Eva and Gerald Gurin, *Participation in Outdoor Recreation:* Factors Affecting Demand Among American Adults. U.S. Government Printing Office, Washington, 1962.

Mueller, Eva and John Lansing, *The Geographic Mobility of Labor in the United States.* Survey Research Center Monograph (in press). Institute for Social Research, University of Michigan, Ann Arbor, 1967.

Mueller, Eva and James Morgan, "Location Decisions of Manufacturers," *American Economic Review,* Vol. 52, May, 1962, pp. 204–217.

Mueller, Eva and Harlow Osborne, "Consumer Time and Savings Balances: Their Role in Family Liquidity," *American Economic Review,* Vol. 55, May, 1965, pp. 265–275.

Mueller, Eva and Jay Schmiedeskamp, *Persistent Unemployment 1957–1961.* Upjohn Institute for Employment Research, Kalamazoo, Mich., 1962.

Mueller, Eva, Arnold Wilken, and Margaret Wood, *Location Decisions and Industrial Mobility in Michigan, 1961.* Survey Research Center, University of Michigan, Ann Arbor, 1962.

National Bureau of Economic Research, *Short Term Economic Forecasting.* Princeton University Press, Princeton, 1955.

National Bureau of Economic Research, *The Quality and Economic Significance of Anticipations Data.* Princeton University Press, Princeton, 1960.

Neter, John and Joseph Waksburg, "A Study of Response Errors in Expenditure Data from Household Surveys," *Journal of the American Statistical Association,* Vol. 54, March, 1964, pp. 18–55.

Neter, John and Joseph Waksburg, "Conditioning Effects from Repeated Household Interviews," *Journal of Marketing,* Vol. 18, April, 1964, pp. 51–56.

Okun, Arthur, "The Value of Anticipations Data in Forecasting National Product," in *The Quality and Economic Significance of Anticipations Data.* Princeton University Press, Princeton, 1960.

Orcutt, Guy, "Simulation of Economic Systems," *American Economic Review,* Vol. 50, December, 1960.

Orcutt, Guy, *et al., Microanalysis of Socioeconomic Systems.* Harper & Bros., New York, 1961.

Pigou, A. C., "The Classical Stationary State," *Economic Journal,* Vol. 53, December, 1943, pp. 343–350.

Prais, S. J. and H. S. Houthakker, *The Analysis of Family Budgets.* Cambridge University Press, Cambridge, 1955.

Projector, Dorothy and Gertrude Weiss, *Survey of Financial Characteristics of Consumers.* Board of Governors of the Federal Reserve System, Washington, 1966.

Rogers, E. M., *Diffusion of Innovations.* Free Press, Glencoe, Ill., 1962.

Rosett, R. N., "Working Wives: An Economic Study," in *Studies in Household Economic Behavior.* Yale University Press, New Haven, 1958.

Sirken, Monroe, E. S. Maynes, and John Frechtling, "The Survey of Consumer Finances and The Census Quality Check," in *An Appraisal of the 1950 Census Income Data.* Princeton University Press, Princeton, 1958.

Sobol, M. G., "Correlates of Present and Expected Future Work Status of Married Women," doctoral thesis, University of Michigan, Ann Arbor, 1960.

Sonquist, John and James Morgan, *The Detection of Interaction Effects.* Monograph

No. 35, Survey Research Center, Institute for Social Research, University of Michigan, Ann Arbor, 1964.

Special Advisory Committee on Employment Statistics *Report.* U.S. Bureau of the Census, 1954.

Steiner, P. O. and Robert Dorfman, *The Economic Status of the Aged.* University of California Press, Berkeley, 1957.

Study of Consumer Expenditures, Incomes and Savings, 18 vols. University of Pennsylvania Press, Philadelphia, 1959.

Stycos, J. M., "Survey Research and Population Control in Latin America," *Public Opinion Quarterly,* Vol. 28, Fall, 1964, pp. 367–372.

Suits, Daniel, "Use of Dummy Variables in Regression Equations," *Journal of American Statistical Association,* Vol. 52, December, 1957, pp. 548–551.

Suits, Daniel, "Forecasting and Analysis with an Econometric Model," *American Economic Review,* Vol. 52, March, 1962, pp. 104–132.

Survey Research Center, *1960 Survey of Consumer Finances.* Institute for Social Research, University of Michigan, Ann Arbor, 1961, and similar volumes for the 1961 through 1966 Surveys of Consumer Finances published in 1962 ff.

Thore, Sten, *Household Saving and the Price Level.* National Institute of Economic Research (Konjunctur Institutet), Stockholm, 1961.

Tobin, James, "On the Predictive Value of Consumer Intentions and Attitudes," *Review of Economics and Statistics,* Vol. 41, February, 1959, pp. 1–11.

Tsumimura, Kotaro and Tamotsa Sato, "Irreversibility of Consumer Behavior in Terms of Numerical Preference Fields," *Review of Economics and Statistics,* Vol. 46, August, 1964, pp. 305–319.

U.S. Bureau of Labor Statistics, *Consumer Expenditures and Income.* (BLS report, 237-xx or U.S. Agriculture Department report CES-xx), U.S. Government Printing Office, 1964–1966.

U.S. Bureau of Labor Statistics, *1935–36 Consumer Expenditure Study,* in various bulletins of the Bureau of Labor Statistics, the W.P.A., and the Dept. of Agriculture.

Vandome, Peter, "Aspects of the Dynamics of Consumer Behavior," *Bulletin of the Oxford University Institute of Statistics,* Vol. 20, February, 1958, pp. 65–105.

Westoff, Charles, *et al., Family Growth in Metropolitan America.* Princeton University Press, Princeton, 1961.

Williams, Faith and C. C. Zimmerman, *Studies of Family Living in the United States and Other Countries:* An Analysis of Material and Method. U.S. Department of Agriculture, Miscellaneous Publication No. 223, Washington, December, 1935.

Wirick, Grover and Robin Barlow, "The Economic and Social Determinants of the Demand for Health Services," in *The Economics of Health and Medical Care.* Proceedings of a conference sponsored by the Bureau of Public Health and the Department of Economics, University of Michigan, Ann Arbor, 1964.

Yang, C. Y., "An International Comparison of Consumption Functions," *Review of Economics and Statistics,* Vol. 56, August, 1964, pp. 279–286.

Survey Research and

Sociocultural
Anthropology

by John W. Bennett
and Gustav Thaiss
Washington University
at St. Louis

Survey Research and Holistic Depiction in Anthropology

Methods in Combination: A Review of the Literature

Community Studies
Urbanization Studies
Applied Anthropology
National Character
Multi-ethnic Field Research
Socialization

Some Marginal Applications

Analytic Comparison
Systematic Ethnography

Conclusion

Sociocultural Anthropology and Survey Research*

T
HIS CONTRIBUTION is an essay on the applicability of survey research methods to various anthropological research modalities[1] and includes a review of current anthropological studies in which survey techniques have been used. We exclude from discussion the fields of archeology and physical anthropology, although it must be noted that the basic technique of survey research—the collection of comparable "bits" of information from a sample of a defined universe—has been utilized in these fields for a long time. However, the human populations investigated by archeologists and physical anthropologists are typically defined not in terms of their observable behavior but in terms of material objects and techniques, and biological phenomena, respectively. New studies of micro-evolutionary processes require the simultaneous investigation of social behavior and biological traits, and here survey methods are of great value. We shall not consider these studies here, but many of our observations pertain to them insofar as we discuss the application of survey methods to the social segment.

This paper will consist of: (1) a discussion of the "holistic-depictive" approach in anthropology and the special difficulties attending the use of

* The writers wish to acknowledge the assistance of their colleague, Don Bushell, Jr., who participated in the development of basic ideas for this paper.
1. We identify these materials as "anthropology" by the professional allegiances of their authors, by the adherence to fieldwork methodology, and by a respect for the largest possible context for the specific data collected. At the same time, we acknowledge strong tendencies toward merging of methodological and theoretical views in the social sciences (e.g., Schwab, W. B. "An Experiment in Methodology in a West African Urban Community," *Human Organization,* Vol. 13, Spring, 1954, pp. 13–19; Sofer, Cyril and Rhona Sofer, *Jinja Transformed:* A Social Survey of a Multiracial Township. East African Studies 4, Kegan Paul, Trench, Trubner, London, 1955; Bennett, J. W. and K. H. Wolff, "Toward Communication Between Sociology and Anthropology," in *Current Anthropology.* Edited by W. L. Thomas, Jr. University of Chicago Press, 1956; Vidich, A. J. and Gilbert Shapiro, "A Comparison of Participant Observation and Survey Data," *American Sociological Review,* Vol. 20, February, 1955, pp. 28–33; Lang, G. O. and Peter Kunstadter, "Survey Research on the Uintah and Ouray Ute Reservation," *American Anthropologist,* Vol. 59, June, 1957, pp. 527–532). However, the separate professions are as distinct as ever, if not more so.

survey methods therein; (2) a review of recent anthropological and near-anthropological studies in which survey techniques have been combined with other methods; and (3) a brief consideration of comparative cultural studies in which elements of survey methodology are present.

Therefore, we are considering survey research in two main contexts: *first,* as a methodological entity in its own right which may be contrasted with another methodological entity—field-holistic or depictive research—in anthropology; and *second,* as a body of specialized techniques which can be adapted to various anthropological objectives. That is, we shall hold that while in certain anthropological research modalities survey methods as an entity, with their distinctive logic and epistemology, are wholly or partly inappropriate, in other contexts one or more of the techniques can be used with profit.

Survey Research and Holistic Depiction in Anthropology

The methodological approach of modern anthropology includes a particular method—fieldwork—and a major objective: a respect for cultural context. This approach consists today of a number of other separable but inter-related objectives and methods, some of which, considered to be in conflict, have contributed to theoretical controversy in the discipline. Thus, anthropological studies include: (a) depictive reconstruction of whole cultures, with an emphasis on intensive observation and informal interviewing methods. The "social systems" constructed by some anthropologists imply somewhat different objectives but in this generalized context can be taken as part of the approach; (b) studies of parts of cultures or social systems, made in pursuit of specialized theoretical objectives, and employing sharply defined techniques as well as the more exploratory techniques; (c) a view of the human subjects of the research as individual persons, with interest in their unique historical qualities (an approach especially associated with (a)); and (d) a view of the human subjects as groups or populations about which to generalize (associated with both (a) and (b), but perhaps especially (b)). Sometimes the sub-approaches (a) and (b) are placed in opposition, as in the controversy between the holistic "cultural character" school and the analytical social anthropologists. Others see no particular conflict between them, and regard the methods and approaches as complementary.

Conceived as an entity, survey research is a method which in essence requires the presentation of a standardized stimulus to a human population selected on the basis of defined criteria. The information sought is generally defined in terms of the stimulus or topic, rather than in terms of the unique qualities of the population. That is, there is typically more interest shown in the topic of the survey than in the population itself, and this concern for the topic requires attention to the methodology and theory of the research in advance of the actual study. Topics to be researched need to be defined with great precision, since complete control over relationships between factors bearing on the topic is desired. Broad theoretical assumptions concerning certain common factors in the populations to be surveyed generally lie behind the research. We shall usually refer to these various techniques with the term "extensive."

The (a) plus (c) modality of field-holistic research can be viewed as a methodological entity, and we shall call it *holistic depiction*. Associated with holistic depiction are a number of data-gathering techniques which have in common a certain exploratory approach, i.e., the movements of the investigator are adjusted to the rhythms of everyday life, and not to the demands of a structured instrument. Among these "intensive" techniques are observation, participant and otherwise; general, "open-ended" interviewing or simple *talk;* visitations of people and events, including photography and sound recording; the keeping of diaries, and kindred devices. These techniques are all adjusted to a residential form of investigation, rather than laboratory or door-to-door. They should not be viewed as "traditional," or "imprecise," as some social scientists have done, but rather as simply another approach to the gaining of knowledge of social behavior.[2] We shall subsequently refer to this entire body of techniques with the term "intensive."

All of the primary data of sociocultural anthropology come from studies made in living societies in their natural setting; and, although not all the studies aim at presenting the literal "whole" of a culture or society, there remains the objective of describing as inclusive a context as possible. Holistic depiction is done in a way which focuses the attention of the anthropologist, and his reader, on the human subjects of the research and their unique milieu or in their milieu conceived as unique for purposes of study. The logic of such studies requires the investigator to consider the individual subjects as persons, and therefore they are not, in any fundamental or ultimate

2. Bennett, J. W., "The Study of Cultures: A Survey of Technique and Methodology in Field Work," *American Sociological Review,* Vol. 13, December, 1948, pp. 672–689.

sense, simply a "population." The relationship of topics to the subject-person is typically complex: classically, in holistic depiction the topics of inquiry flow from the interaction of the investigator with his subjects, and it is felt that neither topics nor particular theoretical concepts should bias the study. An extreme example of this approach is found in Bateson's *Naven,* where the field work phase of social experience with the subjects was prolonged into a post-field work intellectual experience, in search of the problems of the research and their solution.[3] While this case is hypertypical, its general aspects are visible in all the major ethnological treatises. Often actual or pseudonymic names of particular persons studied are used (in contrast to the merged anonymity of the subjects in survey research), and the emergence of problems and methods for their solution in the course of the field work is documented. An example is the graphic presentation, via actual case studies, of the conflicts between matrilineal kinship and father-son relationships in Malinowski's *Sexual Life of Savages in Northwestern Melanesia.*[4]

It has been argued that, notwithstanding fundamental differences in holistic and survey research, extensive survey research techniques can and should make a desirable adjunct to intensive ethnological field work. Major hypotheses, especially those concerning the typicality or representativeness of certain attitudes and behavior patterns, at least could be checked with the use of an instrument providing a standard stimulus applied to carefully selected groups of informants. An example of the application of such methods to what is, on the whole, an ethnological study of a human social group, is Dore's *City Life in Japan.*[5] We do not know whether Dore would answer to the title of "anthropologist" or "sociologist," but in any case he used a carefully constructed interview schedule to obtain responses to important questions in the study. This material is introduced at strategic points in order to illustrate and to buttress conclusions derived from observational and other intensively gathered field data. In a few cases the survey data are themselves the initiators of key interpretations or hypotheses.

3. Bateson, Gregory, *Naven:* A Survey of the Problems Suggested by a Composite Picture of the Culture of a New Guinean Tribe, Drawn from Three Points of View. Cambridge University Press, London, 1936.
4. Malinowski, Bronislaw, *The Sexual Life of Savages in Northwestern Melanesia:* An Ethnographic Account of Courtship, Marriage and Family Life Among the Natives of the Trobriand Islands. Liveright, New York, 1929.
5. Dore, R. P., *City Life in Japan:* The Study of a Tokyo Ward. University of California Press, Berkeley, 1958.

The skillful accommodation between extensive and intensive methods in Dore's study was made possible in part by the fact that he was working within an urban population—a population possibly culturally more integrated than those of most Western cities, but similar in most respects. The methods of survey research are often made easy of application by the existence of populations which can be stratified by various well-known criteria such as education and socio-economic factors. The variables in modern urban or urbanized populations the world over are thus the common ground out of which survey research methodology arises; the fact that some of these population-stratifying characteristics do not exist or cannot be easily determined, being objects of study in themselves in some of the societies studied by anthropologists, can be a practical difficulty in the use of such methods.

A related issue is the difficulty of getting people to respond to questionnaires in the absence of a well-defined cultural tradition of "opinion" or "attitude." In the early post-World War II years, ambitious survey researchers made several international studies of attitudes, using the same schedule in several languages. Some of these studies were failures; others were sharply criticized as unreliable due to the fact that respondents in some countries simply had no understanding of the question-and-answer situation. Societies with strong collectivist patterns, where the person is more a committed member of a group than an autonomous, thinking individual, are exceedingly difficult to survey at the cultural or psychological levels, although surveys of other types of data present no particular difficulty. However, these cultural limitations on interviewing tend to disappear as countries and peoples lacking national institutions begin to acquire them.[6]

The survey researcher, either in his own country or in the form of a native team of interviewers, is generally working within a known cultural con-

---

6. An especially dramatic example of this type of change occurred in Japan immediately after World War II. The Occupation had no difficulty introducing and using public attitude survey techniques, because the Japanese took to them with enthusiasm. The Japanese citizen, newly emancipated, welcomed the opportunity to sound off; and newspaper men, political scientists, psychologists, and others went about the task of finding out about the attitudes of the population with vigor and determination. The long-suppressed tendencies in these directions, developing through the years of industrialization under authoritarian and traditionalist governments, demanded an outlet; and survey research became, for a time, a major public and political symbol of the right to have ideas and the right to find out about them. (See Passin, H., "The Development of Public Opinion Research in Japan," *International Journal of Opinion and Attitude Research*, Vol. 5, 1951, pp. 20–30 for an account.)

text, and assumes that the respondent accepts him as a fellow member of the larger society and responds in an appropriate manner. The anthropologist usually cannot make this assumption, since, at least at the beginning, he is a "foreigner," an outsider, even in cases where he is studying a society or sub-culture of his own tradition: he must assume that the people he talks to will color their remarks to a varying degree on the basis of their perception of his foreignness. Hence, by constant checking of statements and observations, the anthropologist finds it necessary to seek out the "truth"; whereas the survey researcher, on the whole, assumes that he is obtaining it through his tested instrument.

A special difficulty in the use of extensive survey research methods by the holistic-depictive anthropologist lies in the large number of variables with which he habitually concerns himself. The survey instrument is generally confined to a few variables, conceived as related to a limited number of objective dimensions. Answers provided for hypotheses are thus limited in scope: hence the frequent criticism of survey research made by anthropologists as being narrow in content and methodologically constricted. Bateson's *Naven* provides an extreme case once again; the full interpretation of the ceremonial reported in this monograph includes dozens of variables, found related to one another by intensive qualitative analysis. The relevant dimensions of the behavior examined are, moreover, not the typical "objective" and oral "public" data utilized in survey research, but "private" emotive patterns, gestures, states of being, perspectival orientations, and the like. It is difficult to see how survey research could possibly contribute to a complex study, as *Naven* is, of ceremonial transvestitism. This difficulty would inhere even in the case of anthropological studies of economics (supposedly an "objective" topic), where complicated forms of gift-giving, prestige competition, subtle interpersonal exchanges, and so on form the essence of the study.[7]

Still another difficulty centers around the nature of the data regarded by the anthropologist as significant for interpretation. In survey research, the critical interaction takes place between the interviewer and the respondent; in anthropology too this is important, but even more important are interactions between the subjects themselves. That is, the anthropologist *observes* social behavior in the actual social setting (the archetypical case is Bateson-Mead, *Balinese Character*), and interprets the sociocultural whole as much

7. Burling, Robbins, "Maximization Theories and the Study of Economic Anthropology," *American Anthropologist*, Vol. 64, August, 1962, pp. 818–819.

from this type of data as from oral responses to questions. Techniques of observation of subject-subject interactions are not available in a survey approach, and the anthropologist is forced to be skeptical of informants' accounts of such interaction.[8]

Thus, the anthropologist's view of oral statements of informants is sometimes in conflict with the conception held by the survey researcher. By and large, the latter must place considerable trust in the oral report; or he may hold that his sample is constructed in such a way that falsifications are distributed so that they cancel each other. On the other hand, when the anthropologist is concerned with the literal truth of oral statements, he may utilize survey techniques with considerable profit, since these will require him to sample a number of informants, systematically chosen. Actually all good field workers follow a "survey research" approach, in this sense of using more than one informant, whether they construct statistical samples or not.

However, the anthropologist is just as frequently concerned with an entirely different aspect of oral statements—their indirect or oblique representations. Truth is no object here; the concern is for subtle symbolism and negative evidence, or even in the fact of lying as revelatory of cultural stresses.[9] The intensive nature of the methodology in this context leads toward conversation, not survey of opinion, and intensive participation with particular individuals chosen on the basis of their unique or strategic personal qualities and roles. Survey methodology in the strict sense is not appropriate in these situations.

Another argument leveled against survey methods by some anthropologists is based on the small size of the populations studied in many field researches. The small size of the community permits a saturation sample; every individual and family can be talked with at some length. Hence, it is sometimes argued, there is no need for an interview schedule which is seen, in this type of criticism, simply as a device to obtain data from a large number of individuals in a brief period of time. This is one function of a schedule, but by no means the only one. The criticism misses an important point; the schedule is fundamentally a means of obtaining responses to standard-

8. A possible blending of extensive techniques and intensive observation appears to be emerging in the recent methodological approach called by various terms: cognitive analysis, systematic ethnography, componential analysis, ethnoscience. We discuss this approach later.

9. Passin, H. "Tarahumara Prevarication: A Problem in Field Method," *American Anthropologist,* Vol. 44, April, 1942, pp. 235–247.

ized stimuli, so that comparisons between responses can be controlled. Hence, there is no important *theoretical* objection to the use of schedules in small populations when it is desirable to obtain comparative response data on particular topics—whether or not an actual sample is used.

The resistance displayed by many anthropologists to the idea of a sample is also somewhat questionable due to the fact that, even in cases where not everyone in the community is interviewed, the large number that is may come to constitute an adequate sample: there is no reason why this implicit sample should not be treated as such, and the responses analyzed comparatively with the usual survey methods. Kluckhohn used these implicit samples, as well as formal samples, during his many years of work on the Navaho. In some of his publications he used percentages of responses from the implicit or accumulated samples of informants in order to demonstrate salience of attitudes and other phenomena.[10]

Another problem concerns the social atmosphere of field work. The anthropologist is typically concerned with establishing personal relationships with his subjects, not the formal contacts found in survey research. It has been argued that standardized questionnaires, used at the beginning of a field study, provide a suitable means for meeting individuals, and quite often this can be and is done. However, there are other ways of getting acquainted; once a routine is established and channels of information developed, the use of a schedule can disrupt relationships. The field worker may feel that it is too artificial and formal a technique; it violates the personal mood already established.[11] A related objection concerns the rather exten-

10. Kluckhohn, Clyde, "Participation in Ceremonials in a Navaho Community," *American Anthropologist,* Vol. 40, July, 1938, pp. 359–369; Streib, G. F., "The Use of Survey Methods Among the Navaho," *American Anthropologist,* Vol. 54, January, 1952, pp. 30–40; see also, Henry, Jules, "Economics of Pilaga Food Distribution," *American Anthropologist,* Vol. 53, April, 1951, pp. 187–219.

11. One reader of this paper objected that this argument is fallacious insofar as clinical psychologists and psychiatrists use instruments, and do not thereby disrupt relationships with their patients. This point, often voiced by people who have never done intensive field work, misses the important differences between the role situations in medical practice and participant field work. In the former, the relationship is one of doctor and patient, and of course the patient will take a test if the doctor asks him to—it is in his interest to do so. In the field, the informant is the *host,* not the patient, and the field worker the *guest,* not the doctor. The latter sits at the feet of the informant, as it were, and has no control over him. A discussion of the consequences of this relationship is found in E. E. Evans-Pritchard's *The Nuer.* Clarendon Press, Oxford, England, 1940, pp. 9–15.

sive commitment of time required to plan, pre-test, and administer a schedule.

Thus, the informal, probing techniques associated with holistic-depictive research are typically flexible and eclectic, whereas the techniques in survey research are highly disciplined. Field work as a method is typically unpredictable because the movement of the researcher in the natural society is to some extent unpredictable. Hence he may find it difficult to accept the particular discipline of a particular methodological procedure. Rather than resisting discipline, however, he is in a position to try out many different disciplined approaches, discarding or keeping them on the basis of a simple pragmatic test—whether they contribute to general enlightenment, or secure a needed slice of data.

There is, of course, a final issue here—the extent to which intensive methodology is psychologically more congenial for certain types of workers. There seems little doubt, though there is no definite proof, that intensive ethnographic research is a style of operation which requires certain subjective skills for maximum accomplishment; and, conversely, that extensive methodology is best used by individuals who remain at a calculated distance from their human subjects.[12]

Methods in Combination: A Review of the Literature

We have already pointed out that survey methods taken as single techniques can be of use in anthropological research, even when holistic-depictive interests are dominant. However, when anthropological research moves toward the (b) plus (d) modality described on p. 273—that is, toward problem-oriented studies of parts of culture and toward methods which to some degree accept the subjects as groups or populations—the possibilities of fusion of survey and intensive approaches become greater. Perhaps a majority of anthropological work today is carried out in the atmosphere of problem-orientation; and, insofar as this is the case, the use of prepared interview schedules, scales, and analytical procedures becomes more common. A check of the contents of the *American Anthropologist* over the past six years showed that about one-third of the research articles in the field of sociocultural anthropology were based upon data acquired by the use of such instruments. Nearly all of these articles were segments of larger studies, segments in which specific

12. Mead, Margaret and R. B. Metraux, *The Study of Culture at a Distance.* University of Chicago Press, Chicago, 1953, especially chap. 1.

hypotheses were tested with the use of instruments on a survey basis. In many cases, it was not possible to tell whether the hypotheses were formulated in advance of field work or during it, but in any event they *were* formulated and appropriate methods developed. Some of the anthropologists who do this type of work would probably hold to the position that the overall depictive study cannot, in any comprehensive sense, utilize structured survey instruments, but that the segmental studies of particular phases of the research can do so with profit.

Such fusion of methods has characterized social research for many years. Malinowski, for example, in his *Argonauts of the Western Pacific* and *Coral Gardens and Their Magic,* discussed the use of what he called the "method of statistic documentation of concrete evidence."[13] This somewhat cumbersome concept involved, among other things, the use of village censuses to obtain data on the quantifiable aspects of village life, such as the number and type of dwellings, household composition, information on gardening practices, and other similar types of data. Because of Malinowski's great influence in anthropology and especially with regard to field-work methods, most anthropologists have since used one or another technique of this kind. Lists and censuses have become standard in anthropology, useful not only for the data to be collected but also because they enable the anthropologist to get to know the community and establish rapport relatively quickly.[14]

13. Malinowski, Bronislaw, *Argonauts of the Western Pacific:* An Account of Native Enterprise and Adventure in the Archipelagoes of Melanesian New Guinea. Routledge & Kegan Paul, London, 1922; Malinowski, Bronislaw, *Coral Gardens and Their Magic,* Routledge & Kegan Paul, London, 1935.
14. For conflicting statements on "when to use" survey devices in field studies see Landy, David, *Tropical Childhood:* Cultural Transmission and Learning in a Rural Puerto Rican Village. University of North Carolina Press, Chapel Hill, 1959; and Streib, G. F., *op. cit.* Some examples of more recent monographs—such as Mitchell, J. C., *The Yao Village:* A Study in the Social Structure of a Nyasaland Tribe. Manchester University Press, Manchester, 1956; Fraser, T. M., Jr., *Rusembilan:* A Malay Fishing Village in Southern Thailand. Cornell University Press, Ithaca, 1960; Anderson, R. T. and B. G. Anderson, *The Vanishing Village:* A Danish Maritime Community. University of Washington Press, Seattle, 1964—show quite clearly how social survey methods, especially the community census technique, supplement intensive methods in order to establish a clearer picture of the culture under consideration. For discussions of the use of the village census, survey and quantitative methods in anthropology, see Richards, A., "The Village Census in the Study of Culture Contact," *Africa,* Vol. 8, 1935, pp. 20–33; Schapera, I., "Field Methods in the Study of Modern

Anthropologists have also turned to survey methods in their recent move to study "complex societies"—that is, in doing field work in the population aggregates of contemporary nation-societies. This venture has been accompanied by considerable methodological difficulty, insofar as the methods used by anthropologists in the field-holistic tradition have been inappropriate to large populations—or at least, there has been a serious problem of representativeness created by the intensive work with single small population units. Hence survey techniques become necessary and desirable. At the same time, however, the anthropologist chafes under the restrictions created by survey methods, since he desires to pursue his typically complex questions and hypotheses, which contain far more variables than can possibly be handled in surveys, or at least in surveys done on any reasonable basis of time and money.

In any case, the prototype of all survey research combined with intensive field work on modern populations is the *Mass Observation* technique, as it existed in Harrison's original format.[15] Workers were often drawn from the actual social segments to be studied, and then sent back to the field to conduct the interviews and participant observation. The published reports of this work were a matrix of survey tables and participant reports. The "panel study," a somewhat related approach developed in public attitude surveying, combined formal interviewing with personal acquaintance and informal conversation with a constant group of respondents.

An example of problem-oriented segmental research on a modern society, where the community becomes the "sample" rather than the "object" in itself, is recounted in a paper by Vidich and Shapiro on a study of stratification in an American small town by an anthropologist who used participant observation techniques and a sociologist using sur-

---

Culture Contacts," *Africa*, Vol. 8, 1935, pp. 315–326; Schapera, I., "Marriage of Near Kin Among the Tswana," *Africa*, Vol. 27, April, 1957; Firth, R., "Census and Sociology in a Primitive Community," in *Problems and Methods in Demographic Studies of Preliterate Peoples*, Proceedings of World Population Conference, United States, 1954, Paper 6, pp. 105–227; Keller, S., "Der Zensus als Quelle Sozial-anthropologischer Untersuchungen," *Homo*, Vol. 11, No. 1, 1960, p. 2; Schade, H., "Sozial-Anthropologie—Ergebnisse einer Zensus-Untersuchung," *Homo*, Vol. 11, 1960, pp. 1–2.

15. Madge, Charles and Tom Harrison, *Britain by Mass Observation*. Penguin Books, London, 1939.

vey techniques.[16] Both investigators accepted the problem and the general objective of the testing of a "theory" of social stratification as measured by prestige ratings. The anthropologist (Vidich) obtained his prestige ratings by assigning each person in a random sample a rating on the basis of his and his assistant's general knowledge of the community and its residents. The sociologist (Shapiro) obtained his ratings by administering a sociometric-type questionnaire to the same sample. The two systems of ratings agreed on the whole, and each, according to the authors, provided complementary data. The anthropological data gave considerable meaning and depth to the survey data; and the latter secured a more representative spectrum of prestige positions (it was found that the anthropologist apparently had not made adequate contact with lower-class groups). The authors conclude that the two approaches are complementary and should be used in juxtaposition and not in competition.

However, attention should be called again to the fact that *both* investigators accepted the general problem and theoretical objective of the study in a frame described by our (b) plus (d) modality. Consequently, this comparison of field-holistic and survey methods is not complete. A more adequate test would have required the anthropologist to make his own study independently, work out his own system of classifying social groups in his own way and with his own "sample," with the sociologist doing likewise, and their final results compared. It is probably safe to say that the anthropologist *would* have made some sort of stratification analysis, since stratification seems to be an inherent feature of American communities, although one could always argue that one must never make such assumptions, however familiar the context. The holistic-depictive anthropologist would typically question the relevance of all such pre-research constructs as "stratification" since they tend to bias the results by providing categories for data collection which are derived from the observer and not from the observed. It is conceivable, therefore, that the convergence of the results obtained in intensive and extensive methodologies in this case was due to the adherence by the anthropologist to the sociological frame of reference and sampling concept. If this were true, then his prestige ratings were basically the "same" as those obtained by the sociometric survey: they were simply an inspectional survey.

16. Vidich, A. J. and Gilbert Shapiro, *op. cit.* See also Arensberg, C. M., "The Community as Object and as Sample," *American Anthropologist,* Vol. 63, April, 1961, pp. 241–264.

A related example exists in the status data from the two studies of Plainville, made at a fifteen-year interval by Withers and Gallaher.[17] Both studies were done with intensive methods, that is, neither investigator utilized survey instruments in the strict sense to obtain a picture of the stratification situation. Withers, however, identified a definite system of "social classes," whereas Gallaher denied that such a system of definite groups existed, preferring the concept of "status rank," in which every individual is assigned a fluctuating position along an infinitely graded continuum between two extremes. When Withers did his study, the recognition of social class in U.S. society was *de rigeur*. However, we cannot know for sure whether Gallaher is more correct than Withers, since the time interval could have blurred the boundaries of an actual stratification system. In any case, the research points up the need for extreme care in the use of theoretical concepts of classification in holistic research, and the anthropologist has a point when he warns against the pre-commitment to such concepts inherent in the use of many types of survey instruments. Commitment to highly specific theories and hypotheses provides a classification of data in advance of the study and, if the objectives emphasize the "discovery" of the community or culture, flowing out of its existential state into the experiences of the observer, and thus to the write-up, then pre-existing theories may become a filter which prevents much of importance coming through.

On the other hand, the Withers-Gallaher studies suggest a criticism of field methods in which a needed survey-type discipline is lacking. The ambiguity in the differences between the two approaches to stratification and status is due in part to the fact that structured instruments apparently were not used in either study, alone or in combination with the observational field methods. If Withers had used a schedule of some kind, and if this could have been replicated by Gallaher, considerable light would have been shed on the problem discussed above. The case illustrates the potential usefulness of a combination of the extensive survey approach with intensive field investigation. Even more, the case points up the frequent confusion between holistic and problem-oriented research. It is one thing to aim at a holistic depiction of culture with the personalized, exploratory style which is typical of this type of research as a distinct methodological entity. However, whenever theoretical concepts borrowed

17. West, James (Carl Withers), *Plainville, U.S.A.* Columbia University Press, New York, 1945; Gallaher, Art, Jr., *Plainville Fifteen Years Later.* Columbia University Press, New York, 1961.

from external frames of reference are to be used—e.g., "stratification"—then the researcher has an obligation to utilize the instruments and the logic appropriate to these frames, for better or for worse. This type of confusion also existed in the earlier culture-and-personality research, where many of the problems which required disciplined techniques were studied in holistic-depictive style.

At this point we shall present our topical review of current anthropological literature in which survey methods have been used to advantage. The review is not exhaustive, but the majority of important items have been analyzed and presented as typical of the available resources. The purely quantitative surveys usually contain fairly complete information on technique—the choice and reliability of the sample, and the formulation and administration of questionnaires.[18] In reports which combine extensive and intensive techniques, the survey methods are usually (but not always) described, but the intensive methods, hardly ever (i.e., the precise techniques used in participant observation, informal and focused interviewing, etc.).[19]

In anticipation of our conclusions, we may say that the use of survey methods as revealed by the literature suggests that anthropologists use them as they approach certain kinds of problems—those concerned with change, and especially in societies which are part of larger national frameworks. Insofar as anthropologists have done such work, their efforts blend with those of non-anthropologists studying similar phenomena. Thus, we have included a number of scholars from other fields in our review, for example: sociologists Dore, Bose and Lerner, and political scientist Frey.[20] Delving further back into the literature, the study which

18. For example, see Smith, M. G., *West Indian Family Structure*. University of Washington Press, Seattle, 1962.
19. See Wilson, Godfrey, "An Essay in the Economics of Detribalisation in Northern Rhodesia," *Rhodes Livingstone Papers, No. 5 and 6*. Rhodes-Livingstone, Northern Rhodesia, 1941 and 1942. For consideration of the problem of partial reportage of method in anthropological research, see Stavrianos, B. K., "Research Methods in Cultural Anthropology in Relation to Scientific Criteria," *Psychological Review*, Vol. 57, November, 1950, pp. 334–344.
20. Dore, R. P., *op. cit;* Bose, S. P., "Peasant Values and Innovation in India," *American Journal of Sociology*, Vol. 67, March, 1962, pp. 552–560; Lerner, Daniel, *The Passing of Traditional Society: Modernizing the Middle East*. Free Press, Glencoe, Ill., 1958; Frey, F. W., "Surveying Peasant Attitudes in Turkey," *Public Opinion Quarterly*, Vol. 27, Fall, 1963, pp. 335–355.

classically represents this disciplinary fusion is *Middletown*.[21] The Lynds, as sociologists, lived and worked in the community for eighteen months, sharing in its life, collecting abundant survey and statistical materials, and making use of the intensive techniques familiar to the anthropologist.

COMMUNITY STUDIES

After World War II a noticeable shift in research interests took place as more anthropologists became interested in the study of complex societies. Among the major reasons for this trend were the emergence of new nations and the rapid rate of change in developing areas.

The most common form of anthropological research in complex societies has been the community study. This approach, however, has come under serious attack not only from anthropologists but from other social scientists as well. The French sociologist Dumont, writing about recent fieldwork in India, attacks "the uncritical choice of a number of anthropologists of the village as the frame of inquiry," arguing that this approach is a simple heritage of the discipline's classic, tribe-inspired, overemphasis on local groups in contrast to more extensive research.[22] From another perspective, the development economist Higgins, frustrated by the difficulty of determining to what extent the results of community-based studies of economic change in one region of rural Java may be generalized to refer to Indonesia as a whole, complains:

> If anthropologists are to be genuinely helpful to economists seeking to understand the relationship between culture and economic behavior, their scope and method must be substantially changed. . . . They must find short cuts to generalization. The traditional methods of the anthropologists confine them to intensive and prolonged study of small geographic regions. If their scientific standards are to be met, that cannot be helped. But some training in statistical methods, and particularly in sampling techniques, might enable them to distinguish the strategic variables which correlate highly with everything else in the culture and thus characterize it. Thus armed, anthropologists would need less time to find out whether

21. Lynd, R. S. and Helen Lynd, *Middletown: A Study in Contemporary American Culture*. Harcourt, Brace, New York, 1929.
22. Dumont, L. and D. Pocock, eds., *Contributions to Indian Sociology*, Vol. 1. Institute of Social Anthropology. Paris-Oxford, 1957.

neighboring (communities) are different or the same. If they are the same, the anthropologist can move on; if they are different, more prolonged study may be necessary.[23]

While anthropological methods are undergoing re-examination, there remain many anthropologists who will state, with Casagrande, that:

> I am not suggesting that we sell our birthright for statistics and surveys. Both can be instructive, but our distinctive research contribution and our particular strength lies in the intensive study of small groups and I assume that our work will continue to be anchored to the natural community.[24]

Comments of this kind notwithstanding, the investigation of small communities in complex societies often involves a more rigorous and a more self-conscious methodology than has been characteristic of tribal studies. Ryan has used a questionnaire approach in attempting to examine the attitudes of Sinhalese peasants toward modernization, surveying about 100 households in a village near Colombo with respect to their opinions concerning both traditional practices and innovative behavior.[25] A similar but much more ambitious study was undertaken by Frey, a political scientist, who surveyed more than 450 Turkish villages in an attempt to determine the attitudes of Turkish peasants toward modernization. The author, in discussing the reasons for the project, states that:

> The nation is currently in the anxious "second stage" of its contemporary revolution; having largely accomplished the modernization of elite elements, it is attempting to bring its peasantry into active social and political participation on supra-village levels. Information about peasant attitudes and conditions of life—more profound than that obtained by the national census and more general than that garnered from the few good anthropological studies—is urgently required.[26]

23. Higgins, B. H., *Economic Development:* Principles, Problems and Policies. W. W. Norton, New York, 1959.
24. Casagrande, J. B., "Some Observations on the Study of Intermediate Societies," in *Intermediate Societies,* American Ethnological Society Publications. Edited by V. F. Ray. University of Washington Press, Seattle, 1959.
25. Ryan, B., *et al., Sinhalese Village.* University of Miami Press, Coral Gables, 1958.
26. Frey, F. W., *op. cit.*

Frey included eight basic areas of inquiry in the final interviewing schedule: communications, personal background, attitudes toward development, other relevant psychological traits, socialization, position in and conception of environing social structure, politicization, and religiosity.

In his discussion of the way in which patterns of caste ranking are affected by the structure of the local community in which they appear, Marriott used both the results of a survey he had conducted of the opinions of some 300 persons in two Uttar Pradesh villages as to the ranking of 36 locally represented castes, and a correlation based on data from secondary sources of population size and number of castes in 151 villages from five regions in India and Pakistan.[27] In a study of conflict and solidarity in a Guianese plantation, Jayawardena used a combination of formal and informal interviewing methods as well as a survey conducted to elicit information on the demographic and social characteristics of his respondents and to ascertain their degree of involvement with the courts. The author was interested in the study of the factors that cause social conflict, the forms it takes, and the social consequences of such behavior.[28]

The Youngs administered a "structured" questionnaire to a sample of community officials in 24 Mexican villages in connection with their study of rural reactions to the growth of industrialization in one of the states of central Mexico. They then used the results as well as various types of census data to construct a Guttman scale of economic contact between various villages and the factory center, to set up indices of absolute and relative social change in the villages, and to obtain an objective measure of village "morale."[29]

Lerner, combining survey techniques with depth interviews, has produced a typology of "traditional," "transitional," and "modern" societies, derived from studies of communities in the Middle East. It might well serve as a heuristic model of social and cultural change to be tested in other devel-

27. Marriott, McKim, "Caste Ranking and Community Structure in Five Regions of India and Pakistan," Monograph No. 23, Deccan College Post-Graduate and Research Institute, Poona, India, 1960.
28. Jayawardena, Chandra, *Conflict and Solidarity in a Guianese Plantation.* Athlone Press, London, 1963.
29. Young, F. and R. Young, "Social Integration and Change in Twenty-four Mexican Villages," *Economic Development and Cultural Change,* Vol. 8, 1960, pp. 366–377; Young, F. and R. Young, "Two Determinants of Community Reaction to Industrialization in Rural Mexico," *Economic Development and Cultural Change,* Vol. 8, 1960, pp. 257–264.

oping areas. Lerner considers the interrelationship of historic, cultural, economic, and technological factors in the individual drive to modernity. He points to sociocultural regularities in the passing of traditional society and in the psychological processes of transition to modernity, emphasizing the individual desire for change among "transitionals" and elites in the Middle East. He also notes the survey findings that rural people are "unhappier" than urban people, as opposed to conventional dichotomies of urban anomie versus rural stability. Lerner concludes that in the Middle East traditional society is passing because relatively few want to maintain the traditional rules.[30]

A final example of the community study, this one done in India by the sociologist Bose, attempts to test by the use of survey methods certain postulates of Redfield's folk-urban continuum.[31] In Redfield's model the peasant society is considered to be intermediate between the folk society and the urban society. In such a society there are some persons who have the value systems expected in a folk society and there are others who have the value systems of an urban society. In Bose's study, it was postulated that people with folk value systems would resist change in agricultural techniques and those with urban value systems would accept it. To test this hypothesis, a random sample of 80 farmers was selected from a list of owners cultivating three acres of land or more. A questionnaire of 30 items was used for eliciting responses. The results of the study support the hypotheses that the value orientation of a people has a relation to technological change and that people with tradition-oriented, folk-type values are more resistant to change than people with urban-oriented values.

This is an interesting piece of research, but it invites certain basic criticism. It is a matter of doubt as to whether Redfield's categories of "folk" and "urban" can be taken as empirical types or putative types for the purposes of constructing survey instruments. It is not always clear what Redfield himself had in mind, but there seems little doubt that in large part he was concerned with an image of man and human diversity, and not with the empirical typing of actual communities. In a sense Redfield was pointing to features of all societies; all men have both "folk" and "urban" characteristics, just as all men have anxiety in some degree. In part, Bose's study represents an instance where the choice of extensive methods was partly inappro-

30. Lerner, Daniel, *op. cit.*
31. Bose, S. P., *op. cit.*

priate to the particular problem. Intensive, exploratory, and introspective research might have been better adapted to the task. Or if his objective was to type communities quantitatively, types other than "folk" and "urban" would have been more suitable.

URBANIZATION STUDIES

One aspect of the study of complex societies and the anthropology of development—and an area of research which anthropologists have largely ignored until recently—is that of urban society and the process of urbanization. The most extensive research on this topic has been done in Africa by British and British-trained anthropologists. Much of this research is undertaken for practical, administrative objectives, such as collecting information to be of use to the national government or municipality. Other pieces of research are more theoretical in nature and are concerned with the formulation of hypotheses and the provision of material capable of comparative analysis, although they may incidentally provide data useful for administrative objectives. Most of the following studies present combinations of extensive and intensive methods.

Fortes states that the purpose of the Ashanti survey was "to get a broad general picture of the social and political structure of Ashanti today, and to investigate in greater detail those aspects in which ecological and economic factors play the biggest part."[32] In addition to the customary methods of collecting information from selected informants, observation and participation in group activities and so forth, much use was made of questionnaires and other prepared inquiry forms. Fortes notes that the collection of numerical data was necessary not only because of the large scale of the Ashanti survey, but also because of the variability of social relationships in a rapidly changing society. In studying land tenure, for example, the broad principles could be ascertained from discussions with informants, but the actual operation of these principles varied from case to case, owing to the presence of conditions and circumstances not allowed for by the general rules. Hence, it was necessary to attempt to measure the strength of the different forces of change.

Busia, a Ghanaian sociologist, conducted a social survey of Sekondi-Takoradi (Ghana) in 1947–1948. The objectives of the research were pri-

32. Fortes, M., "Ashanti Social Survey: A Preliminary Report," in *Human Problems in British Central Africa*. Edited by M. Gluckman and J. M. Winterbottom. Vol. 6, Rhodes-Livingstone, Northern Rhodesia, 1948, pp. 1–36.

marily practical, to elucidate problems with which the government was concerned, such as urban living conditions, the cost of living, and the effect of crowded urban conditions upon juvenile delinquency. Busia further states that he tried to combine the methods of the social survey with those of the social anthropologist:

> In collecting our information, we have used all the five techniques most generally used in the collection of social data: direct observation of behavior, examination of documents, "free" interview, questionnaires and interview by schedule.[33]

Because the study was designed to elucidate practical problems, the facts were presented as briefly as possible and only those have been included in the monograph which throw light on such problems.

An investigation sponsored by the Institut d'Etudes Centre-Africaines and directed by Balandier, a social anthropologist, had two main objectives: first, the gathering of precise information on the African population of Brazzaville, Congo, and an analysis of the problems which characterize the two main areas of the city; second, the inquiry was conceived as part of a larger research program into the social evolution of the Bacongo peoples. Quantitative methods, based on questionnaires and schedules, were used in collecting all basic data. Other methods included the collection of life histories, and the administering of Rorschach, intelligence, and sociometric tests. No mention is made of direct and participant observations.[34]

Mitchell, an anthropologist on the staff of the Rhodes-Livingstone Institute, conducted a survey of four Copperbelt mining towns in 1953 and 1954. The surveys were designed to give statistical information on such topics as occupation, religion, tribe, marital status, education, wages, and length of residence in the mining towns. A supplementary schedule obtained information on literacy and reading preferences. A 10 per cent random sample of houses in the four towns was used to represent the population. After the surveys were completed, intensive anthropological studies of a selected sub-sample of households were made.[35]

33. Busia, K. A., *Report on a Social Survey of Sekondi-Takoradi*. Crown Agents, London, 1950.
34. Balandier, G., "Approche sociologique des "Brazzavilles noires": étude preliminaire," *Africa*, Vol. 22, No. 1, 1952, pp. 23–34.
35. Mitchell, J. C., "An Estimate of Fertility Among Africans on the Copperbelt of Northern Rhodesia," *Human Problems in British Central Africa*, Vol. 13, 1953, pp.

A study done in East London (South Africa), this one some years later by Pauw, sought information on the family among urbanized Bantu. The first part of the study consisted of the application of a questionnaire to a sample of 202 individuals representing 109 different households. Information was sought on demographic characteristics of the population as well as sociocultural variables dealing with marriage, the household, and the family. Further data were gathered about preceding generations who had moved from the rural areas to the town. After these data were tabulated, 14 households representative of different cultural and structural types were selected for more intensive study.[36]

We shall now turn to two additional African studies whose methods are unusually well described: *Jinja Transformed* by the Sofers, and *An Experiment in Methodology in a West African Urban Community* by Schwab.[37]

According to the authors of the Jinja study:

The study of Jinja had three main objectives: (a) to collect data likely to be of use to government in framing policy; (b) to contribute to the general body of scientific knowledge concerning social process and social relations in urban societies with multi-racial populations; (c) to experiment in methods of social research.[38]

The practical aspect of the study concerned the attempt to gather data on such questions as the effects of the employment of women on African social structure, why African workers prefer monthly to weekly wages, whether tenants in the African housing estate would like to have communal plots to cultivate, whether Africans receive adequate attention at the local hospital, and what fuel Africans use and where they secure it. Statistical information was requested by the government regarding African incomes and rentals, and the number of children in need of educational facilities.

The theoretical aspects of the study attempted to test hypotheses concerning a multi-racial and multi-cultural society undergoing rapid growth and

---

18–29; Mitchell, J. C., "The Distribution of African Labour by Area of Origin on the Copper Mines of Northern Rhodesia," *Human Problems in British Central Africa,* Vol. 14, 1954, pp. 30–36.

36. Pauw, B. A., *The Second Generation:* A Study of the Family Among Urbanized Bantu in East London. Oxford University Press, Fairlawn, N.J., 1963.

37. Sofer, Cyril and Rhona Sofer, *op. cit.*; Schwab, W. B., *op. cit.*

38. Sofer, Cyril and Rhona, *op. cit.*

change. The authors hoped that their findings might be of some use to researchers using comparable methods to build up theories or universal principles applicable to all such societies.

With regard to experimentation in methods of social research, the authors felt that the investigation should be conducted by a combination of the methods of the quantitative social survey and of more intensive field work:

> The employment of sample survey methods becomes necessary when it is desired to collect systematic numerical facts relating to the characteristics of a population as a whole and when that population is large in relation to research resources and heterogeneous in respect of the characteristics in which the investigator is interested. If the population is small, it is possible to investigate all the units involved. . . . (In intensive field work) there is greater concentration on qualitative data not susceptible to expression or analysis in quantitative form. . . .[39]

The Sofers go on to discuss how the data obtained through survey methods for the understanding of the dynamic aspects of town administrative problems is limited in scope:

> If depth of insight is to be obtained into the problem situations and processes of urban life, survey methods need to be supplemented by the intensive fieldwork of the trained observer, involving lengthy and/ or repeated contact with individuals and groups. This necessity can be illustrated with reference to problems associated with immigration. It is possible through survey methods to ascertain such facts as the tribes, religions, age and sex composition, geographical origins, standard of living and occupations of the immigrant population, but less easy to discover significant material relating to the immigrant's transition to urban life, or to the effects of the new environment on his relations with his wife and his control over his children. Again survey methods can establish the labour resources of the population in terms of manpower and training, but can help only to a limited extent to account for the productivity of the labourer, a question not only bound up with nutrition but also with such factors as the social atmosphere of the job and familial incentives to higher production.[40]

39. *Ibid.*
40. Schwab, W. B., *op. cit.*

The Sofers conclude their discussion of methods by stating that it is "valuable to use both groups of methods in urban social research."

Schwab attempted, in his "intensive anthropological survey of the social and economic organization of Oshogbo," to integrate the social survey with intensive anthropological methods.[41] The study was undertaken because it was felt that there was a need to study large, urban areas in Africa which have undergone extensive and systematic contact with Western culture, and which consequently are important foci for cultural change. "Because of the complexity and size of the Oshogbo community and the tremendous variation in and fluidity of norms of present-day Oshogbo social life," the use of quantitative measurement, "however approximate or crude," was necessary. Intensive observational methods were judged inadequate in and of themselves, and had to be augmented by additional techniques which could better sample the complexity and variability of the community. Further, as a consequence of changes taking place in social relationships and value patterns, it became necessary to speak of a continuum of norms existing in the community, since there no longer existed any uniformity of patterns. It was therefore hoped that, by developing sampling and other quantifying devices, Schwab and his associates could get at some measure of isolation of the various dependent and interdependent variables that entered into the changing social relationships and make some effort to assess their strength.

Initially Schwab devoted much effort to getting the consent of the community for the study and establishing effective rapport with the people of Oshogbo. This latter involved several weeks of meeting and talking with as many individuals as possible, until Schwab no longer seemed to be regarded as a stranger. After this period of attempting to allay suspicion, the author began to question and interview people in a more systematic manner:

> The main purpose of these inquiries was not to secure detailed or even, in some instances, very precise information, but to obtain general knowledge necessary for the initiation of a census. Since there were no records available, a sample census was considered essential to secure basic demographic and other social data. The objectives of the sample census were not to enumerate heads, but rather to obtain the characteristics of the community, and to collect reliable and representative data concerning family organization, occupational structure, and

41. *Ibid.*

the religious, educational and age composition of the community. From the census, a sub-sample of families was to be chosen, with selection being made on the basis of economic differentiation of the male heads of the households. These selected families were to be subjected to intensive investigation for the remainder of the survey.[42]

While the research was in progress, Schwab overcame many of the difficulties encountered in doing survey research in underdeveloped areas.[43] Eventually there were 6,241 individuals in the census out of a total population of about 70,000. The data were obtained largely through the use of schedules in the form of guides to the problems under investigation, and also through the use of questionnaires:

> Questionnaires, however, had only a limited scope, for they were employed primarily for the collection of factual data that lent themselves easily to quantification. Thus questionnaires were utilized to obtain such information as the number and percentage of children's deaths, the incidence of divorce, and certain economic data. However, after some experience with questionnaires in the field, it became apparent that they could not be employed in a situation where the material was in any way qualitative or complex, as in the study of the kinship system or other complex institutions. In these circumstances the schedules

42. *Ibid.*
43. We may briefly describe a few of these problems. The inevitable problem of "why me?" arose among respondents because the people of Oshogbo were unable to comprehend why they were chosen in preference to residents of some other compound. As a result they refused, at first, to cooperate. A further problem was that it was necessary to secure the permission of the entire corporate group of which the respondent was a member before interviewing could proceed. In addition, people refused to enumerate wives and children and when they did so, children under five were often omitted since they were not considered permanent members of the family because of the high death rate among young children. Respondents were also frequently chastised by other members of their group or compound for being "informers" and hence others in the area were reluctant to give information. Most of these difficulties were overcome by repeated visits to the compounds and by enlisting further aid from influential leaders of the community. In addition, Schwab was able to convince his population that he had no official government capacity and was in no position to levy taxes or impose laws. See Stycos, J. M., "Sample Surveys for Social Science in Underdeveloped Areas," in Adams, R. N. and J. Preiss, eds., *Human Organization Research:* Field Relations and Techniques. Dorsey Press, Homewood, Ill., 1960, for further discussion of such problems.

were used which suggested the lines the investigation should follow and set the minimum limits for the information required.[44]

Schwab goes on to state that he feels that where questionnaires were used the interviews tended to be directive, but where the guides were used they were non-directive. This may have been disadvantageous since it may have produced uneven results; but, on the other hand, Schwab says that excellent rapport was established which probably led, ultimately, to more complete knowledge.

For another study of urban areas we move to the islands of the West Indies. To determine whether the family systems of three West Indian societies conform to a single model of family and domestic relations, M. G. Smith, an anthropologist, undertook an extensive social survey of three large samples: 224 households of Carriacou, 215 households of Grenada and 1,440 Jamaican households.[45] A tremendous amount of work went into the collection of the data in order to insure representativeness, comparability, and full documentation of all interpretations and analytic statements. The book offers a somewhat different approach to the study of West Indian family life than is usually presented and is also, in part, a criticism and refutation of the methods and results of others who have tackled the same analytic problems. Because of the great variation of family types (at least hypothetically) and because of the sociological and cultural diversity of the populations and their sizes, it was deemed necessary to undertake a social survey. As far as we have been able to discern, depth or intensive observational studies were not made.

APPLIED ANTHROPOLOGY

Anthropologists have also concerned themselves with the role of anthropology in administration and economic development. This role has primarily been advisory and to a large extent, because of the socio-political situation, concerned chiefly with the administration of colonial areas and dependent peoples. The work of the British anthropologists falls into this category and was discussed in the section on urban studies. Here we shall concern ourselves with the few studies which have been done by anthropologists and other social scientists concerned with administration, community development, and health programs in developing areas.

44. Schwab, W. B., *op. cit.*
45. Smith, M. G., *op. cit.*

Lewis, known primarily for his work in rural and urban Mexico, did a study of village life in northern India to gather data which would be useful and enlightening to Indian government administrators.[46] A social survey was conducted in order to determine the demographic and sociocultural variables of the village. Such data as sex, age, clan, caste, and age at betrothal were collected. For those villagers involved in agriculture such variables as amount of land owned, size of cultivated units, amount of land rented in and amount of land rented out, and number of oxen and bullock carts were collected. At the conclusion of the census, a socio-economic scale was developed with the aid of the census data. With this scale Lewis and his colleagues were able to select a sample of 30 households which was representative of all the major socio-economic variables in the village, and undertake an intensive qualitative study.

A similar piece of research was done by Dube in the state of Hyderabad in south-central India.[47] A social survey was carried out in the village of Shamirpet, the data of which were used to select a sample of 120 families representing different castes and levels of income, education, and urban contacts. These families then became the subjects for intensive anthropolitical investigation. Dube also used survey data collected by other specialist members of his research team, including information from a diet and nutritional survey, a survey of village agriculture and its problems, and a survey of animal care and health. These additional data provided important leads for intensive investigation within the sub-sample.

Mangin and his associates, one of whom was an anthropologist, undertook a study of the effects on mental health of migration to urban areas:

> In collaboration with Humberto Rotondo, a psychiatrist from the Ministry of Health, and Jose Matos Mar, an anthropologist from the University of San Marcos (Lima, Peru) a study of one *barriada* (a squatter settlement) was carried out during 1958 and 1959. In addition to traditional anthropological methods such as observation, conversation and participation, we administered five questionnaires, including the Cornell Medical Index, to a selected sample of 65 of the 600 families.[48]

46. Lewis, Oscar, *Village Life in Northern India:* Studies in a Delhi Village. University of Illinois Press, Urbana, 1958.
47. Dube, S. C., *Indian Village*. Routledge & Kegan Paul, London, 1955.
48. Mangin, W., "Mental Health and Migration to Cities: A Peruvian Case," *Annals of the New York Academy of Sciences,* Vol. 84, December, 1960, pp. 911–917.

The author states that the material has not yet been systematically analyzed but he does present tentative findings. For example, in noting that there seemed to be much ambivalence toward marriage and the family, Mangin states:

> A common contradiction that may not be as contradictory as it first appears is that in which one encounters verbalization about happiness and enjoyment only with wife and children from the very same men who habitually beat their wives and children. Violence toward wife and children is the most frequently encountered form of violence in Peru and, in many cases, there was no hint of it in the questionnaires. This was one of the many occasions where the questionnaires became valuable only in conjunction with the observational data of the anthropologist.[49]

Seppilli, of the University of Perugia, Italy, reports on a study of fertility in a rural Mexican community:

> The study of fertility is part of a larger research program designed to examine the dynamics of male and female roles and of family organization in a changing rural society.[50]

Analysis of the phenomena under investigation was achieved through a "dynamic methodology based on an interdisciplinary approach, combining cultural anthropology and other social sciences contributions." A random sample of the population (3,361 inhabitants) was taken with a ratio of 1:6 between the sample and the universe. The final sample—after refusal and absentees—consisted of 143 family units representing 566 individuals. Questionnaires were then administered to the sample. Special questionnaires were also administered to a sample of school children. Additional intensive techniques were carried out in order to integrate and deepen the general data.

And finally, Scotch and Geiger discuss the results of an interdisciplinary cross-cultural study which attempted to establish the relationship between cultural processes or factors and the processes in the pathophysiology of

49. *Ibid.*
50. Seppilli, T., "Social Conditions of Fertility in a Rural Community in Transition in Central Mexico," *Annals of the New York Academy of Sciences,* Vol. 84, December, 1960, pp. 959–962.

disease.[51] The instrument used for the study was the Cornell Medical Index, which was applied to probability samples of two general population groups —urban and rural Zulu. The C.M.I. questionnaire (made up of 195 questions on physical and emotional symptoms) was modified for use in the non-Western setting. Scotch, in another survey study among the Zulu, reports on the relation of sociocultural factors to hypertension.[52] These reports are the result of an extensive epidemiological study conducted in the Union of South Africa.

NATIONAL CHARACTER

National character studies developed out of applied research in World War II, and were initially founded on culture-and-personality theory. In this section we shall discuss a few studies that have made methodological contributions.

In a study of English national character, Gorer used a questionnaire consisting of opinion and attitude questions.[53] His procedure in obtaining respondents was somewhat unique since he introduced the questionnaire in a widely read weekly newspaper asking for cooperation. About 11,000 completed forms were returned, of which some 5,000 were analyzed. Gorer did not submit his questionnaire to other national populations and, in any case, he seems to take it for granted that their answers would be different from those of the English. In 1948 Gorer did a study of *The American People* which was based mainly on rather impressionistic methods.[54] However, he used data from the *Fortune* magazine surveys as a check on certain of his hypotheses.

Lanham sent detailed questionnaires on child training devices to parents in a Japanese community, using the schools as an intermediary.[55] The results convincingly disproved the La Barre and Gorer suppositions on the

51. Scotch, N. A. and H. J. Geiger, "An Index of Symptoms and Disease in Zulu Culture," *Human Organization,* Vol. 22, Winter, 1963–1964, pp. 304–311.

52. Scotch, N. A., "A Preliminary Report on the Relations of Socio-cultural Factors to Hypertension Among the Zulu," *Annals of the New York Academy of Science,* Vol. 84, No. 17, 1960, pp. 1000–1009.

53. Gorer, Geoffrey, *Exploring English Character.* Criterion Books, New York, 1955.

54. Gorer, Geoffrey, *The American People:* A Study in National Character. W. W. Norton, New York, 1948.

55. Lanham, B. B., "Aspects of Child Care in Japan: A Preliminary Report," in *Personal Character and Cultural Milieu,* 3rd rev. ed. Edited by D. G. Haring. Syracuse University Press, Syracuse, 1956.

social pervasiveness of the strictness of Japanese child rearing, especially toilet training.

Stoetzel obtained data on the outlook of Japanese youth after the war, and its attitude toward etiquette (*giri*).[56] Stoetzel's results concerning *giri* deserve special mention since he utilized the survey technique to test certain holistic-depictive findings of Benedict:[57]

> We thus see that contrary to the findings of Benedict's anthropological investigation, the technical interpretation of "giri" is recognized by only a little over one-third of the Japanese people (35%). Moreover, when we consider the distribution according to age and place of residence we find (a) that country-people far more often refrain from defining "giri" than townspeople; (b) that they give technical replies much less often, but give "popular" replies almost equally often; (c) that young people are less familiar with "giri" than their elders, either in the technical sense or in the more usual acceptation. This leads to the conclusion that, if "giri" is really the culture trait so precisely defined in "The Chrysanthemum and the Sword"—a definition endorsed by 35% of present day Japanese—it is a feature which is dying out; at the same time, as it survives to a greater extent in urban than in country communities, it would appear to be an aristocratic rather than a popular feature, spread among the people in the more or less recent past by literary and intellectual means.[58]

In this example, as in the pieces by Bose and Lanham, we may observe the value of survey techniques in attempting to test generalizations and hypotheses obtained by intensive and observational methods. In such studies, the possibility is raised of using surveys as explanatory rather than purely descriptive devices. While anthropologists might benefit greatly from the application of explanatory-type survey methods, considering the ambiguity of some aspects of their own intensive methodology, there are great difficulties

56. Stoetzel, Jean, "The Contributions of Public Opinion Research Techniques to Social Anthropology," *International Social Science Bulletin*, Vol. 5, No. 3, 1953, pp. 494–503; Stoetzel, Jean, *Without the Chrysanthemum and the Sword:* A Study of the Attitudes of Youth in Post-War Japan. Columbia University Press, New York, 1955.
57. Benedict, Ruth, *The Chrysanthemum and the Sword:* Patterns of Japanese Culture. Houghton Mifflin, Boston, 1946.
58. Stoetzel, Jean, *Without the Chrysanthemum . . . , op. cit.*

in refining hypotheses and problems in order to make them amenable to the disciplined technology of survey research. As we noted in the first section of the paper, many of the anthropologist's conclusions are statements of tendency, or global conclusions of great textural complexity, which resist dissection. However this may be, whenever the anthropologist proposes a conclusion of relatively simple and explicit dimensions, he has an obligation to utilize survey research to give it a final test.

MULTI-ETHNIC FIELD RESEARCH

Another important arena for the use of survey research instruments is the comparative multi-ethnic regional field study. Such studies are made in relatively large regions inhabited by a number of different subcultures, ethnic groups, tribes, or neighborhood groups. The objectives are to compare responses of the different groups to the natural environment, the effect of differing cultural traditions on a similar economy, and related problems. Examples are the Harvard Five Cultures studies, the research program directed by Steward on Puerto Rico,[59] and the current study of a region in southwestern Saskatchewan by the senior author of this chapter.

In the last case, a single basic survey instrument—a detailed open-ended interview schedule—was administered to a large sample of persons and families from each of the several ethnic, religious, and occupational groups in the region. This schedule included questions relating to each of the important problem-areas of the research program. A basic regional foundation was thus laid for the interpretation of the very different slices of data obtained by many other methods from the separate cultural groups. The distinctive adaptations and problems of these groups required variant approaches—the Indians were studied as a deprived minority, the ranchers as a problem in the nostalgic persistence of frontier ideology, the farmers as a case of political sophistication in a rural setting, the Hutterites as a problem in the influence of communal organization on economic efficiency, and so on.

59. Steward, J. H., *et al.*, *The People of Puerto Rico:* A Study in Social Anthropology. University of Illinois Press, Urbana, 1956; Kluckhohn, F. R. and F. Strodtbeck, *Variations in Value Orientations*. Row, Peterson, Evanston, Ill., 1961; Vogt, E. Z. and Ethel Albert, *People of Rimrock:* A Study of Values in Five Cultures. Harvard University Press, Cambridge, 1966, contains a complete bibliography of the Five Cultures project, and a review and critique of its methods.

SOCIALIZATION

Landy presents an "exploratory-descriptive ethnographic study of social-ization, or cultural transmission and learning, in a rural Puerto Rican village within the context of its culture and social structure."[60] As to the me-thod of investigation Landy states ". . . contrary to ethnographic tradition, we found it helpful at the outset to take a census of the community or uni-verse. . . ." The census covered many categories of demographic, sociologi-cal, and psychological data and it also proved useful as a means of estab-lishing contacts with every family in the community. From the census data, 18 lower-class families were selected according to certain specific criteria in order to provide representation of this segment of the population, and then subjected to intensive observational and interviewing studies.

GENERAL REMARKS

There appears to be general consensus among the authors examined in this section that the choice of field methods is *not* an either/or proposition. The authors recognize that an adequate field study is not conducted on the basis of a single technique, gathering a single kind of information, but rather that different types of data require different approaches. This is borne out by the methodological sequence displayed by most of the reviewed studies. The investigator's initial approach to the community was designed to obtain general impressions of the culture through personal contacts and observa-tion. When the investigator felt the time was appropriate, a census was con-ducted, its categories based on the qualitative data at hand—that is, the per-ceived cultural and social-structural patterns largely determined the choice of a method of sampling and the structure of the samples, as well as the recruitment of interviewers of various origins and the precautions to be taken in approaching the persons questioned. The pre-tests of the instruments as-sisted in evaluating the initial qualitative judgments. After the completion of the census, a sub-sample was selected for intensive depth studies. In some of the researches, questionnaires and schedules were used as instruments for eliciting responses; in others, intensive observational techniques were used; while in still others, a combination of the two methods was employed.

We noted also that social surveys illustrate the use of quantitative tech-niques in testing anthropological hypotheses—the studies of Bose which

60. Landy, David, *op. cit.*

attempted to test postulates of Redfield's folk-urban continuum, and of Stoetzel concerning the generality of Benedict's conclusions on Japanese culture. Other research opportunities provided by survey data will accrue in the use of the growing number of social survey data archives in the United States and Europe. The data libraries at the University of Michigan, the University of California at Berkeley, Yale University, and the University of Cologne select certain topics or areas for special emphasis. Thus Berkeley specializes in survey data from underdeveloped areas in Asia and Latin America; Ann Arbor emphasizes data based on consumer behavior and political behavior; the Yale collection combines survey data with extensive holdings of demographic and official statistics from many countries.[61] Admittedly there are many problems involved in the use of survey data cross-culturally, but there is considerable scope for experimentation with regard to such matters as the applicability of survey methods developed in Western cultures to non-Western areas, the optimum combination of survey with intensive fieldwork techniques, and the sequence in which both types should be undertaken. Schwab's study provides an excellent example of such experimentation.

Survey methods enable the investigator to define the nature and extent of the various cultural traits and permit an analysis of social differentiation, while intensive methods permit the deepening of knowledge of the "social facts" or approach to, in Malinowski's phrase, "the imponderabilia of actual life."

If anthropology has a message for survey research, it is this: delay the construction of schedules of all kinds until something is known about the cultural context of the phenomenon under study; do not assume that all slices of social actuality are always identically responsive to theoretical constructs; remember that all such constructs are, in the last analysis, human conceptions of the social situation at one place and time, and their relevance to a new situation must always be a problem for investigation.[62]

If survey research has a message for anthropology, it is this: first, often

61. See Scheuch, E., as chairman of a conference on "Data Archives; Problems and Promise," at the Proceedings of the Eighteenth Conference on Public Opinion Research, *Public Opinion Quarterly,* Vol. 27, Winter, 1963, pp. 641–643.
62. Bennett, J. W., "Individual Perspective in Fieldwork," in *Human Organization Research:* Field Relations and Techniques. Edited by R. N. Adams and J. J. Priess. Dorsey Press, Homewood, Ill., 1961.

context can be known in general terms, known sufficiently well to permit the use of instruments which will materially aid in the checking of particular hypotheses, or hasten the collection of certain types of data. It is not always necessary to know the culture in detail; the intelligent and well-educated observer can operate on the basis of our growing comparative knowledge of cultures and social systems. Second, whenever specific hypotheses are to be tested in fieldwork, the anthropologist has an obligation to construct and utilize instruments which will adequately represent the population under study.

Some Marginal Applications

ANALYTIC COMPARISON

Research which aims at a comparison of two or more cultural or institutional systems is often problem-oriented research, which, as we have already seen, is susceptible to the application of survey research methods. Comparison requires the investigator to exert controls over the data in ways which are not needed in depictive studies of single systems. Some comparative studies are *post hoc;* they are performed on data already collected, and this fact also requires the exertion of disciplined control and the logical conception of cultural data as composed of analytical bits, more or less representative of particular "populations."

In anthropology, the comparative approach has a history going back to Tylor, who "surveyed" marriage customs and found "adhesions" which indicated, in his view, historical connections.[63] Another classical instance was Morgan's monumental attempt to study kinship on a comparative basis by sending a questionnaire around the world to missionaries and administrators in contact with non-Western peoples.[64] The "culture element surveys" of the California anthropologists Kroeber and Driver, and their precursors, the "trait analysts" like Spier;[65] the grand-scale comparators like

63. Tylor, E. B., "On a Method of Investigating the Development of Institutions Applied to the Laws of Marriage and Descent," *Journal of the Royal Anthropological Institute,* Vol. 18, 1889, pp. 245–269.
64. Morgan, L. H., "Systems of Consanguinity and Affinity in the Human Family," *Smithsonian Contribution to Knowledge,* Vol. 17. U.S. Government Printing Office, Washington, 1871.
65. Kroeber, A. L. and H. E. Driver, "The Reliability of Culture Element Data," *University of California Anthropological Records,* Vol. 1, 1938; Spier, L., *The Sun*

Hobhouse, Wheeler, and Ginsberg, and their modern descendents, Murdock, Driver, Whiting and others, are all important representatives of this trend.[66]

It is important to note that the comparative analytic survey made on secondary cultural data has always occupied a controversial position in anthropology. During the 1930's, the trait analysis work of the preceding decades was subjected to a detailed criticism which still hangs over it like a cloud.[67] The essence of this criticism was that culture cannot be segregated into simple, single items, since culture is by nature a complex configurational or functional whole—or at least an entity in which the bonds between the parts are so unique that to break them arbitrarily in favor of a rationalistic classification is to falsify the nature of the entity. In spite of criticism, the secondary comparative survey has persisted in anthropology, and has undergone considerable refinement. The extent of this refinement can be grasped from a comparison of the "culture element survey" work done by Driver and Kroeber in the 1930's and 1940's and the recent volumes on the American Indian by Driver.[68] A contemporary study of broader scope, with considerable methodological sophistication, has been done by Swanson.[69]

The criticisms were correct insofar as the analysts attempted to define single cultures as mere assemblages of traits. However, the criticisms missed the point when the comparative dimension of analysis was in view, for it is difficult to compare cultures *as wholes*. Some kind of classification—implicit or explicit—of their elements is necessary. The nature of this classification

---

Dance of the Plains Indians: Its Development and Diffusion. Anthropological Papers, American Museum of Natural History, Vol. 16, Part 7, 1921; Bennett, J. W., "The Development of Ethnological Theory as Illustrated by Studies of the Plains Indian Sun Dance," *American Anthropologist,* Vol. 46, April, 1944, pp. 162–181.

66. Hobhouse, L. T., G. C. Wheeler and Morris Ginsberg, *The Material Culture and Social Institutions of the Simpler Peoples.* Chapman & Hall, London, 1930; Murdock, G. P., *Social Structure.* Macmillan, New York, 1949; Driver, H. E. and W. C. Massey, *Comparative Studies of North American Indians.* Transactions of the American Philosophical Society, New Series, Vol. 47, Part 2, 1957; Whiting, J. W. and I. L. Child, *Child Training and Personality:* A Cross-Cultural Study. Yale University Press, New Haven, 1953.

67. See the review by E. R. Leach of S. H. Udy's *Organization of Work* in *American Sociological Review,* Vol. 25, 1960, pp. 136–138.

68. Kroeber, A. L. and H. E. Driver, *op. cit.;* Driver, H. E. and W. C. Massey, *op. cit.*

69. Swanson, Guy E., *The Birth of the Gods.* University of Michigan Press, Ann Arbor, 1960.

is the vital issue, and it is true enough that the early classificatory schemes like Wissler's "universal pattern" were jejune and biased.[70] However, classifications based on the recognition of enduring or typical functional relationships among institutions, among institutions and habitat, or among interaction patterns associated with recurring status relationships in many societies, are another story altogether. Classifications of this kind should, as a general rule, precede rather than follow analytic comparison: the partnership between the "anthropologist" and the "survey researcher" is thus once more demonstrated.[71]

SYSTEMATIC ETHNOGRAPHY

A related and possibly significant new approach has developed in recent years, especially among linguistic anthropologists, that provides a new approach to the problem of classification. This approach has been labeled "the new ethnography" or "ethnoscience" by its devotees. Essentially, what this new approach involves is the systematic collection of data on how the natives of a given culture themselves classify and structure their material and social universe. Thus, the anthropologists are trying to get at a refinement of the empirical basis of comparative study, by providing more surely valid descriptions of the individual systems on which comparative study must depend. It is the classificatory principles discovered in ethnography which should be compared, not the occurrence of categories defined by arbitrary criteria whose relevance in the cultures described is unknown.[72]

An example here might help to clarify this problem. Murdock, in discussing one of his findings, states that if a tribe, for example, under the influence of a more powerful culture accepts a new method of production, its rule of residence will soon change, for this is the first response to altered conditions.[73] Now, Murdock's categories of residence are based on the conventional ethnological concepts of patrilocal, matrilocal, bilocal, etc.; but the "ethnoscientists" state that the principles by which people choose where

70. Wissler, Clark, *Man and Culture*. T. Y. Crowell, New York, 1923.
71. See Eggan, Fred, "Social Anthropology and the Method of Controlled Comparison," *American Anthropologist*, Vol. 56, October, 1954, pp. 743–763; and Forde, Daryll, "The Anthropological Approach in Social Science," in *Readings in Anthropology*, Vol. 2. Edited by M. H. Fried. Thomas Y. Crowell, New York, 1959, pp. 59–78, for the classic anthropological view of these matters.
72. Goodenough, W. H., "Residence Rules," *Southwestern Journal of Anthropology*, Vol. 12, Spring, 1956, pp. 22–37.
73. Murdock, G. P., *Social Structure, op. cit.*

to reside may involve considerations not only of genealogical tie (which underlie traditional categories) but also features of ecology, social role, and other expectations and obligations.[74] It is therefore essential to resist the temptation to assign an aspect of a native culture too easily to a familiar category. Such methodological errors often result from not investigating the full range of phenomena. In order to correct for these methodological errors, many anthropologists are using standardized stimuli with selected samples in order to control for as many of the variables as possible. In addition, other systematic ethnographers are endeavoring to amend intensive methods of investigation with quantitative techniques. Here the stress is placed upon techniques which can measure the degree of consistency of utterances and behavior at various levels of explicitness. This requires a survey type of approach, with greater care given to problems of representativeness than may be the case for more informal studies.[75]

Conclusion

In this chapter we first described aspects of anthropological research which do not readily conform to the extensive methodology of survey research, and indicated that often this situation becomes the focus of polemic attacks— the "anthropologists" condemning "sociologists" and "behavioral scientists" for meaningless abstractions and excessive counting; the "sociologist" accusing the "anthropologist" of sloppy method and unwarranted generalization. It is clear from the review of problem-oriented research that anthropologists in respectable numbers have abandoned the holistic-depictive approach, and consequently accept whatever methods are useful in pursuing

74. Hymes, D. H., "A Perspective for Linguistic Anthropology," in *Horizons of Anthropology*. Edited by Sol Tax. Aldine Press, Chicago, 1964, pp. 92–107.

75. See Sturtevant, W. C., "Studies in Ethnoscience," *American Anthropologist*, Vol. 66, Part 2, June 1964, pp. 99–131; Romney, A. K. and R. G. D'Andrade, "Cognitive Aspects of English Kin Terms," *American Anthropologist*, Vol. 66, Part 2, June, 1964, pp. 146–170; Frake, C. O., "Notes on Queries in Ethnography," *American Anthropologist*, Vol. 66, Part 2, June, 1964, pp. 132–145; Ackerman, Charles, "Structure and Statistics: The Purum Case," *American Anthropologist*, Vol. 66, February, 1964, pp. 53–66; Burling, Robbins, "Cognition and Componential Analysis: God's Truth or Hocus-Pocus?" *American Anthropologist*, Vol. 66, February, 1964, pp. 20–28; Metzger, Duane and G. E. Williams, "A Formal Ethnographic Analysis of Tenejapa Ladino Weddings," *American Anthropologist*, Vol. 65, October, 1963, pp. 1076–1101; Cancian, Frank, "Informant Error and Native Prestige Ranking in Zinacantan," *American Anthropologist*, Vol. 65, October, 1963, pp. 1068–1075.

the problem of interest. Change and other aspects of dynamics constitute the primary focus of these problems; such interests require more analytic procedures than do the depictive studies.

At the same time, certain continuities in anthropological research regardless of modality are evident and suggest that anthropology for the time being retains a distinctive viewpoint while also showing acceptance of a more self-conscious methodology. The bulk of research has been done on foreign soil and, in nearly all cases, respect for cultural context accompanied the survey operations. These two features—the foreign environment for research and respect for cultural context—are anthropological specialties in the sense that the academic anthropology departments are equipped to foster and train students in the appropriate procedures. Other social sciences, while evincing increased interest in non-Western research, are not so well equipped to handle this type of work and often call upon the anthropologist as a team member in interdisciplinary projects.

Underlying these features are deeper issues, also suggested by some of our early discussion. The nature of the anthropologist's engagement with culture in the context of intensive method carries with it certain sources of insight and understanding which are simply not available in extensive methods. It is hoped that this difference of approach can be preserved in the social sciences. Often the advocates of one grand social science imply, perhaps unconsciously, the abandonment of any type of *verstehen* and the substitution of the computer or the social survey. It matters little whether the torch is kept alight by people who bear the label "anthropologist," or some other; but the need for a *variety* of approaches and methods in the social sciences is critical. Those periods of social science which displayed a marked unity of outlook have been the theoretically sterile periods: the last half of the 19th century, with its "evolutionary" presumptions for all the social sciences, is the most familiar; another was the "historical" period of anthropology, particularly the first two decades of the 20th century. The human reality must be apprehended by a variety of viewpoints, not by one alone, because this very reality is always in part a construct, always in part an image, and only by encouraging difference in perspective and approach can one obtain the needed richness of imagery, and consequently, theory.

Bibliography

Ackerman, Charles, "Structure and Statistics: The Purum Case," *American Anthropologist,* Vol. 66, February, 1964, pp. 53–65.

Adams, R. N. and J. Preiss, eds., *Human Organization Research:* Field Relations and Techniques. Dorsey Press, Homewood, Ill., 1960.

Anderson, R. T. and B. G. Anderson, *The Vanishing Village:* A Danish Maritime Community. University of Washington Press, Seattle, 1964.

Arensberg, C. M., "The Community as Object and as Sample," *American Anthropologist,* Vol. 63, April, 1961, pp. 241–264.

Balandier, G., "Approche Sociologique des 'Brazzavilles noires': étude preliminaire," *Africa,* Vol. 22, No. 1, 1952, pp. 23–34.

Bateson, Gregory, *Naven:* A Survey of the Problems Suggested by a Composite Picture of the Culture of a New Guinean Tribe, Drawn from Three Points of View. Cambridge University Press, London, 1936.

Bateson, Gregory and Margaret Mead, *Balinese Character:* A Photographic Analysis. New York Academy of Sciences, New York, 1942.

Benedict, Ruth, *The Chrysanthemum and the Sword:* Patterns of Japanese Culture. Houghton Mifflin, Boston, 1946.

Bennett, J. W., "The Development of Ethnological Theory as Illustrated by Studies of the Plains Sun Dance," *American Anthropologist,* Vol. 46, April, 1944, pp. 162–181.

Bennett, J. W., "The Study of Cultures: A Survey of Technique and Methodology in Field Work," *American Sociological Review,* Vol. 13, December, 1948, pp. 672–689.

Bennett, J. W., "Individual Perspective in Fieldwork," in *Human Organization Research:* Field Relations and Techniques. Edited by R. N. Adams and J. J. Priess. Dorsey Press, Homewood, Ill., 1961.

Bennett, J. W. and K. H. Wolff, "Toward Communication Between Sociology and Anthropology," in *Current Anthropology.* Edited by W. L. Thomas, Jr. University of Chicago Press, Chicago, 1956.

Blalock, H. M., Jr., *Social Statistics.* McGraw-Hill, New York, 1960.

Bose, S. P., "Peasant Values and Innovation in India," *American Journal of Sociology,* Vol. 67, March, 1962, pp. 552–560.

Burling, Robbins, "Maximization Theories and the Study of Economic Anthropology," *American Anthropologist,* Vol. 64, August, 1962, pp. 802–821.

Burling, Robbins, "Cognition and Componential Analysis: God's Truth or Hocus-Pocus?" *American Anthropologist,* Vol. 66, February, 1964, pp. 20–28.

Busia, K. A., *Report on a Social Survey of Sekondi-Takoradi.* Crown Agents, London, 1950.

Cancian, Frank, "Informant Error and Native Prestige Ranking in Zinacantan," *American Anthropologist,* Vol. 65, October, 1963, pp. 1068–1075.

Casagrande, J. B., "Some Observations on the Study of Intermediate Societies," in *Intermediate Societies,* American Ethnological Society Publications. Edited by V. F. Ray. University of Washington Press, Seattle, 1959.

Dore, R. P., *City Life in Japan:* The Study of a Tokyo Ward. University of California Press, Berkeley, 1958.

Driver, H. E. and W. C. Massey, *Comparative Studies of North American Indians.* Transactions of the American Philosophical Society, New Series, Vol. 47, Part 2, 1957.

Dube, S. C., *Indian Village.* Routledge & Kegan Paul, London, 1955.

Dumont, L. and D. Pocock, eds., *Contributions to Indian Sociology,* Vol. I. Institute of Social Anthropology, Paris-Oxford, 1957.

Eggan, Fred, "Social Anthropology and the Method of Controlled Comparison," *American Anthropologist,* Vol. 56, October, 1954, pp. 743–763.

Eisenstadt, S. N., "Anthropological Studies of Complex Societies," *Current Anthropology,* Vol. 2, No. 3., June, 1961, pp. 201–222.

Evans-Pritchard, E. E., *The Nuer.* Clarendon Press, Oxford, England, 1940.

Firth, R., "Census and Sociology in a Primitive Community," in *Problems and Methods in Demographic Studies of Preliterate Peoples.* Proceedings of World Population Conference, United States, 1954, Paper 6, pp. 105–227.

Forde, Daryll, "The Anthropological Approach in Social Science," in *Readings in Anthropology,* Vol. 2. Edited by M. H. Fried. Thomas Y. Crowell, New York, 1959, pp. 59–78.

Fortes, M., "Ashanti Social Survey: A Preliminary Report," in *Human Problems in British Central Africa.* Edited by M. Gluckman and J. M. Winterbottom. Vol. 6, Rhodes-Livingston, Northern Rhodesia, 1948, pp. 1–36.

Frake, C. O., "Notes on Queries in Ethnography," *American Anthropologist,* Vol. 66, Part 2, June, 1964, pp. 132–145.

Fraser, T. M., Jr., *Rusembilian:* A Malay Fishing Village in Southern Thailand. Cornell University Press, Ithaca, 1960.

Frey, F. W., "Surveying Peasant Attitudes in Turkey," *Public Opinion Quarterly,* Vol. 27, Fall, 1963, pp. 335–355.

Gallaher, Art, Jr., *Plainville Fifteen Years Later.* Columbia University Press, New York, 1961.

Geertz, Clifford, "Studies in Peasant Life: Community and Society," in *Biennial Review of Anthropology, 1961.* Edited by B. J. Siegel. Stanford University Press, 1962.

Goodenough, W. H., "Residence Rules," *Southwestern Journal of Anthropology,* Vol. 12, Spring, 1956, pp. 22–37.

Goodman, L. A. and W. H. Kruskal, "Measures of Association for Cross-Classification," *Journal of the American Statistical Association,* Vol. 49, 1954.

Gorer, Geoffrey, *The American People:* A Study in National Character. W. W. Norton, New York, 1948.

Gorer, Geoffrey, *Exploring English Character.* Criterion Books, New York, 1955.

Gouldner, A. W. and R. A. Peterson, *Notes on Technology and the Moral Order.* Bobbs Merrill, New York, 1962.

Henry, Jules, "Economics of Pilaga Food Distribution," *American Anthropologist,* Vol. 53, April, 1951, pp. 187–219.

Higgins, B. H., *Economic Development:* Principles, Problems and Policies. W. W. Norton, New York, 1959.

Hobhouse, L. T., G. C. Wheeler, and Morris Ginsberg, *The Material Culture and Social Institutions of the Simpler Peoples.* Chapman & Hall, London, 1930.

Hotchkiss, J. C., "Studies of Language and Culture in Highland Chiapas, Mexico," in *Proceedings of the 1963 Annual Spring Meeting of the American Ethnological Society.* Edited by V. E. Garfield. University of Washington, Seattle, 1964.

Hunter, Monica, *Reaction to Conquest:* Effects of Contact with Europeans on the Pondo of South Africa. Part 2: An Urban Community, Oxford University Press, New York, 1936, pp. 434–504.

Hymes, D. H., "A Perspective for Linguistic Anthropology," in *Horizons of Anthropology.* Edited by Sol Tax. Aldine Press, Chicago, 1964, pp. 92–107.

Jay, Paul, "Tahitian Fosterage and the Form of Ethnographic Models," *American Anthropologist,* Vol. 65, 1963, pp. 1027–1046.

Jayawardena, Chandra, *Conflict and Solidarity in a Guianese Plantation.* Athlone Press, London, 1963.

Keller, S., "Der Zensus als Quelle Sozial-anthropologischer Untersuchungen," *Homo,* Vol. 11, No. 1, 1960.

Kluckhohn, Clyde, "Participation in Ceremonials in a Navaho Community," *American Anthropologist,* Vol. 40, July, 1938, pp. 359–369.

Kluckhohn, F. R., and Fred Strodtbeck, *Variations in Value Orientations.* Row, Peterson, Evanston, Ill., 1961.

Kroeber, A. L. and H. E. Driver, "The Reliability of Culture Element Data," *University of California Anthropological Records,* Vol. 1, 1938.

Lancaster, Lorraine, "Some Conceptual Problems in the Study of Family and Kin Ties in the British Isles," *British Journal of Sociology,* Vol. 12, December, 1961, pp. 317–331.

Landy, David, *Tropical Childhood:* Cultural Transmission and Learning in a Rural Puerto Rican Village. University of North Carolina, Chapel Hill, 1959.

Lang, G. O. and Peter Kunstadter, "Survey Research on the Uintah and Ouray Ute Reservation," *American Anthropologist,* Vol. 59, June, 1957, pp. 527–532.

Lanham, B. B., "Aspects of Child Care in Japan: A Preliminary Report," in *Personal Character and Cultural Milieu,* 3rd rev. ed. Edited by D. G. Haring. Syracuse University Press, Syracuse, 1956.

Leach, E. R., Review of S. H. Udy, Jr., *Organization of Work:* A Comparative Analysis of Production Among Non-Industrial Peoples. HRAF Press, New Haven, 1959, appearing in *American Sociological Review,* Vol. 25, 1960, pp. 136–138.

Lerner, Daniel, *The Passing of Traditional Society:* Modernizing the Middle East. Free Press, Glencoe, Ill., 1958.

Lewis, Oscar, *Village Life in Northern India:* Studies in a Delhi Village. University of Illinois, Urbana, 1958.

Lynd, R. S. and Helen Lynd, *Middletown:* A Study in Contemporary American Culture. Harcourt, Brace, New York, 1929.

Madge, Charles and T. H. Harrison, *Britain by Mass Observation.* Penguin Books, London, 1939.

Malinowski, Bronislaw, *Argonauts of the Western Pacific:* An Account of Native

Enterprise and Adventure in the Archipelagoes of Melanesian New Guinea. Routledge & Kegan Paul, London, 1922.

Malinowski, Bronislaw, *The Sexual Life of Savages in North Western Melanesia:* An Ethnographic Account of Courtship, Marriage and Family Life Among the Natives of the Trobriand Islands. Liveright, New York, 1929.

Malinowski, Bronislaw, *Coral Gardens and Their Magic:* Study of Method of Tilling in the Trobriand Islands. Routledge & Kegan Paul, London, 1935.

Mangin, W., "Mental Health and Migration to Cities: A Peruvian Case," *Annals of the New York Academy of Sciences,* Vol. 84, No. 17, December, 1960, pp. 911–917.

Marriott, McKim, "Caste Ranking and Community Structure in Five Regions of India and Pakistan," Monograph No. 23, Deccan College Post-Graduate and Reseach Institute, Poona, India, 1960.

Mead, Margaret and R. B. Metraux, *The Study of Culture at a Distance.* University of Chicago Press, Chicago, 1953.

Metzger, Duane and G. E. Williams, "A Formal Ethnographic Analysis of Tenejapa Ladino Weddings," *American Anthropologist,* Vol. 65, October, 1963, pp. 1076–1101.

Mitchell, J. C., "An Estimate of Fertility Among Africans on the Copperbelt of Northern Rhodesia," *Human Problems in British Central Africa,* Vol. 13, 1953, pp. 18–29.

Mitchell, J. C., "The Distribution of African Labour by Area of Origin on the Copper Mines of Northern Rhodesia," *Human Problems in British Central Africa,* Vol. 14, 1954, pp. 30–36.

Mitchell, J. C., *The Yao Village:* A Study in the Social Structure of a Nyasaland Tribe. Manchester University Press, Manchester, 1956.

Morgan, L. H., "Systems of Consanguinity and Affinity in the Human Family," *Smithsonian Contribution to Knowledge,* Vol. 17. U.S. Government Printing Office, Washington, 1871.

Murdock, G. P., *Social Structure.* Macmillan, New York, 1949.

Murdock, G. P., "World Ethnographic Sample," *American Anthropologist,* Vol. 59, August, 1957, pp. 664–687.

Murdock, G. P., "Introduction to S. H. Udy Jr.," in *Organization of Work.* Human Relations Area Files Press, New Haven, 1959.

Naroll, R., *Data Quality Control:* A New Research Technique. Free Press, Glencoe, Ill., 1962.

Passin, H., "Tarahumara Prevarication: A Problem in Field Method," *American Anthropologist,* Vol. 44, April, 1942, pp. 235–247.

Passin, H., "The Development of Public Opinion Research in Japan," *International Journal of Opinion and Attitude Research,* Vol. 5, 1951, pp. 20–30.

Pauw, B. A., *The Second Generation:* A Study of the Family Among Urbanized Bantu in East London. Oxford University Press, Fairlawn, N.J., 1963.

Pettit, G. A., "Primitive Education in North America," *University of California Publications in American Archeology and Ethnology,* Vol. 43, 1946.

Richards, A., "The Village Census in the Study of Culture Contact," *Africa,* Vol. 8, 1935, pp. 20–33.

Romney, A. K. and R. G. D'Andrade, "Cognitive Aspects of English Kin Terms,"

American Anthropologist, Vol. 66, Part 2, June, 1964, pp. 146–170.

Ryan, B., *et al., Sinhalese Village.* University of Miami Press, Coral Gables, 1958.

Schade, H., "Sozial-Anthropologie—Ergebnisse einer Zensus-Untersuchung," *Homo,* Vol. 11, 1960.

Schapera, I., "Field Methods in the Study of Modern Culture Contacts," *Africa,* Vol. 8, 1935, pp. 315–326.

Schapera, I., "Marriage of Near Kin Among the Tswana," *Africa,* Vol. 27, April, 1957.

Scheuch, E., as chairman of a conference on "Data Archives: Problems and Promise." At the Proceedings of the Eighteenth Conference on Public Opinion Research, *Public Opinion Quarterly,* Vol. 27, Winter, 1963, pp. 641–643.

Schwab, W. B., "An Experiment in Methodology in a West African Urban Community," *Human Organization,* Vol. 13, Spring, 1954, pp. 13–19.

Scotch, N. A., "A Preliminary Report on the Relations of Socio-cultural Factors to Hypertension Among the Zulu," *Annals of the New York Academy of Sciences,* Vol. 84, No. 17, 1960, pp. 1000–1009.

Scotch, N. A. and H. J. Geiger, "An Index of Symptom and Disease in Zulu Culture," *Human Organization,* Vol. 22, Winter, 1963–1964, pp. 304–311.

Seppilli, T., "Social Conditions of Fertility in a Rural Community in Transition in Central Mexico," *Annals of the New York Academy of Sciences,* Vol. 84, December, 1960, pp. 959–962.

Smith, M. G., *West Indian Family Structure.* University of Washington Press, Seattle, 1962.

Sofer, Cyril and Rhona Sofer, *Jinja Transformed:* A Social Survey of a Multiracial Township. East African Studies 4, Kegan Paul, Trench, Trubner, London, 1955.

Spier, L., *The Sun Dance of the Plains Indians:* Its Development and Diffusion. Anthropological Papers, American Museum of Natural History, Vol. 16, Part 7, 1921.

Stavrianos, B. K., "Research Methods in Cultural Anthropology in Relation to Scientific Criteria," *Psychological Review,* Vol. 57, November, 1950, pp. 334–344.

Steward, J. H., *et al., The People of Puerto Rico:* A Study in Social Anthropology. University of Illinois Press, Urbana, 1956.

Stoetzel, Jean, "The Contributions of Public Opinion Research Techniques to Social Anthropology," *International Social Science Bulletin,* Vol. 5, No. 3, 1953, pp. 494–503.

Stoetzel, Jean, *Without the Chrysanthemum and the Sword:* A Study of the Attitudes of Youth in Post-war Japan. Columbia University Press, New York, 1955.

Streib, G. F. "The Use of Survey Methods Among the Navaho," *American Anthropologist,* Vol. 54, January, 1952, pp. 30–40.

Sturtevant, W. C., "Studies in Ethnoscience," *American Anthropologist,* Vol. 66, Part 2, June, 1964, pp. 99–131.

Stycos, J. M. "Sample Surveys for Social Science in Underdeveloped Areas," in *Human Organization Research:* Field Relations and Techniques. Edited by R. N. Adams and J. J. Priess. Dorsey Press, Homewood, Ill., 1960.

Swanson, G. E., *The Birth of the Gods:* The Origin of Primitive Beliefs. University of Michigan Press, Ann Arbor, 1960.

Tylor, E. B., "On a Method of Investigating the Development of Institutions Applied to the Laws of Marriage and Descent," *Journal of the Royal Anthropological Institute,* Vol. 18, 1889, pp. 245–269.

Vidich, A. J. and Gilbert Shapiro, "A Comparison of Participant Observation and Survey Data," *American Sociological Review,* Vol. 20, February, 1955, pp. 28–33.

Vogt, E. Z. and Ethel Albert, *People of Rimrock:* A Study of Values in Five Cultures. Harvard University Press, Cambridge, 1966.

West, James (Carl Withers), *Plainville, U.S.A.* Columbia University Press, New York, 1945.

Whiting, J. W. and I. L. Child, *Child Training and Personality:* A Cross-Cultural Study. Yale University Press, New Haven, 1953.

Wilson, Godfrey, "An Essay in the Economics of Detribalisation in Northern Rhodesia," *Rhodes-Livingstone Papers, Nos. 5 and 6.* Rhodes-Livingstone, Northern Rhodesia, 1941 & 1942.

Wissler, Clark, *Man and Culture.* T. Y. Crowell, New York, 1923.

Young, F. and R. Young, "Two Determinants of Community Reaction to Industrialization in Rural Mexico," *Economic Development and Cultural Change,* Vol. 8, 1960, pp. 257–264.

Young, F. and R. Young, "Social Integration and Change in Twenty-four Mexican Villages," *Economic Development and Cultural Change,* Vol. 8, 1960, pp. 366–377.

Survey Research and

Education

by Martin Trow
University of California
Berkeley

Survey Research and Education

Formal education in the United States comprises an immense network of institutions ranging all the way from nursery schools to the Institute for Advanced Study at Princeton, from the one-room schoolhouse to great universities. Yet this huge institutional complex, so important throughout the history of this country and of paramount importance in an increasingly complex society, has been the object of extraordinarily little systematic study by American sociologists.[1]

The relative neglect of education by sociologists (as compared, say, with their attention to political, economic, familial, and even religious institutions) may be ascribed to a number of factors. First, American sociology has grown and developed most rapidly since the middle 1930's—a period of economic crisis, war and international tensions. All of these events and forces of great urgency have tended to divert attention from the sociology of education. In addition, the chief professional concern with education has been lodged in schools and departments of education and teachers colleges, which have by and large been cut off from the main stream of work in the social sciences. In part cause and in part consequence of this separation, work in the field of "educational sociology" has, with few exceptions, addressed itself to immediate and narrowly defined problems of classroom and school administration, and has had little or no relation (either as consumer or contributor) to the substantive theoretical and methodological advances of academic sociology. Finally, the early and nearly complete identification of scientific research in education with certain kinds of learning and measurement psychology has prevented the stimulus to sociological research which might have arisen had the profession made genuine demands on sociology for information of the kind that is represented by industrial sociology, market research and, more recently, by medical sociology.

These and other forces have ensured that, until fairly recently, educational sociology has had little live relation to either the development or the appli-

1. See Brim, O. G., Jr., *Sociology and the Field of Education.* Russell Sage Foundation, New York, 1958, pp. 8–10; also Gross, Neal, "The Sociology of Education," in *Sociology Today:* Problems and Prospects. Edited by R. K. Merton, Leonard Broom, and L. S. Cottrell. Basic Books, New York, 1959, pp. 128–129.

cation of knowledge and ideas in the main current of sociology. This insulation is most apparent where research methodology has achieved its greatest advances in recent decades—that is, in survey research.

The characteristic modes of data collection and the analytical strategies that go by the name of survey research have developed largely over the past twenty-five years, with their earliest applications and systematic development taking place in the areas of public opinion polling, market research, and studies of the audience and the impact of the mass media. More recently, as other chapters in this volume describe, survey research methods have been applied to almost the full range of empirical problems to which sociologists and other social scientists have turned their attention. But sociological research in education has until recently been largely cut off from these developments in survey methods, for the same reasons it has been insulated from developments in the field of sociology generally.

The "Natural" Appeal of "Survey Research" to Educational Sociology

A cursory glance at the research literature in education may well seem to contradict these assertions. This is because one aspect of survey research, and its most visible characteristic—the structured questionnaire administered to large numbers of individuals whose responses are then tabulated and reported—strongly recommends itself to those interested in research in education. Above all, the economy of the mass questionnaire as a research device recommends it to educators; here in the schools and colleges is the "ideal" population for polling—a convenient, captive, compliant, and literate population, whose members' daily round involves taking tests and answering questions. Students and teachers are, for the most part, the pollster's dream; from the age when they can sit still without squirming until, as professors, they come to believe they know more than the researchers and resist the implied insult of forced choices in the structured question, they provide a continually replenished army of potential respondents.

A host of practical, technical, and methodological problems which bedevil the survey researcher in other areas is simply not present or can be avoided by researchers in schools. In a survey in schools there is no painful trudging to fourth floor coldwater flats in remote parts of a city, or frustrating and troublesome "not at homes"; nor are there the problems of defining the relevant population faced by the student of political behavior or the mass media analyst, nor the resistance met by industrial sociologists whose questionnaire clip-board looks suspiciously like a tool of management. Thousands of masters and doctoral candidates, teachers and researchers, have availed themselves of this immensely convenient source of "scientific" data elicited from captive populations of students, teachers, and school administrators for conversion into theses, articles, books, and monographs on every conceivable subject under the educational sun.

Unfortunately, and perhaps ironically, the very ease of access to a body of respondents available for questioning, and the absence of so many of the practical problems faced by survey researchers in other areas, have allowed every researcher in education using these techniques to be his own survey research expert. While the practical and methodological problems faced by researchers in other areas have stimulated critical thought and increased sophistication in the use of survey research, within education much survey research has been carried on in substantial innocence of these developments. The bulk of survey research in education has been little more than a matter of asking some people some questions, and reporting the distribution of their responses. But this practice, whatever its appeal to the writers of dissertations in education, has serious shortcomings which substantially reduce both the practical and the scientific value of the research thus conducted. The errors and inadequacies of survey research in education appear at many points—from the way problems are initially chosen and defined to the choice of the subject population, the selection of the sample, the design of the individual questions and the questionnaire as a whole, and the analysis of the resulting data. Before turning to some of the more important of these errors, let us consider how "survey research" is presented in the texts on research methods in education—the texts that people in education naturally consult when they contemplate studying problems in education through survey methods.

"Survey Research" in Texts on Methods in Education Research
Survey research, as the term is used in this volume, is almost unknown to the men who have been writing the texts on research methods in education around the country.[2] The names of Lazarsfeld, Stouffer, or Hyman, and

2. The texts on research methods in education mentioned later are: Good, C. V. and D. E. Scates, *Methods of Research:* Educational, Psychological, Sociological. Appleton-Century-Crofts, New York, 1954; Travers, R. M. W., *An Introduction to Educational Research.* Macmillan, New York, 1958; Smith, H. L. and J. R. Smith, *An Introduction to Research in Education.* Educational Publications, Bloomington,

the work associated with these names, are rarely found in the texts under review. What that means is that the advances in survey research in the last two decades, and especially the advances in the analysis of survey data, have found no foothold in the instruction in research methods in education.[3] In some of these texts there is only a cursory reference to "surveys." Where more attention is given to "survey research," the bulk of concern is with the *techniques* of conducting surveys—with questionnaire construction, sampling, and the statistics of relationships, with references to statistical literature where these subjects are discussed. In addition, some texts discuss some field problems, such as how not to weary the respondent. But there is little consideration of the *logic* of survey research—of the larger problems of design, of analytical strategies, or of the interdependence of the elements in the research. Small wonder, then, that these latter concerns are so rarely in evidence in the published research, when survey research is reduced to questionnaire collection and the reporting of distributions.

The backwardness (there is no other word) of survey research in education has, I think, two major sources.[4] The first is that the dominant tradition in educational research is psychological and experimental. This is a

Ind., 1959. Texts similar in their treatment of survey methods include: Barnes, J. B., *Educational Research for Classroom Teachers*. G. P. Putnam's Sons, New York, 1960; Barr, A. S., R. A. Davis, and P. O. Johnson, *Educational Research and Appraisal*. J. B. Lippincott, New York, 1953; Best, J. W., *Research in Education,* 9th printing. Prentice-Hall, Englewood Cliffs, N.J., 1965; Good, C. V., *Introduction to Educational Research*. Appleton-Century-Crofts, New York, 1959; Rummel, J. F., *An Introduction to Research Procedures in Education*, Harper & Bros., New York, 1958; Whitney, F. L., *The Elements of Research*, 3rd ed. Prentice-Hall, New York, 1950.
3. See for example: Lazarsfeld, P. F. and Morris Rosenberg, eds., *The Language of Social Research:* A Reader in the Methodology of Social Research. Free Press, Glencoe, Ill., 1955; Hyman, H. H., *Survey Design and Analysis:* Principles, Cases and Procedures. Free Press, Glencoe, Ill., 1955; Stouffer, S. A., *The American Soldier,* Vol. I. Princeton University Press, Princeton, 1949. Significantly, none of these books is cited in any of the texts under discussion. For other works in survey research and analysis, see the other essays in this volume.
4. Some additional sources of this backwardness are discussed in Lazarsfeld, P. F. and S. D. Sieber, *Organizing Educational Research:* An Exploration. Prentice-Hall, Englewood Cliffs, N.J., 1964, especially chap. 3. The gulf between sociology and "educational sociology" which has contributed to that backwardness is discussed in Brim, O. G., Jr., *op. cit.* The penetrating essay on the writing of the history of American education—in Bailyn, Bernard, *Education in the Forming of American Society:* Needs and Opportunities for Study. University of North Carolina Press, Chapel Hill, 1960—casts light on problems in other areas of educational research as well.

very strong research tradition, and it is not hospitable to another set of procedures whose assumptions are so different, and which seems so subjective,
so imprecise, so uncontrolled as to be hardly "scientific" at all. In one text
in which the experimental tradition is predominant, the author simply
assigns survey research to a very subordinate position in the hierarchy of
research methods, in the process making strong, even if mistaken, assertions
about the inherent limitations of the method. For example:

> Survey studies are mainly of the "what exists" type; that is to say,
> they are designed to determine the nature of an existing state of
> affairs. They may be considered to be research in that they result in
> the accumulation of a certain type of knowledge, not, in a sense, that
> their scientific status may be questioned. The reason for this is that
> scientific knowledge must consist of an organized body of generaliza-
> tions that will permit the prediction of events which have not yet oc-
> curred and which are not predicted on the basis of what might be
> called common sense. The survey does not aspire to develop an or-
> ganized body of scientific laws but provides information useful in the
> solution of local problems. . . .
>
> In many surveys . . . an attempt is made to find the interrelationship
> among events. . . . The study of such relationships is unlikely to pro-
> vide direct evidence concerning causal relationships, and indeed they
> are extremely difficult to interpret. Although religious affiliation, for
> example, may be related to preference for one of the major political
> parties, it is clearly unreasonable to conclude that affiliation with reli-
> gion *causes* the individual to vote for Republican candidates. Yet it is
> clear that such a relationship, if well established, must be a result of the
> complex causal relationships that may produce both phenomena. The
> survey itself is unlikely to establish the nature of the complexities and
> thus is likely to leave the pollster with little except the bare facts which
> form only a basis for speculation.[5]

There is, of course, a vast difference between "establishing the nature of
these complexities" and being left with "little except the bare facts which
form only a basis of speculation," and it is between these poles that survey
research in politics has been conducted.[6] But there is no evidence that

5. Travers, R. M. W., *op. cit.*, pp. 236–237.
6. For example, on the relation of religion to voting behavior, see Berelson, B. R.,
P. F. Lazarsfeld, and W. W. McPhee, *Voting:* A Study of Opinion Formation in a
Presidential Campaign. University of Chicago Press, Chicago, 1954, especially pp. 64–

judgments such as the above of Travers are the result of a critical review of the great body of survey research done in recent decades. Students so trained to this view of survey research are, by a kind of self-fulfilling prophecy, likely to do the kind of survey research which confirms the author's view of it.

In addition, though the word "survey" in education means something rather different from its use in this volume, the educational use of the word "survey" is also often applied to at least some of the procedures of "survey research," without the authors being quite aware they are sliding from one use to another. For example:

> Surveys are conducted to establish the nature of existing conditions.[7]
> The word 'survey' indicates the gathering of data regarding current conditions.[8]

A somewhat lengthier definition ties the "survey" to its practical purposes:

> The term "survey" may be applied to the study and diagnosis of an entire school system, to any single part of that system, or even to only one problem within the system. Regardless of its scope, however, the survey should be actuated by a very definite purpose, growing out of some felt need. . . . It should originate in the actual needs of the school and result in a practical solution of unsolved and conflicting problems.[9]

In most cases authors in education continue immediately with a discussion of the questionnaire, since what better way to gather data about "existing conditions" than by asking people? Of course that is not the only way, and several of the authors make clear that a survey (in the educational sense) may well involve several kinds of data collection and investigation. Thus a "survey" (in the sense of a study involving questionnaire data) is often discussed as part of "the survey" (in the educational sense) until the

---

71; Campbell, Angus, Gerald Gurin, and W. E. Miller, *The Voter Decides*. Row, Peterson, Evanston, Ill., 1954, pp. 71, 77, 79, 211–214; Lipset, S. M., Martin Trow, and James Coleman, *Union Democracy:* The Internal Politics of the International Typographical Union. Free Press, Glencoe, Ill., 1956, pp. 113–120 and 236–331; and Lenski, G. E., *The Religious Factor:* A Sociological Study of Religion's Impact on Politics, Economics and Family Life. Doubleday, New York, 1961, pp. 120–192.

7. Travers, R. M. W., *op. cit.,* p. 231.
8. Good, C. V. and D. E. Scates, *op. cit.,* p. 549.
9. Smith, H. L. and J. R. Smith, *op. cit.,* p. 214–15.

two meanings are hopelessly confused. And there is an odd by-product of this confused identification; the low status in which "survey research" (in the educational sense) is held by experimental psychologists who dominate educational research rubs off on the procedures of "survey research" (in the sense of this volume). For example:

> Surveys are conducted to establish the nature of existing conditions. The survey method represents research at a primitive level. It builds a body of fact that is usually of only local significance. The facts thus collected may contribute to the solution of immediate problems, but rarely do they develop a body of knowledge that can be used in solving future problems. Thus the technique tends to be a one shot method.[10]

Leaving aside the odd causal inversion here (it is a one shot method *because* it can't solve future problems), this view may explain why so little attention is paid to survey research—research at a primitive level hardly deserves serious attention. Another self-fulfilling prophecy.

Of course, what is primitive is not survey research but the conceptions of it presented in the texts on research methods in education. For example, a text published in 1959 advises the student that:

> Generally, in formulating the questions (in a questionnaire), only facts should be requested, not opinions. Opinions do not lend themselves readily to tabulation or generalization and are difficult to handle in a study.[11]

This opinion, it is clear, could hardly have been arrived at after a critical review of the immense literature on opinion research, but rather in ignorance of that literature. These same authors also see as one of the advantages of the questionnaire that:

> It brings about a crystallization of thought on the part of the investigator and also of those answering the questionnaire which is a wholesome attitude to be taken by educators.[12]

If constructing questionnaires and answering them are good in themselves, apart from the information gathered, there is justification for doing "surveys" casually, and without reference to the literature.

10. Travers, R. M. W., *op. cit.*, p. 231.
11. Smith, H. L., and J. R. Smith, *op. cit.*, p. 205.
12. *Ibid.*, p. 206.

Misconceptions in these texts about the nature of survey research occur at many levels. For example, the widely used text by Good and Scates differs with Smith and Smith about the possibility of studying survey methods:

> A questionnaire is a form prepared and distributed to secure responses to certain questions; as a general rule, these questions are factual, intended to obtain information about conditions or practices of which the respondent is presumed to have knowledge. The questionnaire has been used increasingly, however, to inquire into the opinions and attitudes of a group.[13]

While this recognition of the possibility of opinion research is reassuring, the student who reads Good and Scates is scarcely any better off than the student who relies on Smith and Smith. The former may gather a body of responses to questions about attitudes and opinions, but he will have little help when faced with the problem of what to do with it. The authors appear to assume that, with the questionnaires in hand, the task is chiefly to count up the responses to the different questions and report the distributions. In the two and a half pages on "Interpreting Questionnaire Returns," Good and Scates use the term "interpreting" in two senses. First, it means deciding what to do about "problem" responses—where the handwriting is bad, the information supplied too fragmentary, or the categories provided are inappropriate. These are, to be sure, problems which confront every researcher, but their solution is (or ought to be) merely part of preparing the data for analysis and evaluation. The authors also imply that interpretation involves an effort to assess the policy implications of the findings, but here their remarks are no more helpful:

> Interpretations of results which are in the form of frequencies is often inadequate and difficult. If 60 per cent, or even 75 per cent, of a group of administrators replying to a questionnaire indicate that they solve a problem in a certain way, or perform a particular duty once each week or monthly, what should the conclusion be? Is this a desirable means of solving the particular problem? Is it necessarily more effective than another method that comes to light in the survey, of which the majority have not yet thought or heard? How can the investigator determine whether the particular duty is important? Can cruciality be inferred from frequency? Or can the importance of an event or

13. Good, C. V. and D. E. Scates, *op. cit.,* p. 205.

duty for a given individual be inferred from the prevalence of the event or duty for the majority of the group?[14]

The reader finds that these questions are simply left dangling—apart from a passing remark about "putting together many lines of evidence in different parts of the questionnaire."[15] The student is given no guides for handling his distributions of responses or for answering the questions the authors raise.

To give only one example of the sort of guide lines for the analysis of survey data that we have in mind, we find in these texts no discussion of the importance for evaluating distributions of the existence of *standards of comparison*.[16] Taking as an example only the fragmentary illustrations the authors provide us, what does it mean when we learn that 60 per cent of "the group" of administrators report that they "solve a problem in a certain way?" The meaning of this "finding" (both for understanding the situation and for policy implications) is altogether different if in neighboring districts 95 per cent of the administrators solve that problem in that way, or if only 30 per cent do. This kind of *external* comparison would provide some basis for interpreting and evaluating a distribution. Similarly, we may find our comparative norms *within* the sample itself. If we find that in the largest schools 90 per cent of the administrators act in the indicated way, as compared with only 50 per cent of the administrators in the smallest schools, we are provided with additional bases for evaluating our distributions. What comparisons we make in the analysis of descriptive survey data depend largely on what we know about the situation we are studying and how we have defined our problem; if we have some idea of the ways we want to analyze the data—that is, what kinds of comparisons we will want to make between subgroups and categories—we will design our sample and our questionnaire with those comparisons in mind. But in none of these texts is there any indication of the ways in which the proposed analysis and evaluation of survey findings must be taken into account in the initial design of the survey. It is not surprising, when we turn to the published literature of survey research in education, that we find so little interpretation of findings: most commonly "the facts are left to speak for themselves," and most commonly the reader finds they are mute.

Some of the texts under consideration spend considerable space on the

---

14. Good, C. V. and D. E. Scates, *op. cit.*, p. 632.
15. *Ibid.*, p. 633.
16. See Hyman, H. H., *op. cit.*, pp. 126–131.

statistics of variance and measures of relationship, on scaling and sampling and other techniques of measurement and data manipulation. What they do not present is a conception of survey research as a coherent and integrated effort to answer questions and illuminate a problem; they are cookbooks rather than systematic considerations of the elements and types of decisions met in research, and the relationships among those elements and decisions. For example, one author notes that:

> In tabulating the data, "frequency counting" is not always sufficient. It is often necessary and desirable, in addition, to make a full interpretation of the returns. This might involve an evaluation of the entire questionnaire and consideration of the relationships among various items.[17]

At that point the section on the questionnaire ends. The student may well wonder how to make that "evaluation of the entire questionnaire and consideration of the relationships among various items." Several chapters later he finds a discussion of "basic statistical concepts and their computation," and he can hardly be blamed if he proceeds to apply some of the measures there provided, without raising for himself the question of whether those measures and computations are appropriate to his data or his problem. In many cases—I suspect most—he needs to be shown how to make some elementary comparisons between distributions, and how to draw inferences from those comparisons that are relevant to his problem, whether it be for adding to knowledge or for making policy recommendations or both. And this is precisely what he is not shown. The result in the literature is often a mechanical (and inappropriate) statistical treatment of data which yields little enlightenment on the topic under consideration.

Descriptive, Explanatory, and "Pseudo" Surveys

In light of the inadequacy of treatment of survey research methods in the standard methods texts in use in education, it is hardly surprising that these inadequacies should be reflected in the research carried out by the students trained through these texts. The methodological failings of the bulk of this research would comprise a dictionary of error in survey research. In this short review, I will restrict myself to noting and briefly illustrating only the most common and most pernicious of those errors and failings.

We may classify studies which use survey research methods according to the purpose of the study and the kinds of generalized statements that are

17. Rummel, J. F., *op. cit.*, p. 110.

made. With respect to any given study, we may ask the following questions. Does the study generalize to the study population, of which the sample is presumably representative? Or is the author concerned primarily with studying social relationships and processes with the choice of his population subordinate to that purpose? Or is the author concerned with both characterizing a population *and* with uncovering and accounting for patterns and processes within it, doing both at different points within the same study? Studies which are primarily concerned with saying something about the population from which the sample of respondents was drawn, we may call "descriptive surveys"; studies which are primarily concerned with the development of theoretical statements about relationships and processes we may call "explanatory surveys"; and surveys which are concerned with doing *both* within the framework of the same study, we may call "descriptive-explanatory."

Most survey studies can be classified into one or another of these three types, but the typology is not a mere naming device. The distinctions in purpose and function of studies alert us also to different procedures that these different functions and purposes call for. These different kinds of studies, which differ in aim, also necessarily differ in many other ways—in the ways their subject populations are selected, their samples drawn, their instruments designed, their data analyzed, even the ways their findings are discussed and presented. It is not possible here to develop the connections between the "purposes" of a study and its design, broadly conceived, except to note that a methodological critique of a piece of research usefully begins by examining the fitness and suitability of the study's *procedures* for its analytical *purposes*.

While many survey studies (including some in the area of education) may be classified and criticized in terms of the foregoing categories, there is a broad class of "studies" which do not fall into any of these categories. These are studies whose authors are neither interested in saying something about the specific population from which the subject sample was drawn, nor are they pointed toward the uncovering of social relationships and processes. These studies are in effect "pseudo studies," resembling other forms of survey research in their outward characteristics—the collection and manipulation of survey data—but without the functions of research: to contribute dependable knowledge about the subjects of investigation or about some generalized processes which the behavior of the immediate subjects reveal.

For example, one such "study," published in a journal of educational research in 1959, reports a survey of the attitudes and opinions of 569 high school students in the Milwaukee area on a variety of topics—dating, religion, satisfaction with school, future plans, leisure activities, and so forth. The results reported are simply the proportions of students who gave different responses to the questions asked. The students are not drawn from a single high school, nor are they a representative sample of students in the Milwaukee area; nor is the author interested in exploring any relationships among these attitudes, or in any of their social or psychological sources or correlates. Another study, also published in a professional journal, in 1958, is based on a sample of university students enrolled in an introductory course in social science, and discovers that those who were more favorable to the course were more interested in its content. The author has no special interest in the specific population from which the sample was drawn, nor does he illuminate any relationships or processes through an analysis of the data. These are "studies" in name only. In the absence of a guiding interest or purpose, it is not at all clear why they were done.

It is impossible, without extensive comparative evidence which I do not possess, to say whether "pseudo studies" in survey research are more commonly found in the field of education than in other areas where survey research is done—say, in the study of industry or of politics. My impression is that this is the case; if so, it may well flow from the very ease and convenience of survey research in the captive populations of schools and colleges.

Problems and Potentialities of Survey Research in Education

Despite the wholly inadequate discussion of survey research in the textbooks on research methods in education, there exists a rapidly growing body of research in education which fruitfully employs survey methods, exclusively or in conjunction with other modes of data collection and analysis. The following review, which aims at suggesting the potentialities of survey research for education rather than at appraising a body of literature, will stress the nature of the problems studied, with some consideration of the procedures employed and their suitability to the problems. With few exceptions, the procedures used both in data collection and analysis are similar to those used in other substantive areas of research. Unlike research in politics, industrial organization, market research, and the mass media, survey research in education has been a consumer of research methodologies and ideas developed in these other areas, and is interesting for the range of its substantive problems and findings rather than for its methodological contributions. This reflects the fact that the bulk of survey research in education has been done during the past decade by a generation of students who have found the existing procedures more than adequate for the wealth of substantive problems in education that call for study.

The study of education through survey methods is largely (though not exclusively) the study of the formal organizations of education, and of one or more categories of members of those organizations.[18] The designs of these studies vary most notably with respect to (1) whether they are carried out in only one institution, in several (allowing comparisons between institutions), or in a large enough number so that characteristics of the institutions can be analyzed through quantitative techniques; and (2) whether the studies gather data over time in an effort to deal directly with the question of changes either in the institutions or in their participants, or are restricted to data gathered at one moment in time.

STUDIES OF DIFFERENT POPULATIONS

The study of students within a single institution at a given moment in time is certainly the most common form that survey research in education has taken. Surveys are frequently initiated by institutions which want to learn something about themselves and their students; moreover, the relative ease and economy of data collection, and the direct comparability of responses provided by students within the same institution and subject to "the same" environment, make this kind of research possible on small budgets and without the necessity for additional kinds of institutional analysis aimed at studying the variations in contexts.

Some of the very earliest survey research in any field was employed in studies of students within colleges. In 1931 Katz and Allport were already able to say, "Studies of the attitudes, opinions, and practices of college students in this country have been numerous."[19] Their own study, entitled simply *Students' Attitudes,* summarized the preceding work in that area, while itself is the prototype for many similar studies of student opinions and behaviors in the succeeding three decades. Katz gathered over 4,000 questionnaires from substantially the whole of the student body at Syracuse Uni-

18. There is another important, though largely potential, use of survey research in the broad study of education—that is, the study of various "effects" of education in the general population, where the term "education" refers not to specific experiences in specific institutions, but to the amount of formal education completed. We touch on this line of investigation in the last section of this chapter.
19. Katz, Daniel, F. H. Allport, and M. B. Jenness, *Students' Attitudes: A Report of the Syracuse University Reaction Study.* Craftsman Press, Syracuse, N.Y., 1931, p. 374.

versity in 1926, apparently in response to an interest on the part of groups of students and faculty members in the "opinions, practices, and attitudes of students at Syracuse University."[20] The greater part of the book is a report of the responses of students to a variety of questions in different areas. There are chapters on reasons for coming to college, college activities, attitudes toward studies, personal ideals of students, adjustment to the college situation, vocational choice, attitudes toward fraternities, attitudes on cribbing, religious beliefs, and so forth. The book provides a wealth of information regarding student sentiment at Syracuse in the middle 1920's on matters of importance today as well, and might well provide the base point for a study of trends in student opinions. It has been used in this way by Goldsen *et al.* on the question of religious belief.[21]

For the most part, Katz and Allport report their data in the form of percentage distributions of responses to single items within the categories of the several schools within the university—liberal arts, business administration, fine arts, forestry, etc. Unfortunately we are not told a great deal about these different schools, what majors they include, what kinds of people take work in them, and what other differences there are among them that might help explain the differences in distributions of attitude and opinion found in them. But at many points the authors break out of a mechanical or routine tabular form for reporting their data, and introduce cross-tabulations which allow them to make statements about some relationships, at least among the sentiments and attitudes they are exploring. For example, at one point the authors show a relationship between the student's own degree of satisfaction with his studies and his estimate of the degree of academic freedom enjoyed by the faculty at Syracuse: the more dissatisfied students are less likely to believe the faculty member has freedom to express his ideas or convictions in class.[22] The authors then speculate on the relationship: perhaps the students who are dissatisfied and those who don't believe in academic freedom are both members of a "generally cynical" group.[23] Alternatively, perhaps "students think less of their course because they feel, rightly or wrongly, that their professors are hampered in giving utterance to what they really be-

20. *Ibid.,* p. 1.
21. Goldsen, R. K., *et al., What College Students Think.* D. Van Nostrand, Princeton, N.J., 1960.
22. Katz, Daniel, F. H. Allport, and M. B. Jenness, *op. cit.,* p. 63.
23. Cynicism among students is given considerable study in Rosenberg, Morris, *Occupations and Values.* Free Press, Glencoe, Ill., 1958.

lieve. . . . On the other hand, many students who allege a lack of academic freedom may be merely seeking a rationalization for their lack of successful academic adjustment."[24]

This study suggests the level of insight and sophistication with which the authors were discussing survey findings thirty-five years ago; unfortunately, the range of attitudes being studied and the absence of a central problem for investigation tended to prevent the authors from following up lines of investigation and inquiry uncovered by the discovery of relationships of the sort reported. Nevertheless, the nature of the data and its analysis make this a useful descriptive survey of student opinions and attitudes at Syracuse at the time of the study; and, although a clear disclaimer is made regarding generalizations beyond the sample population, the reader may find many points in the analysis and discussion which suggest relationships that may obtain more widely among American college and university students.[25]

Another study done in one educational institution some thirty years later provides an instructive comparison with the Katz-Allport study. The Undergraduate Association of Massachusetts Institute of Technology commissioned the study of a class of M.I.T. freshmen "in order to discover what contributes to a high or low morale among them."[26] Nearly the entire freshman class of 1961 (about 800 men) filled out a mailed questionnaire be-

24. Katz, Daniel, F. H. Allport, and M. B. Jenness, *op. cit.*, p. 63.
25. The authors include two summary chapters which correspond to the distinctions between descriptive and analytical surveys. The first, entitled "Conclusions Bearing upon Problems of College Administration" suggests implications of the findings for the Syracuse University faculty and administration. The second entitled "Suggestions Relating to Psychology, Sociology and Political Science" suggests some of the implications for social science theory in such areas as race and ethnic relations, political attitudes, and the social-psychology of organizations. This procedure recommends itself to students of sociology of education: very often, the same body of data yields information on which both policy recommendations may be made and theoretical propositions developed. Nevertheless, these kinds of "interpretation" involve rather different ways of looking at and assessing the data. A finding of very considerable importance theoretically may have little or no relevance to practical educational problems because, for example, the variables involved are beyond the reach of administrative influence or manipulation. Conversely, an exclusive preoccupation with what is administratively relevant and feasible may restrict the nature of the analysis, and reduce the contribution of the study to basic knowledge about the educational structures and processes. There is much to be said for insulating these sets of concerns from one another and, in effect, writing two sets of reports, one on the practical applications, the other on theoretical implications of the findings.
26. Sussman, Leila, *Freshman Morale at M.I.T.*, Massachusetts Institute of Technology Press, Cambridge, 1960, p. ix.

fore arriving on campus, and a random sample of the same class was interviewed late in the freshman year. This survey data was supplemented by other kinds of data—observations, intensive interviews, daily biographical journals, college records and the like.

In two monographs,[27] the author develops an illuminating picture of what the freshman year at M.I.T. is like, how it is experienced by the students, and how those experiences affect their satisfaction with the school. The advances of this study over the roughly comparable one done at Syracuse thirty years earlier are both methodological and conceptual:

1. The more recent study shows a greater ease and flexibility in the manipulation of the survey data. Where the first study somewhat mechanically presents a series of two-variable tables, the later one presents its data in a variety of ways.

2. The later study has a central problem which gives it a perspective on the data and a basis for deciding what data to present and how to present it.

3. The M.I.T. study has the advantage of a body of knowledge and theory that the earlier study did not possess about organization, and specifically about students and colleges. For example, one section of the study discusses the existence of "output norms" which the students enforce against academic "ratebusters," and does this explicitly in terms of similar norms in industry.[28]

4. The study of M.I.T. freshmen introduces at several points comparable data on another engineering school and another liberal arts college. Both the introduction of theoretical propositions (which are comparable data in concentrated form) and the explicit comparisons with other institutions allow a level of interpretation of the survey findings which would not be possible solely by reference to responses from members within the one institution.

27. Sussman, Leila, *op. cit.;* also Sussman, Leila and G. N. Levine, *The Entering Freshman at M.I.T.* (mimeo). Massachusetts Institute of Technology, Cambridge, 1958.
28. The classic studies in industrial sociology carried out at the Western Electric plant at Hawthorne in the 1920's—Roethlisberger, F. J. and W. J. Dickson, *Management and the Worker*. Harvard University Press, Cambridge, 1937—introduced the concept of restriction of output norms into American sociology and analyzed the social structure that supported it. The M.I.T. study is an example of the way that survey research in education draws the greater part of its conceptual equipment, and its working array of sociological propositions, from the great body of social research conducted in areas other than education.

5. The later study, by gathering data from the *same* individuals at two points in time—before they arrived at M.I.T. and toward the end of their first year—is able to study the nature and processes of change in attitudes, perceptions, and behaviors in ways that the earlier "one-shot" study of the Syracuse student body could not.[29]

6. The later study systematically included non-survey data in its research design. In part, we suspect, this decision grew out of a more sophisticated awareness of the nature of survey data and of the problems that arise in analyzing it. For example, while survey data collected from the same individuals over time give evidence as to changes in attitudes and behaviors, and where in the population the changes occur, they do not shed much light directly on the mechanisms through which these changes take place. Diaries, direct observation, and intensive interviews are more useful for that purpose.

7. The decision in the later study to supplement survey data with other sources of information probably also flowed from a greater awareness of the influences of social structures—both formal and informal—on individual behaviors and sentiments. For example, the later study placed much greater stress on one of the formal structures within the institution which heavily conditioned the attitudes and behaviors of their members—that is, the living groups. While Sussman, like Katz-Allport, was primarily concerned with reporting the distributions of individual behaviors and sentiments which characterized the students in her study, and with showing the relationships among them, she is, at several points, at some pains to show the bearing of the student's living group on his relevant attitudes and behaviors.[30] The earlier study frequently compares students in different colleges within the university—though never making clear why it makes these

29. At a few points in the Katz-Allport study, the comparison of responses by school year approximates a study over time. For example, at one point Katz-Allport note that seniors show relatively more enthusiasm for their academic studies than do freshmen. They observe that this *may* be because students acquire "a more mature and serious appreciation of college work" over their college careers (p. 55). Alternatively, as the authors note, it may be that the students least interested in their studies are eliminated early in their course, leaving the more interested to survive to their senior year. Or still another possibility is that the program of courses offered the seniors is more interesting than that offered the freshmen. The gains and limitations of such cross-class comparisons, in contrast to panel studies which follow the same students over time, are discussed below.

30. See Katz, Elihu and P. F. Lazarsfeld, *Personal Influence: The Part Played by People in the Flow of Mass Communications.* Free Press, Glencoe, Ill., 1955, pp. 25–30.

comparisons, or what relevant features of those divisions of the university might account for any observed differences among their members. By contrast, the later study tries to characterize the four major types of living groups compared, *both* by aggregating the characteristics of their members as learned through the survey data and *also* by reporting certain other characteristics of those groups which were learned in other ways—through the intensive interviews, observations, and the like. Thus, in the later study, the characteristics of the living groups actively enter into the analysis and interpretation, rather than simply providing a set of parallel molds into which the several distributions were poured, as is usually the case in the earlier study.

The major limitations of the M.I.T. study lie in the fact that the sample of students interviewed late in the freshman year was too small to allow a consideration of more than two variables at a time.[31] The total freshman class which filled out questionnaires prior to coming to M.I.T. provided a satisfactory sample size for more intensive analysis to be undertaken with it. It is clear from the report that much of the important information about the students' adjustment to the college could only be learned after they had been on campus for a while; yet the sample interviewed in May numbered only about 140, too small for the simultaneous consideration of more than two variables. Yet while the largest advances in the logic of survey analysis have occurred in connection with multivariate analysis, which the M.I.T. study could not employ, it is impressive how much more enlightening the Sussman report is than the Katz-Allport study, despite the fact that its central analytical tool—the two-variable relationship—is the same as that used in the earlier study. The author of the M.I.T. study is a highly competent sociologist and survey analyst, but the authors of the earlier study were also highly competent social scientists. At least part of the advance of the later study over the earlier must be attributed to advances both in sociological theory and in the methodology of survey research. Unfortunately, these advances are not so apparent in the bulk of contemporary survey research in education, much of which is inferior, both in design and analysis, to the Katz-Allport study done over three decades ago.

A study by Selvin and Hagstrom, done at Berkeley in 1957, is similar to the M.I.T. study in that it is a study of student attitudes and behaviors

---

31. At a few points, three-variable tables are included, but the numbers are too small for any clear findings or decisive results to emerge, as the text admits.

within one institution.[32] It differs in that it does not primarily attempt to characterize the student body in that institution, but is concerned with exploring a set of social and social-psychological forces underlying one specific cluster of attitudes—those having to do with the students' support for civil liberties. With this problem in mind, rather than that of characterizing student opinion or behavior specifically at Berkeley, the authors selected a *purposeful* rather than a representative sample:

> The sample of 894 students was designed to compare significant types of groups—to study the influence of such factors as place of residence and major subject—rather than 'represent' the total student body at this university. In other words, the sample is representative of certain kinds of social backgrounds and campus experiences, rather than of a particular collection of people.[33]

Where the Sussman study is primarily a descriptive survey aimed at characterizing a specific population (with analytical statements generalized to broader substantive or theoretical propositions also present), the Selvin-Hagstrom study is primarily an explanatory survey, concerned chiefly with general social and social-psychological processes (with some additional characterization of the university student population from which it was drawn).

The Selvin-Hagstrom study provides clues to how even "one-shot" studies within one institution can shed light on complex social-psychological processes even in the absence of the qualitative data—the intensive interviews, observations, and diaries—which helped Sussman interpret her survey findings.[34] For example, at one point Selvin and Hagstrom address themselves to the question of the direction and amount of change in libertarian attitudes among Berkeley students in the course of their four years on cam-

32. Selvin, H. C. and W. O. Hagstrom, "Determinants of Support for Civil Liberties," *British Journal of Sociology*, Vol. 1, April, 1960, pp. 51–73.
33. *Ibid.*, p. 52. The authors manage to have it both ways; although they drew their sample with certain theoretical purposes in mind—specifically, to make certain comparisons that would not be possible with a representative sample of the same size—still, their purposeful sample turns out to be sufficiently representative of the Berkeley student body "to permit rough comparisons between our sample and others."
34. However, Selvin did have the benefit of a prior study of student living groups at Berkeley on which to draw, as well as his experience as a faculty member—and thus, in a sense, as a participant observer on the Berkeley campus.

pus. Like Katz and Allport, Selvin and Hagstrom use "year in school" as an approximation of the measurement of students' attitudes at the beginning and end of their college life that would otherwise require a lengthy longitudinal panel study to gather. Their comparisons of the first, second, third, and fourth year students show a steady increase in the proportion of "libertarian" students. Without speculating on the extent to which this represents a real change in Berkeley students' attitudes over the four years, as compared with the extent to which the results are an artifact of disproportionate drop-outs among the less libertarian (or a disproportionate transfer to Berkeley of more libertarian students), the authors turn directly to a consideration of the relationship of students' libertarianism to their social origins, as indicated by their fathers' occupations. They find that sons of manual workers and professional men are most likely to be libertarian, while students from lower middle backgrounds—small business men and lower white collar workers—are least likely to be libertarian. Leaving this interesting finding largely uninterpreted, since their study centers on the influence of college experience and not of prior life experiences on libertarianism, the authors then consider the simultaneous relationship of father's occupation, year in school, and libertarianism.[35] They now find that the very marked difference in libertarianism among students of different social origins originally found is even more marked among lower division (freshman and sophomore) students, but has largely disappeared among upper division (junior and senior) students.[36] This finding has a number of implications. It strengthens the possibility that increases in libertarianism between freshman and senior year are the product of actual changes in attitudes, rather than the result of disproportionate drop-outs among the least libertarian, since the increases are the greatest among those groups originally lowest in libertarianism. But more important, the finding sheds light on one of the most important functions of higher education—its tendency to reduce the influence of prior social statuses and experiences, and forge a new set of shared identities and attitudes among college graduates:

> The University takes in students of varied social backgrounds and attitudes. The difference in attitudes are steadily reduced, so that the

35. The size of the sample requires that they combine students in the first two years for comparison with students in their last two years in college.
36. Selvin, H. C. and W. O. Hagstrom, *op. cit.,* Table X, p. 65.

graduates are appreciably more homogeneous than is the general public. University education "declassifies" students (and then usually reclassifies them). . . . In a very real sense their social statuses are more similar than they were before entering the university and than they will be after graduation. And what is important here, they have lost the support for the beliefs and attitudes they had before entrance. No longer surrounded primarily by people of the same social background, they take on some of the dominant values of their new environment if these were not present in their pre-university environment. Since both the faculty and the students are predominantly libertarian, the result is a marked lessening of the effects of a father's occupation as students move through their four years.[37]

This is a complex web of inferences which says a great deal not only about the particular students under study, but about higher education generally—and also, perhaps, about other quasi-total institutions. For example, there are important implications here for the probable social and political consequences of the mass higher education toward which the country is clearly moving. But the tabulations of survey data on which the interpretations are based are also interesting for methodological reasons. What is the relation between the data and its interpretation? The propositions and inferences are in no sense "proved" by the data—in the sense that a carefully designed controlled experiment can "prove" to a very high order of probability that under the specified conditions certain events have certain consequences. In the passage quoted, which importantly was *suggested* by the data rather than *tested* by it, there is a train of inferences about a set of processes and causal connections for which no data are shown—for example, the assumption that when students go to college they are (a) no longer surrounded by people of the same social background and (b) lose support for the beliefs and attitudes they had before entrance. At most, the interpretation is congruent with data the authors do show, and is not contradicted by it or by other data or relationships turned up during the analysis. The interpretation would gain in plausibility if it were supported by additional evidence bearing either on the major relationships or on some of the inferred, or hypothesized, intervening processes. And one of the central skills of the survey analyst is his ingenuity in linking a complex causal

37. *Ibid.*, p. 61.

chain to his survey data at a number of points—increasing the plausibility of the whole chain of inference as he refines his analysis and illuminates the social processes in more detail.

Of course, qualitative data as well as additional survey material can help the analyst refine and support his interpretation, in somewhat different ways. In the Berkeley study, for example, the interpretation would be stronger if the authors could show, perhaps through students' diaries, *how* students come to modify their earlier views in the course of being exposed to the influences of peers from different social origins, and also to the influences of their teachers. This is not to criticize a modest study done on a tiny budget, but rather to observe that such tentative interpretations, consisting of chains of causal inferences which are keyed at some points but not at others to empirical findings of varying probability, is the contribution survey research makes when it goes beyond reporting the distributions of responses to questions. Survey research in education, as in other fields, is constantly confronted with the alternatives posed years ago by Merton in another connection: to say only what one is quite sure is true, whether or not it is significant, or to say what is significant, without being sure that it is true.[38] Really significant interpretations of survey data almost always run beyond the empirical data to which they are directed and on which they are based (or we might better say, by which they are suggested). There are ways, especially through the use of supplementary non-survey data, to greatly increase the strength of an interpretation in survey research—that is, the probability that the interpretation offered, rather than some other, is a correct account of the processes under consideration. Very often the choice is to say little more than the tabulations directly warrant, or to go beyond them to the underlying social and social-psychological processes which are usually the matters of real interest of which the empirical findings are more or less crude indicators. When the researcher decides for the former alternative —that is, in effect merely to report but not interpret his findings—his study is rarely of value either as a contribution to theory or to educational practice.

A number of studies have been carried out through survey research which differ from the foregoing in that they have gathered data from students in more than one institution. The gain here is that such designs allow the comparison of institutional contexts, and thus the interplay between the charac-

38. Merton, R. K., *Social Theory and Social Structure*, rev. ed. Free Press, Glencoe, Ill., 1957, p. 85.

teristics of individuals, the processes that occur within small groups, and the larger institutional structures within which these processes occur.[39] With more than one school represented in the sample, some of the characteristics of whole organizations can enter into the study as variables and not merely as the name of the place where the study was done.[40]

Studies of students in more than one institution exploit the possibilities for comparative institutional analysis in a variety of ways. In a very large study of undergraduate student attitudes and behaviors in eleven major universities across the country, the authors very often lump the data together "to approximate the flavor of student opinions across the country."[41] The fact that the study was done in eleven different universities is merely part of the effort to get a rough approximation of a national sample of university undergraduates. Elsewhere in the same study the authors report distributions separately for the eleven schools, and in the course of the analysis comparative portraits of the several colleges emerge, but the chief purpose of showing the results separately for the several colleges in that study is to give the reader a sense of the range of climates on various campuses across the country, and also to show that most of the "trends" in student sentiment over the four years were in the same direction in most of the universities studied. Despite the fact that data about students were gathered from the eleven campuses, the authors do not do any comparative contextual analysis; that is, they do not characterize the several colleges and then introduce that information into the analysis to help explain findings, or indicate the conditions under which different relationships were obtained. The different colleges enter the text as names and thus as a series of "replications" which lend great weight to the authors' generalizations about American college students. But they do not tell us much about differences among the colleges and their different influence on their students. Of course, the reader may know something about the several universities studied, and use that knowledge to help explain to himself variations in student attitudes and behaviors reported in the text: for that reason, the tables are infinitely more informative than if the colleges were identified only as university A, B, C, and so

39. Selvin and Hagstrom approximate these multi-school studies by studying different formal organizations within one university.
40. Though the inclusion of more than one organization in a study by no means guarantees that they will enter as more than names, that is, that there will be any genuine comparative study of contexts.
41. Goldsen, R. K., *et al., op. cit.*, p. xxxvi.

forth. The decision about how to treat the comparative data from the several colleges was clearly made with the larger purposes of the study in mind; the authors of this book were simply not interested in the comparative study of institutions, but rather in presenting a descriptive portrait of American university student opinion on a range of important issues, as the title of the volume says plainly. And this they do.

Another study of college students currently under way is interested in the interplay of organizational and individual characteristics, and it will treat the survey data being collected rather differently.[42] Where the Cornell study reports student opinion at various colleges, showing the similarities and differences in student opinion across the country, the study currently under way will report *relationships* and processes as these differ in different institutions, and will try to explain variations in those relationships and processes at least partly in terms of differences in the characteristics of the institutions in which they occur.

Two relatively recent studies of high school students also employ a genuine contextual analysis—that is, introduce characteristics of the schools the students attend into their interpretations of students' sentiments and behavior.[43] Coleman for example, shows that in high schools where athletes are the most prestigeful students, the best academic students are also likely to be athletes; whereas in schools where highest prestige goes to students in student government and other non-athletic extra-curricular activities, the best students are likely to be in those activities. The influence of variations in the normative climate in high schools is also seen in the study by Wilson, who shows that in predominantly working-class schools, the minority of middle-class children are more likely to hold working-class attitudes (toward going to college, etc.) than students from similar backgrounds who attend predominantly middle-class schools. Similarly, students from working-class backgrounds in predominantly middle-class schools are more likely to share the dominant middle-class norms than are students from similar backgrounds in predominantly working-class schools. In these survey studies, the nature of the findings allows us to draw inferences about how char-

42. This is a study of eight colleges and universities currently under way at the Center for the Study of Higher Education, at the University of California, Berkeley.
43. Coleman, James, *The Adolescent Society:* The Social Life of the Teenager and its Impact on Education, Free Press, Glencoe, Ill., 1961; and Wilson, A. B., "Residential Segregation of Social Classes and Aspirations of High School Boys," *American Sociological Review,* Vol. 24, December, 1959, pp. 836–845.

acteristics of the institutional setting affect the relationships between individual characteristics—that is, how the social structure of the school influences interpersonal relationships and processes among students. Needless to say, this lies at the heart of the perennial question of the "impact" of educational institutions on their students.

STUDIES OF THE "IMPACT" OF EDUCATION ON STUDENTS

Of all social institutions, educational institutions are most clearly and strongly committed to effecting changes in most of their members. At the very least, students are expected to grow in the skills and knowledge that are taught in the schools. But much broader changes than those are expected in American schools, which characteristically assume a broader responsibility for more of the students' personal qualities of mind and character than was true in the past or is true today in most other countries. We judge schools and colleges not only on how successfully they teach the subjects in their curriculum, but also on whether students develop attitudes which will make them good citizens in a democracy, productive and creative in their occupations, and men and women who will develop most fully their own individual talents and capacities, both for their own benefit and for that of the larger society. Whether or not we believe these qualities can be taught directly, we are certainly interested in whether the whole experience of education does in fact have an influence on students in these directions.[44] For example, at a time when all kinds of higher intellectual skills are in short supply, many people are concerned to see that bright and able students get the advanced education that will help them convert their potential abilities into realized skills and capacities. Experiences in school are not the only forces which influence students to continue their education into college and beyond, but almost certainly some kinds of schools encourage students to want more education while others do not.

We may be able to assess the purely academic effectiveness of a school program through tests of knowledge and skills in various subject matters. But many other outcomes of education which are of equal importance can often be studied through varieties of survey methods.

Most educators (and others) would agree that education should broaden

44. Though a perennial problem in the study of changes in students over time is to distinguish how much of the observed change is attributable to the experience in school, and how much to experiences quite outside school—for example, to the effects of simply becoming older.

a student's sympathies, reduce his prejudices, and strengthen his commitments to democratic processes and the rule of law. Through studies of students' sentiments and attitudes over time, we can learn about the extent to which students become more tolerant of racial and religious differences, more aware of the sources of those differences, and more deeply committed to the civil rights and liberties that are guaranteed in our Constitution and our laws. A number of studies, most notably one by Stouffer, show that people who have been to college are more likely to be tolerant toward racial and religious groups and to support the civil liberties of unpopular political and religious minorities.[45] But we cannot simply assume that this greater tolerance is the product of a higher education; it may be that the kind of people who go to college—who are, on the whole, from wealthier and better educated backgrounds—are more likely to hold these views independent of their higher education. Moreover, even if higher education does strengthen these attitudes by and large, we know little of what it is about the experience in school or colleges that has this effect, or under what conditions it is likely to occur. Questions like these call for intensive scrutiny of students' attitudes and behaviors in different kinds of schools and colleges, and *over time,* so that we can see them actually in the process of change and learn something of the forces in or outside of school that are actually operative on them.

This kind of study—of students in different situations whose attitudes, orientations, and behaviors are studied over time—has been very little done up to now. Studies involving large numbers of students in several colleges and universities over long periods of time are comparatively expensive, and many of the technical and methodological tools required have only recently been developed. Nevertheless, some efforts to study changes in students over time—and thus, inferentially, the impact of various kinds of education—have been made or are under way.

The great majority of survey studies of students have gathered information at one point in time. How can such studies lead to any knowledge about changes in students over time? As we saw in our discussion of the Katz-Allport study, the first approach that recommends itself to analysts who have data for students over the four years is to compare distributions among freshmen with those for students in the succeeding years. Katz-

45. Stouffer, S. A., *Communism, Conformity and Civil Liberties:* A Cross-Section of the Nation Speaks its Mind. Doubleday, Garden City, N.Y., 1955. See also Hyman, H. H. and P. B. Sheatsley, "Attitudes Toward Desegregation," *Scientific American,* Vol. 195, No. 6, 1956, pp. 35–39.

Allport makes this comparison at a number of points, and shows, for example, that in one institution at one moment in time seniors were less likely to hold an "orthodox" view of God, as a personal Being whose actions can be affected by prayer, than freshmen, with sophomores and juniors in between;[46] that upper classmen were more likely than lower classmen to favor requiring liberal arts courses even for students in vocational majors;[47] and that there was little increase in the proportions of students who had made a definite decision about their future vocations in the course of the four years.

This kind of study, it can be readily seen, makes a number of assumptions when it goes from the simple comparative statement "seniors differ from freshmen in these respects" to the statement inferring individual changes, "students over their four years tend to become, or to feel, or believe. . . ." The central assumption involved is that the seniors are as a group "drawn from the same population" and thus are like the freshmen (and sophomores, etc.) in all respects other than the length of time they have spent in school, and the changes that have occurred in them as a result of their college experience. This assumption may not be warranted for a number of reasons.

1. It may be that a pattern of selective withdrawal and late transfer changes the composition of classes over the four years so that, while none of the students who remain in college over the four years change in the specified way, the class as a whole does, thus giving the misleading impression that the changes in the group are the result of the aggregate changes in its members. For example, let us suppose that less intelligent students are also less likely to be racially and politically tolerant. If large numbers of these students drop out of college over the four years, the seniors would appear to be much more liberal than the freshmen, on the average, without any of its members necessarily having changed their political or racial attitudes over the four years. Similarly, if the transfers to the group in the course of the four years differ from the class they are joining with respect to the attitude in question, the distributions of that attitude will also change in ways that might appear to result from changes in the students, but actually result from the pattern of selective recruitment. For example, if many transfers to a university in the third and fourth years come from junior colleges, and thus are more likely to be from poorer homes than those who started in the

---

46. Katz, Daniel, F. H. Allport and M. B. Jenness, *op. cit.,* p. 268.
47. *Ibid.,* p. 84.

freshman year, these differences will show themselves in a variety of ways in the distribution of attitudes in the junior and senior classes—independent of changes in the students.

2. The comparison of classes also assumes that each successive class entering college represents about the same selection from the population at large. If, for example, a college raises its academic standards for admission very rapidly, as a number of colleges recently have, then the freshmen are likely as a group to be much more able academically than the seniors when they entered and may, for example, be more likely to be planning to continue their studies in graduate school. If we look at the class comparisons on this question and find proportionately fewer seniors than freshmen planning to go to graduate school, we would be tempted, but wrong, to suggest that the four years at this college tends to discourage students from continuing their education.

3. The comparison of classes assumes that the distribution of attitudes on the issues in question in the general population have not changed materially during the four year period of a college generation. For example, let us assume that there has been an increase in political tolerance in the society generally over the past four years. This increase will be reflected in the distributions of attitudes among entering freshmen, who will show higher levels of tolerance than this year's seniors would have when they were freshmen, and thus will conceal part of the growth in tolerance of the present seniors.

4. Another problem of a somewhat different kind arises when comparing students at different stages in their school careers. We may ask a question, say, about attitudes toward studies, assuming that "your studies" means roughly the same thing to freshmen and seniors, and therefore that differences in distributions of attitudes toward "studies" reflect changes in the actual attitudes toward scholarly work generally. But the studies themselves may have changed character between the freshman and senior years —perhaps, as Katz and Allport suggested, senior course work is more interesting—so that an apparent increase in favorable attitudes toward studies among seniors as compared with freshmen may reflect not changes in basic attitudes toward school work, but a more favorable assessment of the specific studies offered in the senior year.

This last problem is not special to the inter-class comparisons we are now discussing, but is implicit in the assumption that the same question must "mean" the same thing to all respondents whose responses to it are compared, and thus is present in panel studies as well as comparative studies of different institutions, or any different categories of students. This is what has been called the "item-indicator" problem—that is, the same item may elicit responses about a different order of experience or point to a different phenomenon among different kinds of students or students in different situations. The simplest illustration of this difficulty is the danger of assuming that a question about participation in "extra-curricular activities" means the same thing in different schools. In one the term may be used to refer only to the formally organized non-academic activities; elsewhere it may include various kinds of regular but informal extra-class activities; in still other schools it may include the student's casual social activities. Clearly, a question about how much interest students have in "extra-curricular activities" will be answered in these different schools from different frames of reference. This will not only mislead an analyst who compares student behavior between schools, but also will distort the analysis of inter-class comparisons which aims to study changes in this kind of interest over time, if the students' definition of extra-curricular activities should itself change over time. The only way of meeting this problem is for the analyst to take pains to learn about variations in the experiences or phenomena he is asking about in the different groups and contexts he is studying, either through other survey questions or by gaining a close familiarity with the situations he is studying. There is no substitute for this kind of intimate knowledge of the situation under investigation, for it is out of his general stock of knowledge of the situation—its structure and processes—as well as his grasp of relevant sociological theory, that the analyst's interpretations will be made.

Despite the many assumptions involved in translating inter-class comparisons into statements about student change, the device is used, and with fruitful results where the analyst is aware of the possible errors. The method recommends itself because questions about student changes are central to many studies which cannot afford to study the same students over time. Moreover, the analyst can discover, or at least infer, the degree to which assumptions underlying inter-class comparisons such as those mentioned above actually operate in his situation. For example, the researcher comparing data collected from freshmen and seniors can often learn something about the gross *amount* of dropping out and transferring over the period he is studying; if there is very little of that in proportion to the size of groups he is studying, then it is less likely that differences he finds between freshmen and seniors result from the special characteristics of the withdrawals and transfers. In addition, he may even be able to learn something about the characteristics of the students who leave and enter during the period across which he is making his comparisons; it may be that they do not differ greatly from the students who remain in the school over that period. Or he may use his knowledge of the characteristics of drop-outs and transfers in yet another way in his analysis; for example, if the drop-outs tend to be the least able students, he may be able to make cross-class comparisons separately among the more able students, who are likely to remain in school for the four years.

The analyst may also make efforts to learn whether the characteristics of entering classes have changed materially over the period across which he is comparing classes. Often the admissions office can give him gross character-izations of entering classes, and also tell him whether there have been changes in admissions policy which would be reflected in the characteristics of the entering classes. In the case of elementary or high schools, the analyst will want to be sure that the neighborhood or area from which the students were drawn had not changed its class or racial character greatly during the period. The analyst will also be more wary of making cross-class com-parisons on issues with respect to which there have been very large shifts in public sentiment over the period the seniors have been in school: he can often learn more about these by inspecting public opinion polls of national samples done during the period.

All of these precautions, and there are others, work to increase the analyst's confidence that the differences he finds, say between seniors and freshmen, in some ways reflect changes in the former over their school careers.[48] While these inter-class comparisons can be highly suggestive of such changes, at their best they nevertheless leave much to be desired in studies primarily concerned with the processes of student change. Even after all precautions are taken to test the assumptions underlying such interpreta-tions, doubts remain that the cross-class differences are the result of changes in the students over their years in school. More important, even if they are, the cross-class comparisons tell the analyst almost nothing about (a) what kinds of students undergo the changes in question and what kinds do not and (b) what the conditions and processes are that are associated with the changes. While the analyst may know that 60 per cent of the seniors as com-pared with only 20 per cent of the freshmen hold tolerant views on certain questions of race relations, and while he may believe that this difference re-

48. While I speak here of inter-class comparisons in college, for convenience, most of what is said applies equally well to studies at other levels of education.

sults from shifts in student attitudes over the four years, he doesn't know which of the tolerant students among the seniors have become so while in college and which were so before entering. Moreover, he doesn't know whether some students may not have become *less* tolerant over the four years while a still larger group were becoming more tolerant, since his figures for the whole class tell him (subject to the above qualifications) only what the net change in the direction of tolerance was. He may be tempted to ask the students about the racial or religious attitudes they held when entering college four years earlier, but the answers would be so distorted by the vagaries of memory that he could attach little confidence to those responses. There *are* subjects that respondents can report on retrospectively after four years with considerable reliability, but most attitudes and sentiments are not among them. Since the analyst doesn't know what students underwent the specific changes, he cannot know very well what conditions or experiences stimulated or hastened or supported those changes, and through what specific processes they occurred. Yet it is precisely this kind of detailed knowledge of the ways in which different aspects of the educational experience have different consequences for specific kinds of students that is often of greatest value to the educator who wants to use such information when he makes plans for changes in curriculum, admissions policy, or some other part of the educational system.

The best and surest way to learn about changes students undergo in the course of some period in school is through a panel study—that is, through the collection of information *from the same students* at different points in time about many of *the same issues* at both points in time.[49] In the study by Goldsen and others, in addition to the "cross-sectional" data from ten other universities, the authors also gathered data from nearly a thousand students at Cornell, first when they were underclassmen, and again two years later when they were juniors and seniors. While the authors make very little use of the panel data[50] probably because they are more concerned to draw a descriptive portrait of student opinion rather than to analyze intensively its sources and the institutional forces making for change, their use of it at a few points illustrates how it differs from the cross-class comparisons

---

49. On some of the problems and potentialities of "panel analysis," see the essays by Lazarsfeld, P. F. *et al.*, and Glock, C. Y., in *The Language of Social Research.* Edited by P. F. Lazarsfeld and Morris Rosenberg. *op. cit.*, pp. 231–242 and 242–251.
50. Rosenberg, Morris, *op. cit.*, makes much greater use of the Cornell panel data than does the summary volume by Goldsen, R. K., *et al.*, *op. cit.*

possible in "one-shot" studies. At one point the authors present cross-class comparisons for seven of their universities which have fraternities, showing a slight tendency for senior fraternity members to be more conservative than freshman fraternity members, while among the independent students at the same universities, there is little evidence of consistent differences between freshmen and seniors in either direction. But we could scarcely tell from this what the influence of fraternities on liberal-conservative sentiments were, since we might suspect that more conservative (that is, pro laissez-faire) students tended to join a fraternity sometime along in their college careers, thus accounting for the smaller proportion of conservatives among first year fraternity men than senior fraternity men. The Cornell panel data allow the authors to look at this in much greater detail; for example, they can look at the students who were originally liberal and see whether belonging to a fraternity or not made any difference to their ideological positions when they were upperclassmen. Similarly, they can look at the students who were originally conservative and see whether there were differences in the proportions of fraternity and non-fraternity members moving to a more liberal position. As we might expect, the conservative students who belonged to fraternities were more likely to remain conservative than those who did not join fraternities, and similarly, the liberal students who joined fraternities were more likely to move toward conservatism than those who did not join fraternities.

These findings based on the panel data serve at least two functions in the Goldsen study. First, they provide more direct and substantial support for the findings of the cross-class comparisons done in the eleven colleges, and thus strengthen the bulk of the discussion which is based on these eleven colleges and which aims to generalize to the American college population in a way that would not be possible solely on the basis of the data from the Cornell students. While only a few of the cross-class findings (from eleven universities) are examined more closely in light of the Cornell panel data, even a few such examinations which provide confirmation that the cross-class comparisons are indeed measuring opinion *change* tends to lend support to all of them. That is the chief gain from panel analysis for the *descriptive* purposes of the study, and it is an important one.

In addition, the examination of panel data in this study sheds light on some of the internal processes through which attitudinal changes of various kinds come about. For example, at one point the authors are able to discuss the functions of "insulating subsystems," of which fraternities are a major

example, which both socialize their members to their dominant value systems (conservative ones, in the case of most fraternities), and also work to
sustain those values by insulating their members against relationships and
identifications whose influences are in contrary directions.[51] This use of the
panel data makes the study at these points *explanatory,* with a consequent
gain to social science theory, since the operation of "insulating subsystems"
has relevance far wider than college situations and the specific attitudes with
which this study was primarily concerned.[52] A characteristic of such analysis
of panel data is that it suggests further analysis of the same data which would
shed even more light on the complex processes involved in the conditions of
change. For example, in the present case we might ask how the initially liberal students who joined fraternities, and thus voluntarily made themselves
part of a conservative insulating system, differed from those who did not and
what the processes of recruitment were. This would probably shed light
on the forces in colleges which work against the academic community and its
liberalizing influences, by showing how certain kinds of students are drawn
out of their liberalizing orbit. Similarly, we might wish to compare the
minority of students who moved in liberal directions despite their fraternity
memberships with the majority for whom fraternity membership preserved
or strengthened initially conservative dispositions. This sort of investigation, to which panel analysis is singularly well-suited, may contribute much
to the study of the actual process through which specific college experiences have specific consequences for students' behaviors, attitudes, and
post-graduate educational and occupational plans.

The decision regarding how far to carry such analysis of panel data, as
with all such decisions, ought to be made in the light of the purposes of the
study as a whole. In the Goldsen study, the purpose was clearly to present a
broadly descriptive portrait of "what college students think" about a range
of important subjects in the middle of the twentieth century. But a study
such as this has value not only for what it tells us directly, but also for the
lines of further inquiry it suggests. Here, as elsewhere, survey findings have

51. Goldsen, R. K., *et al., op. cit.,* pp. 119–124. Selvin and Hagstrom, *op. cit.,* have
analyzed the insulating role of sororities at Berkeley in considerable detail, but
through detailed contextual comparisons together with cross-class comparisons,
rather than through the analysis of panel data. A comparison of the methods used in
these two studies dealing with an almost identical problem is instructive regarding
alternative strategies of survey analysis.
52. This is a problem studied in high schools by Coleman, James, *op. cit.,* using both
contextual and panel analysis.

their greatest value not for what they say about the phenomena they describe, but for the questions they generate which would not be clarified were it not for the empirical findings that suggest them.

Up to this point we have considered a very limited number of studies chiefly to illustrate some of the varieties of research designs and modes of analysis that are employed by survey researchers in the field of education. Our illustrations have been drawn largely from studies of college students, since much, though by no means all, of the best survey research in education has dealt with the college student population. But the scope for survey research in education is infinitely wider, both actually and in potential, than the study of college students. We will now consider some of the kinds of substantive problems in and around education to which survey research may contribute, both by citing survey research studies already done or under way and by pointing to areas in which survey research might be fruitfully employed.

Some Problems of Survey Research
Among Teachers and Administrators

If we are to know anything at all about the nature of an educational system and of what actually goes on within its institutions, we must know something about the men and women who teach within it—the kinds of people they are, how they are recruited, from what parts of society they come, through what paths they come to teaching, what values and attitudes they hold, and their conceptions of themselves, their roles, their students, and the material they teach. These and many other questions are especially, though not exclusively, amenable to study through survey research methods. If they have not been studied, or at least not as fully as have questions about students, it is in part because teachers are more difficult subjects for the survey researcher than are students. They are not subject to the same degree of authority as are students; they are not conveniently assembled and available in classrooms; many of them by the very nature of their profession mistrust survey research and the ways it gathers its data. Teachers, and this is especially true of college teachers, have considerable experience with the complexities of human behavior; moreover, they tend to be thoughtful and reflective by temperament and training. They are or often feel themselves to be "experts" in the problems in education which the survey analyst is often studying when he approaches them. All these factors lead many teachers to resent the structured questions about complicated issues, the forced choices among limited alternatives, above all the sense that they are being studied rather than consulted, through methods that appear to them mechanical and stereotyped.

In what is perhaps the most sophisticated and extensive study of college professors done to date, Lazarsfeld and Thielens were sufficiently concerned about the reliability, validity, and general adequacy of the data collected through structured interviews to ask two experienced social scientists to explore those specific questions by talking in much more informal ways both with a sample of the interviewers and with some of the professors whom they had interviewed.[53] Some of the resentment and suspicion of survey methods held by the professors, who in this study were all teachers in the social sciences, are reported in an appendix to the study.[54] One professor observed:

> "I'm inclined to discount the value and worth of the instrument. . . .
> I've gotten the conviction that attitudes in politics are so infinitely
> complex that a poll can hardly get at them."

And another:

> "I do not like questionnaires in general. I think anything as subtle as
> freedom, academic or otherwise, cannot be reduced to a questionnaire
> the answers to which can be tabulated and reduced to statistics."[55]

But despite all the difficulties associated with interviewing professors of social science on as sensitive and complicated an issue as academic freedom, the study is a major contribution to knowledge about American higher education. The central question to which the study addressed itself was to what extent did the heightened concern for national security following World War II, and the tensions that quickly developed in connection with that concern, affect the teaching of social science in American colleges. In the course of attempting to answer that question, on the basis of interviews with nearly 2,500 social scientists, the authors had to answer many others. Among other things, they had to identify and distinguish substantially different types of

53. Lazarsfeld, P. F., and Wagner Thielens, Jr., *The Academic Mind:* Social Scientists in a Time of Crisis. Free Press, Glencoe, Ill., 1958.
54. The appendix by David Riesman, "Some Observations on the Interviewing in the Teacher Apprehension Study," sheds a great deal of light on many problems met in doing survey research with college professors as respondents. On the general topic of interviewing, see also Hyman, H. H., *et al., Interviewing in Social Research.* University of Chicago Press, Chicago, 1954.
55. Lazarsfeld, P. F. and Wagner Thielens, Jr., *op. cit.,* p. 293.

colleges and universities that make up American higher education, characterize the men who teach social science in them in a variety of ways, and relate the characteristics of both the colleges and the professors to their experience with, perceptions of, and responses to pressures on their teaching of social science flowing from the heightened national concern with loyalty and disloyalty. The effort to deal with these enormously complex questions provides a valuable source of information about American higher education and also a useful demonstration of the analysis of survey data by a leading practitioner of that art.[56]

But survey research lends itself as well to more limited problems. A study by Ward Mason starts from the very practical problem posed by the growing shortage of qualified elementary and high school teachers at a time when the public school population is growing very rapidly.[57] The teacher shortage would certainly be alleviated if fewer trained and qualified teachers left the profession for other work. The study addresses itself to the question of how teachers just beginning their careers view their professional futures and, more specifically, the characteristics of teachers who plan to remain in teaching, as compared with those of the potential teachers who are thinking about getting out of the classroom even before they enter it. The study, done through a mail questionnaire to a representative sample (numbering about 7,500) of all beginning public school teachers in the country, shows that fewer than one in three of the men and fewer than one in six of the women expect to continue teaching until retirement.[58] Half the men hope to move into educational administration, while well over two-thirds of the women

---

56. See also the preliminary reports of a study of the political and professional attitudes and orientations of junior college teachers by Herbert Maccoby, "Controversy, Neutrality, and Higher Education," in *American Sociological Review,* Vol. 25, December, 1960, pp. 844–893.

57. Mason, W. S., *The Beginning Teacher:* Status and Career Orientations. U.S. Government Printing Office, Washington, D.C., 1961.

58. The study was done as part of the regular research program of the United States Office of Education. It is suggestive not only of the kinds of information provided by the U.S.O.E. to students of education, but also of the kinds of studies that the Office might support even if conducted by researchers not in its employ. Needless to say, studies of this and related problems could make substantial contributions, both to educational practice and to social science theory, even if not conducted on a national scale. In fact, a smaller budget might be a positive advantage to research on this (as on many other) subjects in that it would require the researcher to look more closely at the school system and the immediate teaching situation within which his smaller number of respondents worked.

hope to leave teaching at least temporarily for marriage and a family. The study explores further a variety of attitudes associated with their professional commitments and career plans, and concludes with observations about the problems of the retention of teachers that may be of value to school administrators.

This national study of beginning teachers is useful in showing us that the desire of men teachers to leave the classroom for administration is not simply a result of peculiarly unrewarding teaching conditions in one district or one state, and moreover seems to be unrelated to the teachers' satisfactions with their own jobs. On the other hand, both theory and practice would profit from knowledge about the special conditions under which the flow of male teachers out of the classroom is especially low, and this is something that this national survey does not tell us. The Office of Education study suggests that men teachers are especially concerned with the pay and working conditions of teaching, and that it is deficiencies in this regard that lead many to plan to leave the classroom. But we may indeed discover that, within limits, proportionately as many men leave teaching where their pay and working conditions are good as where they are bad, and that their appraisal of their own situations is based not so much on the absolute levels of their pay and working conditions as on their comparisons of their own situations with that of others. For many teachers, the "others" with whom they compare themselves are likely to be school administrators, who are largely recruited from teachers and whose pay and status are very often much higher than that of teachers. It is a hypothesis worthy of test that loss of men teachers from the classroom is related to the size of the *difference* in pay and status between them and their own school administrators. If this is so, then the policy implication is that, to retain more male teachers in the classroom, the difference between the rewards of teachers and administrators must be kept low.[59]

59. Reference group theory holds great potential value for the study of problems of teacher recruitment, retention, and satisfaction; moreover, it lends itself to study through survey research methods. On reference group theory, see Merton, R. K., "Continuities in the Theory of Reference Groups and Social Structure," in *Social Theory and Social Structure. op. cit.,* pp. 281–386; and Kelley, H. H., "Two Functions of Reference Groups," in *Readings in Social Psychology*. Edited by G. E. Swanson, T. M. Newcomb, and E. L. Hartley. Henry Holt, New York, 1952, pp. 410–414; and on its potential applications to very similar problems in industry, Lipset, S. M. and Martin Trow, "Reference Group Theory and Trade Union Wage Policy," in *Common Frontiers of the Social Sciences*. Edited by Mirra Komarovsky. Free Press, Glencoe, Ill., 1957, pp. 391–411.

On When Not to Ask "Why?"

A discussion of research on teacher retention points to one of the most common failings in survey research in education. This is, in brief, a tendency on the part of researchers to abdicate their own functions as analysts and interpreters and, in effect, to ask their respondents to do the analysis for them.[60] They do this, very often, by asking respondents to say *why* they feel or act as they do. Very commonly, in studies of teacher morale or turnover, the researcher will simply ask the teacher not only how he likes his job or what he plans to do but also why he is dissatisfied or is planning to leave his job, and then report the distributions of responses to these questions as if they were an adequate explanation of teacher dissatisfaction or turnover in that school or district. The difficulty is that the forces and conditions that make for variations in the rates of dissatisfaction or turnover, which are usually what the researcher wants to learn about, may not be at all the same as the conscious motives of the individuals whose attitudes and behaviors when aggregated make up those rates. In the study cited above, teachers who hope to leave teaching are not likely to volunteer that they are dissatisfied with the material and status rewards of teaching as compared with that of school administrators; the force and effect of this comparison may only emerge when we see variations in the rates of turnover under conditions which sharpen or ameliorate the comparison. The reasons teachers offer for their own attitudes and behaviors *may* suggest underlying social forces at work, but the researcher will often have to look to social factors outside the awareness of the participants if he is to explain more adequately than they can differences in the rates and frequencies of "individual" sentiment and action.[61]

Most research in education using survey methods is concerned with "sociological" problems—that is, with variations in social patterns and structures and the sources and consequences of these variations. But much of it is done by people who have little or no sociological training, and their approach to the data is often "psychologistic" in that they assume that the

---

60. The U.S. Office of Education study discussed above is far less guilty of this error than are most survey studies in education.
61. On the difference between the sociological concern with the rates of behavior, and the psychologists' interests in the incidence of behavior, see Merton, R. K., "Continuities in the Theory of Social Structure and Anomie," in his *Social Theory and Social Structure*, chap. 5, *op. cit.;* see also Hyman, H. H., *Survey Design . . . , op. cit.,* pp. 254–263.

explanation of social behavior is merely the sum of the explanations of the behaviors of the individuals who contribute to the pattern. Since survey methods can learn relatively little about the idiosyncratic psychological forces at work in each of its respondents, this psychologically-oriented treatment of survey data usually adds up to little more than a summation of the superficial "reasons" that respondents give for their own behaviors and actions. Indeed, much of the disrepute in which survey research is held in education arises from the recognition that it does badly what it ought not to be asked to do at all—that is, to explain why *individuals* hold certain views or do certain things. It is inherently "superficial" only on the level of the explanation of individual behavior; and matters are not improved even if the researcher has collected a hundred thousand questionnaires, if he does not recognize the inherent qualities and limitations of survey research data or, more generally, the differences between sociological and psychological explanations.

Survey research is inherently a tool for sociological and social-psychological investigation; in education it has largely been used by people trained in a predominantly individual-psychological tradition of research. This, it seems to me, lies at the heart of the poor quality of the bulk of survey research in education, and of its understandably low status in the field. Educators who employ survey research methods do *not* need to have had formal training in sociology in order to employ the research method fruitfully, though it helps. They *do,* however, have to have some grasp of the nature of the sociological perspective and, above all, an understanding of the differences in kind between the socially engendered frequencies which their tabulations of survey data provide them and the individual behaviors and sentiments which their respondents report.

Some Potentially Fruitful Areas
for Survey Research in Education

The variety of problems in and around education that can be studied through survey research is limitless. The few cited below serve only to illustrate the range of issues and problems which call for survey research, and are distinguished only in that they have been suggested by work already done, or are close to the writer's own interests.

Recruitment to occupations. Survey research among students in schools and colleges could add much to our knowledge of the nature and processes of social recruitment to occupations and professions. The knowledge we now possess on this is fragmentary and partial. For example, various scattered studies suggest that engineers as a group are recruited from lower socio-economic groups than are natural scientists or students in the liberal arts.[62] Again, at Berkeley we find that over a third of students majoring in the physical sciences come from working-class origins, as compared with only three per cent in the life sciences. Similar scattered data bear on differences in the religious and ethnic backgrounds of students who major in different subjects in college. Systematic data bearing on these questions would provide clues to the ways in which statuses held by one's parents shape life chances and experience which in turn affect the kind and amount of formal education one gets and the kind of work one ends up doing.[63] Such data would enormously increase our detailed knowledge of (a) the nature of social mobility in our society; (b) the influence of the religious, class, and ethnic sub-cultures into which a person is born in shaping his educational and occupational career; and (c) the ways various specific occupations and professions themselves affect and are affected by the patterns of social recruitment to them.

Images of occupations. Related to the foregoing, but of interest in its own right, is the question of the images held of different occupations by students

62. Trow, Martin, "Some Implications of the Social Origins of Engineers," *Scientific Manpower,* National Science Foundation, Washington, D.C., 1958, pp. 67–74. Knowledge in this area has been very greatly advanced by the studies, based on a national survey of college graduates of the class of 1961, conducted by the National Opinion Research Center in Chicago. The findings of these studies are reported in two volumes, both by Davis, J. A., *Great Aspirations:* The Graduate School Plans of America's College Seniors. Aldine, Chicago, 1964, and *Undergraduate Career Decisions:* Correlates of Occupational Choice. Aldine, Chicago, 1965. These books are in many respects models of careful and imaginative survey analysis.

63. In addition to the many studies linking class origins and educational achievement, there are a handful which show its relation to ethnic origins. See for example, Rosen, B. C., "Race, Ethnicity and the Achievement Syndrome," *American Sociological Review.* Vol. 24, February, 1959, pp. 47–60; Strodtbeck, F. L., "Family Integration, Values and Achievement," in *Talent and Society.* Edited by D. C. McClelland, *et al.,* D. Van Nostrand, Princeton, N.J., 1958; McClelland, D. C., *The Achieving Society.* D. Van Nostrand, Princeton, N.J., 1961, chap. 9; Caudill, William and George De Vos, "Achievement, Culture and Personality: The Case of the Japanese-Americans," *American Anthropologist,* Vol. 58, December, 1956, pp. 1102–1126; Toby, Jackson, "Hoodlum or Business Man: An American Dilemma," in *The Jews:* Social Patterns of an American Group. Edited by Marshall Sklare. Free Press, Glencoe, Ill., 1958, pp. 542–550.

from different social origins, and at different stages in their education. We know that some occupations, such as medicine, are enormously more "visible" to people than are others, such as meteorology or biochemistry. And we suspect that the image held of an occupation, including the limiting case of never having heard of it, affects recruitment to it, or, for students, affects the probabilities of doing the things which will eventuate in entering it. But we know almost nothing of how knowledge and beliefs about various occupations vary among different kinds of students, nor how and why such knowledge and beliefs are acquired by some but not others, nor how they really affect educational and occupational plans and choices.[64] These are problems of especial interest and importance at a time when there is great concern in the society with increasing the numbers and quality of people recruited to the natural sciences; but certainly the practical implications of such research is not limited to those concerns.

As another practical contribution, survey research might well be employed to learn more about the educational and vocational guidance people in secondary schools and colleges. What kinds of people are they, what are their social origins, their education, values, orientations? What are *their* images of the occupations about which they advise students: for example, what do they know or believe about the requirements and rewards of different occupations? What are the actual bases on which they decide what advice to give to students? How do their perceptions of students from different backgrounds affect the kind of advice they offer them? Many of these questions are susceptible to study through survey methods, although at various points the survey research would need to be supplemented by information gathered in other ways. The practical implications of such research for improved recruitment, training, and employment of school counseling and guidance people, and for the dissemination of accurate information about occupations, need hardly be elaborated.

64. See Beardslee, David and Donald O'Dowd, "Students and the Occupational World," in *The American College.* Edited by Nevitt Sanford. John Wiley & Sons, New York, 1962, pp. 597–626; also Beardslee, David and Donald O'Dowd, *College Student Images of a Selected Group of Professions and Occupations.* Cooperative Research Project No. 562-8142, U.S. Office of Education, Washington, 1960. Mead, Margaret, and Rhoda Metraux, "The Image of the Scientist among High School Students: A Pilot Study," *Science,* Vol. 126, August, 1957, pp. 384–390; Becker, H. S., and James Carper, "The Elements of Identification with an Occupation," in *The Sociology of Science.* Edited by Bernard Barber and Walter Hirsch. Free Press, Glencoe, Ill., 1962; and Rosenberg, Morris, *Occupations and Values, op. cit.*

The public and public education. American education is more immediately dependent on public support in the local community and state than is education in any other country. Public elementary and secondary schools and the bulk of the junior colleges are heavily dependent on the willingness of people in the local school district or county to tax themselves for their support; half of all funds for American public schools come from the immediate locality, the bulk of the rest from the state. The municipal and state colleges and universities which enroll well over half of all American college students are dependent on appropriations by the representatives of local constituencies. Yet there has been relatively little research on how the American public views education and how these views differ in various parts of the population.[65] To what extent are different parts of the population dissatisfied with their schools? To what extent are they prepared to support larger appropriations or bond issues? What kinds of expenditures—teachers' salaries, supplementary curricular programs, buildings—do they view with greater or less favor? More fundamentally, what is the nature and degree of interest in public education in different parts of the population, and how does this level of interest affect the readiness to support increased appropriations for education, or to take other kinds of direct action to influence the nature and content of public education? More specifically, how do people differently situated in our society view higher education? To what extent do people of varying social and educational experience accept the universities' claim to a high degree of autonomy in the government of their own affairs, and for freedom to pursue the varied goals of higher education even where these are at variance with the sentiments of a majority of those whose taxes support the institutions?

Public opinion is by no means the only force which shapes the relations of educational institutions to local and state governments, but in our society it is immensely important in determining the kinds of educational systems we have.[66] Yet the distribution of public sentiment about the educational

65. As examples, see Carter, R. F., *Voters and Their Schools.* Institute of Communications Research, Stanford, Calif., 1960; Mitchell, R. E. *Voting for Education* (forthcoming); and Morgan, James, *et al., Income and Welfare in the United States.* McGraw-Hill, New York, 1962, pp. 415–424.

66. This is obviously true for elementary and secondary schools. But in addition, "Most state universities are also creatures of the legislature rather than the constitution, or at least subject to such controls as the legislature may choose to impose over their operation. None of these schools can appeal to any system of higher law in justification of their right to enjoy a degree of independence within the framework of the

system, the responsiveness of that opinion to local conditions and campaigns or to national and international events, its direction of development, its links with attitudes toward other public issues and aspects of society, are almost wholly unknown. Here, certainly, survey research can yield knowledge of value to students of public opinion, politics, and education alike, and to educators and administrators who live with the tensions inherent in the multiple and frequently conflicting commitments of different portions of our public to the values of academic freedom, professional responsibility, and public control over education.

Cultural sophistication. The preceding problem area—the study of public sentiments regarding education and its institutions—would bring survey research back to its roots in public opinion research. In recent years survey researchers have turned increasingly away from the study of attitudes and sentiments in the general population, and directed their attention more to the study of formal organizations—armies, business firms, voluntary organizations, trade unions, churches, now schools and colleges—to learn how such organizations function, and how formal structures, informal groups, and individual characteristics and sentiments are linked to one another. This kind of interest grew in part out of a dissatisfaction with public opinion research in the general population; on the theoretical level, a heightened interest in organizational theory and small groups led sociologists and survey researchers to study situations where more could be learned of the immediate social context and its bearing on the sentiments and actions of its participants.

This has been a highly fruitful body of inquiry, and its methods and perspectives are being applied to educational institutions, as some of the studies discussed earlier testify. But there remain important problems for survey research outside the confines of organizations, and some of these problems may be of interest to students of education.

One fruitful approach would go beyond the study of specific attitudes in an attempt to study the distribution, sources, and correlates of a quality of mind that can be called "cultural sophistication" or awareness. Cultural sophistication is perhaps more easily recognized than precisely defined, but

state government. They must make their case for the freedom of higher education in the legislature or in the form of public debate, unprotected by any shield of legal autonomy." Moos, M. C., *et al., The Campus and the State.* Johns Hopkins Press, Baltimore, 1959, p. 19.

it clearly has two components: a degree of knowledge about the society in which we live, its history, organization, and culture; and secondly, and perhaps more important, an awareness of the nature of ideas, some skill in using them to clarify the connections among things, and a tendency to respond to them on their own terms, rather than solely as evaluations or prescriptions for action.[67] This quality of mind is close to what Weber meant when he raised the question of the conditions necessary for different kinds of social action.[68] The development of more complex forms of organized social and political action that are rationally oriented toward the achievement of some shared purposes, he suggests, are linked to "the transparency of the connections" between the causes and consequences of the existing situation.[69] But "the transparency of the connections between causes and consequences" in society is not simply a characteristic of the situation, but also of the observers, and thus is related to "general cultural conditions, especially to those of an intellectual sort."[70] Weber here is pointing to the distribution in a society of certain modes of thought, kinds of knowledge and intellectual skills, and to the connections between these and the possibilities of effective public action rationally oriented to the achievement of shared purposes. In contemporary society, the connections between the causes and consequences of social and political events are very often far from transparent, and a very high order of knowledge and skill is required to trace out those connections, either to assess situations or to act effectively. This kind of knowledge and skill is an important part of "cultural sophistication."

Cultural sophistication is also close to Mannheim's conception of substantial rationality, and it was precisely the increasing complexity of social arrangements in modern society, and the growing opacity of the connections between their causes and consequences, without, in Mannheim's view, a corresponding growth in the distribution of knowledge and intellectual skills, that led him to see substantial rationality as diminishing, and increasingly

67. See the discussion of the concept in Trow, Martin, "Cultural Sophistication and Higher Education," in *Selection and Educational Differentiation.* Field Service Center and Center for the Study of Higher Education, Berkeley, 1959, pp. 107–125.
68. Weber, Max, *From Max Weber.* Translated and edited by H. H. Gerth and C. W. Mills. Oxford University Press, New York, 1946, p. 184.
69. Weber's discussion centered on various forms of class action, and the "existing situation" he referred to was the existing "class situation," but his remarks are applicable to other kinds of situations and to social actions based on other shared interests.
70. *Ibid.*

supplanted by technical or functional rationality which does not involve a grasp of connections outside the narrow sphere of one's job or technical specialty.

Weber and Mannheim wrote when the power of organization and technology was already apparent but when mass education, especially mass higher education as we see it in the U.S., was scarcely imaginable. But the knowledge and skills that enter into cultural sophistication are among the desired outcomes of a liberal higher education and we can scarcely doubt that, by and large, men who have been to college are better equipped to perceive the connections between causes and consequences in social, political, and economic life than those who have not. Formal education is by no means the only kind of experience which equips men with these kinds of knowledge and skills, but in our society it is probably the most important kind.[71] If the growth of mass higher education provides for a substantial part of the population the knowledge and intellectual skills that enable them to understand political problems and assess alternatives, then it may be through a much wider distribution of cultural sophistication that higher education will have the most direct effects on the possibilities of democratic politics in a mass bureaucratic society.

The question of the broad social and political consequences of variations in levels of cultural sophistication—both the consequences for effective democratic politics of variations in cultural level between societies, and the consequences for the political behavior of groups whose cultural levels differ —may properly lie in the sphere of political sociology, and is one of the points where educational policy and outcomes affect political structures.[72]

71. For example, Stouffer, S. A., in *Communism, Conformity and Civil Liberties, loc. cit.*, shows a very marked relationship between formal education and support for civil liberties. Trow, Martin, in "Small Businessmen, Political Tolerance, and Support for McCarthy," *American Journal of Sociology*, Vol. 64, November, 1958, pp. 270–281, found formal education the single most important correlate of opposition to McCarthyism. Ferber, Robert, in "The Effect of Respondent Ignorance on Survey Results," *Journal of the American Statistical Society*, Vol. 51, December, 1956, pp. 576–586, shows a very marked difference in the levels of ignorance and misinformation on current economic and social issues among groups with different amounts of formal education. For a discussion of the relation of formal education to the level of knowledge, sense of political efficacy, and various political attitudes, see Key, V. O., Jr., *Public Opinion and American Democracy*. Alfred A. Knopf, New York, 1961, pp. 315–343.

72. See Lipset, S. M., *Political Man:* The Social Bases of Politics. Doubleday, Garden City, N.Y., 1960, pp. 53–60.

But of much more direct relevance to students of education are the prior questions: (a) what are the social sources of these variations in cultural sophistication among different groups and categories in a society, and (b) to what extent can formal education, and especially higher education, contribute to the cultural sophistication of its students; more specifically, under what conditions and circumstances is this most likely to occur, and for what kinds of students?

Answers to the first of these questions can shed light on how students from different backgrounds and with different kinds of life experience use their educations in different ways. Karl Mannheim suggests that diversity of social experience gives men some detachment from the assumptions of any given perspective, and allows them to see the connections between the assumptions of a particular group and its mode of life:

> For the son of a peasant who has grown up within the narrow confines of his village and spends his whole life in the place of his birth, the mode of thinking and speaking characteristic of that village is something that he takes entirely for granted. But for the country lad who goes to the city and adapts himself gradually to city life, the rural mode of living and thinking ceases to be something to be taken for granted. He has won a certain detachment from it, and he distinguishes now, perhaps quite consciously, between "rural" and "urban" modes of thought and ideas. . . . That which within a given group is accepted as absolute appears to the outsider conditioned by the group situation and recognized as partial, (in this case, as "rural").[73]

This "relational" thinking is clearly a component of "cultural sophistication," for without it men can hardly be aware of the nature of ideas or their usefulness in revealing the connections among causes and consequences in social life. Educators need not be told of the difficulties of advancing the liberal education of children from backgrounds which have not exposed them to a variety of perspectives, whether they come from culturally impoverished slums or from equally encapsulated middle-class environments.

But what are the class, ethnic, religious, regional sub-cultures in our society which provide the variety of experience which make for intellectual awareness, and from which students come able and motivated to use the schools and colleges to further their own liberal education? Conversely,

73. Mannheim, Karl, *Ideology and Utopia*. Harcourt, Brace, New York, 1952, p. 253: see also pp. 6–11.

from what parts of our society do students come indifferent or even hostile to the cultivation of critical and independent thinking through liberal education?

We may get clues to this through survey research in schools by comparing the attitudes, orientations, and cultural habits of students from different social origins. For example, we may note the extraordinary resistance to liberal education among engineering students, and their characteristic lack of the intellectual skills and orientations associated with cultural sophistication. We may note, further, that engineers are disproportionately recruited from lower middle-class backgrounds, and appear to be strongly oriented toward mobility into higher middle-class strata. We may note further that where Orientals comprise a sizable proportion of the student body, as they do at the University of California at Berkeley, Oriental boys are disproportionately enrolled in the engineering courses. While there has been some study of personality variation among students in different major fields,[74] there has been little study of their different social and ethnic origins. But occupations and professions differ in the kinds of students they recruit, and especially in their intellectual and cultural orientations. Survey research on these questions would provide important clues to the links between variations in life experience associated with different social origins, on one hand, and orientations toward education and recruitment into the occupational structure on the other.

In the light of Mannheim's discussion of diversity of social experience, we might be led to believe that social mobility would contribute to the broadening of horizons and the detachment from narrow perspectives that characterizes cultural sophistication. Yet the evidence suggests that in the early phases of social mobility, illustrated by many engineering students, students and their parents view education almost exclusively in vocational terms.[75] A commitment to higher education as a "vocational training" is not congruent with the conception of it as a source of a liberal education.[76] Re-

74. For instance, Bereiter, Carl and M. B. Freedman, "Fields of Study and the People in Them," in *The American College.* Edited by Nevitt Sanford, *op. cit.,* pp. 563–596, and the references there given.
75. See, for example, Kahl, J. A., " 'Common Man' Boys" in *Education, Economy and Society: A Reader in the Sociology of Education.* Edited by A. H. Halsey, Jean Floud and C. A. Anderson. Free Press, Glencoe, Ill., 1961, pp. 348–366.
76. This point is made by Miller, Norman, "Academic Climate and Student Values," paper presented at the Fifty-Fourth Annual Meeting of the American Sociological Society, September, 1959.

search shows that students who see their college education primarily as a vocational training are much less likely to have the kinds of knowledge and habits—for example, doing serious reading aside from school assignments —that are associated with cultural sophistication.[77] There is some reason to believe that intellectual detachment, pleasure in speculative thought, and a playfulness with ideas are all associated with cultural sophistication. Some of these bents of mind seem to require a social and psychological security which is precluded by very strong mobility orientations.[78]

While there is some evidence that students who have the less arduous task of merely *maintaining* high social status are more likely to develop the intellectual habits associated with cultural sophistication than are those who are trying to *achieve* it, there may well be other kinds of social situations and experiences which work in similar directions. Mannheim suggests at one point that it is not *mobile* but *marginal* men who are most likely to achieve detachment from parochial perspectives.[79] Marginal men are posed on the edge of several groups but wholly committed to none of them, whereas mobile people, through anticipatory socialization and powerful "over-commitments" to the groups to which they aspire, may be in the

77. Reinhard Bendix observes that early industrial entrepreneurs in nineteenth century England whose energies were totally committed to their work and their businesses were completely uninterested in and even hostile to speculative thought. Bendix, Reinhard, *Work and Authority in Industry:* Ideologies of Management in the Course of Industrialization. John Wiley & Sons, New York, 1956, p. 88. We find the same hostility to ideas today in those deeply oriented to action and to striving to get ahead. Erikson's work on identity formation in late adolescence sheds light on another dimension of this; he observes that vocationalism and early career choice is an aspect of "premature" foreclosure of identity formation, and an end to identity play. Erikson, E. H., "The Problem of Ego Identity," *Journal of the American Psychoanalytic Association.* Vol. 4, 1956, pp. 56–121. Early marriage can also be a reflection of this premature foreclosure of intellectual and emotional growth, and is seen by Margaret Mead and others as antithetical to the purposes of liberal education. Mead, Margaret, *et al.,* "Marrying in Haste in College," *Columbia University Forum,* Spring, 1960, pp. 31–34. The trend toward early marriage among college students thus poses a problem for the colleges in which it occurs.
78. On the relation of creativity among children and a playfulness with ideas, see Getzels, J. W. and P. W. Jackson, *Creativity and Intelligence:* Explorations with Gifted Students. John Wiley & Sons, New York, 1962. There is some suggestion in this research that this kind of playfulness is less likely to be found among children who are strongly oriented toward achievement.
79. Mannheim, Karl, *op. cit.,* pp. 136–144.

process of acquiring a new perspective, rather than broadening their horizons by gaining detachment from any of them.

Can we distinguish marginal from mobile students through survey methods? We may look to the literature on ethnic and religious subgroups in our population—on Jews, Japanese, Catholics, Mexicans, Italians—to learn something of the relation of these subgroups to the larger society, and then see what variations there are in the orientations toward education, occupational aspirations, cultural habits, and levels and varieties of cultural sophistication among students from these backgrounds. Or we may look to various kinds of detachment and "alienation" of students in different situations and look, through survey data, for differences in their social origins and early life experience.[80]

The question about the extent to which higher education actually contributes to the social and cultural awareness of those who experience it, directs our attention back to the colleges and universities and to what goes on within them. To some extent, differences in levels of social and cultural awareness between the student bodies at different colleges reflect a selective recruitment from the general population to higher education and to specific institutions. We need to distinguish the differences in attitudes and perspectives that flow from selective recruitment from those which reflect the impact of the college experience itself. Having done that, we may then go on to look, through survey research, for the specific experiences in college which seem to inhibit or contribute to the growth of intellectual sophistication. Riesman has suggested that the cultural impact of college is greater if students leave home and live at the college than if they live at home.[81] Presumably, living at home insulates students from the full effect of exposure to the new ideas and relationships in college. The Selvin-Hagstrom research at Berkeley indicates that residential sororities can serve the same function of insulating their members against the liberalizing influences of the college environment.[82] We may also look at the time at which students make their decisions about major fields or future occupation, compare students who

80. See Hajda, Jan, "Intellectual Orientations of Graduate Students," paper read at the Fifty-Fourth Annual Meeting of the American Sociological Society, Chicago, September, 1959. Also Clark, B. R. and Martin Trow, "The Organizational Context," in *College Peer Groups*. Edited by T. M. Newcomb and E. K. Wilson. Aldine, Chicago, 1966.
81. Riesman, David and Christopher Jencks, "The Viability of the American College," in *The American College*. Edited by Nevitt Sanford, *op. cit.,* pp. 105–106.
82. Selvin, H. C. and W. O. Hagstrom, *op. cit.*

make those decisions early with those who make them late in their careers, and look especially at those who change their major fields and occupational choices in the course of their college careers. The time, as well as the nature, of the choice of major subject and occupation may be related both to the student's social origins and his orientations toward education, and may give clues to the processes underlying the growth of new perspectives and cultural sophistication.

Survey research among students may well shed light on matters as subtle as the nature and sources of the qualities of mind that we have been discussing. Research could contribute both to knowledge about the impact of different kinds of educational experiences on different kinds of students, and also to knowledge about developments in the "general cultural conditions, especially of an intellectual sort" which Weber linked to the whole political and social life of a society. Student populations in schools and colleges provide a strategic population for inquiry into these problems, and survey techniques may be the most useful research method of investigating these issues.

On the Relevance of Survey Research to Educational Practice

Every applied field faces the problem of the right relationship between professional practice and the systematic knowledge and theory whose application distinguishes a profession from any other art or occupation. Most often, the desirable relationship is boldness on the part of the scientist and scholar, caution and prudence on the part of the administrator and practitioner. In education and educational research, the relationship has been too often the reverse—excessive caution and timidity in the research, and insufficient caution in the application of the "findings" of this research on the part of the educators. This reversal has clear implications for those who carry out and use survey research in education.

There are many ways in which we can characterize studies which use survey research methods. We can distinguish them as we have earlier by how they generalize their findings, whether and how they study processes of change, whether or not they are carried on within comparative contexts, and the extent to which the characteristics of those contexts enter into the analysis of the survey data itself. There is yet another way of characterizing survey research studies, along a dimension which cuts across these others— that is, the boldness or caution with which such studies treat the survey data, and the readiness of their authors to impose themselves on their data and draw general conclusions from them.

At one extreme, the most cautious approach to survey data is to "let the facts speak for themselves," and to do little more than to translate the tabulations into words. Researchers with this commitment work within an austerely self-inhibiting set of rules; they say nothing that the data do not directly support, they tend not to generalize beyond the population from which the sample was drawn or the theoretical propositions directly involved in the research, and they implicitly accept the dictum that the burden of proof falls on him who makes an assertion. As a corollary, they try very hard not to be wrong in what they say, and the way not to be "wrong" (i.e., vulnerable to criticism) is (a) to pay very great attention to the techniques of sample design and data collection, and (b) to say little beyond what the data show directly.

The alternative to the doctrine of caution in survey research is a style of empirical and analytical boldness which accepts *provisionally* any proposition that plausibly accounts for a set of systematic observations and is part of a more general set of interpretive ideas about the phenomenon. This style, which characterizes the best explanatory research using survey methods, subordinates the techniques of data collection and manipulation to the substantive or theoretical problem at hand, assessing those techniques not independently but only as they affect the research itself, recognizing also that the statistics of probability are not the only criteria of the validity of empirical relationships and should affect but not determine the interpretation of the survey findings. This style assumes that all propositions in science are provisional, and are ultimately tested not within the confines of the research out of which they arise but rather within the whole body of related research of which they are part and to which they contribute. In this perspective, by contrast with that of the doctrine of caution, the burden of "proof," in its etymological sense of "test," rests not primarily on the researcher but rather on those who read and use the research.

Styles of research ought properly to be appraised in terms of their consequences. Where the doctrine of caution in the analysis of survey data tends to inhibit the study of significant issues, and represses the interplay of research findings with more general ideas and questions as it simultaneously encourages an overemphasis on technique, the doctrine of boldness in survey research encourages fresh ideas and new perspectives on familiar issues. It provides the climate of freedom within which the researcher can relate his data to more general problems and ideas even where a rigorous demonstration of the connection cannot be made. This juxtaposition of general ideas and rather special data that do not bear directly on those ideas can nevertheless serve to generate questions and problems for further research. Such questions, generated out of research rather than imposed on it, are in many cases more valuable than the specific empirical findings of a given study. But such questions do not arise nearly so frequently out of research dominated by an overly anxious concern to demonstrate that what is reported is in fact so.

I have been saying that the doctrine of boldness in research creates a climate encouraging greater freedom for inventiveness and creative thought on the part of the research man himself. At least as important are its consequences for the reader and user of research. Where there is considerable tolerance for the reporting of highly provisional findings and interpretations, there is more likely to be a healthy skepticism and mistrust on the part of the reader, a state of mind much more likely to lead to replications and further related research aiming to see if the findings are in fact as reported, under what conditions they obtain, and so on. Research in the tradition of boldness accepts, or rather insists on, the provisional quality of research findings, and encourages, almost requires, a critical and skeptical stance on the part of reader and practitioner. This is in contrast to the passive absorption and consumption of research findings encouraged by "cautious" research, with its implicit and often unwarranted assertion of certainty.

The findings of the cautious school are far more provisional than they appear, and assume the spurious status of "facts" on which recommendations for practice can be based. For example, one study finds that women, on the average, report that they "decided" to become teachers earlier in their academic careers than did the men. On this basis, the writer recommends that:

> For the girls, recruitment should be rather intensive in high school and extend through the freshman and sophomore years of college; while for the boys recruitment should not be completely ignored in high school, but intensified in the lower division of college and extended into the upper division and graduate years.[83]

The author observes that more research is needed to see if, as his findings suggest, teaching is more often a first choice for women, while often a second or even a third choice for men; but presumably, if this is so, it is all the

83. Jantzen, J. M., "An Opinionaire on Why College Students Choose to Teach," *Journal of Educational Research.* 53, September, 1959, pp. 13–17.

more reason to "recruit" actively for men later along in college. The trouble is that the writer's horizon is limited by his survey data; he does not consider that the processes of occupational choice are more complicated than the respondent's reports on when they "decided" to become teachers would indicate; or that the kinds of men and women who "decide" early in their schooling to prepare for teaching may differ importantly from those who decide late; or that men for whom teaching is a second or third choice may not be the best recruits; or that since the great majority of all men who are "recruited" to teaching seem to want nothing so much as to get out of the classroom,[84] a simple effort to recruit more men to "teaching" may be less useful than an effort to learn what kinds of men may in fact want to teach and not merely use the classroom as a stepping stone to other things. Those questions would, of course, have taken the author of the survey in question "far beyond the bounds" of his modest and cautious study; but we may ask what value his study has if it does not raise these questions, and what contribution to educational practice it will have if incorporated as a "research finding" into a program for the recruitment of future teachers in high school and college.

The explicitly and highly provisional status of findings out of the bolder style of survey research encourages, paradoxically, a more cautious application of these findings in practice. Survey research cannot relieve the teacher or administrator of the responsibility of acting in his own situation on the best information he has. The findings of survey research may provide an additional body of knowledge for the practitioner, but its being called "research" and surrounded by a scientific methodology do not make it necessarily true or useful for the practitioner, nor does it relieve him of assessing its relevance to his situation.

Conclusion

The purpose of this review of survey research in education is to contribute to the realization of its potential contribution to sound knowledge and fruitful theory about the institutions and processes of education. Much survey research that is now done in education does not realize its potential, which is just another way of saying that much of it is bad research. How can it be made better?

First, there is no substitute for knowledge by the survey researcher of the

---

84. Mason, W. S., *op. cit.*

nature of his research instrument—knowledge about the variety of information it can provide, as well as about the kinds of phenomena that are better studied through other methods. This means that the survey researcher in education must become familiar with the considerable body of work that has advanced the methodology of survey research, especially in the past few decades, and with the analysis of survey data, as well as with the better-known subjects of sample design and questionnaire construction. Perhaps the best source of knowledge about survey research are books and monographs which use the method to illuminate substantive problems and advance social science theory. At the present time, this requires the student of education to go outside the literature on education to studies in political behavior, mass communications, public health, and military life to find the best examples of survey research.[85]

Second, the survey researcher in education must have a grasp of the "sociological perspective," that is, a sense of the ways in which the distributions of sentiments and behaviors which his tabulations provide are more than mere aggregations of the sentiments and behaviors of the individuals that make up his sample, but point to forces and processes which are to some extent independent of any of the individuals in the study. A student of education with no formal training in sociology can gain a sense of this sociological perspective by reading and study in the sociological literature; formal course work in sociology helps.

And finally, survey research in education needs the freedom to be wrong. The curse of much survey work in education is timidity, and not so much a personal as an institutionalized timidity. At least part of the source of that timidity is a desire to produce "findings" which are of direct practical usefulness to educators.[86] If someone is going to put what one says into practice uncritically, then the costs of error are too high for analytical boldness. The only sure way to reduce the risks of being wrong in research is to be cautious—to say nothing one isn't very sure of. But this is usually what people already know; it may also, as a "research finding," have an undeserved status as certified truth, even where it does not take other facts into account which might lead to quite different policy recommendations.

85. This is less true every day. Since this chapter was written, some excellent survey research in education has been completed, most notably the nation-wide study by James Coleman *et al., Equality of Educational Opportunity.* U.S. Government Printing Office, Washington, D.C., 1966.
86. Lazarsfeld, P. F. and S. D. Sieber, *op. cit.,* point to the emphasis in educational research on improving education over understanding it.

Illuminating contributions to knowledge about education through survey research, as through other research methods, require that the researcher have the freedom to be wrong, be psychologically prepared to take that risk, and be professionally supported in that risk-taking. This means he cannot be held responsible for the practical applications of his provisional findings. He must be responsible solely to his discipline and to his fellow social scientists. The quality of research in education depends in part on the readiness of the educator and school administrator to accept responsibility for educational policy and practice. Uncritical acceptance of research findings by educators and analytical timidity by researchers in education are opposite sides of the same coin: both inhibit the freedom and boldness of the researcher, and prevent him from taking the necessary risks that are required for genuine discovery.[87]

The growing importance of education in the developing countries and in "post-industrial" societies like our own is paralleled by the expansion of social science research into new areas of concern. These trends, in society and in social science, ensure that the quantity of survey research in education will grow very rapidly in the immediate future. If it is to make a contribution to knowledge and to practice at all commensurate with the resources put into it, men with skills in survey research will have to learn about the problems of education, while men who know and live with the problems of education will have to acquire the skills in survey research that will illuminate them. The most pressing immediate need is the recognition that neither the problems of education nor the skills of survey research are self-evident and matters of common sense.

87. It may be suggested that these remarks apply more properly to explanatory studies than to "simple" descriptive studies, which aim modestly to find out "what is," but on close inspection, "descriptive" studies are the first phases (and thus incomplete forms) of a special kind of analytical study—the kind that wants to generalize its findings to a very specific population and situation. In other respects descriptive studies are like analytical studies in that they have built into them notions about the causal connections among the elements of the situation. But since these notions are implicit in descriptive studies rather than explicit as in analytical studies, they are usually assumed in the former rather than taken as problematic and studied as in the latter.

Bibliography

Bailyn, Bernard, *Education in the Forming of American Society*. University of North Carolina Press, Chapel Hill, 1960.

Barnes, J. B., *Educational Research for Classroom Teachers*. G. P. Putnam's Sons, New York, 1960.

Barr, A. S., R. A. Davis, and P. O. Johnson, *Educational Research and Appraisal*. J. B. Lippincott, New York, 1953.

Beardslee, David and Donald O'Dowd, *College Student Images of a Selected Group of Professions and Occupations*. Cooperative Research Project No. 562-8142, U.S. Office of Education, Washington, 1960.

Beardslee, David and Donald O'Dowd, "Students and the Occupational World," in *The American College:* A Psychological and Social Interpretation of Higher Learning. Edited by Nevitt Sanford. John Wiley & Sons, New York, 1962, pp. 597–626.

Becker, H. S. and James Carper, "The Elements of Identification with an Occupation," in *The Sociology of Science*. Edited by Bernard Barber and Walter Hirsch. Free Press, Glencoe, Ill., 1962.

Bendix, Reinhard, *Work and Authority in Industry:* Ideologies of Management in the Course of Industrialization. John Wiley & Sons, New York, 1956.

Bereiter, Carl and M. B. Freedman, "Fields of Study and the People in Them," in *The American College*. Edited by Nevitt Sanford, John Wiley & Sons, New York, 1962, pp. 563–626.

Berelson, B. R., P. F. Lazarsfeld, and W. W. McPhee, *Voting:* A Study of Opinion Formation in a Presidential Campaign. University of Chicago Press, Chicago, 1954.

Best, J. W., *Research in Education,* 9th printing. Prentice-Hall, Englewood Cliffs, N.J., 1965.

Brim, O. G. Jr., *Sociology and the Field of Education*. Russell Sage Foundation, New York, 1958.

Campbell, Angus, Gerald Gurin, and W. E. Miller, *The Voter Decides*. Row, Peterson, Evanston, Ill., 1954. See chap. 2, and pp. 71, 77, 79, 211–214.

Carter, R. F., *Voters and Their Schools*. Institute of Communications Research, Stanford, Calif. 1960.

Caudill, William and George De Vos, "Achievement, Culture, and Personality: The Case of the Japanese-Americans," *American Anthropologist,* Vol. 58, December, 1956, pp. 1102–1126.

Clark, B. R. and Martin Trow, "The Organizational Context," in *College Peer Groups*. Edited by T. M. Newcomb and E. K. Wilson. Aldine, Chicago, 1966.

Coleman, James, *The Adolescent Society:* The Social Life of the Teenager and Its Impact on Education. Free Press, Glencoe, Ill., 1961.

Coleman, James, *et al., Equality of Educational Opportunity*. U.S. Government Printing Office, Washington, 1966.

Davis, J. A., *Great Aspirations:* The Graduate School Plans of America's College Seniors. Aldine, Chicago, 1964.

Davis, J. A., *Undergraduate Career Decisions:* Correlates of Occupational Choice. Aldine, Chicago, 1965.

Erikson, E. H., "The Problem of Ego Identity," *Journal of the American Psycho-analytic Association,* Vol. 4, 1956, pp. 56–121.

Ferber, Robert, "The Effect of Respondent Ignorance on Survey Results," *Journal of the American Statistical Society,* Vol. 51, December, 1956, pp. 576–586.

Getzels, J. W. and P. W. Jackson, *Creativity and Intelligence:* Explorations with Gifted Students. John Wiley & Sons, New York, 1962.

Goldsen, R. K., *et al., What College Students Think.* Van Nostrand, Princeton, N.J., 1960.

Good, C. V., *Introduction to Educational Research.* Appleton-Century-Crofts, New York, 1959.

Good, C. V. and D. E. Scates, *Methods of Research:* Educational, Psychological, Sociological. Appleton-Century-Crofts, New York, 1954.

Gross, Neal, "The Sociology of Education," in *Sociology Today:* Problems and Prospects. Edited by R. K. Merton, Leonard Broom, and L. S. Cottrell. Basic Books, New York, 1959.

Hajda, Jan, "Intellectual Orientations of Graduate Students," paper read at the Fifty-Fourth Annual Meeting of the American Sociological Society, Chicago, September, 1959.

Hyman, H. H., *Survey Design and Analysis:* Principles, Cases and Procedures. Free Press, Glencoe, Ill., 1955.

Hyman, H. H. and P. B. Sheatsley, "Attitudes Toward Desegregation," *Scientific American,* Vol. 195, No. 6, 1956, pp. 35–39.

Hyman, H. H., *et al., Interviewing in Social Research.* University of Chicago Press, Chicago, 1954.

Jantzen, J. M., "An Opinionaire on Why College Students Choose to Teach," *Journal of Educational Research,* Vol. 53, September, 1959, pp. 13–17.

Kahl, J. A., " 'Common Man' Boys," in *Education, Economy and Society:* A Reader in the Sociology of Education. Edited by A. H. Halsey, Jean Floud, and C. A. Anderson. Free Press, Glencoe, Ill., 1961, pp. 348–366.

Katz, Daniel, F. H. Allport, and M. B. Jenness, *Students' Attitudes:* A Report of the Syracuse University Reaction Study. Craftsman Press, Syracuse, N.Y., 1931.

Katz, Elihu and P. F. Lazarsfeld, *Personal Influence:* The Part Played by People in the Flow of Mass Communications. Free Press, Glencoe, Ill., 1955, pp. 25–30.

Kelley, H. H., "Two Functions of Reference Groups," in *Readings in Social Psychology.* Edited by G. E. Swanson, T. M. Newcomb and E. L. Hartley. Henry Holt, New York, 1952, pp. 410–414.

Key, V. O., Jr., *Public Opinion and American Democracy.* Alfred A. Knopf, New York, 1961, pp. 315–343.

Lazarsfeld, P. F. and Morris Rosenberg, eds., *The Language of Social Research:* A Reader in the Methodology of Social Research. Free Press, Glencoe, Ill., 1955.

Lazarsfeld, P. F. and S. D. Sieber, *Organizing Educational Research:* An Exploration. Prentice-Hall, Englewood Cliffs, N.J., 1964.

Lazarsfeld, P. F. and Wagner Thielens, Jr., *The Academic Mind:* Social Scientists in a Time of Crisis. Free Press, Glencoe, Ill., 1958.

Lenski, G. E., *The Religious Factor:* A Sociological Study of Religion's Impact on Politics, Economics and Family Life. Doubleday, New York, 1961, pp. 120–192.

Lipset, S. M., *Political Man:* The Social Bases of Politics. Doubleday, Garden City, N.Y., 1960, pp. 53–60.

Lipset, S. M. and Martin Trow, "Reference Group Theory and Trade Union Wage Policy," in *Common Frontiers of the Social Sciences*. Edited by Mirra Komarovsky. Free Press, Glencoe, Ill., 1957, pp. 391–411.

Lipset, S. M., Martin Trow, and James Coleman, *Union Democracy:* The Internal Politics of the International Typographical Union. Free Press, Glencoe, Ill., 1956, pp. 113–120 and 236–331.

McClelland, D. C., *The Achieving Society*. D. Van Nostrand, Princeton, N.J., 1961, pp. 356–373.

Maccoby, Herbert, "Controversy, Neutrality, and Higher Education," *American Sociological Review*, Vol. 25, December, 1960, pp. 844–893.

Mannheim, Karl, *Ideology and Utopia*. Harcourt, Brace, New York, 1952.

Mason, W. S., *The Beginning Teacher:* Status and Career Orientations. U.S. Government Printing Office, Washington, 1961.

Mead, Margaret and Rhoda Metraux, "The Image of the Scientist Among High-School Students: A Pilot Study," *Science*, Vol. 126, August, 1957, pp. 384–390.

Mead, Margaret, *et al.*, "Marrying in Haste in College," *Columbia University Forum*, Spring, 1960, pp. 31–34.

Merton, R. K., *Social Theory and Social Structure*, rev. ed. Free Press, Glencoe, Ill., 1957.

Miller, Norman, "Academic Climate and Student Values," paper presented at the Fifty-Fourth Annual Meeting of the American Sociological Society, Chicago, September, 1959.

Mitchell, R. E., *Voting for Education* (forthcoming.)

Moos, M. C., *et al.*, *The Campus and the State*. Johns Hopkins Press, Baltimore, 1959.

Morgan, James, *et al.*, *Income and Welfare in the United States*. McGraw-Hill, New York, 1962, pp. 415–424.

Riesman, David, "Some Observations on the Interviewing in the Teacher Apprehension Study," in *The Academic Mind:* Social Scientists in a Time of Crisis. Edited by P. F. Lazarsfeld and Wagner Thielens, Jr. Free Press, Glencoe, Ill., 1958.

Riesman, David and Christopher Jencks, "The Viability of the American College," in *The American College*. Edited by Nevitt Sanford. John Wiley & Sons, New York, 1962, pp. 105–106.

Roethlisberger, F. J. and W. J. Dickson, *Management and Worker*. Harvard University Press, Cambridge, 1937.

Rosen, B. C., "Race, Ethnicity and the Achievement Syndrome," *American Sociological Review*, Vol. 24, February, 1959, pp. 47–60.

Rosenberg, Morris, *Occupations and Values*. Free Press, Glencoe, Ill., 1958.

Rummel, J. F., *An Introduction to Research Procedures in Education*. Harper & Bros., New York, 1958.

Sanford, Nevitt, ed., *The American College*. John Wiley & Sons, New York, 1962.

Selvin, H. C. and W. O. Hagstrom, "Determinants of Support for Civil Liberties," *British Journal of Sociology*, Vol. 1, April, 1960, pp. 51–73.

Smith, H. L. and J. R. Smith, *An Introduction to Research in Education.* Educational Publications, Bloomington, Ind., 1959.

Stouffer, S. A., *The American Soldier:* Adjustment During Army Life, Vol. 1. Princeton University Press, Princeton, 1949.

Stouffer, S. A., *Communism, Conformity and Civil Liberties:* A Cross-Section of the Nation Speaks its Mind. Doubleday, Garden City, N.Y., 1955.

Strodtbeck, F. L., "Family Integration, Values and Achievement," in *Talent and Society.* Edited by D. C. McClelland, *et al.* D. Van Nostrand, Princeton, N.J., 1958.

Sussman, Leila and G. N. Levine, *The Entering Freshman at M.I.T.* (mimeo). Massachusetts Institute of Technology, Cambridge, 1958.

Sussman, Leila, *Freshman Morale at M.I.T.* Massachusetts Institute of Technology Press, Cambridge, 1960.

Toby, Jackson, "Hoodlum or Business Man: An American Dilemma," in *The Jews: Social Patterns of an American Group.* Edited by Marshall Sklare. Free Press, Glencoe, Ill., 1958, pp. 542–550.

Travers, R. M. W., *An Introduction to Educational Research.* Macmillan, New York, 1958.

Trow, Martin, "Some Implications of the Social Origins of Engineers," *Scientific Manpower,* National Science Foundation, Washington, D.C., 1958, pp. 67–74.

Trow, Martin, "Small Businessmen, Political Tolerance, and Support for McCarthy," *American Journal of Sociology,* Vol. 64, November, 1958, pp. 270–281.

Trow, Martin, "Cultural Sophistication and Higher Education," in *Selection and Educational Differentiation.* Field Service Center and Center for the Study of Higher Education. Berkeley, 1959, pp. 107–125.

Weber, Max, *From Max Weber:* Essays in Sociology. Translated and edited by H. H. Gerth and C. W. Mills. Oxford University Press, New York, 1946, chap. 2.

Whitney, F. L., *The Elements of Research,* 3rd. ed. Prentice-Hall, New York, 1950.

Wilson, A. B., "Residential Segregation of Social Classes and Aspirations of High School Boys," *American Sociological Review,* Vol. 24, December, 1959, pp. 836–845.

The Survey Method in

Social Work:
Past, Present, and Potential

by Fred Massarik
University of California,
Los Angeles

A Historical Prelude

The Position of Survey Methods in Social Work Research

The Changing Survey Concept

Obstacles to the Use of the Survey Method in Social Work

Emphasis on Individual Uniqueness. Problems in Manpower and Training. Pragmatic Short-Term Research Orientation

Recent Applications of the Survey Method in Social Work Research

The Client as Focus of Survey Research

Surveys of Need. Surveys of "Clients in Process." Surveys of Effect

Social Work's Professional, Occupational, and Organizational Matrix as Focus of Survey Research

Surveys of the Practicing Social Worker. Surveys of Entry into, Training for, and Exit from the Social Work Profession. Surveys of Clients and Public Concerning Social Worker and Social Work. Surveys of Agency Operations and Organizational Effectiveness

The Unfulfilled Potential

When Not to Use the Survey

Sampling: Whom Should We Study?

Field Work: "One-Shot" or "Multi-Shot" Surveys?

Data Analysis and Re-analysis: Can We Become More Flexible?

The Survey Report: Final or Open?

Conclusions

The Survey Method in Social Work:
Past, Present, and Potential*

T HIS CHAPTER examines the role the survey plays in research in social work—its historical background, current use, and especially its promise for the future. The task is complicated by the fact that rigid boundaries cannot, and should not be drawn around fields of practice or inquiry. Where "social work" leaves off and where other disciplines begin is a matter of some conjecture, although the baselines of social work can be drawn with a measure of success.

As a working guide, it is convenient to distinguish "social work" from "social welfare." The former may be regarded as a discipline of professional practice, with particular institutional settings and specific modes for helping people to meet personal and social needs. Social agencies—private and public—and planning councils are typical social work institutions. Social group work and casework are characteristic modes, or practice specialities. Areas such as community organization are developing their own identities within social work.

Social welfare goes beyond social work, to encompass other helping approaches—for instance, aspects of vocational guidance and public health—and the early non-professional views of social reform. As we consider survey approaches in the historical review that follows, we are concerned properly with "social welfare," and with the varied attempts to improve community conditions as influenced by the results of surveys.

Subsequently, however, the focus of our attention will be on "social work" as a specific discipline, and our concern with survey research will be limited primarily to surveys conducted by social work researchers, for use within the profession. This means that studies published in social work journals on problems of casework and group work will be emphasized

*Special thanks are due to Ernest Greenwood for his detailed and helpful comments, both written and verbal, at all stages of this project, and to Charles Y. Glock for his incisive but supportive evaluations, no less than for his unfailing patience. I should also like to express my appreciation to Byron W. Evans, David Franklin, Eugene Bender, Bertram Gold, Eugene Levine, Olive Stone, Harold Moncrief, Leonard S. Cottrell, and other staff of the Russell Sage Foundation for their helpful suggestions.

more than investigations reported in the sociological literature. Many interesting publications in neighboring fields, notably in sociology and social psychology (on topics such as delinquency or group dynamics), are beyond the bounds of our review, and working reports which are not generally available, whatever their merits, are also not cited. These delimitations are intended to highlight the most authoritative part of the literature on applications of the survey method to professional social work, rather than its peripheral areas.

The plan for the chapter is simple. Following a *historical prelude, the position of survey methods* in social work will be assessed. We will note how the concept "survey" in social welfare has changed over the years, shifting emphasis from social reform to systematic research methodology. Here, we shall also consider a number of obstacles to the effective employment of the method. Next we will review *recent applications of the survey method* in social work, particularly research on clients, and on professional, occupational, and organizational problems. The review will be selective and illustrative, seeking to provide some indication of the range of survey uses, some more and others less rigorous, some large-scale and others small-scale. Finally, we will speculate about the survey method's *unfulfilled potential* in social work research and suggest how the method might be used to greater advantage.

It is well to make clear at the outset that no amount of improvement in technique or methodology can take the place of adequate formulation of concept and theory. The survey method will prove to be optimally useful only when underlying theory on topics such as need, process and effect of social work is clarified, and when creative conceptual frameworks and insightful hypotheses become available as bases for investigation.

A Historical Prelude

No single definition of the "survey method" remains fixed for all time. The terms "survey" and "survey method" antedate by centuries the development of social work as a field of professional practice. Even ancient Egypt and the Greece of Herodotus reputedly made use of survey-like procedures. But as we focus on social welfare, we note especially in the 18th and 19th century outpouring of "survey" approaches to the study of social life. These inquiries primarily sought to establish a factual basis for achieving human betterment or, if you will, for raising the level of social welfare. Young, in her research methods text *Scientific Social Surveys and Research,* reviews the pioneering efforts of John Howard, Frederic LePlay, Charles

Booth, B. S. Rowntree, Arthur Bowley, and Hubert Llewelyn Smith.[1] The *leitmotiv* of these early surveys was the compilation of facts relating to social problems, primarily to establish a basis for social reform. Howard dealt with the study of prison conditions; LePlay was concerned with the lot of the working man; Charles Booth, in his studies of the *Life and Labor of the People of London,* centered his investigations on poverty, a subject which also motivated the work of Rowntree, Bowley, and H. L. Smith.

The survey's early stress on social reform persists in Young's definition which emphasizes social welfare objectives, not methodology or theory. Young notes the survey's concern with ". . . the formulation of *a constructive program of social reform and ameliorization* of . . . current or immediate conditions of a social pathological nature, which have definite geographic limits and definite social implications and social significance." Only then does she allude to method, observing that ". . . these conditions can be *measured and compared* with situations which can be accepted as a model." (ital. mine).[2]

The beginnings of the survey method in social welfare drew vigor from direct, often zealous, concern with a troubled social environment. The pioneers of the survey did not choose an abstract theoretical approach, nor were they preoccupied with system and rigor as ends in themselves. Nonetheless, these early investigators made important contributions to method. Their orientation was empirical rather than speculative; data-gathering in the field was its essence. Statistical application appeared, including innovative uses of probability theory as in Bowley's sampling procedures.[3]

While this work was progressing in England, interest in the survey as an approach to social change was also growing dramatically in the United States. No history of social research, and surely no review of research in social welfare or social work, can afford to ignore the Pittsburgh survey begun under the direction of Paul Kellogg in 1909.[4]

The Pittsburgh survey's substantive focus was the condition of the steel

1. Young, P. V., *Scientific Social Surveys and Research,* 2nd ed., Prentice-Hall, Englewood Cliffs, N.J., 1949.
2. *Ibid.,* p. 20.
3. Bowley's work circa 1912 established the pattern of developing a list of housing units in a specified geographic area, selecting for interview every *n*th unit. Bowley's writings on this and related topics span about three decades.
4. Kellogg, P. V., ed., *The Pittsburgh Survey,* 6 vols. Russell Sage Foundation, New York, 1914; Klein, Philip, *et al., A Social Study in Pittsburgh:* Community Problems and Social Services in Allegheny County. Columbia University Press, New York, 1938.

workers affected by the forces of urban life. Its approach was interdisciplinary. Its choice of methods was eclectic, including unstructured and controlled observation, the use of informants and interviews. In its own way, following the 19th century tradition of study as a tool of social reform, the Pittsburgh survey set the pattern for a vast number of later researches on American social conditions.

Another particularly significant milestone in the development of the survey in social welfare and social work was the subsequent *Social Study of Pittsburgh*. This "new" Pittsburgh survey, directed by Philip Klein, placed heavy emphasis on the analysis of the community's network of social, health and welfare agencies. But no matter how significant Klein's study proved to be in influencing thinking about social agency structure, function, and co-ordination, it added little by way of new methods.

The intimate tie between the survey concept and the development of social work in the United States was demonstrated further by the work of the Russell Sage Foundation. Kellogg's Pittsburgh survey (1909) was financed by Russell Sage soon after its organization in 1907. A great number of important subsequent publications in social work appeared under its imprint.[5]

When the Russell Sage Foundation established a Department of Surveys and Exhibits in 1912, it did so with something of a missionary intent, asserting that "the two main objectives which the department set for itself were the spreading of the survey idea and the further development of survey methods." That it was successful, directly through its own efforts and indirectly by furthering a survey-conscious *Zeitgeist,* is attested by Eaton and Harrison's massive bibliography, published in 1930 and containing references to no fewer than 2,775 surveys.[6]

As a symbol for professional communication, the word "survey" looms

5. Among others, the historically basic, Richmond, M. E., *Social Diagnosis.* Russell Sage Foundation, New York, 1917.

6. Eaton, E. A. and S. M. Harrison, *A Bibliography of Social Surveys.* Russell Sage Foundation, New York, 1930. Shelby M. Harrison's name is associated more than any other with the development of the survey under Russell Sage Foundation auspices. Harrison was instrumental in establishing the foundation's Department of Surveys and Exhibits; for many years he gave leadership to it and eventually to the foundation as a whole. It is interesting to note that some of the roots of interest in the survey method as represented by the Russell Sage Foundation's work go back directly to the work of Bowley, referred to earlier. Margaret Hogg, a Russell Sage Foundation staff member, also worked with Bowley during the 1920's; see Bowley, A. L. and Margaret Hogg, *Has Poverty Diminished?* P. S. King, London, 1925.

large in the history of American social work. Evolving from the journal *Charities and Commons,* there eventually developed the *Survey Graphic* and *Survey Midmonthly,* for many years the field's "trade organs."

In view of this long and richly-diversified history of the "survey" in social work, one might expect to find many examples of imaginative and technically advanced survey methodology in current social work research. Unfortunately, the expectations are not fulfilled. In some sense, the early views of what the suvey is, and what it is not, may have retarded the development of a rigorous survey method in social work today.

The Position of Survey Methods in Social Work Research

Konopka has noted that "In general we can say that until 1940, surveys dominated the field of social research."[7] In the 1960's, survey applications continue to abound. In order to assess the current "state of the art," we must re-examine the nature of the concept "survey" as it was first formulated, and as its emphasis has shifted in the last several decades.

THE CHANGING SURVEY CONCEPT

The term "survey," after all, originally referred to a *general* view, or to a view on *all* sides. True to this intent, many early surveys tried to encompass an extremely broad range of social phenomena. Even a cursory examination of works such as those of Booth, Kellogg, or Klein reveals the wide scope of subject matter covered. This tendency to deal with the vast and complex through the device of the survey is reflected in the textbooks of some decades ago. For example, in *Technique of Social Surveys,* Elmer develops a "general outline for a comprehensive social survey," which includes, among others, the following topics: population density and distribution, nationality, domestic life and vital statistics, the community's distribution of wealth and industries, group relationships, political organizations, legislative functions, the courts, the entire range of charitable institutions (child care facilities, agencies serving homeless men, juvenile delinquents, etc.), recreation and amusements, education, libraries, music and art, and the press.[8] It is evident that the survey indeed aspired to become a "general view" and a "view on all sides."

But the meaning of the term "survey" has changed considerably. In

7. See Konopka, Gisela, "Changing Definitions and Areas of Social Work Interest," *Social Work Journal,* Vol. 36, April, 1955, p. 57.
8. Elmer, M. C., *Technique of Social Surveys.* Jesse Ray Miller, Los Angeles, 1927, pp. 26–27.

present social research usage it is viewed with a more precise methodological focus. For instance, Glock points out that the survey seeks *"standardized* information from or about the subjects being studied."[9] Writers like
Campbell and Katona stress *"systematic* collection of data from populations
or samples of populations through the use of personal interviews or other
data-gathering devices."[10]

Thus, the "survey" of former days and the survey as it evolved through
the 1940's are but distant cousins, related by a common heritage of empirical commitment, but differing significantly in their research technologies.
The massive "let's study everything" survey has come to be relatively rare
though probably not quite extinct, to be replaced for the most part by
more delimited exercises in survey method.

OBSTACLES TO THE USE OF THE SURVEY METHOD IN SOCIAL WORK

Emphasis on individual uniqueness. The specific character that social work
has assumed as a field of professional practice has created certain barriers to
the full realization of the survey technique's potential. A major complication
is created by the fact that individual uniqueness, rather than generalization, is emphasized. In a classic statement of casework method (1917),
Richmond spoke of the purpose of social casework as "the social treatment
of *individuals.*"[11] In recent time, a synthesis of individual- and group-oriented
methods has evolved; but in spite of new vistas in family therapy, for instance, the individual continues to receive the major share of attention.

It may be assumed that since the basic working unit of the survey is
typically the individual—a respondent sought out by the interviewer—the
individual-oriented casework approach would establish a climate sympathetic to the use of survey methodology. Certainly the notion of interaction
with another person in an interview setting is very familiar to the social
worker. The stressing of individual uniqueness with its clinical overtones
has, however, tended to retard development of methods in social work that
seek broad generalization and that *abstract* from individual behavior. Because much research generally, and surveys in particular, employ response
categories amenable to statistical manipulation, many practitioners regard

9. See p. xvi.
10. See Campbell, Angus and George Katona, "The Sample Survey: A Technique for
Social Science Research," in *Research Methods in the Behavioral Sciences.* Edited by
Leon Festinger and Daniel Katz. Dryden Press, New York, 1953, pp. 16–17.
11. Richmond, M. E., *op. cit.* Ital. mine.

such approaches as mechanical, and as poor substitutes for exploration-in-depth of individual dynamics.[12]

Problems in manpower and training. Another obstacle relates to manpower and training for social work research. The number of social work researchers is insufficient and many of those in the field are not well trained in survey techniques. Among recent social work graduates but a small fraction are specifically attracted to research. Although special programs, such as one supported by the Eli Lilly Foundation at the University of California (Berkeley) and another by the Russell Sage Foundation at the University of Michigan and at Columbia, have endeavored to improve the situation, *less than one per cent* of the 1963 social work graduates were employed in the field's research work.

The most active social work researchers, the members of the Research Council of the National Association of Social Workers, come from very diverse academic specializations. This diversity has had a mixed impact on how much and how well survey methods are used. Scholars with varying kinds of backgrounds are, of course, guided by differing intellectual assumptions and research philosophies. Some are very familiar with survey methods, particularly those recently trained. Others lean toward qualitative, clinical approaches and shy away from formal survey methodology, which they find to be overly rigid and intellectually uncomfortable.

Pragmatic short-term research orientation. Finally, there is the not unmixed blessing of the uses to which social work research is put. Many of the investigations serve primarily as a basis for planning and action. Guided by a short-term, pragmatic orientation, large numbers of these studies fail to find their way into the printed monograph, book, or journal. Welfare planning councils notably, and other agencies, conduct substantial inquiries without, however, doing much more than distributing reports on a "by re-

12. This tendency should be considered in the light of occupational trends in social work. It is clear that the practice specialty particularly concerned with individual uniqueness—social casework—will continue to be a very substantial component of the profession. A recent publication of the National Association of Social Workers (*Personnel Information,* Vol. 8, January, 1965, p. 35) shows that 67 per cent of male social work graduates and 79 per cent of female graduates are employed in direct service casework positions. When Richmond attempted a similar computation nearly fifty years ago, her estimate of social workers in New York City employed in casework was about 56 per cent: Richmond, M. E., *op. cit.,* p. 25.

quest" basis.[13] Because of the prevalence of such "fugitive" publications, it becomes difficult to assess the total picture, and many surveys lie buried in relatively inaccessible places. Further, the publication style of most social work journals is such that little is said about details of method. Specifics of sample design and statistical procedures often are unreported. Evaluating the results and building on the work of others thus becomes difficult.

The net effect of the several factors cited has been to retard the effective use of the survey method in social work research.

Recent Applications of the Survey Method in Social Work Research

Maas and Polansky, both influential members of the social work research community, stress the importance of the survey as a method, commenting that ". . . the ability to plan and conduct an adequate survey is an essential part of the equipment of every professional social work researcher."[14] While noting its prevalence in the collection of original data, Maas and Polansky focus on the descriptive function of the survey, "by and large, the purpose of any survey is to get a valid *description* of a situation of interest" (ital. theirs).[15]

Along similar lines, Young says, "(the) social *surveyor* . . . does not formulate hypotheses nor suppositions about social phenomena, as a social *researcher* does; rather the social survey proceeds from known and established facts. Neither does he, as does the social researcher, formulate theories or laws in an attempt to explain processes, patterns, similarities or dissimilarities which apply to all typical phenomena. . ." (ital. mine).[16]

Wolins observes that, "survey research comes early in the development of the profession. There is a search for relationships in the face of general ignorance, and a descriptive survey is started which seeks to find out what has happened and to whom. When this information becomes available, the

13. For comments on organizations sponsoring surveys and other research in social work, see Karpf, M. J., "Surveys and Research in Present-Day Social Work," in *Scientific Social Surveys and Research*. Edited by P. V. Young, *op. cit.*, p. 65ff; and Finestone, Samuel, "Some Requirements for Agency-Based Research," *Social Casework*, Vol. 44, March 1963, pp. 132–136.
14. See Maas, H. S. and N. A. Polansky, "Collecting Original Data," in *Social Work Research*. Edited by N. A. Polansky. University of Chicago Press, Chicago, 1960, p. 142.
15. *Ibid.*, p. 142.
16. Young, P. V., *op. cit.*, pp. 115–116.

focus shifts: 'what was done?' or 'why did it happen?' Then the descriptive survey with its broad sweep and relatively shallow inquiry becomes inadequate; case studies and experimental studies usually follow."[17]

The positions of Maas, Polansky, Young, and Wolins, who generally regard the survey as blandly empirical, exploratory, and superficial—a systematic reportorial technique which examines a natural environment, largely without conceptual constraint or manipulation of data—still appear to be widely held in social work. The survey's capacity to assist in *explaining* human phenomena remains relatively undeveloped.

The point that the survey has potential for purposes other than description has been made elsewhere in this volume. Even its link to the experiment is closer than customarily thought. Whether the survey seeks its data by direct, personal interview or indirectly as through the mail questionnaire, whether it selects samples or covers entire populations, whether it is structured or unstructured, the survey provides data that lend themselves to *ex post facto* experimentation.[18] This procedure permits the re-examination of available data in a kind of "on-paper" simulation of experimental conditions. Methods such as these are particularly promising in social work where intentional experimental manipulations still are rare, costly, and complex.

But it is also possible to administer data-gathering instruments normally identified with the sampling survey, such as the interview, in situations embodying conventional experimental designs. For instance, one may conceive of a series of laboratory experiments involving the behavior of a large number of individuals in a large number of groups, in which original data are obtained by conducting interviews with a sample of individuals in a sample of the experimental groups. In this sense, the individuals taking part in an experiment may themselves become subjects of a sample survey, and survey results may help to "explain" experimental outcomes.

THE CLIENT AS FOCUS OF SURVEY RESEARCH

Clients—the recipients of social work services—continue to be the favorite subject of the survey in social work. They are surveyed at all stages of their relationship to the social work process. Sometimes they are studied as *potential* clients. This is often the case in surveys seeking to measure

17. Polansky, N. A., ed., *op. cit.,* p. 252.
18. See Greenwood, Ernest, *Experimental Sociology:* A Study in Method. King's Crown Press, New York, 1945.

need for a service. They may be *active* clients, and then the survey may focus on their present perceptions of family adjustment or on their views of social worker and service effectiveness. And as *past* clients, they may be interviewed in follow-up studies examining the imputed long-range effects of the social work experience.

Accepting the temporal relationship between clients and social work, we shall consider three major survey emphases: surveys of *need* for service; surveys of client characteristics and events occurring during the social work *process*; and surveys of *effect* or outcome.[19]

Surveys of need. The concept of "need" in social work is used widely in planning and in research but, in spite of several efforts to define it rigorously, it continues to be employed with a variety of meanings. Need has been viewed as a gap existing between services offered and services required; it has been measured by indices based on census characteristics suggesting the existence of undesirable community conditions; and it has been studied in terms of the demands of one or another group of people for a particular program. These approaches focus in common on some population—its characteristics or perceptions—as a basis for the measurement of need. This concern with population characteristics may be the key factor in the wide use of the survey as a tool in the study of need. The range and potential of its applications is suggested by a review of need studies prepared by Carter.[20] Of the several studies Carter selects as illustrative of research in this area, nearly all make use of some form of survey methodology:

19. Basically, these are study types 1, 2, and 3 of the classification proposed by Klein, Philip and I. C. Merriam, *The Contribution of Research to Social Work.* American Association of Social Workers, New York, 1948; as used, for instance, in the section on "Research in Social Work," in Kurtz, R. H., ed., *Social Work Yearbook.* National Association of Social Workers, New York, 1960, p. 508. For other categorizations of social work research, see Konopka, Gisela, *op. cit.,* p. 59, and Greenwood, Ernest, "Social Work Research: The Role of the Schools," *Social Service Review,* June, 1958. Also of interest is the classification system used by Owen, M. I., ed., *Inventory of Research,* published by the National Association of Social Workers in 1960; it distinguishes major subject matter rubrics of practice methodology, program activities, agency structure and administration, and community processes and epidemiology. Further, it focuses on quantitative and qualitative descriptive studies (including surveys), experimental design studies, measurement design studies, case method studies, and historical studies.
20. Carter, G. W., "Measurement of Need," in *Social Work Research.* Edited by N. A. Polansky, *op. cit.,* pp. 201–222.

The first study, concerned with maternity and infant care, employed interviews with servicemen's wives in a specified geographic area who had given birth during a sample week or month. For study of this group, "a 25% stratified probability sample was chosen from a population of 286 cases."

The second study, concerned with needs for a therapeutic nursery, was based on a series of related samples, one composed of pediatricians, clinical psychologists and psychiatrists—50% included in a mail sample survey, with a sub-sample reached by personal follow-up interviews—and samples of agency executives and staffs.

The third study, concerned with the assessment of need for a dental clinic in a large urban center, employed a variety of interview and questionnaire approaches, as well as ratios and other indices to measure the gap existing between available resources and demand for service.

A fourth study, focusing on needs for Jewish child care programs, primarily employed case records analysis, in its own way—as we shall note later—a distant relative of the survey method.

Finally, a study of the needs of adolescent girls, conducted by the University of Michigan Survey Research Center rather than by social work researchers, made use of a multi-stage probability sample of some 1,900 girls in grades 6 through 12, with responses obtained by several questionnaire forms.[21]

Sampling methods employed in need surveys range from relatively informal approaches, such as the interviews with agency executives in the study of Jewish child care needs, to highly systematic procedures, like those used in the multi-stage probability sample of adolescent girls. While it is common enough to break down need survey results by various general cate-

21. *Ibid*, pp. 208–214. The specific references cited by Carter are (in alphabetical order): Carter, G., E. Reznick, and G. Roman, "Maternity and Infant Care Provisions for Servicemen's Dependents," *Journal of the American Medical Association*, Vol. 153, 1953, pp. 51–54; Federation of Jewish Philanthropies of New York, *To Serve the Children Best*. New York, 1956; Massarik, Fred, *A Study of Needs for a Specialized Nursery School Program*. Los Angeles Jewish Community Council, Research Service Bureau, Los Angeles, 1958; Survey Research Center, Institute for Social Research, *Adolescent Girls: A Nationwide Study of Girls Between Eleven and Eighteen Years of Age Made for the Girl Scouts of the United States*. University of Michigan Press, Ann Arbor, 1956; and Welfare Council of Metropolitan Chicago, *Survey of Dental Clinics in Metropolitan Chicago, 1956–57*. Chicago, 1958.

gories—age, sex, geographic location, etc.—the studies noted leave something to be desired by way of sophistication in treatment of the data. This lack may be accounted for in large part by the scantiness of theoretical formulation underpinning many research designs. Often devised on an *ad hoc* basis, typically under auspices of a welfare planning council or agency to deal with some immediate problem of community concern, need surveys tend to focus on relatively obvious variables, pragmatically defined and superficially "reasonable" in the eyes of community organization workers, agency executive, or lay committee. Theoretic schemata of significant generality and explanatory power still are rare in the literature of the need survey, and little systematic knowledge has accumulated from this kind of inquiry.

In the studies concerned with client characteristics, attitudes, and the like, the focus typically is on the individual client, separate from others—as though the researcher were examing a pebble in a pile of pebbles. This is so even though these characteristics and attitudes may include the client's perception of relationships that link him to the social world around him. For instance, in the study of adolescent girls, some questions dealt with dating; however, rarely was an effort made to survey the *reciprocal* perceptions of the boys involved, or the perceptions of the girls' parents. And though the social context as defined, for instance, by school or community, becomes a useful device in delimiting or specifying the study population, there is little use of school, community, or of any other broader configuration as more than a descriptive concept in survey analysis. There are few studies that systematically sample from among some specified group of agencies, neighborhoods, or cities.[22]

In addition to the inquiries on relatively specific needs, such as therapeutic nursery or infant care needs, the literature abounds with more general across-the-board studies, exploring the needs for welfare services in some rather large geographic area. In intent representing the tradition of the early "surveys," these are "community studies" or "population studies." Prompted sometimes by major shifts in society, such as "flight to the suburbs" or the increasing number of aged, or in response to some acute problem, such as an alarming rise in delinquency, studies of this kind seek a

22. However, for an approach using "community" matching to take into account variables relevant to a study design, see Maas, H. S., and R. E. Engler, Jr., *Children in Need of Parents*. Columbia University Press, New York, 1959, especially pp. 406–407.

comprehensive background of facts to guide many aspects of welfare planning. The survey technique is a "natural" for this sort of research, especially as actual and potential clients residing in a certain geographic area constitute the population of major interest.

Two somewhat different approaches to population or community study are illustrated by a project conducted in Cleveland, Ohio, and by a study conducted by the Jewish Community Federation of Greater Lynn, Massachusetts.[23] The Hough area study of Cleveland is characteristic of straightforward sociological research applied to social work planning problems. It employed a random sample of some 400 families, drawn from a total of about 21,000 dwelling units. Noting the growth of Negro population in the area, from 5 per cent in 1950 to 52 per cent in 1957, and the shift from middle-class to lower social rank, the study falls clearly under the rubric "descriptive." It represents the typical population survey method—cross-sectional sampling of people in a specific locality, whose characteristics are relevant inputs for the social welfare planning process.

A different strategy is illustrated by the Lynn, Massachusetts study. With the objective of reaching *all* of the community's estimated 3,200 Jewish families, the telephone interview was chosen as the primary technique. With the aid of 150 volunteers, an excellent response rate was reported—better than 91 per cent by telephone and an additional 5 per cent by direct interview. It was recognized that the complete coverage telephone technique would place constraints on the depth of the interviews and that inquiries would need to be confined to specific, modestly delimited information.

The Hough and Lynn studies both examined the characteristics of relatively large, undifferentiated populations—the former, all people living in the community, the latter, an area's entire Jewish population. There is little advance formulation of hypotheses concerning the particular response patterns expected and of their implications for specifying one or another welfare need. The study population is treated initially as something of a homogeneous entity whose characteristics are elicited by the survey itself. Such studies often provide guidance for social welfare planning only through vague, inductive "conclusions" at their very end. They may crudely paint

23. See White, R. C. and M. B. Sussman, *Hough, Cleveland, Ohio:* The Study of Social Life and Change. Western Reserve University Press, Cleveland, 1959; and Stein, A. M., "The Population Study as A Tool in the Community Planning Process," *Journal of Jewish Communal Service,* Vol. 34, Fall, 1957, pp. 78–83.

the background for general social planning, but rarely examine in depth any one planning problem.

Surveys of "clients in process." In the course of studies such as those cited above, current recipients of services may be reached, but their inclusion is incidental and their special characteristics are rarely focused upon or elucidated. But what about surveys specifically dealing with people who are agency clients *at the time of study?*

There is considerable feeling in the social work community, perhaps particularly by casework practitioners, that to "do research" on the client *while he is a client* may be a dangerous practice; the assumption is that to use the client as a "guinea pig" while he is involved in a helping relationship with the agency interferes with the helping process itself. As a result, the client has been studied *indirectly,* most frequently as seen through the eyes of the caseworker. Perhaps somewhat less reluctance has been displayed with respect to the study of the client in group work, though such studies also are few.[24]

However, even in casework, surveys of clients while they are clients are not entirely lacking. For example, a study covering agencies affiliated with the Family Service Association of America obtained nearly perfect (99.7 per cent) coverage of a one-day sample of applicants for casework service. While not probing deeply, this inquiry provided a significant overall view of the characteristics of a large client population, including typical demographic variables specifically germane to the casework process (e.g., referral source, the nature of the client's problem, and social class patterns).[25]

A rather different approach is illustrated by Vincent's study of unmarried mothers. After locating his respondents through physicians and other sources, Vincent collected data by direct personal interview and psychological testing.[26] This study shows considerable methodological sophistication,

24. See for instance, Shyne, A. W., "Casework Research: Past and Present," *Social Casework,* Vol. 43, November, 1962, pp. 467–473, especially p. 469. Shyne comments that "research on the client has been restricted by the fact that the principal source of data has been the caseworker or the case record. Exclusive reliance on caseworker's judgments as data seems, however, decreasing."
25. Family Service Association of America, *Patterns in Use of Family Agency Service.* New York, 1962.
26. Vincent, C. E., *Unmarried Mothers.* Free Press of Glencoe, New York, 1961.

considering the differential significance of clients' characteristics that may be related to the pregnancy, as contrasted with those that may reflect stable, long-term patterns. Further, Vincent's design skillfully deals with problems of sampling representativeness uniquely arising in the study of a condition often kept secret because of a prevailing social stigma.

Still another illustration of survey research on clients during the period of their clienthood is furnished by a recent study of young adult participation in community center programs.[27] This study, sampling community center members and non-members (as well as agency board members, staff, and community leaders), furnished data that made possible comparisons between persons actively involved in a community center program and those who did not participate. The previously mentioned study of applicants for casework service provided comparisons of clients with the general non-client population by means of census data, while the study of community center clients made it possible, by means of sub-samples, to contrast the characteristics of center clients and non-clients. Designs providing such comparisons add significantly to the explanatory power of the study and to its capacity for facilitating useful interpretations.

Surveys of effect. Next we consider the survey as an approach to studies of effect or outcome. Wolins illustrates the nature of surveys of effect, citing a number of studies varying considerably in sophistication of design and precision of measurement.[28] Among others, he refers to early unsystematic evaluative surveys such as those conducted during the last quarter of the 19th century. One of these inquired somewhat vaguely into the success of placement in "kindly, Christian homes of wayward boys from the streets of New York." Wolins also reviews more recent effect studies, including investigations of the amount of personal and social change presumably attributable to casework.[29] Of special relevance to surveys of effect are a num-

27. Specht, Harvey, "Report on the Findings of the Study of Jewish Young Adults and the Jewish Community Center," *Journal of Jewish Communal Service*, Vol. 41, Winter, 1964, pp. 175–185.

28. Wolins, Martin, "Measuring the Effect of Social Work Intervention," in *Social Work Research*. Edited by N. A. Polansky, *op. cit.*, pp. 252–254.

29. Though primarily of methodological rather than substantive significance, still the best known research concerning the effects of casework is that of Hunt, J. McV., L. S. Kogan, and Margaret Blenkner, *Testing Results in Social Casework: A Field-Test of the Movement Scale.* Family Service Association of America, New York, 1950; and Hunt, J. McV. and L. S. Kogan, *Measuring Results in Social Casework: A Manual*

ber of fundamental questions raised by Hill concerning use of secondary sources, such as case records, as raw material for the study of social work outcomes. He asks, for instance, "Is the evidence discerned by the case-worker and recorded in his case record accurate and sufficiently complete to support valid judgments . . . ?"[30]

Much evaluative research, especially in casework, rests squarely upon the case record as a data source and upon an expert, or "judge," as the instrument of evaluation. In a broad sense, the case record shares certain common elements with the interview schedule or protocol of conventional survey research. Though unlike the survey interview in that it is not normally fully systematic or standardized, the case record is a written record documenting events that transpired in an interview situation.[31] The use of case records for research purposes, therefore, is in some measure analogous to certain survey research procedures, particularly those involved in analysis of protocols resulting from open-ended interviews and unstructured questions.[32] When a technician employing content analysis is required to impose a systematic classification or rating, he performs a function similar to that of a "judge" making determinations of degree of movement in evaluating casework outcome.[33]

Occasionally, efforts are made to develop the case record as a standardized abstract of what occurred in the course of the casework process. Here,

---

on Judging Movement. Family Service Association of America, New York, 1950; and a number of subsequent publications. This approach and its variants, though of some interest here because of its concern with past clients, probably doesn't fit readily within the usual definition of "survey method" as used in this paper. An example of a rigorous experimental evaluation of outcomes is Meyer, H. J., E. F. Borgatta, and W. C. Jones, *Girls at Vocational High:* An Experiment in Social Work Intervention. Russell Sage Foundation, New York, 1965.

30. In French, D. G., *An Approach to Measuring Results in Social Work.* Columbia University Press, New York, 1952, p. 150.

31. The typical survey interview, of course, does not have a therapeutic intent though incidentally, and without such intent by the survey researcher, it may turn out to have therapeutic side effects. On the other hand, the social work interview ordinarily does not seek to gather systematic data for research purposes.

32. For a useful view of content analysis as a method, see Pool, I. deS., ed., *Trends in Content Analysis.* University of Illinois Press, Urbana, 1959.

33. Concerning this problem, see Shyne, A. W., ed., *Use of Judgments as Data in Social Work Research.* National Association of Social Workers, New York, 1959; and especially, Hunt, J. McV., "On the Judgment of Social Workers as a Source for Information in Social Work Research," in *ibid.,* pp. 38–54.

more than ever, the record conceptually resembles a special kind of survey interview schedule.[34] Problems of accuracy and uniformity of recording by caseworkers (analogous to uniformity among survey interviewers) become of interest. These matters, as well as broader issues relating to evaluative research, are noted by Elizabeth Herzog as she considers alternative approaches to the assessment of change in social work.[35] Indeed, she raises the classic questions of measurement in general. How trustworthy are the categories and measurements employed? How reliable and how valid are they? The use of the case record in evaluative research places the caseworker in a role rather like that of a survey interviewer; the client may be regarded as a special kind of respondent, and the judge (or rater) performs functions similar to those of the content analyst. Thus, the case record turns out to be a relative of the interview protocol in open-ended or unstructured survey questions. Further, any sort of information, especially more objective items, may be transferred from a case record to separate forms, coded, and then treated as survey data.

Still, the hazards of using case records, prepared for purposes quite different from those of the systematic survey, are great indeed. In the past too much evaluative research has placed undue reliance on fortuitously available documents.

Studies of clients *after* they have concluded their relationship with the agency now more and more often make use of procedures other than the retrospective analysis of case records. A typical direct approach is the *follow-up study,* ranging in complexity from the small local study of clients in one agency to the ambitious, broad-scale inquiry dealing with a large category of clients scattered across the country. The follow-up study surveys the population of interest at one or several points in time after a social work process has ended. Its goal often is the assessment of effects or measurement of outcomes. In its concern with results, therefore, it resembles the analysis of case records and movement scales.

In some instances, the follow-up study may seek simply to describe the

34. See for instance the Standardized Case Recording Form (SCRF) developed by Fred Massarik and Byron Evans in connection with a study of unmarried fathers, Vista Del Mar Child Care Service and Research Service Bureau, Jewish Federation-Council, Los Angeles, 1964.
35. Herzog, Elizabeth, *Some Guidelines for Evaluative Research.* U.S. Department of Health, Education, and Welfare, Social Security Administration, Children's Bureau, Washington, 1959.

client's attitudes and behaviors. The problems of this kind of small-scale follow-up are illustrated in a recent article by Varon.[36] In Varon's inquiry "interviews were held with former clients and non-clients in order to obtain data on factors that affected their perception of the agency, and the standards and values to which the agency worker would have to accommodate himself in order to communicate with clients." Although it was the researcher's intent to reach the total population of former clients (n=24), only slightly more than half of this number were contacted successfully. Varon notes that the ex-client's response dealt primarily with the social worker rather than with the social agency; but, in view of the problems of non-response and considering the limited size of the sample, even if response had been complete, it would have been difficult to generalize this kind of finding to broader client populations.

A competent large-scale follow-up study is *Independent Adoptions*.[37] While approaching its subject matter from a variety of vantage points— including the analysis of records and a review of legal background and school information—interviews conducted in the homes of the adoptive parents made up the core of the study design. These interviews, with an average length of two to three hours, were guided by a topical outline, assuring coverage of specified items. A sample of 500 non-relative independent adoptions was the initial study focus. The sample plan considered the child's age (no child could be younger than nine years at the time of the interview), race (white children only were included in view of the relative rarity of independent adoptions of children of other races in Florida at the time of the study), and locatability (only adoptive families residing in Florida were included). Of 665 children whom the researchers tried to locate, 484, or 73 per cent, were found to be living in Florida. Careful analyses were made, especially on the basis of available records, comparing respondents located to those who could not be found: while some differences appeared, the study's authors concluded that "none of the available comparisons suggest that the distribution of outcomes would be substantially different if information had been obtained about the nonlocated families." For those contacted, a refusal rate of 10 per cent was recorded. The authors of *Independent Adoptions* were aware of the pitfalls inherent in sampling relatively mobile and occasionally unavailable clients years after

36. Varon, Edith, "Communication: Client, Community and Agency," *Social Work*, Vol. 9, April, 1964, pp. 51–57.
37. Witmer, Helen, *et al.*, *Independent Adoptions*—A Follow-Up Study. Russell Sage Foundation, New York, 1963.

the social work process under study (the independent adoption) had taken place.

Much of the analysis reports rather straightforward relationships between two variables (e.g. the parents' description of the child's temperament, and an analysis of children's handicaps), as detectable and as in fact noted by parents before or after adoption.[38] A number of multivariate analyses are reported or implied: there is, for example, an exploration of the interconnections between the way in which adoption was arranged, the socio-economic characteristics of the parents involved, parents' education, and placement age.[39] Further, sociometric data, highly relevant to meeting the study's objectives—though representing an administratively difficult survey application—as well as test results, are reported. *Independent Adoptions* illustrates the use of the survey method in social work at a high level of technical competence and with a degree of sophistication rarely encountered in this field.

Even under favorable circumstances, follow-up studies using survey method face a variety of vexing problems. Locating respondents is a persistent source of difficulty, particularly in residentially-mobile urban areas. However, in some cases the possibility of obtaining virtually complete coverage has been demonstrated.[40]

When mobility and distance prevent direct interviewing of respondents, even if they have been located, comparisons between respondents interviewed and those beyond the interviewers' reach often are made on the basis of data on objective characteristics. Data such as age and occupation, usually available in case records prepared during an early contact with the client-respondent, may prove helpful in this context. The lack of significant differences in a limited number of characteristics between those reached and those not reached is, at best, only indirect evidence that no such differences would appear in major substantive survey results.

SOCIAL WORK'S PROFESSIONAL, OCCUPATIONAL, AND
ORGANIZATIONAL MATRIX AS FOCUS OF SURVEY RESEARCH

Social work has demonstrated a continuing concern with its status as a profession, perhaps because of its relatively recent ascendancy in professionalization, or perhaps because practical problems in training, salary

38. *Ibid.,* tables 19 and 22.
39. *Ibid.,* pp. 94–95.
40. Skeels, H. M. and Marie Skodak, "Techniques for a High-Yield Follow Up Study in the Field," *Public Health Reports,* Vol. 80, March 1965, pp. 249–257.

standards, and personnel practices have persisted in the discourse throughout the years of the field's emergence.[41] But regrettably, empirical research
that might seek wider and deeper understanding of the social work profession has in fact had a halting, *ad hoc* character, accumulating data now and
then but doing little to place them into a broader theoretic context. In spite
of the existence of a variety of inquiries, mainly of the survey type, it was
noted by the chairman of a social work practice commission as recently as
1961 that:

> ... the commission was especially struck by ... the sparseness of data
> about ... membership with respect to employment, experience, educa-
> tion, salaries, ... and by the complete lack of any objective data con-
> cerning aspects of practice ... which (the National Association of
> Social Workers) ... has considered in formulating national policy.[42]

Surveys of the practicing social worker. While antedated by more or less
informal approaches, including statistical reviews of salary distribution and
background, systematic surveys of social workers began to appear in the
1930's.[43] These studies typically relied on mail questionnaires and often
sought to reach *all* the social workers in a specific grouping, rather than employing samples. Interview surveys have come into wider use in more
recent years, but the mail survey, now often on a sampling basis, persists as
the dominant method. Although subject to the major drawback of mail surveys—the difficulty of generalizing from returns received to include the
characteristics of those who fail to reply—the rate of response in studies
such as these is usually very satisfactory, often exceeding 60 per cent and

41. See for instance, the much-cited Flexner, Abraham, "Is Social Work a Profession?" *Proceedings of the National Conference of Charities and Corrections.* University of Chicago Press, Chicago, 1915, pp. 576–590; Addams, Jane, "Social Workers
and the Other Professions," *Proceedings of the National Conference of Social Workers,* University of Chicago Press, Chicago, 1930, pp. 50–54; Cockerill, Eleanor, "The
Interdependence of the Professions in Helping People," *The Social Welfare Forum,*
Columbia University Press, New York, 1953, pp. 137–147; Bowers, Swithun, "Social
Work as a Helping and Healing Profession," *Social Work,* Vol. 2, January, 1957, pp.
57–62; and Greenwood, Ernest, "Attributes of a Profession," *Social Work,* Vol. 2,
July, 1957, pp. 45–55.
42. Reece, S. A., "Social Work Practice: An Exploratory Study," *Social Work,* Vol. 6,
July, 1961, p. 59.
43. See, for example, "Report on Salary Scale Standards," *The Compass,* Vol. 21,
December, 1939, pp. 7–13.

going as high as a remarkable 92 per cent.[44] These impressive response rates no doubt reflect in large measure the saliency and personal significance of the subject matter—social work salaries and recommended action toward improvement of salary standards—under investigation by the generally trusted auspices of a professional membership association, such as the National Association of Social Workers. Further, these topics lend themselves to concise, objective formulation, especially suitable to mail questionnaire reply.

In addition to inquiries dealing with the economically important facts of compensation, surveys of social workers as practicing professionals explore various aspects of social work education and employment background. These include degrees received, field of practice, type of employer (e.g. agency or private practice), and years of experience.

The personal background of social workers, their ages, socio-economic characteristics, and religious preferences, have been studied, both descriptively and in their relation to aspects of practice.

Sample size often has been small in the more sophisticated designs, though substantial in the less interesting descriptive projects. Data obtained in small-scale but well-designed studies of social worker background may add much to knowledge of practice. For instance, a study by Briar indicates that the interplay between practitioner and client is affected significantly by the socio-cultural characteristics of the interacting participants.[45] Studies of relationships between the social worker's personal background and what the worker sees and does in his contact with the client no doubt have more to contribute than the simple recitations of demographic and salary characteristics that now abound.

44. Reece, S. A., *op. cit.*, p. 60; Golden, Deborah, "Selected Characteristics of NASW Members: The Second Study," *Personnel Information* (National Association of Social Workers), Vol. 8, July, 1965, p. 1 and pp. 32–35; and Becker, R. R., "NASW Salary Minimum a Reality but Maximum Still a Goal," *Personnel Information*, Vol. 4, November, 1961, p. 1 and pp. 21–24.

45. See, for example, Briar's study of a social work student population, examining interrelationship between social class membership and practice orientation: Briar, Scott, "Use of Theory in Studying Effects of Client Social Class on Students' Judgment," *Social Work*, Vol. 6, July, 1961, pp. 91–97. For a conceptual consideration of culture conflict between client and caseworker, see Pollak, Otto, "Cultural Dynamics in Casework," in *Social Casework in the Fifties*. Edited by Cora Kasius. Family Service Association of America, New York, 1962, pp. 83–92 (or in *Social Casework*, July, 1953).

Encountered less frequently, but of much interest, are surveys of social workers' attitudes toward their personal practice styles and job activities. What about the worker's view of how he actually carries out his duties, whether and how he supervises and is supervised, and the technical orientation that guides him? Though these topics certainly are more subtle than matters of dollar-and-cents and sheepskins, carefully written questions and cautious interpretation of findings derived from mail questionnaires can provide valuable, though tentative, insights into social work practice itself.[46] However, it is clear that the personal interview furnishes greater opportunity for probing intensively the crucial issues of the social worker's perception of his professional activity.

A somewhat different survey approach to the study of attitudes relating to practice is illustrated by Rawley's work in the 1950's.[47] Focusing on a small sample of "experts" (members of the Family Service Association's Committee of Study of Basic Concepts in Casework Practice, and others), he examined the extent to which there is agreement in functional or diagnostic practice orientations. He investigated not the attitudes held by the worker himself, but rather those of a sample of "informants," or raters, who indicated agreement or disagreement with general concepts and principles guiding social work practice.

Another topic of broad significance is that of attitudes toward social work as an occupation. Polansky and his associates interviewed a sample of paid-up members of a number of social work organizations in Detroit with respect to their attitudes toward the role of the social worker and toward "conflict and frustration" in the profession.[48] Although the interviews elicited much more than could have been attained by mail questionnaire, the authors were led to comment on the necessity of conducting more intensive inquiries to probe the worker's inner experience and personal dynamics. One highly significant aspect of this experience is, of course, the social worker's pattern of feelings toward the clients with whom he works. In this vein, Borgatta, Fanshel, and Meyer investigated the way in which a population of caseworkers perceived the social and personality characteris-

---

46. Reece, S. A., *op. cit.,* pp. 62–67.
47. Rawley, Callman, "A Sampling of Expert Opinion on Some Principles of Casework," *Social Casework,* Vol. 35, April, 1954, pp. 154–161.
48. Polansky, N. A., *et al.,* "Social Workers in Society: Results of a Sampling Study," *Social Casework,* Vol. 34, April, 1953, pp. 74–80.

tics of a group of clients.[49] This kind of systematic look at the social work process through the worker's eyes is very much in order, but it needs to be augmented by studies of the client's reciprocal perceptions of worker and agency.[50]

Surveys of entry into, training for, and exit from the social work profession. While surveys of social workers have considered primarily the professional actively engaged in a field of practice, there remains another set of significant questions relating to the nature of the profession as, for instance, those posed by White. He asked, "What kind of people are drawn into social work, and how does the discipline of education and practice mold them into the typical representative of the profession?"[51]

In the logic of study design, surveys of students about to enter the profession are similar to surveys of practicing social workers. But since the quest for information on salary patterns and professional status is lacking, and since it is somewhat inconvenient to construct samples from class rosters provided by geographically-separated institutions, less is known about social work students than about the professional social worker. There are the routine administratively-oriented surveys of relatively sizable student groups; but, more importantly, there are a number of small-sample inquiries examining personal and psychological characteristics of students that affect their future professional performance, and studies of the process by which a student acquires the values of the profession. Bruck, for example, explored the relationship between students' self-concepts and their casework competence (n=18), and Varley sought to identify changes in students' values attributable to social work education (n=61, beginning and graduating students).[52]

Varley's method—the comparison of student populations at different

49. Borgatta, E. F., David Fanshel, and H. J. Meyer, *Social Workers' Perceptions of Clients.* Russell Sage Foundation, New York, 1960.
50. It has been pointed out to me that recent work by Helen Perlman deals with several of these issues.
51. White, R. C., "Social Workers in Society: Some Further Evidence," *Social Casework,* Vol. 34, October, 1953, pp. 161–164.
52. Bruck, Max, "The Relationships between Student Anxiety, Self-Concept, and Students' Competence in Casework," *Social Casework,* Vol. 44, March, 1963, pp. 132–136; Varley, Barbara, "Socialization in Social Work Practice," *Social Work,* Vol. 8, July, 1963, pp. 102–109.

stages of their academic careers—suggests the potential of survey designs requiring systematic comparisons among groups for which significant differences may be expected. The use of such comparative designs is illustrated further by the work of Reid which throws light on changes in approach to casework practice that may be associated with early exposure to and later experience in social work training.[53]

To examine the reasons that people leave social work or a given agency, the exit survey, adapted from personnel administration, has been used occasionally. For example, the Girl Scouts of the U.S.A. investigated reasons for the severance of workers who left the organization in the course of an eighteen-month period.[54] With a response rate of 73 per cent, an open-end questionnaire yielded a parsimonious configuration of reasons for voluntary severance, including such factors as marriage, spouse's need to relocate, salary, supervision and volunteer-professional relationships. Little is available by way of long-range, follow-up studies that trace what happens to workers after separation from an agency, their eventual re-employment by another agency, their establishment in private practice, or their long-range career patterns.

Surveys of clients and public concerning social worker and social work. Perlman has noted that, "It is remarkable how little attention we have paid to the question of who and what the applicant (for casework services) has presumed the caseworker and agency to be."[55] But work in this area is on the upswing. In an article exploring approaches to family service research, the research director of the Family Service Association of America could cite a number of survey-type studies in which clients served as respondents, reacting to service, worker, or agency.[56] In community organization re-

53. Reid, William, "An Experimental Study of Methods Used in Casework Treatment," doctoral dissertation (D.S.W.), Columbia University, New York, June, 1963, abstracted in *Social Service Review*, Vol. 37, September, 1963, p. 349. Strictly speaking, Reid's study is not an experiment, but a survey focusing on contrasting groups, and interpreting the results in an experimental paradigm.

54. See *An Exit Study of Local Professional Workers in Girl Scouting*, Girl Scouts of the U.S.A., New York, 1954.

55. Perlman, H. H., "Intake and Some Role Considerations," *Social Casework of the Fifties*. Edited by Cora Kasius, *op. cit.*, p. 169.

56. Beck, D. F., "Potential Approaches to Research in the Family Service Field." *Social Casework*, Vol. 40, July, 1959, p. 390; citing, for instance, Polansky, N.A. and Jacob Kounin, "Clients' Reactions to Initial Interviews: A Field Study," *Human Relations*, Vol. 9, No. 3, 1956, pp. 237–264.

search, clients' views of the agency and professional setting also appear occasionally.

Now and then a general sociological investigation, particularly in the field of social stratification, incidentally includes evaluations of social work by a broad population. However, there exists a dearth of survey material on the views of the general public about social work and its functions. A recent exception, hopefully a harbinger of a trend, is a study by Bailey of a random probability sample of 1,660 adults in "Midtown," exploring their views of social casework.[57] Studies of general and student populations' perceptions of social work as a profession have been begun by Ernest Greenwood at the University of California, Berkeley.

Surveys of agency operations and organizational effectiveness. Ultimately, the setting that serves as "home base" for the social worker and within which (or from which) he performs his professional functions is the agency or some other organization.[58] In recent years, a large literature, encompassing a variety of disciplinary viewpoints, has considered the organization concept.[59] The most comprehensive treatment relating to social work is the monograph *Research in Social Welfare Administration,* edited by Fanshel.[60] As survey methods have been found to be generally helpful in the study of organizational behavior, so it is apparent that such methods deserve attention in the study of social agency operations. Stein, in his essay on organizational effectiveness, considers the concept of organization goals.[61] By means of the survey it becomes possible to make operational the nature of goals, as they are held by community leaders, agency executives, practitioners, and clients. In addition, the survey allows assessment of differential

57. Bailey, M. B., "Community Orientations Toward Social Casework," *Social Work,* Vol. 4, July, 1959, pp. 60–66. There are, however, numerous studies with a public relations focus, largely unpublished, concerning agency "image" as it affects philanthropic fund-raising campaigns.

58. A possible exception: the individual social worker, in private practice, without associates or assistants.

59. See, for instance, Litterer, J. A., *The Analysis of Organizations.* John Wiley & Sons, New York, 1965; and Schein, E. H., *Organizational Psychology.* Prentice-Hall, Englewood Cliffs, N.J., 1965, among many others.

60. Fanshel, David, ed., *Research in Social Welfare Administration.* National Association of Social Workers, New York, 1962.

61. Stein, H. B., "The Study of Organizational Effectiveness," in *Research in Social Welfare Administration.* Edited by David Fanshel, *op. cit.,* pp. 22–32.

perceptions of goals as they exist or "should" exist, and of their relative attainment. Stein also proposes longitudinal studies of agency behavior, noting the potential usefulness of survey approaches to the study of intra-organizational strains. And in mundane, but administratively vital areas such as the analysis of social welfare expenditures, the survey once more shows its usefulness. Fanshel notes Hylton's cost study which employed survey methodology, interviewing a sample of executives in residential treatment institutions.[62]

Though empirical survey applications in the study of agency operations are still relatively rare, some research in this area is finding its way into the literature. In at least one instance, survey data collected in a social work setting are reported in a volume that constitutes a contribution to organization theory in general. This is the work of Blau and Scott on the effects of supervisory style in two casework agencies.[63] In many respects, the Blau and Scott findings corroborate those obtained in industrial situations.

Examining another aspect of the organizational nexus in social work, Nettler contrasts the views of board members and those of social work personnel toward various aspects of practice and agency operations. He notes, among other things, that board members generally hold more punitive attitudes.[64] Unfortunately, while displaying many methodological and conceptual virtues, the results of Nettler's study are difficult to generalize because of the failure of nearly one-half of the original sample of community leaders to respond to the questionnaire.

A hopeful trend, but one showing only modest beginnings to date, is that of the "institutional study" in which specific relationships among persons interacting within the agency are the center of attention. For example, Piliavin studied attitudes characterizing relations between cottage parents and caseworkers in two treatment institutions.[65] His study design employed interviews yielding data on *mutual* perceptions and provides a significant insight into the nature of conflict in institutional settings.

As one contrasts studies such as the one by Piliavin with the mail ques-

62. *Ibid.,* p. 19.
63. Blau, P. M. and W. R. Scott, *Formal Organizations:* A Comparative Approach. Chandler, San Francisco, 1962, especially p. 97, p. 148, p. 160, and pp. 254–257.
64. Nettler, Gwynn, "Ideology and Welfare Policy," *Social Problems,* Vol. 6, 1959, pp. 203–212; see also Fanshel, David, "Research in Child Welfare: A Critical Analysis," *Child Welfare,* Vol. XLI, December, 1962, p. 449.
65. Piliavin, Irving, "Conflict Between Cottage Parents and Caseworkers." *Social Service Review,* Vol. 37, March, 1963, pp. 17–25.

tionnaire survey usual in the study of salary trends, one notes that, apart from the obvious difference in purpose, there exist considerable differences in complexity of conception and in size of sample. Generally an inverse relationship appears between these two elements; while the conceptually more interesting designs are limited by their modest sample sizes, the relatively simple, reportorial inquiries have the benefit of a good number of cases. This is no accident. It is easier to distribute a simple questionnaire to a large number of people than to examine complicated interpersonal relationships in going enterprises. Still, one wishes that the large-scale sampling surveys in social work might raise their sights toward greater conceptual refinement, while the institutional study and other well-conceived survey applications might reach out to encompass a broader range of social phenomena by coverage of larger representative samples.

The Unfulfilled Potential

Our review of the survey method in social work suggests that the most widespread use of the method has been in the study of clients and potential clients, especially in the assessment of need and, to a lesser extent, of effects of service. Many broad studies attempt to assess community need. Others concentrate on a client population, examining its characteristics at some stage before, during, or after receiving social work service. Frequently, it is the casework client who is the center of attention, but now more and more attention is being paid to the group work client.[66] So far, however, the potential participant in group work has been studied most often in the course of surveys focusing on a large, relatively undifferentiated population, such as people living in a certain geographic area or persons in certain age brackets. Some more recent surveys have been concerned with the social work profession and agency operations, ranging from relatively simple personnel censuses to small-scale but sophisticated institutional studies.

As we evaluate this panorama of survey applications to social work subject matter, we observe that there are some examples of imaginative, well-conceived, and carefully conducted survey research, but that the overall picture is still dominated by routine data collection, covering routinely defined, often unrepresentative samples of various populations, culminating in reports providing one or another set of descriptive statements. And

66. The National Jewish Welfare Board now has established a research center on group work at Brandeis University that, under the direction of Bernard Lazerwitz, has a strong orientation in the direction of survey use.

unfortunately with us still are the pseudo-surveys—the unsystematic, haphazard collections of data from vaguely-defined congeries of respondents by means of poorly conceived questionnaires and interviews.

Having reviewed the method's present uses, we now consider how the survey can be made a *more* effective tool in social work research. A number of methodological problems deserve special attention. (1) There is the fundamental question as to *the survey's appropriate range* of application: under what conditions is it a desirable research tool and when is it mere camouflage or inadequate surrogate for some other, more fitting method? (2) *What populations* should be the subjects of survey? Is it enough to look exclusively at the characteristics of individuals, as has been done in the past, or is it advisable to shift to the study of relationships, as between clients and social workers, or clients and their families? And would there not be increasing pay-off in surveys of entire social units, such as agencies and institutions, and of a variety of populations, each of which may contribute a somewhat different perspective to the understanding of a social work problem? (3) How about *repeated measurements* of conditions of need and of the effects of service, rather than the more usual "one-shot" approaches? Would not the careful study of change add more to our knowledge than the conventional, single cross-section at any one moment in time? (4) What about the creative use of data for purposes other than those for which they were initially collected? Can we do more by way of *ex post facto experimentation and secondary analysis,* rather than permitting to lie fallow considerable amounts of potentially useful survey data? And (5) how can we plan the *survey report* so that it becomes an open, living document instead of a way of terminating discourse.

WHEN NOT TO USE THE SURVEY

The researcher needs to improve his judgment as to when the survey should *not* be employed. Too often the terms "survey" and "study" become synonymous. It is still all too common for a social agency executive when confronted by a request for information—say, concerning accounting procedures or the amount of disability insurance in force—to announce to his board that he will "do a survey" of the situation. What he has in mind has little to do with systematic survey procedure. Further, especially in the context of "the let's look at everything" tradition, there exists the ever present temptation to "do some interviews," or to send out a questionnaire, whatever the issue at hand. As a result, though there are many survey applications in social work, the quality of these applications is, as we have suggested, not necessarily a lofty one.

Behind the query "to survey or not to survey" lies a broader area of concern that cannot be dealt with in detail in this essay—the exploration of the concepts that guide the design of research in social work. Progress has been made in specifying notions such as "need" by, for instance, Wolin's excellent paper exploring the conceptual base of community welfare studies.[67] Concepts such as "effect" or "evaluation" of social work services require further sharpening and elaboration. The nature of the social work process, though the subject of many discourses, still remains vague in many respects, so that the development of clear-cut research designs, including survey designs, is hampered.

For qualitative insights into unique social phenomena, the case method continues to be appropriate, whatever its difficulties of generalization. For the rigorous testing of causal linkages, requiring the purposeful manipulation of clearly-definable variables, the experiment continues as the method par excellence. Yet, much more remains to be done with the survey. Most of all, there is the challenge to shift emphasis from prevailing, often unimaginative and mechanical procedures to survey applications with greater explanatory power.

SAMPLING: WHOM SHOULD WE STUDY?

An early strategic issue in increasing the usefulness of the survey as a social work research tool concerns the choice of sampling units. Too often there seems to be an apparent inevitability in the selection of the individual *qua* individual as the sole unit of sampling. This preoccupation with the sampling of individuals, of course, follows the conventional pattern of survey research as it has evolved in the last few decades, especially through the polling approach. Yet it is becoming increasingly clear, on conceptual as well as on practical grounds, that the individual represents but one of many relevant realities that may be studied productively by survey techniques. The increasing concern with group methods of counseling and with family therapy suggests that the social work profession, more than ever before, recognizes the significance of group and family contexts.

It may be advisable to replace the individual as basic sampling unit, especially in research in casework and group work, with a unit that might

67. Wolins, Martin, "A Base for Community Welfare Studies," in *The Social Welfare Forum,* Columbia University Press, New York, 1954, pp. 216–233.

be designated as the *"client-in-a-relationship."* For some studies in group work, the appropriate sampling unit may be "the client-and-his-fellow-club members"; elsewhere we may want to take a systematic look at "the campaign volunteer viv-à-vis the campaign leadership," "the client and his family," or "the client and the caseworker." Further, more complex relationship links such as "client, social worker, agency" or "group worker, supervisor, agency executive" may become productive research foci. In design terms, this change in strategy would lead the researcher to seek data not simply from a given client or other individual, but also from persons in this individual's social world with whom he is engaged in particular relationships. Operationally, careful mapping of social configurations involving clients and others will be required to define the more complicated "universe" of social units, each composed of several interacting persons, which ultimately will be sampled.

Methodologically, it remains necessary in most cases to interview *individual* people, rather than groups of people gathered together at one time. The conceptual difficulties of untangling responses obtained in the group interview remain formidable, though for some problems where a group-consensual response is sought, group interviews eventually may emerge as an appropriate and manageable technique.

The development of such relational samples is not an easy matter. In the first place, it requires contacts with a substantially greater number of persons than conventional surveys—namely, all those who are involved in the relationships studied. Secondly, as the social contexts vary among individuals, issues of comparability of relational patterns among such varied sample units must be resolved. For example, in a study with a family emphasis, analyses may need to take into account different family constellations. And finally, there are the practical problems of obtaining responses from persons who may be involved only peripherally in the process under study. This may give rise to higher refusal rates, especially if these respondents are asked to discuss intimate personal relationships. Even a few instances of non-response, especially in sociometric surveys, may leave gaps in the matrix of relationships that limit severely the significance of the results.

In spite of these difficulties, a strong case can be made that the inclusion of relationship and social context as integral elements of sample design is of particular importance in social work research. The number of concepts in the behavioral sciences that have an interpersonal emphasis and that are significant for social work practice is great indeed. One needs only to consider a concept such as "role set" with its emphasis on systems of reciprocal and normative expectations among individuals, or the idea of "rapport" with its implications for client-social worker contact, to be quickly reminded of the importance of this interpersonal perspective. Family role, sick role, the role of the caseworker vis-à-vis the client—these and many other situations involving interrelated persons are highly relevant in social work. In group work, the network of interpersonal relationships, implicit in concepts such as group structure and group process, is an example of a topic that can be investigated effectively by relational sampling. This design strategy encompassing the people around the people who are usually studied may be one way to breathe life into the concept "social" in social work research.

In addition to regarding these other persons as "independent variables" with the client remaining the "dependent variable," it is possible to look upon the interpersonal context as a dependent variable in its own right. In studies of the group work process, for example, the sample unit of primary concern may be the group itself. Here it becomes appropriate to define a population composed of groups which, in turn, is sampled. Interview data, then, are obtained from the individual members of groups included in the sample, but their results are "pooled" or otherwise combined in order to provide parameters characterizing each *group* included in the sample. Development of sample survey approaches to populations of groups, and the study of group characteristics by this means to reflect the differential nature and outcomes of group work processes, constitute potentially promising kinds of survey application largely overlooked so far.

Another appropriate area for sampling units other than individuals is social work administration.[68] In search of better understanding of the internal administrative process in social agencies, we may conceive of a population whose members are not individuals but the agencies themselves. We may regard this population as being divided into a suitable number of strata, distinguishing, for example, private from public agencies, group-work from casework agencies, and agencies of varying size. For this "agency population," we may construct the necessary samples, employing research designs dealing with the administrative process itself. In the course of working out designs such as these, we may choose to test various theories of organizational functioning—for instance, those proposed by March and Simon and others—probing the nature of the administrative system,

68. See Fanshel, David, ed., *Research in Social Welfare Administration, op. cit.*

worker motivation, differential effects of supervisory techniques and executive personalities, and so forth.[69]

The proposal that samples of agencies be designed, eschewing exclusive conceptual focus on individual social workers, practitioners, or administrators, rests on the contention that the agency is a *system* of interlocking relationships, which can be understood only if it is treated as a total unit. The *interrelations* of individuals that give meaning to the systems concept become the principal study concern. Obviously, it will not do here to study individuals who have no mutual links to one another and who are scattered here and there in separate agency settings.

Sampling agencies and other institutions has its problems. This kind of research is expensive, requiring contact with substantial numbers of individuals in social units that are distant from one another, though in large urban communities it is occasionally possible to sample among units located there. Further, though some sub-sampling may be possible, it is necessary in most cases to include all personnel in the social system so that sociometric and other interpersonal patterns may be examined fully. Though designs of this kind appear ambitious, they should make possible insights into social work administration which at present are largely unavailable. Our current perceptions rest on rather ambiguous scraps of information, often derived from studies in disparate fields, that are generalized at considerable risk. Surveys dealing specifically with social agencies as systems may help to rectify the situation.

As if the task were not difficult enough, one may readily complicate it by recognizing the ever-widening ripples of interpersonal contexts within which a given social unit functions. For example, one may conceive of research designs in social agency administration which, upon sampling agencies and their personnel, move into further sampling of lay leadership, volunteer workers, and committees which are associated with these agencies.[70]

Long overdue are well-designed sampling studies of reciprocal perceptions among social workers, lay leaders, colleagues in related professions (such as psychologists, psychiatrists, and other medical doctors), and the

69. March, J. G. and H. A. Simon, *Organizations*. John Wiley & Sons, New York, 1958. For specific hypotheses, see for instance, pp. 100–101, pp. 127–128.
70. For a study in this area, see Massarik, Fred and Leo Okin, *Patterns of Center Leadership*. Jewish Centers Association and Research Service Bureau, Los Angeles, 1964.

general public. All these require sample designs aiming at relationships rather than simple collations of individual responses.

Another consideration affecting sample design relates to the concept of need for social welfare services and thence to the kinds of people who should be sampled. It is well to remind ourselves that the concept of need ultimately rests on the value systems held by a variety of relevant publics—by several definable population strata.

Often we tend to take for granted the value system that happens to be our own or that establishes a pervasive community atmosphere. Yet is is evident that the "need" for recreation, for example, is based on some value assumption that recreation is "good" because of its imputed promotion of physical and emotional health. A given value related to some condition of need stands necessarily in some hierarchic relationship to other values in the eyes of a given public: is recreation more or less important than, for instance, family counseling? It may be sobering for the board of an agency to realize that to certain potential clients a particular service—of apparent vital import as viewed by the board—appears quite unnecessary to a significant public. Of course, one may argue that potential clients are not the best judges of what is required, or that some other group in the community ought to be the judge of what is and what is not needed. But regardless of exactly who is considered to be the appropriate judge of prevailing needs, *some* group (or groups) of persons necessarily act as arbiters in specifying need. Thus, the survey method becomes a logical tool for examining systematically the views held concerning the importance of various services and programs. For example, concurrent sampling surveys may be performed to probe the attitudes toward particular needs held by groups such as (1) the lay leadership of a community planning body—for example, the board of a welfare planning council, (2) clients actually or potentially reached by the program or service, and (3) professional social workers and other specialists. Comparisons of values held by these groups, as related to services and programs, would add richness of meaning that generally is lacking when need definition is based solely on an interpretation of some set of "facts" unilaterally by one or another leadership group in the social welfare community. In studies of effect, the examination of outcome as seen by client, worker and family member simultaneously, rather than reliance on any one evaluative assessment, also should prove productive.

Similarly, in studies of the social work profession as seen through the eyes of people in the community, designs calling for samples of several strata—such as persons in other helping professions (e.g., physicians and psychologists), lay leadership bodies, and present or past recipients of service—would provide a basis for significant comparisons of views of social work's emerging professional status.

FIELD WORK: "ONE-SHOT" OR "MULTI-SHOT" SURVEYS?

In social work as elsewhere, change is the law of life; but survey applications in social work, especially the typical need studies, often reflect a "one-shot" philosophy that implicitly assumes static conditions. Many studies of need arise in response to a vaguely sensed social condition, as articulated by one or more presumably informed publics. At present, the survey design in a need study usually seeks to provide specific information which will "validate" the existence of the need, or which may indicate that the need fails to exist. The group(s) concerned with the matter expect to arrive at a definite "answer"—a yes-no conclusion. Once the decision has been made, the matter is usually dropped. It is re-opened only when some major new development or obvious cry for help makes a re-examination urgent. Though need studies are intermittent events in the stream of community planning, needs themselves, however defined, are in continuing flux.

Community planning and its research activities would profit by a philosophy that clearly recognizes this process of change. Instead of responding solely to actual or imagined crises, calling for the expansion of some service or for its retrenchment or elimination, it would be well to institute *continuing* approaches to need assessment. At least two major alternative research strategies are available.

First, programs of *successive* cross-sectional surveys could probe in standardized fashion the factors deemed to be significant in specifying need. Survey applications of this kind are not new in fields such as marketing research and political polling. Newspapers and advertisers, for example, conduct continuing home audits, examining use and acceptance of various products; the successive sample surveys, showing net changes in attitude toward one or another political candidate prior to an election, are commonplace. Yet, social work research has made little use of analogous, carefully planned, repeated need assessments.

Second is the even more promising design alternative of the *"panel"* study. Instead of selecting samples composed of different individuals in successive surveys, the study seeks to maintain contact with the *same* individuals over a period of time. This has the advantage that the process of change in viewpoint and behavior of any individual or group may be examined. Considering that need-related characteristics of communities and individuals do change over time, panel designs no doubt would be highly useful in keeping social work agencies abreast of changes in need for services.[71]

The study of clients in process, and the study of effects of social work service, constitute further opportunities for application of successive cross-sectional and panel survey plans. What transpires while social work proceeds and in its aftermath, implies change over time. Brief casework, involving only an interview or two during a short period, may not provide an adequate opportunity for repeated data collection. But if active clients increasingly become "legitimate" subjects for research interviews, a client group, defined by intake during a specified week or month, becomes an ideal panel that may reflect from time to time changes in self-concept, attitude toward worker or agency, or personal adjustment.

Re-interviewing effects and optimum spacing of the survey interviews need to be considered carefully, however, if results of such panel studies are to be interpreted meaningfully. Further, for studies of clients in casework, there remains the complex question of possible interinfluence that might prevail between the interviews conducted for research purposes and those conducted in the "helping" process.

In studies of effect, there is no reason to assume that a particular outcome at a given time is necessarily representative of future (or prior) outcomes. In some sense, then, the use of follow-up interviews at *several* time points would serve to measure the relative permanence of outcomes by hedging against temporary idiosyncratic variations, and by assessing short-term and long-term impact. The matter of longitudinal research, whether by survey or by other techniques, is, of course, an extraordinarily complicated matter.[72] It seems certain, however, that if based on adequate theory, multiple administrations of survey interviews (or occasionally of questionnaires)

71. A number of technical problems are involved in panel design. The fact that respondents move away, that they die, that they lose interest in the study, are among obstacles to the complete and efficient execution of panel studies.
72. A recent attempt to conceptualize the problems of follow-up studies and evaluations of impact of service in a related field appears in Massarik, Fred, *A Sensitivity Training Impact Model:* Some First (and Second) Thoughts on the Evaluation of Sensitivity Training. National Training Laboratories, Washington, 1965.

to the same or sequentially-chosen clients (and social workers) would strengthen significantly the study of social work process and outcome.

It may be very ambitious to contemplate survey applications in the study of need and effect that would employ continuing measurements of views held by the several different publics—and of objective, personal, and social conditions—by means of successive cross-sectional panel survey designs. Still, such massive survey approaches would go a long way toward providing the kind of dynamic and realistic information that is necessary.

DATA ANALYSIS AND RE-ANALYSIS: CAN WE BECOME MORE FLEXIBLE?

As a further step in realizing the untapped potential of the survey method in social work, it would be useful to discard the straight-jacket that treats each survey as a discrete, self-contained unit which proceeds in rather stilted motions from the formulation of a research question, to delimitation of the population, sample design, interviewing, data analysis and report preparation—the last being apparently the final, fixed end product of the survey process. These phases of design and study procedure are, of course, necessary and appropriate and deserve the methodological attention they have received. To the extent to which they take on the appearance of an immutable chain of events with little tie-in to what has gone on before and with little carry-over to the future, however, they impose unnecessary limitations. If the conceptual foundations are well constructed and if "the sample is ample" the potential value of secondary analysis of data, perhaps long after the initial survey is ostensibly completed, can hardly be exaggerated.[73]

Earlier, we alluded to *ex post facto* experimentation which permits the creation of near-experimental conditions by the manipulation of data after they have been collected. In a general survey of needs of the aged, if the number of cases is sufficient and if the design is otherwise sound, one may proceed later with data rearrangements that make it possible to contrast matched groups of aged (further controlling for sex, socio-economic status, religion, etc.), in examining, for instance, adjustment patterns of a hypothetical "experimental group" composed of participants in a Golden Age group work program, and non-participants in a contrived "control group." Here, the experimental variable is the participation in the group work program, while the outcome variable may be made operational by measures of social adjustment or by indices such as applications for admissions to homes for the aged, hospital clinic visits for minor ailments, and the like.

73. Secondary analysis involves the re-examination of data at a time later than the initial study, for purposes other than those originally intended.

Further, the secondary analysis of survey data can help to spec:
variables which seem to have the greatest potential predictive or explanatory
power in a research problem other than the one originally under study. In a
survey of volunteers working in a United Fund Campaign, intended primarily to assess their effectiveness as campaign solicitors, the question may
be posed later as to what factors in their background and attitude relate to
their own levels of philanthropic giving. Here, the data may be reanalyzed
in a manner different from that employed in the test of the initial hypothesis. Now attention shifts to establishing the degree and nature of association
between such factors as the volunteer's age, length of involvement in the
United Fund Campaign, annual income and religion, on one hand, and
giving level on the other. Though a given sample may permit only limited
and tentative measures of the patterns of association, this kind of secondary
analysis may provide clues pointing to significant empirical relationships
and theoretic constructs which in turn lay the groundwork for more definitive studies.

Under these circumstances, it is indeed true that no one survey remains
an island unto itself. In the classic tradition of scientific inquiry, carry-over
of hypothesis and data from one investigation to another becomes possible,
and data increase their effective life span with future retrieval and reanalysis continuously possible. There is nothing very new about this strategy; it
is simply surprising—and depressing—that, though considerable bodies of
survey data in social work have been accumulated, there has been so little
skillful reanalysis, particularly in search of explanation and prediction.
Further, though there have been numerous efforts to abstract research in
social work (notably under the auspices of the research bodies of the
National Association of Social Workers, by the Family Service Association
of America and by the Department of Health Education and Welfare), no
comprehensive synthesis of survey findings has been attempted.

As the level of theory formulation and design in social work research im-
proves, and as social work researchers become increasingly adept in the use
of more powerful data-handling techniques—especially in their facility with
the omnipresent computer—we may look for more thorough exploitation
of available data and for more productive cumulation of findings from one
study to another.

THE SURVEY REPORT: FINAL OR OPEN?

A word must be said about the survey report itself. The view that this
report ought not to be a *final* document but rather a beginning of a process

is of significance, particularly in community planning. Often, though the study is regarded as a planning tool, the report, with its aura of authority and complexity, cannot be used with ease by the community planner. Frequently, it needs to be "translated" if it is to be truly useful. Further, it may act as a "group Rorschach," permitting each interpreter of the results to project on to it his own expectations and values. Obviously, there must be survey reports, yet the case can be made that such reports should embody a degree of openness much greater than that in evidence in current publications. This would be in order both for scientific reasons and for the practical reason that an excess sense of "closure" interferes with the actual use of research results in planning. Rather than reading impressive documents, the survey consumer in social work needs to understand thoroughly what kinds of data are available, how they were gathered, and, most important, how they may be reshaped to yield answers to new questions that may arise in the course of the planning process.

Conclusions

As a closing caveat we may note that "the survey" is a research tool of misleading simplicity. To the neophyte researcher, and now and then even to the more knowledgeable, setting up some kind of sample and doing some kind of interview appears to be the royal road to scientific legitimacy. Though the survey, variously defined, has a long and respectable history in social work, and though it has made many contributions in recent years, particularly in studies of need and effect, it has far to go toward becoming a truly mature social work research method. Most of all, it requires an increasingly powerful conceptual basis. This is a task more appropriate for the theory builder in social work than for the survey methodologist, but methodological progress, too, must grow from an improved conceptual base.

New ways of defining populations for sampling must be considered. Samples of "clients-in-relationship" need to replace individual, fragmented approaches. Agencies, groups, and contextual variables need to be included in study designs. One-shot study approaches need to be replaced with more dynamic research strategies, including successive cross-sectional and panel surveys. And data need to be available for retrieval and reanalysis, to be treated in secondary analysis designs of greater sophistication.

If all goes well, survey designs in social work will move toward greater flexibility of conception, doing more with the resources at hand. Sampling plans will become less mechanical and conventional. Analysis methods will move from naive counting to more insightful, multivariate searches for explanation. And findings will become more significant and integrative, not only elucidating narrowly-defined, pragmatic social planning issues, but also making further contributions to the solution of the field's basic theoretic and practical problems.

Much more can be done with the survey method in social work. It remains a tool of wide applicability and promise. The time now seems ripe to move into a "new generation" of surveys that may realize this promise, helping us to learn more about the things that really matter concerning clients, social workers, institutions, and communities. It is by these more creative approaches that we may deepen our understanding of the complex relationships among people that are at the heart of social work's helping process.

Bibliography

Addams, Jane, "Social Workers and the Other Professions," *Proceedings of the National Conference of Social Workers,* University of Chicago Press, 1930, pp. 50–54.

Bailey, M. B., "Community Orientations Toward Social Casework," *Social Work,* Vol. 4, July, 1959, pp. 60–66.

Beck, D. F., "Potential Approaches to Research in the Family Service Field," *Social Casework,* Vol. 40, July, 1959, p. 390 *ff.*

Becker, R. R., "NASW Salary Minimum a Reality but Maximum Still a Goal," *Personnel Information,* Vol. 4, November, 1961, p. 1 and pp. 21–24.

Blau, P. M. and W. R. Scott, *Formal Organizations: A* Comparative Approach. Chandler, San Francisco, 1962.

Bogue, D. J., *Skid Row in American Cities.* Community and Family Study Center, Chicago, 1963.

Borgatta, E. F., David Fanshel, and H. J. Meyer, *Social Workers' Perceptions of Clients.* Russell Sage Foundation, New York, 1960.

Bowers, Swithun, "Social Work as a Helping and Healing Profession," *Social Work,* Vol. 2, January, 1957, pp. 57–62.

Bowley, A. L. and Margaret Hogg, *Has Poverty Diminished?* P. S. King, London, 1925.

Briar, Scott, "Use of Theory in Studying Effects of Client Social Class on Students' Judgment," *Social Work,* Vol. 6, July, 1961, pp. 91–97.

Bruck, Max, "The Relationships Between Student Anxiety, Self Concept, and Students' Competence in Casework," *Social Casework,* Vol. 44, March, 1963, pp. 132–136.

Campbell, Angus and George Katona, "The Sample Survey: A Technique for Social Science Research," in *Research Methods in the Behavioral Sciences.* Edited by Leon Festinger and Daniel Katz. Dryden Press, New York, 1953.

Carter, G. W., "Measurement of Need," in *Social Work Research.* Edited by N. A. Polansky. University of Chicago Press, Chicago, 1960.

Cockerill, Eleanor, "The Interdependence of the Professions in Helping People," in *The Social Welfare Forum.* Columbia University Press, New York, 1953, pp. 137–147.

The Compass, "Report on Salary Scale Standards," Vol. 21, December, 1939, pp. 7–13.

Eaton, E. A. and S. M. Harrison, *A Bibliography of Social Surveys.* Russell Sage Foundation, New York, 1930.

Elmer, M. C., *Technique of Social Surveys.* Jesse Ray Miller, Los Angeles, 1927.

Family Service Association of America, *Patterns in Use of Family Agency Service.* New York, 1962.

Fanshel, David, "Research in Child Welfare: A Critical Analysis," *Child Welfare,* Vol. XLI, December, 1962.

Fanshel, David, ed., *Research in Social Welfare Administration.* National Association of Social Workers, New York, 1962.

Finestone, Samuel, "Some Requirements for Agency-Based Research," *Social Casework,* Vol. 44, March, 1963, pp. 132–136.

Flexner, Abraham, "Is Social Work a Profession?" *Proceedings of the National Conference of Charities and Corrections.* University of Chicago Press, 1915, pp. 576–590.

French, D. G., *An Approach to Measuring Results in Social Work.* Columbia University Press, New York, 1952.

Girl Scouts of the U.S.A., *An Exit Study of Local Professional Workers in Girl Scouting.* Girl Scouts of the U.S.A., New York, 1954.

Golden, Deborah, "Selected Characteristics of NASW Members: The Second Study," *Personnel Information,* Vol. 8, July, 1965, p. 1 and pp. 32–35.

Greenwood, Ernest, *Experimental Sociology:* A Study in Method. King's Crown Press, New York, 1945.

Greenwood, Ernest, "Attributes of a Profession," *Social Work,* Vol. 2, July, 1957, pp. 45–55.

Greenwood, Ernest, "Social Work Research: The Role of the Schools," *Social Service Review,* June, 1958.

Herzog, Elizabeth, *Some Guidelines for Evaluative Research.* U.S. Department of Health, Education and Welfare, Social Security Administration, Children's Bureau, Washington, D.C., 1959.

Hollis, Florence, *Casework—A Psychosocial Therapy.* Random House, New York, 1964.

Hunt, J. McV., "On the Judgment of Social Workers as a Source for Information on Social Work Research," in *Use of Judgments as Data in Social Work Research.* Edited by A. W. Shyne. National Association of Social Workers, New York, 1959, pp. 38–54.

Hunt, J. McV. and Leonard S. Kogan, *Measuring Results in Social Casework:* A Manual on Judging Movement. Family Service Association of America, New York, 1950.

Hunt, J. McV., L. S. Kogan, and Margaret Blenkner, *Testing Results in Social Casework:* A Field-Test of the Movement Scale. Family Service Association of America, New York, 1950.

Hunter, Floyd, *Community Power Structure Study of Decision Makers.* Anchor Books, Garden City, New York, 1963.

Karpf, M. J., "Surveys and Research in Present-Day Social Work," in *Scientific Social Surveys and Research,* 2nd ed. Edited by P. V. Young. Prentice-Hall, Englewood Cliffs, N.J., 1949.

Kasius, Cora, ed., *Social Casework in the Fifties.* Family Service Association of America, New York, 1962.

Kellogg, P. V., ed., *The Pittsburgh Survey,* 6 vols. Russell Sage Foundation, New York, 1914.

Klein, Philip, *et al., A Social Study of Pittsburgh:* Community Problems and Social Services in Allegheny County. Columbia University Press, New York, 1938.

Klein, Philip and I. C. Merriam, *The Contribution of Research to Social Work*. American Association of Social Workers, New York, 1948.

Konopka, Gisela, "Changing Definitions and Areas of Social Work Interest," *Social Work Journal*, Vol. 36, April, 1955.

Kurtz, R. H., ed., *Social Work Yearbook*. National Association of Social Workers, New York, 1960.

Kutner, Bernard, *et al.*, *Five Hundred Over Sixty*. Russell Sage Foundation, New York, 1956.

Litterer, J. A., *The Analysis of Organizations*. John Wiley & Sons, New York, 1965.

Maas, H. S. and R. E. Engler, Jr., *Children in Need of Parents*. Columbia University Press, New York, 1959.

Maas, H. S. and N. A. Polansky, "Collecting Original Data," in *Social Work Research*. Edited by N. A. Polansky. University of Chicago Press, Chicago, 1960.

March, J. G. and H. A. Simon, *Organizations*. John Wiley & Sons, New York, 1958.

Massarik, Fred, *A Sensitivity Training Impact Model:* Some First (and Second) Thoughts on the Evaluation of Sensitivity Training. National Training Laboratories, Washington, 1965.

Massarik, Fred and Leo Okin, *Patterns of Center Leadership*. Jewish Centers Association and Research Service Bureau, Los Angeles, 1964.

Meyer, H. J., E. F. Borgatta, and W. C. Jones, *Girls at Vocational High:* An Experiment in Social Work Intervention. Russell Sage Foundation, New York, 1965.

National Association of Social Workers, *Personnel Information*. Vol. 8, January, 1965.

Nettler, Gwynn, "Ideology and Welfare Policy," *Social Problems*, Vol. 6, 1959, pp. 203–212.

Owen, M. I., ed., *Inventory of Research*. National Association of Social Workers, Social Work Research Section, New York, 1960.

Parnisky, J. J. and Richard Onken, "Survey of Selected Characteristics of Deaf-Blind Adults in New York State," abstracted in *Inventory of Research*. Edited by M. I. Owen. National Association of Social Workers, Social Work Research Section, New York, 1960.

Perlman, H. H., "Intake and Some Role Considerations," in *Social Casework in the Fifties*. Edited by Cora Kasius. Family Service Association of America, New York, 1962.

Piliavin, Irving, "Conflict Between Cottage Parents and Caseworkers," *Social Service Review*, Vol. 37, March, 1963, pp. 17–25.

Polansky, N. A., ed., *Social Work Research*. University of Chicago Press, Chicago, 1960.

Polansky, N. A. and J. S. Kounin, "Clients' Reactions to Initial Interviews: A Field Study," *Human Relations*, Vol. 9, No. 3, 1956, pp. 237–264.

Polansky, N. A., *et al.*, "Social Workers in Society: Results of a Sampling Study," *Social Casework*, Vol. 34, April, 1953, pp. 74–80.

Pollak, Otto, "Cultural Dynamics in Casework," in *Social Casework in the Fifties*. Edited by Cora Kasius. Family Service Association of America, New York, 1962, pp. 83–92 (or in *Social Casework*, July, 1953).

Pool, I. de S., ed., *Trends in Content Analysis*. University of Illinois Press, Urbana, 1959.

Rawley, Callman, "A Sampling of Expert Opinion on Some Principles of Casework," *Social Casework,* Vol. 35, April, 1954, pp. 154–161.

Reece, S. A., "Social Work Practice: An Exploratory Study," *Social Work,* Vol. 6, July, 1961.

Reid, William, "An Experimental Study of Methods Used in Casework Treatment," doctoral dissertation (D.S.W.), Columbia University, June, 1963, abstracted in *Social Service Review,* Vol. 37, September, 1963, p. 349.

Richmond, M. E., *Social Diagnosis.* Russell Sage Foundation, New York, 1917.

Rothman, Jack, "Community Organization as Applied to Social Science," *Sociology and Social Research,* Vol. 48, April, 1964, pp. 315–373.

Schwartz, William, "Strategy of Group Work Practice." *Social Service Review,* Vol. 36, September, 1962.

Schein, E. H., *Organizational Psychology.* Prentice-Hall, Englewood Cliffs, N.J., 1965.

Shyne, A. W., ed., *Use of Judgments as Data in Social Work Research.* National Association of Social Workers, New York, 1959.

Shyne, A. W., "Casework Research: Past and Present," *Social Casework,* Vol. 43, November, 1962, pp. 467–473.

Sills, D. L., *The Volunteers:* Means and Ends in a National Organization. Free Press of Glencoe, Chicago, 1957.

Skeels, H. M. and Marie Skodak, "Techniques for a High-Yield Follow Up Study in the Field," *Public Health Reports,* Vol. 80, March, 1965, pp. 249–257.

Specht, Harvey, "Report on the Findings of the Study of Jewish Young Adults and the Jewish Community Center," *Journal of Jewish Communal Service,* Vol. 41, Winter, 1964, pp. 175–185.

Stein, A. M., "The Population Study as a Tool in the Community Planning Process," *Journal of Jewish Communal Service,* Vol. 34, Fall, 1957, pp. 78–83.

Stein, H. B., "Research in Social Welfare Administration," in *The Social Welfare Forum.* Columbia University Press, New York, 1954.

Stein, H. B., "The Study of Organizational Effectiveness," in *Research in Social Welfare Administration.* Edited by David Fanshel. National Association of Social Workers, New York, 1962.

Varley, Barbara, "Socialization in Social Work Practice," *Social Work,* Vol. 8, July, 1963, pp. 102–109.

Varon, Edith, "Communication: Client, Community and Agency," *Social Work,* Vol. 9, April, 1964, pp. 51–57.

Vincent, C. E., *Unmarried Mothers.* Free Press of Glencoe, New York, 1961.

Warner, W. K. and S. J. Miller, "Organizational Problems in Two Types of Voluntary Associations," *American Journal of Sociology,* Vol. 69, May, 1964, pp. 654–657.

White, R. C., "Social Workers in Society: Some Further Evidence," *Social Casework,* Vol. 34, October, 1953, pp. 161–164.

White, R. C. and M. B. Sussman, *Hough, Cleveland, Ohio:* The Study of Social Life and Change. Western Reserve University Press, Cleveland, 1959.

Witmer, Helen, *et al., Independent Adoptions*—A Follow-Up Study. Russell Sage Foundation, New York, 1963.

Wolins, Martin, "A Base for Community Welfare Studies," in *The Social Welfare Forum,* Columbia University Press, New York, 1954, pp. 216–233.

Wolins, Martin, "Measuring the Effect of Social Work Intervention," in *Social Work Research*. Edited by N. A. Polansky. University of Chicago Press, Chicago, 1960.
Young, P. V., *Scientific Social Surveys and Research,* 2nd ed. Prentice-Hall, Englewood Cliffs, N.J., 1949.

The Survey Method
Applied to

Public Health
and Medicine

by Edward A. Suchman
University of Pittsburgh

The Behavioral Sciences and Health Research

The Nature of Survey Research in Public Health and Medicine

The Major Applications of Survey Method

Ecology and Etiology
Morbidity or health status surveys. Social epidemiological surveys.
Variations in Response to Illness and the Maintenance of Health
Surveys of public information, attitudes, and behavior. Surveys of health needs, resources, and utilization.
The Health Professions and Organizations
Surveys of the health professions. Surveys of health organizations.

The Conduct of Surveys in Health and Medicine

Conclusion

The Survey Method Applied to
Public Health and Medicine

DISEASE is a phenomenon which distributes itself unequally throughout a population. To some extent, chance alone will be the major factor determining both who will be stricken and who will survive. But many more purposive forces enter the picture to increase or decrease the probability of one's becoming ill and dying. Degree and type of exposure, the organism's ability to resist, the virulence of the disease-causing agent, the availability and use of preventive measures, the quality of medical care, and other factors combine to produce this differential occurrence of and reaction to disease—and it is the study of these variations in rates of morbidity and mortality and in the behavior of the ill that is the basic contribution of the survey method to health and medical research.[1]

The use of the survey method in the health and medical field probably goes back to the beginnings of medicine as a scientific discipline. The collection of mortality statistics as an index of health status, the determination of differential rates of illness to identify foci of disease, the comparison of exposed and unexposed or of treated and untreated groups in the population, the evaluation of community public health programs—in short, the approach to medicine which demanded reliable and valid proof that what the medical practitioner did actually affected the course of disease—necessitated the systematic collection of data concerning health and illness from carefully defined population groups.

Medical and health research may be classified according to three main approaches.[2] First, and probably most traditional, is the *clinical* observation of the sick individual in terms of symptom development, the natural history of the disease, the biological and physical sequelae of abnormal bodily struc-

1. This report will not attempt any systematic differentiation between the various sub-areas of public health and private medicine. Our focus will be upon the general use of surveys in relation to all types of health problems and health programs regardless of the particular public health organization or branch of medicine involved.
2. For a good introduction to the major forms and areas of medical research, see Green, D. E. and E. W. Knox, eds., *Research in Medical Science*. Macmillan, New York, 1950.

ture or function, and the response to various forms of medical treatment. Second, beginning with the great bacteriological discoveries, came *laboratory* experiments involving attempts to define and isolate the disease-causing agents and to find the means of combating them. Third, and most current, are *epidemiological* studies of population groups in the field in an effort to determine the differential distribution of disease among various subgroups of the population and to analyze the various host, agent, and environmental factors that affect the development of the disease. All three approaches are complementary to each other and each attempts to use the scientific method in its design of research and in the collection and analysis of its data.[3]

Our concern in this chapter is obviously with the most recent of these methods—the field or population survey. When medical and health research moved out of the clinic and laboratory to study man where he lived, it turned to the survey method for techniques of sampling, questionnaire construction, interviewing, and analysis of data. Today, medical and health surveys occupy an established place in both the basic search for new medical knowledge and the application of this knowledge to the care of the ill. The growth in importance of the chronic diseases with their multiple etiologies, slow degenerative processes, and their long-term therapy, the development of the modern public health movement with its increased emphasis upon public opinion and securing community cooperation and participation, and the reorganization of medical services into more sophisticated and complex means of providing medical care have raised a host of new questions, the answers to which must come, to a large extent, from carefully designed cross-sectional sampling surveys.

The Behavioral Sciences and Health Research

The relevance of the survey method for health and medical research strongly reflects the increasingly close relationship between the behavioral sciences and the fields of medicine and public health. Traditionally, medical research has been conducted in the laboratory or clinic, largely confined to the biological and physical sciences. But a number of new developments in disease states and in the provision of medical care have forced the medical researcher to look beyond his test tubes and experimental subjects to the community at large.

3. Leavell, H. R. and G. E. Clark, *Preventive Medicine for the Doctor in His Community:* An Epidemiologic Approach. McGraw-Hill, New York, 1958.

First, and perhaps of greatest significance, is the increasing predominance of the chronic diseases as major causes of sickness and death. The tremendous success of medical research in dealing with the communicable infectious diseases in the United States has resulted in a drastic decrease in the importance of many of these diseases as major threats to the public's health. In the place of such once-deadly diseases as smallpox, typhoid, malaria, and diphtheria, we now find the modern killers of heart disease, cancer, and diabetes. In addition, we have an increase in importance of the behavioral and addictive disorders such as mental illness, alcoholism, and narcotics addiction.

There is a radical difference between the communicable diseases and the chronic and addictive diseases which has great significance for survey research. This difference applies to the entire disease process from etiology to treatment and prevention and affects both the theoretical basis of disease and the methodological approach to its study. In place of specific infectious agents which often could be isolated as single causes and treated with specific remedies, we now have a complex interaction of multiple causes involving social and psychological factors as well as biological ones. Furthermore, both the prevention and treatment of these chronic diseases and behavioral disorders can much less frequently be accomplished with a single specific preventive or therapeutic agent; much more often, long-term and drastic changes in the individual's way of life are required.

These dramatic shifts in disease patterns have far-reaching implications for the relationship of medicine to the social sciences, both conceptually and methodologically. The medical researcher must now learn to deal with social and psychological factors in the etiology and treatment of disease. The social environment becomes as important as the physical environment, while the individual's own behavior may make him both the recipient host and the causative agent.[4] Increasingly, medical data will have to come from surveys of groups of individuals in the community at large. These data will deal with such variables as social and psychological stress, group memberships, interpersonal relationships, personality, and attitudes. Questionnaires and interviews will take their place alongside laboratory tests and clinical records as basic sources of data. The analysis of these data will take on increased complexity involving statistical inference and correlations based on

4. Suchman, E. A., "The Addictive Disorders as Socio-Environmental Health Problems," in *Handbook of Medical Sociology*. Edited by H. E. Freeman, Sol Levine and L. G. Reeder. Prentice-Hall, Englewood Cliffs, N.J., 1963, pp. 123–143.

multivariate analysis as opposed to the experimental identification of single causes.

A second major development that has led to an increased convergence of the medical and social sciences is the reorganization of medical care. The traditional general practitioner with a close personal relationship with his patients on a fee-for-service basis is giving way to increased specialization as medical care becomes more complex (reflecting some of the disease trends discussed above), and to new administrative arrangements such as group insurance plans and group practice, as medical costs and shortages of personnel and facilities continue to mount. The field of administrative medicine, dealing with the economic and administrative aspects of medical care, opens a whole new area of research, more social than medical, requiring surveys of medical expenditures, the availability and utilization of facilities, doctor-patient relationships, and a host of other data related to society's provision of medical care.

A third trend, reflecting the above major developments, concerns the changing nature of the field of public health. Initially established as official agencies concerned with the control of the communicable diseases through environmental sanitation and immunization, departments of health are now involved in such activities as mass screening programs for the chronic diseases, rehabilitation, well-baby clinics, public health education, and a host of other programs aimed not only at fighting disease but, as proclaimed by the World Health Organization, at producing "a state of complete physical, mental, and social well-being."

To accomplish this goal, public health has recognized its strong alliance with the theories and methods of the social sciences. The provision of community health services requires a knowledge of community structure and function. The participation of the public in mass detection and immunization programs calls for a knowledge of public information, attitudes, and behavior. Legal sanctions and coercion so predominant in the early control of the communicable diseases have had to give way to voluntary cooperation in the case of the chronic diseases. Cultural barriers have to be overcome, public support has to be secured for community health measures, individuals have to be motivated to change their habits of living; in short, public health must now be marketed and the best marketing research techniques are needed to reach the consumer.[5]

5. Hanlon offers the following picture of the field of public health—a description which shows quite clearly the significance of survey research on health behavior:
It is well to give constant consideration to these social and environmental influ-

To the above major changes in the health and medical field could be added many other developments which increasingly have brought the medical and social sciences closer together. This trend has been recognized by many medical historians. Anderson and Rosen, in an analysis of five major patterns of disease over the past one thousand years, predict that pattern number six will be a period of disease characterized by the emergence of social and psychological factors as major forces in health, illness, and medical care.[6] Gregg divides public health history into three major eras, concluding with the modern era in which the whole patient and the community, rather than the disease entity, becomes the focal point of medical attention.[7] Perhaps in recognition of this trend, the United States Public Health Service in 1962 established a National Institute of Child Health and Human Development whose "attention is not focused on any one disease or part of the body, but rather on the whole person," while the National Institute of Mental Health gives substantial support to research on the behavioral aspects of health.[8] The Health Information Foundation Inventory of Social and Economic Research in Health, issued annually, listed 1,035 projects for the year 1960.[9] These studies were divided into three categories: 212 dealt with research related to health levels, 437 with research related to behavioral aspects of health, and 386 with research related to health resources

---

ences in order to emphasize the importance of regarding public health work for what it really is, i.e., an applied social science, to which is brought to bear appropriate medical, engineering, nursing, educational, and many other disciplines. It is only by considering the social and environmental conditions under which people live, sleep, work, recreate, procreate, and rear their young, that we can hope to understand and control disease in the most complete sense.

Hanlon, J. J., *Principles of Public Health Administration,* 3rd ed. C. V. Mosby, St. Louis, 1960, p. 140. This volume contains two excellent chapters dealing with the behavioral sciences and social pathology.

6. Anderson, Odin W. and George Rosen, *An Examination of the Concept of Preventive Medicine.* Research Series No. 12, Health Information Foundation, Chicago, 1960, pp. 4–6.

7. Gregg, Alan, "The Future Health Officer's Responsibility—Past, Present, and Future," *American Journal of Public Health,* Vol. 46, November, 1956, pp. 1384–1389.

8. U.S. Public Health Service, *National Institutes of Health,* Publication No. 81, U.S. Government Printing Office, Washington, revised 1963, p. 14.

9. Health Information Foundation, *An Inventory of Social and Economic Research in Health,* New York, 1960. This was the last year during which a cumulative list was made. Since 1960, annual inventories have presented only new projects, totaling about 200 to 250 each year.

and economic aspects of health. An overwhelming majority of these studies made use of the sampling survey method for the collection of data.

Responding to this convergence of subject matter and research method between the medical and social sciences, an increasing number of social scientists are entering the health field.[10] The sociologist finds a close affinity between the problems and methods of epidemiology and those of the sampling survey, especially in relation to the investigation of social factors in disease. The psychologist's interests in public opinion, with emphasis on motivational factors in changing attitudes and behavior in regard to health programs, puts him in an advantageous position to study the effects of mass communications upon public health education and participation in health campaigns through means of the public opinion survey. The anthropologist can bring his knowledge of cultural values and community forces to bear upon the problem of cultural resistances to the adoption of health innovations, especially in the underdeveloped areas of the world. The economist will find, in the problems of health expenditures and the matching of supply and demand, a challenge to his best theoretical formulations and data collection and analysis methods. Finally, the growth of governmental and public interest and participation in decisions concerning the ways and means of providing medical care has created a political arena of natural interest to the political scientist. In all of these instances, research has barely gotten under way and there is ample opportunity to make use of the sampling survey technique.

The fields of medicine and public health have turned to the social scientists with mixed feelings of need and suspicion. Many medical and public health schools have added social scientists to their faculty, and some medical organizations and departments of health have social scientists on their staffs.[11] While recognizing that many of the major problems they face today involve social variables and that research on these problems necessitates the

10. For example, a survey in 1961 by the American Sociological Association showed "Medical Sociology" with the highest percentage gain as the major field of competence of its members (723 per cent or an absolute increase from 26 to 188 members): Riley, M. W., "Membership of the American Sociological Association, 1950–1959," *American Sociological Review,* Vol. 26, December, 1961, p. 925; see also, Anderson, Odin W. and Milvoy Seacat, *The Behavioral Scientists and Research in the Health Field.* Bulletin #1, Health Information Foundation, Chicago, 1957.

11. Straus, Robert, "The Nature and Status of Medical Sociology," *American Sociological Review,* Vol. 22, April 1957, pp. 200–204. A brief but comprehensive account of the current status of medical sociology is given in Freeman, Howard, Sol Levine, and L. G. Reeder, eds., *Handbook of Medical Sociology, op. cit.,* pp. 473–491.

use of social research techniques, especially the large-scale sampling survey, medical people are ill at ease with what appears to be a lack of scientific method in research design and in the collection and analysis of data.[12] To some extent this distrust is justified since there still remains much to be desired in the rigorousness of a great deal of current survey research in the health field. Nevertheless, there is a growing recognition and acceptance on the part of medical and public health personnel that modern diseases and modern health problems are complex in nature and that research on their causes, treatment, and consequences must involve the simultaneous analysis of multiple variables—many of which can only be measured subjectively and crudely by means of large-scale surveys, with results that will always consist of statistical associations rather than definitive proof.

The Nature of Survey Research in Public Health and Medicine

There are a number of different ways one might classify the kinds of surveys that are being or could be made in the field of health and medical research. These include the purpose of the survey, i.e., basic or applied research; the subject matter being investigated, i.e., the disease entity or health problem; the population being surveyed, i.e., the public as a whole, patients in hospitals, or professional workers; or the method being used, i.e., prospective or retrospective survey. Probably the one most commonly used classification deals with the substantive content or subject matter of the survey. These content subdivisions can serve a useful function insofar as they highlight the kinds of problem areas which are subject to investigation by social survey techniques.

A fairly comprehensive bibliography of "Health Studies of Human Populations" dealing with the use of the survey method in health and medical research offers the following classification: (1) nature and extent of sickness, (2) receipt of medical services, (3) information and attitudes about use of health services, (4) health in relation to social and economic characteristics, (5) growth and processes of aging, (6) specific diseases or conditions, (7) nutrition, (8) harmful elements in the physical environment, (9) demonstrations and evaluations, (10) field trials.[13] These categories are

12. For a brief description of current methods of social research in the medical field, see Elinson, Jack, "Methods of Socio-Medical Research," *ibid.*, pp. 449–471.
13. U.S. Public Health Service, *Health Studies of Human Populations*. Public Health Bibliography Series, No. 38, U.S. Government Printing Office, Washington, 1962. This publication also offers an annotated bibliography of methodological problems in health surveys.

obviously neither complete nor mutually exclusive and involve a mixture of surveys focused on people, on services, on disease entities, on causes of disease, and on methodology. They do, however, indicate the wide range of subject matter capable of being investigated by the survey method.

A more logical, problem-oriented classification is offered by Kendall and Merton, who subdivide the field of social research in health into four categories: (1) etiology and ecology, (2) response to illness and maintenance of health, (3) organization of health facilities, and (4) professional education and training.[14] This classification does, by and large, cover the main content areas of survey research today. We might group the first two into surveys "*in* medicine" and the last two into surveys "*of* medicine," following a distinction developed by Straus for differentiating between research dealing with illness itself and research dealing with the practice of medicine.[15] In the present section, we will briefly characterize these four main types of health and medical surveys, postponing our critical evaluation for the next section in which we will describe and analyze specific examples of major surveys in each of these areas.[16]

Surveys on etiology and ecology constitute what is perhaps the most significant contribution that survey research has to offer to basic medical science. This is the study of the patterns of distribution of disease in different geographical areas and among different groups of individuals. From these data, one can compute the morbidity and mortality rates necessary for judging the health status of a community or nation, for determining trends in disease states, and for comparing the demographic characteristics of individuals with different diseases. These studies provide the point of departure for more detailed research on etiological factors and constitute the basis of the rapidly expanding field of social epidemiology.

The study of variations in response to illness and the maintenance of

---

14. Kendall, P. L. and R. K. Merton, "Medical Education as a Social Process," in *Patients, Physicians and Illness*. Edited by E. J. Jaco. Free Press, Glencoe, Ill., 1958, pp. 321–350.
15. Straus, Robert, "The Nature and Status. . . ," *op. cit.*, pp. 201–202.
16. A comprehensive bibliography of the literature on social research in health and medicine contains several hundreds of references to survey research divided as follows: (I) General Statements; (II) The Sociology of Illness; (III) Practitioners, Patients, and Medical Settings; (IV) Sociology of Medical Care; and (V) Strategy, Method, and Status. Simmons, Ozzie G., "Social Research in Health and Medicine: A Bibliography." In Freeman, H. E., Sol Levine and L. G. Reeder, eds., *op. cit.*, pp. 493–581.

health encompasses a vast area that might be characterized as the marketing aspects of health and medical care. Preventive health measures and medical treatment must be sold to the consuming public like any other product; and knowledge of the public's information, attitudes, and behavior is as necessary in the health field as in any other large scale merchandising enterprise. These surveys range from the pedestrian, but essential, studies of who utilizes what medical facilities to the rather abstract and theoretical analyses of the cultural meaning of illness.

Undoubtedly, the greatest number of current studies in the health and medical field are of this latter type. Literally hundreds of surveys are made each year in the field of health education to determine what the public knows about different diseases, preventive measures, and medical care facilities.[17] Most of these surveys, like so much marketing research, are limited in scope to particular health messages or campaigns, but an increasing number are probing more deeply into motivations for health action and resistances to changes in behavior. Such problems as patient delay in seeking medical care, public apathy to mass screening programs, and political opposition to new health measures are receiving increased attention. Gradually, a body of data is being accumulated which should serve as a basis for the more rational planning and development of health programs.

The third major application of surveys has been within the field of health itself, in an effort to understand better the structure and functioning of health organizations. The institutional arrangements for the provision of medical care in modern society are quite complex. Responsibility for the health of the public is shared by official governmental agencies, voluntary non-profit organizations, large commercial enterprises, and individual practitioners. Medical services are dispersed in hospitals, both large and small, in clinics, in health centers, and in private offices. The administrative arrangements for providing medical care and the interpersonal relations that develop within different medical and health organizations have been the subject of a number of surveys, especially of local health agencies and mental hospitals. On the whole, however, this is a relatively neglected area

17. A content analysis of several hundred studies related to health education practice produced the following classification: (I) What People Know, Believe, and Do About Health; (II) Some Major Psycho-Social and Cultural Factors Relevant to Health Education Practice; (III) Methods and Materials in Health Education (Communication); and (IV) Program Planning and Evaluation. "Review of Research Related to Health Education Practices," *Health Education Monographs,* Supplement No. 1, 1963.

of social survey research, probably reflecting its sensitivity to examination by outsiders.

The final area of survey research concerns the study of the recruitment, training, placement, and performance of medical and health personnel. In a field plagued by extreme shortages of qualified personnel, it is only natural that attempts be made to find out who enters the medical and health field and why. A number of major surveys have been made of prospective nurses, student nurses, and practicing nurses to determine their satisfactions and dissatisfactions, their motivations and expectations, their prospects and plans. Rather extensive surveys have been made of the education and "socialization" of the doctor, the dentist, the nurse, and the public health officer. Studies of professional "images" have been conducted to help understand occupational roles and statuses. Some of the best survey research has been done in this area and it is not too unlikely that we know more about the medical and health profession than about any other occupational group in our society.

Thus, we find that the survey research method has achieved an established place in almost all aspects of health and medical research. It is a fundamental tool for the study of both basic processes in disease causation and applied programs of medical care. In the following section, we will elaborate upon some of these major uses of the survey method, pointing out current strengths and weaknesses and discussing possibilities for the even more productive application of survey techniques to health problems.

The Major Applications of Survey Method

The area of health and medical care comprises one of the major activities of any social system. All societies are concerned with maintaining the health of their members through the prevention and treatment of disease. Every social system has developed its own set of cultural values regarding health, which helps determine the definition of and attitudes towards illness within that society and the prescribed behavior of the sick individual. In each society, we also find institutional arrangements for "legitimizing" illness and for providing medical care. Thus it is no wonder that research in the health and medical field should ramify into almost all aspects of the social system and that the use of the survey method in the conduct of such research should be extended toward a myriad of different health and medical problems.

In this section, we cannot hope to discuss in any detail each of the dozens of different applications of the survey method. Instead, we have chosen to single out three major areas of general concern, to describe briefly the kinds of research questions being asked in these areas, and then to evaluate the state of the survey research that is currently being conducted. In line with the classifications offered in the previous section, we have divided these applications of the survey method into the following major sub-groups:

Ecology and Etiology
1. Morbidity or health status surveys
2. Social epidemiological surveys
Variations in Response to Illness and Maintenance of Health
1. Surveys of public information, attitudes, and behavior regarding illness and disease
2. Health needs, resources, utilization, and evaluation surveys
Health Personnel and Organizations
1. Surveys of health personnel
2. Structure and function of health organizations

The first division concentrates on surveys of *disease* states, the second on surveys of the *patient or public,* and the third on surveys of the *profession.* We will not attempt a complete coverage of the multitude of surveys that have been made in each area, but will select a few representative examples for critical evaluation. Our primary purpose is an analysis of the theoretical and methodological bases for the use of the survey method in each of these major areas of health and medical research. Hopefully, this analysis will point the way toward a more sophisticated, rigorous, and creative use of the survey method in seeking answers to the problems raised in each area.

ECOLOGY AND ETIOLOGY

The ecological approach to health and illness is founded on the proposition that disease constitutes a maladjustment of the human organism to his environment. This environment includes the physical, biological, and social forces which surround the individual and which represent a balance between man and nature. Disturbance of this balance may result in the initiation of the disease process. As defined by Rogers, "Ecology is the study of the relations between organisms and their environment. Human ecology, then, is the study of the relations between man and his environment, both as it affects him and as he affects it."[18]

Basic to the ecological approach are the interrelationships of man, his environment, and the agents of disease. This triad of host, agent, and environment constitutes the principal conceptual model for the epidemiological approach to the study of disease. The *host*, through his inherent and acquired characteristics, presents a target of variable susceptibility to the disease *agent*, which represents that substance or element whose presence initiates the disease process. The *environment* consists of those external conditions—physical, biological and social—which affect both the resistance of the host and the virulence of the agent. As we shall see in our analysis of the social epidemiological survey, this classification of host, agent, and environment is rather artificial and, in actuality, the interrelationship between these three categories is so complex as to make them almost inseparable.

Through the use of surveys which determine the distribution of illness and disease according to different geographical and demographic groupings of the population, the ecological method attempts to locate focal points of high and low incidence.[19] The methodological rationale is that the comparison of high and low risk groups and areas will help the medical researcher to discover clues to the etiology and development of disease in those host, agent, and environmental factors which underlie these observed differences.

The different functions of the ecological survey relate to this determination of comparative rates of disease. As described by the U.S. Public Health Service, medical ecology is considered as having three major subdivisions:

1. The establishing of norms for traits of human populations of different ages, sexes, and races, including norms for the growth process;
2. Population dynamics, including problems of fertility and natural selection;

18. Rogers, Edward S., *Human Ecology and Health*. Macmillan, New York, 1960, p. vii; and his "Man, Ecology, and the Control of Disease," *Public Health Reports*, Vol. 77, September, 1962, pp. 755–762. Rogers notes that the term "human ecology" was first introduced by two sociologists, Burgess and Clark, in 1921.
19. For example, see Sauer, H. I., "Epidemiology of Cardiovascular Mortality— Geographic and Ethnic," *American Journal of Public Health*, Vol. 52, January, 1952, pp. 94–105.

3. The etiology of disease and injury (including inheritance patterns of specific diseases), and emotional and social disorders.[20]

Thus, ecological surveys cover a wide range of activities, including morbidity and mortality surveys, demographic surveys of the physical and social characteristics of population groupings, fertility and population growth surveys, migration surveys, surveys of socio-environmental conditions, and epidemiological surveys. These surveys supply much of the basic data for medical and health research. They provide the basic measurements of the changing health status of a population, and they are a major area of health research today.

While, to a large extent, ecological analysis makes use of already existing records and statistics, an ever-increasing proportion of such research is being conducted through large-scale field surveys. This movement toward the collection of original data reflects both the desire for increased reliability and validity, and the need for more detailed information than could be supplied by official records. The sampling survey offers the medical ecologist, the demographer and the epidemiologist an opportunity to collect facts systematically. One of the major weaknesses of much existing data on population and disease trends lies in the incompleteness of these data and the unknown representativeness of the population base. These data, furthermore, are often collected without the use of standardized instruments, and involve varying definitions of the factors being studied and differing procedures for the collection of the data.[21]

Comparisons between groups are subject to a high degree of possible bias resulting from differing methods of data collection. One must be cautious, therefore, in interpreting variations as reflecting real differences in the groups being compared rather than spurious artifacts of the method being used. Thus, for example, it is difficult to know whether differential rates of

20. Tibbitts, H. G., and Thomas D. Dublin, *Public Health Service Supported Research in Medical Ecology*. U.S. Public Health Service, Division of Research Grants, Working Paper, p. 7.
21. Sanders lists the following factors as interfering with the reliability and validity of morbidity rates based on reported cases: 1) Individuals who see a doctor are self-selected; 2) Doctors vary in their diagnostic competence, and this variation is not random; 3) Both patient and doctor are primarily interested in relieving the patient, not assessing general health. This article also contains an excellent bibliography of 122 articles dealing with methodology problems in medical diagnoses. Sanders, B. S., "Completeness and Reliability of Diagnoses in Therapeutic Practice," *Journal of Health and Human Behavior*, Vol. 5, Summer-Fall, 1964, pp. 84–94.

heart disease or mental illness in rural and urban areas, or among low vs. high income groups, represent true differences due to geographical location or socio-economic status, or spurious differences stemming from different methods of defining, finding, and reporting these diseases. The sampling survey has been embraced by the medical ecologist as a valuable scientific tool for determining with greater reliability and validity the incidence and prevalence of disease in different population groups. This use of the survey method for measuring health status probably reflects the largest and most significant area of current activity in the health field and will be discussed in detail below.

A second major shortcoming of ecological analysis based on existing records concerns the very limited content of these records. For the most part, data are collected on such gross demographic variables as sex, age, race, and marital status. While these variables are essential for "medical bookkeeping," they are only the beginnings of a search for causes. One must look behind these observed differences for the underlying etiological process. *Why* do men have more heart disease than women, or why is the rate of tuberculosis higher among Negroes than whites? The demographic categories are simply labels for a complex combination of differing inherent and acquired individual characteristics and of differing socio-environmental conditions.[22] The search for these underlying etiological factors requires the design of special surveys which go beyond the available records. This is largely the function of the epidemiological survey, which will be the second major area of survey research to be evaluated below.

Morbidity or health status surveys. The morbidity survey is basically a means for describing and evaluating the health status of a population. In its simplest form, it represents a frequency count of the different kinds of illness and disease present in the community. In its more complex formulation, it may involve not only the measurement of the prevalence of disease, but also such additional health data as the presence of symptoms or conditions, the utilization of medical facilities, and the costs and disabling consequences of illness. For example, the California Health Survey lists the following six major objectives:

22. See, for example, Stockwell, E. G., "A Critical Examination of the Relationship Between Socio-Economic Status and Mortality," *American Journal of Public Health,* Vol. 53, June 1963, pp. 956–964.

1. *Demography*—a description of the population, including the pattern of its household composition, occupation, income levels, racial characteristics, age, sex, and marital status.
2. *Broad Picture of Community Health*—the amount of social disruption due to disability from disease and the major types of illness and accidents.
3. *Knowledge of Diseases Themselves*—the distribution of disease among different population groups extended beyond the usual sources of obtaining such information.
4. *Utilization of Health Services*—the extent to which persons use hospitals, visit physicians or obtain home nursing care.
5. *Rosters for Detailed Epidemiologic Study*—rosters of individual cases of selected chronic diseases for intensive study.
6. *Data on Causative Factors*—data bearing directly on etiologic hypotheses, e.g., cigarette smoking as a factor in chronic disease.[23]

This broad use of the health survey is quite recent. Collection of data on morbidity or illness from samples of the population via the household interview was stimulated largely by the inadequacy of available mortality or death statistics as an index of the health of a nation. Mortality statistics have been collected for a long time by almost all nations; today, these are collated according to an international code of causes of death by the World Health Organization. However, such statistics are becoming increasingly inadequate as chronic diseases gradually supplant communicable diseases in importance. Sudden death or complete cure are the natural outcome of many acute infectious diseases; while, in the case of chronic diseases, there is usually a slow degenerative process with little hope of any complete cure. In general, mortality statistics reflect only what is happening to less than one per cent of the population in a given year. A much more significant measure today is the incidence of chronic illness and the presence of medical symptoms or conditions. The health of a community today is more accurately reflected in its sick rather than in its dead.

The determination of illness is much more difficult than the counting of deaths. The latter is definable and reportable, while the former contains

23. Breslow, Lester, "Uses and Limitations of the California Health Survey for Studying the Epidemiology of Chronic Disease," *American Journal of Public Health,* Vol. 47, February 1957, pp. 168–172.

many problems both in identification and notification.[24] Where a disease has a gradual developmental history, it is difficult to determine when it is or is not present.[25] Even with the appearance of clear-cut symptoms, it is not always easy to diagnose the proper disease entity. Furthermore, there are apt to be great differences in who comes to the attention of medical authorities. Not all individuals with the same medical condition are equally likely to seek and find medical care. Thus, morbidity data from official medical sources are notably biased both in terms of the types of conditions reported and the characteristics of the individuals with these conditions.

The household morbidity survey has developed in the past few decades as an attempt to collect information about illness and disease from a representative cross-section of the population.[26] Until the development of the sampling survey method, there did not seem to be any practical way of counting and describing illness and disease in a society. As Dorn observed, "Our present knowledge of nonfatal illness in the United States is no further advanced than the knowledge of fatal illness at the beginning of the century."[27] And so the health population survey was born—at first, an infant content to count medical conditions as reported by a representative sample of respondents; then a child curious about such additional factors as medical care being received, disabling effects, and cost; and, hopefully, some day a mature adult, searching for etiological factors, evaluating treatment programs, testing preventive measures, and measuring medical and social consequences.

The first morbidity surveys were initiated by the United States Public Health Service in 1921 on a single community basis in Hagerstown, Mary-

24. For example, a study in New York City revealed that at least 65 per cent of the gonorrhea cases and 40 per cent of syphilis cases were not reported despite a law requiring such reports by private physicians. Gelman, A. C., J. E. Vandow, and Nathan Sobel, "Current Status of Venereal Disease in New York City: A Survey of 6,649 Physicians," *American Journal of Public Health,* Vol. 53, December, 1963, pp. 1903–1918.

25. Dunn proposes an ingenious method for taking into account disease-development time in health surveys. Dunn, J. E., "The Use of Incidence and Prevalence in the Study of Disease Development in a Population," *American Journal of Public Health,* Vol. 52, July, 1963, pp. 1107–1118.

26. For a good introduction to the household health survey and its relationship to laboratory and clinical research, see Lilienfeld, Abraham M., "The Distribution of Disease in the Population," *Journal of Chronic Diseases,* Vol. 11, 1960, pp. 471–483.

27. Dorn, H. F., "Some Problems for Research in Mortality and Morbidity," *Public Health Reports,* Vol. 71, January, 1956.

land, using personal interviews of 1,822 white families at intervals of 6 to 8 weeks for 29 months—perhaps the first "panel" or longitudinal health survey ever to be made. Data were gathered on acute and chronic illnesses, whether non-disabling or disabling.[28] It is interesting to note that this first health survey was already concerned about the static nature of the "one-shot" survey and expressed the desire to determine changes in health status over time. As Syndenstricker pointed out forty years ago, this longitudinal approach was necessary to determine the *incidence* of new illness as well as the *prevalence* of illness at any single instant in time.[29]

As if to underscore this highly significant principle in survey research, the Hagerstown survey was repeated 20 years later among 1,943 of the approximately 5,000 individuals who had been free of chronic disease in the 1921–1924 survey.[30] This highly ambitious endeavor to determine changes in chronic disease incidence over time produced some valuable lessons on the limitations of the longitudinal survey—such as the unfortunate but inevitable loss of original cases and the resulting bias in representativeness of the follow-up population, the unknown effect of using different interviewers, and the change in meaning of concepts over time, in this case diagnostic terminology, etc. These limitations, however, were more than balanced by the overwhelming advantages of studying the course of illness, of observing the time sequence of causal and consequent events, of comparing the results of different kinds of treatment, of discovering the characteristics of high-risk and low-risk groups, of determining delay in seeking medical care and many other aspects of illness and patient behavior.

The Hagerstown health survey was followed by other community surveys: a study of illness and medical costs among 9,000 families in 130

28. Sydenstricker, Edgar, *Hagerstown Morbidity Studies—A Study of Illness in a Typical Population Group* (a collection of 12 reprints from *Public Health Reports*). U.S. Government Printing Office, Washington, 1930; see also, Turner, V. B., *Hagerstown Health Studies:* An Annotated Bibliography. Public Health Service Publication No. 148, U.S. Government Printing Office, Washington, 1952.
29. For a discussion of longitudinal surveys of health status, see Downes, Jean, "Method of Statistical Analysis of Chronic Illness in a Longitudinal Study of Illness," *Milbank Memorial Fund Quarterly*, Vol. 29, October, 1951, pp. 404–422.
30. Lawrence, P. S., "An Estimate of the Incidence of Chronic Disease," *Public Health Reports*, Vol. 63, January 16, 1948, pp. 69–82. For an informative analysis of the order of events in the relationship between illness and socio-economic status, see also, Lawrence, P. S., "Chronic Illness and Socio-Economic Status," *Public Health Reports*, Vol. 63, 1948, pp. 1507–1521.

localities[31] and studies of Chattaraugus County and Syracuse, New York, and the Eastern Health District of Baltimore.[32] These studies resulted in the first comprehensive volume on sickness experience in relation to demographic and social characteristics.[33] It was only natural that this type of morbidity survey be extended to the United States as a whole and in 1935–1936 the first National Health Survey was organized by the U.S. Public Health Service covering 800,000 families by means of household interviews. Data were collected on the prevalence and incidence of acute and chronic disabling illnesses and death, the receipt of medical care from physicians, health clinics, sanitoriums and public health nursing services related to such factors as sex, color, income, age, occupation, employment status, housing conditions and amount of time lost from usual activities. These data have been used for such purposes as estimating health status changes resulting from population shifts and for evaluating community needs for health services. The findings have served as the basis for some 200 reports, articles, and comparative studies.[34]

In 1949 and 1950, the Current Population Survey of the Bureau of the Census included several questions on the prevalence of disabling illness.[35] This was followed by a series of studies under the guidance of the Commission on Chronic Illness which culminated in four major volumes: (1) Prevention of Chronic Illness; (2) Care of the Long-Term Patient; (3) Chronic Illness in a Rural Area; and (4) Chronic Illness in a Large

31. Collins, S. D., *The Incidence of Illness and the Volume of Medical Services Among 9,000 Canvassed Families* (a collection of 23 reprints). U.S. Government Printing Office, Washington, 1944.

32. Morbidity Survey in Baltimore, 1938–43, *Collected Papers on a Five-Year Study of Illness in the Eastern Health District of Baltimore.* Milbank Memorial Fund, New York, 1957.

33. Collins, S. D., *et al., Sickness Experience in Selected Areas of the United States.* Public Health Monograph No. 25, PHS Publication No. 390, U.S. Government Printing Office, Washington, 1955.

34. U.S. Government Printing Office, *Illness and Medical Care Among 2,500,000 Persons in 83 Cities, with Special Reference to Socio-Economic Factors* (a collection of 27 reprints). Washington, 1945. For a discussion of survey methodology, see U.S. Public Health Service, Division of Public Health Methods, *The National Health Survey, 1935–36.* National Institute of Health, Washington, 1938.

35. Woolsey, T. D., *Estimates of Disabling Illness Prevalence in the United States.* Public Health Monograph No. 14, Public Health Service Publication No. 181, U.S. Government Printing Office, Washington, 1953.

City.[36] These studies represent a bench mark in the development of survey methodology for the study of health status. In addition to determining the volume and character of chronic disease, they also investigated the public's need for care and rehabilitation. Not satisfied with the individual's own report on his health status, the Commission instituted a "clinical evaluation" consisting of a review of existing medical information obtained from hospitals and private physicians; a complete diagnostic examination including all indicated laboratory tests; and, for a special group, an evaluation of social, nursing, and rehabilitation needs by a team composed of a physician, a nurse, a social worker, and a vocational counselor. These actual physical examinations provided the opportunity for comparing the subjective reports of respondents with the much more objective diagnosis of physicians. A major portion of the reports of these studies is devoted to methodological analyses, constituting a basic contribution to survey research techniques.

Benefiting greatly from the experiences of the first National Health Survey and from the studies of the Commission on Chronic Illness, a second and current National Health Survey was launched in 1956. This program of research encompasses a continuing household interview survey of national cross-sections of families, a series of sub-studies on special populations utilizing existing medical records and conducting specially designed medical examinations and laboratory tests, and a number of carefully designed methodological studies of such problems as respondent understanding and cooperation.[37] The objective of the survey is to provide continuing data on the incidence and prevalence of diseases, injuries, and impairments, and the disabilities resulting from such conditions, the patterns of medical care, the utilization of health facilities and related types of information analyzed according to such significant demographic variables as sex, age, geographical location, and race.[38] There can be little doubt that the National Health Survey

36. Reports by Commission on Chronic Illness, *Chronic Illness in the United States,* 4 vols. Harvard University Press, Cambridge, 1956–1957.
37. National Center for Health Statistics, *Cycle 1 of the Health Examination Survey: Sample and Response.* Public Health Service Publication No. 1000, Series 11, No. 1, Washington, 1964.
38. Reports of findings are appearing regularly on such topics as chronic respiratory conditions, heart conditions and hypertension, peptic ulcers, accidents, disability, and hospitalization patterns, as well as a special series of reports on technical and methodological aspects of health surveys. U.S. Public Health Service, *Origin and Programs of the U.S. National Health Survey,* U.S. Public Health Service, Publication No. 584-

will provide the basic information on the health status of the American people for many years to come.

The above description of health status surveys is by no means complete. To these major studies would have to be added a number of large-scale local surveys (e.g., the Kansas Health Survey), foundation surveys (e.g., Health Information Foundation), university surveys (e.g., Cornell University Medical School), and literally hundreds of smaller surveys of particular subgroups of the population such as industrial workers, armed forces personnel, veterans, health insurance plan members, and university students.[39] Morbidity surveys have also been conducted in other countries: notably the Survey of Sickness conducted for a number of years by the Ministry of Health of Great Britain, the Danish National Morbidity Survey of 1950, and surveys of health status in Japan and Canada.[40]

All of these morbidity surveys add up to a tremendous amount of activity in the health and medical field. We may well ask how good they are and what use they have. To the social scientist, they are apt to appear dull and insignificant—the collection of a myriad of facts lacking in any systematic framework and aimed at the testing of few, if any, specific hypotheses. To many demographers and public health statisticians, however, they constitute the basic data out of which will grow the disease expectancy tables, the identification of groups with high and low risk of disease, the determination of health needs and resources, the evaluation of preventive and therapeutic health measures, the cost in money and disability of illness, the utilization of health facilities, and the first indications of where to look and what to look

A-1, U.S. Government Printing Office, Washington, May, 1958. These reports are divided into two series: (A) deals with methodological problems while (B) presents substantive findings.

39. Hood, T. R. and Virginia Pence, "Community Health Studies in Kansas," *American Journal of Public Health,* Vol. 50, October, 1960, pp. 1560–1569; Anderson, O. W. and Monroe Lerner, *Measuring Health Levels in the United States 1900–1958.* Research Series No. 11, Health Information Foundation, New York, 1960. This series contains a number of reports based on health surveys; Srole, Leo, *et al., Mental Health in the Metropolis.* McGraw-Hill, New York, 1962.

40. See for example, Ministry of Health and Welfare, Division of Health and Welfare Statistics: *Vital and Health Statistics in Japan,* 2 vols., Tokyo, 1953; The Committee on the Morbidity Survey, "The Danish National Morbidity Survey in 1950." Communication No. 7, *Danish Medical Bulletin,* Vol. 2, 1955, pp. 148–152; Jackson, F. W., "The Canadian Sickness Survey." *Research in Public Health,* Milbank Memorial Fund, New York, 1952, pp. 214–222.

for in the search for the causes of disease.[41] Perhaps their very strength lies in the broad array of the facts they collect and in their lack of adherence to any specific hypothesis. They provide the raw material from which many different analyses can be made.

Future household morbidity surveys will probably be broader in content coverage and pay increased attention to the methodological problems of sampling and the measurement of illness. The community population laboratory, with its emphasis on continuous surveys of cross-sections of the community, will provide much of the data on health status and medical behavior of the community. These data will deal with basic medical research problems of epidemiology and applied administrative problems concerning the provision and utilization of health facilities and services.

A promising example of this broader use of the continuing population health survey may be found in the current application of this method by the Puerto Rico Department of Health. At regular quarterly intervals throughout the year, representative cross-sections containing a continuing core of families for purposes of panel analysis are being interviewed with the following objectives in mind: (1) an aid in overall planning, evaluation, and assessment of priorities by providing quantitative island-wide information, not available through routinely collected statistics; (2) an opportunity for directors of programs to do research on their specific programs; (3) a way of identifying areas of health needs not adequately met by current programs and to suggest activities to meet these needs; and (4) a procedure for certain kinds of epidemiologic and social research on chronic conditions and related health problems. An interesting feature in the research design of these continuous surveys is the division into a common core of repeated questions to permit studies of change, and a special section devoted to some specific health program or problem.

Elinson points out several advantages of such community population laboratories:

1. Cumulative as against "one-shot" data about a community population.
2. Opportunity to establish bench marks for periodic appraisal of health programs and studies of change over a long time period.

41. Tayback, Matthew and T. M. Frazier, "Continuous Health Surveys, a Necessity for Health Administration," *Public Health Reports*, Vol. 77, September, 1962, pp. 763–771.

3. Operational benefits in terms of economy, quality and speed of research.
4. Feedback to health and service organizations in the community for program development and evaluation.
5. Development and testing of new research techniques and approaches.[42]

The organization and function of such community population laboratories is currently under review by the U.S. Public Health Service. It appears extremely likely that such laboratories for the conduct of community health surveys will be established in many communities throughout the United States.[43]

Methodologically, the household morbidity survey faces serious problems of sampling and measurement.[44] Many current community health surveys suffer from a high rate of sample mortality. This is especially true in large urban areas with high proportions of racial or ethnic subgroups. There is good reason to believe that these socially and economically deprived groups of the population constitute focal points of illness which are largely escaping current medical detection or treatment. This problem of differential sample mortality is particularly troublesome when attempting to correlate variables within specific sub-populations.[45]

The problem of sample mortality is especially acute in relation to health surveys which make use of medical examinations.[46] Refusals to cooperate

42. Elinson, Jack, "Community Population Laboratories," address to the New York Chapter of the American Statistical Association, April 28, 1960.

43. There is a danger that unless these health surveys become more focused upon specific health problems, they will produce what one public health administrator termed, "a monotonous similarity of findings." Fleck, A. C., "A Public Administrator Looks at Chronic Illness Surveys," *Public Health Reports,* Vol. 77, December, 1962, pp. 1077–1080.

44. Mooney, H. W., "Methodology in Two California Health Surveys: San Jose (1952) and Statewide (1954–55)," *Public Health Monographs,* Vol. 70, 1963, pp. 1–143; Napier, J. A., "Field Methods and Response Rates in the Tecumseh Community Health Study," *American Journal of Public Health,* Vol. 52, February, 1962, pp. 208–216; Woolsey, T. D., P. S. Lawrence, and Eva Balamuth, "An Evaluation of Chronic Disease Prevalence Data from the Health Interview Survey," *American Journal of Public Health,* Vol. 52, October, 1962, pp. 1631–1637.

45. Lilienfeld, A. M., "Epidemiological Methods and Inferences in Studies of Non-Infectious Diseases," *Public Health Reports,* Vol. 72, No. 51, 1957.

46. Cobb, Sidney, Stanley King, and Edith Chen, "Differences Between Respondents and Non-Respondents in a Morbidity Survey Involving Clinical Examination," *Journal of Chronic Diseases,* Vol. 6, August, 1957, pp. 95–108.

may run as high as 40 per cent, although the success of the health examination program of the National Health Survey indicates that this percentage can be lowered considerably.[47] Again, the crucial danger lies in the probability that people who refuse medical examinations have different health problems than those who cooperate.[48] The use of these detailed medical examinations, including laboratory tests, provides an interesting example of surveys based on objective measurements rather than subjective responses.

The need for diagnostic medical examinations to determine the presence of illness is underscored by the generally low correlations found between illness as reported by the respondent and illness as diagnosed by a qualified physician.[49] These inconsistencies point to one of the major methodological problems of morbidity surveys, namely, what is a valid diagnosis? The difficulty in answering this question lies in both the conceptual problem of defining what is meant by illness and disease and the methodological problem of measuring the actual state of an individual's health. These problems are relatively simple in regard to physical handicaps or the acute communicable diseases where some specific infectious agent is involved and where the episode of illness lasts only for a limited period of time.[50] In the large majority of cases, there is little doubt of a medical diagnosis of

---

47. Dawber, T. R. and F. N. Moore, "Longitudinal Study of Heart Disease in Framingham, Massachusetts," Research in Public Health, *Milbank Memorial Fund Quarterly,* New York, 1952; Trussell, R. E., Jack Elinson and M. L. Levin, "Comparison of Various Methods of Estimating the Prevalence of Chronic Disease in a Community—The Hunterdon County Study," *American Journal of Public Health,* Vol. 46, No. 173, 1956.

48. For example, an analysis of refusals to take medical examinations in a study on arthritis in Pittsburgh concluded: "The confirmed non-participants are notable for their minimal use of medical care and their belief that they are in good health." Chen, Edith and Sidney Cobb, "Further Study of Non-Participation Problems in a Morbidity Survey Involving Clinical Examination," *Journal of Chronic Diseases,* Vol. 7, April, 1958, pp. 321–331.

49. Two large-scale, carefully conducted surveys of chronic illness by the Commission on Chronic Illness found that three out of four of the clinically determined cases of chronic illness failed to be detected by the household interview. Commission on Chronic Illness, *op. cit.:* Vol. 3, *Chronic Illness in a Rural Area* and Vol. 4, *Chronic Illness in a Large City.* The reader is referred to the extensive appendices of these studies for a comprehensive analysis of the methodological problems encountered in the household morbidity survey.

50. Banas, P. A. and R. V. Davis, "Identifying the Physically Handicapped Through Survey Methods," *American Journal of Public Health,* Vol. 52, March, 1962, pp. 443–449.

measles, typhoid, or diphtheria, and most respondents can report accurately whether or not they have had or are having these diseases. But the picture changes radically in the case of the chronic degenerative diseases, where both medical diagnosis is uncertain and the respondent's subjective reports of symptoms often become the main basis for deciding whether he is sick or well.[51] This is especially true for mental disease and the addictive disorders such as alcoholism and narcotics addiction.[52]

To this indefiniteness of diagnosis must be added the absence of any clear-cut time span for the duration of the illness. First, the chronic diseases have a long period of onset so that they may very well be present before they can be clinically observed. Second, these diseases continue over long periods of time during which symptoms may come and go so that measures made at different times may result in different medical appraisals. Finally, there are often valid differences of opinion among medical practitioners themselves as to the diagnosis of a chronic illness. For example, the major studies of chronic illness in rural and urban areas mentioned previously found considerable variability among the diagnoses made by different qualified medical examiners.

Part of the difficulty of defining and measuring illness and disease stems from the failure to distinguish adequately between these two concepts. They are often used interchangeably, whereas it might help matters if disease were limited to some abnormal, observable physical or physiological condition, while illness represented the more subjective feelings of sickness or discomfort resulting from the diseased state. Several research workers have pointed out the need to distinguish between what the individual feels in terms of pain and discomfort and what actual disease state may be present.[53] Trussell and Elinson attribute "a major deficiency in the Hunterdon

51. Maddox, G. L., "Self-Assessment of Health Status: A Longitudinal Study of Selected Elderly Subjects," *Journal of Chronic Diseases,* Vol. 17, May 1964, pp. 449–460.

52. Gordon, C., A. R. Emerson and J. Simpson, "The Cornell-Medical Index Questionnaire as a Measure of Health in Socio-Medical Research," *Journal of Gerontology,* Vol. 14, July, 1959, pp. 305–308.

53. Woolsey, T. D. and H. Nisselman, "Some Problems in Statistical Measurement of Chronic Disease," in *Improving the Quality of Statistical Surveys.* Edited by American Statistical Association, 1956. For a good discussion of problems of disease diagnosis in epidemiological studies, see Acheson, R. M., ed., *Comparability in International Epidemiology.* Milbank Memorial Fund, New York, 1964, pp. 32–39, 90–106, 161–168.

County study, in its companion study in Baltimore, and in virtually all household or family interview surveys of morbidity" to "the failure adequately to conceptualize, make clear, and take account of the distinction between disease and illness."[54]

The conceptual analysis of the difference between disease and illness, and the further differentiation of these two states from that of good health poses many complex problems. Operationally, however, we might make a useful distinction between disease as detected by clinical examination, diagnosed condition as appraised by a physician, symptoms as observed by a physician, and feelings of sickness as reported by the respondent.[55] Which of these operational measures is used will depend a great deal upon the purpose of the survey.[56] If the morbidity survey proposes to develop incidence and prevalence rates of disease in a population, then it would seem quite clear that the emphasis must be upon the actual clinical examination and physician's diagnosis. However, if the purpose of the survey is to study the behavior of sick individuals or to investigate the personal and social consequences of ill health, then it may well be that the respondent's own perception of himself as "ill" or "well" will be more valid.[57] We will examine this problem in more detail later when we discuss surveys of patient behavior.

A great deal of methodological research remains to be done on the morbidity survey.[58] An excellent overall review of problems needing solu-

54. Trussell, R. E., Jack Elinson, and M. L. Levin, *op. cit.,* p. 55.

55. Elinson offers a useful differentiation of six types of measures of morbidity ranging from confirmed tissue alteration to individual feeling states. He observes that each has its own validity and suggests the empirical investigation of correlations among the various measures. Elinson, Jack, "Methods of Socio-Medical Research," *op. cit.,* pp. 454–456.

56. The U.S. National Health Survey introduces the interesting conceptual definition of morbidity as including an "awareness of illness and the taking of some action." Thus it places particular emphasis upon symptoms and the seeking of medical care as indicative of illness. Woolsey, T. D., P. S. Lawrence, and Eva Balamuth, *op. cit.*

57. Suchman, E. A., Bernard Phillips, and G. Streib, "An Analysis of the Validity of Health Questionnaires," *Social Forces,* Vol. 36, March, 1958, pp. 223–232.

58. See Kassebaum, G. G., "Response Set: A Methodological Problem in Complaint Inventories," *American Journal of Public Health,* Vol. 51, March, 1961, pp. 446–449, Cartwright, Ann, "Memory Errors in a Morbidity Survey," *Milbank Memorial Fund Quarterly,* Vol. 41, January, 1963, pp. 5–24; Croog, S. H., "Ethnic Origins, Educational Level, and Response to a Health Questionnaire." *Human Organization,* Vol. 20, Summer, 1961, pp. 65–69; Simmons, W. R. and E. E. Bryant, "An Evaluation of

tion is offered by Feldman.[59] Among the major problems he discusses are single-visit versus periodic-visit surveys related to the cyclic character of many of the chronic diseases which show quiescent and active periods, self-respondent versus household informants related to the bias introduced when health data are collected about persons other than the respondent, specificity of diagnostic categories related to the problem of global assessment as opposed to the presence or absence of specific symptoms, standards of diagnostic validity related to the use of subjective reports or medical records and examinations. On the basis of the record to date, Feldman concludes that: "The potential of the household interview survey as a technique for the direct collection of data usable in medical research has in the past been overrated by at least some investigators." Among the more promising solutions he proposes are the categorization of illness in terms of symptoms and disabilities rather than clinical categories and the use of a standardized battery of screening items for symptoms and conditions.

There can be little doubt that the morbidity survey is *not* an adequate substitute for clinical examination. But there can be even less doubt that the morbidity survey is the only currently feasible method of determining the health status of an entire population. Given the proper precautions, this application of the survey method to medical and health research can produce many of the basic facts concerning individual and group differences in health status so necessary to an understanding of health and illness.[60]

While the attention given to sampling problems in population health surveys more than matches similar concern in other areas of survey application, it does seem that in the future, more carefully planned and designed

---

Hospitalization Data from the Health Interview Survey," *American Journal of Public Health,* Vol. 52, October, 1962, pp. 638–647; Hopkins, C. E., *et al.,* "Intrafamily Correlation and Its Significance in the Interpretation of Sample Surveys," *American Journal of Public Health,* Vol. 53, July, 1963, pp. 1112–1120; Hutchison, G. B., Sam Shapiro, and Paul Densen, "Evaluation of a Mailed Health Questionnaire," *American Journal of Public Health,* Vol. 52, November, 1962, pp. 1894–1917.

59. Feldman, J. J., "The Household Interview Survey as a Technique for the Collection of Morbidity Data," *Journal of Chronic Diseases,* Vol. 2, May, 1960, pp. 535–557.

60. As predicted by one public health researcher, "It is perhaps not too great an exaggeration to say that the National Health Survey offers the potential for prompting as great an advance in epidemiologic knowledge in this country as did the introduction of death registration in London four hundred years ago." MacMahon, Brian, T. F. Pugh, and Johannes Ipsen, *Epidemiologic Methods.* Little, Brown, Boston, 1960, p. 85.

health status surveys should aim at special problems, perhaps even testing specific hypotheses. While "medical bookkeeping" will continue to demand the routine determination of standardized incidence and prevalence rates, population health surveys such as those of Leighton in Canada and Srole in New York[61] point the way toward the utilization of such surveys for greater understanding of the causes and consequences of illness. For example, symptoms or conditions can be subjected to multivariate analysis techniques to determine major configurations rather than simple, specific diagnostic labels. These symptoms could include individual feeling states as well as organic manifestations. Similarly, expanding the approach offered by the National Health Survey, a scale of "awareness" of illness coupled with the interference of such illness with normal activities could broaden the concept of morbidity to include sickness as well as disease occurrence.

In addition to such potentially significant changes in the "subject" of morbidity surveys, more refined analyses would include new and more sophisticated demographic characteristics—moving beyond the customary sex, age, occupation, and geographical factors to include family composition, organizational membership, social class, group cohesion—and would analyze these variables not so much for purposes of description as for an understanding of why and how they contribute to variations in the rate of disease. The use of contextual analysis to determine individual variation within different social and geographical "climates," including the greater use of "natural" communities as opposed to current political and census districts, can add much to a truly ecological approach. Comparative analysis techniques which employ cross-community and cross-national comparisons need to be improved to provide greater equivalence of data and concepts that cut across cultural lines.[62] Longitudinal studies using continuing panels of respondents offer an opportunity for determining incidence as opposed to prevalence rates and for relating changes in physical and social environment to changes in health status.

In summary, the morbidity survey provides an excellent means of increasing our understanding as well as our awareness of a population's health status. As we shall see in the next section, this is the fundamental rationale

61. Leighton, A. H., *My Name is Legion*. Basic Books, New York, 1959, and other volumes in the series; Srole, Leo, *et al., op. cit.,* and other volumes in the series.
62. Suchman, E. A., "The Comparative Method in Social Research." *Rural Sociology,* Vol. 29, June, 1964, pp. 123–137.

of the epidemiological survey and, to be sure, more and more morbidity surveys are adding such epidemiological features.

Social epidemiological surveys. The morbidity survey discussed above may be equated with the "descriptive" type of survey. The epidemiological survey, on the other hand, represents the "explanatory" type of survey. Differences in the incidence and prevalence of disease become the jumping off point in the search for "causes" of disease. Consequently, the epidemiological survey has a different logical basis than the morbidity survey and requires a much more complex research design to begin with and a more sophisticated analytic treatment of the data. Thus, as we shall see, the epidemiological survey offers many challenges to the best that survey research methodology has to offer and, not surprisingly, has become a major focus of interest for survey researchers entering the health field.

"Epidemiology in its modern sense is human medical ecology."[63] Disease is studied from the point of view of the mutual interaction and balance of three main sets of factors: the *host* or human individual varying in genetic resistance, susceptibility, and degree of immunity to the disease; the *agent* or carrier of the disease, including any adverse process whether it be an excess, deficiency, or interference of a microbial, toxic, or metabolic factor and varying according to infectivity, virulence, and pathogenesis; and the *environment* or surrounding medium, social as well as physical, which affects the susceptibility of the host, the virulence of the agent or the disease process, and the quantity and quality of contact between host and agent.[64] The basic unit of study is the population group and the objective of epidemiological research is to discover and account for variations in the distribution of disease among different subgroups of the population.[65]

A conference on epidemiology of cardiovascular diseases methodology listed five basic requirements for epidemiological studies:

63. James, George and Morris Greenberg, "The Medical Officer's Bookshelf on Epidemiology and Evaluation," *American Journal of Public Health,* Vol. 47, April, 1957, p. 402. This review offers a good basic bibliography on epidemiology.
64. Paul, J. R., "Epidemiology," in *Research in Medical Science.* Edited by D. E. Green and E. W. Knox. Macmillan, New York, 1950, pp. 53–54.
65. For a good discussion of current conceptual and methodological problems in epidemiology, see Terris, Milton, "The Scope and Methods of Epidemiology," *American Journal of Public Health,* Vol. 52, September, 1962, pp. 1371–1376; also Acheson, R. M., ed., *op. cit.*

1. The subjects studied include not only persons known to have the disease but also persons who are free of it. This makes possible the search for factors which differentiate the two groups.
2. Knowledge of the parent population and the way in which the sample subjects were drawn are essential in evaluating limitations on generalizability.
3. The first aim is to identify characteristics of individuals and of their environment which are associated with the existence or occurrence of disease.
4. It is rarely appropriate to study a single factor; usually, multiple factors and associations are studied.
5. No attempt is made to alter the characteristics of the group under study or to assign individuals at random to "treatment" and "control" groups (two important elements of the clinical or laboratory experiment).[66]

The similarity between this brief characterization of epidemiological research and the social survey method is striking. In both cases, the research process originates with a hypothesis concerning variations in some phenomenon according to different social characteristics. These observed correlations then become the target of a series of statistically controlled comparisons in an attempt to modify or destroy the initial correlation. Thus, for example, a difference may be observed in the frequency of occurrence of cancer of the cervix among Jewish as compared to non-Jewish women. The question for epidemiological research now becomes one of determining why this difference occurs. The search for an answer to this question requires one to compare Jewish and non-Jewish women on those characteristics which are hypothesized as "causing" the observed difference. If the hypothesized characteristics are causally involved in the disease process, and if it is differentially distributed among Jewish and non-Jewish women, then controlling or matching the two groups of women on these characteristics should produce a change in the original correlation. This is the basic logic of the explanatory social survey and the underlying rationale of the epidemiological survey. As in the case of the social survey, causation is

66. "Epidemiology of Cardiovascular Diseases Methodology," *American Journal of Public Health,* Vol. 50, October, 1960, Supplement, pp. 10–11.

viewed as involving many different factors present in the host, the agent, and the environment.[67]

This concept of multiple causation and of necessary but not sufficient causal factors is essential to both the epidemiological and social survey. Unlike the "single factor" closed-system, mechanistic theories of disease so prevalent during the bacteriological era of medical research, the current approach to the epidemiology of the chronic diseases demands an open-system, naturalistic model of multiple causes which envisions a continuous chain of causes in which any single factor can only modify but not prevent the natural process of disease. Given this model, the epidemiological survey, like the social survey, becomes a powerful tool for research on the etiology of disease. However, it is necessary for the epidemiological survey to recognize that the discovery of group differences raises rather than answers the problem of causation. The search for the "intervening" variables which produce the group differences, and the reconstruction of the causal nexus by which these intervening variables are linked, are as essential in social epidemiology as in social research. More and more, social epidemiology must substitute the testing of specific hypotheses concerning underlying causal variables for the general collection of group differences in the distribution of disease.

Epidemiology, like medicine in general, has traditionally concentrated upon the discovery of infectious agents. However, the shift from communicable to chronic diseases has witnessed a parallel shift from agent to host and social environment factors, and the growth of what is now called social epidemiology. As defined by Gordon, epidemiology today is becoming increasingly concerned with "the social component of environment [as] that part which results from the association of man with his fellow man [including] the attainments, beliefs, customs, traditions and like features of a people [that] range from housing to food supply; and from education to the provisions made for medical care."[68] In the absence of any discernible infectious agent, the host may become the agent of his own destruction, while the social environment so defines the position of the host as to be almost indistinguishable from the host himself.

67. For a more detailed discussion, see Suchman, E. A., *Sociology and the Field of Public Health*. Russell Sage Foundation, New York, 1963, pp. 96–98.
68. Gordon, J. E., "The Twentieth Century—Yesterday, Today, and Tomorrow (1920–   )," in *The History of American Epidemiology*. Edited by F. H. Top. C. V. Mosby, St. Louis, 1952, pp. 124–125. Contains a comprehensive bibliography and discussion of modern developments.

There are several significant questions concerning social factors as causes of disease. These questions underlie much of the current controversy over the use and validity of social epidemiological surveys for medical research. The approach to social factors as causes of disease is largely dependent upon the acceptance of the model of multiple causality discussed previously. Given this model, social factors may be studied as direct causes of disease in the sense of social stress acting as a catalytic or potentiating agent in psychosomatic illness, or as indirect causes of disease insofar as they affect either (1) the environment of the individual so as to increase or decrease the presence or virulence of the disease-causing agents, or (2) the host so as to increase or decrease his vulnerability or degree of exposure. As described by Gotjahn early in this century:

> The social basis of disease may be considered under the following heads: Social conditions (a) may create or favor a predisposition for a disease; (b) may themselves cause disease directly; (c) may transmit the causes of disease; and (d) may influence the course of disease.[69]

King offers a much more sophisticated analysis of the channels whereby social factors produce illness in terms of the effects of social forces upon physiological balance, biological or physical disease agents and host vulnerability.[70]

Social epidemiology, through the use of the survey method, is concerned with determining which social factors affect the occurrence of disease and through which process. Its kinship to the social survey is quite apparent. In fact, one of the earliest social surveys was basically an epidemiological survey—that of Durkheim in his study of differential rates of suicide.[71] Beginning with observed differences of suicide rates in different countries, Durkheim attempted to explain these differences in terms of the "causal" factor of social cohesion. Perhaps it would be more appropriate to describe this

69. Gotjahn, Alfred, *Soziale Pathologie,* 1915, as quoted in Rosen, George, *Approaches to a Concept of Social Medicine:* A Historical Survey. Milbank Memorial Fund, New York, 1949, p. 18.
70. King, S. H., "Social Psychological Factors in Illness," in *Handbook of Medical Sociology.* Edited by H. E. Freeman, Sol Levine, and L. G. Reeder, *op. cit.,* pp. 99–121. This chapter offers a summary of various theories concerning the relationship of social factors to disease.
71. Durkheim, Emile, *Suicide:* A Study in Sociology. Translated by J. A. Spaulding and George Simpson. Free Press, Chicago, 1951.

study as a social survey of a health problem, a distinction which is becoming more tenuous every day, especially in relation to behavioral disorders.

The early epidemiological surveys consisted primarily of what is now referred to as "descriptive" epidemiology. Their major focus was upon the straightforward determination of the incidence and prevalence of disease rather than the analysis of its causes. Largely aimed at the prevention of infectious diseases, these descriptive epidemiological surveys were more concerned with locating the focal points of disease concentration for preventive action than with etiology. This emphasis, of course, stemmed from the original source of epidemiological interest in the study of epidemics. Excellent examples of this type of epidemiological survey which still stand today as methodological models are those of Snow on cholera and Goldberger on pellagra.[72] The latter provides a good illustration of the logic of epidemiological analysis, beginning with a geographical difference in the occurrence of a disease, followed by a field survey which discovered associated behavioral differences in diet, and finally a series of laboratory experiments which proved the cause to be a niacin deficiency.

Today, however, epidemics of infectious diseases are few and far between and the epidemiologist's role in the study of chronic degenerative diseases has moved him almost entirely away from pure description to a search for explanation. One of the earliest examples of the use of epidemiology for explanatory purposes is the work of Ackerknecht on malaria. Both a physician and an anthropologist, Ackerknecht explained an observed difference in malaria between settlements of French and Americans in similarly infected geographical areas in terms of the different cultural patterns of living of the two groups.[73]

Today, descriptive epidemiological surveys have been conducted for almost all diseases.[74] The morbidity surveys discussed previously are a major source of descriptive epidemiological data, since most of them report

72. Snow, John, *On the Mode of Communication of Cholera.* John Churchill, London, 1855 (reprinted by the Commonwealth Fund, New York, 1936); Goldberger, J., G. A. Wheeler, and E. Sydenstricker, "A Study of the Relation of Diet to Pellagra Incidence in Seven Textile Mill Communities in South Carolina in 1916." *Public Health Reports,* Vol. 35, No. 648, 1920.
73. Ackerknecht, E. H., "Malaria in the Upper Mississippi Valley, 1760–1900," *Bulletin of the History of Medicine,* Supplement No. 4, Johns Hopkins Press, 1945, pp. 1–142.
74. Clausen, J. A., "Social Factors in Disease," *Annals of the American Academy of Political and Social Science,* Vol. 346, March, 1963, pp. 138–148.

their results according to demographic groupings. Of more interest to us at the moment are those epidemiological surveys which deliberately set out to search for causes. Major social epidemiological surveys, surpassing many of the most ambitious social surveys, have been conducted for heart disease, cancer, mental disease, and arthritis, to mention only a few.[75] In this brief review, it is impossible to deal with these in any detail, but excellent summaries and evaluations have been prepared by Glock and Lennard on hypertension, Graham on cancer, Felix and Kramer on mental illness, Scotch and Geiger on arthritis, Mishler and Scotch on schizophrenia, and Suchman and Scherzer on childhood accidents.[76]

Each of the social epidemiological studies mentioned has attempted first to discover differences in incidence and prevalence of the disease among different demographic or geographical subgroups, and then to explain these differences in terms of underlying social or psychological factors.[77] Perhaps one of the most detailed attempts to analyze the social forces lying

75. Dawber, T. R., *et al.,* "Some Factors Associated with the Development of Coronary Artery Disease," *American Journal of Public Health,* Vol. 49, 1959, pp. 1349–1356; Wynder, E. L., *et al.,* "A Study of Environmental Factors in Carcinoma of the Cervix," *American Journal of Obstetrics and Gynecology,* Vol. 68, 1954, pp. 1016–1047; Jaco, E. G., *The Social Epidemiology of Mental Disorders.* Russell Sage Foundation, New York, 1960; King, S. H. and Sidney Cobb, "Psychological Factors in the Epidemiology of Rheumatoid Arthritis," *Journal of Chronic Diseases,* Vol. 7, June, 1958, pp. 466–475; Johnson, B. C., *et al.,* "Distribution and Familial Studies of Blood Pressure and Serum Cholesterol Levels in a Total Community—Tecumseh, Michigan," *Journal of Chronic Diseases,* Vol. 18, 1965, pp. 147–160.
76. Glock, C. Y. and H. L. Lennard, "Psychological Factors in Hypertension: An Interpretative Review," *Journal of Chronic Diseases,* February 1957, pp. 178–184; Graham, Saxon, "Social Factors in the Epidemiology of Cancer at Various Sites," *Annals of the New York Academy of Sciences,* Vol. 84, December 8, 1960, pp. 807–815; Felix, R. H., and M. Kramer, "Research in Epidemiology of Mental Illness," *Public Health Reports,* Vol. 67, February, 1952, pp. 152–160; Scotch, N. A., and J. J. Geiger, "The Epidemiology of Rheumatoid Arthritis: A Review with Special Attention to Social Factors," *Journal of Chronic Diseases,* Vol. 15, November, 1962, pp. 1037–1067; Mishler, E. G., and N. A. Scotch, "Socio-Cultural Factors in the Epidemiology of Schizophrenia," *Psychiatry: Journal for the Study of Inter-personal Processes,* Vol. 26, November, 1963, pp. 315–351; Suchman, E. A. and Alfred Scherzer, *Current Research in Childhood Accidents.* Association for the Aid of Crippled Children, New York, 1960.
77. Pemberton, John, ed., *Epidemiology:* Reports on Research and Teaching. Oxford University Press, London, 1963. This collection of articles offers an excellent summary of current epidemiology data and research.

behind an observed demographic group difference is that of Hollingshead and Redlich in regard to social class and mental illness.[78] The major mental health surveys in New York City by Srole and in Canada by Leighton, mentioned previously, are also highly sophisticated conceptually and methodologically in their attempt to interpret correlations between social class and mental illness. As a major social variable, socio-economic status plays a significant role in almost all social epidemiology surveys.

As more and more data of a general nature are accumulated concerning variations in the distribution of disease according to social factors, an increasing number of epidemiological surveys have begun to concentrate upon the testing of specific hypotheses. Thus, for example, several large-scale surveys have been conducted on the effects of social and psychological stress upon the occurrence of several different diseases.[79] While the measurement of stress continues to be one of the most difficult problems in social medical research, surveys of mental illness, heart disease, tuberculosis, arthritis, ulcers, alcoholism, diabetes and many other diseases have all indicated the greater occurrence of such diseases under stressful conditions.[80]

A particularly interesting example of survey research on a specific causal factor concerns the relationship of smoking to lung cancer.[81] Many surveys have demonstrated statistically the existence of this relationship but, perhaps because of the economic interests involved, the demand continues for direct laboratory evidence rather than "merely associational" statistical proof.

These social epidemiological surveys have for the most part used household interviews involving detailed questionnaires aimed at establishing the state of disease and uncovering factors related to its occurrence. Several of them have employed the repeated interview technique with a panel of respondents, notably the panel study of heart disease in Framingham, Massachusetts. These surveys have been conducted with rigorously selected

78. Hollingshead, A. B. and F. C. Redlich, *Social Class and Mental Illness.* John Wiley & Sons, New York, 1958.

79. Wardwell, W. I., Merton Hyman, and C. B. Bahnson, "Stress and Coronary Heart Disease in Three Field Studies," *Journal of Chronic Diseases,* Vol. 17, 1964, pp. 73–84.

80. For a general review, see Milbank Memorial Fund, "Inter-relations Between the Social Environment and Psychiatric Disorders." Milbank Memorial Fund, New York, 1953.

81. Dorn, H. F., and S. J. Cutler, *Morbidity from Cancer in the United States.* Public Health Monograph 46, U.S. Government Printing Office, Washington, 1958.

samples, using highly skilled interviewers and carefully pre-tested questionnaires. They rank among the best health surveys in design, execution, and analysis.

This does not mean that they are free of faults any more than the best of our present social surveys are. In a review of epidemiological surveys of rheumatoid arthritis, Scotch concludes rather critically: "In summary, this section on research in social factors in rheumatoid arthritis makes one fact dramatically clear: there have been very few studies that meet even minimal criteria for scientific evidence and inference." Among the inadequacies he discusses are those of sampling (non-representativeness, mortality, and absence of non-diseased control groups), procedure (bias in the collection and analysis of data) and instrumentation (lack of reliability or validity in the measurement of both the disease state and the causal variables).[82] These are all serious limitations but, in this writer's opinion, their solution depends as much, if not more, on the further methodological progress of the survey technique than on the skills and resources of the research worker.

An excellent methodological analysis by the committee on design and analysis of studies of the previously mentioned conference on epidemiology of cardiovascular diseases methodology discusses some of the major methodological problems in current social epidemiological research.[83] Four of these are particularly relevant to the use of the survey method for studying the etiology of disease:—

(1) *The time reference.* Many current surveys are based upon retrospective recall which introduces serious problems of memory as well as sampling bias, e.g., they deal only with survivors. A major methodological advance in answer to these problems involves the use of prospective studies, or as they are often called in social research, panel studies. Using this method, a population is selected for study without prior knowledge of the disease status of the individuals included. This population is then examined and classified as diseased or free of disease. Data are also collected on possible causal or related factors. The individuals free of disease are considered to be the population at risk, and are observed over some time period. At the end of this period, those individuals who have developed the disease are then compared with those who are still disease-free, both on past and present charac-

82. Scotch, N. A. and J. J. Geiger, *op. cit.*
83. "Epidemiology of Cardiovascular Diseases Methodology," *American Journal of Public Health, op. cit.*

teristics. Significant differences in hypothesized "causal" variables and the occurrence of the disease are taken as suggestive of etiological factors.

(2) *Selection of comparison groups.* The logic of the ideal experimental design provides for the random assignment of cases to an experimental and a control group. This is not possible in the epidemiological survey and there is always a serious danger that the disease and disease-free groups are not matched. There is no way of fully overcoming this inherent weakness, but what can be done is to insure that the two groups being compared are as much alike as possible with respect to factors which are known in advance to differentiate the two groups. The use of matched "controls" affords some approximation to the experimental design.

(3) *The problem of non-response.* As in all surveys, incomplete response introduces a strong possibility of biased results since those individuals who refuse to cooperate or who drop out of a survey cannot be assumed to have the same characteristics as those who are included in the final sample. Special sample surveys of non-respondents aimed at determining how they differ from respondents afford some measure of control of this problem.

(4) *The definition of the disease.* We have already noted the difficulties of a reliable and valid diagnosis of disease through survey methods. This problem is particularly acute for epidemiological surveys of specific diseases, since the correct identification of the diseased group is essential to further analysis. A combination of clinical examinations and medical diagnoses, with medical histories and descriptions of symptoms, seems most likely to produce valid results. The successful use of a Rheumatoid Arthritis Index based on a series of symptom questions indicates the potential utility of such indices for epidemiological surveys.[84] Such composite indices have also been employed by Leighton and Srole in their studies of mental illness. These disease indices can also be used as a method for preliminary screening of potentially positive cases who could then be followed up with medical examinations.

To the above major problems in the epidemiological survey can also be added the dozens of minor problems that deal with instrument construction and field administration. For example, methodological studies have shown that the number and type of diseases obtained in an interview vary with both

84. King, S. H. and Sidney Cobb, *op. cit.*

question wording and interviewer. These are standard problems in survey research, however, and need not be elaborated upon here.[85]

Of greatest current significance is the need to develop a conceptual or analytical model whereby social factors can be linked to disease processes in such a way as to provide guidelines for the testing of specific hypotheses concerning the etiology of different diseases. At the present time, epidemiological research lacks such models and is largely limited to the essential but largely unimaginative search for correlations between disparate social factors and disease. The prevalent host-agent-environment classification of etiological factors, while useful for descriptive purposes, is limited in explanatory power. A promising approach to the study of social and cultural processes of significance to health is offered by Cassel *et al.,* on the basis of a linked open system. The general proposition underlying their research is worth quoting as an illustration of the greater depth of explanation provided by such an approach:

> The process of socio-culture change as manifested in migration from a rural to an urban industrial setting raises the probability of incongruity between the culture of the migrant and the social situation in which he lives. Such incongruities place excessive adjustive burdens on the social groups in which the migrant interacts and on the personality systems of individual migrants. Insofar as these stresses are not absorbed by small group systems and/or the personality system, recent migrants to the industrial city are likely to manifest increased rates of psychological, somatic, and social ill health.[86]

According to Cassel, epidemiologists must increasingly turn to social science theory as the source for their hypotheses.[87] He largely discounts the germ theory of disease as no longer profitable in the case of the chronic diseases where social and cultural factors appear most relevant. He proposes that, instead of focusing upon the disease entity and studying its antecedents, epidemiologists begin with people exposed to relevant social proc-

85. Wardwell, W. I., and C. B. Bahnson, "Problems Encountered in Behavioral Science Research in Epidemiological Studies," *American Journal of Public Health,* Vol. 54, June, 1964, pp. 972–981.

86. Cassel, John, R. Patrick, and D. Jenkins, "Epidemiological Analysis of the Health Implications of Cultural Change: A Conceptual Model," *Annals of the New York Academy of Sciences,* Vol. 84, December 8, 1960, p. 944.

87. Cassel, John, "Social and Cultural Considerations in Health Innovations," *Annals of the New York Academy of Medicine,* Vol. 107, May 22, 1963, p. 741.

esses and determine the spectrum of resulting disorders rather than any specific disease. He also points out the highly significant fact that those factors which are responsible for the onset of an illness condition may be very different from those affecting recovery from the condition.[88]

Approaches to explanation, based upon decision-making processes in risk-taking situations, are currently being developed in accident surveys.[89] As social epidemiology continues to develop such "causal" models, the epidemiological survey will progress far beyond the current concentration upon host, agent and environmental factors, as has social survey research in general.

Another major direction of growth combines individual respondents and ecological surveys. As Clausen and Kohn, among others, have pointed out, the assumptions concerning causation based upon variations in overall rates for total areas or groups is subject to challenge.[90] An area may have a high rate of disease and a high rate of social disorganization without the two being necessarily connected. A much more promising approach is afforded by the idea of "contextual" analysis in social survey research, which would involve the location of areas or groups of high and low incidence and then the study of differences in disease occurrence and related factors separately within each area. Thus, for example, it may well be that the relationship between psychological stress and narcotics addiction will be different in an area in which narcotics addiction is a fairly well known and accepted phenomenon than in one where it is not.[91] Studies of mental disease in Canada provide an excellent example, combining case studies, clinical examinations, and epidemiological surveys within areas of high and low social disorganization.[92]

One final example of more advanced survey techniques in epidemiological research is the use of scale and latent-structure analysis for the multi-

88. Cassel, John, "Social Science Theory as a Source of Hypotheses in Epidemiological Research." *American Journal of Public Health,* Vol. 54, September, 1964, 1482–1488.

89. Suchman, E. A., "A Conceptual Analysis of the Accident Phenomenon," *Social Problems,* Vol. 8, Winter, 1960–61, pp. 241–253.

90. Clausen, J. A. and M. L. Kohn, "The Ecological Approach in Social Psychiatry," *American Journal of Sociology,* Vol. 60, September, 1954, pp. 140–151.

91. Chein, Isador, *et al., The Road to H:* Narcotics, Delinquency and Social Policy. Basic Books, New York, 1964.

92. Hughes, Charles, *et al., People of Cove and Woodlot.* Basic Books, New York, 1960.

variate analysis of symptoms. As we have seen, the definition of an illness or a disease is a major problem in both morbidity and epidemiological surveys. Some attempts have been made to develop indices based on a series of diagnostic items.[93] The analysis of such items in terms of unidimensionality or latent structure might produce more reliable and valid measures of both gradations of seriousness and types of illness. This scaling approach to the analysis of symptoms has been analyzed in some detail by Stouffer *et al.* in relation to the screening of psychoneurotics in the armed forces.[94]

There are many other ways in which epidemiological and social surveys can share their mutual conceptual and methodological problems. As the chronic diseases, especially the mental and addictive disorders, continue to grow in importance, we may expect more and more attention to be paid to social and psychological factors with a consequent narrowing of the gap between social and medical research. The search for etiological factors in the chronic diseases is bound to force the medical researcher to supplement his laboratory experiments with field surveys both as source and proof of his hypotheses.

VARIATIONS IN RESPONSE TO ILLNESS AND THE MAINTENANCE OF HEALTH

Not only do social and psychological forces influence the occurrence of disease in society, but these factors also determine the behavior of the public in response to illness. The study of how and why people behave the way they do in relation to health problems comprises a major portion of current survey research in the health field.[95] After all, the provision of medical care to the public, like the supply of any other basic commodity in society, represents a highly complex marketing situation. Involved are many different types of medical services rendered by a wide variety of professional and non-professional personnel, under differing public and private auspices, aimed at varying segments of the public, and performed in highly diverse organizational settings. The maintenance of health in modern times is a

93. Langer, T. S., "A Twenty-Two Item Screening Score of Psychiatric Symptoms Indicating Impairment," *Journal of Health and Human Behavior,* Vol. 3, Winter, 1962, pp. 269–276.
94. Stouffer, S. A., *et al., Measurement and Prediction,* Vol. IV of *Studies in Social Psychology in World War II,* Princeton University Press, Princeton, 1950, chap. 13 and 14. This volume contains an excellent analysis of different scaling procedures.
95. For a fairly comprehensive listing of surveys in this area, see "What People Know, Believe, and Do About Health." *Health Education Monographs,* Supplement No. 1, 1963.

combination of big business and big government, and health surveys perform an essential function in studying the relationships between private medicine, government, and the public.

In addition to the study of individual responses to illness, an important area of current health research concerns community factors in both the definition of what are to be considered health problems and the organization of community forces to meet these problems. As pointed out by James: "Effective public health programs can only rarely be conducted in the present era, unless the community attitude toward them is satisfactory. Community attitude may include public opinion (as expressed, for example, in a referendum on fluoridation), or professional custom (as, for example, underreporting of venereal disease by practicing physicians)."[96] Included in this area of health research are community surveys of public opinion, the analysis of special interest groups in the health field, the study of different forms of health communication, and the evaluation of informational or propaganda campaigns.

Surveys of problems encountered in the provision of medical care are aimed at (1) an understanding of the basic processes of human behavior such as in the prevention of illness, the seeking of medical care, and the adjustment to illness, or community forces such as leadership structure, forms of power, and group organization; and (2) the more *applied* problems of public health and medical care program operation and administration. These surveys reflect the increased need for reliable and valid data on health problems resulting from the changing nature of public health and medicine. Chronic disease control requires much more voluntary activity on the part of the public than does the control of the acute communicable diseases. Both in the prevention and the treatment of these chronic diseases, the individual has to take greater initiative in recognizing symptoms, in seeking medical care, and in following through with medical treatment. He can no longer be required by law to take preventive immunizations, since none exist for the chronic diseases; nor can he be forcibly quarantined or treated, since the chronically ill person does not constitute as obvious a threat to the safety of the public as does an individual with a communicable disease. He can only be educated to change his basic habits of living and eating, to recognize the insidious onset of chronic disease symptoms, to cooperate in mass detection or screening programs, to seek proper medical

96. James, George, "The Present Status and Future Development of Community Health Research—A Critique from the Viewpoint of Community Health Agencies," *Annals of the New York Academy of Science,* Vol. 107, May 22, 1963, p. 761.

advice, to utilize existing treatment facilities and, often, to accept a changed way of life as the the only adjustment to an incurable, progressively degenerative disease. Similarly, community support for health programs in the chronic disease area can no longer be taken for granted as fulfilling an obvious health need. The emphasis is only rarely upon the dramatic prevention of epidemics, much more often consisting of such undramatic requirements as mass screening and early detection.

Another trend which has increased the demand for survey research in this area concerns the changing nature of medical practice. The old-time family general practitioner who performed his duties on a personal fee-for-service basis is giving way to specialized medical care, with its greater formality of doctor-patient relationship and its more complex and technical tools for diagnosis and treatment.[97] The result has been a change in patterns of provision and utilization of medical facilities, the growth of new forms of medical group practice, and the development of new methods of payment.[98] To help plan and evaluate these new approaches, surveys have been undertaken on medical care needs and resources, on the utilization of medical facilities, and on the costs and methods of financing medical care.[99]

In an attempt to meet the challenges of a changed disease picture and new methods of providing medical care, the official public health units throughout the country have developed many new programs of prevention, treatment, and rehabilitation. Much greater emphasis is being placed upon "reaching out" to the public with such services as well-baby clinics, home care programs, mass screening and detection programs, rehabilitative and restorative services, and school health programs. Survey research occupies a prominent place today in the planning, operation, and evaluation of these new public health services and programs.[100]

97. Davis, Michael M., *Medical Care for Tomorrow*. Harper and Bros., New York, 1955.
98. For an excellent collection of articles dealing with changes in the provision of medical care, see *Medical Care in Transition*, Vols. 1 and 2. Public Health Service Publication No. 1128, U.S. Government Printing Office, Washington, 1955.
99. A detailed bibliography of research in this area may be found in Simmons, O. G., "Social Research in Health and Medicine," *op. cit.*, and his "Sociology of Medical Care," in *Handbook of Medical Sociology*. Edited by H. E. Freeman, Sol Levine, and L. G. Reeder, *op. cit.*, pp. 536–577.
100. See for example, *Evaluation in Public Health*. Public Health Services Publication No. 413, U.S. Government Printing Office, Washington, 1958; and bibliography by Getting, V. A., "Evaluation," *American Journal of Public Health*, Vol. 47, April, 1957, pp. 408–413.

In the remainder of this section, we will examine and evaluate some of the major surveys that have been conducted in two main areas of current concern: (1) public information, attitudes, and behavior, and (2) health needs, resources, and utilization. These two areas are closely interrelated and there will obviously be a great deal of overlap among the surveys conducted in them. However, for the purpose of analyzing the differing natures of the problem in each area and evaluating the contribution of survey research to them, we will treat each area separately.

Surveys of public information, attitudes, and behavior. A New York State Commissioner of Health is credited with saying: "Public health is what the public wants"—and he might have gone on to paraphrase Abraham Lincoln and state that his job was to find out what this was. We will not get into the complicated question here of the proper role of surveys of public opinion in determining medical policy, but there is little doubt that a great deal of survey research in the public health field concerns finding out what the public does want.[101]

This has been the subject of investigation on such diverse topics as fluoridation, choice of medical personnel, operation of a public health program, community health facilities, hospital care, medical payment, drugs and prescriptions, the behavior of physicians, and health and medical care in general.[102] These public opinion surveys have shown that there is a great

101. As pointed out by James, "We know surprisingly little about how to motivate people . . . we know little about convincing them to come to clinics, we even fall short in getting them to take vaccines. We shall have to do a great deal of research in how to motivate people to act for their health's sake." James, George, "The Present Status . . . ," *op. cit.,* p. 767.

102. Davis, Morris, "Community Attitudes Toward Fluoridation," *Public Opinion Quarterly,* Vol. 23, Winter, 1959–60, pp. 474–482; Freidson, Eliot, *Patient's Views of Medical Practice.* Russell Sage Foundation, New York, 1961; Metzner, C. A. and Gerald Gurin, *Personal Response and Social Organization in a Health Campaign.* Bureau of Public Health Economics, Research Series No. 9, University of Michigan, 1960; Koos, E. L., "Metropolis—What City People Think of Their Medical Services," *American Journal of Public Health,* Vol. 45, December, 1955, pp. 1551–1557; Freidson, Eliot and J. J. Feldman, *The Public Looks at Hospitals.* Health Information Foundation, Research Series No. 4, New York, 1958; Caldwell, B. J., "Employees Study Patients' Complaints," *Modern Hospital,* May, 1956; Freidson, Eliot and J. J. Feldman, *Public Attitudes Toward Health Insurance.* Health Information Foundation Research Series No. 5, New York, 1958; National Opinion Research Center, *Public Attitudes Toward Prescription Costs and the Drug Industry.* Health Information Foundation, New York, October, 1955; American Medical Association, *What Americans*

deal of variation in public opinion concerning these different health topics and that, as might be expected, these variations are related to the different group memberships, social roles and statuses, and information, attitudes, and experiences of the individual.

Many of these surveys suffer from a lack of sufficient attention to the analysis of the public opinion process and consist of rather straightforward descriptive rather than explanatory studies. Despite the fact that this area represents, in general, one of the most advanced developments of survey technique, public opinion studies in the health field have not made adequate use of such features as panel designs for measuring change, comparative studies to determine cross-community variation, contextual analyses to investigate "health climates of opinion," and special group surveys to determine leadership and community power structure. Furthermore, in very few cases have knowledge and attitudes been measured by means of scales or latent-structure analysis, or been adequately related to behavior.

There are exceptions. A series of public opinion studies undertaken by the National Opinion Research Center for the Health Information Foundation did attempt to relate public information and attitudes to health behavior. These studies employed an interesting sample design involving interlocking samples. Each member of the general public sample was asked to name his regular physician and pharmacist. A subsample of these professionals was then interviewed permitting a comparison of the attitudes and behavior of the respondent with those of his physician or pharmacist.[103] One comparison, for example, showed contradictory reports from the public and the physicians concerning satisfaction with hospital care, with the physicians believing that their patients were much more dissatisfied than they reported themselves to be.[104]

A rather extensive series of public opinion surveys has been conducted on the issue of fluoridation, which provides an excellent example of the

Think of the Medical Profession, American Medical Association, Chicago, 1956; Haldeman, Jack C., "What the American Public Wants in Health Care," *Public Health Reports,* Vol. 77, April, 1962, pp. 301–306; Sheatsley, Paul B., *Public Attitudes Toward Aspects of Health.* Health Information Foundation, New York, 1956; Bugbee, George, *Public Attitudes Toward Use of Medical Care,* Health Information Foundation, New York, 1956.

103. Feldman, Jacob J., "Problems in the Study of Health Attitudes and Practice," paper read at the 1956 Annual Conference of the American Association for Public Opinion Research.

104. Sheatsley, Paul, "Public Attitudes Toward Hospitals," *Hospitals,* May 16, 1957.

potential conflict between the value system of certain segments of the community and the professional judgment of the public health authorities. As observed at one conference:

> Fluoridation appears to be an excellent problem for the juncture of social science and medicine, since it involves entire communities and brings to the fore many aspects of response to health programs. Among the ways of viewing fluoridation as a community decision are: classification of populations according to their gross characteristics such as age, education, income, etc.; studies of community organization; analysis of fluoridation decisions as processes, including sequential patterns and reconstructions of decision-making. . . . Fluoridation, being a widespread phenomenon, also affords opportunities for comparative studies (of communities).[105]

A special issue of the *Journal of Social Issues* brought together a number of these surveys of public opinion and community attitudes toward fluoridation. They reveal the motivational base of the opponents and proponents, the alignment of power within the community, and the relative effectiveness of various approaches toward instituting fluoridation. This collection of studies, together with Paul's introduction and Kegeles' evaluation of them, offers an excellent illustration of public opinion at work in the field of health.[106]

The most detailed surveys of the relationship of community forces and cultural values to health action have been undertaken by sociologists and anthropologists concerned with the introduction of new health techniques or programs. In the United States, community surveys have been made in North Carolina, Massachusetts, and Michigan, as well as in other states.[107] These studies have demonstrated the important roles played by public

---

105. *Conference on Preventive Medicine and Social Science Research,* Social Science Research Council, Skytop, Pa., June 22–27, 1958, mimeographed.

106. Paul, B. D., *et al.,* eds., "Trigger for Community Conflict: The Case of Fluoridation," *Journal of Social Issues,* Vol. 17, No. 4, 1961 (entire issue); Garrison, W. A. and C. G. Lindberg, "An Annotated Bibliography of Social Science Aspects of Fluoridation," *Health Education Journal,* Vol. 19, November, 1961, pp. 209–230.

107. See Kimball, S. T. and Marion Pearsall, *The Talledega Story:* A Study in Community Process. University of Alabama Press, Tuscaloosa, 1954; Hunter, Floyd, R. C. Schaffer, and C. G. Sheps, *Community Organization:* Action and Inaction, University of North Carolina Press, Chapel Hill, 1956; Sower, Christopher, *Community Involvement.* Free Press, Glencoe, Ill., 1957.

opinion and the community power structure in the development of health programs. An analysis by Rossi of differential influence, power, and authority in a community, concludes: "Citizen participation is a good way for a professional to operate to get things done, but there is no superior wisdom in the local masses, merely superior strength."[108] This statement points to the great need to view mass opinions within the broader context of community power in general. The current emphasis upon the superficial polling of information and attitudes has resulted in a generally negative appraisal of the utility of public opinion surveys by the health professions. The study of these opinions within the broader context of community action should do much to remedy this criticism.

A large number of community studies, many involving population surveys, by behavioral scientists in the underdeveloped areas of the world have underscored the intimate relationship between health behavior and cultural values.[109] The use of survey techniques for research on health problems in the underdeveloped countries offers a highly promising area for future research.[110] The success of such surveys will depend a great deal upon the development of reliable and valid survey techniques for making cross-cultural comparisons.[111] While traditional anthropological techniques have proven productive in dealing with small communities, research in such mass societies as India and South America demand the use of modern survey techniques.

Perhaps the greatest number, and also the poorest, of health surveys have been made in connection with measuring public knowledge and information regarding disease and medical care. A working paper for a World Health Organization conference on health and health education mentions "thousands of survey studies with some relevance for health education practice reported in the literature." These studies range from large nation-

---

108. Rossi, P. H., "What Makes Communities Tick," *Public Health Reports,* Vol. 77, February, 1962, pp. 117–124.

109. Paul, B. D., ed., *Health, Culture, and Community.* Russell Sage Foundation, New York, 1955; Rubin, Vera, ed., "Culture, Society, and Health," *Annals of the New York Academy of Science,* Vol. 84, December 8, 1960; Polgar, Steven, "Health Action in Cross-Cultural Perspective," in *Handbook of Medical Sociology.* Edited by H. E. Freeman, Sol Levine and L. G. Reeder, *op. cit.,* pp. 397–419.

110. Jenney, E. R. and O. G. Simmons, "Human Relations and Technical Assistance in Public Health," *Scientific Monthly,* Vol. 78, June, 1954, pp. 365–371.

111. Chance, N. A., "Conceptual and Methodological Problems in Cross-Cultural Health Research," *American Journal of Public Health,* Vol. 52, March, 1962, pp. 410–417.

wide surveys of information concerning nutrition to small classroom surveys on specific health facts. As listed by Kaplan:

> Polling methods have many applications in public health education, chief among which are (a) in planning, conducting, and evaluating health education programs; (b) in gathering information useful to volunteer health groups in the conduct of fund-raising and educational campaigns; (c) in determining the usefulness of materials published by health agencies; (d) in obtaining public support for health programs; (e) in gathering information essential to the understanding of the health needs of a community; (f) in ascertaining knowledge of available health facilities.[112]

An analysis of health education research in the *Research Quarterly* for the ten-year period 1951–60 showed that three out of four studies reported used the survey method.[113] A review of these surveys, however, shows most of them to be highly deficient in design or execution. In general, the field of public health education has not made use of many of the current concepts and methods in public opinion and communications research. Unrepresentative samples, poorly constructed questionnaires, unskilled interviewing, and inadequate analysis are the rule rather than the exception.

Several excellent surveys have been conducted, however, on attempts to change attitudes and behavior through information. A large-scale health education campaign by the Edinburgh Public Health Department to inform the public on the risks of lung cancer associated with cigarette smoking failed to show any changes, according to a well-designed before-and-after survey.[114] An attempt to change mental health information and attitudes in a Canadian community through extensive public health education techniques showed a similar lack of success; in fact, there was evidence to indicate an increase in anxiety. This survey revealed the following characteristic public response to mental illness:

112. Kaplan, Oscar J., "Evaluation of Health Education Activities by Opinion Poll Techniques," *American Journal of Public Health,* Vol. 41, August, 1951, Supplement No. 1.
113. Russell, R. D., "An Analysis of the Health and Health Education Research in the Research Quarterly, 1951–60," *Research Quarterly,* Vol. 33, 1962, pp. 137–140.
114. Cartwright, Ann, F. M. Martin and J. J. Thomson, "Efficacy of an Anti-Smoking Campaign," *The Lancet,* February, 1960, p. 329.

. . . first, denial of mental illness; second, isolation of the affected person in a hospital where mental illness can no longer be denied, with concomitant rationalization of this isolation with beliefs that the hospital is a wonderful place, capable of curing mental illness, if it can be cured at all, which is doubtful; and finally, isolation of the whole vexing problem by a secondary denial that a problem exists insofar as it needs solving by ordinary citizens.[115]

The preliminary study of the community, the careful and painstaking introduction of the program, and the well-planned surveys of public reactions before and after the campaign mark this study as a model of evaluation research.

A nation-wide interview survey of attitudes toward mental illness by the Joint Commission on Mental Illness and Health pointed to the continuing stigma of mental illness in present day society.[116] This survey represents one of the few methodologically sound health surveys aimed at a specific illness and including an analysis of the interrelationship between knowledge, attitudes, and behavior. The public was found to lack an awareness of the nature of mental illness and to view the mentally ill individual with disapproval. The attitude of the public toward mental disease was also found to affect the seeking of medical care for mental illness. Other surveys on the meaning of mental illness to a family showed that the way in which mental illness was defined influenced the individual's coming into contact with medical care and his reception after treatment.[117]

Many surveys conducted on the meaning of illness in general in our society support the definition of disease to be found, of all places, in a medical text on physiology: "Health and disease are primarily sociological concepts; they generally mean that a man can or cannot carry on his normal

115. Cumming, Elaine and John Cumming, *Closed Ranks:* An Experiment in Mental Health Education. Harvard University Press, 1957, pp. 122–123.
116. Joint Commission on Mental Illness and Health, *Action for Mental Health,* 1961. See also Gurin, Gerald, Joseph Veroff and Sheila Feld, *Americans View Their Mental Health.* Basic Books, New York, 1960. An excellent review of opinion surveys in the mental health field is given in Halpert, H. P., *Public Opinions and Attitudes about Mental Health.* Public Health Service Publication No. 1045, U.S. Government Printing Office, Washington, May, 1963.
117. Yarrow, M. R., *et al.,* "The Psychological Meaning of Mental Illness in the Family," *Journal of Social Issues,* Vol. 11, No. 4, 1955, pp. 12–24, and Simmons, O. G. and Howard Freeman, *The Mental Patient Comes Home.* John Wiley & Sons, New York, 1963.

occupation."[118] Koos, in a cross-sectional survey of some of the commonly held beliefs and practices about health in one American community, using repeated interviews of 500 families over a four-year period, found marked differences between the social classes in the symptoms they felt indicated the need for medical care. The method of seeking medical care was also affected by social class position.[119] This relationship of social class to knowledge, attitudes, and behavior in response to illness has been supported by a large number of social surveys.[120]

Quite a few rather detailed and fairly rigorous surveys have been made on the process of seeking, finding, and adjusting to medical care. In fact, the sophistication of the theoretical formulations on this aspect of medical behavior is fairly well advanced. Largely based upon the conceptual analysis of Parsons of the "sick role" and the need for "legitimization" by professional medical personnel, these surveys of medical behavior seek to determine when, how, why, and where individuals perceive themselves as sick and proceed to seek and carry out medical treatment.[121] Freidson makes an interesting distinction between the "professional referral structure" and the "lay referral structure" in his survey of a sample of hospital patients: "Indeed, the whole process of seeking help involves a network of potential consultants, from the intimate and informal confines of the nuclear family through successively more select, distant, and authoritative laymen, until the 'professional' is reached."[122]

118. Winton, F. R. and L. E. Bayliss, *Human Physiology,* 4th ed. Little, Brown, Boston, 1955, p. 1.
119. Koos, Earl L., *The Health of Regionville.* Columbia University Press, New York, 1954.
120. Badgley, R. F. and R. W. Heterington, "Medical Care and Social Class in Wheatville," *Canadian Journal of Public Health,* Vol. 53, October, 1962, pp. 425–431; Ross, J. A., "Social Class and Medical Care," *Journal of Health and Human Behavior,* Vol. 3, Spring, 1962, pp. 288–292; Rosenblatt, Daniel and Edward A. Suchman, "Blue Collar Attitudes and Information Toward Health and Illness," in *Blue Collar World.* Edited by A. B. Shostak and William Gomberg. University of Pittsburgh Press, Pittsburgh, 1964.
121. Parsons, Talcott, *The Social System.* Free Press, Glencoe, Ill., 1951, pp. 428–473; see also his "Social Change and Medical Organization in the United States: A Sociological Perspective," *Annals of the American Academy of Political and Social Science,* Vol. 346, March, 1963, pp. 21–33.
122. Freidson, Eliot and George Silver, "Social Science in Family Medical Care," *Public Health Reports,* Vol. 75, 1960, pp. 489–493. See also Freidson, Eliot, *Patients' Views of Medical Practice, op. cit.*

A survey of over 2,000 families by the New York City Department of Health divided the illness episode into five different stages:

1. *The symptom experience stage:* when the symptoms are a) recognized, b) interpreted as to their seriousness, possible cause and their import or meaning, c) reacted to with varying degrees of concern.
2. *The sick seeking status stage:* when the potentially ill person begins to seek symptom alleviation, information and advice, and provisional validation.
3. *The medical contact stage:* when one or more sources of medical care are contacted to ascertain a diagnosis and discover what courses of treatment will be recommended.
4. *The dependent-patient role stage:* when the individual has committed himself into the hands of a doctor and surrendered certain prerogatives and decisions, and accepted care.
5. *The rehabilitation stage:* when the individual returns to his normal role functioning.[123]

This survey found a significant relationship between the health orientation of the sick individual and his medical behavior. For example, individuals with a "scientific" as opposed to a "folk" orientation to medical care were more likely to pay attention to initial symptoms, to seek professional medical attention more quickly, to follow medical advice more faithfully, and to adjust to illness more adequately. Other surveys of patients experiencing illness have, in general, documented the importance of acceptance of the sick role as a prerequisite to "rational" health behavior.[124] A nationwide survey of the role of anxiety in motivating the individual to seek medical care found the better educated and more informed respondents less anxious about their illness.[125] Another survey of a sample of college students with a history of rheumatic fever found that prophylaxis behavior

123. Suchman, E. A., "Stages of Illness and Medical Care," *Journal of Health and Human Behavior,* Vol. 6, Fall, 1965, pp. 114–128.
124. Davis, Milton S. and R. L. Eichhorn, "Compliance with Medical Regimens: A Panel Study," *Journal of Health and Human Behavior,* Vol. 4, Winter, 1963, 240–249; for a good review of these studies see Stoeckle, J. D., I. K. Zola and G. E. Davidson, "On Going to See the Doctor: The Contributions of the Patient to the Decision to Seek Medical Aid," *Journal of Chronic Diseases,* Vol. 16, 1963, pp. 975–989.
125. Levine, G. N., "Anxiety About Illness; Psychological and Social Bases," *Journal of Health and Human Behavior,* Vol. 3, Spring, 1962, pp. 30–34.

was better in cases of perceived susceptibility, a self-definition of serious-ness, knowledge of the disease, and a belief in the benefits of treatment.[126]

A number of longitudinal or panel surveys have attempted to study ad-justment to illness during the course of an actual illness. Using carefully selected samples and well tested instruments, two studies of individuals with heart disease were able to evaluate the effect of this type of chronic ailment upon the patient and his family. Following a sample of 326 farmers over four years, one study found that changes in work behavior were most likely to be made to the extent that the individual *perceived* himself as having a heart condition regardless of objective evidence. As concluded by the in-vestigators, ". . . the belief that one was diseased, rather than the presence of clinically diagnosed heart disease, most influenced the farmer's be-havior."[127] It is this subjectivity of sickness-feelings which gives a crucial importance to survey research using attitudinal questions for understanding and predicting illness behavior. A panel study of family adjustment to myocardial infarction pointed up the familiar problems in longitudinal studies created by a loss of respondents, in this case about 50 per cent.[128]

The use of the panel survey design is particularly appropriate for the study of the course of an illness. The seeking, finding, and carrying out of medical care involve a number of critical decision-points which may well spell the difference between life or death. Here, indeed, is an excellent opportunity to apply the latest models of decision-making theory utilizing survey research designs similar to those developed for the study of voting behavior. At the present time, we know very little about the interrelation-ship of factors which enter into medical decisions. The author has proposed the following model, based upon an illness-behavior survey of a representa-tive cross-section of 1,883 respondents, linking social factors to health behavior.[129]

126. Heinzelmann, Fred, "Factors in Prophylaxis Behavior in Treating Rheumatic Fever: An Exploratory Study," *Journal of Health and Human Behavior*, Vol. 3, Sum-mer, 1962, pp. 73–81.
127. Eichhorn, R. L. and Ronald M. Anderson, "Changes in Personal Adjustment to Perceived and Medically Established Heart Disease," *Journal of Health and Human Behavior*, Vol. 3, Winter, 1962, p. 248.
128. Johnson, Walter L., "Longitudinal Study of Family Adjustment to Myocardial Infarction," *Nursing Research*, Vol. 12, Fall, 1963, pp. 242–247.
129. Suchman, E. A., "Social Patterns of Illness and Medical Care," *Journal of Health and Human Behavior*, Vol. 6, Spring, 1965, pp. 2–15. The arrows indicating the

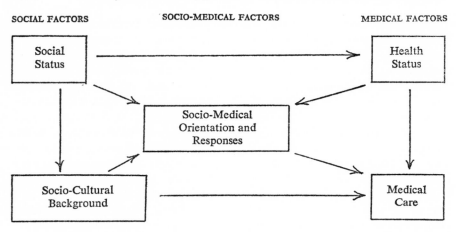

Closely allied to surveys on seeking medical care are a number of surveys which attempt to study the interpersonal relations between physician and patient. The reciprocal roles developed by these two actors in the medical drama constitute an interesting example of how the expectations, perception, and definition of a situation by the persons involved are considered "acceptable and appropriate."[130] As yet, however, few surveys have attempted to study both the doctor and his patient as a dyad. Social and cultural differences have been found to have a marked effect upon communication and understanding between the practitioner of medical care and

---

direction of causality are, of course, largely arbitrary, but, as Freeman, Levine and Reeder have pointed out, "Often, of course, the ordering of variables is purely arbitrary and 'casual sequence' is not a relevant issue. Nevertheless, from the standpoint of the field of medicine, knowledge becomes relatively useless unless some ordering can be identified or at least assumed." Freeman, H. E., Sol Levine, and L. G. Reeder, "Present Status of Medical Sociology," in *Handbook of Medical Sociology.* Edited by H. E. Freeman, L. G. Reeder, and Sol Levine. *op. cit.,* pp. 484–485. The need for the development of such theoretical frameworks in the field of medical sociology has been stressed by many writers. See Polgar, Steven, "Health and Human Behavior: Areas of Interest Common to Social and Medical Sciences," *Current Anthropology,* Vol. 3, April, 1962, pp. 159–205.

130. Bloom, S. W., *The Doctor and His Patient.* Russell Sage Foundation, New York, 1963; Wilson, R. N., "Patient-Practitioner Relationships," in *Handbook of Medical Sociology.* Edited by Freeman, Howard, Sol Levine and L. G. Reeder *op. cit.,* pp. 273–295.

his client.[131] Goffman offers a particularly interesting approach for the analysis of interpersonal relations between physician and patient in terms of the various rituals that develop in daily medical practice, both in the private office and the medical institution.[132] A large number of surveys have been made of interpersonal relations between staff and patients in hospitals.[133] These surveys have also underscored the different expectations and definitions of medical and lay personnel.

One area of public health research that has proven particularly amenable to the survey method is the study of public participation in mass health campaigns. Increasingly, public health programs involve the voluntary cooperation of large portions of the public in mass screening, detection, and immunization drives. The public opinion and behavior surveys that have been conducted in this area have been generally well-designed and executed. Many have employed before-and-after research designs, and carefully formulated hypotheses or conceptual models of collective behavior. An excellent survey of the effectiveness of a mass X-ray campaign in New York City found that participation was not so much a matter of adequate motivation as of convenience. Furthermore, attempts to secure community organization support failed for the simple reason that the slum neighborhoods of New York City were almost completely lacking in social organization.[134] Other studies by Hochbaum, Rosenstock, and Kegeles point to a combination of personal-readiness factors consisting of perceived susceptibility and recognition of threat, and situational factors such as timing and convenience, as significant in determining the degree of public participation.[135] A survey

131. Saunders, Lyle, *Cultural Differences and Medical Care,* Russell Sage Foundation, New York, 1954.
132. Goffman, Irving, *The Presentation of Self in Everyday Life.* University of Edinburgh Social Sicence Research Center, Edinburgh, 1958.
133. Burling, Temple, E. M. Lentz, and R. N. Wilson, *The Give and Take in Hospitals:* A Study of Human Organization in Hospitals. G. P. Putnam's Sons, New York, 1956.
134. Metzner, C. A. and Gerald Gurin, *op. cit.*
135. Hochbaum, G. M., *Public Participation in Medical Screening Programs:* A Socio-Psychological Study. Public Health Service Publication No. 572, U.S. Government Printing Office, Washington, 1958; Rosenstock, I. M., *et al.,* "Why People Fail to Seek Poliomyelitis Vaccination," *Public Health Reports,* Vol. 74, February, 1959, pp. 98–104, and Rosenstock, I. M., *et al., The Impact of Asian Influenza on Community Life.* Public Health Service Publication No. 766, U.S. Government Printing Office, Washington, 1960; Kegeles, S. S., "Why People Seek Dental Care: A Test of a Conceptual Formulation," *Journal of Health and Human Behavior,* Vol. 4, Fall, 1963, pp. 166–173.

of public responses to a poliomyelitis vaccination campaign in Florida utilized a highly sophisticated approach to study the interrelationship of psychological motivational factors and sociological pressures. This study concluded: "Belief that one's friends had taken the new vaccine had a particularly strong association with the respondent's own vaccine status. These informal interpersonal factors, membership in social organizations, social class, and education were the variables found by this survey to be the most powerful predictors of vaccine acceptance and rejection."[136] Here is an example of the social survey disentangling the relative importance of social vs. psychological factors in public behavior.

There can be little doubt that one of the most promising contributions that survey research can make to health and medicine lies in the study of the process whereby individuals and communities decide to undertake health action. The decision whether, when, where, and how to act has been found by many surveys in this area to be largely due to the interaction of such factors as social or cultural definitions of illness, recognition of symptoms, psychological readiness to seek medical care, perception of threat to life, expectations concerning the treatment process, and availability of resources. Survey research provides an excellent opportunity for the further development and evaluation of theories of medical behavior. These concepts and hypotheses will spring from and contribute to existing approaches to the understanding of human behavior. Their formulation and testing offers one of the greatest current challenges to social and medical researchers.

Surveys of health needs, resources, and utilization. The rational planning of health facilities to meet existing needs requires a knowledge of the demand for health services, the availability of health personnel and facilities, and current patterns of utilization. The high cost of medical care combined with a scarcity of resources makes the allocation of priorities an important administrative problem in the fields of medicine and public health. The increased role of the government in supplying funds for the construction of community health facilities has lent impetus to research on needs and resources.

One result of this trend has been the rapid growth and expansion in recent years of the field of administrative medicine concerned with the study of how a society distributes its medical resources. One of the major concerns of public health and medicine today is with the ways in which health and

136. Johnson, A. L. *et al., Epidemiology of Polio Vaccine Acceptance,* Monograph No. 3, Florida State Board of Health, 1962, p. 98.

medical care services are organized and delivered. Too often, these services are either over-utilized or under-utilized, fragmented, lacking in continuity and comprehensiveness, and of low quality. Many of these problems represent a "cultural lag" between modern medical technology and traditional means of medical practice.[137] The rapid advance of medical science today has created serious problems of communicating the latest discoveries to the medical practitioner. An interesting survey revealed that a major factor in the physician's adoption of new drugs was not the scientific literature on the drug but the personal influence of the physician's own colleagues.[138]

A number of large-scale surveys have been conducted in an attempt to determine community needs and resources, and to develop plans for the more effective distribution of medical services.[139] As described in a review of such surveys, "The health survey has gained an important place in public health practice as a useful administrative, evaluative, and planning device and as a means of focusing attention upon critical needs and problems."[140]

One of the most extensive of these surveys was carried out by the Columbia University School of Public Health and Administrative Medicine for the Commonwealth of Puerto Rico. This study was aimed at the development of a total medical care plan for Puerto Rico, including the reorganiza-

---

137. This conflict between medical progress and cultural resistance was clearly recognized by Stern as early as 1941. Stern, B. J., *Society and Medical Progress*. Princeton University Press, Princeton, 1941. See also Mackintosh, J. M., "Health, Medicine, and Social Change," *Canadian Journal of Public Health,* Vol. 52, November, 1961, pp. 455–462.

138. Coleman, James, H. Menzel, and E. Katz, "Social Processes in Physicians' Adoption of a New Drug," *Journal of Chronic Diseases,* Vol. 91, January, 1959, pp. 1–19. See also pp. 20–40.

139. Public Health Service, *U.S. National Health Survey, Health Statistics.* Public Health Service Publication Series, U.S. Government Printing Office, Washington, a continuing series of reports dealing with utilization of medical facilities. See especially, *Medical Economics: Present Status and Recommendations for Additional Data,* Public Health Service Publication No. 1125, U.S. Government Printing Office, Washington, January, 1964. This volume deals with current and future needs for surveys of manpower resources, facility resources, utilization of services, consumer expenditures, medical care insurance, quality of medical care. See also, Rosen, George, "Medical Care: Health Needs and Resources in the United States," *New England Journal of Medicine,* Vol. 270, January, 1964, pp. 81–89.

140. "Review of Research Related to Health Education Practice." *Health Education Monographs,* Supplement No. 1, 1963, p. 18. See also Tayback, Matthew and T. M. Frazier, "Continuous Health Surveys, A Necessity for Health Administration," *Public Health Reports, op. cit.,* pp. 763–771.

tion of services, the training of personnel, and the financing of medical care. Cross-sectional household surveys were made to determine current utilization rates and patterns; manpower surveys, including personal interviews, were made with physicians and nurses; financial surveys were made of medical costs; hospital facilities were appraised; and medical audits were made on the quality of medical care. The results of these integrated surveys served as the basis for a major reorganization plan for medical services in Puerto Rico.[141]

Similar surveys of health needs and resources have been made in a number of communities and constitute a highly significant force in the planning and development of medical facilities and services.[142] The American Public Health Association is currently attempting to develop a "Guide to a Community Health Study" which would permit each community to conduct surveys of their own needs and resources.[143] This guide calls for a series of sampling surveys in relation to each of the major areas of medical care and public health. While this type of self-survey may have some value in building community concern and involvement, the lack of methodological rigor and the subjective involvement of the research workers could make them useless, and perhaps even harmful, for planning purposes.[144]

In several instances, community health surveys have been successful in uncovering unmet needs, especially in relation to those health conditions and subgroups of the population that escape the attention of established medical channels.[145] This is also true for such behavioral disorders as men-

141. Puerto Rico Department of Health, *Medical and Hospital Care in Puerto Rico.* Commonwealth of Puerto Rico, 1962.
142. Harting, D., *et al.,* "Public Health Needs and Practices in a Great Plains County," *American Journal of Public Health,* Vol. 49, December, 1959, pp. 1591–1595; Kimball, S. T., "An Alabama Town Surveys Its Health Needs," in *Health, Culture, and Community.* Edited by B. D. Paul, *op. cit.,* pp. 269–294. Hoffer, C. R., *et al. Health Needs and Health Care in Michigan.* Special Bulletin No. 365, Michigan Agricultural Experiment Stations, Michigan State College, East Lansing, Mich., 1950. See also Special Bulletins Nos. 370 and 377.
143. American Public Health Association, *Guide to a Community Health Study,* revised 1961. Getting, Vlado A., "Community Self-Study in a Changing Society," *American Journal of Public Health,* Vol. 52, June, 1962, pp. 970–975.
144. The inherent dangers of evaluating public health activities on the basis of self-surveys are convincingly discussed in Ciocco, Antonio, "On Indices for the Appraisal of Health Department Activities," *Journal of Chronic Diseases,* Vol. 11, May, 1960, pp. 509–522.
145. Phillips, H. T. and Camille Lambert, "Survey of Health Needs of Older Citizens

tal illness, alcoholism, and narcotics addiction, where the sick individual and his family may actually avoid professional medical care.[146] However, the population survey of health needs has also been valuable in discovering unknown cases for such non-stigmatic diseases as diabetes and such medical conditions as physical disabilities.[147] Some of these case-finding surveys have made valuable contributions to survey methodology, both in their comparison of results obtained through the use of different methods such as mail, telephone, and personal interview and in their checks on the validity of responses in terms of actual physical examinations.[148] A methodological study of hospital utilization revealed little loss from use of survey method in constructing accurate configurations of medical care in out-patient clinics.[149]

Surveys of health needs have also demonstrated the well-known sociological fact that the minority groups in an American community are apt to live and move outside the normal channels of social action, including medical care.[150] These surveys have shown that the lower income groups in general, and the minority groups in particular, in the large cities have a lower rate of utilization of health facilities and lower participation in mass detection or immunization programs at the same time that they have a higher

---

and Their Potentials in Home Health Work," *Public Health Reports,* Vol. 79, July, 1964, pp. 571–576; Lowry, S. G., C. M. Selz and D. G. Hay, "Factors Associated with the Acceptance of Health Care Practice Among Rural Families," *Rural Sociology,* Vol. 23, June, 1958, pp. 198–202.

146. Mechanic, David, "Some Implications of Illness Behavior for Medical Sampling," *New England Journal of Medicine,* Vol. 269, August, 1963, pp. 244–247. Mechanic points out that, "Those with similar medical conditions who are not under stress may not seek medical advice. For some illnesses, at least, appearance in medical statistics may be a result as much of patterns of illness behavior and situational events as of the symptoms experiences," p. 246.

147. Hochbaum, G. M., *op. cit.*

148. Banas, P. A. and R. V. Davis, "Identifying the Physically Handicapped . . . ," *op. cit.;* Kruger, P. E., "Measurement of Prevalence of Chronic Diseases by Household Interviews and Clinical Evaluations," *American Journal of Public Health,* Vol. 47, No. 8, 1900, pp. 953–960.

149. Solon, J. A., *et al.,* "Patterns of Medical Care: Validity of Interview Information on Use of Hospital Clinics," *Journal of Health and Human Behavior,* Vol. 3, Spring, 1962, pp. 21–29.

150. Suchman, Edward A., "Socio-Medical Variations Among Ethnic Groups," *American Journal of Sociology,* Vol. 70, November, 1964, pp. 319–331.

need for medical attention.[151] The cultural barriers that keep these groups out of the main stream of American community life also block their participation in the American medical care system.[152]

Another significant survey finding in relation to the utilization of medical facilities concerns the concept of the "multi-problem family." In an extensive survey of health care in St. Paul, Buell found that 6 per cent of the families were utilizing well over half of all the health services.[153] Combine this with another survey finding by Hinkle and Plummer, that about one-third of the population can account for three-fourths of all episodes of illness, and the significance of the survey method becomes apparent.[154]

The relationship of utilization rates to the costs of medical care has been the subject of a number of extensive surveys. The National Health Survey now provides detailed utilization data according to various demographic subgroupings.[155] These nation-wide surveys reveal the fact that health expenses for a child in a small, well-to-do family (income of $7,000 a year or over) are *five times* greater than those for a child in a large, poor family (income less than $2,000). These surveys also examine the type of medical service used, duration of use, and the degree of disability created by the illness. Consistently, these utilization surveys have substantiated the greater need of and lower utilization by the lower socio-economic groups.[156] Polgar

151. Simmons, O. G., *Social Status and Public Health,* Social Science Research Council, New York, 1958; Cornely, P. B. and S. K. Bigman, "Some Considerations in Changing Health Attitudes," *Children,* Vol. 10, January–February, 1963, pp. 23–28; Rosenblatt, Daniel and E. A. Suchman, "The Underutilization of Medical Care Among Blue Collarites," in *Blue Collar World.* Edited by A. B. Shostak and William Gomberg, *op. cit.*

152. Suchman, E. A. and Lois Alksne, "Communicating Across Cultural Barriers," *The American Catholic Sociological Review,* Winter, 1961, pp. 306–313; Cornely, P. B. and S. K. Bigman, "Acquaintance with Municipal Government Health Services in a Low-Income Urban Population." *American Journal of Public Health,* Vol. 52, November, 1962, pp. 1877–1886; Pond, M. A., "Inter-relationship of Poverty and Disease," *Public Health Reports,* Vol. 76, November, 1961, pp. 967–974.

153. Buell, Bradley, *et al., Community Planning for Human Services.* Columbia University Press, New York, 1952.

154. Hinkle, Lawrence and N. Plummer, "Life Stress and Industrialism—The Concentration of Illness and Absenteeism in One Segment of a Working Population," *Industrial Medicine and Surgery,* Vol. 21, 1952, pp. 365–375.

155. National Center for Health Statistics, "Medical Care, Health Status, and Family Income," *Vital and Health Statistics,* Series 10, No. 9, May 1964, Washington.

156. Graham, Saxon, "Socio-Economic Status, Illness, and the Use of Medical

attributes this relationship to variation in risk, accessibility, and concern.[157] Many other surveys have found that the various subgroups of the population make differential use of medical facilities. A nation-wide survey of illness and the utilization of medical care by the aged indicates the complex interplay of perceived need, costs, and expenditures:

> The majority of older people do not think they are sick enough to see a doctor, (that) most older people are managing current medical costs, although almost half of all people could not manage a medical bill as large as $500, and (that) a relatively small group in the older population comprises the heavy users of medical care.[158]

Surveys of financial expenditures for medical care are particularly relevant to the current political controversy concerning the government's role in health insurance.[159] There can be little question that the costs of medical care have spiraled upward as a result of long-term chronic illness and of the need for specialized treatment and rehabilitation, combined with a general rise in the costs of labor, construction, and supplies. Furthermore, people today seem to turn much more readily to physicians and hospitals when they are not feeling well. The admission rate to general hospitals in the United States was 130 per 1,000 population in 1957 as compared to only 59 per 1,000 in 1935.[160] Physician visits have similarly increased from 2.6 out-of-hospital visits per person in a year during 1928–1931 to 5.3 for the period 1957–1958. The role of voluntary health insurance plans in paying for medical care has been studied by a number of surveys. These studies have shown, in general, that membership in a health insurance plan does

---

Services," in *Patients, Physicians and Illness.* Edited by E. G. Jaco. Free Press, Glencoe, Ill., 1958, pp. 129–134; Kriesberg, Louis, and B. R. Treiman, "Socio-Economic Status and the Utilization of Dentists' Services," *Journal of the American College of Dentists,* September, 1960, p. 164.

157. Polgar, Steven, "Health and Human Behavior . . . ," *op. cit.,* with bibliography.

158. Shanas, Ethel, "Reported Illness and Utilization of Medical Care," *Public Welfare,* April, 1960.

159. Anderson, O. W. and J. J. Feldman, *Family Medical Costs and Voluntary Health Insurance:* A Nationwide Survey. McGraw-Hill, New York, 1956; Reed, L. S., and D. P. Rice, "Private Medical Care Expenditures and Voluntary Health Insurance, 1948–61," *Social Security Bulletin,* Vol. 25, December, 1962, pp. 3–13; U.S. Department of Commerce, *Survey of Current Business,* Vol. 43, July, 1963.

160. Health Information Foundation, "The Changing Patterns of Hospital Use," *Progress in Health Services,* May, 1958; *Hospital Utilization Studies,* Public Health Service Publication No. 930-G-4, U.S. Government Printing Office, Washington, 1962.

lead to a slight increase in the utilization of services.[161] But whether this is desirable or undesirable is subject to debate.

Anderson presents an excellent review of variations by geographical area and demographic characteristics as determined by surveys of medical expenditures.[162] These patterns of expenditures show substantial differences. As estimated by Anderson, the medical dollar may be distributed as follows:

Hospital Care	23%
Physicians' Services	34
Medicines	20
Dentists' Services	15
All Other	8
	100%

Of these expenditures, 60 per cent are made by families and individuals, 20 per cent by some form of voluntary health insurance, and 20 per cent by various levels of government.

While surveys dealing with community and individual behavior toward preventive, therapeutic, and rehabilitative health programs lie at the heart of medical and public health program planning, operation, and evaluation, this crucial area of survey research has not received the rigorousness of study it deserves. Most of the current and past surveys of needs, resources, and utilization have been content to be descriptive only. *Why* variations in expenditures and utilization occur in terms of social, psychological, and economic forces has not been extensively studied. There is ample opportunity for the use of the survey method in explaining differences in expenditures and utilization and in evaluating the relative costs and quality of services of different modes of financing and organization. Such explanatory surveys would be of great use in the planning of health services and in shedding light on some of the current controversies regarding the best way to organize medical care.

We can mention only a few examples of challenging new uses of survey research in this area. First, and perhaps foremost, is the greater use of the survey method, especially the panel design, for evaluating existing medical and health programs. In an era marked by rapidly changing health needs

161. *Health and Medical Care in New York City,* Harvard University Press, Cambridge, 1957.
162. Anderson, Odin W., "The Utilization of Health Services," in *Handbook of Medical Sociology*. Edited by H. E. Freeman, Sol Levine, and L. G. Reeder, *op. cit.,* pp. 349–367.

and services, there is a constant pressure to develop new programs and to evaluate old programs. While the current health literature abounds with reports on evaluation studies and discussions of the increasing need for "scientific" evaluation, little progress is actually being made in the use of statistically controlled field studies involving preliminary population surveys to plan programs, and experimental population surveys to measure effectiveness of programs.[163] What is especially needed is greater attention to the measurement of "effectiveness" as opposed to "effort" and to the analysis of why programs succeed or fail.[164] A good example of a survey which included both a measure of effectiveness and an analysis of process is that of a mental health campaign in Canada.[165] This type of evaluation survey is particularly appropriate for studying the effectiveness of specific mass screening and detection programs and special health services.[166] The survey method would also be applicable in carefully designed field experiments to test the effectiveness of specific communication media or types of appeals. An excellent example and methodological model for such surveys of communication materials is given by Greenberg and Mattison, who indicate some of the different forms which evaluation surveys can take.[167]

Our final comment on the state of survey research on problems of program planning, operation, and evaluation would stress the need to orient these surveys more toward policy and less toward "bookkeeping." The col-

163. See for example, Herzog, Elizabeth, *Some Guide Lines for Evaluative Research.* Children's Bureau, U.S. Department of Health, Education, and Welfare, 1959; and *Planning Evaluations of Mental Health Programs,* Millbank Memorial Fund, New York, 1958.
164. An excellent methodological discussion of evaluation also applicable to health research is given in Hyman, H. H., T. W. Hopkins and Charles Wright, *Applications of Methods of Evaluation:* A Study of the Encampment for Leadership. University of California Press, Berkeley, 1961.
165. Cumming, Elaine and John Cumming, *op. cit.*
166. Enterline, P. E. and Bernard Kordan, "A Controlled Evaluation of Mass Surveys for Tuberculosis and Heart Disease," *Public Health Reports,* Vol. 73, October, 1958, p. 867; Robb, G. L., H. S. Elwood and R. J. Haggerty, "Evaluation of a Poison Center," *American Journal of Public Health,* Vol. 53, November, 1963, pp. 1751–1760: as stated by this questionnaire survey of 800 calls, "We must conclude that such centers are probably saving few lives, but that their activities have met with satisfied acceptance by both the public and the physician." This demonstrates the problem of constructing the criteria of evaluation. Tayback, Matthew and Lillian Scally, "An Evaluation of Community Nursing Services in the Care of the Mentally Ill," *American Journal of Public Health,* Vol. 53, August, 1963, pp. 1260–1268.
167. Greenberg, B. G. and B. F. Mattison, "The Whys and Wherefores of Program Evaluation," *Canadian Journal of Public Health,* Vol. 46, July, 1955, pp. 293–299. A

lection of data on health services has tended to become routinized into statistical reports which actually have very little utility for determining policy, the data becoming ends in themselves instead of means toward program improvement.

To some degree, many social surveys on health needs and resources have tended to imitate such medical bookkeeping and have failed to fulfill their unique contribution of providing data for policy-making purposes. Roemer takes the social scientist to task for failing to apply his research techniques to the study of the more basic issues in health and medical care:

> In current work by sociologists and anthropologists, there is an enormous preoccupation with the internal psychological mechanisms of the current social institution of medicine. Within this, there is heavy concentration on the phenomena of interpersonal relations; the relationship of patient to doctor, of doctor to nurse, of lower to upper echelons in a hospital, of the family to a voluntary or official agency, etc. Attitudes, and changes in attitudes; decisions and feelings that determine them—these are the popular units of study. . . . On the other hand, the social organization of these health services, the forces that shape it, the degree to which present patterns actually meet social needs, and the lines that might be followed to readjust patterns to meet needs are subjects getting scant attention from sociologists and anthropologists.[168]

Perhaps the survey research of the future will address itself to some of these more basic policy issues on the social organization of health services. Here, indeed, is an outstanding opportunity for national and international surveys comparing and evaluating the social, economic, and political factors, both as causes and consequences, in different patterns of organization for the provision of medical care.[169]

---

highly instructive analysis of some of the methodological problems in evaluation surveys is given in MacMahon, Brion, T. F. Pugh, and G. B. Hutchison, "Principles in the Evaluation of Community Health Programs," *American Journal of Public Health,* Vol. 51, July, 1961, pp. 963–968.

168. Roemer, M. I., "Social Science and Organized Health Services," *Human Organization,* Vol. 18, No. 2, 1959, pp. 75–77.

169. For a good analysis of the current state and potential contribution of social research to major policy issues in the medical care field, see Roemer, M. I., and R. H. Elling, "Sociological Research on Medical Care," *Journal of Health and Human Behavior,* Vol. 4, Spring, 1963, pp. 49–68.

THE HEALTH PROFESSIONS AND ORGANIZATIONS

The previous two areas of application of survey methodology dealt with problems *in* health and illness; the present section will include a review and evaluation of surveys designed to study problems *of* the health field itself, particularly those of its personnel and its organization. The provision of health services is a complex operation involving a large number of professional, semi-professional, and ancillary personnel and many different kinds of organizations and agencies for the administration of health services. The selection, training, and performance of these personnel and the structure and function of the medical organization are important topics for current survey research.

The research stimulated in these two areas is again both basic and applied. Social scientists have found the study of medical personnel particularly appropriate for understanding the process of professionalization, while the hospital has furnished an excellent testing ground for social theories concerning bureaucratic organization. On the other hand, shortages of personnel and facilities have led the medical educators and administrators to study problems of recruitment, training, and job performance, and the more effective organization of medical services. As in the case of the disease process itself and the behavior of the sick individual, this combination of basic and applied interests has proven mutually advantageous.

Surveys of the health professions. The health and medical field is composed of a wide variety of different occupations. These range from the highly skilled medical specialist to the relatively unskilled nurse's aid, from the universally accepted physician to the marginal chiropractor and the dubious faith healer. The major emphasis of survey research has naturally been upon the more legitimate of these occupational categories—the physician, the dentist, the nurse, and the pharmacist—although some occupational surveys have been made of such health-related groups as chiropractors.[170]

When we consider the large number of important health-related occupational groups such as podiatrists, optometrists, audiologists, and osteopaths, who have not been studied in any detail, we can agree with Wardwell who,

170. Croatman, Wallace and P. B. Sheatsley, *The Prescription Pharmacist Today.* Research Series No. 3, Health Information Foundation, New York, 1958; McCormack, T. H., "The Druggists' Dilemma: Problems of a Marginal Occupation," *American Journal of Sociology,* Vol. 61, January, 1956, pp. 308–315; Barsalow, F. W., *et al., Chiropractic in California.* Haynes Foundation, Los Angeles, 1960.

after an analysis of limited, marginal, and quasi-practitioners in the health field, concludes: "Nearly all the types of research that have been done on the medical profession could be replicated on limited, marginal, and quasi-practitioners with great theoretical and practical benefit."[171] Despite the lack of official recognition by the orthodox medical profession, these groups play a significant role in the treatment of health conditions, and we need to know more about their selection, training, and practice problems as well as their relations to the public and to the other health occupations.

(1) *Selection.* One of the major areas of survey research concerns the choice of medicine, dentistry, or nursing for a career. These surveys have examined who enters the profession, why they enter, what their attitudes and values are both in general and specifically related to the health occupation, and what their expectations and plans are in regard to the future. Such occupational surveys attempt to determine the relevant factors in the decision to become a doctor, dentist, or nurse, and the factors which aid or interfere with the carrying out of this decision. Thus, for example, several studies have found that upward social mobility was a major factor in the decision of many lower social class girls to become nurses,[172] the desire for autonomy was a primary motivating factor in the choice of dentistry,[173] many medical students come from families with doctors,[174] and, in the case of sanitary engineers, many of the prospective engineers left the field before they even entered it due to poor recruitment techniques.[175] Other surveys have investigated the timing of the decision to enter medicine, the difference between medical and law students in their choice of a career, and the particular dilemma of osteopathic students.[176]

171. Wardwell, W. I., "Limited, Marginal, and Quasi-Practitioners," in *Handbook of Medical Sociology*. Edited by H. E. Freeman, Sol Levine, and L. G. Reeder, *op. cit.*, p. 234.
172. Hughes, E. C., H. M. Hughes, and Irwin Deutscher, *Twenty Thousand Nurses Tell Their Story: A Report on Studies of Nursing Functions Sponsored by the American Nurses' Association.* J. B. Lippincott, Philadelphia, 1958.
173. More, D. M. and Nathan Kohn, "Some Motives for Entering Dentistry," *American Journal of Sociology,* Vol. 66, July, 1960, pp. 48–53.
174. Adams, Stuart, "Trends in Occupational Origins of Physicians," *American Sociological Review,* Vol. 18, August, 1953, pp. 404–410.
175. Rosenstock, I. M. and A. P. Miller, *Why Some Sanitary Engineers Leave the Field.* Public Health Service Publication No. 359, U.S. Government Printing Office, Washington, 1954.
176. Rogoff, Natalie, "The Decision to Study Medicine," in *The Student Physician.* Edited by R. K. Merton, G. G. Reeder and P. L. Kendall. Harvard University Press,

Perhaps because it is the area of greatest demand and shortest supply, the largest number and most comprehensive recruitment surveys have been made in the field of nursing. In general, these surveys indicate that nursing, as an occupation, has relatively high status and prestige.[177] Attitudes toward standards of nursing and length of training are generally favorable.[178] Effective recruitment techniques include personal influences of friends and family, mass media, brochures and other literature on nursing.[179] These surveys also tell us who the prospective nurses are and where they come from. Considering the fact that one out of every sixteen girls who graduates from high school enters nursing, these surveys of the choice of nursing provide valuable data on career choices among women in general.

Surveys of occupational choice in the health and medical field are among the best in the field of survey research. Many of them employ sophisticated research designs, the sampling is good (usually of "captive" high school populations) often using people who choose other occupations for comparative purposes, the questionnaires are carefully constructed and pre-tested, and many contain attitude scales based on Thurstone, Likert, Guttman, or Lazarsfeld models of scale construction. In several cases, notably the work of Taves, Corwin and Haas,[180] the research has involved the development of decision-making and role-conception models. The results of these surveys have advanced our understanding of the relationship between occupational choice and personality, of the growth of professional images, and of the decision-making process. In addition, these surveys have proven of practical value in the planning and execution of recruitment campaigns in medicine and nursing.

(2) *Education and training.* The education of the prospective doctor or nurse has been the subject of a number of intensive surveys of medical and

---

Cambridge, 1957, pp. 109–130; Thielens, Wagner, Jr., "Some Comparisons of Entrants to Medical and Law School," *ibid.,* pp. 131–152; New, P. K., "The Osteopathic Students: A Study in Dilemma," in *Patients, Physicians and Illness.* Edited by E. G. Jaco, *op. cit.,* pp. 413–421.

177. Bullock, R. P., *What Do Nurses Think of Their Profession?* Ohio State University Research Foundation, Columbus, 1954, pp. 27–62.

178. Berkowitz, J. E. and N. H. Berkowitz, "Nursing Education and Role Conception," *Nursing Research,* Vol. 9, Fall, 1960, pp. 218–219.

179. Mayo, A. A., ed., "Student Recruitment Is Underway," *American Journal of Nursing,* Vol. 49, April, 1949, pp. 242–245.

180. Taves, Marvis, R. G. Corwin, and E. J. Haas, *Role Conception and Vocational Success and Satisfaction.* Bureau of Business Research, Columbus, Ohio, 1964.

nursing students which have dealt with such diverse topics as satisfactions and dissatisfactions with schooling,[181] student-faculty relationships,[182] career interests and expectations,[183] choice of a specialty,[184] the development of professional values and orientations,[185] the growth of a self-image,[186] attitudes and values[187] and reasons for withdrawal or dropping-out.[188] We probably know more about the educational process for doctors and nurses than for any other professional group.

Out of the myriad of different surveys that have been conducted among medical and nursing students, we will select the subject of "socialization" of medical students for specific comment. Probably because of its greater theoretical interest for social scientists, this topic has received a great deal of attention. Two major studies utilizing survey techniques have been made among medical students at Cornell University Medical College and the University of Kansas Medical School.[189] These studies have followed medical students through the four years of medical school and have employed a variety of techniques—including participant observation and case studies—in conjunction with the survey method for the collection of data. They stand as successful models of social research linking well-formulated theory and sociological conceptualization with rigorous research methodology.

181. Ingmire, A. E., "Attitudes of Student Nurses at the University of California," *Nursing Research,* Vol. 1, October, 1952, pp. 36–39.
182. Caplovitz, David, "Student-Faculty Relations in Medical School," unpublished doctoral thesis, Columbia University, New York, 1960.
183. Cahalan, Don, *et al.,* "Career Interests and Expectations of U.S. Medical Students," *Journal of Medical Education,* Vol. 32, August, 1957, pp. 557–563.
184. Back, K. W., Robert Coker, and T. G. Donnelly, "Public Health as a Career in Medicine: Secondary Choice Within a Profession," *American Sociological Review,* Vol. 23, October, 1958, pp. 533–541.
185. Becker, Howard, *et al., Boys in White:* Student Culture in Medical School. University of Chicago Press, Chicago, 1961; Meyer, G. R., "Conflict and Harmony in Nursing Values," *Nursing Outlook,* Vol. 7, July, 1959, pp. 298–299.
186. Huntington, M. J., "The Development of a Professional Self-Image," in *The Student Physician.* Edited by R. K. Merton, G. G. Reader and P. L. Kendall, *op. cit.,* pp. 179–187.
187. Deutscher, Irwin and Ann Montague, "Professional Education and Conflicting Value Systems: The Role of Religious Schools in the Educational Aspirations of Nursing Students." *Social Forces,* Vol. 35, December, 1956, pp. 126–131.
188. Middlewood, E. L., "Why Do Students Drop Out?" *American Journal of Nursing,* Vol. 46, December, 1946, pp. 838–840.
189. Merton, R. K., *et al.,* eds., *The Student Physician, op. cit.;* Becker, Howard, *et al., Boys in White, op. cit.*

The objective of these studies was to determine, among other things, how the medical student develops his professional self-image and learns to think and behave like a physician. The definition of socialization used by the Cornell study was:

> (a) The process through which the individual develops his "professional self" with his characteristic values, attitudes, knowledge and skills, fusing these into a more or less consistent set of dispositions which govern his behavior in a wide variety of professional (and extra-professional) situations; (b) the processes by which neophytes come to acquire in patterned but selective fashion the attitudes and values, skills and knowledge, and ways of life established in the professional subculture.

These studies demonstrate the importance of the socialization process during the training period whereby students come to think of themselves as professionals. Becker and Geer point to an increase in cynicism among medical students as they progress through medical school.[190] Studies of nurses stress the growth of disillusionment with the humanitarian aspects of nursing.[191] To what extent these values and images developed in professional school carry over to actual practice is not known. Future survey research might usefully investigate the extent to which the behavior of the practicing physician and nurse is based upon these values, and the actual situations in practice which produce value conflicts for the physician and nurse.[192]

(3) *Job performance.* The types, quantity, and quality of activities carried on by medical personnel have been the subject matter of a number of job analyses and performance surveys. These surveys have been extremely useful in helping to define the duties and functions of the various personnel groups, of determining their proficiency and efficiency, of assessing the degree of job satisfaction and dissatisfaction, and of studying communication and interaction. As in the case of training, they have advanced

190. Becker, Howard and Blanche Geer, "Medical Education," in *Handbook of Medical Sociology.* Edited by H. E. Freeman, Sol Levine, and L. G. Reeder, *op. cit.,* pp. 169–186.
191. Williams, T. R. and M. Williams, "The Socialization of the Student Nurse," *Nursing Research,* Vol. 8, Winter, 1959, pp. 18–25; and Corwin, R. G., M. Taves and E. J. Haas, "Professional Disillusionment," *Nursing Research,* Vol. 10, Summer, 1951, pp. 141–144.
192. Skipper, J. K., "Functional Significance of the Nurse Role: An Evaluation," *Journal of Health and Human Behavior,* Vol. 3, Spring, 1962, pp. 41–45.

our knowledge of basic factors influencing worker morale and determining status and interpersonal relationships, as well as provided practical answers to the formulation of tasks, the division of labor, and the management of personnel relations and working conditions in the "big business" of medical care.

In the field of nursing, a major focus of survey research has been upon an analysis of the kinds of tasks and activities that make up nursing care, and the attitudes of nurses toward these tasks.[193] There is much disagreement and conflict among nurses as to the proper responsibilities of nurses, their subordinates and their supervisors, of doctors and of ancillary personnel.[194] However, in general, morale appears remarkably high and, while nurses often appear to have only a tentative commitment to remaining in nursing,[195] they seem satisfied with their choice of a career.[196] Perhaps because of this kind of conflict between low commitment and high morale, the nursing profession offers a particularly interesting group for occupational analysis via the survey method.[197]

The professional responsibilities and performance of physicians have not been as subject to survey research as have nurses. This is probably due to their higher professional status, the individual nature of their practice, and the greater difficulty of interviewing them. A comprehensive survey of how physicians worked and lived, including an evaluation of the quality of medical care, has been conducted by Peterson *et al.*[198] In general, this survey found that many private physicians were not practicing as high a quality

193. Pollak, O., C. Westoff, and M. Bressler, "Pilot Study of Nursing Functions," *Nursing Research,* Vol. 2, June, 1953, pp. 15–22.

194. Reissman, Leonard and J. H. Rohrer, eds., *Changes and Dilemma in the Nursing Profession:* Studies of Nursing Services in a Large General Hospital. G. P. Putnam's Sons, New York, 1957.

195. Orzack, Louis, *Work as a Central Life Interest of Professionals.* Reprint No. 8, Industrial Relations Center, University of Wisconsin, Madison, 1960, p. 127.

196. Bressler, M. and W. Kephart, "Career Dynamics," Pennsylvania Nurses Association, 1955.

197. Corwin and Taves stress the following factors in the nurses' search for professional identity: 1) a drive for prestige; 2) disparities between ideology and the actual job experience of nurses; and 3) competing expectations of role performance. Corwin, R. G. and M. Taves, "Nursing and Other Health Professions," in *Handbook of Medical Sociology.* Edited by H. E. Freeman, Sol Levine and L. G. Reeder, *op. cit.,* pp. 187–212.

198. Peterson, Osler, *et al.,* "An Analytical Study of North Carolina General Practice, 1953–54," *Journal of Medical Education,* Vol. 3, December, 1956, part 2.

of medical care as they might. An unusual survey of the criteria used by physicians in choosing physicians and surgeons for themselves and their families showed wide discrepancies in whom doctors would choose for themselves as compared to recommendations for their patients.[199] We have already noted some of the surveys dealing with the doctor-patient relationship. A recent survey of medical school faculty, students, and practitioners revealed that the physician's satisfaction from his work stemmed from his personal relationships and ability to help his patients, while his major dissatisfactions were attributed to his lack of control over the treatment situation, largely due to patient disobedience.[200] A survey of nurses showed them to be concerned with such work problems as pattern-maintenance and tension-management, as well as patient recovery.[201] A survey of job satisfaction among physicians and nurses in child health stations stressed the lack of professional gratification in this type of clinic work.[202]

Several surveys have investigated the influence of specific factors upon medical practice. For example, Kutner has shown that the reference group of a surgeon has considerable influence upon his technological orientation, while Straus attributes the private practitioner's neglect of the alcoholic patient to similar prestige factors.[203]

Several surveys have been made of the membership of professional associations—for example, the American Nurses' Association and the American Public Health Association—in an attempt to determine the composition of the society and the attitudes and practices of its members.[204]

199. Maloney, M., R. Trussell, and Jack Elinson, "Physicians Choose Medical Care: A Sociometric Approach to Quality Appraisal," *American Journal of Public Health,* Vol. 50, November, 1960, pp. 1678–1686.

200. Ort, R. S., A. B. Ford and R. E. Liske, "The Doctor-Patient Relationship as Described by Physicians and Medical Students," *Journal of Health and Human Behavior,* Vol. 5, Spring, 1965, pp. 25–34.

201. Skipper, J. K., "Functional Significance of the Nurse Role . . . ," *op. cit.*

202. Goldman, M., *et al.,* "Child Health Station Personnel: A Profile," *American Journal of Public Health,* Vol. 54, August, 1964, pp. 1302–1311.

203. Kutner, B., "Surgeons and Their Patients: A Study in Social Perception," in *Patients, Physicians and Illness.* Edited by E. G. Jaco, *op. cit.,* pp. 384–397. Straus, Robert, "Medical Practice and the Alcoholic," *Annals of the American Academy of Political and Social Science,* Vol. 315, 1958, pp. 117–124.

204. Deutscher, Irwin, *A Survey of the Occupational Characteristics of a Metropolitan Nurse Complement.* Community Studies, Kansas City, Missouri, 1956. Hilleboe, H. E. and W. E. Boek, "An Opinion Survey of the American Public Health Association by New York State Public Health Association Members," *American Journal of Public Health,* Vol. 44, 1954, pp. 64–76.

The American Dental Association has made an extremely comprehensive survey of all aspects of dental practice.[205]

The use of the survey method for increased knowledge concerning the health professions—or any other profession—can be rewarding. The significance of such research for the recruitment, selection, training, and performance evaluation of the various occupational groupings makes it of immediate practical value. The research can be done comparatively easily because of the limited membership and relatively easy accessibility of the professions for study. The respondents have a personal interest in the content of the survey and cooperation is not too difficult to obtain.

Given these natural substantive and methodological advantages, the survey researcher can expand his current interests beyond recruitment, training, and performance problems into more complex areas such as relationships among the professional groups[206] and between them and their patients and the community at large,[207] the influence of professional associations on private and public policy,[208] the conflict between private and public service,[209] the determinants of the quality of professional service,[210] and the relationship between education and practice.[211] In addition, survey research could be of greater value in studying interpersonal conflicts within the medical field, especially personnel relations between medical workers and health organizations. The level of personnel surveys in the medical field is currently far below that of industry in general. As medical care continues

205. American Dental Association, Bureau of Economic Research and Statistics, "The 1962 Survey of Dental Practice," *Journal of the American Dental Association,* Vols. 66 and 67, 1963–1964 (seven parts, other parts to be published).

206. Arnold, M. F., "Perception of Professional Role Activities in the Local Health Department," *Public Health Reports,* Vol. 77, January, 1962, pp. 80–88.

207. Willie, C. V., "The Social Class of Patients that Public Health Nurses Prefer to Some," *American Journal of Public Health,* Vol. 50, 1960, pp. 1126–1136.

208. Klerman, L. V. and Camille Lambert, "Attitudes of Private Dentists Toward a Public Dental Care Program," *The Journal of the American Dental Association,* Vol. 68, March, 1964, pp. 416–423.

209. Elinson, Jack, "The Physician's Dilemma in Puerto Rico," *Journal of Health and Human Behavior,* Vol. 3, Spring, 1962, pp. 14–20; and Ben-David, Joseph, "The Professional Role of the Physician in Bureaucratized Medicine: A Study in Role Conflict," *Human Relations,* Vol. 11, No. 3, 1958, pp. 255–274.

210. Hawley, P. R., "Evaluation of the Quality of Patient Care," *American Journal of Public Health,* Vol. 45, December, 1955.

211. Cohart, E. M. and I. V. Hiscock, "A Profile of the Public Health Worker," *American Journal of Public Health,* Vol. 45, December, 1955, pp. 1525–1532.

to become more and more a matter of big business, personnel and marketing surveys will become increasingly appropriate and useful.

Surveys of health organizations. In the United States, the number and types of organizations concerned with health are almost overwhelming. They exist on a national and local level, they represent official and private sponsorship, they deal with prevention, treatment, and rehabilitation and they run the gamut of all possible medical conditions. In general, they can be grouped into four main types, although these are not mutually exclusive: (1) official or public agencies, (2) voluntary or non-profit agencies, (3) hospitals and nursing homes, and (4) health-related organizations. Many of these health organizations have employed the survey method for internal research on their own problems of structure and function, and for external research on their clients and on the effectiveness of their programs, as discussed previously. Our present concern will be with the use of the survey method for studying problems of internal organization.

Many different surveys have been made of and by these various health organizations of their personnel, their organizational problems, and the operation of their programs.[212] A large-scale survey of 130 different health and welfare agencies and their patterns of interaction with each other and with the community has been conducted in four Northeastern communities.[213] This study discusses the various barriers to greater interorganizational cooperation arising out of the current "laissez-faire" policy, a policy which has been vividly described by Crabtree: "If one could imagine the fields of public education, safety, highways, law enforcement, fire protection, and public libraries functionally splintered as here described for public health, the situation would be labelled as containing most of the ingredients of chaos."[214] Levine and others offer the following six recommendations, each of which could well serve as the basis for comprehensive surveys of organi-

212. An excellent description and analysis of the various types of health organizations from a social research point of view is contained in Levine, Sol and P. E. White, "The Community of Health Organizations," in *Handbook of Medical Sociology.* Edited by H. E. Freeman, Sol Levine, and L. G. Reeder, *op. cit.,* pp. 321–347.

213. Levine, Sol and P. E. White, "Exchange as a Conceptual Framework for the Study of Inter-organizational Relationships," *Administrative Science Quarterly,* Vol. 5, March, 1961, pp. 583–601.

214. Levine, Sol and P. E. White, "Problems of Voluntary Health and Welfare Agencies," School of Public Health, Harvard University, mimeographed. Crabtree, J. A., "Plans for Tomorrow's Needs in Local Public Health Administration," *American Journal of Public Health,* Vol. 53, August, 1963, p. 1178.

zational problems in community health: 1) use more state and national resources and organization; 2) improve mutual knowledge of problems, goals, and functions; 3) recognize, analyse, and set up mechanisms to deal with domain differences and related tensions; 4) reorient board and community leaders to recognize interdependence, need for cooperation; 5) introduce incentives for personnel in different agencies to work together; 6) establish formal mechanisms for charging specific professionals with responsibility for coordination.[215]

To meet staffing problems, many health agencies have turned to volunteers from the community. An intensive survey of such volunteers with the National Health Foundation examines who they are, why and how they were recruited, and the gratifications they receive from their work.[216] This survey found that only 10 per cent of the volunteers joined on their own initiative, the majority having been recruited through personal influences. This is an excellent survey and deserves repetition within other types of agencies employing voluntary help.

Perhaps the most significant survey research on organizational problems has been conducted in regard to hospitals, especially mental hospitals.[217] This is not difficult to understand since the modern hospital is a highly complex organization whose administration is rapidly becoming a specialized field in medical care. Hospitals differ greatly in type of service, type of financial control, and type of administration, as well as in physical size and staff composition. The dimensions of the hospital "business"—the nation's fifth largest industry—can be estimated from the fact that there are over 7,000 hospitals in the United States, employing about 1,500,000 full-time workers and admitting approximately 25,000,000 patients each year.[218]

Considering the rather haphazard development of hospital organization, it is little wonder that there is currently so much demand for research and reform. This need is being aggravated by the rapidly changing nature of illness and medical care as discussed previously. Wesson points up the implications of these changes for the organization of medical care:

215. Levine, Sol, P. E. White, and Benjamin Paul, "Community Inter-organizational Problems in Providing Medical Care and Social Services," *American Journal of Public Health,* Vol. 53, August, 1963, pp. 1183–1195.
216. Sills, D. L., *The Volunteers.* Free Press, Glencoe, Ill., 1957.
217. For a good review of recent mental hospital surveys, see Clausen, J. A., "The Sociology of Mental Illness," in *Sociology Today.* Edited by R. K. Merton, L. Broom and L. S. Cottrell. Basic Books, New York, 1959, pp. 485–508.
218. *Hospitals,* Vol. 35, August 1, 1961, Guide Issue.

Developments in medical science have also greatly altered the pattern of medical practice. Hospitals have become broader in scope and more complex in organization; specialization has threatened to fragment medical care as it has increased its technical efficiency; the number of health organizations and services in the average city has become legion. Individualistic patterns are being supplanted by collaborative ones; the emergence of the "team" concept in the hospital, the development of group practices in medicine and the widespread diffusion of third-party payment plans are manifestations of a more general trend. Accordingly, understanding of complex organizational patterns is becoming increasingly important for intelligent medical practice.[219]

One of the most comprehensive studies of the general hospital was conducted by Burling, Lentz and Wilson in six private, non-profit hospitals.[220] This study examined both the internal structure of these hospitals and the problems of staff interaction and communication. The complexity of the hospital, with its strong differentiation of tasks, creates serious problems of communication. In an excellent analysis of interpersonal relations in medical settings, Croog discerns three main problems: (1) what variables determine the form and structure of interpersonal relationships in hospital settings; (2) what is the nature of the processes of social interaction; and (3) what is the relationship between staff interaction and the success of medical care.[221]

Some answers to these problems have come from several detailed studies of staff interaction and patterns of patient care in mental and general hospitals.[222] Several of these surveys of interpersonal relationships between staff members and the progress of the patient have shown that conflict and low morale among the staff can be a deterrent to the improvement of the patient.[223] In an attempt to relate the structure of hospital organization to

219. Bloom, S. W., *et al.*, "The Sociologist as a Medical Educator: A Discussion," *American Sociological Review*, Vol. 25, February, 1960, pp. 96–101.
220. Burling, Temple, E. M. Lentz, and R. N. Wilson, *op. cit.*
221. Croog, S. H., "Interpersonal Relations in Medical Settings," in *Handbook of Medical Sociology*. Edited by H. E. Freeman, Sol Levine, and L. G. Reeder, *op. cit.*, pp. 241–271.
222. Several of these studies are reported in Greenblatt, Milton, *et al.*, eds., *The Patient and the Mental Hospital*. Free Press, Glencoe, Ill., 1957; and Freidson, Eliot, ed., *The Hospital in Modern Society*, Macmillan, New York, 1963.
223. Stanton, A. H. and M. S. Schwartz, *The Mental Hospital:* A Study of Institutional Participation in Psychiatric Illness and Treatment. Basic Books, New York, 1954.

the performance of medical tasks, Seeman and Evans found that high stratification tended to interfere with communication to and about the patient.[224] Several interesting experiments have been carried out which substantiate the improvement in patient care which can be brought about by changing lines of authority and communication.

The nature of the interaction among hospital staff members has been found to be strongly influenced by formal administrative arrangements. The dual system of authority, one professional and one administrative, creates many conflicts of both ideology and practice.[225] The performance of the many diverse and complicated hospital tasks is greatly impeded by an authority system in which a single hospital worker may be subordinate to a number of different chiefs.[226] A good illustration of conflicting types of authority structure and their effect upon staff interaction is afforded by Coser's study of medical vs. surgical wards.[227]

The nature and importance of "ward culture" within the hospital has been the subject of a number of specific surveys. Surveys of different types of hospital wards have shown that there are marked differences in the way these wards are organized and operated. Different wards will be organized according to varying levels of "permissiveness" for both staff and patient. The importance of the type of "therapeutic environment" to the progress of the patient has been found to be especially pronounced for mental wards.[228]

Two areas of hospital life particularly suited to research using the survey method are the attitudes and beliefs of the medical staff and of the patients. Several surveys have shown that the attitudes and ideology of staff members differ widely and that a relationship exists between what the staff believes and the type of medical care rendered. A study by Rapoport of a planned mental hospital community demonstrates the importance of the value system of the staff in relation to the degree of freedom permitted the mental

224. Seeman, Melvin and J. W. Evans, "Stratification and Hospital Care: I. The Performance of the Medical Interne," *American Sociological Review,* Vol. 26, February, 1961, pp. 67–80.

225. Smith, Harvey L., "Two Lines of Authority: The Hospital Dilemma," *The Modern Hospital,* Vol. 84, March, 1955, pp. 59–64.

226. Henry, Jules, "Types of Institutional Structure," *Psychiatry,* Vol. 20, February, 1957, pp. 47–60.

227. Coser, R. L., "Authority and Decision-Making in a Hospital," *American Sociological Review,* Vol. 23, February, 1958, pp. 56–63.

228. Dunham, H. W. and S. K. Weinberg, *The Culture of the State Mental Hospital.* Wayne State University Press, Detroit, 1960.

patient.[229] Another study of the out-patient department in a hospital found that there were wide differences in the perceptions and attitudes of physicians, nurses and social workers related to the professional ideologies of these three groups and affecting their treatment of the patient.[230] Personality characteristics of the medical staff were also found to relate to the "custodial" or "humanistic" approach of the staff to the treatment of the patient.[231]

Surveys of patients' attitudes and beliefs have shown similar variation and relationship to behavior. We have already noted that the definition by an individual of himself as "sick" is an important determinant of his behavior as a patient. When he enters the hospital, his expectations concerning hospital "life" and his attitudes toward medical care continue to influence his behavior. Learning to be a hospital patient is a new experience and a number of studies have focused upon the process of hospital adjustment.[232] Studies of the development of informal organizations among ward patients have shown that patient cliques can develop which may be detrimental to the therapeutic goals of the institution.[233] The leadership structure of patient groups and the degree of participation have been found to reflect the social status which the individuals bring from the outside world.[234]

These surveys of the attitudes and behavior of hospital staff and patients, as well as the previously mentioned studies of hospital organization and operation, point to a highly significant area for future survey research. Unfortunately, to date, most of the surveys made have not taken full advantage of the conceptual and methodological tools available. By and large, they are characterized by small, poorly selected samples, a lack of control cases, limitation to individual situations, and an emphasis upon impressionistic evidence. Considering the wide range of medical treatment settings, it is obvious

229. Rapoport, R. N., Rhona Rapoport, and Irving Roscow, *Community vs. Doctor.* Tavistock Publications, London, 1959.

230. Solon, Jerry, *et al.,* "Staff Perceptions of Patients' Use of a Hospital Out-Patient Department," *Journal of Medical Education,* Vol. 33, January, 1958, pp. 10–21.

231. Carstairs, G. M. and A. Baron, "The Social Environment of Mental Hospital Patients: A Measure of Staff Attitudes," in *The Patient and the Mental Hospital.* Edited by Milton Greenblatt, *et al., op. cit.,* pp. 218–229.

232. Reader, G. G., L. Pratt, and M. C. Mudd, "What Patients Expect from Their Doctors," *Modern Hospital,* Vol. 89, 1957, pp. 88–94.

233. Caudill, William, *The Psychiatric Hospital as a Small Society.* Harvard Universiy Press, Cambridge, 1958.

234. Croog, S. H., "Patient Government—Some Aspects of Participation and Social Background on Two Psychiatric Wards," *Psychiatry,* Vol. 19, May, 1956, pp. 203–297.

that much remains to be done in this area. There is a great need for long-term studies employing the panel technique to compare medical organizations. The use of contextual analysis would be particularly appropriate to the study of staff and patient attitudes and behavior within the varying social climates created by different therapeutic environments and medical care systems.[235]

A further need is for survey research on the many different types of health organizations and personnel that have not yet been studied. For example, there has been no organizational study of an official public health agency, despite the tremendous importance of these local units in the current health picture.[236]

Finally, we need more research on the many voluntary health and welfare agencies that constitute such a major force in the health field today. How are they organized, what functions do they perform, where do they get their support, how do they relate to each other and to official agencies, are examples of topics about which we know very little today. The proper role of these voluntary agencies is under great debate at the moment.[237] The increased activity of the government in medical research, and the broadening of the goals of local official health units, have raised serious questions concerning the continued functioning of these voluntary health organizations. Survey research which examines the total health picture of a community in terms of current needs and resources would contribute significantly to the most efficient allocation of responsibility to each of the various health agencies in the community.

The Conduct of Surveys in Health and Medicine

It should be obvious, even from this brief description of the applications of survey research to health and medical problems, that the survey method has found its way into almost every aspect of public health and medicine. According to the subject index of the 1960 Inventory of Social and Economic Research in Health of the Health Information Foundation, over 1,000 different topics were studied, from "Absenteeism, industrial, organizational

235. Anderson, Odin W., "Medical Care: Its Social and Organizational Aspects: Health-Service Systems in the United States and Other Countries—Critical Comparisons." *New England Journal of Medicine*, Vol. 269, October 17 and 24, 1963, pp. 239–243 and pp. 896–900.

236. Roemer, M. I., "Health Service Organization as a Task in Applied Social Science," *Canadian Journal of Public Health*, Vol. 45, April, 1954, pp. 133–145.

237. Hamlin, R. H., *Voluntary Health and Welfare Agencies in the United States.* Schoolmasters' Press, New York, 1961.

factors and problem drinking, interrelationships of" to "Zulu of S. Africa, hypertension among, socio-cultural factors related to urban, nutrition and blood pressure among."[238] If we examine these surveys for the populations being studied, we find that almost no group has escaped being selected by the sampler or questioned by the interviewer. Both the medical clients and the practitioners have been examined from many different perspectives. Practically no group of patients, or would-be patients, or should-be patients, whether at home, on the street, or in the hospital, has been overlooked. Even their families and neighbors have been caught in the sampling net of the survey researcher. No community has been completely immune, from the smallest to the largest, from rural Africa to urban New York. Few professional, or semi-professional, or pseudo-professional workers, whether ordained or prospective, have been entirely neglected. No major type of medical organization or institution has failed to come under the questioning gaze of the survey researcher.

Looking briefly at the agencies and individuals making these surveys, again we find a wide range, from the U.S. Public Health Service to the Oahu (Hawaii) TB and Health Association, from the medical research director of a large public health department to a social science student at a small college. Almost all official and voluntary public health agencies engage in survey research related to their program of health activities. Several of the large state and city health departments—e.g. California, New York, Pennsylvania, New York City, Philadelphia, Cambridge—have social science research programs which employ survey researchers to study both the basic problems of social epidemiology and the applied problems of program evaluation.[239] A number of the large national voluntary health agencies such as the National Heart Association, the National Council on Alcoholism, and the American Social Health Association, directly support and conduct health surveys in their area of interest. Many of the professional schools—medicine, nursing, public health, dentistry—and many universities conduct active programs on health problems using the survey method extensively. Various community agencies (e.g. Community Service Society of New York, Community Welfare Council of Greater Milwaukee) and local hospitals (e.g. Montefiore Hospital of New York, Children's Medical Center of Boston) engage in survey research of their own patients or clientele. In fact, it would be difficult to find any major health organization which has not

238. Health Information Foundation, *An Inventory of Social . . . , op. cit.*
239. For a more detailed analysis of social science programs in the field of public health, see Suchman, E. A., *Sociology and the Field . . . , op. cit.,* pp. 130–174.

turned to the survey method for research on its basic or administrative problems.

The field of health survey research is a rapidly expanding one—probably more surveys are being made in this area than in any other professional field. Perhaps because of this rapid development, the quality of research is very uneven. Some organizations have well-trained staffs of their own under highly qualified professional guidance, while many, perhaps the majority, are comparative amateurs in their use of the survey method. In general, there is a shortage of qualified survey researchers and there is a great need for recruitment and training programs. In several cases, the cooperation of social science departments of local colleges and universities has been enlisted in joint undertakings. As more and more trained students enter the field, it is to be hoped that the quality of survey research will improve.

The health field does offer excellent opportunities to the social survey researcher. While there are bound to be areas of conflict whenever professional workers from different disciplines come together, there is a kind of natural affinity between the social scientist and the health researcher.[240] Both groups are greatly concerned with the development of a scientific approach for studying the behavior of people. The professional worker in health and medicine has a long tradition of medical science to support his desire for empirical proof of theoretical assumptions and will be receptive to the need for carefully designed and well-conducted survey research projects. His greatest difficulty will come in recognizing and accepting the need for the general type of survey research not aimed at the testing of a specific hypothesis. The inherent complexity of social factors in human behavior will often, to him, seem to reflect the survey researcher's own lack of rigor rather than the natural social process. Multiple causation, subjective attitude measurement, the use of indirect indices of behavior, the variability of response from subjects, the dependence upon correlational analysis, and many other inherent problems of survey research will often lead to confusion and distrust. A mutual education and growth process is necessary: the survey researcher must continue to strive to make his techniques more rigorous—including the recognition and acknowledgment of the limitations of his data—and to report his findings in terms that are understandable to the non-social scientist, while the health professional must learn to accept the different nature of social as opposed to biological or physical research

240. Cottrell, L. S. and E. B. Sheldon, "Problems of Collaboration Between Social Scientists and the Practicing Professions," *Annals of the American Academy of Political and Social Science,* Vol. 346, March, 1963, pp. 126–137.

and to understand better the meaning and significance of basic social concepts. The survey researcher's desire to look behind the straightforward demographic correlation for its meaning in terms of status and role performance is really an attempt to explain the significance of these observed relationships in terms of human behavior variables and not just "sociological jargon." Hopefully, some day, these social and psychological variables will replace the demographic characteristics as more direct measures of variations in the disease process.

To the above basic scientific problems of causal models and the measurement of variables must be added the usual problems in collaboration between the survey researcher in an applied field and the program administrator. These are probably no different in the health field than in any other endeavor to apply survey techniques to the solution of specific operational problems. A symposium of social research personnel and health administrators showed how deeply differences in orientation and approach can be between these two groups.[241] As described by Warren, a basic source of conflict concerned the goal of "understanding" as opposed to "action." The survey researcher is more likely to emphasize the significance of his findings for an increased understanding of basic human behavior, while the health administrator will be looking for answers to practical, operational problems—even based on inadequate data. Foster describes this conflict of interests:

> Not only are the aims of disciplines and professions distinct, but the ego-satisfying criteria are also different. Public health personnel feel gratified when they know they have raised the level of health in their jurisdiction through their efforts, and that this success is recognized by their colleagues. Behavioral scientists feel gratified when they feel they have made new contributions to basic science, and when these contributions are acknowledged by their colleagues.[242]

This is not a new problem, however, and need not concern us here, although it is a basic problem in the application of survey research techniques to professional areas of activity.

241. State Charities Aid Association, *Social Research in Health and Welfare Agencies.* June, 1960.
242. Foster, George, "Public Health and Behavioral Science: The Problem of Teamwork," *American Journal of Public Health,* Vol. 51, September, 1961, p. 1288.

Conclusion

This report on the use of surveys in health and medicine has stressed three main areas of application: (1) the study of the *disease* itself—its distribution throughout the population and its etiology; (2) the study of the *individual*—his knowledge, attitudes, and behavior in relation to illness and his utilization of health services; and (3) the study of the *profession*—its organization and personnel. In each of these areas, surveys were found to play an important role in advancing basic knowledge and in providing useful information for the solution of applied problems in the prevention and treatment of disease and disease-related conditions.

There are other areas of application of the survey method in health and medical research that we have not been able to develop in any detail. Among the more important of these are the effects of illness and disease on society and the individual, the social problems related to health, intercultural and international comparisons of health problems and action, and evaluation surveys of health programs. Each of these areas provides many examples of the successful use of the survey method for both basic research on social and medical processes and applied research on practical problems of health management.

The world of health is a big wide world. It encompasses all individuals and societies and constitutes a major area of personal concern and social activity. It involves all branches of science—physical, biological, and social. Its problems arise from natural causes and from man's attempts to deal with these inevitable processes of life.

Research in the area of health, therefore, means the study of man—how and where he lives, what he does, and why he does it. As one of modern science's essential tools for the study of man, the survey method has found a natural application to research on health problems. As the chronic diseases increase in importance and as the organization of medical care becomes even more complex, social and behavioral factors will assume greater and greater significance. The past has given us some promising glimpses of what survey research can contribute to the understanding and solution of social and behavioral health problems; the future will undoubtedly witness the continued development and expansion of survey research in the health and medical field as new techniques are perfected and new areas are opened for study.

Bibliography

Acheson, R. M., ed., *Comparability in International Epidemiology*. Milbank Memorial Fund, New York, 1964, pp. 32–39, 90–106, 161–168.

Ackerknecht, E. H., "Malaria in the Upper Mississippi Valley, 1760–1900," *Bulletin of the History of Medicine*, Supplement No. 4, Johns Hopkins Press, 1945, pp. 1–142.

Adams, Stuart, "Trends in Occupational Origins of Physicians," *American Sociological Review*, Vol. 18, August, 1953, pp. 404–410.

American Dental Association, Bureau of Economic Research and Statistics, "The 1962 Survey of Dental Practice," *Journal of the American Dental Association*, Vols. 66 and 67, 1963–1964.

American Medical Association, *What Americans Think of the Medical Profession*. American Medical Association, Chicago, 1956.

American Public Health Association, *Guide to a Community Health Study*, revised 1961.

Anderson, O. W., "Medical Care: Its Social and Organizational Aspects: Health-Service Systems in the United States and Other Countries—Critical Comparisons," *New England Journal of Medicine*, Vol. 269, October 17 and 24, 1963, pp. 239–243 and pp. 896–900.

Anderson, O. W., "The Utilization of Health Services," in *Handbook of Medical Sociology*. Edited by H. E. Freeman, Sol Levine and L. G. Reeder. Prentice-Hall, Englewood Cliffs, N.J., 1963, pp. 349–367.

Anderson, O. W. and J. J. Feldman, *Family Medical Costs and Voluntary Health Insurance:* A Nationwide Survey. McGraw-Hill, New York, 1956.

Anderson, O. W. and Monroe Lerner, *Measuring Health Levels in the United States 1900–1958*. Research Series No. 11, Health Information Foundation, New York, 1960.

Anderson, O. W. and George Rosen, *An Examination of the Concept of Preventive Medicine*. Research Series No. 12, Health Information Foundation, Chicago, 1960, pp. 4–6.

Anderson, O. W. and Milvoy Seacat, *The Behavioral Scientists and Research in the Health Field*. Bulletin #1, Health Information Foundation Research Series, Chicago, 1957.

Arnold, M. F., "Perception of Professional Role Activities in the Local Health Department," *Public Health Reports*, Vol. 77, January, 1962, pp. 80–88.

Back, K. W., Robert Coker, and T. G. Donnelly, "Public Health as a Career in Medicine: Secondary Choice Within A Profession," *American Sociological Review*, Vol. 23, October, 1958, pp. 533–541.

Badgley, R. F. and R. W. Heterington, "Medical Care and Social Class in Wheatville," *Canadian Journal of Public Health*, Vol. 53, October, 1962, pp. 425–431.

Banas, P. A. and R. V. Davis, "Identifying the Physically Handicapped Through

Survey Methods," *American Journal of Public Health,* Vol. 52, March, 1962, pp. 443–449.

Barsalow, F. W., *et al., Chiropractic in California.* Haynes Foundation, Los Angeles, 1960.

Becker, Howard, *et al., Boys in White:* Student Culture in Medical School. University of Chicago Press, Chicago, 1961.

Becker, Howard and Blanche Geer, "Medical Education," in *Handbook of Medical Sociology.* Edited by H. E. Freeman, Sol Levine and L. G. Reeder. Prentice-Hall, Englewood Cliffs, N.J., 1963, pp. 169–186.

Ben-David, Joseph, "The Professional Role of the Physician in Bureaucratized Medicine: A Study in Role Conflict," *Human Relations,* Vol. 11, No. 3, 1958, pp. 255–274.

Berkowitz, J. E. and N. H. Berkowitz, "Nursing Education and Role Conception," *Nursing Research,* Vol. 9, Fall, 1960, pp. 218–219.

Bloom, S. W., *The Doctor and His Patient.* Russell Sage Foundation, New York, 1963.

Bloom, S. W., *et al.,* "The Sociologist as a Medical Educator: A Discussion," *American Sociological Review,* Vol. 25, February, 1960, pp. 96–101.

Breslow, Lester, "Uses and Limitations of the California Health Survey for Studying the Epidemiology of Chronic Disease," *American Journal of Public Health,* Vol. 47, February, 1957, pp. 168–172.

Bressler, M. and W. Kephart, "Career Dynamics," Pennsylvania Nurses Association, 1955.

Buell, Bradley, *et al., Community Planning for Human Services.* Columbia University Press, New York, 1952.

Bugbee, George, *Public Attitudes Toward Use of Medical Care.* Health Information Foundation, New York, 1956.

Bullock, R. P., *What Do Nurses Think of Their Profession?* Ohio State University Research Foundation, Columbus, 1954, pp. 27–62.

Burling, Temple, E. M. Lentz, and R. N. Wilson, *The Give and Take in Hospitals:* A Study of Human Organization in Hospitals. G. P. Putnam's Sons, New York, 1956.

Cahalan, Don, *et al.,* "Career Interests and Expectations of U.S. Medical Students," *Journal of Medical Education,* Vol. 32, August, 1957, pp. 557–563.

Caldwell, B. J., "Employees Study Patients' Complaints," *Modern Hospital,* May, 1956.

Caplovitz, David, "Student-Faculty Relations in Medical School," unpublished doctoral thesis, Columbia University, New York, 1960.

Carstairs, G. M. and A. Baron, "The Social Environment of Mental Hospital Patients: A Measure of Staff Attitudes," in *The Patient and the Mental Hospital.* Edited by Milton Greenblatt, *et al.* Free Press, Glencoe, Ill., 1957.

Cartwright, Ann, "Memory Errors in a Morbidity Survey," *Milbank Memorial Fund Quarterly,* Vol. 41, January, 1963, pp. 5–24.

Cartwright, Anna, F. M. Martin, and J. J. Thomson, "Efficacy of an Anti-Smoking Campaign," *The Lancet,* February, 1960.

Cassel, John, "Social and Cultural Considerations in Health Innovations," *Annals of the New York Academy of Medicine,* Vol. 107, May 22, 1963.

Cassel, John, "Social Science Theory as a Source of Hypotheses in Epidemiological Research," *American Journal of Public Health,* Vol. 54, September, 1964, pp. 1482–1488.

Cassel, John, R. Patrick, and D. Jenkins, "Epidemiological Analysis of the Health Implications of Cultural Change: A Conceptual Model," *Annals of the New York Academy of Sciences,* Vol. 84, December 8, 1960.

Caudill, William, *The Psychiatric Hospital as a Small Society,* Harvard University Press, Cambridge, 1958.

Chance, N. A., "Conceptual and Methodological Problems in Cross-Cultural Health Research," *American Journal of Public Health,* Vol. 52, March, 1962, pp. 410–417.

Chein, Isador, *et al., The Road to H:* Narcotics, Delinquency and Social Policy. Basic Books, New York, 1964.

Chen, Edith and Sidney Cobb, "Further Study of Non-Participation Problems in a Morbidity Survey Involving Clinical Examination," *Journal of Chronic Diseases,* Vol. 7, April, 1958, pp. 321–331.

Ciocco, Antonio, "On Indices for the Appraisal of Health Department Activities," *Journal of Chronic Diseases,* Vol. 11, May, 1960, pp. 509–522.

Clausen, J. A., "The Sociology of Mental Illness," in *Sociology Today.* Edited by R. K. Merton, L. Broom, and L. S. Cottrell. Basic Books, New York, 1959, pp. 485–508.

Clausen, J. A., "Social Factors in Disease," *Annals of the American Academy of Political and Social Science,* Vol. 346, March, 1963, pp. 138–148.

Clausen, J. A. and M. L. Kohn, "The Ecological Approach in Social Psychiatry," *American Journal of Sociology,* Vol. 60, September, 1954, pp. 140–151.

Cobb, Sidney, Stanley King, and Edith Chen, "Differences Between Respondents and Non-Respondents in a Morbidity Survey Involving Clinical Examination," *Journal of Chronic Diseases,* Vol. 6, August, 1957, pp. 95–108.

Cohart, E. M. and I. V. Hiscock, "A Profile of the Public Health Worker," *American Journal of Public Health,* Vol. 45, December, 1955, pp. 1525–1532.

Coleman, James, H. Menzel, and E. Katz, "Social Processes in Physicians' Adoption of a New Drug," *Journal of Chronic Diseases,* Vol. 91, January, 1959, pp. 1–40.

Collins, S. D., *The Incidence of Illness and the Volume of Medical Services Among 9,000 Canvassed Families,* (a collection of 23 reprints). U.S. Government Printing Office, Washington, 1944.

Collins, S. D., *et al., Sickness Experience in Selected Areas of the United States.* Public Health Monograph No. 25, Public Health Service Publication No. 390, U.S. Government Printing Office, Washington, 1955.

Commission on Chronic Illness, *Chronic Illness in the United States,* 4 vols. Harvard University Press, Cambridge, 1956–1957.

Committee on the Morbidity Survey, "The Danish National Morbidity Survey in 1950." Communication No. 7, *Danish Medical Bulletin,* Vol. 2, 1955, pp. 148–152.

Conference on Preventive Medicine and Social Science Research, Social Science Research Council, Skytop, Pa., June 22–27, 1958, mimeographed.

Cornely, P. B. and S. K. Bigman, "Acquaintance with Municipal Government Health Services in a Low-Income Urban Population," *American Journal of Public Health,* Vol. 52, November, 1962, pp. 1877–1886.

Cornely, P. B. and S. K. Bigman, "Some Considerations in Changing Health Attitudes," *Children,* Vol. 10, January–February, 1963, pp. 23–28.

Corwin, R. G. and M. Taves, "Nursing and Other Health Professions," in *Handbook of Medical Sociology.* Edited by H. E. Freeman, Sol Levine and L. G. Reeder. Prentice-Hall, Englewood Cliffs, N.J., 1963, pp. 187–212.

Corwin, R. G., M. Taves, and E. J. Haas, "Professional Disillusionment," *Nursing Research,* Vol. 10, Summer, 1961, pp. 141–144.

Coser, R. L., "Authority and Decision-Making in a Hospital," *American Sociological Review,* Vol. 23, February, 1958, pp. 56–63.

Cottrell, L. S. and E. B. Sheldon, "Problems of Collaboration Between Social Scientists and the Practicing Professions," *Annals of the American Academy of Political and Social Science,* Vol. 346, March, 1963, pp. 126–137.

Crabtree, J. A., "Plans for Tomorrow's Needs in Local Public Health Administration," *American Journal of Public Health,* Vol. 53, August, 1963.

Croatman, Wallace and P. B. Sheatsley, *The Prescription Pharmacist Today.* Health Information Foundation, Research Series No. 3, New York, 1958.

Croog, S. H., "Patient Government—Some Aspects of Participation and Social Background on Two Psychiatric Wards," *Psychiatry,* Vol. 19, May, 1956, pp. 203–297.

Croog, S. H., "Ethnic Origins, Educational Level, and Response to a Health Questionnaire," *Human Organization,* Vol. 20, Summer. 1961, pp. 65–69.

Croog, S. H., "Interpersonal Relations in Medical Settings," in *Handbook of Medical Sociology.* Edited by H. E. Freeman, Sol Levine and L. G. Reeder. Prentice-Hall, Englewood Cliffs, N.J., 1963, pp. 241–271.

Cumming, Elaine and John Cumming, *Closed Ranks:* An Experiment in Mental Health Education. Harvard University Press, Cambridge, 1957.

Davis, Michael M., *Medical Care for Tomorrow,* Harper & Bros., New York, 1955.

Davis, Milton S. and R. L. Eichhorn, "Compliance with Medical Regimens: A Panel Study," *Journal of Health and Human Behavior,* Vol. 4, Winter, 1963, pp. 240–249.

Davis, Morris, "Community Attitudes Toward Fluoridation," *Public Opinion Quarterly,* Vol. 23, Winter, 1959–1960, pp. 474–482.

Dawber, T. R. and F. N. Moore, "Longitudinal Study of Heart Disease in Framingham, Massachusetts," Research in Public Health, *Milbank Memorial Fund Quarterly,* New York, 1952.

Dawber, T. R., *et al.,* "Some Factors Associated with the Development of Coronary Artery Disease," *American Journal of Public Health,* Vol. 49, 1959, pp. 1349–1356.

Deutscher, Irwin, *A Survey of the Occupational Characteristics of a Metropolitan Nurse Complement.* Community Studies, Kansas City, Missouri, 1956.

Deutscher, Irwin and Ann Montague, "Professional Education and Conflicting Value Systems: The Role of Religious Schools in the Educational Aspirations of Nursing Students," *Social Forces,* Vol. 35, December, 1956, pp. 126–131.

Dorn, H. F., "Some Problems for Research in Mortality and Morbidity," *Public Health Reports,* Vol. 71, January, 1956.

Dorn, H. F. and S. J. Cutler, *Morbidity from Cancer in the United States,* Public Health Monograph 46. U.S. Government Printing Office, Washington, 1958.

Downes, Jean, "Method of Statistical Analysis of Chronic Illness in a Longitudinal Study of Illness," *Milbank Memorial Fund Quarterly,* Vol. 29, October, 1951, pp. 404–422.

Dunham, H. W. and S. K. Weinberg, *The Culture of the State Mental Hospital.* Wayne State University Press, Detroit, 1960.

Dunn, J. E., "The Use of Incidence and Prevalence in the Study of Disease Development in a Population," *American Journal of Public Health,* Vol. 52, July, 1963, pp. 1107–1118.

Durkheim, Emile, *Suicide:* A Study in Sociology. Translated by J. S. Spaulding and George Simpson. Free Press, Chicago, 1951. Paris, 1930 ed.

Eichhorn, R. L. and R. M. Anderson, "Changes in Personal Adjustment to Perceived and Medically Established Heart Disease," *Journal of Health and Human Behavior,* Vol. 3, Winter, 1962.

Elinson, Jack, "Community Population Laboratories," address to the New York Chapter of the American Statistical Association, April 28, 1960.

Elinson, Jack, "The Physician's Dilemma in Puerto Rico," *Journal of Health and Human Behavior,* Vol. 3, Spring, 1962, pp. 14–20.

Elinson, Jack, "Methods of Socio-Medical Research," in *Handbook of Medical Sociology.* Edited by H. E. Freeman, Sol Levine, and L. G. Reeder. Prentice-Hall, Englewood Cliffs, N.J., 1963, pp. 449–471.

Enterline, P. E. and Bernard Kordan, "A Controlled Evaluation of Mass Surveys for Tuberculosis and Heart Disease," *Public Health Reports,* Vol. 73, October, 1958.

"Epidemiology of Cardiovascular Diseases Methodology," *American Journal of Public Health,* Vol. 50, October, 1960, Supplement, pp. 10–11.

Feldman, J. J., "Problems in the Study of Health Attitudes and Practice," paper given at 1956 Annual Conference of the American Association for Public Opinion Research.

Feldman, J. J., "The Household Interview Survey as a Technique for the Collection of Morbidity Data," *Journal of Chronic Diseases,* Vol. 2, May, 1960, pp. 535–557.

Felix, R. H. and M. Kramer, "Research in Epidemiology of Mental Illness," *Public Health Reports,* Vol. 67, February, 1952, pp. 152–160.

Fleck, A. C., "A Public Administrator Looks at Chronic Illness Surveys," *Public Health Reports,* Vol. 77, December, 1962, pp. 1077–1080.

Foster, George, "Public Health and Behavioral Science: The Problem of Teamwork," *American Journal of Public Health,* Vol. 51, September, 1961.

Freeman, H. E., Sol Levine, and L. G. Reeder, eds., *Handbook of Medical Sociology.* Prentice-Hall, Englewood Cliffs, N.J., 1963.

Freidson, Eliot, *Patients' Views of Medical Practice.* Russell Sage Foundation, New York, 1961.

Freidson, Eliot and J. J. Feldman, *The Public Looks at Hospitals.* Health Information Foundation, Research Series No. 4, New York, 1958.

Freidson, Eliot and J. J. Feldman, *Public Attitudes Toward Health Insurance.* Health Information Foundation, Research Series No. 5, New York, 1958.

Freidson, Eliot and George Silver, "Social Science in Family Medical Care," *Public Health Reports,* Vol. 75, 1960, pp. 489–493.

Freidson, Eliot, ed., *The Hospital in Modern Society.* Macmillan, New York, 1963.

Garrison, W. A. and C. F. Lindberg, "An Annotated Bibliography of Social Science Aspects of Fluoridation," *Health Education Journal,* Vol. 19, November, 1961, pp. 209–230.

Gelman, A. C., J. E. Vandow and Nathan Sobel, "Current Status of Venereal Disease in New York City: A Survey of 6,649 Physicians," *American Journal of Public Health,* Vol. 53, December, 1963, pp. 1903–1918.

Getting, V. A., "Evaluation," *American Journal of Public Health,* Vol. 47, April, 1957, pp. 408–413.

Getting, V. A., "Community Self-Study in a Changing Society," *American Journal of Public Health,* Vol. 52, June, 1962, pp. 970–975.

Glock, C. Y. and H. L. Lennard, "Psychological Factors in Hypertension: An Interpretative Review," *Journal of Chronic Disease,* Vol. 5, February, 1957, pp. 178–184.

Goffman, Irving, *The Presentation of Self in Everyday Life.* University of Edinburgh Social Science Research Center, Edinburgh, 1958.

Goldberger, J., G. A. Wheeler, and Edgar Sydenstricker, "A Study of the Relation of Diet to Pellagra Incidence in Seven Textile Mill Communities in South Carolina in 1916," *Public Health Reports,* Vol. 35, No. 648, 1920.

Goldman, M., *et al.,* "Child Health Station Personnel: A Profile," *American Journal of Public Health,* Vol. 54, August, 1964, pp. 1302–1311.

Gordon, C., A. R. Emerson, and J. Simpson, "The Cornell-Medical Index Questionnaire as a Measure of Health in Socio-Medical Research," *Journal of Gerontology,* Vol. 14, July, 1959, pp. 305–308.

Gordon, J. E., "The Twentieth Century—Yesterday, Today, and Tomorrow (1920–)," in *The History of American Epidemiology.* Edited by F. H. Top. C. V. Mosby, St. Louis, 1952, pp. 124–125.

Graham, Saxon, "Socio-Economic Status, Illness, and the Use of Medical Services," in *Patients, Physicians, and Illness.* Edited by E. G. Jaco. Free Press, Glencoe, Ill., 1958, pp. 129–134.

Graham, Saxon, "Social Factors in the Epidemiology of Cancer at Various Sites," *Annals of the New York Academy of Sciences,* Vol. 84, December 8, 1960, pp. 807–815.

Green, D. E. and E. W. Knox, eds., *Research in Medical Science.* Macmillan, New York, 1950.

Greenberg, B. G. and B. F. Mattison, "The Whys and Wherefores of Program Evaluation," *Canadian Journal of Public Health,* Vol. 46, July, 1955, pp. 293–299.

Greenblatt, Milton, *et al.,* eds., *The Patient and the Mental Hospital.* Free Press, Glencoe, Ill., 1957.

Gregg, Alan, "The Future Health Officer's Responsibility—Past, Present, and Future," *American Journal of Public Health,* Vol. 46, November, 1956, pp. 1384–1389.

Gurin, Gerald, Joseph Veroff, and Sheila Feld, *Americans View Their Mental Health.* Basic Books, New York, 1960.

Haldeman, J. C., "What the American Public Wants in Health Care," *Public Health Reports,* Vol. 77, April, 1962, pp. 301–306.

Halpert, H. P., *Public Opinions and Attitudes about Mental Health.* Public Health Service Publication No. 1045, U.S. Government Printing Office, Washington, May, 1963.

Hamlin, R. H., *Voluntary Health and Welfare Agencies in the United States.* School-masters' Press, New York, 1961.

Hanlon, J. J., *Principles of Public Health Administration,* 3rd ed. C. V. Mosby, St. Louis, 1960.

Harting, D., *et al.,* "Public Health Needs and Practices in a Great Plains County," *American Journal of Public Health,* Vol. 49, December, 1959, pp. 1591–1595.

Harvard University Press, *Health and Medical Care in New York City.* Cambridge, 1957.

Hawley, P. R., "Evaluation of the Quality of Patient Care," *American Journal of Public Health,* Vol. 45, December, 1955.

Health Education Monographs, "Review of Research Related to Health Education Practices," Supplement No. 1, 1963.

Health Education Monographs, "What People Know, Believe, and Do About Health," Supplement No. 1, 1963.

Health Information Foundation, "The Changing Patterns of Hospital Use," *Progress in Health Services,* May, 1958.

Health Information Foundation, *An Inventory of Social and Economic Research in Health.* New York, 1960.

Heinzelmann, Fred, "Factors in Prophylaxis Behavior in Treating Rheumatic Fever: An Exploratory Study," *Journal of Health and Human Behavior,* Vol. 3, Summer, 1962, pp. 73–81.

Henry, Jules, "Types of Institutional Structure," *Psychiatry,* Vol. 20, February, 1957, pp. 47–60.

Herzog, Elizabeth, *Some Guide Lines for Evaluative Research.* Children's Bureau, U.S. Department of Health, Education, and Welfare, 1959.

Hilleboe, H. E. and W. E. Boek, "An Opinion Survey of the American Public Health Association by New York State Public Health Association Members," *American Journal of Public Health,* Vol. 44, 1954, pp. 64–76.

Hinkle, Lawrence and N. Plummer, "Life Stress and Industrialism—The Concentration of Illness and Absenteeism in One Segment of a Working Population," *Industrial Medicine and Surgery,* Vol. 21, 1952, pp. 365–375.

Hochbaum, G. M., *Public Participation in Medical Screening Programs:* A Socio-Psychological Study. Public Health Service Publication No. 572, U.S. Government Printing Office, Washington, 1958.

Hoffer, C. R., *et al., Health Needs and Health Care in Michigan.* Special Bulletin No. 365 (see also Special Bulletins Nos. 370 and 377), Michigan Agricultural Experiment Stations, Michigan State College, East Lansing, 1950.

Hollingshead, A. B. and F. C. Redlich, *Social Class and Mental Illness.* John Wiley & Sons, New York, 1958.

Hood, T. R. and Virginia Pence, "Community Health Studies in Kansas," *American Journal of Public Health,* Vol. 50, October, 1960, pp. 1560–1569.

Hopkins, C. E., *et al.,* "Intra-Family Correlation and Its Significance in the Interpretation of Sample Surveys," *American Journal of Public Health,* Vol. 53, July, 1963, pp. 1112–1120.

Hospitals, Vol. 35, August 1, 1961, Guide Issue.

Hughes, Charles, *et al., People of Cove and Woodlot.* Basic Books, New York, 1960.

Hughes, E. V., H. M. Hughes, and Irwin Deutscher, *Twenty Thousand Nurses Tell Their Story:* A Report on Studies of Nursing Functions Sponsored by the American Nurses' Association. J. B. Lippincott, Philadelphia, 1958.

Hunter, Floyd, R. C. Schaffer, and C. G. Sheps, *Community Organization:* Action and Inaction. University of North Carolina Press, Chapel Hill, 1956.

Huntington, M. J., "The Development of a Professional Self-Image," in *The Student Physician.* Edited by R. K. Merton, G. G. Reader and P. L. Kendall. Harvard University Press, Cambridge, 1957, pp. 179–187.

Hutchison, G. B., Sam Shapiro, and Paul Denson, "Evaluation of a Mailed Health Questionnaire," *American Journal of Public Health,* Vol. 52, November, 1962, pp. 1894–1917.

Hyman, H. H., T. W. Hopkins and Charles Wright, *Applications of Methods of Evaluation:* A Study of the Encampment for Leadership. University of California Press, Berkeley, 1961.

Ingmire, A. E., "Attitudes of Student Nurses at the University of California," *Nursing Research,* Vol. 1, October, 1952, pp. 36–39.

Jackson, F. W., "The Canadian Sickness Survey." *Research in Public Health,* Milbank Memorial Fund, New York, 1952, pp. 214–222.

Jaco, E. G., ed., *Patients, Physicians and Illness.* Free Press, Glencoe, Ill., 1958.

Jaco, E. G., *The Social Epidemiology of Mental Disorders.* Russell Sage Foundation, New York, 1960.

James, George, "The Present Status and Future Development of Community Health Research—A Critique from the Viewpoint of Community Health Agencies," *Annals of the New York Academy of Science,* Vol. 107, May 22, 1963.

James, George and Morris Greenberg, "The Medical Officer's Handbook on Epidemiology and Evaluation," *American Journal of Public Health,* Vol. 47, April, 1957.

Jenney, E. R. and O. G. Simmons, "Human Relations and Technical Assistance in Public Health," *Scientific Monthly,* Vol. 78, June, 1954, pp. 365–371.

Japan: Ministry of Health and Welfare, Division of Health and Welfare Statistics, *Vital and Health Statistics in Japan.* 2 vols., Tokyo, 1953.

Johnson, A. L., *et al., Epidemiology of Polio Vaccine Acceptance.* Monograph No. 3, Florida State Board of Health, 1962.

Johnson, B. C., *et al.,* "Distribution and Familial Studies of Blood Pressure and Serum Cholesteral Levels in a Total Community—Tecumseh, Michigan," *Journal of Chronic Diseases,* Vol. 18, 1965, pp. 147–160.

Johnson, Walter L., "Longitudinal Study of Family Adjustment to Myocardial Infarction," *Nursing Research,* Vol. 12, Fall, 1963, pp. 242–247.

Kaplan, O. J., "Evaluation of Health Education Activities by Opinion Poll Techniques," *American Journal of Public Health,* Vol. 41, August, 1951, Supplement No. 1.

Kassebaum, G. G., "Response Set: A Methodological Problem in Complaint Inventories," *American Journal of Public Health,* Vol. 51, March, 1961, pp. 446–449.

Kegeles, S. S., "Why People Seek Dental Care: A Test of a Conceptual Formulation," *Journal of Health and Human Behavior,* Vol. 4, Fall, 1963, pp. 166–173.

Kendall, P. L. and R. K. Merton, "Medical Education as a Social Process," in *Patients,*

Physicians and Illness. Edited by E. G. Jaco. Free Press, Glencoe, Ill., 1958, pp. 321–350.

Kimball, S. T., "An Alabama Town Surveys Its Health Needs," in *Health, Culture, and Community.* Edited by B. D. Paul. Russell Sage Foundation, New York, 1955, pp. 269–294.

Kimball, S. T. and Marion Pearsall, *The Talledega Story:* A Study in Community Process. University of Alabama Press, Tuscaloosa, 1954.

King, S. H., "Social Psychological Factors in Illness," in *Handbook of Medical Sociology.* Edited by H. E. Freeman, Sol Levine and L. G. Reeder. Prentice-Hall, Englewood Cliffs, N.J., 1963, pp. 99–121.

King, S. H. and Sidney Cobb, "Psychological Factors in the Epidemiology of Rheumatoid Arthritis," *Journal of Chronic Diseases,* Vol. 7, June, 1958, pp. 466–475.

Klerman, L. V. and Camille Lambert, "Attitudes of Private Dentists Toward a Public Dental Care Program," *Journal of the American Dental Association,* Vol. 68, March, 1964, pp. 416–423.

Koos, E. L., *The Health of Regionville.* Columbia University Press, New York, 1954.

Koos, E. L., "Metropolis—What City People Think of Their Medical Services," *American Journal of Public Health,* Vol. 45, December, 1955, pp. 1551–1557.

Kriesberg, Louis and B. R. Treiman, "Socio-Economic Status and the Utilization of Dentists' Services," *Journal of the American College of Dentists,* September, 1960.

Kruger, P. E., "Measurement of Prevalence of Chronic Diseases by Household Interviews and Clinical Evaluations," *American Journal of Public Health,* Vol. 47, No. 8, 1900, pp. 953–960.

Kutner, B., "Surgeons and Their Patients: A Study in Social Perception," in *Patients, Physicians and Illness.* Edited by E. G. Jaco. Free Press, Glencoe, Ill., 1958, pp. 384–397.

Langner, T. S., "A Twenty-Two Item Screening Score of Psychiatric Symptoms Indicating Impairment," *Journal of Health and Human Behavior,* Vol. 3, Winter, 1962, pp. 269–276.

Lawrence, P. S., "An Estimate of the Incidence of Chronic Disease," *Public Health Reports,* Vol. 63, January 16, 1948, pp. 69–82.

Lawrence, P. S., "Chronic Illness and Socio-Economic Status," *Public Health Reports,* Vol. 63, 1948, 1507–1521.

Leavell, H. R., and G. E. Clark, *Preventive Medicine for the Doctor in His Community:* An Epidemiologic Approach. McGraw-Hill, New York, 1958.

Leighton, A. H., *My Name is Legion.* Basic Books, New York, 1959.

Levine, G. N., "Anxiety About Illness: Psychological and Social Bases," *Journal of Health and Human Behavior,* Vol. 3, Spring, 1962, pp. 30–34.

Levine, Sol and P. E. White, "Exchange as a Conceptual Framework for the Study of Inter-organizational Relationships," *Administrative Science Quarterly,* Vol. 5, March, 1961, pp. 583–601.

Levine, Sol and P. E. White, "The Community of Health Organizations," in *Handbook of Medical Sociology.* Edited by H. E. Freeman, Sol Levine and L. G. Reeder. Prentice-Hall, Englewood Cliffs, N.J., 1963, pp. 321–347.

Levine, Sol and P. E. White, "Problems of Voluntary Health and Welfare Agencies" (mimeographed), School of Public Health, Harvard University.

Levine, Sol, P. E. White, and Benjamin Paul, "Community Inter-organizational Problems in Providing Medical Care and Social Services," *American Journal of Public Health,* Vol. 53, August, 1963, pp. 1183–1195.

Lilienfeld, A. M., "Epidemiological Methods and Inferences in Studies of Non-Infectious Diseases," *Public Health Reports,* Vol. 72, No. 51, 1957.

Lilienfeld, A. M., "The Distribution of Disease in the Population," *Journal of Chronic Diseases,* Vol. 11, 1960, pp. 471–483.

Lowry, S. G., C. M. Selz, and D. G. Hay, "Factors Associated with the Acceptance of Health Care Practice Among Rural Families," *Rural Sociology,* Vol. 23, June, 1958, pp. 198–202.

McCormack, T. H., "The Druggists' Dilemma: Problems of a Marginal Occupation," *American Journal of Sociology,* Vol. 61, January, 1956, pp. 308–315.

Mackintosh, J. M., "Health, Medicine and Social Change," *Canadian Journal of Public Health,* Vol. 52, November, 1961, pp. 455–462.

MacMahon, Brian, T. F. Pugh, and G. B. Hutchison, "Principles in the Evaluation of Community Health Programs," *American Journal of Public Health,* Vol. 51, July, 1961, pp. 963–968.

MacMahon, Brian, T. F. Pugh, and Johannes Ipsen, *Epidemiologic Methods.* Little, Brown, Boston, 1960.

Maddox, G. L., "Self-Assessment of Health Status: A Longitudinal Study of Selected Elderly Subjects," *Journal of Chronic Diseases,* Vol. 17, May, 1964, pp. 449–460.

Maloney, M., R. Trussel, and Jack Elinson, "Physicians Choose Medical Care: A Sociometric Approach to Quality Appraisal," *American Journal of Public Health* Vol. 50, November, 1960, pp. 1678–1686.

Mayo, A. A., ed., "Student Recruitment Is Underway," *American Journal of Nursing,* Vol. 49, April, 1949, pp. 242–245.

Mechanic, David, "Some Implications of Illness Behavior for Medical Sampling," *New England Journal of Medicine,* Vol. 269, August, 1963, pp. 244–247.

Merton, R. K., G. G. Reader, and P. L. Kendall, eds., *The Student Physician.* Harvard University Press, Cambridge, 1957.

Metzner, C. A. and Gerald Gurin, *Personal Response and Social Organization in a Health Campaign.* Bureau of Public Health Economics, Research Series No. 9, University of Michigan, Ann Arbor, 1960.

Meyer, G. R., "Conflict and Harmony in Nursing Values," *Nursing Outlook,* Vol. 7, July, 1959, pp. 298–299.

Middlewood, E. L., "Why Do Students Drop Out?" *American Journal of Nursing,* Vol. 46, December, 1946, pp. 838–840.

Milbank Memorial Fund, *Collected Papers on a Five-Year Study of Illness in the Eastern Health District of Baltimore.* Morbidity Survey in Baltimore, 1938–1943. New York, 1957.

Milbank Memorial Fund, "Inter-relations Between the Social Environment and Psychiatric Disorders," New York, 1953.

Milbank Memorial Fund, *Planning Evaluations of Mental Health Programs.* New York, 1958.

Mishler, E. G. and N. A. Scotch, "Socio-Cultural Factors in the Epidemiology of Schizophrenia," *Psychiatry: Journal for the Study of Inter-personal Processes,* Vol. 26, November, 1963, pp. 315–351.

Mooney, H. W., "Methodology in Two California Health Surveys: San Jose (1952) and Statewide (1954–55)." *Public Health Monographs,* Vol. 70, 1963, pp. 1–143.

More, D. M. and Nathan Kohn, "Some Motives for Entering Dentistry," *American Journal of Sociology,* Vol. 66, July, 1960, pp. 48–53.

Napier, J. A., "Field Methods and Response Rates in the Tecumseh Community Health Study," *American Journal of Public Health,* Vol. 52, February, 1962, pp. 208–216.

National Center for Health Statistics, "Medical Care, Health Status and Family Income," *Vital and Health Statistics,* Series 10, No. 9, May, 1964, Washington.

National Center for Health Statistics, *Cycle 1 of the Health Examination Survey: Sample and Response.* Public Health Service Publication No. 1000, Series 11, No. 1, Washngton, 1964.

National Opinion Research Center, *Public Attitudes Toward Prescription Costs and the Drug Industry.* Health Information Foundation, New York, October, 1955.

New, P. K., "The Osteopathic Students: A Study in Dilemma," in *Patients, Physicians and Illness.* Edited by E. G. Jaco. Free Press, Glencoe, Ill., 1958, pp. 413–421.

Ort, R. S., A. B. Ford, and R. E. Liske, "The Doctor-Patient Relationship as Described by Physicians and Medical Students," *Journal of Health and Human Behavior,* Vol. 5, Spring, 1965, pp. 25–34.

Orzack, Louis, *Work as a Central Life Interest of Professionals.* Reprint No. 8, Industrial Relations Center, University of Wisconsin, Madison, 1960.

Parsons, Talcott, *The Social System.* Free Press, Glencoe, Ill., 1951, pp. 428–473.

Parsons, Talcott, "Social Change and Medical Organization in the United States: A Sociological Perspective," *Annals of the American Academy of Political and Social Science,* Vol. 346, March, 1963, pp. 21–33.

Paul, B. D., ed., *Health, Culture, and Community.* Russell Sage Foundation, New York, 1955.

Paul, B. D., *et al.,* eds., "Trigger for Community Conflict: The Case of Fluoridation," *Journal of Social Issues,* Vol. 17, No. 4, 1961.

Paul, J. R., "Epidemiology," in *Research in Medical Science.* Edited by D. E. Green and E. W. Knox. Macmillan, New York, 1950.

Pemberton, John, ed., *Epidemiology:* Reports on Research and Teaching. Oxford University Press, London, 1963.

Peterson, Osler, *et al.,* "An Analytical Study of North Carolina General Practice, 1953–54," *Journal of Medical Education,* Vol. 3, December, 1956, part 2.

Phillips, H. T. and Camille Lambert, "Survey of Health Needs of Older Citizens and Their Potentials in Home Health Work," *Public Health Reports,* Vol. 79, July, 1964, pp. 571–576.

Polgar, Steven, "Health and Human Behavior: Areas of Interest Common to Social and Medical Sciences," *Current Anthropology,* Vol. 3, April, 1962, pp. 159–205.

Polgar, Steven, "Health Action in Cross-Cultural Perspective," in *Handbook of Medical Sociology.* Edited by H. E. Freeman, Sol Levine, and L. G. Reeder. Prentice-Hall, Englewood Cliffs, N.J., 1963, pp. 397–419.

Pollak, O., C. Westoff, and M. Bressler, "Pilot Study of Nursing Functions," *Nursing Research,* Vol. 2, June, 1953, pp. 15–22.

Pond, M. A., "Inter-relationship of Poverty and Disease," *Public Health Reports,* Vol. 76, November, 1961, pp. 967–974.

Puerto Rico: Department of Health, *Medical and Hospital Care in Puerto Rico.* Commonwealth of Puerto Rico, 1962.

Rapoport, R. N., Rhona Rapoport and Irving Roscow, *Community vs. Doctor.* Tavistock Publications, London, 1959.

Reader, G. G., L. Pratt, and M. C. Mudd, "What Patients Expect from Their Doctors," *Modern Hospital,* Vol. 89, 1957, pp. 88–94.

Reed, L. S. and D. P. Rice, "Private Medical Care Expenditures and Voluntary Health Insurance, 1948–61," *Social Security Bulletin,* Vol. 25, December, 1962, pp. 3–13.

Reissman, Leonard and J. H. Rohrer, eds., *Changes and Dilemma in the Nursing Profession:* Studies of Nursing Services in a Large General Hospital. G. P. Putnam's Sons, New York, 1957.

Riley, M. W., "Membership of the American Sociological Association, 1950–1959," *American Sociological Review,* Vol. 26, December, 1961.

Robb, G. L., H. S. Elwood, and R. J. Haggerty, "Evaluation of a Poison Center," *American Journal of Public Health,* Vol. 53, November, 1963, pp. 1751–1760.

Roemer, M. I., "Health Service Organization as a Task in Applied Social Science," *Canadian Journal of Public Health,* Vol. 45, April, 1954, pp. 133–145.

Roemer, M. I., "Social Science and Organized Health Services," *Human Organization,* Vol. 18, No. 2, 1959, pp. 75–77.

Roemer, M. I. and R. H. Elling, "Sociological Research on Medical Care," *Journal of Health and Human Behavior,* Vol. 4, Spring, 1963, pp. 49–68.

Rogers, E. S., *Human Ecology and Health.* Macmillan, New York, 1960.

Rogers, E. S., "Man, Ecology and the Control of Disease," *Public Health Reports,* Vol. 77, September, 1962, pp. 755–762.

Rogoff, Natalie, "The Decision to Study Medicine," in *The Student Physician.* Edited by R. K. Merton, G. G. Reader, and P. L. Kendall. Harvard University Press, Cambridge, 1957, pp. 109–130.

Rosen, George, *Approaches to a Concept of Social Medicine:* A Historical Survey. Milbank Memorial Fund, New York, 1949.

Rosen, George, "Medical Care: Health Needs and Resources in the United States," *New England Journal of Medicine,* Vol. 270, January, 1964, pp. 81–89.

Rosenblatt, Daniel and E. A. Suchman, "Blue Collar Attitudes and Information Toward Health and Illness," in *Blue Collar World.* Edited by A. B. Shostak and William Gomberg. University of Pittsburgh Press, Pittsburgh, 1964.

Rosenblatt, Daniel and E. A. Suchman, "The Underutilization of Medical Care Among Blue Collarites," in *Blue Collar World.* Edited by A. B. Shostak and William Gomberg. University of Pittsburgh Press, Pittsburgh, 1964.

Rosenstock, I. M. and A. P. Miller, *Why Some Sanitary Engineers Leave the Field.* Public Health Service Publication No. 359, U.S. Government Printing Office, Washington, 1954.

Rosenstock, I. M., *et al.*, "Why People Fail to Seek Poliomyelitis Vaccination," *Public Health Reports,* Vol. 74, February, 1959, pp. 98–104.

Rosenstock, I. M., *et al., The Impact of Asian Influenza on Community Life.* Public Health Service Publication No. 766, U.S. Government Printing Office, Washington, 1960.

Ross, J. A., "Social Class and Medical Care," *Journal of Health and Human Behavior,* Vol. 3, Spring, 1962, pp. 288–292.

Rossi, P. H., "What Makes Communities Tick," *Public Health Reports,* Vol. 77, February, 1962, pp. 117–124.

Rubin, Theodore, Joseph Rosenbaum, and Sidney Cobb, "The Use of Interview Data for the Detection of Associations in Field Studies," *Journal of Chronic Diseases,* Vol. 4, 1956, pp. 253–266.

Rubin, Vera, ed., "Culture, Society and Health," *Annals of the New York Academy of Science,* Vol. 84, December 8, 1960.

Russell, R. D., "An Analysis of the Health and Health Education Research in the Research Quarterly, 1951–60," *Research Quarterly,* Vol. 33, 1962, pp. 137–140.

Sanders, B. S., "Completeness and Reliability of Diagnoses in Therapeutic Practice," *Journal of Health and Human Behavior,* Vol. 5, Summer-Fall, 1964, pp. 84–94.

Sauer, H. I., "Epidemiology of Cardiovascular Mortality—Geographic and Ethnic," *American Journal of Public Health,* Vol. 52, January, 1952, pp. 94–105.

Saunders, Lyle, *Cultural Differences and Medical Care.* Russell Sage Foundation, New York, 1954.

Scotch, N. A. and J. J. Geiger, "The Epidemiology of Rheumatoid Arthritis: A Review with Special Attention to Social Factors," *Journal of Chronic Diseases,* Vol. 15, November, 1962, pp. 1037–1067.

Seeman, Melvin and J. W. Evans, "Stratification and Hospital Care: I. The Performance of the Medical Interne," *American Sociological Review,* Vol. 26, February, 1961, pp. 67–80.

Shanas, Ethel, "Reported Illness and Utilization of Medical Care," *Public Welfare,* April, 1960.

Sheatsley, P. B., *Public Attitudes Toward Aspects of Health.* Health Information Foundation, New York, 1956.

Sheatsley, P. B., "Public Attitudes Toward Hospitals," *Hospitals,* May 16, 1957.

Sills, D. L., *The Volunteers.* Free Press, Glencoe, Ill., 1957.

Simmons, O. G., *Social Status and Public Health.* Social Science Research Council, New York, 1958.

Simmons, O. G., "Social Research in Health and Medicine: A Bibliography," and "Sociology of Medical Care," in *Handbook of Medical Sociology.* Edited by H. E. Freeman, Sol Levine and L. G. Reeder. Prentice-Hall, Englewood Cliffs, N.J., 1963.

Simmons, O. G. and Howard Freeman, *The Mental Patient Comes Home.* John Wiley & Sons, New York, 1963.

Simmons, W. R. and E. E. Bryant, "An Evaluation of Hospitalization Data from the Health Interview Survey," *American Journal of Public Health,* Vol. 52, October, 1962, pp. 638–647.

Skipper, J. K., "Functional Significance of the Nurse Role: An Evaluation," *Journal of Health and Human Behavior,* Vol. 35, Spring, 1962, pp. 41–45.

Smith, Harvey L., "Two Lines of Authority: The Hospital Dilemma," *The Modern Hospital*, Vol. 84, March, 1955, pp. 59–64.

Snow, John, *On the Mode of Communication of Cholera*. John Churchill, London, 1855. Reprinted by the Commonwealth Fund, New York, 1936.

Solon, J. A., *et al.*, "Staff Perceptions of Patients' Use of a Hospital Out-Patient Department," *Journal of Medical Education*, Vol. 33, January, 1958, pp. 10–21.

Solon, J. A., *et al.*, "Patterns of Medical Care: Validity of Interview Information on Use of Hospital Clinics," *Journal of Health and Human Behavior*, Vol. 3, Spring, 1962, pp. 21–29.

Somers, H. H. and A. R. Somers, *Doctors, Patients, and Health Insurance*. Brookings Institution, Washington, 1961.

Sower, Christopher, *Community Involvement*. Free Press, Glencoe, Ill., 1957.

Srole, Leo, *et al.*, *Mental Health in the Metropolis*. McGraw-Hill, New York, 1962.

Stanford Research Institute, *Chiropractic in California*. Haynes Foundation, Los Angeles, 1960.

Stanton, A. H. and M. S. Schwartz, *The Mental Hospital:* A Study of Institutional Participation in Psychiatric Illness and Treatment. Basic Books, New York, 1954.

State Charities Aid Association, *Social Research in Health and Welfare Agencies*. June, 1960.

Stern, B. J., *Society and Medical Progress*. Princeton University Press, Princeton, 1941.

Stockwell, E. G., "A Critical Examination of the Relationship Between Socio-Economic Status and Mortality," *American Journal of Public Health*, Vol. 53, June, 1963, pp. 956–964.

Stoeckle, J. D., I. K. Zola, and G. E. Davidson, "On Going to See the Doctor: The Contributions of the Patient to the Decision to Seek Medical Aid," *Journal of Chronic Diseases*, Vol. 16, 1963, pp. 975–989.

Stouffer, S. A., *et al.*, *Measurement and Prediction*. Vol. IV of *Studies in Social Psychology in World War II*. Princeton University Press, Princeton, 1950, chap. 13 and 14.

Straus, Robert, "The Nature and Status of Medical Sociology," *American Sociological Review*, Vol. 22, April, 1957, pp. 200–204.

Straus, Robert, "Medical Practice and the Alcoholic," *Annals of the American Academy of Political and Social Science*, Vol. 315, 1958, pp. 117–124.

Suchman, E. A., "A Conceptual Analysis of the Accident Phenomenon," *Social Problems*, Vol. 8, Winter, 1960–61, pp. 241–253.

Suchman, E. A., "The Addictive Disorders as Socio-Environmental Health Problems," in Handbook of Medical Sociology. Edited by H. E. Freeman, Sol Levine and L. G. Reeder. Prentice-Hall, Englewood Cliffs, N.J., 1963, pp. 123–143.

Suchman, E. A., *Sociology and the Field of Public Health*. Russell Sage Foundation, New York, 1963.

Suchman, E. A., "The Comparative Method in Social Research," *Rural Sociology*, Vol. 29, June, 1964, pp. 123–137.

Suchman, E. A., "Socio-Medical Variations Among Ethnic Groups," *American Journal of Sociology*, Vol. 70, November, 1964, pp. 319–331.

Suchman, E. A., "Stages of Illness and Medical Care," *Journal of Health and Human Behavior,* Vol. 6, Fall, 1965, pp. 114–128.

Suchman, E. A., "Social Patterns of Illness and Medical Care," *Journal of Health and Human Behavior,* Vol. 6, Spring, 1965, pp. 2–15.

Suchman, E. A. and Lois Alksne, "Communicating Across Cultural Barriers," *The American Catholic Sociological Review,* Winter, 1961, pp. 306–313.

Suchman, E. A. and Alfred Scherzer, *Current Research in Childhood Accidents.* Association for the Aid of Crippled Children, New York, 1960.

Suchman, E. A., Bernard Phillips, and G. Streib, "An Analysis of the Validity of Health Questionnaires," *Social Forces,* Vol. 36, March, 1958, pp. 223–232.

Sydenstricker, Edgar, *Hagerstown Morbidity Studies—A Study of Illness in a Typical Population Group.* U.S. Government Printing Office, Washington, 1930.

Taves, Marvis, R. G. Corwin and E. J. Haas, *Role Conception and Vocational Success and Satisfaction.* Bureau of Business Research, Columbus, Ohio, 1964.

Tayback, Matthew and T. M. Frazier, "Continuous Health Surveys, A Necessity for Health Administration," *Public Health Reports,* Vol. 77, September, 1962, pp. 763–771.

Tayback, Matthew and Lillian Scally, "An Evaluation of Community Nursing Services in the Care of the Mentally Ill," *American Journal of Public Health,* Vol. 53, August, 1963, pp. 1260–1268.

Terris, Milton, "The Scope and Methods of Epidemiology," *American Journal of Public Health,* Vol. 52, September, 1962, pp. 1371–1376.

Thielens, Wagner, Jr., "Some Comparisons of Entrants to Medical and Law School," in *The Student Physician.* Edited by R. K. Merton, G. G. Reader, and P. L. Kendall. Harvard University Press, Cambridge, 1957, pp. 131–152.

Tibbitts, H. G. and T. D. Dublin, *Public Health Service Supported Research in Medical Ecology.* U.S. Public Health Service, Division of Research Grants, Working Paper, p. 7.

Trussel, R. E., Jack Elinson and M. L. Levin, "Comparison of Various Methods of Estimating the Prevalence of Chronic Disease in a Community—The Hunterdon County Study," *American Journal of Public Health,* Vol. 46, No. 173, 1956.

Turner, V. B., *Hagerstown Health Studies:* An Annotated Bibliography. Public Health Service Publication No. 148, U.S. Government Printing Office, Washington, 1952.

U.S. Department of Commerce, *Survey of Current Business.* Vol. 43, July, 1963.

U.S. Government Printing Office, *Illness and Medical Care Among 2,500,000 Persons in 83 Cities, with Special Reference to Socio-Economic Factors* (see fn. 34) (a collection of 27 reprints). Wahington, 1945.

U.S. Public Health Service, *U.S. National Health Survey, Health Statistics.* Public Health Service Publication Series, U.S. Government Printing Office, Washington, a continuing series including No. 1125: *Medical Economics:* Present Status and Recommendations for Additional Data.

U.S. Public Health Service, *Evaluation in Public Health.* Public Health Service Publication No. 413, U.S. Government Printing Office, Washington, 1958.

U.S. Public Health Service, *Medical Care in Transition.* Vols. 1 and 2. Public Health Service Publication No. 1128, U.S. Government Printing Office, Washington, 1955.

U.S. Public Health Service, *Origin and Programs of the U.S. National Health Survey.* Public Health Service Publication No. 584-A1, U.S. Government Printing Office, Washington, May, 1958.

U.S. Public Health Service, *Health Studies of Human Populations.* Public Health Bibliography Series, No. 38, U.S. Government Printing Office, Washington, 1962.

U.S. Public Health Service, *Hospital Utilization Studies.* Publication No. 930-G-4, U.S. Government Printing Office, Washington, 1962.

U.S. Public Health Service, *National Institutes of Health.* Publication No. 81, U.S. Government Printing Office, Washington, revised 1963.

U.S. Public Health Service, Division of Public Health Methods, *The National Health Survey, 1935–36.* National Institute of Health, Washington, 1938.

Wardwell, W. I., "Limited, Marginal, and Quasi-Practitioners," in *Handbook of Medical Sociology.* Edited by H. E. Freeman, Sol Levine and L. G. Reeder. Prentice-Hall, Englewoods Cliffs, N.J., 1963.

Wardwell, W. I. and C. B. Bahnson, "Problems Encountered in Behavioral Science Research in Epidemiological Studies," *American Journal of Public Health,* Vol. 54, June, 1964, pp. 972–981.

Wardwell, W. I., Merton Hyman, and C. B. Bahnson, "Stress and Coronary Heart Disease in Three Field Studies," *Journal of Chronic Disease,* Vol. 17, 1964, pp. 73–84.

Williams, T. R. and M. Williams, "The Socialization of the Student Nurse," *Nursing Research,* Vol. 8, Winter, 1959, pp. 18–25.

Willie, C. V., "The Social Class of Patients that Public Health Nurses Prefer to Some," *American Journal of Public Health,* Vol. 50, 1960, pp. 1126–1136.

Wilson, R. N., "Patient-Practiner Relationships," in *Handbook of Medical Sociology.* Edited by H. E. Freeman, Sol Levine, and L. G. Reeder. Printice-Hall, Englewood Cliffs, N.J., 1963, pp. 273–295.

Winton, F. R. and L. E. Bayliss, *Human Physiology,* 4th ed. Little, Brown, Boston, 1955.

Woolsey, T. D., *Estimates of Disabling Illness Prevalence in the United States.* Public Health Monograph, No. 14, Public Health Service Publication No. 181, U.S. Government Printing Office, Washington, 1953.

Woolsey, T. D. and H. Nisselman, "Some Problems in Statistical Measurement of Chronic Disease," in *Improving the Quality of Statistical Surveys.* Edited by American Statistical Association, 1956.

Woolsey, T. D., P. S. Lawrence, and Eva Balamuth, "An Evaluation of Chronic Disease Prevalence Data from the Health Interview Survey," *American Journal of Public Health,* Vol. 52, October, 1962, pp. 1631–1637.

Wynder, E. L., *et al.,* "A Study of Environmental Factors in Carcinoma of the Cervix," *American Journal of Obstetrics and Gynecology,* Vol. 68, 1954, pp. 1016–1047.

Yarrow, M. R., *et al.,* "The Psychological Meaning of Mental Illness in the Family," *Journal of Social Issues,* Vol. 11, No. 4, 1955, pp. 12–24.

Name Index

Subject Index